Lecture Notes in Computer Science 8377

Commenced Publication in 1973
Founding and Former Series Editors:
Gerhard Goos, Juris Hartmanis, and Jan van Leeuwen

Editorial Board

David Hutchison, UK
Josef Kittler, UK
Alfred Kobsa, USA
John C. Mitchell, USA
Oscar Nierstrasz, Switzerland
Bernhard Steffen, Germany
Demetri Terzopoulos, USA
Gerhard Weikum, Germany
Takeo Kanade, USA
Jon M. Kleinberg, USA
Friedemann Mattern, Switzerland
Moni Naor, Israel
C. Pandu Rangan, India
Doug Ty

Services Science

Subline of Lectures Notes in Computer Science

Subline Editors-in-Chief

Robert J.T. Morris, *IBM Research, USA*
Michael P. Papazoglou, *University of Tilburg, The Netherlands*
Darrell Williamson, *CSIRO, Sydney, Australia*

Subline Editorial Board

Boualem Bentallah, Australia
Athman Bouguettaya, Australia
Murthy Devarakonda, USA
Carlo Ghezzi, Italy
Chi-Hung Chi, China
Hani Jamjoom, USA
Paul Klingt, The Netherlands
Ingolf Krueger, USA
Paul Maglio, USA
Christos Nikolaou, Greece
Klaus Pohl, Germany
Stefan Tai, Germany
Yuzuru Tanaka, Japan
Christopher Ward, USA

Alessio R. Lomuscio   Surya Nepal
Fabio Patrizi   Boualem Benatallah
Ivona Brandić (Eds.)

Service-Oriented Computing– ICSOC 2013 Workshops

CCSA, CSB, PASCEB, SWESE, WESOA,
and PhD Symposium
Berlin, Germany, December 2-5, 2013
Revised Selected Papers

Volume Editors

Alessio R. Lomuscio
Imperial College London, UK
E-mail: a.lomuscio@imperial.ac.uk

Surya Nepal
CSIRO Computational Informatics, Marsfield, NSW, Australia
E-mail: surya.nepal@csiro.au

Fabio Patrizi
Sapienza Università di Roma, Italy
E-mail: patrizi@dis.uniroma1.it

Boualem Benatallah
The University of New South Wales, Sydney, NSW, Australia
E-mail: boualem@cse.unsw.edu.au

Ivona Brandić
Vienna University of Technology, Austria
E-mail: ivona@infosys.tuwien.ac.at

ISSN 0302-9743 e-ISSN 1611-3349
ISBN 978-3-319-06858-9 e-ISBN 978-3-319-06859-6
DOI 10.1007/978-3-319-06859-6
Springer Cham Heidelberg New York Dordrecht London

Library of Congress Control Number: 2014937671

LNCS Sublibrary: SL 2 – Programming and Software Engineering

© Springer International Publishing Switzerland 2014
This work is subject to copyright. All rights are reserved by the Publisher, whether the whole or part of the material is concerned, specifically the rights of translation, reprinting, reuse of illustrations, recitation, broadcasting, reproduction on microfilms or in any other physical way, and transmission or information storage and retrieval, electronic adaptation, computer software, or by similar or dissimilar methodology now known or hereafter developed. Exempted from this legal reservation are brief excerpts in connection with reviews or scholarly analysis or material supplied specifically for the purpose of being entered and executed on a computer system, for exclusive use by the purchaser of the work. Duplication of this publication or parts thereof is permitted only under the provisions of the Copyright Law of the Publisher's location, in ist current version, and permission for use must always be obtained from Springer. Permissions for use may be obtained through RightsLink at the Copyright Clearance Center. Violations are liable to prosecution under the respective Copyright Law.
The use of general descriptive names, registered names, trademarks, service marks, etc. in this publication does not imply, even in the absence of a specific statement, that such names are exempt from the relevant protective laws and regulations and therefore free for general use.
While the advice and information in this book are believed to be true and accurate at the date of publication, neither the authors nor the editors nor the publisher can accept any legal responsibility for any errors or omissions that may be made. The publisher makes no warranty, express or implied, with respect to the material contained herein.

Typesetting: Camera-ready by author, data conversion by Scientific Publishing Services, Chennai, India

Printed on acid-free paper

Springer is part of Springer Science+Business Media (www.springer.com)

Preface

This volume contains the proceedings of the satellite events that were held in conjunction with the 2013 International Conference on Service-Oriented Computing (ICSOC 2013), which took place in Berlin, Germany, December 2-5, 2013. The satellite events provide venues for specialist groups to engage in focused discussions on specific sub-areas within service-oriented computing. The satellite events significantly helped to enrich the main conference both by expanding the scope of the scientific topics discussed at the conference and by attracting participants from the wider community. The selected scientific satellite events consisted of two tracks: a workshop track and a PhD symposium track.

The ICSOC 2013 workshop track consisted of five workshops on a range of topics in the area of service-oriented computing. The workshops were held on December 2, 2013. Each workshop had its own chairs and Program Committee who were responsible for the selection of papers. The overall organization for the workshop program, including the selection of the workshop proposals, was carried out by Alessio Lomuscio and Surya Nepal. The following workshops were held:

- Third International Workshop on Cloud Computing and Scientific Applications (CCSA 2013)
- First International Workshop on Cloud Service Brokerage (CSB 2013)
- First International Workshop on Pervasive Analytical Service Clouds for the Enterprise and Beyond (PASCEB 2013)
- 9th international workshop on Semantic Web-Enabled Software Engineering (SWESE 2013)
- 9th International Workshop on Engineering Service-Oriented Applications (WESOA 2013)

The ICSOC 2013 PhD Symposium Track provided a forum for PhD students to present and discuss their research among their peers. It also provided PhD students with an opportunity to get advice and share experiences on their approach to research and thesis planning. The PhD symposium Track was chaired by Fabio Patrizi, Boualem Benatallah, and Ivona Brandic.

As editors of the volume we wish to thank the workshop and symposium authors and panelists, as well as the workshop Organizing Committees, who contributed to this important aspect of the conference. We hope the proceedings will serve as a valuable reference for researchers and practitioners working in the service-oriented computing domain and its emerging applications.

February 2014

Alessio Lomuscio
Surya Nepal
Fabio Patrizi
Boualem Benatallah
Ivona Brandic

Organization

ICSOC Workshop Co-chairs

Alessio R. Lomuscio	Imperial College London, UK
Surya Nepal	CSIRO, Australia

PhD Symposium Chairs

Boualem Benatallah	University of New South Wales, Australia
Ivona Brandić	Vienna University of Technology, Austria
Fabio Patrizi	Sapienza University of Rome, Italy

Organizers

Third International Workshop on Cloud Computing and Scientific Applications (CCSA)

Suraj Pandey	IBM Research, Australia
Surya Nepal	CSIRO, Australia

9th International Workshop on Engineering Service-Oriented Applications (WESOA 2013)

George Feuerlicht	HCTD, University of Technology, Sydney, Australia
Winfried Lamersdorf	University of Hamburg, Germany
Guadalupe Ortiz	University of Cádiz, Spain
Christian Zirpins	SEEBURGER AG, Germany

First International Workshop on Cloud Service Brokerage CSB 2013

Gregoris Mentzas	National Technical University of Athens, Greece
Anthony J.H. Simons	University of Sheffield, UK
Iraklis Paraskakis	South-East European Research Centre, Thessaloniki, Greece

9th International Workshop on Semantic Web-Enabled Software Engineering (SWESE 2013)

Gerd Gröner	Institute for Web Science and Technologies, University of Koblenz-Landau, Germany
Jeff Z. Pan	Department of Computing Science, University of Aberdeen, UK
Yuting Zhao	Department of computing science, University of Aberdeen, UK
Elisa F. Kendall	Sandpiper Software, Inc., USA

First International Workshop on Pervasive Analytical Service Clouds for the Enterprise and Beyond (PACEB 2013)

Alex Norta	Independent Researcher, Finland
Claudia-Melania Chituc	Eindhoven University of Technology (TU/e), The Netherlands
Roman Vaculín	IBM Research - Watson Lab, USA
Hong-Linh Truong	Vienna University of Technology, Austria
Lam-Son Lê	University of Wollongong, Australia
Weishan Zhang	China University of Petroleum, China
Klaus Marius Hansen	University of Copenhagen, Denmark
Paolo Bellavista	DEIS, Università di Bologna, Italy
JieHan Zhou	Uniersity of Oulu, Finland
Yu Deng	IBM T.J. Watson Research Center, USA
Liangzhao Zeng	IBM T.J. Watson Research Center, USA

Table of Contents

Engineering Service-Oriented Applications WESOA 2013

Cloud Service Brokerage CSB 2013

Semantic Web Enabled Software Engineering SWESE 2013

Cloud Computing and Scientific Applications CCSA 2013

Pervasive Analytical Service Clouds for the Enterprise and Beyond PACEB 2013

PhD Symposium

Introduction to the 9th International Workshop on Engineering Service-Oriented Applications (WESOA'13)

George Feuerlicht[1,2], Winfried Lamersdorf[3], Guadalupe Ortiz[4], and Christian Zirpins[5]

[1] Prague University of Economics
jirif@vse.cz
[2] University of Technology, Sydney
george.feuerlicht@uts.edu.au
[3] University of Hamburg
lamersdorf@informatik.unihamburg.de
[4] University of Cádiz
guadalupe.ortiz@uca.es
[5] SEEBURGER AG
c.zirpins@seeburger.de

The Workshop on Engineering Service Oriented Applications (WESOA'13) focuses on core service software engineering issues keeping pace with new developments such as methods for engineering of cloud services. Over the past nine years the WESOA workshop has been able to attract high-quality contributions across a range of service engineering topics with recent proceedings published by Springer in the LNCS series. The ninth Workshop on Engineering Service Oriented Applications (WESOA'13) was held in Berlin, Germany on 2 December 2013. We have received twenty-four submissions and following review of each paper by at least three reviewers we accepted ten papers for presentation at the workshop and publication in the ICSOC'2013 Workshop Proceedings. The workshop included an excellent keynote presentation by Tom Baeyens, the CEO of Effektif.com titled "A decade of open API's", followed by ten papers organized into three sessions. The first session focused on Business Processes and I.T. Services Management and included papers titled: *From Process Models to Business Process Architectures: Connecting the Layers* by Rami-Habib Eid-Sabbagh and Mathias Weske, *Integrating Service Release Management with Service Solutioning Processes* by Heiko Ludwig, Juan Cappi, Valeria Becker, Bairbre Stewart and Susan Meade, and *Practical Compiler-based User Support during the Development of Business Processes* by Thomas M. Prinz and Wolfram Amme. The second session focused on Automating Process Discovery and Composition and included papers titled: *Towards Automating the Detection of Event Sources* by Nico Herzberg, Oleh Khovalko, Anne Baumgrass, and Mathias Weske, *Discovering Pattern-Based Mediator Services from Communication Logs* by Christian Gierds and Dirk Fahland, and *Goal-driven Composition of Business Process Models* by Benjamin Nagel, Christian Gerth, and Gregor Engels. The final session included papers on Modelling Service-Oriented and Adaptive Systems: *Model Checking GSM-Based Multi-Agent Systems* by Pavel Gonzalez, Andreas Griesmayer, and Alessio Lomuscio, *Towards Modelling and Execution of Collective Adaptive*

A.R. Lomuscio et al. (Eds.): ICSOC 2013 Workshops, LNCS 8377, pp. 1–3, 2014.
© Springer International Publishing Switzerland 2014

Systems by Vasilios Andrikopoulos, Antonio Bucchiarone, Santiago Gomez Saez, Dimka Karastoyanova, and Claudio Antares Mezzina, *A Requirements-based Model for Effort Estimation in Service-oriented Systems* by Bertrand Verlaine, Ivan J. Jureta, and Stephane Faulkner, and *Augmenting Complex Problem Solving with Hybrid Compute Units* by Hong-Linh Truong, Hoa Khanh Dam, Aditya Ghose and Schahram Dustdar. The workshop provided an effective platform for exchange of ideas and extensive discussion of topics covered by paper presentations.

Workshop Organizers

George Feuerlicht, University of Technology, Sydney, Australia, Prague University of Economics, Czech Republic
Winfried Lamersdorf, University of Hamburg, Germany
Guadalupe Ortiz, University of Cádiz, Spain
Christian Zirpins, SEEBURGER AG, Germany

Program Committee

Marco Aiello, University of Groningen, The Netherlands
Vasilios Andrikopoulos, University of Stuttgart, Germany
Muneera Bano, University of Technology, Sydney, Australia
Alena Buchalcevova, Prague University of Economics, Czech Republic
Anis Charfi, SAP Research CEC Darmstadt, Germany
Javier Cubo, University of Malaga, Spain
Daniel Florian, University of Trento, Italy
Valeria de Castro, Universidad Rey Juan Carlos, Spain
Laura Gonzalez, Universidad de la República, Uruguay
Paul Greenfield, CSIRO, Australia
Dimka Karastoyanova, University of Stuttgart, Germany
Agnes Koschmieder, Karlsruhe Institute of Technology, Germany
Mark Little, Red Hat, United States
Leszek Maciaszek, Wroclaw University of Economics, Poland
Michael Maximilien, IBM Almaden Research, United States
Massimo Mecella, Univ. Roma LA SAPIENZA, Italy
Daniel Moldt, University of Hamburg, Germany
Rebecca Parsons, ThoughtWorks, United States
Achille Peternier, Università della Svizzera Italiana, Switzerland
Pierluigi Plebani, Politecnico di Milano, Italy
Franco Raimondi, Middlesex University, United Kingdom
Wolfgang Reisig, Humboldt-University Berlin, Germany
Norbert Ritter, University of Hamburg, Germany
Nelly Schuster, FZI Forschungszentrum Informatik, Germany
Yi Wei, University of Notre Dame, United States of America
Olaf Zimmermann, ABB, Switzerland
Didar Zowghi, University of Technology, Sydney, Australia

Acknowledgements. Guadalupe Ortiz thanks for the support from Ministerio de Ciencia e Innovación (TIN2011-27242). George Feuerlicht wishes to acknowledge the support of GAČR (Grant Agency, Czech Republic) grant No. P403/11/0574 and ARC Grant Design of Service Interfaces (2004000242).

The organizers of the WESOA'13 workshop would like to thank all authors for their contributions to this workshop, and members of the program committee whose expert input made this workshop possible. Finally, we thank ICSOC'13 workshop chairs Alessio Lomuscio and Surya Nepal for their direction and guidance.

From Process Models to Business Process Architectures: Connecting the Layers

Rami-Habib Eid-Sabbagh and Mathias Weske

Hasso Plattner Institute at the University of Potsdam
{rami.eidsabbagh,mathias.weske}@hpi.uni-potsdam.de

Abstract. Business process management has become a standard commodity to manage and improve business operations in organisations. Large process model collections emerged. Managing, and maintaining them has become a major area of research. Business process architectures (BPAs) have been introduced to support this task focusing on interdependencies between processes. Both the process and BPA layer are often modeled independently, creating inconsistencies between both layers. However, a consistent overview on process interdependencies on BPA level is of high importance, especially in regard to assessing the impact of change when optimising business process collaborations. In this paper, we propose a formal approach to extract BPAs from process model collections connecting process layer and BPA layer for assuring consistency between them. Interdependencies between process models will be reflected in trigger and message flows on BPA level giving a high level overview of process collaboration as well as allowing its formal verification with existing approaches. We will show the extraction of BPAs from process model collections on a running example modeled in BPMN.

1 Introduction

In the last decade business process management has become prevalent in public and private organisations for managing, maintaining, and improving business operations. Large process collections emerge that consist of hundreds or thousands of process models [1]. The large amount of processes requires to provide process managers with an overview of the process model collection. Business process architectures have been introduced to provide an overview on the processes in an organisation and their interdependencies. In most business process architecture (BPA) approaches, processes are only listed along organisational, object-based or function-based aspects so that process and BPA layer are modeled independently, leading to inconsistencies between both layers.

However, the production of goods or the delivery of services often is the result of a complex interaction of many processes that each contribute a part to the final result. Fig. 1 shows a simple example from the public administration that consists of three processes. An architect applies for a construction permit by submitting the relevant documents to the building authority. After an initial evaluation of the documents the building authority involves several experts depending on the

A.R. Lomuscio et al. (Eds.): ICSOC 2013 Workshops, LNCS 8377, pp. 4–15, 2014.
© Springer International Publishing Switzerland 2014

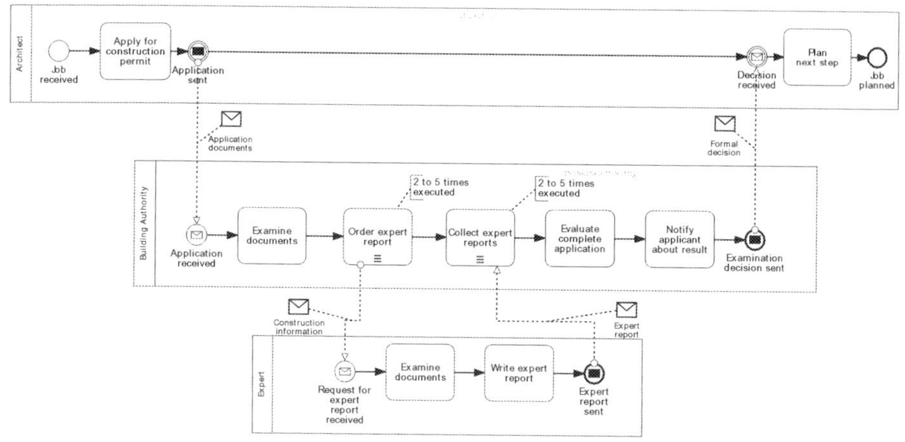

Fig. 1. Simple Construction Permit Application

complexity of the construction project. After the experts provide their evaluation of the case, the building authority decides on the application and informs the architect about it.

To depict such interdependencies between processes on a higher level, we propose a formal approach to extract BPAs proposed by [2,3] from process model collections and connect process model layer and BPA layer in a consistent way. The resulting BPA provides an overview on the underlying complex process interdependencies for evaluating the resources required in regard to process instances, and the impact of change in regard to process optimisation. It also allows for initial correctness analysis on BPA level with approaches presented in [2,3].

The remainder of this paper is structured as follows: Section 2 introduces the formal foundations of process model collections, process models and BPAs. Section 3 presents process structures that depict the interdependencies between processes, namely, trigger and message flows, as well as their multiplicity aspects. Section 4 describes the BPA extraction algorithm from process model collections. Section 5 embeds our approach into current research, followed by Section 6 that concludes the paper.

2 Foundations

This section introduces the formal concepts for the extraction of business process architectures from business process model collections. First, we will introduce the formal definition of process models and process model collections. Then we present the formal definition of BPAs that depict the interdependencies of the process models in the process collection on an abstract level.

A process model describes a business process in an organisation. It consists of nodes (i.e., events, activities, and gateways), data objects, and sequence flows.

Definition 1 (Process Model). *A process model M is a tuple $(N, \mathcal{D}, CF)$ in which:*

- $N \subseteq A \cup G \cup E$ is the set of nodes being activities A, XOR-gateways G, and events E
- $\mathcal{D}$ is a finite non-empty set of data objects.
- N and $\mathcal{D}$ are disjoint.
- $CF \subseteq N \times N$ is the sequence flow between the nodes
- $\bullet n, n\bullet$ describe the preset, respectively postset of a node n that contains the predecessor, respectively successor nodes of n.

In this initial approach we assume and limit our process models to be sequences (including simple cycles), and structurally and behaviorally sound, i.e., that each process model has only one start and end node, and that each remaining node is on a path between those two nodes.

By PM we denote a process model collection. In the following we introduce the definition of a process model collection and the message flow relations that depict the interdependencies between processes in a process model collection.

Definition 2 (Process Model Collection). Let $\mathcal{M} = (M_1, ..., M_n)$ be a set of process models. The tuple $PM = (\mathcal{M}, O, F)$ is a tuple consisting of a set of process models describing a process model collection in which

- M_i depicts each process model in PM, the process model collection.
- $O_i \subseteq A_i \cup E_i$ is a subset of nodes consisting of only activities and events which take part in the interaction between two or more processes.
- $MF_{i,j} \subseteq O_i \times O_j, i \neq j$ describes the message flow relation between two process models where $(o_1, o_2) \in MF$ with $o_1 \in M_1$ and $o_2 \in M_2$, i.e., the nodes belong to two different process models.
- $F \subseteq CF \cup MF$ is the overall set of flows in the process model collection where CF and MF are disjoint.

Process model collections usually contain hundreds or thousands of process models that describe the operations of a company [1]. The production of goods or the delivery of services often is the result of a collaboration between several processes that are loosely connected through message flows or data interdependencies. However, not all processes are connected with each other.

Business process architectures describe all processes of an organisation and their interdependencies on an abstract level giving an overview of the process interdependencies in a process model collection. A BPA consists of *BPA subsets* that all together form the BPA of the process model collection. Each *BPA subset* describes a group of processes that, e.g., produce a good or deliver a service in collaboration. These groups can be found on the first level of a business process architecture. On a lower level, process models describe the control flow of processes in a detailed and explicit way.

Each extracted BPA process is understood as a sequence of events, which are interconnected by message and trigger flows, depicting the process interaction. The interaction found on process model level needs to be mapped to two concepts on BPA level, trigger and message flows. Trigger flows explicitly show the instantiation of processes, i.e., that one process instantiates another process by sending it a trigger flow without that, it could not start. Message flows depict the interaction between two or more instantiated processes. To be able to show and analyse the amount of instances required in a business process collaboration BPAs allow to model multiple instances in various ways by BPA multiplicties. This term subsumes the sending and receiving of variably many messages and triggers to and fro multiple process instances of several processes. In [3] correctness criteria for BPAs with multiplicities were proposed as well as a transformation into Petri nets for model checking them. In the following we present the formal definition of BPAs.

Definition 3 (Business Process Architecture, Based on [2,3]). A Business Process Architecture is a tuple $(E, V, L, I, \chi, \mu, =)$, in which:

- E is a set of events, partitioned in start events, E^S, end events E^E, intermediate throwing events E^T, and intermediate catching events E^C.
- V is a partition of E representing a set of business processes.
- $v \in V$ is a sequence of events, $v = \langle e_1, ..., e_n \rangle$ such that $e_1 \in E^S$ is a start event, $e_n \in E^E$ an end event, and $e_i \in E^C \cup E^T$ for $1 < i < n$ are intermediate events.
- $L \subseteq (E^T \cup E^E) \times E^C$ is a message flow relation.
- $I \subseteq (E^T \cup E^E) \times E^S$ is a trigger relation.
- $\chi \subseteq \{((e, e_1), (e, e_2)) \mid (e, e_1), (e, e_2) \in L \cup I\}$ is a conflict relation indicating flows that are mutually exclusive.
- $\mu : E \to \mathcal{P}(\mathbb{N}_0)$ denotes the multiplicity set of an event.
- $= \subseteq (E^T \times E^C) \cup (E^C \times E^T)$ is an equivalence relation between events of the same process, demanding they send resp. receive the same number of messages. ◇

The conflict relation χ describes an alternative between two flows from one event e that exclude each other. E.g., if sending event e has two flows $(e, e_1), (e, e_2) \in I$ and $(e, e_1) \chi (e, e_2)$, then it sends a trigger flow to either e_1 or e_2, instantiating only one of the two processes [3]. The multiplicity set μ contains all valid numbers of messages or trigger signals an event can send or receive. $\mu(e) = \{1\}$ is called *trivial* and is omitted in graphical representation. The preset $\bullet e = \{e' \in E^E \cup E^T \mid (e', e) \in I \cup L\}$ of e contains the events with an outgoing relation to $e \in E$. The set $e\bullet = \{e' \in E^S \cup E^C \mid (e, e') \in I \cup L\}$, called *postset of* e, consists of the events with an incoming relation from $e \in E$ [2,3].

3 Process Model Elements and Process Structures Involved in Process Interdependencies

In this section, we present different elements of process models and process structures that are involved in the interaction between process models showing their interdependency. We examined process models modeled in different process modeling notations as Event Driven Process Chains (EPCs) or the Business Process Modeling Notation (BPMN) [4]. An excerpt of the most common structures observed will be presented and explained in detail.

3.1 Basic Process Elements

EPCs and BPMN are the most prevalent process modeling languages for BPM. EPCs in general are rather underspecified and lack well defined syntax and semantics [5]. They consist of only few elements.

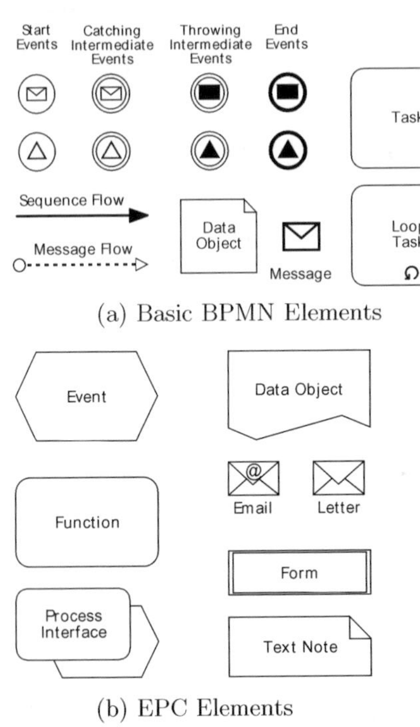

(a) Basic BPMN Elements

(b) EPC Elements

Fig. 2. Selected BPMN and EPC Elements

BPMN has become a de facto standard for BPM and eases the modeling of complex business operations with a variety of elements [6]. Fig. 2 shows selected BPMN (Fig. 2(a)) and EPC (Fig. 2(b)) elements that are used for modeling interaction or referring to interdependencies between several process models.

The interaction between processes often is depicted by events, e.g. "document received", or by activities, e.g. "send documents". More hidden, but also commonly found, data access depicts an interaction between processes in regard to writing and later reading of the same data object.

In Fig. 2(a) a small selection of the various BPMN start, intermediate, and end events are depicted. Start and catching intermediate events can be grouped as receiving events, that receive a trigger (start event) or some information (intermediate catching event) from an external source. Throwing intermediate events and end events can be regarded as sending events, that send information to other processes. In Fig. 2(a) only message and signal events were depicted as representation of the various sending and receiving event types of BPMN 2.0. In many cases the sending of information is also depicted by a task symbol, e.g. labeled with "send documents" and a message flow that connects to another process. BPMN differs between sequence flow (the internal control flow) and the message flow that depicts the interaction with other processes. Fig. 2(a) shows also the message and normal data object.

The EPC elements in Fig. 2(b) are events, functions, and a group of symbols representing data objects. EPC function elements are the equivalent to BPMN tasks. Similarly, they can be used to depict external communication by their label, e.g., when labeled "receive documents". In EPCs there are several data object elements that are depicted on the right part of Fig. 2(b), showing the data objects form, or normal data object among others. In EPCs there is no specific message flow symbol, hence in many cases the interaction between processes

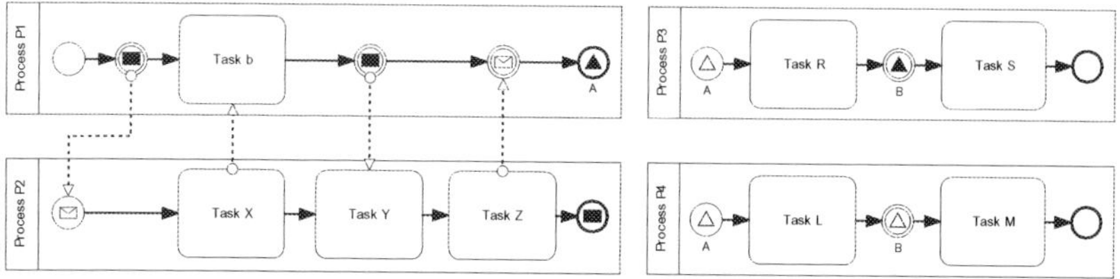

Fig. 3. Exemplary Patterns Found in BPMN Process Models

can only be detected by the data objects, events, labels of activities, or the process interface symbol. The process interface elements can be considered as special event that instantiates other processes and in this way also expresses an interdependency between processes.

3.2 Process Interaction Structures

While examining business process models we identified several process structures that depict business process interdependencies that should be reflected in a BPA. Fig. 3 shows some exemplary process structures that can be found in BPMN models but are not restricted to them. In Fig. 3 we see four process models P_1, P_2, P_3, and P_4. Processes P_1 and P_2 depict different ways of message exchange. First process P_1 sends a message to process P_2 via an intermediate throwing event. Process P_2, receiving it via its start event, is instantiated by this message. The further information exchange between both processes is performed by a combination of sending and receiving tasks, and sending and receiving events. In BPMN this exchange is always associated by a message flow, a dotted arc, that connects the communicating nodes.

Looking at the signal end event of process P_1 one can hardly notice from the process model that it is connected to the start signal events of processes P_3 and P_4 by matching labels. Labels of nodes in process models need to be considered for depicting the interdependency between processes on BPA level. In Fig. 3 process P_1 broadcasts a signal and instantiates both processes P_3 and P_4. We consider such relations also message flows, although they are hidden in the visual representation and assume them given for the BPA extraction.

For EPCs this is rather common as they do not have the concept of message flow between processes. Intermediate sending and receiving events are hard to identify which can only be done by matching their labels. EPC process interfaces are used for describing a message flow or instantiating other processes in some cases. These aspects need to be considered when extracting a BPA from a process model collection. We regard them as message flow and assume them to be given when extracting BPAs.

Data objects play an important role and are another source of interdependency between processes. In BPMN and EPCs the reading and writing of a data object can be expressed. This needs to be reflected in a given BPA concept. The writing and reading of a data object can be considered the sending and receiving of

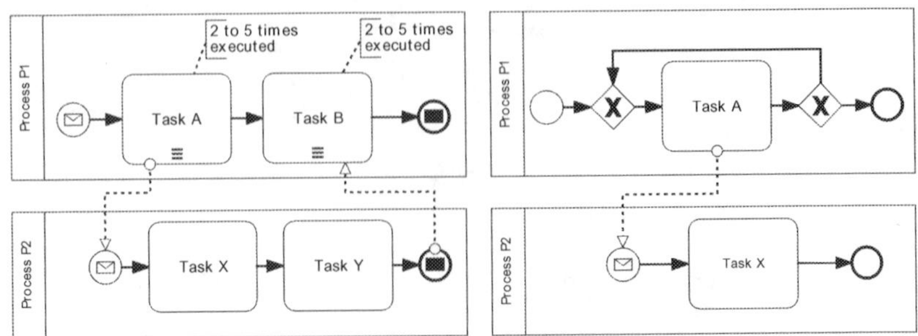

Fig. 4. Loops and Multiplicity Aspects in Process Models

an information. Generally this is modeled by the sending of a message that in the end contains the reference to the according data object. Depending on the occurrence of this operation in the process model this can be mapped to a trigger or message flow on BPA level.

To result in a complete BPA we need to assign multiplicities to BPA process events. Fig. 4 shows on the left hand side the sending of several messages through a multi-instance task by process P_1 that instantiates process P_2 several times and the receiving of answer messages from several process instances of P_2.

The diagram on the right side shows a similar concept, a simple loop construct in the BPMN model. Task A of process P_1 is executed several times instantiating multiple instances of process P_2. Both patterns need to be extracted and transformed to BPA process event multiplicities. In Fig. 1 the multi-instance activities have an annotation that sets the lower and upper bound of execution times of that task. Currently we consider only such simple loop and multi-instance constructs that can easily be mapped to BPA multiplicities. We assume that the lower and upper bound of multi-instance activities and loops is given and can be extracted from the process model elements.

4 Extraction of BPAs

This section describes how a business process architecture is extracted from a process model collection. This is performed in two steps. First, BPA processes are derived from the process models in the process model collection. Second, the interdependencies between the processes in regard to trigger and message flows are inserted into the BPA, based on the interactions detected in the process model collection. The result is a BPA showing the content of the process model collection in an abstract way and highlighting the complex interdependencies for optimisation and restructuring efforts for example.

Extraction of BPA processes from process models. To derive a BPA process from a process model in the process model collection we need to detect the elements that interact with other processes that were introduced in Section 3. Fig. 5 shows the extraction of a BPA from a process model.

Each process model has one start and one end node that can be an activity or an event. Those nodes do not have a preset or postset respectively in regard to their control flow. The first node of a process model being an event or activity maps to the the start event of the BPA process. Similarly the end node of a process model maps to the end event of the BPA process. Of all intermediary nodes of the process model only those nodes that take part in a message flow will be mapped to the according BPA process event. E.g. in 5(a) the intermediate throwing event "Application sent" of the process is mapped to the intermediate throwing event e_2 in the BPA process. If the node was a sending activity it would also be mapped to an intermediate throwing event. In general all sending nodes, be it events, activities, or written data objects, forms, documents, that are read from another process in a later step, will be mapped to an intermediate throwing event of a BPA process. In a similar way receiving elements are mapped to intermediate catching events of the BPA process, e.g. the catching intermediate event "Decision received" is mapped to the intermediate catching event e_3 of the BPA process.

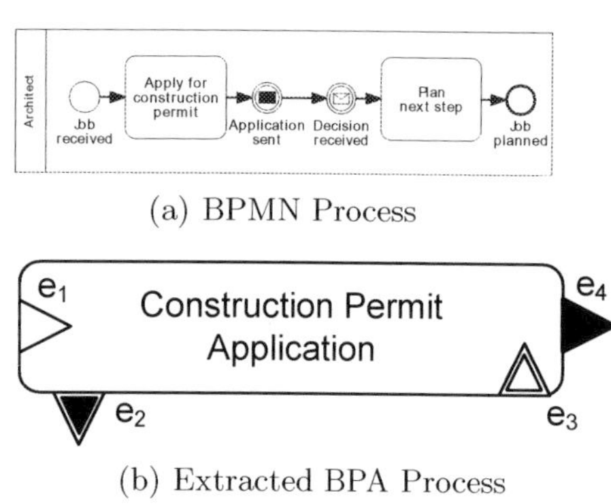

(a) BPMN Process

(b) Extracted BPA Process

Fig. 5. Extraction of BPA Process

All other nodes that are neither a start or end node, nor a node taking part in a message flow, are ignored and not represented in the BPA process as only elements that depict interaction are of interest. E.g., the task node "Apply for construction permit" is not mapped to an intermediate event in the BPA process as it does not take part in any interaction. If the node to be extracted to a BPA process event is a loop activity, or taking part in a simple loop as in Fig. 4 depicted, then the BPA process's event is annotated with the according multiplicity, the lower and upper bound of that loop, or that loop activity. If the node is just executed once in the process model we assign a trivial multiplicity to the event in the BPA process. The trivial multiplicity is not depicted in a BPA process diagram.

Extracting interdependencies between process models. After having performed the extraction of all processes in the process model collection we need to add the trigger and message flows that connect the BPA processes in a BPA. The interdependencies between processes can be attributed to specific elements in the process models introduced in the previous section. The main construct are message flows that connect combinations of the activity and event nodes of process models. Data interdependency are encapsulated in message flows and also need to be transformed into according BPA trigger and message flows. We consider matching signal events in BPMN, and matching events and process interfaces in EPCs as message flows in our formalism that will be introduced in the next paragraph. All message flows between process models that have a start node as receiving partner are mapped to a BPA trigger flow. All message flows between process models that have an intermediate node as receiving partner are mapped to a BPA message flow. For each message flow pair found in the process model collection we introduce the according trigger or message flow in the BPA by connecting the according sending and receiving events of the BPA processes.

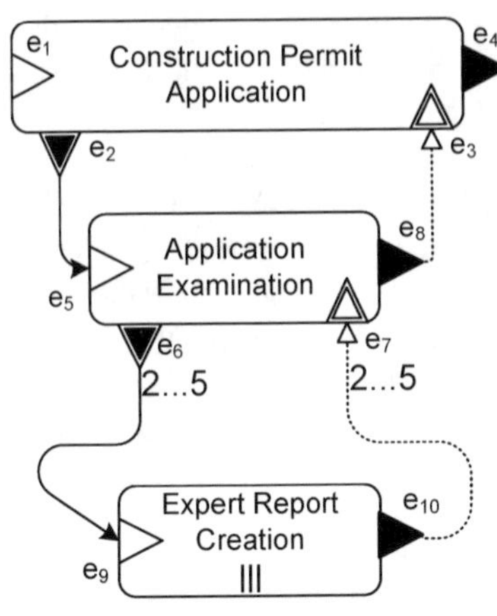

Fig. 6. Extracted BPA construction permit application

Fig. 6 shows the extracted BPA from the introductory scenario in Fig. 1. Each process model was transformed to a BPA process that only consists of the elements that interact with other processes. The start node and end node are always extracted to a BPA process as they show the instantiation and termination of a process. If the start event of a BPA process is not in relation with any other process then the process is instantiated by an external stimulus, in our scenario the architect receiving a job. All other nodes, e.g., tasks that are only performed internally are ignored and not extracted to the BPA level, e.g. the "Examine documents" task of the building authority process was not transferred to BPA level as it concerns no other process. All interdependencies in form of message flows were transformed to either trigger or message flows on BPA level. E.g., the sending activity "Order expert report" that targets the message start event of the "Expert report" process was transformed into a trigger flow in the BPA. The multiplicity annotation of process two was reflected in the multiplicity set of the according events.

BPA extraction formalism. The following definition describes the extraction of BPA processes from process models in a formal way.

Definition 4 (Process Model to BPA Process Transformation). Let $M = (N, \mathcal{D}, CF)$ be a sequential process model of a process collection PM. Let $M' = (N', \mathcal{D}', CF')$ be a second process model that interacts with M. Let $V = (S, T, C, Z)$ be a BPA process model, where S is the set of start events, T the set of throwing intermediate events, C the set of catching intermediate events, and Z the set of end events. The transformation from a process model into a BPA process is defined as follows:

- $S = \{e_s \in E | n \in N \wedge \bullet n = \emptyset\}$
- $T = \{e_t \in E | n \in N \wedge n\bullet, \bullet n \neq \emptyset \wedge (n, n') \in MF, n' \in M'\}$
- $C = \{e_c \in E | n \in N \wedge n\bullet, \bullet n \neq \emptyset \wedge (n', n) \in MF, n' \in M'\}$
- $Z = \{e_e \in E | n \in N \cap M \wedge n\bullet = \emptyset \wedge (n, n') \in MF, n' \in M'\}$
- $mult(n) = \mu(e)$ denotes that the multiplicity of a BPA event is equal to the execution times of the process model's node.

◇

In the following we describe the consistency criteria between BPA and process model layer of a process model collection in a formal way. In summary, the formalism requires that each BPA element of a process collection's BPA must have a partner element on the lower more detailed process model layer.

Definition 5 (Consistency Criteria). *Let* $\mathcal{M} = (M_1, ..., M_n)$ *be a set of process models. Let* $PM = (\mathcal{M}, MF)$ *be a process model collection. Let*$\mathcal{A} = \bigcup_{M_i \in \mathcal{M}} A_i$, $\mathcal{E} = \bigcup_{M_i \in \mathcal{M}} E_i$. *The according* $BPA = (E, V, L, I, \mu, \chi, =)$ *needs to comply to the following consistency criteria.*

- $MF \rightarrow L \cup I$ *is a function that maps the message interaction on process model level to trigger and message flows on BPA level.*
- $E^S = \{n \in (A_i \cup E_i) : \bullet n = \emptyset \wedge n \neq \bullet\emptyset\}$
- $E^T = \{n \in (A_i \cup E_i) : \bullet n, n\bullet \neq \emptyset \wedge \exists b \in A_j \cup E_j, i \neq j : (n, b) \in MF\}$
- $E^C = \{n \in (A_i \cup E_i) : \bullet n, n\bullet \neq \emptyset \wedge \exists b \in A_j \cup E_j, i \neq j : (b, n) \in MF\}$
- $E^E = \{n \in (A_i \cup E_i) : \bullet n \neq \emptyset \wedge n\bullet = \emptyset\}$
- $I = \{(n_1, n_2) \in MF : \nexists n_3 \in N : (n_3, n_2) \in CF\}$
- $L = \{(n_1, n_2) \in MF : \exists n_3 \in N : (n_3, n_2) \in CF\}$

◇

The setting of the conflict relation between two processes and the setting equivalence relation has to be performed by an process expert as such information is difficult to gather from process models. [7] propose to use data objects and their data object lifecycles to derive conflict relations between processes in Business Process Data Architectures.

5 Related Work

In in the last decade the research on BPAs has re-gained attention. Dijkman et al. [8] present an extensive survey of BPA approaches. They provide descriptive examples how to design BPAs for each of the five main BPA categories, function based, goal-based, action-based, object-based, and reference-based. However, the approaches presented do not formally link the lower process model level to the BPA level. Fettke et al. [9] present a survey on BPA approaches that are business process reference model based. Their focus is rather the evaluation of classifications of process models than the actual design of BPAs.

Scheer et al. [10] present a BPA approach that consist of four levels; process engineering, process planning and control, workflow control, and application systems. They describe how the layers are interconnected but do not provide a methodology to maintain the layers in a consistent way. Business process models are classified into categories but their interdependencies are not clearly depicted.

Green and Ould [11] describe and evaluate the RIVA process architecture, a BPA methodology they developed. They also provide guidelines on how to create a BPA according to the RIVA methodology. The steps described do not represent any concrete algorithm to create a consistent BPA for a process model collection.

[12] propose a value based methodology to provide an overview on business collaboration and to examine the value of the collaboration for each participant. Their aim is to depict the value exchange on a higher level providing consistency rules for their different representation layer. In a similar way our consistency criteria assure that all elements in the BPA also have a counterpart on process model level.

Smirnov et al. [13,14] present a methodology for process model abstraction. Similar to BPAs their aim is to provide an overview on the most important aspects of a complex process model. Their approach provides a formal definition for abstracting process elements of a process model. Instead of having a single view our BPA concentrates on extracting an overview about interdependent processes and their interaction.

The importance of depicting and analysing service interaction and business process choreographies are elaborated in [15,16]. Decker and Weske [15] present an approach to examine the behavioral consistency and compatibility of interacting processes in process choreographies. Using Bi-simulation they identify if two services have consistent behavior. They focus rather on the interaction behavior and one to one interaction between two processes rather than considering larger process collaborations.

Our BPA concept touches before presented approaches. Similarly to [15,16] it looks at interaction but with a broader scope and on more abstract level. In reference to other BPA approaches it also gives an overview on a process model collections focusing on trigger and message flows dependencies, an important aspect for maintaining and optimising process collaboration. The extraction approach presented in this paper provides a novel method to generate a BPA from a process model collection that is consistent with the lower and more detailed business process layer.

6 Conclusion

Large process model collections need a compact overview for process managers to easily grasp the interdependencies between process models. Many BPA approaches provide such an overview but usually do not assure consistency between the BPA and the process model layer. To be able to look at interdependencies between process models in regard to instantiation and message flow, we introduced an approach to extract a BPA for a process model collection from its inherent process models. For this we presented process model elements of EPCs and BPMN models that partake in process interaction and described often occurring process structures that depict process instantiation and message flows. Based on those findings we presented an algorithm and formalism to extract BPA processes and BPA trigger and message flows from the process models in a process model collection resulting in a consistent BPA.

This was an initial approach that showed the extraction of BPAs from process model collections with sequential processes. In future work we will look at more complex process models and develop an approach to map those to our BPA concept. We also currently work on tool support for BPAs.

References

1. Weske, M.: Business Process Management: Concepts, Languages, Architectures, 2nd edn. Springer (2012)
2. Eid-Sabbagh, R.-H., Weske, M.: Analyzing Business Process Architectures. In: Salinesi, C., Norrie, M.C., Pastor, Ó. (eds.) CAiSE 2013. LNCS, vol. 7908, pp. 208–223. Springer, Heidelberg (2013)
3. Eid-Sabbagh, R.-H., Hewelt, M., Weske, M.: Business Process Architectures with Multiplicities: Transformation and Correctness. In: Daniel, F., Wang, J., Weber, B. (eds.) BPM 2013. LNCS, vol. 8094, pp. 227–234. Springer, Heidelberg (2013)
4. OMG: Business Process Model and Notation (BPMN), Version 2.0 (2011)
5. van der Aalst, W.M.P.: Formalization and verification of event-driven process chains. Information and Software Technology 41(10), 639–650 (1999)
6. Dijkman, R.M., Dumas, M., Ouyang, C.: Semantics and analysis of business process models in BPMN. Inf. Softw. Technol. 50(12), 1281–1294 (2008)
7. Eid-Sabbagh, R.-H., Hewelt, M., Meyer, A., Weske, M.: Deriving Business Process Data Architecturesfrom Process Model Collections. In: Basu, S., Pautasso, C., Zhang, L., Fu, X. (eds.) ICSOC 2013. LNCS, vol. 8274, pp. 533–540. Springer, Heidelberg (2013)
8. Dijkman, R.M., Vanderfeesten, I., Reijers, H.A.: The Road to a Business Process Architecture: An Overview of Approaches and their Use. BETA Working Paper WP-350, Eindhoven University of Technology, The Netherlands (2011)
9. Fettke, P., Loos, P.: Classification of reference models: a methodology and its application. Information Systems and e-Business Management 1(1), 35–53 (2003)
10. Scheer, A.W., Nüttgens, M.: ARIS Architecture and Reference Models for Business Process Management. In: van der Aalst, W., Desel, J., Oberweis, A. (eds.) Business Process Management. LNCS, vol. 1806, pp. 376–389. Springer, Heidelberg (2000)
11. Green, S., Ould, M.A.: The Primacy of Process Architecture. In: CAiSE Workshops (2), pp. 154–159 (2004)
12. Zlatev, Z., Wombacher, A.: Consistency Between e 3 -value Models and Activity Diagrams in a Multi-perspective Development Method. In: Meersman, R., Tari, Z. (eds.) OTM 2005. LNCS, vol. 3760, pp. 520–538. Springer, Heidelberg (2005)
13. Smirnov, S., Reijers, H.A., Nugteren, T., Weske, M.: Business process model abstraction: theory and practice. Universitätsverlag Potsdam (2010)
14. Smirnov, S., Reijers, H.A., Weske, M.: A semantic approach for business process model abstraction. In: Mouratidis, H., Rolland, C. (eds.) CAiSE 2011. LNCS, vol. 6741, pp. 497–511. Springer, Heidelberg (2011)
15. Decker, G., Weske, M.: Behavioral consistency for B2B process integration. In: Krogstie, J., Opdahl, A.L., Sindre, G. (eds.) CAiSE 2007 and WES 2007. LNCS, vol. 4495, pp. 81–95. Springer, Heidelberg (2007)
16. van der Aalst, W.M.P., Mooij, A.J., Stahl, C., Wolf, K.: Service Interaction: Patterns, Formalization, and Analysis. In: Bernardo, M., Padovani, L., Zavattaro, G. (eds.) SFM 2009. LNCS, vol. 5569, pp. 42–88. Springer, Heidelberg (2009)

Goal-Driven Composition of Business Process Models

Benjamin Nagel, Christian Gerth, and Gregor Engels

s-lab - Software Quality Lab
University of Paderborn
Zukunftsmeile 1
33102 Paderborn, Germany
{bnagel,gerth,engels}@s-lab.upb.de

Abstract. Goal-driven requirements engineering is a well-known approach for the systematic elicitation and specification of strategic business goals in early phases of software engineering processes. From these goals concrete operations can be derived that are composed in terms of a business process model. Lacking consistency between goal models and derived business processes especially with respect to the dependencies between goals can result in an implementation that is not in line with the actual business objectives. Hence, constraints indicated from these dependencies need to be considered in the derivation of business process models. In previous work, we introduced the extended goal modeling language Kaos4SOA that provides comprehensive modeling capabilities for temporal and logical dependencies among goals. Further, we presented an approach to validate the consistency between goal models and business process models regarding these dependencies. Extending the previous work, this paper presents a constructive approach for the derivation of consistent business processes from goal models. We introduce an algorithm that calculates logically encapsulated business process fragments from a given goal model and describe how these fragments can be composed to a business process model that fulfills the given temporal constraints.

Keywords: Requirements engineering, goal models, business process models, business process composition.

1 Introduction

Goal-driven requirements engineering has emerged as a paradigm for the elicitation and specification of requirements in an early phase of the software lifecycle [9,19]. Goal models support the systematic definition of objectives in terms of goals that are structured hierarchically in a goal tree. In the domain of service-oriented enterprise applications these goal models are usually used to capture business goals that need to be achieved. By the iterative refinement of these goals, concrete operations are identified, that need to be performed to achieve

A.R. Lomuscio et al. (Eds.): ICSOC 2013 Workshops, LNCS 8377, pp. 16–27, 2014.
© Springer International Publishing Switzerland 2014

the defined goals [1,20]. These operations are used as input for the definition of business processes composing these operations to a sequence of activities.

Recent research addresses the relations between goal models and business process models by different approaches that explicitly consider the links and relationships between elements in goal models and business process models [6,8]. The explicit consideration of these links ensures completeness and traceability among both models.

However, the initial composition of operations to business processes is still an open challenge. The identified operations cannot be composed in an arbitrary way, since the different types of relationships between goals (AND-, OR-decompositions) need to be considered. In addition, domain-specific knowledge of stakeholders about dependencies between goal, e.g. the order in which goals need to be achieved, have to be considered as well.

In previous work we contributed two extensions addressing this topic. In [14] we presented an extension of KAOS goal models, termed Kaos4SOA. This approach enables the specification of temporal and logical dependencies among goals. Hereby, we enable the elicitation and modeling of the stakeholders' knowledge about dependencies among goals that need to be considered in the derivation of business processes. Further, we presented a consistency validation approach in [13]. We demonstrated the generation of formalized business process quality constraints from these goal dependencies and showed how a derived business process model can be validated against these constraints.

Extending the previous work, we introduce a constructive approach for the systematic derivation of consistent business process models from Kaos4SOA goal models. To solve the composition problem in a sufficient way we state the following requirements to our approach. First, it can not be guaranteed that all operations are constrained in a way, that they can be composed unambiguously, i.e. there is no unique valid business process model that achieves the goals and fulfills the defined quality constraints. Second, the usage of model-checking provides a high degree of automation, but the computational complexity often raises performance issues especially for large business process models with a high number of constraints to be validated. To enable an efficient usage of model-checking that guides the process designers, the number of process elements and constraints that are validated need to be reduced.

Addressing these requirements, we present a goal-driven approach that enables the systematic derivation of consistent business process models from goal models. By analyzing the logical decompositions through the goal model, business process fragments are calculated encapsulating a set of dependent operations. Applying a set of business process patterns, the operations in each fragment are composed considering the dependencies among them. Dependencies between these fragments are calculated and finally, the fragments are composed to a business process model according to the temporal dependencies by using model-checking techniques.

By realizing the presented solution our approach makes the following contributions:

1. A method for the automatic identification and clustering of business process fragments from a given goal model.
2. A pattern-based approach for the composition of operations in fragments.
3. An model-checking approach for the composition of business process models based on fragments, which are significantly smaller than the business process itself.

The remainder of the paper is structured as follows. In Section 2 we introduce the foundations for our work. Our approach for the goal-driven composition of business processes is presented in Section 3. Related work is discussed in Section 4 and finally Section 5 concludes this paper.

2 Foundations

2.1 Goal Models

Recent research in goal-driven requirements engineering brought up several approaches for the elicitation and specification of goal models. For the expression of these goal models, different notations, like KAOS [5], Tropos [4] and i* [21] have been developed, that provide languages for the definition of goals and relationships among them. Due to its expressiveness and understandability KAOS has been adopted by several approaches [3,8] to specify goal models in the domain of service-oriented systems.

To illustrate the modeling capabilities of KAOS, an example is depicted in Figure 1 that defines a simplified goal model from the scenario introduced in [10]. *Fulfill book order* is the overall root goal that is decomposed to four subgoals. The AND-decomposition expresses that all subgoals need to be achieved in order to achieve the higher-level goal. These subgoals can be further decomposed as exemplary shown for the goal *Payment received*. This goal is OR-decomposed to the subsubgoals *Payment via credit card* and *Payment via money order*, which means that the payment can be received by either credit card or money order.

As illustrated by the ellipses, each leaf goal is operationalized to one or more operations. For example the goal *Book delivered* is achieved by performing the operations *Deliver to courier* and *Courier delivers to customer*. That means all operations assigned to a leaf goal need to be performed in order to achieve it sufficiently.

In previous work we extended KAOS by a concept for expressing temporal relationships between goals and a more precise definition of logical decompositions. To avoid an increasing complexity of the goal models, the temporal dependencies are expressed by goal annotations. The dependency predecessor/successor between two goals G_1 and G_2 expresses that a goal needs to be achieved before or after another goal. Temporal dependencies can only be defined between goals that are AND-decomposed through the whole hierarchy of the goal model, because it is not feasible to define a mandatory temporal dependency among alternative goals in an OR-decomposition.

An example of an order dependency for the goal model depicted in Figure 1 is the dependency between goal *Books delivered* and *Books available* that states

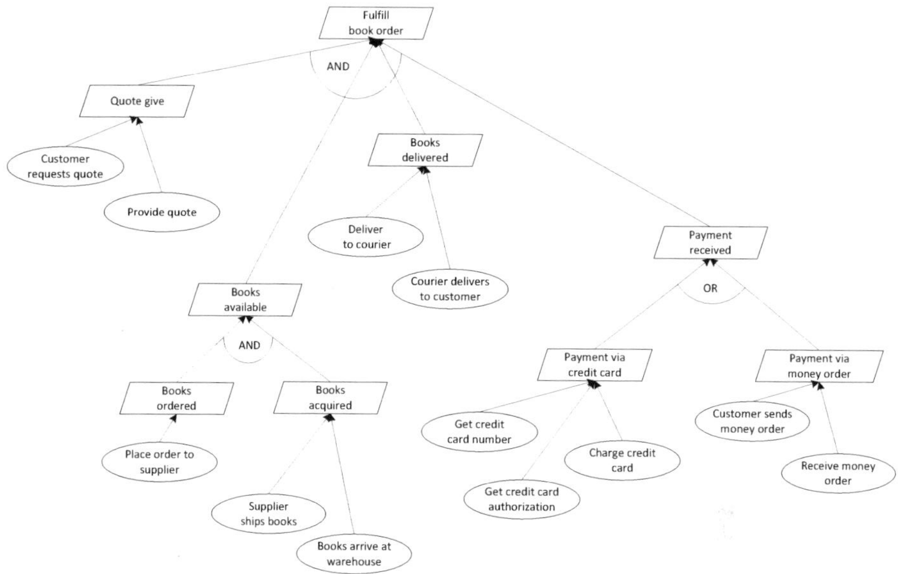

Fig. 1. Exemplary KAOS Goal Model

that the books cannot be delivered until they are available. To express this dependency the goal *Books delivered* is annotated with `Order.Predecessor` *Books available.* A temporal succeeding dependency can be specified between the goals *Payment received* and *Books delivered.* To make sure that the books are delivered after the payment has been received the following annotation can be used. The strict order dependency is expressed with the annotation `Order.Successor` *Books delivered.*

To enable a more precise specification of the decomposition relations between goals we introduced the XOR-decomposition for the explicit distinction of dependencies from the inclusive-OR provided by the KAOS notation. Applied to our running example the OR-decomposition of goal *Payment received* is not precise enough, since the OR-decomposition between subgoals *Payment via credit card* and *Payment via money order* should be exclusive as the customer will pay either by credit card or money order and not both. The updated decomposition with the corresponding conditions is depicted in Figure 2. Our extension also facilitates the definition of conditions for inclusive-OR decompositions.

2.2 Business Process Modeling

Business process models provide visual representations for business processes by describing sequences of activities and gateways connected by edges, defining the order in which the activities are performed. These models enable a common understanding, the analysis of business processes, and also define the required composition of services. To precisely specify business process models in an

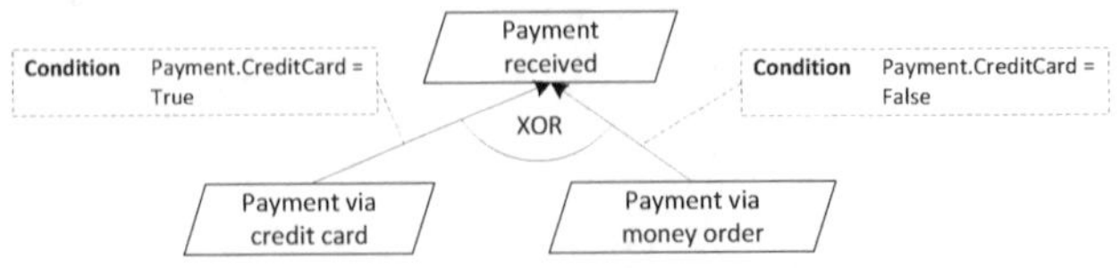

Fig. 2. Exemplary Definition of XOR-decomposition

understandable way, existing process modeling languages like BPMN [16] or UML activity diagrams [15] can be used.

In our approach, we leverage the generic business process modeling language introduced in [7]. Business process models defined in this language can be translated to BPMN. Hence, the usage of this language does not reduce the applicability of our approach. Compared to existing modeling languages this notation supports the explicit definition of business process fragments. A business process fragment encloses a set of business process model elements. These fragments are single-entry-single-exit fragments, that means they have a unique single entry node and a unique one exit node.

3 Approach

To enable the derivation of business process models from goal models, we introduce the goal-driven approach illustrated in Figure 3. As input for our approach we use a given goal model following the Kaos4SOA notation and a set of CTL constraints. These constraints are formal representations of the temporal and logical dependencies that are identified and defined by the approach presented in [13]. By an iterative refinement the used CTL constraints are expressed on the level of operations, i.e. they express constraints between operations.

In the first step, business process fragments which cluster logically related operations are identifed from the goal model. The operations in each fragment are composed using a set of business process patterns according to their logical dependencies in the goal model. By using the given CTL constraint, temporal dependencies between fragments are calculated based on the clustered operations. Using these constraints the fragments are composed to a valid business process model. The three steps of our approach are explained in the following.

3.1 Clustering of Business Process Fragments

The first step of our approach calculates business process fragments from a given goal model. To that extent, we identify operations that can be clustered in fragments. The operations in the fragments can be composed by applying a set of defined business process patterns based on their logical relationships. For this purpose, all decomposition links through the goal model need to be considered for each operation. Therefore we provide a top-down approach starting from the root goal that considers the complete hierarchy of decomposition links.

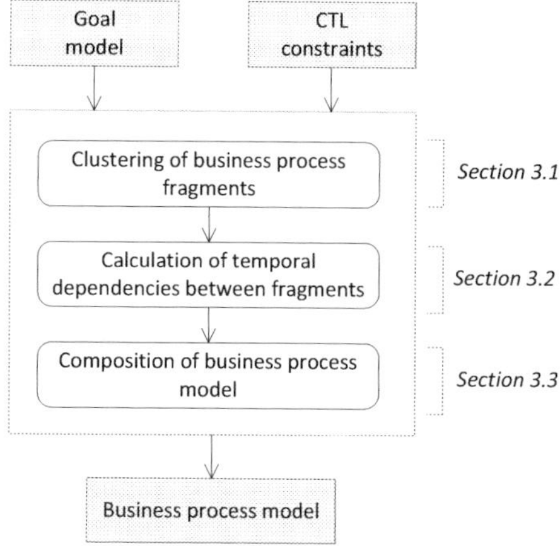

Fig. 3. Conceptual Overview of the proposed Approach

The clustering algorithm is specified in Algorithm 1 and explained in the following. Starting from the root goal, the first fragment is created representing the overall business process that is composed. Then, for each child-goal the algorithm is executed recursively. For each child, that is not a leaf-goal, the further processing depends on the type of decomposition that the goal is part of.

Following the KAOS semantics all goals and it's assigned operations are considered in the business process composition, but of course some goals may be optional, e.g. in an OR-decision. Hence, an AND-decomposition does not intend an additional logical dependency despite the fact that all goals need to be considered. That means, we are able to create logically independent fragments for each goal in an AND-decomposition. The composition of the different fragments with respect to the temporal dependencies among them is part of the following steps.

In our approach the goals are used as temporary elements in the business process model that are refined to subgoals and finally replaced by the operations fulfilling these goals. To compose the goals and operations according to their logical relations, we leverage the business process patterns proposed in [18]. An overview of the patterns used in our algorithm is given in Figure 4. Goals in an OR-decomposition are composed by applying an inclusive-OR gateway (P3). In the case of an conditional OR-decomposition the defined conditions are added to the OR-gateway and pattern P4 is applied. The goals in an XOR-decomposition are composed by an exclusive OR gateway using pattern P5.

Algorithm 1. Cluster Business Process Fragments

```
function CLUSTERFRAGMENTS(Goal goal, Fragment frag)
    if goal.isRootGoal() then
        processModel = createProcessModel(goal.name)
        for all childGoal in goal.getChildGoals() do
            CLUSTERFRAGMENTS(childGoal, processModel)
    else if goal.isLeafGoal() then
        for all operation in goal.getOperations() do
            newFrag.addElement(operation)
            if goal.getOperations().count() ≥ 2 then
                if operation canBeParallelizedWithOperationIn(newFrag) then
                    composition = applyProcessPattern(P2)
                else
                    composition = applyProcessPattern(P1)
                replace(goal, composition)
            else
                replace(goal,operation)
    else
        if goal.isPartOfORDecomposition then
            applyProcessFragment(P3)
        else if goal.isPartOfCondORDecomposition then
            applyProcessFragment(P4)
        else if goal.isPartOfXORDecomposition then
            applyProcessPattern(P5)
        else                                            ▷ AND-decomposition
            newFrag = createFragment(goal.name)
            frag.addElement(newFrag)
        for all childGoal in goal.childGoals do
            CLUSTERFRAGMENTS(childGoal, newFrag)
```

Following the algorithm each goal in the model is refined until a leaf goal is reached. Finally, each goal is replaced by its operations. If a goal is operationalized by exactly one operation, it is replaced by it. More than one operation means that all operations need to be performed to achieve the stated goal. In this case it is checked if the execution of the operations can be parallized. Depending on that, the pattern P2 (parallel execution possible) or P1 (no parallel execution possible) is applied to compose the operations. The order in which the operations need to be performed in a sequence (P1) is decided manually by the business process designer.

An exemplary execution of the algorithm for an excerpt of the running example is shown in Figure 5, which uses the running example introduced in Section 2.1 with the XOR decomposition depicted in Figure 2. Following the decomposition links in the goal model, a new fragment *Payment received* is created and added to the process *Fulfill book order*. The two subgoals are added to the fragment by applying pattern P5, adding an exclusive OR. The temporary goal construct is then replaced by its operations. In this example the goal *Payment*

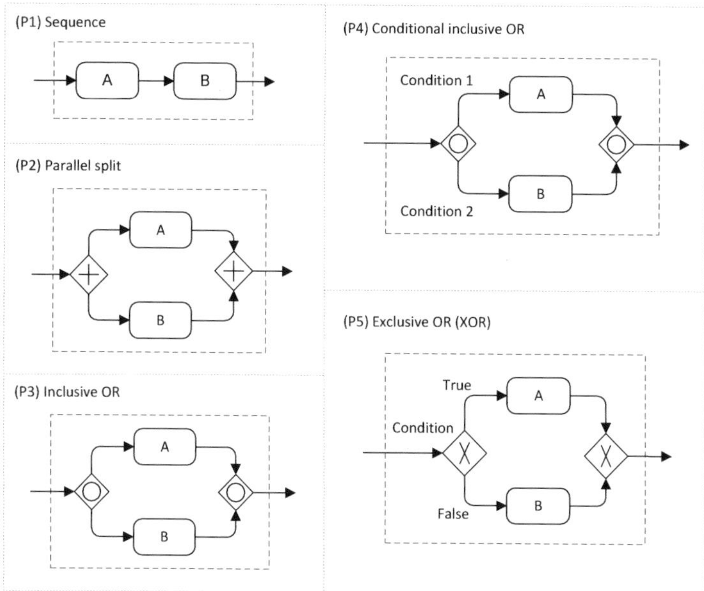

Fig. 4. Business Process Patterns (based on [18])

via credit card is replaced by three operations composed as a sequence (pattern P1).

The result of the presented algorithm is a frame for a business process model that encapsulates all required operations clustered in business process fragments. To complete the business process model, the fragments need to be composed. For this purpose, we first calculate temporal dependencies between these fragments (Section 3.2) and provide a composition approach based on model-checking (Section 3.3).

3.2 Calculation of Temporal Dependencies between Fragments

To enable the composition of the clustered fragments temporal dependencies between operations contained in the fragments need to be considered. As discussed in Section 2.1 temporal dependencies can only be defined between goals in AND-decompositions. Following Algorithm 1 the goals in AND-decompositions are encapsulated in different fragment, which means that temporal dependencies are always stated between operations in different business process fragments.

Algorithm 2 provides a precise definition of the proposed calculation approach. The algorithm iterates through all stated temporal constraints. Each constraint is defined by expressing temporal relations between two or more operations. To derive constraints for fragments, each operation in the constraint is replaced by the business process fragment it is assigned to.

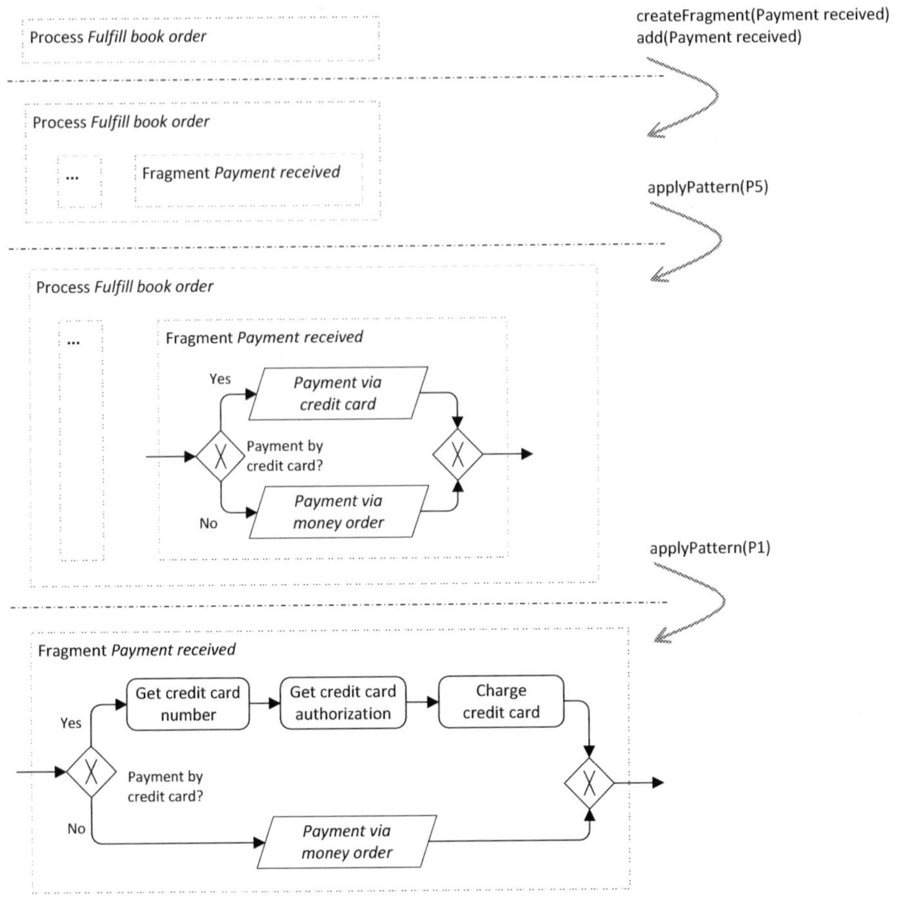

Fig. 5. Exemplary Execution of Composition Algorithm

Algorithm 2. Calculate Temporal Dependencies between Fragments

function CALCULATEFRAGDEPENDENCIES(TempConstraints *tempConstraints*)
  for all *tempConstraint* in *tempConstraints* **do**
    operations = *tempConstraint*.getElements()
    for all *operation* in *operations* **do**
      tempConstraint.replace*operation*, *operation*.getFragment()

As a result, the algorithm provides a set of CTL constraints that define temporal dependencies among the clustered business process fragments. For example, the temporal succeeding dependency between two fragments F_1 and F_2 is expressed in CTL as follows: $AG(F_1 \rightarrow AF(F_2))$. In the next step, the identified fragments and the dependencies among them are used to compose a valid business process model that fulfills the given constraints.

3.3 Composition of Business Process Model

Depending on the specification in the goal model, the number of constraints itself as well as the number of constrained fragments can vary. That means, not all business process fragments do have temporal relations with other fragments. As a consequence, in some cases only parts of the business process model can be composed automatically based on the given constraints. For all unconstrained fragments our approach favors the manual composition rather than automatically choose an arbitrary position.

Therefore, the composition of the business process model in our approach comprises two steps. In the first step, a valid composition of the constrained business fragments is calculated automatically. Second, the unconstrained fragment are integrated manually into the business process model.

For the constructive composition of a business process based on a set of constraints the possible combinations need to be validated. Details for the definition of possible compositions and their verification can be found, e.g. in [17]. The advantage of our approach is that not all combinations of all available operations need to be considered. By using the clustered business process fragments, the number of elements that need to composed and as consequence the number of combinations that need to be verified can be reduced significantly.

After a valid composition has been identified, the unconstrained fragments need to integrated into the business process model as well. We consider this a completely manual step based on the domain knowledge of the business analyst.

4 Related Work

The derivation of operationalized requirements and architectural models has been addressed by recent research [12,20] which does not specificly address the composition of business process models. In [22] a pattern-based approach is presented that supports the derivation of component diagrams from goal models. While this work focuses on structural aspects the derivation of business process models is not considered in terms of a concrete algorithm for the calculation of a process composition.

For the domain of adaptive, service-oriented system the work in [2] introduces an approach for the automated service composition by matching pre- and postconditions of operations from goal models. This approach requires an exact matching of these conditions to provide a complete composition.

In [11] an approach for the derivation of business process models from goal models is proposed. By presenting a defined procedure this work provides methodical guidance for the identification of services and their compositions, but does not provide any kind of automated composition capabilities. Based on a qualitative preference analysis, the framework presented in [17] automatically calculates service compositions. Compared to our approach this framework does not consider temporal constraints for the composition and does not address the problem of checking constraints for evolving business process models. In contrast, our approach explicitly considers the efficient validation against constraints. The improvement of the efficiency is achieved by applying the concept of business process fragments. By defining the constraints on the level of these fragments, the number of required validations can be reduced significantly.

5 Conclusion and Future Work

In this paper, we presented an approach for the guided composition of business process models in a goal-driven way. We proposed an algorithm that identifies and clusters related operations to business process fragments and we describe how these fragments can be composed to a business process model by using model-checking techniques. In summary, we provide an approach that provides a high degree of automation but also considers involvement of domain experts and business analysts during the composition.

As future work, we aim for a tool implementation of the presented approach. Based on the existing workbench presented in [13,14] the composition algorithm will be implemented by integrating a model checker (e.g. NuSMV[1]). Using this tool support we will perform comprehensive case studies to evaluate the efficiency and applicability of our approach. A main aspect in the evaluation will be the investigation of the actual improvement of the model-checking scalability by using the business fragments.

References

1. Alrajeh, D., Kramer, J., Russo, A., Uchitel, S.: Learning operational requirements from goal models. In: Proc. of the 31st Int. Conf. on Software Engineering, ICSE 2009, pp. 265–275. IEEE Computer Society (2009)
2. Baresi, L., Pasquale, L.: Adaptive Goals for Self-Adaptive Service Compositions. In: 2010 IEEE International Conference on Web Services (ICWS), pp. 353–360. IEEE (2010)
3. Baresi, L., Pasquale, L.: Adaptation Goals for Adaptive Service-oriented Architectures. In: Relating Software Requirements and Architecture, pp. 161–181. Springer, Heidelberg (2011)
4. Bresciani, P., Giorgini, P., Giunchiglia, F., Mylopoulos, J., Perini, A.: TROPOS: An agent-oriented software development methodology. Autonomous Agents and Multi-Agent Systems (2004)
5. Dardenne, A., Fickas, S., van Lamsweerde, A.: Goal-directed concept acquisition in requirements elicitation. In: Proceedings of the 6th International Workshop on Software Specification and Design, IWSSD 1991, pp. 14–21. IEEE Computer Society Press (1991)
6. Dubois, E., Petit, M., Yu, E.: From Early to Late Formal Requirements: A Process-Control Case Study. In: Proc. of the 9th Int. Workshop on Software Specification and Design, p. 34. IEEE Computer Society (1998)
7. Gerth, C., Küster, J.M., Engels, G.: Language-Independent Change Management of Process Models. In: Schürr, A., Selic, B. (eds.) MODELS 2009. LNCS, vol. 5795, pp. 152–166. Springer, Heidelberg (2009)

[1] `http://nusmv.fbk.eu/`

8. Koliadis, G., Ghose, A.: Relating Business Process Models to Goal-Oriented Requirements Models in KAOS. In: Hoffmann, A., Kang, B.-H., Richards, D., Tsumoto, S. (eds.) PKAW 2006. LNCS (LNAI), vol. 4303, pp. 25–39. Springer, Heidelberg (2006)
9. Lapouchnian, A.: Goal-Oriented Requirements Engineering: An Overview of the Current Research. Requirements Engineering 8(3), 32 (2005)
10. Liaskos, S., McIlraith, S., Sohrabi, S., Mylopoulos, J.: Integrating preferences into goal models for requirements engineering. In: 2010 18th IEEE International Requirements Engineering Conference (RE), pp. 135–144 (2010)
11. Lo, A., Yu, E.: From Business Models to Service-Oriented Design: A Reference Catalog Approach. In: Parent, C., Schewe, K.-D., Storey, V.C., Thalheim, B. (eds.) ER 2007. LNCS, vol. 4801, pp. 87–101. Springer, Heidelberg (2007)
12. Martínez, A., Pastor, Ó., Mylopoulos, J., Giorgini, P.: From Early to Late Requirements: A Goal-Based Approach. In: Kolp, M., Henderson-Sellers, B., Mouratidis, H., Garcia, A., Ghose, A.K., Bresciani, P. (eds.) AOIS 2006. LNCS (LNAI), vol. 4898, pp. 123–142. Springer, Heidelberg (2008)
13. Nagel, B., Gerth, C., Post, J., Engels, G.: Ensuring Consistency among Business Goals and Business Process Models. In: Proceedings of 16th IEEE International Enterprise Distributed Object Computing Conference (EDOC), pp. 17–26 (2013)
14. Nagel, B., Gerth, C., Post, J., Engels, G.: Kaos4SOA - Extending KAOS Models with Temporal and Logical Dependencies. In: Proceedings of the CAiSE 2013 Forum at the 25th International Conference on Advanced Information Systems Engineering (CAiSE), pp. 9–16 (2013)
15. OMG. OMG Unified Modeling Language (OMG UML) Superstructure (2010)
16. OMG. Business Process Model and Notation (BPMN) (2011)
17. Oster, Z.J., Ali, S.A., Santhanam, G.R., Basu, S., Roop, P.S.: A service composition framework based on goal-oriented requirements engineering, model checking, and qualitative preference analysis. In: Liu, C., Ludwig, H., Toumani, F., Yu, Q. (eds.) ICSOC 2012. LNCS, vol. 7636, pp. 283–297. Springer, Heidelberg (2012)
18. Russell, N., Hofstede, A.H.M.T., Mulyar, N.: Workflow ControlFlow patterns: A revised view. Technical report (2006)
19. van Lamsweerde, A.: Goal-oriented requirements engineering: a guided tour. In: Proceedings of the Fifth IEEE International Symposium on Requirements Engineering, pp. 249–262 (2001)
20. van Lamsweerde, A.: From System Goals to Software Architecture. In: Bernardo, M., Inverardi, P. (eds.) SFM 2003. LNCS, vol. 2804, pp. 25–43. Springer, Heidelberg (2003)
21. Yu, E.S.-K.: Towards Modeling and Reasoning Support for Early-Phase Requirements Engineering. In: Proc. of the 3rd IEEE Int. Symposium on Requirements Engineering, pp. 226–235. IEEE Computer Society (1997)
22. Yu, Y., Lapouchnian, A., Liaskos, S., Mylopoulos, J., Leite, J.: From Goals to High-Variability Software Design. In: Foundations of Intelligent Systems, pp. 1–16 (2008)

Integrating Service Release Management with Service Solution Design

Heiko Ludwig*, Juan Cappi, Valeria Becker, Bairbre Stewart, and Susan Meade

IBM Almaden Research Center and IBM Global Technology Services
650 Harry Road, San Jose, CA 95120, USA
{hludwig,jmcappi,beckerv}@us.ibm.com
http://www.almaden.ibm.com/

Abstract. Web-delivered services such as Web or Cloud services are often made available to users in a fast cadence of releases, taking advantage of the single deployment environment of a centrally controlled service. This enables organizations to bring service enhancements to customers in a timely way and respond quickly to market demands. Organizations use multiple Web-delivered services by one or multiple vendors to compose complex solutions to their business problems in conjunction with standard applications and custom implementation and delivery services. Designing these complex solutions often takes considerable time and multiple new releases of a service and a changed service roadmap may have influence on a customer's solution design. Existing IT service management and software development best practices do not consider the relationship between service release management and service design sufficiently to address frequent releases and changes to a service roadmap. This paper discusses the relationship from both the point of view of the service provider and the service customer and proposes an approach to manage those interdependencies between service design and release management.

Keywords: Release management, service management, cloud services, web services, best practices, service solution design.

1 Introduction

Being based on a virtualization layer and being accessed online, Web and Cloud services can be and typically are continuously improved with new features by their providers, often employing an "agile" method and following the paradigm of *continuous delivery* [1]. This enables service providers to bring service enhancements to customers in a timely way and respond quickly to market demands. Facebook, for example, upgrades its service multiple times per month. This holds for Web services and all abstraction levels of a Cloud, from infrastructure to software. While this high-frequency approach to release management enables clients

* Thanks to Tim Kensing and John Hallowell of IBM Global Technology Services for their guidance.

A.R. Lomuscio et al. (Eds.): ICSOC 2013 Workshops, LNCS 8377, pp. 28–39, 2014.
© Springer International Publishing Switzerland 2014

to take advantage of improvements immediately it requires a deployment process different from the deployment to a traditional, more static service delivery environment.

In typical traditional service management settings this has not been an issue. In an in-house service management situation, adding new functionality would have been part of a global change process in which all stakeholders would have been consulted. This would include ongoing solution development using these services, which we refer to in this paper as *solutioning*. Solutioning refers to the process of designing a service in all its aspects, including its use of services, planning the purchasing of hardware and software as well as planning software development and deployment. Best practices from multiple bodies have been defined to address this issue such as the IT Infrastructure Library volume on Service Transition (ITIL) [2] or the CobiT process "Manage Changes" [3]. Service users can weigh in on service priorities and the details of features needed or the evolution of existing features. Release management and change management are part of service transition in the ITIL sense, where a number of changes being associate with a release.

Web or Cloud services to be consumed by outsiders mostly consider release management from a go-to-market and from an operational perspective. Software product (line) management and - more recently and derived from it - service product management identify and organize features of services and group them into releases according to technical synergy and market demand [4]. Services are launched to the market or tested beforehand with key customers, potentially adjusting service features based on feedback. Several approaches exist to manage changes to existing services in a way that includes current users, e.g. [5] and, more generally [6]. However, service management best practices and the service product management discipline do not offer adequate guidance how to relate a complex service solution design process - or a set of them - defining a comprehensive service implementation project with fast-paced release processes.

Different approaches such as [7] have been proposed to reconcile an agile development approach with software product management. This generally entails extending SCRUM principles to the software product process but does not address how to provide guidance to service designers planning to use the process nor how to use the planned service solution designs as inputs to the product design.

The objective of this paper is to discuss the interdependencies of solutioning and service release processes, propose a mechanism to manage these interdependencies, and outline how both service provider and a service client defining a solution benefits from this approach. Along these lines the paper is organized as follows: In the next section we discuss issue of integrating solutioning and release management. Subsequently, we provide a model of the interdependent artifacts and sketch how the interdependent processes can be managed. This is followed by a description of an example implementation. Finally, we conclude discussing the benefits for stakeholders.

2 Issues Integrating Service Solution Design with Release Management

As discussed in the introduction of this paper, the solutioning or service design process traditionally considers designing higher-level services or applications as a service composition or a service implementation. This can be based on one or more services being provided by potentially different service providers. Using services from differing parties has become quite common practice, for example, Web or mobile applications integrating login services, payment services or Cloud services, performing their own capacity management. The advent of fast release cycles, in part driven by agile development approaches or just the advantage to build on a single deployment platform, brought with it the need to deal with frequent releases and potential changes of release plans.

Core to any integration of the solutioning and release management processes is the notion of the *roadmap* of future releases. Releases have a release date associated with them and a set of *features*, which are available from the time of the release date on. New roadmaps can be published by a service provider, changing feature assignments to releases, release dates and introducing new features and releases.

Dealing with a roadmap in a fast-paced environment raises issues both from a perspective of the solutioning process as well as from the release management perspective: How to put together a *good* roadmap for the overall benefit of the service provider? How to design the best solution given the roadmaps for a given set of services available?

2.1 Complex Solution Design in a Context of Fast-Evolving Services

Complex solutioning is usually conducted in a team that plans a technical implementation - the solution - for a problem and also considers how it can be delivered from a timing and business perspective. It is conducted in the form of a structured process that adds different technical, managerial, and business specialists to the team as needed. The deliverables of the solutioning process typically include:

- a list of resources to be used, including Web-delivered services, software and hardware products, as well as implementation labor;
- a solution design that outlines how all the different services and products will deliver the final result;
- a project plan that identifies which resources are needed at which point in time;
- a business case justifying the investment.

Solution design decisions related to service usage depend on the set of features the services will provide. For example, if a solutioning team is considering using an infrastructure-as-a-service Cloud service to run its application it might need to also use a backup service. If the Cloud service provides an image backup feature the solution may take this into consideration in their solution design. If the Cloud service does not provide this feature, the solution might plan for a separate backup service. The Cloud service's roadmap may plan for image-level backup in the future. If the project plan foresees this feature at the time of need this service can be used. Else another backup service may be used in the interim. A planned feature may justify using a more expensive service - in our case for the Cloud service - if the future feature availability makes the additional backup service obsolete. As this example shows, the understanding of a service's roadmap is important for the solutioning process using fast-evolving services.

Solutioning using a set of services that are rapidly adding features faces different challenges depending on the context in which the solutioning is performed. The way solutioning and release management integrate depends on who the service roadmap – or its parts – is known to.

If the solutioning team is part of the same organization than the service provider the roadmap can be fully visible to the solutioning team. While frequent roadmap changes might be disruptive to the solutioning processes, this is acceptable since no external client commitment has been made to a client. A provider-side solutioning process offers more flexibility to the service release management. However, provider-side solutioning is often not possible or desirable from a client perspective wanting to build solutions based on multiple providers' services.

If the solutioning team in not in the provider organization it is either a user organization or a 3rd party designing a solution for the commissioning organization. In this scenario the solutioning team wants to understand the roadmaps of all services under consideration. Disruptive changes to the roadmap such as moving out feature release dates or removal of features from the roadmap altogether are undesirable and reflect negatively on the service provider. A service provider has to trade off announcing its features ahead of time, attracting client, with the potential need of withdrawing a feature or moving it out if unforeseen obstacles to feature implementation occur. This may include underestimated technical effort, service capacity problems or changes in product strategy.

Once a solution has been created containing Web-delivered services the client organization wants to obtain a commitment regarding the roadmap to be able to implement its project plan. If a roadmap of a service changes when solution implementation started a change process with adequate mitigation to the changes in feature availability has to performed. Both, service provider and client will want to avoid such a roadmap change.

2.2 Release Management with Roadmaps

While a service user benefits from having service roadmap information available early and reliably a service provider benefits from understanding which clients plan to use features of its service, maybe also for which purpose. Specific client plans to use features enables much more accurate analysis about feature demand than traditional methods of elicitation such as collecting requirements from existing clients, focus groups and other marketing instruments. This enables a service provider to prioritize features and design the roadmap correspondingly. If the number of clients is sufficient a provider's release management can perform further analysis of feature demand such as feature correlation etc., leading to better input for release planning.

As mentioned in the previous section, the benefit of collecting information of planned feature use must be traded off with the risk of disappointing potential clients from a service provider release management's point of view. The further back planned releases are the more susceptible their features are to delays or changes. Also, release management may learn that certain features it published may not be very popular after all and move them back or remove them from the roadmap. This might cause opposition from the few customers that planned using them and needs to be mitigated. In any case, the service provider's release management can analyze impact of changes to a roadmap based on solutioning projects underway and those already committed to a customer.

3 Approach to Manage Solution and Feature Interdependencies

Coordinating the interdependence between solutioning and release management relies on a shared model of roadmaps, solutions and their relationships. Based on this shared model stakeholders in the service can coordinate how to best fit solutions onto services and how to best shape the service roadmap given feature demand by solutions.

3.1 Model of Dependencies

The notion of a roadmap in the proposed approach is taken from the service and software management disciplines: Features are associated with releases. Releases have a release date. A roadmap is a set of releases published as a version at a specific time. The structure is represented as a graph whose leaf nodes are features as illustrated in figure 1.

The example shows a roadmap V1 for a Cloud service with three planned releases, each labeled with the calendar week of the planned release. Each release has two or three features associated with it.

New versions can be made available by the service provider's Release Managers (RMs) when release plans change, resulting in a new version of the graph. Changes to roadmaps may contain changed release dates, moves of features from one release to another, addition and removal of features as well as feature merges, splits and changes to a feature's scope. Figure 2 illustrates possible roadmap changes.

In this example the new version of the roadmap includes multiple changes: Feature F3 has been moved from Release 1 to Release 2. Feature 5 has been removed from the roadmap. A new feature - F8, (CentOS support) - has been added to Release 3 and the release date of Release 3 has been moved from the 2nd week to the 4th week of 2014.

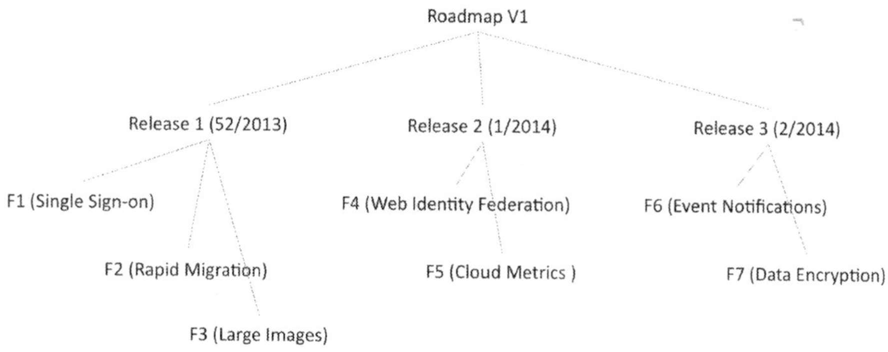

Fig. 1. Roadmap graph

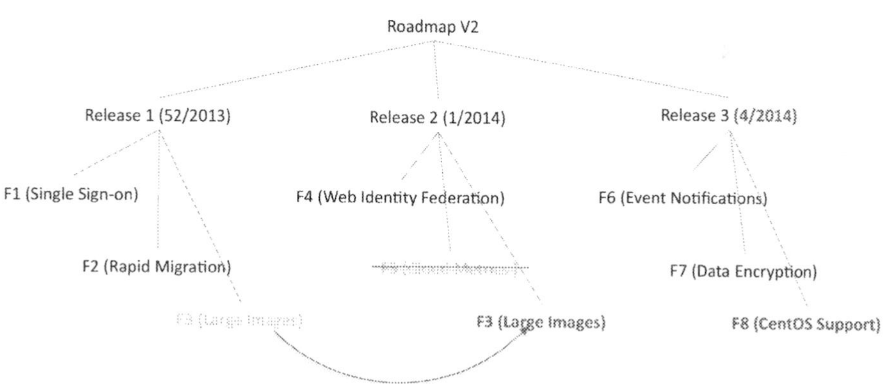

Fig. 2. Modified, new version of a roadmap graph

Interdependencies between features of a service roadmap and solutioning processes are represented in the dependency matrix of this service. The relationship of a solutioning process and a feature is a need and is associated with a specific need data when the project plan of the solution requires it to be available.

Figure 3 illustrates the dependency matrix of our example roadmap - the feature set of roadmap V1 and 4 assumed solutions. Each solution requires a different set of features for its specific solution, each at specific dates. Solutions in the examples are labeled with their state, planned or committed. The dependency matrix is updated each time a new roadmap version is published or a new solution is added.

In addition to feature need dates, solutioning teams may also provide more information about their solution for the purpose of analyzing better the impact of roadmap changes onto solutions affected. The set of attributes depends on the specific service domain but may include the number of users using the solution, the cost or revenue associated with it, metrics of the quantity of service

	Solution 1 (planned)	Solution 2 (committed)	Solution 3 (planned)	Solution 4 (committed)
F1 (Single Sign-on)	2/2014			
F2 (Rapid Migration)	2/2014			2/2014
F3 (Large Images)	3/2014	1/2014		
F4 (Web Identity Federation)				
F5 (Cloud Metrics)	45/2013		4/2014	49/2013
F6 (Event Notifications)				3/2014
F7 (Data Encryption)	49/2013	1/2014		49/2013

Fig. 3. Dependency matrix

consumption such as the number of VMs in a Cloud scenario and so forth. This enables to better assess the impact of roadmap changes in terms of those metrics meaningful to release management and solutioning teams.

A solution that works with multiple services - and hence multiple roadmaps - must consolidate these roadmaps for an overall point of view. Likewise, a service provider publishing roadmaps for different services individually also needs to consolidate the respective dependency matrices.

3.2 Managing Interdependencies

Managing interdependencies falls into 3 settings: The solutioning team self-manages its roadmap dependencies; the release management assess its roadmap impact; a coordination board comprising both solutioning and release management to make solution commitments and to resolves issues.

1. As solutioning teams add their solutions to the dependency matrix they can analyze themselves whether their project plan is feasible with their solution design they have chosen and the feature dependencies it entails. If changes occur to the roadmap they can choose to change their solution design to, say, take advent of a new feature or mitigate the postponement of another feature. This self-service approach entails small coordination overhead and self-enables solutioning teams.
2. Release managers can use information from the dependency matrix for their roadmap planning. Based on the time of need, features can be assigned to later releases if not much need has been articulated yet or moved to earlier ones if there is significant demand. Features can also be prioritized based on properties of the solution that plans to use them, e.g., the number of VMs or the associated revenue, as discussed above.

This roadmap-based approach brings a significant advantage to release management that a traditional, market research-based approach does not have; roadmaps can be based, in part, on actual planned or committed demand.

3. The Coordination Board is the collective of release management and other service delivery representatives as well as the solutioning teams. It is the body that commits to planned solutions and thereby moves them from panned to committed states. This typically entails a commitment to a client, e.g., a sale or statement of work.

   In some cases solutioning teams will disagree with roadmap decisions of release management that are to the disadvantage of their solutioning project. The solutioning process and release management have to reconcile their differences and find roadmap adjustments, short term solutions or alternate solution designs to address the needs of service users. In current practice this is a quite common occurrence and many service providers spend much time on board meetings if roadmaps are used, which is primarily the case for provider-internal solution teams. Managing a dependency matrix will enable a more fact-based discussion based on total feature demand by solutions.

By maintaining the dependency matrix along with roadmap and solution information significantly reduces the coordination effort between solutioning and release management based on this shared, available information.

4 Implementation

The proposed approach has been implemented for evaluation in current practice in the Cloud space. The system is a Web 2.0 application which is divided in several modules customized for the primary stakeholders release management, solutioning and coordination board, as shown in Figure 4.

The Roadmap Module provides functionality for release managers to record when a release plan changes, creating a new version of the roadmap. A new version will be in draft state until it is published. When the roadmap is in draft state, release managers are able to enter a new release by applying changes to the previous one, e.g., change release dates, move features from one release to another, as well as add and remove features from the roadmap. Once the changes are done the new version can be published and it will be available for solutioning teams.

The Customer Solution Module provides functionality for solutioning teams to create their projects using the features from the most recent roadmap available. Solutioning teams can specify solution attributes such as the client name, organization, geography, the VM capacity as well as the planned time of need of the features. The system allows solutioning teams to check the consistency of their project with the Cloud service roadmap, highlighting feature need dates prior to, or close to, availability time in red, green, yellow colors. After all properties and needs are included in the project, solution teams can send planned solutions to the Coordination Board for commitment.

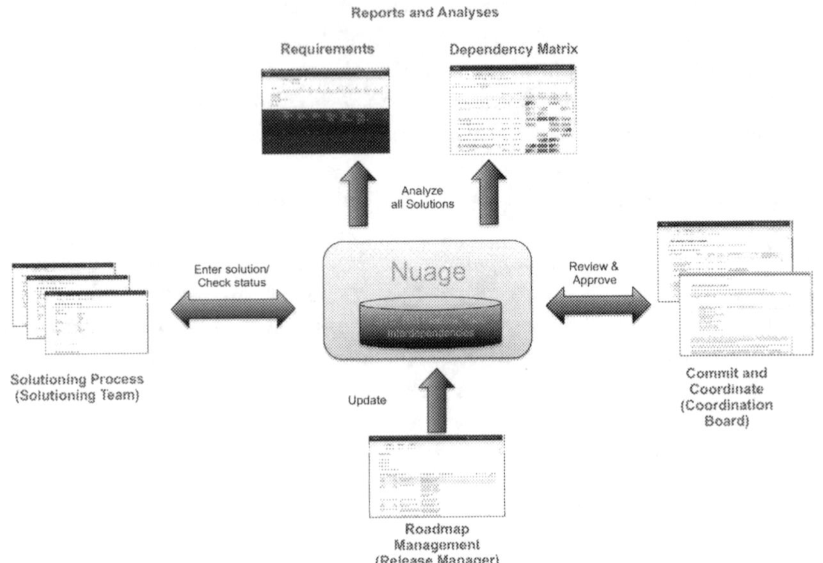

Fig. 4. High-level architecture and interactions

The Customer Solution Review Module provides functionality for the Board Review to analyze the requirements for each project. The system allows Board Review to check when the project was created, which version of the roadmap has been used, highlighting feature need dates prior to, or close to, availability time in red, green, yellow colors. The system helps the Board Review to create an assessment for solutioning teams for the final commitment decision or ask for additional information from the solution team lead.

The Reports and Analysis Module provides different reports for the Coordination board and Release Management, e.g. Requirements and Affected Solutions or a Summary of Commitments. The system uses the dependency matrix of features and solutioning projects to inform the status of deployment projects base on changes on the roadmap, see Figure 5.

As mentioned before, release managers can publish a new roadmap version changing feature assignments to releases, release dates and introducing new features and releases or taking features off the roadmap. It could affect solutions already approved by the Coordination Board. Summary of Commits helps to visualize graphically and in one single page the impact of roadmaps changes on customers commitments.

The Summary of Commits reports shows a view on the dependency matrix in the form of an impact matrix with all features on the left side and solutions on the top. The first column is the feature title, followed by release number and availability date. The rest of the columns are the clients with the actual state

Fig. 5. Screen capture of the dependency matrix implementation

and each cell shows the need date of the feature for the particular Customer and previous and actual state of the feature requirement. Full coloring means no impact with the most recent roadmap changes. The split color means the most recent roadmap change has impacted in the committed feature for the client, showing previous/new state from left to right. For example, a green cell represents a commitment for that feature and solution that has not been affected. A split cell green/red is a feature which has changed the availability date and now the customer will not have it by the date required. Grey feature text and light coloring means that this feature has ben removed.

The implementation is deploying at the time of writing. We collect data for future evaluation of the effectiveness of the approach.

5 Related Work and Discussion

This paper addresses the novel issue of interlinking the design of complex service solutions with a fast-paces service release process. Software product line management has addressed the issue of releasing new version of a software product [4]. Fast-paced release cycles lead to the adoption of agile approaches such as [7]. [8] describe a case study on the adoption of agile software product line management. While the latter approach envisions fast response to stakeholder requirements in an agile way, it does not address the issue of how to enable complex service solution design and use this type of information for roadmap prioritization.

The roadmap graph used in the approach proposed in this paper borrows from feature modeling, an established technique of product line management. Feature models represent the relationships between features of a software or service product and can be analyzed to give guidance product managers as well as those using the product [9]. The roadmap graph of this paper does not capture this semantics but assigns features releases and captures roadmap changes as graph transformations. While containing features as elements the edge semantics is different and it adds releases and changes to the graph model. [10] propose to reverse engineer feature models from feature use. This is related to our approach but we consider planned use and add the timing prospective to our roadmap model.

Coordinating different service management processes has been subject to the creation of best practices such as [2] and [3]. The issue of fast release cycles, cross-organizational use and the need to integrate with complex solution design processes are not covered by those standards. While [6] and [5] address the issue of fast pace and crossing organizational boundaries they do not address the integration with solutioning and do not consider the feature perspective of a planned change of service.

While different proposed approaches provide pieces to the puzzle the this paper proposes a reliable interlink between release management and service solution design processes.

6 Summary and Conclusion

While frequent improvements to a services platform like a Cloud or Web service provides a great opportunity for users to benefit from these improvements in a timely way the approach proposed in this paper enables users to take advantage of new features in a systematic and coordinated way. In addition, service release managers can take advantage of the additional information of how their cloud platform is planned to be used by their clients, enabling them to adjust to client demand and to provide new services based on specific client needs, not marketing projections. The core concepts on which our approach is based is the roadmap and the dependency matrix to solutioning projects, providing the foundation to coordinating the interrelationship between release management and solutioning processes.

Conceptually, the proposed approach complements related work in software and service product line management and in service management, bridging the gap between them in this new, fast-paced environment.

The paper describes work in progress. The feasibility of the approach has been shown in the implementation of the approach. Its effectiveness is currently being studied from service solution designers' and release managers' point of views.

References

1. Humble, J., Farley, D.: Continuous delivery: reliable software releases through build, test, and deployment automation. Pearson Education (2010)
2. Lacy, S., McFarlane, I.: Service Transitions, ITIL, Version 3 (2007)
3. IT Governance Institute: CobiT 4.1. (2007)
4. Pohl, K., Böckle, G., van der Linden, F.: Software Product Line Engineering. Springer (2005)

5. Wassermann, B., Ludwig, H., Laredo, J., Bhattacharya, K., Pasquale, L.: Distributed cross-domain change management. In: Proceedings of the International Conference on Web Services (2009)
6. Ludwig, H., Laredo, J., Bhattacharya, K., Pasquale, L., Wassermann, B.: REST-based management of loosely coupled services. In: Proceedings of the 18th International Conference on World Wide Web (2009)
7. Vlaanderen, K., Jansen, S., Brinkkemper, S., Jaspers, E.: The agile requirements refinery: Applying scrum principles to software product management. Information and Software Technology 53(1), 58–70 (2011)
8. Hanssen, G.K., Fægri, T.E.: Process fusion: An industrial case study on agile software product line engineering. Journal of Systems and Software 81(6), 843–854 (2008)
9. Benavides, D., Trinidad, P., Ruiz-Cortés, A.: Automated reasoning on feature models. In: Pastor, Ó., Falcão e Cunha, J. (eds.) CAiSE 2005. LNCS, vol. 3520, pp. 491–503. Springer, Heidelberg (2005)
10. She, S., Lotufo, R., Berger, T., Wasowski, A., Czarnecki, K.: Reverse engineering feature models. In: 2011 33rd International Conference on Software Engineering (ICSE), pp. 461–470. IEEE (2011)

Practical Compiler-Based User Support during the Development of Business Processes

Thomas M. Prinz and Wolfram Amme

Friedrich Schiller University Jena
07743 Jena, Germany
{Thomas.Prinz,Wolfram.Amme}@uni-jena.de

Abstract. An erroneous execution of business processes causes high costs and could damage the prestige of the providing company. Therefore, validation of the correctness of business processes is essential. In general, business processes are described with Petri nets semantics, even though this kind of description allows only algorithms with a worse processing time and bad failure information to this moment.

In this paper, we describe new compiler-based techniques that could be used instead of Petri net algorithms for the verification of business processes. Basic idea of our approach is, to start analyses on different points of workflow graphs and to find potential structural errors. These developed techniques improved other known approaches, as it guarantees a precise visualization and explanation of all determined structural errors, which substantially supports the development of business processes.

1 Introduction

Business processes, e.g., service orchestrations, can have two kinds of structural errors: *deadlocks* and *lack of synchronization* [1], whereas deadlocks are situations in which the execution within business processes blocks partly, and lack of synchronization are situations in which parts of business processes are executed twice unintentionally. The absence of deadlocks and lack of synchronization in business processes is called *soundness* in the literature [2,3], whereas we prefer to call it structural correctness like Sadiq and Orloswka [1], since soundness describes the overall correctness.

Current soundness checker tools are based on Petri nets, or on workflow graphs, which are similar to control flow graphs using explicit parallelism. Most Petri net-based techniques [4,5] use state space exploration to determine structural errors. This allows the determination of exactly one runtime error, which even could be unsolvable, since it could be caused by a previous error. Take the business process in BPMN notation of Fig. 1 as example. It is possible, that after the execution of the parallel diverging gateway $F1$ the parallel converging gateway $J1$ will be executed, however, the task $T1$ has still a control flow, since there is a classical lack of synchronization situation. If this control flow arrives at $J1$, then there is a deadlock situation. The state space exploration could find the deadlock situation firstly, however, bug-fixing this deadlock seems not to be the

A.R. Lomuscio et al. (Eds.): ICSOC 2013 Workshops, LNCS 8377, pp. 40–53, 2014.
© Springer International Publishing Switzerland 2014

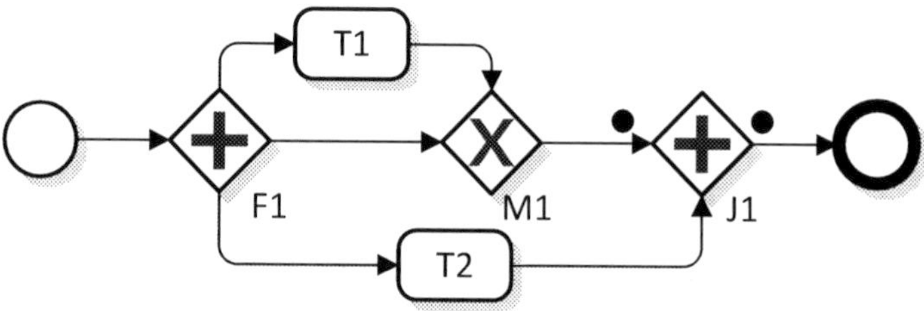

Fig. 1. A lack of synchronization causes a deadlock

best solution to get a correct business process. Therefore, such an information is useless in development tools. Furthermore, state space exploration can lead to an exponential processing time in the size of the Petri net in general. Summarized, they are rather unusable within development tools for business processes.

The best known technique is the SESE decomposition [6], which works on workflow graphs and decomposes the graph into subgraphs called *fragments*. For each fragment only a single error may be detected, and this error can be visualized by highlighting the corresponding fragment. In other words, the SESE decomposition cannot find all structural errors in a fragment. Furthermore, there are some complex fragments, which cannot be addressed by this approach.

Overall, there is no development support tool for business processes being fast, complete and informative. In this paper, we describe new compiler-based techniques, which work directly on workflow graphs and statically determine deadlocks and lack of synchronization, i.e., independent of previously executed workflow graph parts. Compared to other techniques, it guarantees a precise visualization and explanation of all structural errors, which considerabily assists the development of business processes and fulfilles most of the requirements.

This paper is structured as follows. In Section 2, we refresh the definitions of workflow graphs and structural correctness, followed by an informal description of our approach (Section 3). Section 4 describes the properties of structural errors, whereas Section 5 applying them for determination. The approach will be evaluated in Section 6 and compared to other techniques in Section 7. Eventually, Section 8 concludes the paper.

2 Preliminaries

Formally, a *workflow graph* is a directed graph $WFG = (N, E)$ such that N consists of activities $N_{activities}$, forks N_{forks}, joins N_{joins}, splits N_{splits}, merges N_{merges}, one *start*, and *end* node. The end node, each activity, split, and fork has exactly one incoming edge; whereas the start node, each activity, merge, and join has exactly one outgoing edge. Splits and forks have at least two outgoing edges, and merges and joins have at least two incoming edges. Furthermore, each node lies on a path from the start to the end node. A workflow graph is called *simple* if for each edge $e = (n_1, n_2) \in E$ the source n_1 or the target n_2 is an activity.

Figure 2 shows an example workflow graph. The start and end node are depicted as (thick) circles, and an activity is depicted as rectangle. Forks and joins are illustrated as thin rectangles, whereas splits and merges are depicted as (thick) diamonds.

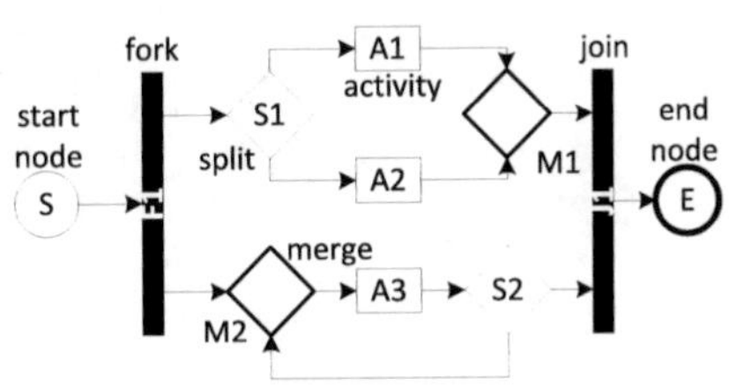

Fig. 2. A workflow graph

The semantics of workflow graphs used in this paper is similar to the semantics of control flow graphs. The execution of a workflow graph begins at the start node and follows the flow described by the directed graph. An activity, a split, a merge, a fork, and the end node can be executed when a control flow reaches an incoming edge of these nodes, whereas a join can only fire if all incoming edges are reached by a control flow. After executing a split, it decides *nondeterministically*, which outgoing edge will be followed by the control flow in workflow graphs without data aspects. After the execution of a fork, parallel control flows will be built for each outgoing edge.

Without loss of generality, we assume each workflow graph is *simple* for the remainder of this paper, since there is a fast transformation from common to simple workflow graphs, e.g., by placing a new activity on each edge. This allows a description of the incoming and outgoing edges of a node with the direct predecessor and direct successor nodes. We write $\bullet n$ to describe the set of direct predecessor nodes of n, i.e., $\forall n_p \in \bullet n : (n_p, n) \in E$. Furthermore, we write $n\bullet$ to describe the set of direct successor nodes of n, i.e., $\forall n_s \in n\bullet : (n, n_s) \in E$.

Paths will be used to describe control flows within workflow graphs. Formally, a *path* $P = (n_1, n_2, \ldots, n_{m-1}, n_m)$ is a sequence of nodes of N such that $\forall i \in \{1, \ldots, m-1\} : (n_i, n_{i+1}) \in E$. A path is called *direct* if $n_2, \ldots, n_{m-1} \neq n_1, n_m$; and *simple* if all nodes on the path are pairwise different.

The structural correctness will be defined by the absence of deadlocks and lack of synchronization. Thereby, a *deadlock* in a join can be reached if it was not executed as often as each of its direct predecessor nodes and cannot fire in future. Furthermore, a reachable fork causes a *lack of synchronization* when its execution may cause a node to be executed twice in series. A workflow graph is structurally correct if it has neither deadlocks nor lack of synchronization.

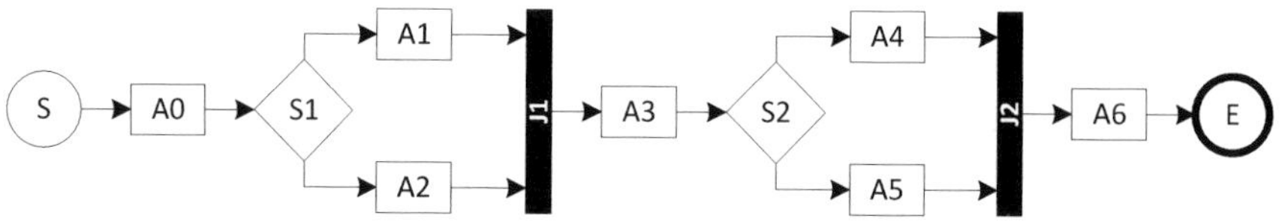

Fig. 3. An unreachable deadlock in join $J2$

3 Informal Description

The basic idea of our approach is to start the analysis for structural correctness on different points (nodes) of the workflow graph, called entrypoints. It is comparable to a compiler, which tries to find a next safe program point to find further errors after a compile time error was found. For example, Figure 3 shows a workflow graph containing two deadlocks. Starting an analysis in the start node shows only a deadlock at the join $J1$, whereas restarting the analysis at the split $S2$ detects another deadlock in join $J2$.

Each node of a workflow graph can be an entrypoint. In order to avoid wrong analysis results, the entrypoints have to be chosen carefully. For example, the activity $A4$ of Fig. 3 is not a good entrypoint to show a possible deadlock in join $J2$, because it has no path to all direct predecessor nodes of this join. To find suitable entrypoints, they will be chosen with regard to another node, e.g., a join.

Definition 1 (Entrypoint). *A node n_1 is an* entrypoint *of a node n_2 if after an execution of n_1 the execution of n_2* could *follow.*

An entrypoint n_1 of a node n_2 is called safe *if after each execution of n_1 the execution of n_2 follows. Furthermore, an entrypoint n_1 of a node n_2 is called* closest *if on at least one path from n_1 to n_2 lies no other entrypoint of n_2.*

For example, the entrypoints of activity $A1$ are the nodes S, $A0$ and $S1$ in Fig. 3. $A1$ has $S1$ as closest but not safe entrypoint, since not each execution of $S1$ causes $A1$ to be executed. A safe and closest entrypoint of the split $S1$ is the activity $A0$. The joins $J1$ and $J2$ have no entrypoints, since no node within the workflow graph could cause the joins to be executed.

4 Properties of Structural Errors

In this section, we show some properties of structural errors. The proofs are out of the scope of this paper, however, the interested reader may find them in the technical report [7].

Safe entrypoints of joins are excellent entrypoints for the determination of deadlocks, referred to as *activation points.*

Definition 2 (Activation Point). *A node n_1 is an (closest) activation point of a node n_2 if n_1 is a (closest) safe entrypoint of n_2.*

With regard to activation points and to joins, the following lemma combines some properties of a join.

Lemma 1 (Properties of a Join). *Let WFG be a workflow graph. Then, the following holds:*

1. *each activation point of a join is an activation point of the joins direct predecessor nodes.*
2. *each closest activation point of a join is a fork.*

Summarized, all closest activation points of a join should be forks and are activation points of all direct predecessor nodes of that join. Knowing these properties, the following theorem could be used for the determination of deadlocks within workflow graphs without lack of synchronization.

Theorem 1 (Deadlock). *Let WFG be a workflow graph, which is free of lack of synchronization.*

$$join \in N_{joins} \text{ has a deadlock}$$
$$\Rightarrow$$

on at least one path from the start node to join or from join to itself lies no activation point of join.

In other words, before any control flow ever arrives at a join within a workflow graph free of lack of synchronization, an activation point of this join must be executed to prevent a deadlock. The basic idea of the proof is to show that after each execution of an activation point, the join will be executed and a remaining deadlock is only caused by lack of synchronization.

The entrypoints for the determination of lack of synchronization are forks, since only forks build more than one control flow, that can cause an execution of a node twice in series. Indeed, control flows will be described by paths within workflow graphs.

Definition 3 (Intersection Point). *Let $fork \in N_{forks}$ and $suc_1, suc_2 \in fork\bullet$, $suc_1 \neq suc_2$.*

An intersection point *of suc_1 and suc_2 is a node $\cap$-point with a direct path from suc_1 and suc_2 to $\cap$-point without node $fork$. It is called* closest *if it is the first common node of such two direct paths. We write $\bar{\iota}(suc_1, suc_2)$ for all closest intersection points of suc_1 and suc_2.*

Intersection points can be used to determine lack of synchronization, since they represent combination points of control flows. Furthermore, all control flows from the same fork have to be combined in joins, before the fork can be executed again or the end node is reached. This fact will be used in the following theorem.

Theorem 2 (Lack of Synchronization). *Let WFG be a workflow graph, end its end node and $fork \in N_{forks}$. Furthermore, let $stop_1, stop_2 \in \{fork, end\}$.*

$$\begin{gathered} \textit{from the execution of fork follows a lack of synchronization} \\ \Rightarrow \\ \exists suc_1, suc_2 \in fork\bullet, suc_1 \neq suc_2: \\ \bar{\iota}(suc_1, suc_2) \nsubseteq N_{joins}, \textit{ or} \\ \exists \textit{ direct } path_1 = (suc_1, \ldots, stop_1),\ path_2 = (suc_2, \ldots, stop_2): \\ path_1 \cap path_2 = \emptyset. \end{gathered}$$

The basic idea of the proof is to show that no two control flows built by a fork can ever execute the same node twice in series.

The conditions used in Theorem 1 and 2 describe a superset of deadlocks and lack of synchronisation, since parts of it never occur at runtime, because forgoing deadlocks will prevent their execution. Therefore, we call them *potential*.

Nevertheless, the structural correctness of a business process can be proven if we can show that no potential deadlock and lack of synchronization arise in its corresponding workflow graph. In addition, with the successive elimination of deadlocks and lack of synchronization during the development process, a moment will be reached at which the set of potential errors equals the set of real errors. In this sense, based on conditions used in Theorem 1 and 2, a finite development process could be defined, which eventually can be used for the determination of real deadlocks and real lack of synchronization.

5 Determination of Structural Errors

The basic idea of the overall algorithm for detecting structural errors is the iteration over two steps until the workflow graph is structurally correct. The first step determines potential lack of synchronization, which are then bug-fixed by the user. Afterwards, the potential deadlocks will be determined, which will also be bug-fixed.

Basically, to determine potential deadlocks, each path from the start node to a join and from this join to itself is checked, whether it contains a fork as a closest activation point. If this does not hold true for a certain join, then this join has a potential deadlock. The determination of potential lack of synchronization is straightforward to Theorem 2, i.e., all paths from direct successor nodes of a fork to the end node and to the fork itself will be determined and pairwise examined: if both paths of all pairs have a first common node and this is a join, the fork is said to be free of causing lack of synchronization.

5.1 Determination of Potential Deadlocks

In the following, let $join \in N_{joins}$. The first step of the algorithm finds all entrypoints for $join$. Thereby, the focus lies on entrypoints which are forks. Afterwards, the closest entrypoints of $join$ will be determined. These closest entrypoints have to be checked to be safe, i.e., they are activation points. Eventually, the algorithm checks the conditions of Theorem 1.

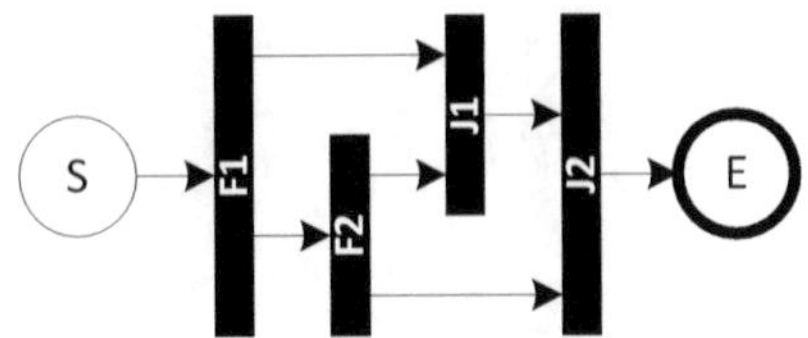

Fig. 4. Two forks and two joins

1. Determine the entrypoints. With regard to Lemma 1, closest activation points of node *join* can only be forks, which have a direct path to each direct predecessor node of *join*. But this basic lemma is not sufficient to proof that a fork is an entrypoint of a join.

For example, a look on Fig. 4 shows, that the fork $F2$ is no entrypoint of $J2$, because no execution of $F2$ follows an execution of $J2$. The execution will be stopped by the join $J1$, because $F2$ is not an entrypoint of $J1$.

Instead of searching the entrypoints for *join*, we determine for each fork the set of nodes for which it is an entrypoint, called the *scope* of a fork.

Definition 4 (Scope of Forks). *Let $fork \in N_{forks}$. The* scope $\sigma(fork)$ *is a set of nodes with $\sigma(fork) = \{n : fork \text{ is an entrypoint of } n\}$.*

A fork *fork* is an entrypoint of each of its direct successor nodes, since the workflow graph is simple. Furthermore, if a node n is not a join and has a direct predecessor node for which *fork* is an entrypoint, then n has *fork* also as entrypoint, since n can be executed if at least one predecessor node was executed. At last, if the node n is a join and each of its direct predecessor nodes has *fork* as entrypoint, then *fork* is also an entrypoint of n, since n can be executed when all of its direct predecessor nodes were executed. Hence, the scope $\sigma(fork)$ of a *fork* could be determined recursively with the algorithm in Fig. 5.

```
Input: A fork fork and σ(fork) ← ∅
Output: The scope σ(fork) of fork
for all suc ∈ fork• do
    determineScope(suc)

function DETERMINESCOPE(current)
    if current ∉ σ(fork) then
        if current ∉ N_joins then
            commonCase(current)
        else
            joinCase(current)

function COMMONCASE(current)
    σ(fork) ← σ(fork) ∪ {current}
    for all suc ∈ current• do
        determineScope(suc)

function JOINCASE(current)
    if •current ⊆ σ(fork) then
        σ(fork) ← σ(fork) ∪ {current}
        for all suc ∈ current• do
            determineScope(suc)
```

Fig. 5. Determine the scope of a fork

A fork is an entrypoint of a join if the join is within the scope of the fork. After the determination of each scope of each fork, the set $\Sigma(join)$ can be determined containing all entrypoints being forks of $join$. If $\Sigma(join)$ is empty for $join$, then $join$ cannot have closest activation points, i.e., $join$ has a potential deadlock.

2. Determine closest entrypoints. From the definition of closest entrypoints, there has to be at least one path from an entrypoint of a node n to this node n, which contains no other entrypoint of n. The closest entrypoints $\Sigma_{closest}(join) \subseteq \Sigma(join)$ can be determined efficiently with a backward depth-first search. It searches the entrypoints of $join$. If such an entrypoint was reached, then this entrypoint is marked as a closest entrypoint of $join$, and the depth-first search stops the ongoing traverse of this path. If the start node or $join$ was reached, then $join$ has a potential deadlock.

3. Determine closest activation points. Referring to Lemma 1, the closest entrypoint $fork$ is a closest activation point for $join$ if $fork$ is an activation point for each $pre \in \bullet join$. As mentioned before, $fork$ is an activation point of a $pre \in \bullet join$ when the execution of pre follows after the execution of $fork$. More specifically, there is a direct path from $fork$ to pre which will be guaranteed to be executed. In general, there could be more than one path from $fork$ to pre, e.g., the paths start of different direct successor nodes of $fork$; or decisions (splits) creates a divergence. Therefore, we merge all the direct paths starting in the same direct successor node of $fork$ and ending in pre. This union of paths is called *deliverer*, because it describes how a control could be delivered from a direct successor node of $fork$ to pre.

Definition 5 (Deliverer). *Let $join \in N_{joins}$, $pre \in \bullet join$, $fork \in N_{forks}$ is a closest entrypoint of $join$, and $suc \in fork\bullet$, which has a direct path to pre.*

A deliverer of $join$ between suc and pre is a set of nodes $\delta(fork, join, suc, pre) = \{n$: n lies on a direct path from $fork$ to $join$ containing suc and $pre\}$.

With the help of the definition of deliverers, the safeness of a closest entrypoint, i.e., the closest activation points, could be formulated as follows.

Lemma 2 (Safeness). *Let $join \in N_{joins}$, and $fork$ be a closest entrypoint of $join$.*

$fork$ is a safe and closest entrypoint of $join$ iff $\forall pre \in \bullet join$, $\exists suc \in fork\bullet$: $\delta(fork, join, suc, pre)$ will be guaranteed to be executed.

A deliverer $\delta(fork, join, suc, pre)$ will be guarenteed to be executed if it neither contains a deadlock nor control flows can leave it. Since $fork$ must be a closest activation point of $join$, it has to be an activation point of all joins within this deliverer. Without loss of generality, we assume that $fork$ is an activation point of all these joins.

Furthermore, an execution of $\delta(fork, join, suc, pre)$ is given if the control flow cannot leave this deliverer. The only node where it is possible to leave a

Input: a workflow graph $WFG = (N, E)$
Output: all joins with a potential deadlock

determine scope σ for all forks and entrypoints Σ for all joins
for all $join \in N_{joins}$ **do**
    determine the last entrypoints $\Sigma_{last}(join)$ with a backward depth-first search
    for all $entrypoint \in \Sigma_{last}(join)$ **do**
        determine all deliverers $\Delta(entrypoint, join)$ for each direct successor node of $entrypoint$ and predecessor node of $join$
        for all $\delta(entrypoint, join, suc, pre) \in \Delta(entrypoint, join)$ **do**
            determine guaranteed execution of $\delta(entrypoint, join, suc, pre)$
            if $\delta(entrypoint, join, suc, pre)$ is guaranteed to be executed **then**
                mark pre as $safe$ for $entrypoint$
        if not all $pre \in \bullet join$ are marked as $safe$ for $entrypoint$ **then**
            eliminate $entrypoint$ from $\Sigma_{last}(join)$
    do a backward depth-first search with begin in $join$ and which stops in a traversation of a path on a $fork \in \Sigma_{last}(join)$
    if the start node or $join$ were reached by the depth-first search **then**
        mark $join$ as deadlock

Fig. 6. Determine potential deadlocks

deliverer is a split. Thus, if $\delta(fork, join, suc, pre)$ contains a split, which has a path outside this deliverer, then an execution is not guaranteed.

Lemma 3 (Guaranteed execution). *Let $\delta(fork, join, suc, pre)$ be a deliverer whose $fork$ is an activation point of all inner joins.*

The execution of $\delta(fork, join, suc, pre)$ is guaranteed iff $\forall split \in (\delta(fork, join, suc, pre) \cap N_{splits})\colon\ split\bullet \subseteq \delta(fork, join, suc, pre)$.

Summarized, the safeness of each closest entrypoint of a join can be determined, i.e., the set $\Sigma_{activation}(n_{join})$.

4. Check the conditions of Theorem 1. This could be proved easily by a backward depth-first search with begin at $join$. It searches the closest activation points of $join$. If such an activation point was found, it stops the further traverse of this path. If it reaches the start node or $join$ itself, $join$ has a potential deadlock.

The overall algorithm is shown in Fig. 6 and has a cubic runtime complexity, although faster implementations are possible.

5.2 Determination of Potential Lack of Synchronization

In the following, let $suc_1, suc_2 \in fork\bullet, suc_1 \neq suc_2$. Furthermore, let $path_1 = (suc_1, \ldots, stop_1)$ and $path_2 = (suc_2, \ldots, stop_2)$ be two direct paths with $stop_1, stop_2 \in \{fork, end\}$, whereas end is the end node. Note, Theorem 2 states that a lack of synchronization will be caused directly by $fork$ if there are two paths with $path1 \cap path2 = \emptyset$, or the closest common node of them is not a join.

Since forks are the entrypoints for the determination of potential lack of synchronzation, the analysis is done for each $fork$. The first step of the algorithm determines for each direct successor node suc of $fork$ the set of all direct paths $paths(suc)$ from suc to $fork$ and from suc to the end node. The next step checks for each pair (suc_1, suc_2) if there is a pair $(path_1, path_2) \in paths(suc_1) \times paths(suc_2)$, where paths $path_1, path_2$ are disjoint or have a closest intersection point not being a join.

1. Find the sets $paths(suc_1), paths(suc_2)$. As mentioned before, for a $suc \in fork\bullet$ holds that $paths(suc) = \{p : p$ is a direct path from suc to $fork$ or from suc to the end node $\}$. Theoretically, there could be any number of such paths, because the workflow graph may contain loops. To address this fact, only the simple paths from a $suc \in fork\bullet$ to $fork$ and to the end node will be determined.

Finding all simple paths between two nodes in a directed graph is called an *all simple paths* problem and a fast algorithm can be found in Pahl et al. [8].

2. Checks done for each $(path_1, path_2) \in paths(suc_1) \times paths(suc_2)$. The check $path_1 \cap path_2 = \emptyset$ will be done first guaranteeing the absence of closest intersection points. If $path_1 \cap path_2 = \emptyset$, $fork$ has a potential lack of synchronization.

For the second check, it holds that $path_1 \cap path_2 \neq \emptyset$. Furthermore, each node of $path_1 \cap path_2$ is an intersection point of suc_1, suc_2. An intersection point $\cap$*-point* of suc_1, suc_2 in $path_1 \cap path_2$ is closest by definition, when it has a $pre \in \bullet \cap$*-point* with $pre \in path_1$ and $pre \notin path_2$, and vice versa.

Summarized, the closest intersection point of suc_1, suc_2 within $path_1$ and $path_2$ can be determined by iterating over each intersection point within $path_1 \cap path_2$ and applying the definition. If the found closest intersection point is not a join, then $fork$ has a potential lack of synchronization.

The overall algorithm will be shown in Fig. 7. This implementation of the algorithm was presented at this point for a better understanding. Although the runtime complexity of the algorithm looks inacceptable, it is possible to build an algorithm which runs in quadratic time, like used in our implementation [7,9].

6 Evaluation

We have implemented the algorithms in Java to detect structural errors in workflow graphs. To check the practical application of the approach, we have evaluated it twice, (1) in the Activiti BPMN 2.0 designer, a modeler for business processes, and (2) as a soundness verification tool. Tools and benchmarks are available on `www.bpmn-compiler.org` and `https://sourceforge.net/projects/bpmojo`

Activiti BPMN 2.0 designer. To verify the usability of the structural correctness approach, we have implemented the algorithms for the Activiti BPMN 2.0 designer (`http://activiti.org`).

Input: a workflow graph $WFG = (N, E)$
Output: all forks which could cause a potential lack of synchronization

for all $fork \in N_{forks}$ **do**
  for all $suc \in fork\bullet$ **do**
    determine $paths(suc)$
  for all $(suc_1, suc_2) \in (fork \bullet \times fork\bullet), suc_1 \neq suc_2$ **do**
    for all $(path_1, path_2) \in paths(suc_1) \times paths(suc_2)$ **do**
      if $path_1 \cap path_2 = \emptyset$ **then**
        mark $fork$ as lack of synchronization
      else
        Find closest intersection point $\cap$-*point* within $path_1$ and $path_2$
        if $\cap\text{-}point \notin N_{joins}$ **then**
          mark $fork$ as lack of synchronization

Fig. 7. Determine potential lack of synchronization

Figure 8 depicts an illustration of the tool highlighting a detected lack of synchronization within the graphical model, and showing a list of all errors. Practically, the structural correctness analysis is upon every change to the graphical model without a visible delay.

Soundness verification tool. The comparison of the processing time to other soundness verification approaches was the primary goal of the evaluation of the algorithms as soundness verification tool. The benchmark contains real-world business processes of IBM [3]. It is splitted in 5 libraries, i.e., A, B1, B2, B3 and C. This benchmark was also used by Fahland et al. [3]. A PNML [10] file was used as input describing a Petri net and then transformed into a workflow graph. By using Petri nets, we can directly compare the results with other tools like LoLA [5].

For benchmark evaluation, we have changed our algorithms to stop structural analysis upon first error. Furthermore, the algorithm was tuned to answer the yes-no question if the workflow graph is structurally correct or incorrect.

Our runtime environment was a 64 bit Intel® Core™2 CPU E6300 processor and 2 GB main memory Linux 3.1.0 system. We ran each of the 5 libraries 10 times, removed the two best and worst results and calculated the average time.

We have chosen LoLA to compare our solution with existing tools. The SESE decomposition approach is hard to compare, because a standalone implementation was not available and it depends on other soundness verification approachs. Table 1 shows the results of the benchmark evaluation.

Compared to LoLA, our algorithm is 150 times faster. This is not the major result, since LoLA was not build to verify business processes. Fahland et al. [3] have shown that SESE decomposition and the Woflan tool have comparable runtimes like LoLA. Summarized, our approach is faster than the state-of-the-art tools compared by Fahland et al. [3].

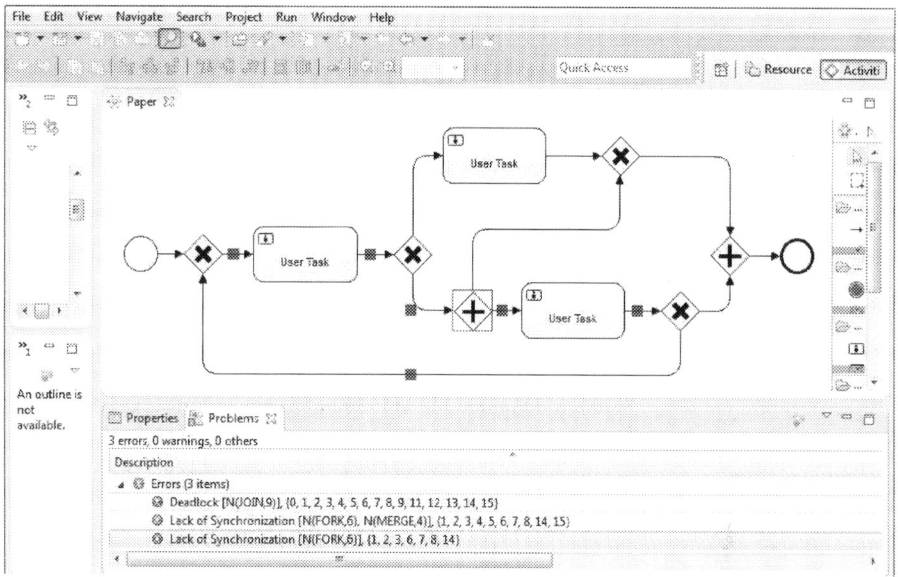

Fig. 8. Visualizing control-flow errors in Activiti

Table 1. Results of the benchmark evaluation

Library:	A	B1	B2	B3	C
Analysis time [ms]	16.4	15.4	20.7	28.4	1.7
Analysis time LoLA [ms]	2373.0	2395.9	3126.1	3651.3	303.8
Per process avg./max. [ms]	0.06/0.28	0.06/0.36	0.06/0.47	0.07/0.69	0.06/0.31
Per process LoLA avg. [ms]	8.5	8.4	8.7	8.7	9.5

7 Related Work

The fastest free choice Petri net soundness verification approach uses the rank theorem [2], i.e., a mathematical theorem of linear algebra. It has at least a cubical time complexity in the size of the workflow graph, but does not provide diagnostic information. The other approach to determine the soundness of free choice Petri nets is model checking with tools like Woflan [4] or LoLA [5]. Thus, a search on the state space of the free choice Petri net will be performed. This technique can lead to an exponential processing time in the size of the free choice Petri net. However, it supplies a failure trace (or execution sequence) that leads to the first error found. It is not possible to detect all failures with this technique.

Primarily, techniques working directly on the workflow graph restrict them to acyclic or restricted, e.g., Perumal and Mahanti [11]. Although they could have a very fast processing time and could provide very detailed failure information, they restrict the completeness of the soundness checking tool directly, rendering it inapplicable. An exception and the best known technique for soundness checking is performing a SESE decomposition [6]. It decompose the workflow graph in subgraphs which have a single entry and a single exit. This decomposition could be done in linear time complexity by constructing a Refined Process Structure Tree [12]. Each of the subgraphs will be checked first by the application of heuristics. Uncovered subgraphs then will be checked by other techniques, like space state exploration. Because subgraphs are usually smaller than the entire workflow graph, the state space exploration performs fast [3]. However, an exponentially processing time in the size of the workflow graph is still possible. Summarized, the SESE decomposition in addition to the heuristics works fast and gives detailed and localized failure information, but the heuristics do not cover all cases.

Our new approach to verify structural correctness is comparable to the SESE decomposition approach of Vanhatalo et al. [6]. Both techniques find failures in isolation. However, the SESE decomposition found only one failure per fragment, while our approach found all potential errors. Furthermore, the SESE decomposition does not always find the structural reason of failures. Therefore, an user cannot repair these structures. In conclusion, our approach is complete, i.e., it finds all structural failures.

8 Conclusion

In this paper, new compiler-based techniques to determine the structural correctness, i.e., the soundness, of a workflow graph were introduced. They directly work on workflow graphs, in order to guarantee a precise visualization and explanation of all determined structural errors, which substantially supports building business processes. Furthermore, the delevoped techniques demonstrate that well-known compiler techniques can be used for business processes. It is possible to perform a structural correctness analysis in each development step, which directly visualizes errors within the editor and shows only failures which must be fixed.

Major issues for future work are including data aspects in our techniques by transforming business processes into CSSA-based workflow graphs [13,14].

References

1. Sadiq, W., Orlowska, M.E.: Analyzing process models using graph reduction techniques. Inf. Syst. 25(2), 117–134 (2000)
2. van der Aalst, W.M.P., Hirnschall, A., Verbeek, H.M.W(E.): An alternative way to analyze workflow graphs. In: Pidduck, A.B., Mylopoulos, J., Woo, C.C., Ozsu, M.T. (eds.) CAiSE 2002. LNCS, vol. 2348, pp. 535–552. Springer, Heidelberg (2002)
3. Fahland, D., Favre, C., Koehler, J., Lohmann, N., Völzer, H., Wolf, K.: Analysis on demand: Instantaneous soundness checking of industrial business process models. Data Knowl. Eng. 70(5), 448–466 (2011)
4. Verbeek, H.M.W(E.), van der Aalst, W.M.P.: Woflan 2.0 A petri-net-based workflow diagnosis tool. In: Nielsen, M., Simpson, D. (eds.) ICATPN 2000. LNCS, vol. 1825, pp. 475–484. Springer, Heidelberg (2000)

5. Wolf, K.: Generating petri net state spaces. In: Kleijn, J., Yakovlev, A. (eds.) ICATPN 2007. LNCS, vol. 4546, pp. 29–42. Springer, Heidelberg (2007)
6. Vanhatalo, J., Völzer, H., Leymann, F.: Faster and more focused control-flow analysis for business process models through SESE decomposition. In: Krämer, B.J., Lin, K.-J., Narasimhan, P. (eds.) ICSOC 2007. LNCS, vol. 4749, pp. 43–55. Springer, Heidelberg (2007)
7. Prinz, T.M., Amme, W.: Practical compiler-based user support during the development of business processes. Technical Report Math/Inf/02/13. (June 2013), `http://www.bpmn-compiler.org`
8. Pahl, P.J., Damrath, R.: Mathematical Foundations of Computational Engineering: A Handbook, 1st edn. Springer, Heidelberg (2001)
9. Prinz, T.M., Spieß, N., Amme, W.: A first step towards a compiler for business processes. In: Cohen, A. (ed.) CC 2014 (ETAPS). LNCS, vol. 8409, pp. 238–243. Springer, Heidelberg (to be published, 2014)
10. Billington, J., Christensen, S., van Hee, K.M., Kindler, E., Kummer, O., Petrucci, L., Post, R., Stehno, C., Weber, M.: The petri net markup language: Concepts, technology, and tools. In: van der Aalst, W.M.P., Best, E. (eds.) ICATPN 2003. LNCS, vol. 2679, pp. 483–505. Springer, Heidelberg (2003)
11. Perumal, S., Mahanti, A.: A graph-search based algorithm for verifying workflow graphs. In: 2012 23rd International Workshop on Database and Expert Systems Applications, pp. 992–996 (2005)
12. Vanhatalo, J., Völzer, H., Koehler, J.: The refined process structure tree. In: Dumas, M., Reichert, M., Shan, M.-C. (eds.) BPM 2008. LNCS, vol. 5240, pp. 100–115. Springer, Heidelberg (2008)
13. Amme, W., Martens, A., Moser, S.: Advanced verification of distributed ws-bpel business processes incorporating cssa-based data flow analysis. International Journal of Business Process Integration and Management 4(1), 47–59 (2009)
14. Heinze, T.S., Amme, W., Moser, S.: A restructuring method for WS-BPEL business processes based on extended workflow graphs. In: Dayal, U., Eder, J., Koehler, J., Reijers, H.A. (eds.) BPM 2009. LNCS, vol. 5701, pp. 211–228. Springer, Heidelberg (2009)

Model Checking GSM-Based Multi-Agent Systems*

Pavel Gonzalez[1], Andreas Griesmayer[2], and Alessio Lomuscio[1]

[1] Department of Computing, Imperial College, London
{pavel.gonzalez09,a.lomuscio}@imperial.ac.uk
[2] ARM, Cambridge
andreas.griesmayer@arm.com

Abstract. Artifact systems are a novel paradigm for implementing service oriented computing. Business artifacts include both data and process descriptions at interface level thereby providing more sophisticated and powerful service inter-operation capabilities. In this paper we put forward a technique for the practical verification of business artifacts in the context of multi-agent systems. We extend GSM, a modelling language for artifact systems, to multi-agent systems and map it into a variant of AC-MAS, a semantics for reasoning about artifact systems. We introduce a symbolic model checker for verifying GSM-based multi-agent systems. We evaluate the tool on a scenario from the service community.

1 Introduction

It has long been argued [1, 2] that agents are a fitting paradigm for service oriented computing (SOC). Indeed, agent-based research has contributed a wealth of techniques ranging from verification [3], protocols [4] and actual prototype implementations [5]. SOC is currently a fast moving research area with significant industrial involvement where highly scalable implementations play a key role. Agent-based solutions can shape developments in SOC if they remain anchored to emerging paradigms being put forward by the leading players in the area.

An increasingly popular paradigm being investigated in SOC is that of *business artifacts* [6]. In this approach *data*, not only processes, play a key part in the service description and implementations. While in traditional service composition processes are advertised at interface level, in the artifact approach both processes and the data structures are given equal prominence. Guard-Stage-Milestone (GSM) has recently been put forward [7] as a language for implementing business artifacts. GSM is a declarative language that provides a description of *stages*, which are clusters of activity pertaining to some artifact data-structure. Stages

* This research was supported by the EU FP7 projects ACSI (FP7-ICT-257593). Work by the author Andreas Griesmayer was conducted in part at Imperial College London and supported by the Marie Curie Fellowship "DiVerMAS" (FP7-PEOPLE-252184). Alessio Lomuscio acknowledges support from the UK EPSRC through the Leadership Fellowship grant "Trusted Autonomous Systems" (EP/I00520X/1).

A.R. Lomuscio et al. (Eds.): ICSOC 2013 Workshops, LNCS 8377, pp. 54–68, 2014.
© Springer International Publishing Switzerland 2014

are governed by *guards* controlling their activation and *milestones* determining whether or not the stage goals have been reached. The Guard-Stage-Milestone (GSM) approach to artifact systems [7] is particularly suitable for large unstructured processes where users have the freedom to decide what actions they perform and in what order. GSM is substantially influencing the emerging Case Management Modelling Notation standard [8]. IBM Watson developed `Barcelona`, a web-based application for modelling and execution of GSM-based artifact systems [7]. `Barcelona` provides a fully model-driven environment where a business operations model of an artifact system is created in a web-based design editor component, and then directly used for deployment on an execution engine.

While business artifacts are an attractive methodology for developing business processes and GSM-based services are a rapidly evolving area of research, they lack fully-fledged automatic methodologies for verification, orchestration and choreography. In this paper we put forward a technique and an implementation for the practical verification of business artifacts from a multi-agent system perspective. Specifically, we give a MAS-based formal model to GSM systems and define the model checking problem on this model. We observe the problem is undecidable in general, but note that as long as we can show the system operates within bounds, the problem is decidable. Within these parameters the methodology we report is sound and complete. We have built an implementation to verify automatically whether a GSM system, including a number of agents, satisfies given temporal-epistemic specifications which may include quantification over artifact instances. We test the technique against a noteworthy application developed by IBM.

Several contributions have so far studied the verification problem from a theoretical perspective [9–12]. The results obtained identify fragments of decidable settings either through restrictions on the specification language or the semantics. While these results are certainly valuable, they provide no methodology for the practical verification of GSM-based systems.

The work presented in this paper is based on [13] where `GSMC`, a model checker for GSM, is introduced. However, the semantics of the underlying formalism is one of plain transition systems and no support for agents in the system is provided. With no agents being present, no support is offered for views and windows, two key concepts that we fully support here. Additionally, as their concern is focused purely on the artifact system, the specification language only supports temporal logic, thereby making impossible to verify the information-theoretic properties of agents throughout an exchange as we do here.

2 The Guard-Stage-Milestone Artifact Model

Artifact systems form a conceptual basis for modelling and implementing business processes [6] and are given in terms of *artifact types*, which correspond to classes of key business entities. Each type has a *lifecycle model*, which describes the structure of the business process, and an *information model*, which gives an integrated view of the business data and the progress of the business process.

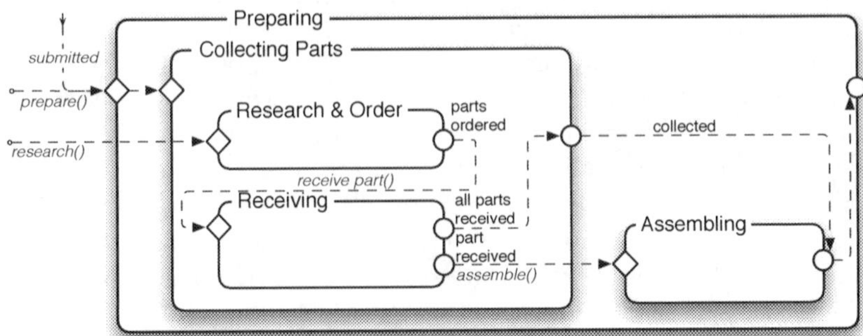

Fig. 1. A lifecycle model

The artifact system interacts with its environment via *events*. Our formal model of GSM is in line with [7].

GSM provides a declarative, hierarchical mechanism for specifying *lifecycle models*. Figure 1 gives a portion of the lifecycle of a manufacturing process and represents the core concepts: The boxes denote *stages*, which represent clusters of activity designed to achieve milestones ($\circ$) that represent operational objectives. A *guard* ($\diamond$) triggers activities in a stage when a certain condition is fulfilled. Stages are organised hierarchically, where the roots are called *top-level stages*, the leaves are called *atomic stages* and the non-leaf nodes are called *composite stages*. Atomic stages contain *tasks* that perform automated actions. Stages can run in parallel and own at least one milestone and one guard, while both milestones and guards belong to exactly one stage. A stage becomes *open* when one of its guards is fulfilled and *closed* when one of its milestones is *achieved*.

The example above gives the portion of the lifecycle of a manufacturing process that handles the procuring of the required building parts and the organisation of the assembly. When a new order is received by the manufacturer, the *submitted* event is sent to the artifact system, which triggers the guard of the *Preparing* stage, and in turn starts with *Collecting Parts*. When this stage is open, an employee of the manufacturer researches the required components and sends the *research* event to the artifact system which in turn processes the order of the required parts. When a part is received (event *part received*), the *Assembling* of the available parts is triggered; when *all parts* are *received* and *collected*, the *Preparing* stage can be closed. More details on this lifecycle will be discussed in Section 6.

Formally, an artifact system holds a number of *artifact instances* ι of *artifact type* $AT = \langle R, Att, Lcyc \rangle$, with R the *name* of the artifact type; Att the *information model* as set of *attributes*; and $Lcyc$ the *lifecycle model*. The *information model* Att is partitioned into the set Att_{data} of *data attributes* to hold business data and the set Att_{status} of *status attributes* to capture the state of the lifecycle model. Each stage (resp. milestone), has a Boolean status attribute in Att_{status}, which is true iff the stage is *active* (resp. the milestone has been *achieved*). Both milestones and guards are controlled declaratively through *sentries*. A sentry of an artifact instance ι is an expression $\chi(\iota)$ in terms of incoming events and the status of the instance.

The progress of the lifecycle is driven by incoming events containing payloads, which are called *applicable* if the lifecycle is ready to consume them. An event with a specific payload is called a *typed external event*.

Definition 1 (Event Type). *An* event type ET *is a tuple* $ET = \langle E, AT, A_1, \ldots, A_l \rangle$*, where* E *is the* name *of the event type,* AT *is an artifact type, and* $A_i \in Att_{data}$*, where* Att_{data} *is the set of data attributes of* AT*.*

In addition, the opening of an atomic stage activates a task associated with the stage. It either performs an *automated system task*, such as the creation of a new instance, or corresponds to an operation outside the artifact system. Agents are not directly present in the GSM model, but it is assumed that human or artificial entities perform *tasks* and generate events for the system.

Definition 2 (GSM Model). *A* GSM model Γ *is a set of* n *artifact types* AT_i *for* $1 \leq i \leq n$ *and* m *event types* ET_j *for* $1 \leq j \leq m$*.*

Definition 3 (Snapshot of GSM Model). *A* pre-snapshot *of* Γ *is an assignment* Σ *that maps each attribute* $A \in Att_\iota$ *of each active artifact instance* ι *to an element in the domain of* A*. A* snapshot *of* Γ *is a pre-snapshot that satisfies the following GSM invariants: all sub-stages of a closed stage are closed; all milestones of an open stage are not achieved; at most one milestone of a stage can be achieved at any time.*

The operational semantics for GSM is based on the notion of a *business step* (B-step). This is an atomic unit that corresponds to the effect of processing one incoming event into the state of the artifact system. A B-step is computed by so called PAC rules which are formed from the sentries of the GSM model and has the form of a tuple $(\Sigma, e, \Sigma', Gen)$, where Σ, Σ' are snapshots, e is an incoming external event, and Gen is a set of outgoing external events generated by opening atomic stages during the B-step. For more details on the computation of a B-step please refer to [13].

3 Agent-Based GSM

A GSM program only deals with the machinery related to the artifact system but does not provide a description of the agents interacting with it. To conduct the verification of agent-based GSM systems via model checking, we define Agent-Based GSM (A-GSM) as an extension of GSM with a set of external agents.

The artifact system and agents communicate using events, where the available events for an agent depend on the current state. The system progresses by non-deterministically selecting an agent, which sends an event and triggers the execution of the AS. Selection of the event and execution of the AS are seen as one step, a stable state has no pending events.

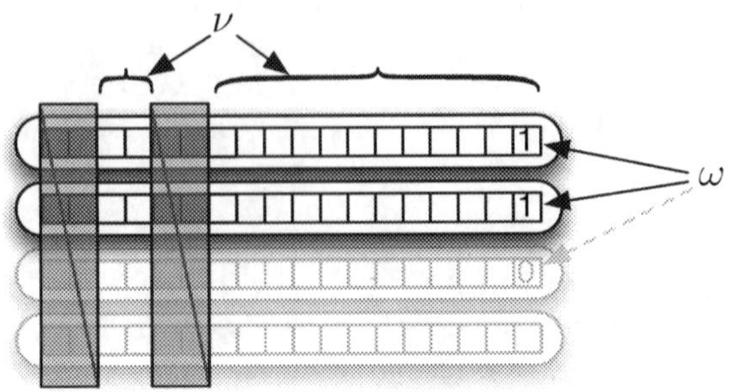

Fig. 2. Static and Dynamic visibility in A-GSM

3.1 Agent Description

Here we outline how the agents are specified and interact with GSM, thereby defining an *A-GSM instance.* The behaviour of an agent is determined by the permitted access to the artifact system AS and by local decisions regarding events to send. The former is determined by an agent's *role*, while the latter are defined for each agent individually.

The *role* is defined using the *view* ν for the visible attributes, the *window* ω to select the visible instances, and the *set of events* ϵ that are accepted by AS. While ν and ϵ are simple lists, $\omega_i(\iota)$ is a formula that is evaluated for a specific artifact instance ι and an agent i. The instance is exposed to the agent only if $\omega_i(\iota)$ evaluates to *true*. In addition to the role, the description of an agent also contains a *protocol* $\wp$ to determine its behaviour depending on the visible state of the AS, the agent's unique ID, and its private variables.

The concepts of ν, ω and ϵ are powerful tools to define the aspects agents can see and the ways they can interact with an artifact system. In Figure 2 the lines correspond to artifact instances that were created during run-time and the columns correspond to data attributes. ν defines a *static view* of the system, as it hides for each agent a fixed set of attributes depending on his role. For example, a *Customer* can only see that the state of an order moved from assembling to shipping, while a *Manufacturer* sees more detail, e.g., on suppliers. In contrast, ω gives a *dynamic* selection of the parts of the AS an agent can access in terms of the state of artifact instances as it hides complete instances depending on the current state. For instance, a *Manufacturer* may only see instances that represent unfinished orders while the window of a *Customer* can use the ID to restrict access to its own orders only.

Figure 3 gives an example of agent's description file. Visible data attributes are listed in the `view` field. The `window` field contains the formula for $\omega_i(\iota)$, where `$$` is a placeholder for the agent's ID. The field `instantiation` lists all artifact types that agents of this role may instantiate; the corresponding instantiation events are added to ϵ. To specify the status attributes and events that are added to ν and ϵ, the field `transformation` holds a set of GSM

```
role Customer {
 view: CustomerId, ManufacturerId;
 window: CustomerId == $$;
 instantiation: CO;
 transformation: condense_stage(CO, Preparing);
};

agent Diogenes {
 role:  Customer;
 vars:  bool cancelled = false;
 protocol:
  Create_CO: CustomerId == "Diogenes" -> cancelled = cancelled,
  OnCancel: true -> cancelled = true;
};
```

Fig. 3. An agent definition file

operators that allow to hide parts of the GSM model Γ. Valid commands here are `hide_stage_status("S")` and `hide_milestone("m")` to hide the status attributes of stage S and milestone m respectively, and `delegate_sentry("s")` to remove events from ϵ_i if they are only used in sentry s. For convenience, the macro operators `condense_stage("S")` and `eliminate_stage("S")` hide all sub-stages or all information including guards and milestones respectively.

The private variables of an agent are defined in a list `var` of variable names $\overline{x}$ with their type and initial value. The `protocol` lists entries of the form `e :` γ `->` μ for all events e the agent can send. Multiple entries for the same event are treated as a disjunction. The condition γ is given in terms of data attributes of the instance ι, the payload, and the private variables. It defines the protocol function $\wp_i(\iota, \overline{x})$, which gives the set of events e with their respective payloads that can be sent in the current state. The protocol also gives an update function $\mu_i(e, \overline{x})$, which computes new assignments for the local variables depending on the selected event and the local state of the agent. By imposing conditions on the *payload* of an event e, $\wp$ also allows the agent to assign a specific value to its parameters, e.g., `CustomerId` is a parameter of `Create_CO`.

To handle *automated tasks*, we define an *AutoAgent*, which handles service calls and computations in the GSM model Γ and returns the result to the artifact system in form of an event. The *AutoAgent* holds pending tasks in a buffer t, has full access to Γ, and can send the return messages at any time, but is otherwise handled like any other agent.

4 Artifact-Centric Multi-Agent Systems

To analyse interactions within a GSM-based artifact system, we use artifact-centric multi-agent systems (AC-MAS) [10, 14], a semantics based on interpreted systems [15, 16]. As a GSM system supports multiple active artifact instances, we require a limited form of quantification. We therefore introduce IQ-CTLK, an extended version of CTLK, which is frequently used to describe agents that share a common environment. IQ-CTLK is a temporal-epistemic specification language with quantification over artifact instances. We give a formal mapping $f : A\text{-}GSM \rightarrow AC\text{-}MAS$, such that f preserves satisfaction of formulas in the specification language IQ-CTLK.

4.1 Formal Model

In an AC-MAS a set of agents $\mathcal{A}$ share an environment E constituted by the artifact system, i.e., the underlying elements of the environment are evolving artifacts of type R. The environment and an agent $i \in A$ have a local state (L_E and L_i respectively), where the agent can observe parts of the environment (i.e., some of the artifact instances in it). The local state of an agent thus comprises private data for the agent and observable aspects of the artifact system. We write $l_E(s)$ to represent the local state of the environment in the global state s, and $l_i(s)$ to represent the local state of agent i.

Definition 4 (Environment). *The* environment *represents an artifact system AS and is a tuple* $E = \langle L_E, Act_E, P_E\rangle$, *where* L_E *is the set of* local states*;* Act_E *is the set of* local actions, *which correspond to the interface of the AS; and* $P_E : L_E \rightarrow 2^{Act_E}$ *is the environment's* protocol function, *which enables actions to be executed depending on the local state of the AS.*

An agent is defined formally as:

Definition 5 (Agent). *An* agent *in an AS is a tuple* $i = \langle L_i, Act_i, P_i\rangle$, *where* L_i *is the set of* local states *including the observable aspect of the AS;* Act_i *is the set of* local actions *corresponding to events that can be sent by the agent onto the AS and including an action skip for performing a null action; and* $P_i : L_i \rightarrow 2^{Act_i}$ *is the local* protocol function.

An agent i and the environment E communicate by synchronisation on actions, where Act_E corresponds to events enabled by the artifact system, and $Act_i \subseteq Act_E \cup \{skip\}$ is the set of *local actions* corresponding to events that can be executed by the agent and the idle action *skip*. Given the relation between notions of *action* in interpreted systems and *event* in GSM, we use these terms interchangeably in the rest of the paper. As in plain interpreted systems, protocols are used to select the actions performed in a given state.

Following the terminology of [14] we define an AC-MAS as the composition of the environment and a number of agents as follows:

Definition 6 (AC-MAS). *Given an environment* E *and a set of agents* $\mathcal{A}$, *an* artifact-centric multi-agent system *is a tuple* $\mathcal{P} = \langle S, \mathcal{I}, \tau\rangle$, *where* $S \subseteq L_E \times L_1 \times \cdots \times L_n$ *is the set of* reachable global states*;* $\mathcal{I}$ *is the* initial state*; and* $\tau : S \times Act \rightarrow 2^S$ *with* $Act = Act_E \times Act_1 \times \cdots \times Act_n$ *is the* global transition relation*. The transition* $\tau(s, \alpha)$ *is defined for* $\alpha = \langle a_E, a_1, \ldots, a_n\rangle$ *iff* $a_E \in P_E(l_E(s))$, *and* $\exists_{0 \leq i < n} : a_i \in P_i(l_i(s))$, $a_E = a_i \wedge \forall_{j \neq i} : a_j = skip$.

Intuitively, the conditions on the transition relation limit the communication between agents and environment such that environment and agent agree on the same action. The environment enables actions when the artifact system is ready to consume them, while the agent i decides on the actions to execute depending on a local strategy encoded in P_i. Only one agent can interact with the environment at a time while the others are idle.

We write $s \to s'$ iff there exists an action α, such that $s' \in \tau(s, \alpha)$, and call s' the *successor* of s. A *run* r from s is an infinite sequence $s^0 \to s^1 \to \ldots$ with $s^0 = s$. We write $r[i]$ for the i-th state in the run and r_s for the set of all runs starting from s. A state s' is *reachable* from s if there is a run from s that contains s'. In line with the semantics of epistemic logic [16], we say that the states s and s' are *epistemically indistinguishable* for agent i, or $\sim_i$, iff $l_i(s) = l_i(s')$.

4.2 The Logic IQ-CTLK

We are interested in specifying temporal-epistemic properties of agents interacting with the artifact system, as well as the system itself. Since GSM supports the dynamic creation of unnamed artifacts, the properties need to be independent of the actual number or possible IDs of artifact instances in the system. To specify such properties we here define a temporal-epistemic logic that supports quantification over the artifact instances. We call the logic IQ-CTLK, for *Instance Quantified CTLK*, where CTLK is the usual epistemic logic on branching time. It is a subset of FO-CTLK where quantification can only be over artifact instances but not data. The syntax is defined in BNF notation as follows:

$$\begin{aligned}\varphi ::= & \; p \mid \neg\varphi \mid \varphi \vee \varphi \mid EX\varphi \mid EG\varphi \mid E(\varphi U \varphi) \\ & \mid K_i\varphi \mid \forall x : R\ \varphi \mid \exists x : R\ \varphi\end{aligned}$$

where R is the name of an artifact type and p is an atomic proposition over the agents' private data and the attributes of active instances that are specified in terms of *instance variables* bound by the quantification operators. The quantified instance variables range over the active instances of a given artifact type R in the state where the quantification is evaluated and must be bound. We write $R(s)$ for the set of instances of type R in s.

The defined operators are read as follows: $EX\varphi$ means *there is a next state in which φ holds*; $EG\varphi$ conveys *there is a run where φ holds in every state*; $E(\varphi U \psi)$ denotes *there is a run in which φ holds until ψ holds*; $K_i\varphi$: expresses *agent i knows φ*; $\forall x : R$ represents *for all instances of type R*; and $\exists x : R$ says *there is an instance of type R*. The remaining CTL operators can be constructed by combination of the ones given above in the standard way. For example, $AG\ \forall x : Order AF\ K_i x.sent$ encodes the property expressing that in any reachable state, agent i will eventually know that the attribute *sent* is set to true for every active instance of type *Order*.

We inductively define the semantics of IQ-CTLK over an AC-MAS $\mathcal{P}$ as follows. A formula φ is true in a state s of $\mathcal{P}$, written $(\mathcal{P}, s) \models \varphi$, iff:

$$
\begin{array}{ll}
(\mathcal{P}, s) \models p & \textit{iff } p \in s \\
(\mathcal{P}, s) \models \neg\varphi & \textit{iff it is not the case that} (\mathcal{P}, s) \models \varphi \\
(\mathcal{P}, s) \models \varphi_1 \vee \varphi_2 & \textit{iff } (\mathcal{P}, s) \models \varphi_1 \textit{ or } (\mathcal{P}, s) \models \varphi_2 \\
(\mathcal{P}, s) \models EX\varphi & \textit{iff } \exists_{s'} : s \to s' \textit{ and } (\mathcal{P}, s') \models \varphi \\
(\mathcal{P}, s) \models EG\varphi & \textit{iff } \exists_{r \in r_s} : \forall_{i \geq 0} : (\mathcal{P}, r[i]) \models \varphi \\
(\mathcal{P}, s) \models E(\varphi U \psi) & \textit{iff } \exists_{r \in r_s} : \exists_{k \geq 0} : (\mathcal{P}, r[k]) \models \psi \textit{ and} \\
& \quad \forall_{j<k} (\mathcal{P}, r[j]) \models \varphi \\
(\mathcal{P}, s) \models K_i\varphi & \textit{iff } \forall s' \in S : s \sim_i s' \textit{ implies } (\mathcal{P}, s') \models \varphi \\
(\mathcal{P}, s) \models \forall x : R\ \varphi & \textit{iff } \forall u \in R(s) : (\mathcal{P}, s) \models \varphi[u/x] \\
(\mathcal{P}, s) \models \exists x : R\ \varphi & \textit{iff } \exists u \in R(s) : (\mathcal{P}, s) \models \varphi[u/x]
\end{array}
$$

The above semantics provides an information-theoretic definition of knowledge, i.e., K_i expresses what agent i can infer from the information available to him. An agent *knows* that φ is true in state s if φ is true in all states s', which the agent cannot distinguish from s. Finally, given an AC-MAS model $\mathcal{P}$ and an IQ-CTLK specification φ, the model checking problem concerns the decision as to whether the formula φ holds at the initial state of $\mathcal{P}$.

Note that the above semantics provides an information-theoretic definition of knowledge, i.e., K_i expresses what agent i can infer from the information available to him. An agent *knows* that φ is true in state s if φ is true in all states s', which the agent cannot distinguish from s. This means the agent does not need to build a knowledge base, from which he can deduce new information, since he already knows everything he could possibly deduce in a certain situation.

Given an AC-MAS model $\mathcal{P}$ and an IQ-CTLK specification φ, the model checking problem concerns establishing whether the formula φ holds at the initial state of $\mathcal{P}$, written $\mathcal{P} \models \varphi$. In the context of our formal model, an AC-MAS $\mathcal{P}$ satisfies φ if $(\mathcal{P}, \mathcal{I}) \models \varphi$. Intuitively this means that the model $\mathcal{P}$ satisfies φ if φ is true in the initial state of $\mathcal{P}$.

This was shown to be undecidable on similar semantic structures and more expressive logics [11]. In the following sections, we will achieve decidability by bounding the data and the number of instances present. We will also show the implementation of the technique to demonstrate its feasibility.

4.3 Mapping to Agent-Based GSM to AC-MAS

We now establish the formal mapping f : *A-GSM* $\to$ *AC-MAS*. Note that the semantics for the local states and protocols of agents in A-GSM are given in terms of AC-MAS. We define the map by constructing the environment $\langle L_E, Act_E, P_E \rangle$ from the GSM model Γ of a given artifact system and create an agent $\langle L_0, Act_0, P_0 \rangle$ for the *AutoAgent*, and $\langle L_i, Act_i, P_i \rangle$ with $1 \leq i \leq n$

for each external A-GSM agent. We identify a GSM event e with an AC-MAS action a and will omit the conversion in the following for ease of presentation. The sets of actions Act_E, Act_0, and Act_i are thus directly defined by the events the AS provides and the permissions of the agents.

Global state: To construct a global AC-MAS state $\langle l_E, l_0, \ldots, l_n \rangle \in S$ from an snapshot Σ, an *AutoAgent* buffer t and the local agent states x_i, we identify l_E with Σ and l_0 with t. The local states $l_1, \ldots, l_n$ of the external agent comprise the state of the private variables x_i and the *projections* $\Sigma_{|i}$ of the environment snapshot such that:

$$\Sigma_{|i} = \{\iota \mid \exists_{\iota' \in \Sigma} : \omega_i(\iota') \wedge \iota = \iota'_{|\nu_i}\}$$

where $\iota'_{|\nu_i}$ is the restriction of the artifact instance ι' to the variables in ν_i (variables not in ν_i are replaced by $\perp$).

The initial state $\mathcal{I}$ is the empty state without any artifact instances in Σ or pending tasks in l_0. Private variables are initialised to their initial value.

Protocol: By construction, GSM executes only *applicable* events and blocks all others. Artifact instantiation events are always permitted. This is reflected in the environment protocol P_E:

$$P_E(\Sigma) = \{a \mid \exists_{\iota \in \Sigma} : (\chi \in X(\Gamma) \wedge \chi(\iota, a)) \vee a \in \mathit{inst}\}$$

where $X(\Gamma)$ is the set of all sentries in the milestones and guards of Γ and $\chi(\iota, a)$ is the evaluation of a sentry χ with respect to the action a and status attributes $Att_{status} \in \iota$. We write *inst* for the set of artifact instantiation events. The *AutoAgent* stores the set of pending tasks in its buffer t and sends them at a later point to Γ. Thus, the protocol simply selects any pending task from its buffer by using the expression $P_0(t) = \{a | a \in t\}$. The protocol of an agent i gives the set of actions that are available in visible instances of its local state and satisfy its local protocol:

$$P_i(l_i) = \{a \mid \exists_{\iota \in l_i} : a \in \epsilon_i(\iota) \cap \wp_i(\iota, x_i)\}$$

These components suffice to instantiate a full AC-MAS from Definition 6. With these details in place we conclude the formal map from *A-GSM* to *AC-MAS*. In the remainder of the paper we present an implementation of a model checker for *IQ-CTLK* on *AC-MAS*.

5 Implementation

To perform AC-MAS model checking, we have extended `GSMC` [13] model checking. The new version, numbered 0.8.5[1], is written in C++ and uses the CUDD

[1] The pre-compiled binaries of the tool can be downloaded from `http://www.doc.ic.ac.uk/~pg809/gsmc/0.8.5.tar.gz`

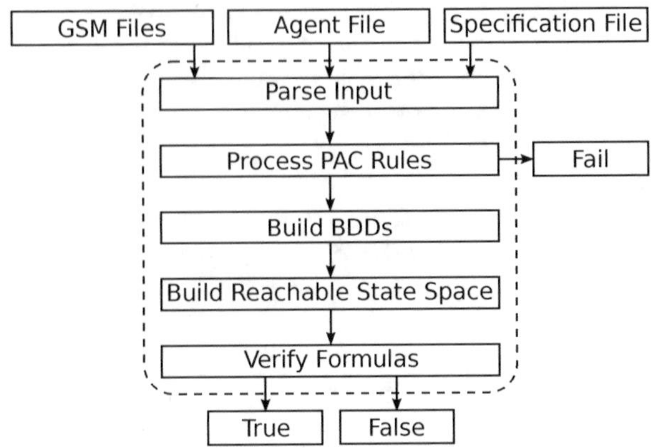

Fig. 4. Architecture of GSMC

library [17] for the back-end symbolic computations. GSMC builds the model and the transition relation and performs a symbolic state space exploration based on BDDs. The GSM model and the specification of the *AutoAgent* are directly loaded from the Barcelona XML input file; agent definitions are given in form of a configuration file as shown in Figure 3. The internal architecture of the model checker is illustrated in Figure 4.

To obtain finite state models, we introduce a *bound* on the number of instances that can be generated and use abstraction to create finite data; an *overflow* flag indicates if the bound was reached during a run. We allocate BDD variables for the states of the agents and the maximum number of artifact instances present in a run. The basic layout of the BDD data structure is shown in Figure 5. We introduce an *Overflow* flag that indicates if the number of instances or data values were exceeded in a run. We pay special attention to this case because some of the results of the check may be unsound and require a re-check with higher bounds. We also capture the *Event ID* and *Payload* of the next action a that is to be executed. The artifact instances correspond to Σ. The actual number and size of these fields depend on the artifact type and the bounds that are fixed at the start of the verification. The special flag *Created* in each artifact instance indicates whether it was instantiated in the corresponding run. The task buffer fields t with a *Pending* flag and the corresponding payload belong conceptually to the *AutoAgent*, but are stored in the artifact state space for technical reasons. Private variables of agents complete the data structure.

Any IQ-CTLK formula φ to be verified is first rewritten by replacing the quantification operators with formulas that range over the actual instances. However, because artifact instances are created dynamically at run-time, the number of *active* instances is not known *a priori* and needs to be considered in the formula.

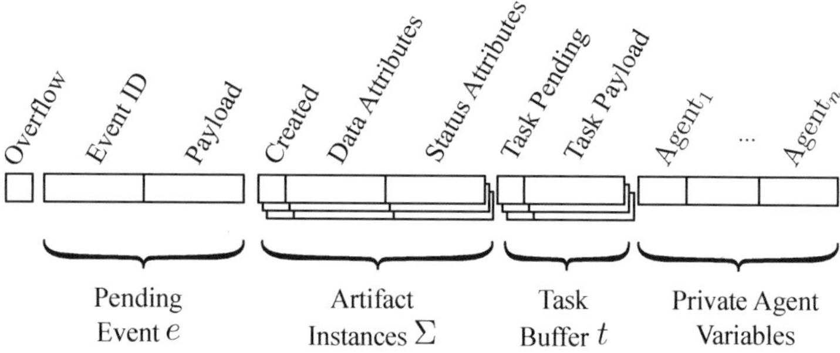

Fig. 5. Layout of the BDD data structure

We use the expression *created*(ι) to check if an instance was created (the *Created* flag is set) and rewrite the quantified formulas as follows:

$$\forall x : \varphi \Rightarrow \bigwedge_{\iota \in \Gamma} created(\iota) \rightarrow \varphi$$

$$\exists x : \varphi \Rightarrow \bigvee_{\iota \in \Gamma} created(\iota) \wedge \varphi$$

Note that, for any existential formula to be valid, at least one of the artifact instances needs to be active; this is not the case in the initial state because no artifact instance has been created yet. Quantifiers can be arbitrarily nested and are resolved recursively. Once the details above are considered, GSMC follows existing methodologies to perform the verification of temporal-epistemic formulas [18].

5.1 Limitations

The bound in the number of instances restricts the possible behaviour of the system, while data abstraction leads to an over approximation. This may lead to loss of soundness or completeness when the limit of artifact instances is reached. The exact outcome depends on the type of the property considered. A violation of a universal property, for instance, does denote a violation on the full unbounded model even if the bound was exceeded during the computation. If an existential property is not satisfied, no conclusion can be drawn regarding the full model in general. These are limitations in the technique at present but, as we show in the following, interesting scenarios can still be analysed.

6 Experimental Results

We evaluated GSMC on the Order-to-Cash scenario, a simplified version of the IBM back-end order management application supplied by IBM Research [7]. In this scenario a manufacturer schedules the assembly of a product based on a

Table 1. Properties of the Order-To-Cash case study

$$AG\ \forall x : CO((x.BId = Dio \land \neg x.Cancelled) \rightarrow K_{Dio}\ EF\ x.Received) \quad (1)$$

$$EF\ \exists x : CO(x.BId \neq Dio \land K_{Dio}\ x.Received) \quad (2)$$

$$AG\ \forall x : CO((x.BId = Dio \land x.Ready) \rightarrow K_{Dio} x.Parts = 3) \quad (3)$$

$$EF\ \exists x : CO(x.BId = Dio \land x.Cancelled \land \neg Dio.cancelled) \quad (4)$$

confirmed purchase order from a customer. Typically, a product requires several components that are sourced from different suppliers. After all components have been delivered the product is assembled and shipped to the customer.

The GSM program is specified in the form of a single-artifact `Barcelona` schema consisting of 9 stages and 11 milestones. To verify the model we performed small modifications to abstract from concrete products and created three agent roles for the above scenario: 1) a *Customer* who creates an artifact instance that represents the order and can only see instances they created; 2) a *Manufacturer* who fulfils the order and can see only uncompleted instances of orders sent to him by a customer; and 3) a *Carrier* who ships the finished product to the customer, and who can see only instances of orders that are to be shipped via them.

Figure 1 gives the lifecycle of the *Preparing* stage. It is controlled solely by the manufacturer, who, upon receiving the order, launches a research process to identify suitable suppliers and orders the required components. The assembling process can begin when the first component is received and remains active until all the components are collected. This is modelled by introducing a counter; the process is considered complete when 3 components have arrived.

Table 1 reports the properties we checked for different numbers of agents and artifact instances, where *Dio* is a customer agent (*Diogenes*) and *CO* stands for the *CustomerOrder* artifact type. Property (1) represents that *Diogenes* knows that, unless he cancels an order, the product can always be received in all of his orders. (i.e., that there is no deadlock in processing an order: An order can always be delivered or is cancelled). To check that the order is private to the customer, property (2) expresses that *Diogenes* may know a product is received for an order with different owner. Property (3) encodes the ability of an agent to deduce information it can not directly observe by checking if *Diogenes* always knows there are 3 *Parts* collected in all of his orders when the milestone *Ready* is achieved. Property (4) implies that an agent other than *Diogenes* can cancel an order that belongs to *Diogenes*. This is done by using a private variable, which is set true only if *Diogenes* executed the *Cancelled* event.

We ran the tests on a 64-bit Fedora 17 Linux machine with a 2.10GHz Intel Core i7 processor and 4GB RAM and measured the number of reachable states, memory used, and CPU time required. The model checker evaluated the properties (1) and (3) to be true and the properties (2) and (4) to be false in the model. This is in line with our intuition of the model and shows that the GSM program of Order-to-Cash application is indeed correct with respect to the requirements.

Table 2. Reachable states, memory and time usage for different numbers of artifact instances ι and agents

	3 agents			15 agents		
$\#\iota$	#states	MB	s	#states	MB	s
1	1.17 e2	27	0.1	2.92 e3	31	0.2
2	3.71 e3	52	0.7	4.16 e6	70	4.9
3	1.16 e5	64	5.9	5.82 e9	84	65.5
4	3.67 e6	96	42.1	8.01 e12	222	360.2
5	1.18 e8	195	176.7	1.09 e16	539	1419.6

Table 2 reports the performance for 3 agents (one for each role) and 15 agents respectively (6 customers, 5 manufacturers, and 4 carriers). We see that the run-time grows exponentially with the number of artifact instances, while the number of agents influences the resource usage only moderately. This is because additional agents add fewer states than additional artifact instances. The results show that the tool has the ability to effectively handle large state spaces, which is required to model realistic artifact systems with complex agent interactions.

7 Conclusions

In this paper we put forward a technique for the practical verification of GSM-based MAS. The approach consists of defining a formal map from the declarative, executable language GSM to an extension of previously studied artifact-centric MAS, a semantics for reasoning about MAS in a quantified setting of the artifact system environment. We reported on a fully-fledged model checker that implements this formal map and supports temporal-epistemic specifications in which quantification is allowed over artifact instances. The experimental results obtained against the Order-to-Cash application led us to conclude that the practical verification of reasonably sophisticated GSM-based MAS is feasible and scalable in valuable scenarios in business processes and services. However, GSM and Barcelona are still a topic of active research and development and sophisticated and stable models are hard to come by.

We plan to extend the work reported here in a number of ways, including the support of limited quantification over data. Theoretical studies [10, 14] point to high-undecidability in settings where unbounded data is present. For this reason we will work on existential abstraction and data abstraction to achieve a transfer of the verification outcome from abstract to concrete models. In particular we work on 3 valued abstraction [19], an abstraction technique that supports the detection of insufficient information in the abstraction.

References

1. Singh, M., Rao, A.S., Georgeff, M.: Formal methods in DAI: Logic-based representation and reasoning. In: Weiß, G. (ed.) Multiagent Systems: A Modern Approach to Distributed Artifical Intelligence, pp. 331–376. MIT Press (1999)
2. Bultan, T., Su, J., Fu, X.: Analyzing conversations of web services. IEEE Internet Computing 10(1), 18–25 (2006)
3. Lomuscio, A., Qu, H., Solanki, M.: Towards verifying contract regulated service composition. Autonomous Agents and Multi-Agent Systems 24(3), 345–373 (2012)
4. Singh, M.P., Huhns, M.N.: Service-oriented computing - semantics, processes, agents. Wiley (2005)
5. Baldoni, M., Baroglio, C., Mascardi, V.: Special issue: Agents, web services and ontologies: Integrated methodologies. Multiagent and Grid Systems 6(2), 103–104 (2010)
6. Cohn, D., Hull, R.: Business artifacts: A data-centric approach to modeling business operations and processes. Bulletin of the IEEE Computer Society Technical Committee on Data Engineering 32(3), 3–9 (2009)
7. Hull, R., Damaggio, E., De Masellis, R., et al.: Business artifacts with guard-stage-milestone lifecycles: managing artifact interactions with conditions and events. In: Proceedings of the International Conference on Distributed Event-Based Systems (DEBS 2011), pp. 51–62 (2011)
8. Object Management Group: Proposal for: Case management modeling and notation (CMMN) specification 1.0, Document bmi/12-02-09 (February 2012)
9. Deutsch, A., Sui, L., Vianu, V.: Specification and verification of data-driven web applications. Journal of Computer and System Sciences 73(3), 442–474 (2007)
10. Hariri, B.B., Calvanese, D., Giacomo, G.D., Deutsch, A., Montali, M.: Verification of relational data-centric dynamic systems with external services. CoRR (2012)
11. Belardinelli, F., Lomuscio, A., Patrizi, F.: Verification of deployed artifact systems via data abstraction. In: Kappel, G., Maamar, Z., Motahari-Nezhad, H.R. (eds.) ICSOC 2011. LNCS, vol. 7084, pp. 142–156. Springer, Heidelberg (2011)
12. Belardinelli, F., Lomuscio, A., Patrizi, F.: Verification of GSM-based artifact-centric systems through finite abstraction. In: Liu, C., Ludwig, H., Toumani, F., Yu, Q. (eds.) ICSOC 2012. LNCS, vol. 7636, pp. 17–31. Springer, Heidelberg (2012)
13. Gonzalez, P., Griesmayer, A., Lomuscio, A.: Verifying GSM-based business artifacts. In: Proceedings of ICWS 2012, pp. 25–32 (2012)
14. Belardinelli, F., Lomuscio, A., Patrizi, F.: An abstraction technique for the verification of artifact-centric systems. In: Proceedings of Principles of Knowledge Representation and Reasoning (KR 2012), pp. 319–328 (2012)
15. Parikh, R., Ramanujam, R.: Distributed processes and the logic of knowledge. In: Parikh, R. (ed.) Logic of Programs 1985. LNCS, vol. 193, pp. 256–268. Springer, Heidelberg (1985)
16. Fagin, R., Halpern, J.Y., Moses, Y., Vardi, M.Y.: Reasoning About Knowledge. The MIT Press (1995)
17. Somenzi, F.: CUDD: CU decision diagram package - release 2.5.0 (2012), `http://vlsi.colorado.edu/~fabio/CUDD/` (January 2013)
18. Lomuscio, A., Qu, H., Raimondi, F.: Mcmas: A model checker for the verification of multi-agent systems. In: Bouajjani, A., Maler, O. (eds.) CAV 2009. LNCS, vol. 5643, pp. 682–688. Springer, Heidelberg (2009)
19. Shoham, S., Grumberg, O.: 3-valued abstraction: More precision at less cost. Information and Computation 206(11), 1313–1333 (2008)

Towards Modeling and Execution of Collective Adaptive Systems

Vasilios Andrikopoulos[1], Antonio Bucchiarone[2], Santiago Gómez Sáez[1], Dimka Karastoyanova[1], and Claudio Antares Mezzina[2]

[1] IAAS, University of Stuttgart
Universitaetsstr. 38, 70569 Stuttgart, Germany
{andrikopoulos,karastoyanova,gomez-saez}@iaas.uni-stuttgart.de
[2] Fondazione Bruno Kessler, Via Sommarive, 18, Trento, Italy
{bucchiarone,mezzina}@fbk.eu

Abstract. Collective Adaptive Systems comprise large numbers of heterogeneous entities that can join and leave the system at any time depending on their own objectives. In the scope of pervasive computing, both physical and virtual entities may exist, e.g., buses and their passengers using mobile devices, as well as city-wide traffic coordination systems. In this paper we introduce a novel conceptual framework that enables Collective Adaptive Systems based on well-founded and widely accepted paradigms and technologies like service orientation, distributed systems, context-aware computing and adaptation of composite systems. Toward achieving this goal, we also present an architecture that underpins the envisioned framework, discuss the current state of our implementation effort, and we outline the open issues and challenges in the field.

1 Introduction

Collective systems comprise heterogeneous entities collaborating towards the achievement of their own objectives, and the overall objective of the collective. Such systems are usually large scale, typically consisting of both physical and virtual entities distributed both organizationally and geographically. In this sense, collective systems exhibit characteristics of both service-oriented and pervasive computing. Furthermore, due to the dynamic nature of the environment they operate in, they have to possess adaptation capabilities.

In our previous work in the ALLOW project, we enabled orchestrations of physical entities [8,16] as the model for individual entities in a collective system. A single entity is modeled using a pervasive flow modeling its functionality, the services it exposes and the functionality a partner entity needs to implement in order to interact with the physical entity. Moreover, the pervasive flows are adaptable in terms of abstract tasks/activities, which can be refined during the execution depending on the goal of the entity. However, this work relies on a model restricting the capabilities of entities to a single behavioral description in terms of Adaptive Pervasive Flows (APFs), and ignores the collaborative aspect in their behavior.

For this purpose, in the current work as part of the ALLOW Ensembles project[1], we aim at defining a Collective Adaptive System (CAS) [19], and the underpinning

[1] ALLOW Ensembles: http://www.allow-ensembles.eu

A.R. Lomuscio et al. (Eds.): ICSOC 2013 Workshops, LNCS 8377, pp. 69–81, 2014.
© Springer International Publishing Switzerland 2014

concepts supporting modeling, execution and adaptation of CAS entities, and their interactions. Toward this goal, we use an approach inspired by biological systems. In particular, we propose to model and manage entities as collections of cells encapsulating their functionality. Entities collaborate with each other to achieve their objectives in the context of ensembles describing the interactions among them.

The contributions of this work can therefore be summarized as follows:

1. Starting from a motivating scenario (Section 2), we introduce a CAS framework (Section 3) defining a conceptual model and the life cycle of systems realizing this model.
2. We introduce an architecture enabling the modeling, execution and adaptation of CAS as distributed, large scale, pervasive systems and we discuss its implementation based on well-established technologies (Section 4).

The paper closes with a summary of related work (Section 5), and concludes with an outline of research challenges and future work (Section 6).

2 Motivating Scenario

Supporting citizens mobility within the urban environment is a priority for municipalities worldwide. Although a network of multi-modal transportation systems (e.g., buses, trains, metro), services (e.g., car sharing, bike sharing, car pooling), and smart technologies (e.g., sensors for parking availability, smart traffic lights, integrated transport pass) are necessary to better manage mobility, they are not sufficient. Citizens must be offered accurate travel information, where and when such information is needed to take decisions that will make their journeys more efficient and enjoyable. In order to deliver "smart services" to citizens, available systems should be interconnected in a synergistic manner constituting a system of systems. The FlexiBus scenario is a case of such system. The goal is to develop a system to support the management and operation of FlexiBuses (FlexiBus Management System (FBMS)), where actors (i.e., passengers, buses, route managers, bus assistance manager etc.) need to cooperate with each other towards fulfilling both individual and collective goals and procedures. As shown in Fig. 1, the system must be able to manage different routes at the same time (e.g. blue and red) set by passengers by allowing pre-booking of pick up points.

More specifically, each *Passenger* can request a trip to one of the predefined destinations in the system, asking to start at a certain time and from a preferred pickup point. The system should manage also special requests from each passenger like traveling with normal or extra sized luggage, or disability related requirements. Each passenger can pay their trip directly in the bus (cash, with a credit card or a monthly pass) or through the FlexiBus company web site. Furthermore, during the route execution, each passenger waiting for a bus can be notified for problems on a selected route (e.g. bus delays, accidents, etc.) Each *Bus Driver* is assigned by the FBMS a precise route to execute, including the list of passengers assigned to it, and a unique final destination (e.g. Trento city center in Fig. 1). During the route realization, each flexibus can also accept passengers that have not booked only if there are available seats. Bus drivers communicate with an assigned *Route Manager* to ask for the next pick-up point and to communicate

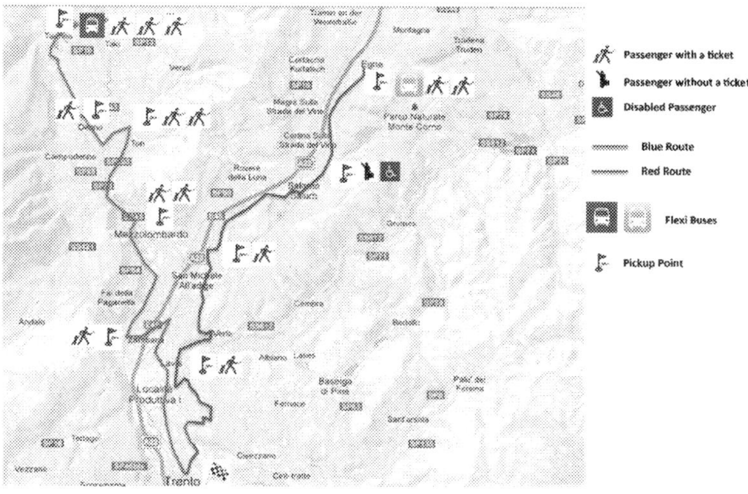

Fig. 1. The FlexiBus Scenario

information like passengers check-in. Different routes are created by a *Route Planner* that organizes them to satisfy all passenger requirements (i.e. arrival time and destination) and to optimize bus costs (i.e. shorter distance, less energy consumptions, etc.). To find the set of possible routes, the Route Planner communicates with the *FlexiBus Manager* in order to collect necessary information (i.e. traffic, closed roads, events, etc.) and available resources (i.e. available buses), and to generate alternative routes. A *Bus Assistance Service* is also available for bus drivers to report problems that occur along one route and request for advice/specific activities to be performed (e.g. notify police for an accident, pickup a bus for repair). Finally, a *Payment Service* is the entity that interfaces with various payment systems in order to ensure that ticket purchases are handled correctly.

The system needs to deal with the *dynamic* nature of the scenario, both in terms of the *variability of the actors involved and of their goals*, and of the exogenous *context changes*, e.g. bus damages, passenger requests cancellations, traffic jams, roads closed due to accidents, etc. affecting its operation. Moreover, some of the tasks executed by the actors *require customization* for different environmental situations, like passenger preferences and requirements (e.g. payment with cash or credit card, trip together with a friend, etc.).

3 Overall Framework for CAS

In this section we present our framework to model and execute Collective Adaptive Systems like the FBMS described above.

3.1 Conceptual Model

We model a CAS as a set of *entities* that can collaborate with each other in order to accomplish their business objectives and in some cases common objectives, and for

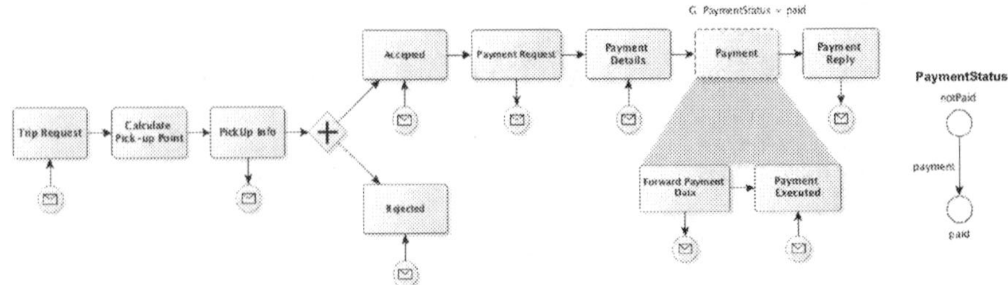

Fig. 2. The Trip Booking Cell Flow

that form one or more *ensembles*. Moreover, to enable interaction among entities, each entity exposes one or more *cells*.

Cells are uniquely identifiable building blocks representing a concrete functionality in a larger, multi-cellular system. Implementing the functionality may involve interacting with other cells through pre-defined protocols. Therefore each cell is defined in terms of its *behavior* (flow) and *protocol*, describing the interaction with other cells and exposed process fragments [15]. For example, the passenger trip booking in the FlexiBus scenario is performed by a specific functionality of the Route Manager entity and it is an example of a cell in the FBMS (see Fig. 2). Among the activities that comprise this flow is Payment, which is marked as an *abstract activity*, in the sense that it requires another cell, or a composition of cells, to implement this functionality. Selecting these cells can be done either during design or run time of the cell at hand.

Cells can be created from each other through differentiation. *Cell differentiation* is the process of modifying/adapting the protocol or flow of an existing cell, resulting in a new cell with more specific functionality. Differentiation can take place either during the instantiation of the cell, or during its lifetime (i.e. in runtime). Accepting only credit cards as part of the Payment activity in Fig. 2 is a case of cell differentiation from the generic cell able to handle different payment options into a cell with more specific functionality. The actual functionality of the Payment activity can actually be provided by another cell, e.g. by the Payment Manager/Service.

After instantiation in the CAS cell instances belong to distinct *entities* and each cell instance belongs to exactly one entity. An entity is a physical or virtual organizational unit aggregating a set of cells. Cells can either be unique in an entity, or they can be replicated by the entity through instantiation as many times as necessary. The Route Manager in the FlexiBus scenario, for example, is an entity containing the Trip Booking cell (Fig. 2) and a Route Assignment cell (Fig. 3a) managing the execution of the route. Each entity has a *context* in which it operates, expressed as a set of stateful properties representing the status of the environment of the entity, e.g. PaymentStatus in Fig. 2. The entity context is accessible and shared by its cells and cells may keep cell specific context. In addition, an entity has a set of *goals*, e.g. ensure that the PaymentStatus context property is set to "paid" at the end of the cell flow execution, that it attempts to fulfill by initiating or participating in one or more ensembles.

An *ensemble* is a set of cells from different entities collaborating with each other to fulfill the objectives of the various entities. Each ensemble is initiated and terminated

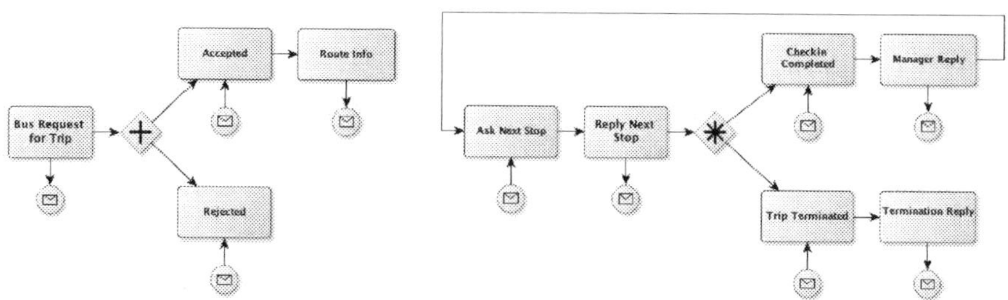

(a) Route Assignment Cell Flow (Route Manager)

(b) Route Execution Cell Flow (Bus Driver)

Fig. 3. Examples of Cells and Associated Entities

by one entity, but more than one entities are expected and allowed to join and leave through the ensemble's lifetime. The Route Assignment cell of the Route Manager entity (Fig. 3a) for example, forms an ensemble with the Route Execution Cell of the Bus Driver entity (Fig. 3b) to successfully coordinate the two entities in executing a (FlexiBus) route. Note that one entity may be involved in more than one ensembles simultaneously.

3.2 Lifecycle

The lifecycle of ensembles is depicted in Fig. 4. We distinguish two major phases: design time and run time. During the *design time* phase the ensembles of a CAS are modeled as choreographies and the cells are expressed as Adaptive Pervasive Flows (APFs) [8]. Modeling choreographies implies defining the visible behavior of the participants (i.e. cell protocols), the sequence of exchanged messages, and the types of the exchanged data. During the *Generation & Refinement* step the resulting choreography definition is first transformed into APF skeletons — one for each participant — which also contain the functionality required to support the defined interaction protocol (i.e. sending and receiving messages from partners, data structures for storing the data, etc.). In the subsequent refinement, each APF is edited so that it is completed to an executable APF. Note that the design time phase of choreography subsumes the design time for APFs, i.e. participant implementations/processes. Any kind of adaptation during the design phase of APFs realizes a differentiation of cells. The possible adaptation actions are inserting, deleting and substituting activities and control flow connectors in the APF, changing the data dependencies, editing the context model, and injecting a process fragment that specifies the functionality of an abstract activity.

The *deployment* step uses the APF skeletons from the previous step, their service interfaces, and deployment information about the binding strategies for each of the services to be used. After the deployment the choreography can be executed collectively by APF instances, i.e. the APFs are made available for instantiation by the execution environment. The instantiation of one of the APFs initiates the choreography, which is the beginning of the *run time phase* for the choreography. More than one APF model may be designated as an initiating one, e.g. the Route ensemble may be initiated by a

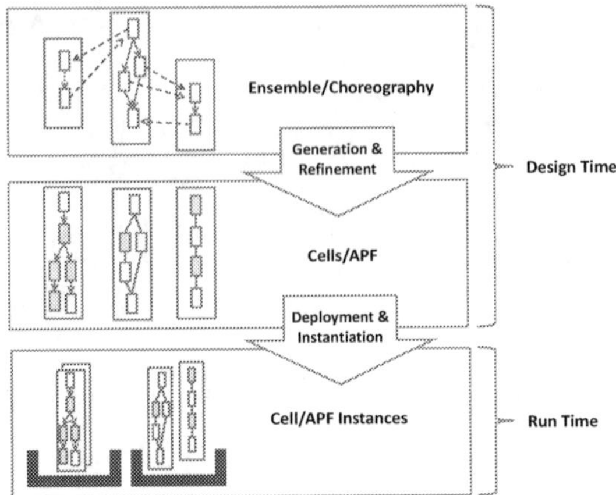

Fig. 4. Lifecycle of Ensembles

cell of the bus or by a cell in a passenger entity. However, if an instance of one APF initiates a choreography, instances of the other participating APFs can only join the initiated choreography, e.g. if a bus cell has started the Route ensemble, passengers can only join the initiated choreography following the predefined rules for passenger check in.

The choreography is completed successfully when the objectives of the entities participating in the ensemble are achieved through executing all APFs in it successfully, or even if some of the cells/APFs have abandoned the ensemble, e.g. if a passenger leaves the bus and moves to another transportation vehicle due to changes in their objectives. For the latter case, fault handling and/or adaptation steps may need to be performed. A choreography is completed abnormally if all participant APFs have been terminated. In this case either the choreography has reached a state for which a termination has been predefined (e.g. the bus breaks down and there is no available one to substitute it, therefore passengers have to join another ensemble, i.e. wait for the next FlexiBus or use an alternative transportation means), or none of the fault handling and/or adaptation steps have been able to complete the choreography successfully. The runtime phase subsumes monitoring and adaptation of choreographies, as well as the runtime and monitoring and adaptation phases of APFs. Adaptation of choreographies is done through adaptation of the visible behavior of the cells and through a change of the interaction protocol among them, including message exchange sequence and message types. Adaptation of an APF may not entail adaptation of the choreography.

4 Realization

4.1 Architecture

The architecture for the modeling and execution of CAS comprises two major component groups (see Fig. 5) which cover the phases of the CAS lifecycle discussed in Section 3.2. More specifically, the *Modeling Tool* comprises three major components:

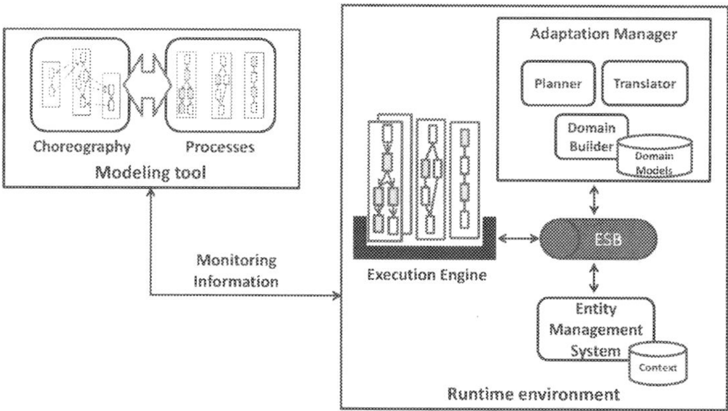

Fig. 5. Architecture overview

a *Choreography Modeler* to create choreography models for the ensembles, a *Transformer* to generate the APF skeletons that can be completed to executable processes by the participant organizations using the APF Editor component, and an *APF Editor* (also called process editor) to allow the visualization and modification of APF models.

The *Runtime Environment* enacts the choreographies. In particular this means that the resulting executable APF models are deployed on one or more *Execution Engines* and can be instantiated at any time. The *Deployment & Instantiation* steps are implementation-specific for each Execution Engine. In order to support the execution of APFs containing abstract activities, the Execution Engine has to be able to start the execution of incomplete processes, allowing the injection of additional activities into APFs. Furthermore, the Execution Engine has to provide fault handling capabilities, both for pre-defined fault and compensation handlers in the APF models, and for failures in the Runtime Environment like service failures and unavailability of other components in the Environment. The Execution Engine has to support user-defined ad hoc control flow changes (e.g. deletion, insertion, substitution of one more activities in the flow). Some of these adaptations require one or more planning steps, for example, in order to resolve abstract activities into concrete ones and to handle the reaction to not pre-modeled faults occurring during the execution of the APF. The component providing this planning functionality is the *Adaptation Manager*.

Once the Adaptation Manager is notified about an execution problem, a change in the context or goals of cells, it decides on the adaptation strategy to be used (horizontal adaptation, vertical adaptation, other adaptation strategies etc. [9]). The choice of the adaptation strategy determines the adaptation goal, which is passed to the *Domain Builder* together with the information about the current context. The *Domain Builder* builds an initial version of the adaptation problem consisting of a context model, a set of available annotated fragments, current context configuration (i.e. the state of context properties), and a set of goal context configurations. The Domain Builder extracts all necessary specification from a repository of *Domain Models*. Taking into account the current context and adaptation goals, the Domain Builder simplifies the context model by pruning all unreachable configurations and removes all services that are useless for the specified goal. With this optimization the size of the planning domain is significantly reduced. The *Translator* component translates an adaptation problem into a planning problem, which is resolved by the *Planner*. It is also responsible for transforming the results of the Planner into executable APF fragments. Finally, the resulting APF fragment expressing the actions necessary for realizing the adaptation strategy is sent to the Execution Engine, that integrates it into the APF instance.

The *Entity Management System (EMS)* deals with all aspects of entity management: persistence storage and management of APF models and associated entities, access control of APF models and instances, and context provisioning and management. When the EMS creates a new entity, it deploys the entity APFs to the execution engine, adds corresponding context properties to the entity context model, and puts all the entity-related specifications (such as fragments models and the context property diagrams provided by the entity) into the Domain Models storage. When the entity "exits" the CAS, inverse actions are performed. The EMS is responsible for storing the system context (i.e. a set of context properties of all active entities) and constantly synchronizes its current configuration with the application domain by monitoring the environment of the entity. Note that the system context is a simplified view of the application domain. The EMS allows the Adaptation Manager to access the APF models and instances needed for the planning step. Context information is used by the Execution Engine for different purposes: as part of the execution of the APFs, as a trigger for adaptation, and as a configuration parameter for the planning step.

All components (Execution Engine, EMS, Adaptation Manager) should be provided as services and communicate through an *Enterprise Service Bus (ESB)* solution to facilitate their integration. Given the fact that multiple organizational domains may use the *Runtime Environment*, it is necessary to offer multi-tenancy capabilities out of the box for all components in the Environment. Furthermore, the Runtime Environment may contain more than one instances of its components, distributed across on-premises and off-premises Cloud infrastructures, for scalability purposes. This has to be taken into consideration during the integration of the individual components.

4.2 Implementation

In the following we present the status of the implementation of the presented architecture. In particular, we have developed the modeling tool as an Eclipse Graphical Editor. For purposes of expressing choreographies we use the BPEL4Chor language [13] (which is an extension of the WS-BPEL language), and WS-BPEL [25] for implementing the APFs. The user can model the participants in the choreography/ensemble as separate entities and define the interaction among them, including the abstract data types used and the sequence of exchanged messages. BPEL4Chor code is automatically generated by the tool for the choreography, for the list of participants in the choreography and the data exchanged among them. The components implementing the transformation from choreography definition in BPEL4Chor to BPEL process skeletons for each participant and their service interfaces in WSDL, presented in [32], are part of the tool as well as the Eclipse perspective for modeling and editing BPEL processes. The BPEL modeling perspective is an extension of the BPEL Eclipse designer [28]. It is used to view the BPEL skeletons and include additional process elements in order to define the participants implementation of the choreography role (e.g. bus, passenger, route manager processes). This manual refinement step is simplified by allowing to use predefined process fragments, which are available in the tool catalogue and stored and managed in the process fragment library Fragmento [27].

Additionally, we have extended the tool with a monitoring component for processes, so that during the execution of the APF instances the user can view their status and also adapt manually the instance that is currently being monitored. For this purpose the modeling tool uses run time information from the execution engine provided via its monitoring component. The interaction between the modeling tool, monitoring component and execution engine supports also the runtime adaptation of APFs processes using mechanisms like control flow change (inserting, deleting or substituting process activities and control connectors), changes in the data used in the process instance, and triggering re-execution of some of the already executed activities through [29].

The additional tasks of the Adaptation Manager component are realized by ASTRO-CAptEvo[2] [26], a comprehensive framework for defining highly adaptable service-based systems (SBSs) and supporting their context-aware execution. It can deal with two different adaptation needs: the need to refine an abstract activity within a process instance (i.e. vertical adaptation), and the need to resolve the violation of a context precondition of an activity that has to be executed (i.e. horizontal adaptation). In the second case, the aim of adaptation is to solve the violation by bringing the system to a situation where the process execution can be resumed. Both adaptation mechanisms rely on sophisticated AI planning techniques for the automated composition of services [5]. Moreover, it is able to execute complex *adaptation strategies* that are realized through combining a few adaptation mechanisms and executing them in a precise order, enabling support for addressing complex adaptation problems that cannot be resolved by a single adaptation mechanism [10].

The execution engine for APFs, i.e. the executable processes of the participants in the choreography, is an extended Apache ODE Engine[3], an open source implementation of BPEL. We have extended the engine to support the integration with the modeling tool for the purposes of monitoring, the adaptation mechanisms mentioned above as well as with the ability to stop, suspend and resume a process instance in the engine from the modeling tool [28]. For the ESB component of the architecture we use the ESB^{MT} multi-tenant aware ESB solution, as presented in [30,31]. ESB^{MT} enhances the Apache ServiceMix solution[4] with multi-tenant communication support within service endpoints deployed in the ESB, and multi-tenant aware dynamic endpoint deployment and management capabilities.

The Entity Management System manages all active entities within a CAS. Currently both the entity management and context management parts of the EMS are under construction. Our CAS modeling tool is also missing features supporting modeling of context in the choreographies and APFs. Adaptation mechanisms performing a reaction to context change or driven by context information are also not yet designed and implemented. Our execution engine prototype does not currently support the injection of

[2] `http://www.astroproject.org/captevo`

[3] Apache ODE: `http://ode.apache.org/`

[4] Apache ServiceMix: `http://servicemix.apache.org`

fragments directly into the process instance; note that this is possible for the design time phase. This is due to the fact that the previously presented implementation [26] of this mechanism needs to be integrated in the current implementation. Currently we are also working towards implementation of multi-tenancy of the APF execution engine.

5 Related Work

Collective or adaptive aspects of complex systems have been studied in various domains. For example in *Swarm Intelligence* entities are essentially homogeneous and are able to adapt their behavior considering only local knowledge [11,22]. In existing systems from *Autonomic computing* the entity types are typically limited and the adaptation is guided by predefined policies with the objective to optimize the system rather than evolve it [1,7,23]. In *Service-based systems* utilized on *Internet of Things*, entities are hidden behind the basic abstraction of services, which are designed independently by different service providers, and approaches to automatically compose services to achieve a predefined goal like user specific [18] and/or business goals [24] are the focus. *Multi-agent based systems* concentrate on defining the rules (norms) for regulating the collective work of different agents [12,21]. Most of the results obtained in these domains are tailored to solve problems specific for the domain at hand using a specific language or model but do not present a generic solution for all aspects of collective adaptive systems.

Different *choreography modeling* approaches have been proposed in [3,14,17,20]. Two key approaches followed when modeling choreographies are interaction and interconnection modeling [3]. The former has interaction activities supporting atomic interactions between participants, while the latter interconnects the communication activities of each participant in a choreography. WS-CDL [17] is a choreography language following the interaction modeling approach. It exhibits however a strong dependency between semantic and syntactic aspects, specifically in the definition requirement of message exchange formats between participants at design time [4], lacks support for describing choreographies with an unknown participants number [20], and does not define guidelines for mapping between the choreography modeling language and existing orchestration languages, such as WS-BPEL [25]. The Savara[5] project for example is based on behavior specification and choreography specification using WS-CDL, and behavior simulation, and generation and implementation of business processes using BPEL and Web services. Despite the similarities in some of the used technologies with our approach however, and due to the use of the interaction modeling approach requiring explicit specifications of choreographies and orchestrations, the Savara approach does not allow for dynamically joining and leaving the choreography.

An example of an interconnection modeling approach is the CHOReOS Integrated Development and Runtime Environment which focuses on the implementation and enactment of ultra large scale choreographies of services[6]. By exploiting the notion of models and models@runtime [6] techniques, the CHOReOS Environment provides support

[5] `http://www.jboss.org/savara`

[6] CHOReOS: Large Scale Choreographies for the Future Internet: `http://www.choreos.eu/`

for a top-down and cross-cutting choreographies incorporating the design, enactment, and adaptation of services during runtime. The adaptation requirements addressed in the CHOReOS Environment (react to participants unavailability, or when the SLA is not accomplished) are only a subset of the requirements on ensembles, where context changes in pervasive environments, structural changes in the ensemble, or cells leaving the ensemble, adapting to utility fluctuations etc. are of interest. In the scope of the Open Knowledge European project[7], the interconnection modeling approach is supported by using the Multiagent Protocol (MAP) Web service choreography language for specifying the interaction between peers, which are connected to the services participating in the choreography. Services must be deployed prior to the choreography enactment and the MAP language does not focus on adaptation features. These features present clear deficits with respect to modeling CAS adaptation and the runtime reaction to changes in a service-oriented pervasive environment.

The interaction modeling approach called BPEL^{gold} [20] is based on BPEL4Chor [14]. The coordination logic of participants in choreographies is enabled by an ESB. Both BPEL4Chor and BPEL^{gold} decouple the choreography specification from communication specific details, allowing for dynamic ensemble adaptation during runtime. However, while these approaches possess the required flexibility for defining ensembles no execution environment is currently available for them.

6 Conclusion and Future Work

Collective Adaptive Systems (CAS) are characterized by heterogeneous entities that can join and leave the system at any time towards fulfilling their own objectives. These entities may be physical or virtual, and interact with each other as part of the collective. CAS systems are naturally distributed, both in terms of the participating entities (i.e. geographical location and/or organizational affiliation), and the required infrastructure to support them. In order to enable CAS exhibiting these properties, in this work we introduce a conceptual model inspired by biological systems which comprises collections of cells (functional building blocks) organized into entities (organizational units), interacting with each other in ensembles (collaborations between cells).

In order to discuss the realization of this model, we map its elements to existing technologies and present a lifecycle for the ensembles based on them. We also introduce an architecture for a CAS that ensures complete coverage of the lifecycle, and present the current status of its implementation. Future work focuses on creating an improved context model and provisioning techniques for entities participating in ensembles in different application domains, e.g. in eScience [2], and managing the adaptation of choreographies. Consequently, the components of the prototype implementation discussed in the previous sections have to be extended, and all the remaining components integrated. In addition, different distribution and deployment options for the Runtime Environment will be investigated in order to identify the optimal solution for different CAS.

Acknowledgment. This work is partially funded by the FP7 EU-FET project 600792 ALLOW Ensembles.

[7] Open Knowledge: `http://www.openk.org/`

References

1. Abeywickrama, D.B., Bicocchi, N., Zambonelli, F.: SOTA: Towards a General Model for Self-Adaptive Systems. In: WETICE, pp. 48–53 (2012)
2. Andrikopoulos, V., Gómez Sáez, S., Karastoyanova, D., Weiß, A.: Towards Collaborative, Dynamic & Complex Systems. In: Proceedings of SOCA 2013. IEEE (December 2013) (to appear)
3. Barker, A., Walton, C.D., Robertson, D.: Choreographing Web Services. IEEE Transactions on Services Computing 2, 152–166 (2009)
4. Barros, A., Dumas, M., Oaks, P.: A Critical Overview of the Web Services Choreography Description Language (WS-CDL). BPTrends (March 2005), http://www.bptrends.com/
5. Bertoli, P., Pistore, M., Traverso, P.: Automated composition of Web services via planning in asynchronous domains. Artif. Intell. 174(3-4), 316–361 (2010)
6. Blair, G., Bencomo, N., France, R.B.: Models@run.time. Computer 42, 22–27 (2009)
7. Bruni, R., Corradini, A., Gadducci, F., Lluch Lafuente, A., Vandin, A.: A Conceptual Framework for Adaptation. In: de Lara, J., Zisman, A. (eds.) FASE 2012. LNCS, vol. 7212, pp. 240–254. Springer, Heidelberg (2012)
8. Bucchiarone, A., Lafuente, A.L., Marconi, A., Pistore, M.: A Formalisation of Adaptable Pervasive Flows. In: Laneve, C., Su, J. (eds.) WS-FM 2009. LNCS, vol. 6194, pp. 61–75. Springer, Heidelberg (2010)
9. Bucchiarone, A., Marconi, A., Pistore, M., Raik, H.: Dynamic Adaptation of Fragment-Based and Context-Aware Business Processes. In: Proceedings of ICWS 2012, pp. 33–41 (2012)
10. Bucchiarone, A., Marconi, A., Pistore, M., Traveso, P., Bertoli, P., Kazhamiakin, R.: Domain Objects for Continuous Context-Aware Adaptation of Service-based Systems. In: Proceedings of ICWS 2013, pp. 571–578 (2013) (to appear)
11. Pinciroli, C., et al.: ARGoS: A modular, multi-engine simulator for heterogeneous swarm robotics. In: Proceedings of IROS. pp. 5027–5034 (2011)
12. Cabri, G., Puviani, M., Zambonelli, F.: Towards a taxonomy of adaptive agent-based collaboration patterns for autonomic service ensembles. In: CTS, pp. 508–515 (2011)
13. Decker, G., Kopp, O., Leymann, F., Pfitzner, K., Weske, M.: Modeling Service Choreographies Using BPMN and BPEL4Chor. In: Bellahsène, Z., Léonard, M. (eds.) CAiSE 2008. LNCS, vol. 5074, pp. 79–93. Springer, Heidelberg (2008)
14. Decker, G., Kopp, O., Leymann, F., Weske, M.: BPEL4Chor: Extending BPEL for Modeling Choreographies. In: Proceedings of ICWS 2007 (2007)
15. Eberle, H., Unger, T., Leymann, F.: Process Fragments. In: Meersman, R., Dillon, T., Herrero, P. (eds.) OTM 2009, Part I. LNCS, vol. 5870, pp. 398–405. Springer, Heidelberg (2009)
16. Herrmann, K., Rothermel, K., Kortuem, G., Dulay, N.: Adaptable Pervasive Flows - An Emerging Technology for Pervasive Adaptation. In: Proceedings of PerAda 2008. IEEE (2008)
17. Kavantzas, N., Burdett, D., Ritzinger, G., Fletcher, T., Lafon, Y., Barreto, C.: Web Services Choreography Description Language Version 1.0 (November 2005)
18. Kazhamiakin, R., Paolucci, M., Pistore, M., Raik, H.: Modelling and Automated Composition of User-Centric Services. In: Meersman, R., Dillon, T.S., Herrero, P. (eds.) OTM 2010, Part I. LNCS, vol. 6426, pp. 291–308. Springer, Heidelberg (2010)
19. Kernbach, S., Schmickl, T., Timmis, J.: Collective Adaptive Systems: Challenges Beyond Evolvability. ACM Computing Research Repository (CoRR) (August 2011)

20. Kopp, O., Engler, L., van Lessen, T., Leymann, F., Nitzsche, J.: Interaction Choreography Models in BPEL: Choreographies on the Enterprise Service Bus. In: Fleischmann, A., Schmidt, W., Singer, R., Seese, D. (eds.) S-BPM ONE 2010. CCIS, vol. 138, pp. 36–53. Springer, Heidelberg (2011)
21. Lavinal, E., Desprats, T., Raynaud, Y.: A generic multi-agent conceptual framework towards self-management. In: NOMS, pp. 394–403 (2006)
22. Levi, P., Kernbach, S.: Symbiotic Multi-Robot Organisms: Reliability, Adaptability, Evolution. Springer (2010)
23. Lewis, P., Platzner, M., Yao, X.: An outlook for self-awareness in computing systems. Awareness Magazine (2012)
24. Marconi, A., Pistore, M., Traverso, P.: Automated Composition of Web Services: The ASTRO Approach. IEEE Data Eng. Bull. 31(3), 23–26 (2008)
25. OASIS: Web Services Business Process Execution Language Version 2.0 (April 2007)
26. Raik, H., Bucchiarone, A., Khurshid, N., Marconi, A., Pistore, M.: ASTRO-CAptEvo: Dynamic Context-Aware Adaptation for Service-Based Systems. In: Proceedings of SERVICES, pp. 385–392 (2012)
27. Schumm, D., Karastoyanova, D., Leymann, F., Strauch, S.: Fragmento: Advanced Process Fragment Library. In: Proceedings of ISD 2010, pp. 659–670. Springer (2010)
28. Sonntag, M., Hahn, M., Karastoyanova, D.: Mayflower - Explorative Modeling of Scientific Workflows with BPEL. In: Proceedings of the Demo Track of BPM 2012. CEUR Workshop Proceedings, pp. 1–5 (2012)
29. Sonntag, M., Karastoyanova, D.: Ad hoc Iteration and Re-execution of Activities in Workflows. International Journal on Advances in Software 5(1&2), 91–109 (2012)
30. Strauch, S., Andrikopoulos, V., Leymann, F., Muhler, D.: ESB^{MT}: Enabling Multi-Tenancy in Enterprise Service Buses. In: Proceedings of CloudCom 2012, pp. 456–463. IEEE Computer Society Press (December 2012)
31. Strauch, S., Andrikopoulos, V., Sáez, S.G., Leymann, F., Muhler, D.: Enabling Tenant-Aware Administration and Management for JBI Environments. In: Proceedings of SOCA 2012, pp. 206–213. IEEE Computer Society Conference Publishing Services (December 2012)
32. Weiß, A., Andrikopoulos, V., Gómez Sáez, S., Karastoyanova, D., Vukojevic-Haupt, K.: Modeling Choreographies using the BPEL4Chor Designer: An Evaluation Based on Case Studies. Tech. Rep. 2013/03, IAAS, University of Stuttgart (2013)

A Requirements-Based Model for Effort Estimation in Service-Oriented Systems

Bertrand Verlaine, Ivan J. Jureta, and Stéphane Faulkner

PReCISE Research Center, University of Namur
Rempart de la Vierge, 8, BE-5000 Namur, Belgium
{bertrand.verlaine,ivan.jureta,stephane.faulkner}@unamur.be

Abstract. Assessing the development costs of an application remains an arduous task for many project managers. Using new technologies and specific software architectures makes this job even more complicated. In order to help people in charge of this kind of work, we propose a model for estimating the effort required to implement a service-oriented system. Its starting point lies in the requirements and the specifications of the system-to-be. It is able to provide an estimate of the development effort needed. The latter is expressed in a temporal measurement unit, easily convertible into a monetary value. The model proposed takes into account the three types of system complexity, i.e., the structural, the conceptual and the computational complexity.

Keywords: Software Engineering, Service-oriented Computing, Development Costs Estimation.

1 Introduction

"*How much will it cost to develop a given Information System* (IS)?" remains one of the main issues for project managers. The rapid evolution of technologies as well as some new IS development paradigms do not often facilitate this work. In this paper, we focus on Service-oriented Systems (SoS), i.e., ISs based on the Service-oriented Computing (SoC) paradigm. Its main component, the service, is a black box: only messages sent and received are known. Consequently, some software features are no longer programmed while the exchanges of messages must be developed. As recently underlined, assessing the cost of SOA development deserves more attention: "Current approaches to costing [SOA] projects are very limited and have only been applied to specific types of SOA such as Service Development or SOA Application Development" [1]. In response, we propose a requirements-based model for estimating *a priori* the effort needed to develop a SoS. To do so, we adapt and extend an existing model to best suit to the service-oriented paradigm. The results provided consists of an estimation of the development effort required to carry out the SoS implementation. This estimate is based on the three types of software complexity, i.e., the structural, the computational and the conceptual complexity [2, Chap. 5]. The measurement unit of the estimate provided is temporal in order to avoid focussing on a specific social policy applied in a given country.

This paper proceeds by first analysing the related literature based on which we conclude that an adapted model for SoS is needed (§2). Then, the methodology followed

A.R. Lomuscio et al. (Eds.): ICSOC 2013 Workshops, LNCS 8377, pp. 82–94, 2014.
© Springer International Publishing Switzerland 2014

is detailed (§3) and the model is developed accordingly (§4). In §5, an example case illustrates the use of the model. Conclusion and future work are presented in §6.

2 Related Work

Existing methods used for estimating a priori the software development costs are either experts-based methods or model-based methods. Model-based methods use algorithms, heuristics computations and/or old projects data. Experts-based methods rely on human expertise and depend on experts' intuition, knowledge and unconscious processes. We decide to focus on a model-based approach in the scope of this work.

Model-based estimation techniques are principally grounded on analogies, empirical studies and/or system-to-be analysis. To be effective, the first kind of techniques needs lots of data collected during previous projects. The objective is to find the similarities with the current project. This technique is close to experts-based methods but it is applied with much more formalism and, often, the use of probabilistic principles. Analogy-based techniques, e.g., [3, 4], face a recurring issue: they need highly skilled workers and they cannot be applied in young organizations because of a lack of historical data. That could be a problem in SoC seeing that it is a young paradigm which evolves quickly.

The second kind of techniques is based on empirical research, whereby situation-based models are proposed. In some sense, they generalize analogy techniques. One well-known initiative is COCOMO [5]. The core idea is that the development costs grow exponentially when the system-to-be grows in size. The problem is that the development of a SoS often combines several development strategies and processes: the underlying services can communicate without any restrictions on their own development technologies. As a result, COCOMO models and similar techniques are often over-calibrated as underlined by Tansey & Stroulia [6]. These authors attempted unsuccessfully to propose an empirical model based on COCOMO to estimate SoS development costs. They were constrained to conclude that SoS development also involves developing and adapting declarative composition specifications, which leads to fundamentally different processes.

The third kind of techniques consists of an analysis of the system-to-be structure in order to measure its characteristics impacting the development costs. One well-known technique is the use of function points based on which the software size is estimated. It is a measurement unit which captures the amount of functionalities of an IS [7, 8]. In this way, Santillo uses the COSMIC measurement method and, actually, he mainly focuses on the determination of the boundary of an SoS [9]. He also identifies one critical issue: from a functional point of view, SoC is different from traditional software architectures. New measurement methods are therefore essential for sizing SoS: we need new rules and new attributes appropriate to the SoC paradigm [9]. Nevertheless, the idea of using the function points deserves further research, which is what we aim for this paper.

2.1 Software Development Costs Estimation in Service-Oriented Computing

In [10], the authors use the Work Breakdown Structure (WBS) for costing SoS. This is a decomposition technique that tries to make a granular list of planned tasks often represented as a tree. It helps to reduce the mean relative error and possible slippages in

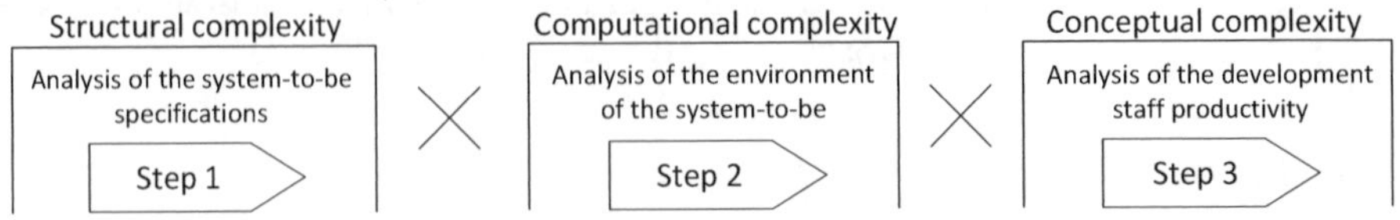

Fig. 1. Illustration of the proposed model structure and its main components

project deliverables. After the SoS decomposition in atomic tasks, the authors propose an algorithm to estimate the development costs of the system-to-be.

A second related work tackles the defect prediction issue in SoS [11]. To do so, the authors use COCOMO to estimate the size of the future SoS. The paper does not solve the main issue explained above, i.e., different strategies and processes can be used during a SoC project, and one variable used in their model –the infrastructure factor– is not clearly defined. It seems they use a COCOMO coefficient estimated based on common software.

In [12], the authors propose an estimation framework for SoS by reducing the total software complexity. They propose to decompose the SoS into smaller parts. Then, each of them is separately estimated. However, it is not clear how all the values resulting from the individual estimation are aggregated to provide a single figure.

3 Methodology Followed

Instead of measuring the SoS development costs –which depend on many unrelated variables such as the wage level– we propose to measure the effort needed, i.e., the number of staff per period needed to carry out the development tasks. To do this, we first evaluate the SoS complexity from which we can deduce the total effort needed. We take into account the three main sources of software complexity [2, Chap. 5]. The *structural complexity* refers to the software design and structure such as the quantity of data stored, the operations achieved, the user interfaces required and so on. As show in Fig. 1, the structural complexity is captured in our model through the analysis of the SoS specifications. This step is the starting point. Specifying the SoS could be achieved thanks to a modelling language, e.g., UML, or with a framework such as IEEE SRS[1]. In the scope of this work, that choice is not important as long as one is able to identify the significant factors –defined below– impacting the structural complexity. The *computational complexity* refers to the way that the computation is being performed. This kind of complexity is captured via an analysis of the system-to-be environment (the second step in Fig. 1). The *conceptual complexity* is related to the difficulty to understand the system-to-be objectives and its requirements. It refers to the cognitive processes and the capabilities of the programmers. In our model, the effort estimation is adjusted to the development staff productivity (the third step in Fig. 1).

[1] The IEEE SRS framework was consulted the last time in February 2013 at `http://standards.ieee.org/findstds/standard/829-2008.html`

Table 1. Characteristics of the SoS Complexity Model along with their acronyms

Acronym	Description
IC	(Input Complexity): Complexity due to data inputs received by the system-to-be.
OC	(Output Complexity): Complexity due to the data outputs that the system-to-be has to send to its environment.
DSC	(Data Storage Complexity): Complexity due to persistent data that the SoS has to store.
WS	(Weight Source): Weight allocated to an input or output source type (see Table 2).
WT	(Weight Type): Weight allocated to a specific type of input or output (see Table 2).
WST	(Weight Storage Type): Weight allocated to a type of storage destination (see Table 2).
IOC	(Input Output Complexity): Sum of the IC, OC and DSC.
FRC	(Functional Requirements Complexity): Complexity due to the implementation of functional stakeholder's needs.
NFRC	(Non-Functional Requirements Complexity): Complexity due to the implementation of non-functional stakeholder's needs.
FI	(Functions to Implement): Features that have to be entirely implemented in the system-to-be.
FS	(Functions as a Service): Features that will not be coded because services will be used instead.
QA	(Quality Attribute): Primary characteristics coming from the non-functional requirements which state how the functional requirements will be delivered.
QSA	(Quality Sub-Attribute): Secondary characteristics refining each QA.
RC	(Requirements Complexity): Sum of the FRC and NFRC.
PC	(Product Complexity): Complexity of the SoS due to the tasks that it will perform; it sums the IOC and RC.
DCI	(Design Constraints Imposed): Complexity due to constraints and rules to follow during the system-to-be development.
C	(Constraint): Any environment characteristic of the development work or of the system-to-be that limits and/or control what the development team can do.
IFC	(Interface Complexity): Complexity due to the interfaces to implement in the system-to-be.
I	(Interface): Integration with another IS or creation of a user interface.
SDLC	(Software Deployment Location Complexity): Complexity due to the type of users who will access to the SoS as well as their location.
UC	(User Class weight): Weight associated with a user class.
L	(Location): Number of the different access locations for a specific user class.
SFC	(System Feature Complexity): Complexity due to specific features to be added to the system-to-be.
FE	(Feature): Distinguishing characteristic of a software item aiming at enhancing its look or its feel.

4 A Model for Effort Estimation in SoS Development

4.1 Software-Intrinsic Complexity Estimation in Service-Oriented Systems

The SoS Complexity Model. The model proposed should first help to estimate the structural complexity of the SoS (see the first step in Fig. 1). To do so, we adapt and improve an existing model [13]. The latter allows to compute the software-intrinsic complexity before its coding. It analyses stakeholders' requirements expressed in natural language and categorizes them into three groups –critical, optional and normal

Table 2. Sources and type weights for the input, output and data storage complexity

Parameter	Description	Weight
Input/Output Sources	External Input/Output through Devices	1
	Input/Output from files, databases and other pieces of software	2
	Input/Output from outside systems	3
Input/Output Types	Text, string, integer and float	1
	Image, picture, graphic and animation	2
	Audio and video	3
Data Storage Types	Local data storage	1
	Remote data storage	2

requirements– according to eleven axioms. The "normal category" is the default category when the classification algorithm does not succeed to select one of the two other categories. From our point of view, this method faces two problems. First of all, the requirements categorization is complex and imprecise (cf. the default category used when no decision is made). Secondly, the complexity estimation does not take into account some specific features of the SoC such as the use of external services to provide system features. In [13], once a requirement is specified, all of its underlying features increase the software complexity. Despite these two flaws, this model performs well during the tests and comparisons with similar initiatives [13–15]. This is why it is a sound basis on which a specific model for the SoC could be built.

In the rest of this section, we identify the characteristics –defined in Table 1– of SoS and how they increase structural complexity based on the model proposed in [13].

Input Output Complexity. The Input Output Complexity (IOC) gathers the complexity of the input (IC), output (OC) and data storage complexity (DSC) together. Table 2 lists the different weights, picked up from [13], for the types and sources of IC, OC and DSC.

$$IC = \sum_{i=1}^{3}\sum_{j=1}^{3} I_{ij} \times WS_i \times WT_j \tag{1}$$

where I_{ij} is the number of inputs of the source i and being of the type j identified in the system-to-be specifications; WS_i and WT_j are respectively the weight of the input source i and the input weight of the type j as listed in Table 2. In order to compute the OC value, you substitute the variable I_{ij} by O_{ij} in Equation 1.

The use of services to perform some functionalities involves data exchanges between the providers and the consumers of services. The WSDL technology is commonly used for describing service capabilities and communication processes [16]. Two versions of the WSDL protocol currently exit (WSDL 1.1 and 2.0), but their relevant parts for our model are identical. *<operation/>* tags define service functions. Each operation consists of one or several input and output tag(s), i.e., messages exchanges, which must be considered as an input/output source from outside systems. Most of the time, the type to apply is "text" seeing that messages exchanged are XML documents.

Equation 2 states how to compute the DSC.

$$DSC = \sum_{i=1}^{2} S_i \times WST_i \tag{2}$$

where S_i is the number of data storage of type i and WST_i is the weight of the type i.

The IOC value is the addition of the IC, OC and DSC values.

Requirement Complexity. The Functional Requirements Complexity (FRC) value captures the complexity of a given functionality. As some functions can be fulfilled thanks to the use of (composite) services, they should not all be taken into account for the computation of the FRC complexity value. Let F be the set which includes all the SoS' functions. F contains two sub-sets: FI and FS for, respectively, the *Functions to Implement* set and the *Functions as Services* set which will not be fully developed because (composite) services will be used instead. They do not increase the RFC value as stated in Equation 3.

$$FRC = \sum_{i=1}^{n}\sum_{j=1}^{m} FI_i \times SF_{ij} + \sum_{k=1}^{k} FS_k \quad (3)$$

where FI_i is the ith function of FI and SF_{ij} is the jth sub-function obtained after the decomposition of the function FI_i. FS_k is the kth function of FS outsourced as services. In this case, only the main function –i.e., the (composite) service being used– increases the FRC value. Although its computational complexity is hidden, developers have to implement the exchanges of messages between the service used and the SoS.

Non-functional requirements are criteria related to the way the functional requirements will be performed; its complexity value can be computed as stated in Equation 4.

$$NFRC = \sum_{i=1}^{6}\sum_{i=1}^{n} QA_i \times QSA_j \quad (4)$$

where QA_i is the main quality attribute i and QSA_j is the quality sub-attributes j related to QA_i. The quality attributes proposed are those of the ISO/IEC-9126 standard[2] [17].

The Requirement Complexity (RC) is the addition of the FRC and the NFRC.

Product Complexity. The Product Complexity (PC) captures the SoS complexity based on its overall computations. It is obtained by multiplying the IOC and the RC values [13].

Design Constraints Imposed. The Design Constraints Imposed (DCI) refers to the number of constraints to consider during the development of the SoS such as regulations, hardware to reuse, database structures, imposed development languages, etc. Of course, the constraints imposed on the software modules used as services are not taken into account. These services are black boxes for service customers, only the constraints concerning the communication are relevant for the computation of the DCI.

$$DCI = \sum_{i=1}^{n} C_i \quad (5)$$

where C_i is the ith constraint type imposed; its value is to number of constraints i.

[2] The main quality attributes of the ISO/IEC-9126 standard are *Functionality, Reliability, Usability, Efficiency, Maintainability* and *Portability*. See [17] for more information.

Interface Complexity. The Interface Complexity (IFC) is computed based on the number of external integrations and user interfaces needed in the future software.

$$IFC = \sum_{i=1}^{n} I_i \tag{6}$$

where I_i is the ith external interface to develop. I_i has a value ranging from one to x depending of the number of integrations to carry out: a user interface has a value of one while the value of an interface used to integrate multiple systems corresponds to the number of ISs to interconnect. Each service used counts for one interface.

Software Deployment Location Complexity. The Software Deployment Location Complexity (SDLC) is the software complexity due to the types of users accessing the system-to-be combined with the different locations from where they will access it.

$$SDLC = \sum_{i=1}^{4} UC_i \times L_i \tag{7}$$

where UC_i is the user class weight and L_i is the number of locations from which the user belonging to the user class i will access the software. User classes are [13]: casual end users occasionally accessing the SOS (weight of 1), naive or parametric users dealing with the database in preconfigured processes (weight of 2), sophisticated users using applications aligned with complex requirements and/or infrequent business processes (weight of 3), and standalone users working with specific software by using ready-made program packages (weight of 4).

System Feature Complexity. The System Feature Complexity (SFC) refers to specific features to be added to enhance the look and the feel of the system-to-be.

$$SFC = \sum_{i=1}^{n} FE_i \tag{8}$$

where FE_i is the feature i with a weight of 1.

Computation of the SOS RBC *value.* The Service-Oriented System Requirements-based Complexity (SOS RBC) value can be computed as follows:

$$SOS\ RBC = (PC + DCI + IFC + SFC) \times SDLC \tag{9}$$

Note Sharma & Kushwaha also include the "personal complexity attribute" (PCA) in their complexity measurement model [13, 18]. However, the structural complexity measure should only take into account the software structure and not the capabilities of the development staff. The latter should only impact the development effort needed.

Validation of the Complexity Model. Here is a theoretical validation of the model we proposed in this section based on the validation framework for the software complexity measurement process of Kitchenham et al. [19].

Property 1: *For an attribute to be measurable, it must allow different entities [i.e., different specifications of systems-to-be] to be distinguished from one other.*

All attributes used in the Equations 1 to 9 are clearly defined and distinguishable from each other (see Table 1). They cover the specifications of a SoS. Therefore, the SOS RBC model should give different values for different SoS specifications.

Property 2: *A valid measure must obey the representation condition, i.e., it must preserve our intuitive notions about the attribute and the way in which it distinguishes entities.*

This property refers to the psychological complexity, also called conceptual complexity, –i.e., the complexity due to the efforts needed for a given human being to understand and to perform a specific software development task– which cannot interfere with the structural complexity . The latter is the kind of complexity that the SOS RBC model has to capture. All the attributes used are only related to countable and distinguishable intrinsic characteristics of the system-to-be without any relations with the development staff capabilities. We conclude that this property is respected by the SOS RBC model.

Property 3: *Each unit of an attribute contributing to a valid measure is equivalent.*

Each identical attribute in the system-to-be will have the same weight and importance in the estimation regardless its position in the specifications.

These three properties are necessary to validate a complexity measurement process, but not sufficient [19]. Indirect measurements must also respect properties 4 and 5.

Property 4: *For indirect measurements processes, the measure computed must be based on a dimensionally consistent model, with consistent measurement units while avoiding any unexpected discontinuities.*

Our model aims at measuring the complexity of software specifications. All the attributes evaluated to compute the model are intrinsic features of the SoS impacting its complexity.

Property 5: *To validate a measurement instrument, we need to confirm that the measurement instrument accurately measures attribute values in a given unit.*

This property asks for a definition of the measured attributes and their unit. In this paper, we propose a semi-formal definition of the measurement instrument –the best solution is to propose a formal one– based on both mathematical tools and literal definitions.

4.2 Estimation of the Total Intrinsic Size of the System-to-be

In order to estimate the total development effort needed, the model is adjusted with the Technical Complexity Factors (TCF) [7, 8]. They are used to capture the computational complexity (see the second step in Fig. 1). The TCFs are significant characteristics of the software development project which influence the amount of work needed. Each TCF is associated to a Degree of Influence (DI) ranging from 0 (*no influence*) to 5 (*strong influence*). They must be estimated by the development team based on the requirements and on the system-to-be environment[3].

Equation 10 expresses TCF value (TCFV) in a mathematical form [8].

[3] The sixteen TFCs are Complex processing, Data communication, Distributed functions, End user efficiency, Facilitate change, Heavily used configuration, Installation ease, Multiple sites, On-line data entry, On-line update, Operational ease, Performance, Reusability, Security concerns, Third parties IS and Transaction rate. See [7, 8] in order to have more details about the TCF's and the process to follow in order to estimate the appropriate DI for a TCF.

$$TCFV = 0.65 + 0.01 \times \sum_{i=1}^{16} DI_i \tag{10}$$

where DI_i is the degree of influence of the ith TCF.

The adjusted SOS RBC (A-SOS RBC) is the SOS RBC value times the TCFV [8].

$$\textit{A-SOS RBC} = SOS\ RBC \times TCFV \tag{11}$$

4.3 Estimation of the Total Development Work Needed

The estimation of the SoS Requirements-based Effort (SOS RBE) value is based on the A-SOS RBC. The SOS RBE is significantly related to the productivity of the development staff –it captures the conceptual complexity (see the third step in Fig. 1). The staff productivity is the ratio between the number of code lines written and the time required. It depends on the language used since the latter can be more or less complex, expressive, flexible, etc. The Quantitative Software Management firm (QSM), specialized in quantitative aspects of software, makes available the productivity of development staff for many languages. These values result from empirical research achieved on more than 2190 projects. For all the studied languages, QSM proposes the average value, the median as well as the lowest and the highest value of the number of lines of code needed[4]. For instance, the values of the J2EE language are, respectively, 46, 49, 15 and 67.

Equation 12 states how to compute the SOS RBE.

$$SOS\ RBE = \frac{(\textit{A-SOS RBC} \times L)}{P} \tag{12}$$

where L is the number of code lines needed per function point as stated by the QSM company. P is the productivity of the development staff express in lines of code per period. The SOS RBE value estimates the number of periods needed for the implementation of the SoS. The unit of the SOS RBE is the same than the period unit of P. The development productivity variables P and L may lack of precision. There are two more sophisticated approaches. The first one lies in calculating the ratio between the number of code lines and development time needed for previous internal projects (see, e.g., [20]). A second approach is to use a parametric estimation model built upon empirical data (see, e.g., [21]). A complete discussion of this topic is out of the scope of this paper.

5 Example Case of the Proposed Effort Estimation Model

A company active in the food industry would like a new IS in order to improve the purchase management. With the new IS, a significant amount of orders should be automatically sent. Currently, workers have to manually carry out all the orders. It exists a legacy IS which manages the outgoing orders. Only its main function will be kept and exposed as a service –it estimates the stock level needed.

[4] All the results of this research are available at `http://www.qsm.com/resources/function-point-languages-table`. Last consultation in July 2013, the 3rd.

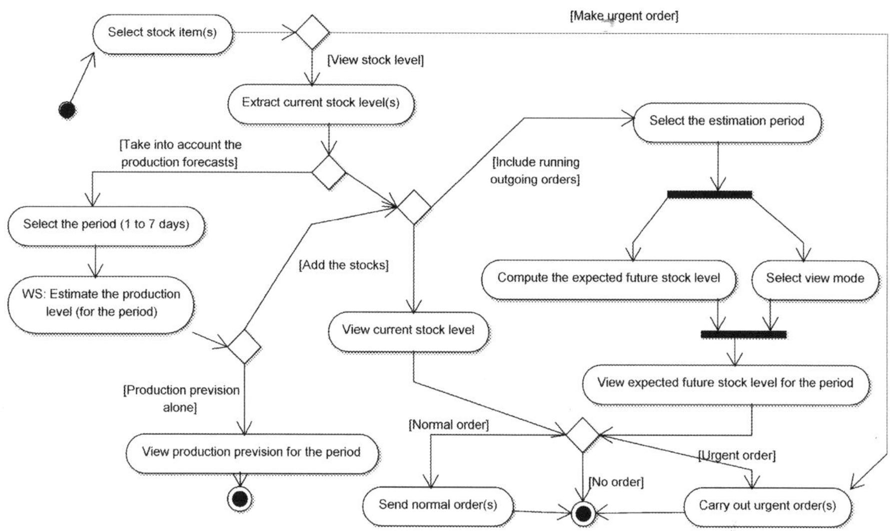

Fig. 2. Activity diagram of the use case *View stock level*

First, the system-to-be specified with UML has to satisfy the following main use cases. *View stock level*: the system-to-be should enable the purchase department to consult the stock levels for all existing products. *Carry out analysis of purchases*: the stock manager would like to have a specific interface to analyse the purchases made (mainly with descriptive statistics and underlying graphic illustrations). *Manage order error*: the purchase manager is in charge of the errors management detected when outgoing orders are delivered and encoded by a warehouse worker. *Send automatic order*: one of the main requirements of the company is to enable automatic sending of orders when a given threshold is reached. The use cases were refined with other UML diagrams. As an example, Fig. 2 represents the Activity diagram refining the use case: *View stock level*.

The IOC identified in the studied Activity diagram is 13: the IC is 5, the OC is 13 and the DSC is 0. E.g., for the activity "*Select stock item(s)*", the OC is 2×1 because of the request in the database (source weight is 2) allowing to display all the possible stock item(s) stored as string (type weigh is 1). The IC is 1×1 because of the selection made by the user through a device, e.g., the mouse or the keyboard.

Concerning the FRC, the use cases compose the functions set; their sub-functions are the steps of their respective Activity diagrams. The FRC value for the studied Activity diagram is 10 $(1 \times 9 + 1)$; 1 because we study here the sub-functions of only one main function, i.e., one use case, 9 because there are nine sub-functions –*send normal order(s)* and *carry out urgent order(s)* are extends use cases and thus refined in other Activity diagrams; the activity *Estimate the production level (for the period)* will be achieved through the use of a Web Service (WS) (+1).

Based on the stakeholders' non-functional requirements, the NFRC value is 10. The total RC value identified in this Activity Diagram is 20 $(10 + 10)$.

The stakeholders explain they want to use the J2EE development platform (one constraint) and the WS technologies –WSDL, SOAP and HTTP (three constraints)– in order to reuse the legacy application. Last but not least, the SOS will be hosted on the existing application server (one constraint). The total DCI value is $5\ (1+3+1)$.

The IFC value identified in the studied Activity Diagram is 16. There is one interface with the Warehouse Management IS, one with the 13 provider ISs, one user interface for the workers at the purchase department and one interface for the WS used.

In this example, two user classes were identified: the workers at the Purchase Department and their manager. Both of these two classes are parametric users (weight of 2). They should access the system-to-be from their company offices. The SDLC value is 2 (2×1).

No additional system features were required for this Activity. The SFC value is thus 0.

Once this work done for all the SOS specifications, the SOS RBC value can be computed. The result of this analysis based on Equations 1 to 9 is[5]: SOS RBC $= 5170$.

The SOS RBC value is then adjusted with the TCF's applicable to this system-to-be such as, e.g., *Distributed functions*, *Facilitate change* and *Third parties* IS, with a DI value of, respectively, 2, 1 and 5 evaluated as described in [7, 8]. The TCFV is: $0.65 + 0.01 \times 27 = 0.96$. The A-SOS RBC value is: $5170 \times 0.92 = 4756.4$.

The last step is the computation of the total work needed for the implementation of the system-to-be. The reference language used is J2EE: $L = 46$ (cf. §4.3). The productivity of the staff development has been estimated to 37 lines per hour thanks to an analysis of previous projects. So, the total development effort needed is: SOS RBE $= \frac{4756.4 \times 46}{37} \cong 5790$ hours. Once the average cost per hour known, the financial forecasting of the total development costs of the system-to-be can be drawn up.

6 Conclusions and Future Work

The model proposed, based on the specifications of a SOS, enables to compute the estimated development effort needed for its development. Eliciting, modelling and specifying correctly the requirements remain a significant success factor in the use of our model.

As underlined in §3, the three sources of software complexity –i.e., the structural, the conceptual and the computational complexity– are covered by the estimation model proposed. The analysis of the system-to-be specifications identifies the different software attributes of the structural complexity and put values behind each one (cf. Equations 1 to 9 from which the SOS RBC value can be computed). The TCFs used to adjust the SOS RBC value (cf. Equation 11) aim at adding the computational complexity to the1 model proposed. Indeed, they refer to the way that the stakeholders' requirements will be processed in the system-to-be according to its environment. Lastly, the third step in the model use takes into account the conceptual complexity. This is achieved thanks to Equation 12 in which the productivity of the development staff is added comparatively to the development language chosen for the project.

However, we put aside some difficulties. First, the system-to-be can be coded with more than one language while allowing the use of other programming languages for

[5] The detailed calculation is: $((IC + OC + DSC) \times (FRC + NFRC) + DCI + IFC + SFC) \times SDLC = ((21 + 33 + 5) \times (33 + 10) + 8 + 39 + 1) \times 2 = 5170$.

implementing the services used. Secondly, the productivity of the development staff deserves more attention. Although this problem is out of the scope of this work, one significant question remains unsolved: Is the productivity of development staff the same for SoC projects than for projects in line with other computing paradigms? To the best of our knowledge, there is no clear answer to this question.

References

1. O'Brien, L.: Keynote Talk: Scope, cost and effort estimation for SOA projects. In: Proceedings of the 12th IEEE International Enterprise Distributed Object Computing Conference Workshop (EDOCW), p. 254. IEEE Computer Society (2009)
2. Laird, L.M., Brennan, M.C.: Software Measurement and Estimation: A Practical Approach. Quantitative Software Engineering Series. Wiley - IEEE Computer Society (2007)
3. Bielak, J.: Improving Size Estimates Using Historical Data. IEEE Software 17(6), 27–35 (2000)
4. Pendharkar, P.C.: Probabilistic estimation of software size and effort. Expert Systems with Applications 37(6), 4435–4440 (2010)
5. Boehm, B.: Software Engineering Economics. Prentice-Hall (1981)
6. Tansey, B., Stroulia, E.: Valuating Software Service Development: Integrating COCOMO II and Real Options Theory. In: Proceedings of the First International Workshop on Economics of Software and Computation, pp. 8–10. IEEE Computer Society (2007)
7. Albrecht, A.J.: Function points as a measure of productivity. In: GUIDE 53 Meeting (1981)
8. Symons, C.R.: Function Point Analysis: Difficulties and Improvements. IEEE Transactions on Software Engineering 14, 2–11 (1988)
9. Santillo, L.: Seizing and sizing SOA applications with COSMIC Function Points. In: Proceedings of the 4th Software Measurement European Forum (SMEF 2007), pp. 155–166 (2007)
10. Oladimeji, Y.L., Folorunso, O., Taofeek, A.A., Adejumobi, A.I.: A Framework for Costing Service-Oriented Architecture (SOA) Projects Using Work Breakdown Structure (WBS) Approach. Global Journal of Computer Science and Technology 11, 35–47 (2011)
11. Liu, J., Xu, Z., Qiao, J., Lin, S.: A defect prediction model for software based on service oriented architecture using EXPERT COCOMO. In: Proceedings of the 21st Annual International Conference on Chinese Control and Decision Conference (CCDC 2009), pp. 2639–2642. IEEE Computer Society (2009)
12. Li, Z., Keung, J.: Software Cost Estimation Framework for Service-Oriented Architecture Systems Using Divide-and-Conquer Approach. In: The Fifth IEEE International Symposium on Service-Oriented System Engineering (SOSE 2010), pp. 47–54. IEEE Computer Society (2010)
13. Sharma, A., Kushwaha, D.S.: Natural language based component extraction from requirement engineering document and its complexity analysis. ACM SIGSOFT Software Engineering Notes 36(1), 1–14 (2011)
14. Sharma, A., Kushwaha, D.S.: Complexity measure based on requirement engineering document and its validation. In: International Conference on Computer and Communication Technology (ICCCT 2010), pp. 608–615. IEEE Computer Society (2010)
15. Sharma, A., Kushwaha, D.S.: A complexity measure based on requirement engineering document. Journal of Computer Science and Engineering 1(1), 112–117 (2010)
16. Papazoglou, M.P., Georgakopoulos, D.: Service-oriented Computing. Communications of the ACM 46(10), 24–28 (2003)

17. ISO/IEC: 25010 - Systems and software engineering - Systems and software Quality Requirements and Evaluation (SQuaRE) - System and software quality models. Technical report, The International Organization for Standardization (2010)
18. Sharma, A., Kushwaha, D.S.: An Improved SRS Document Based Software Complexity Estimation and Its Robustness Analysis. In: Computer Networks and Information Technologies. CCIS, vol. 142, pp. 111–117. Springer, Heidelberg (2011)
19. Kitchenham, B., Pfleeger, S.L., Fenton, N.E.: Towards a Framework for Software Measurement Validation. IEEE Transactions on Software Engineering 21(12), 929–943 (1995)
20. Nguyen, V., Deeds-Rubin, S., Tan, T., Boehm, B.: A SLOC counting standard. In: The 22nd International Annual Forum on COCOMO and Systems/Software Cost Modeling (2007)
21. Cataldo, M., Herbsleb, J.D., Carley, K.M.: Socio-technical Congruence: A Framework for Assessing the Impact of Technical and Work Dependencies on Software Development Productivity. In: Proceedings of the Second ACM-IEEE International Symposium on Empirical Software Engineering and Measurement (ESEM), pp. 2–11. ACM Press (2008)

Augmenting Complex Problem Solving with Hybrid Compute Units

Hong-Linh Truong[1], Hoa Khanh Dam[2], Aditya Ghose[2], and Schahram Dustdar[1]

[1] Distributed Systems Group, Vienna University of Technology, Austria
{truong,dustdar}@dsg.tuwien.ac.at
[2] University of Wollongong, Australia
{hoa,aditya}@uow.edu.au

Abstract. Combining software-based and human-based services is crucial for several complex problems that cannot be solved using software-based services alone. In this paper, we present novel methods for modeling and developing hybrid compute units of software-based and human-based services. We discuss high-level programming elements for different types of software- and human-based service units and their relationships. In particular, we focus on novel programming elements reflecting hybridity, collectiveness and adaptiveness properties, such as elasticity and social connection dependencies, and on-demand and pay-per-use economic properties, such as cost, quality and benefits, for complex problem solving. Based on these programming elements, we present programming constructs and patterns for building complex applications using hybrid services.

1 Introduction

Recently, several novel concepts have been introduced to exploit human computing capabilities together with machine computing capabilities. This combination has introduced a new form of "computing model" that includes both machine-based and human-based "computers". In this emerging computing model, machine-based and human-based computing elements are interconnected in different ways, thus it is possible to support different programming models built on top of them.

Indeed, there are different ways to develop applications atop such a new computing model. In the current research approaches, human-based capabilities are usually provisioned via "crowdsourcing" platforms [1] or specific human-task plug-ins [2,3]. These approaches achieve human and software integration mainly using (specific) platform integration. The main programming model is mostly the workflow which is however not flexible enough for programming different types of interactions among multiple types of services. In these approaches, essential programming elements representing software-based services (SBS) and human-based services (HBS) cannot be programmed directly into applications. Furthermore, these approaches do not provide a uniform view of SBS and HBS, and let the developer perform the complex tasks of establishing relationships between SBS and HBS. In addition, although SBS and HBS can be provisioned using cloud provisioning models (thus they can be requested and initiated on-demand under

A.R. Lomuscio et al. (Eds.): ICSOC 2013 Workshops, LNCS 8377, pp. 95–110, 2014.
© Springer International Publishing Switzerland 2014

different quality, cost and benefit models), there is a lack of mechanisms to program explicitly quality, cost, and benefit constraints for complex elastic applications.

In this paper, we view the "new computing model" as a collection of diverse and heterogeneous SBS and HBS that can be provisioned (e.g., by cloud computing models) on-demand under different cost, benefits and quality models. This view is very different from human-based workflows of which tasks and flows are (statically) mapped to humans. More specifically, our model considers humans as a service unit, like software service units, and takes into account diverse types of relationships among human-based and software-based service units, quality, cost and benefit properties. Our approach provides concepts for developing such applications where *hybrid service units*, their *relationships*, and *cost, quality and benefits* are first-class programming elements. Hence, our approach provides a higher level of abstraction and a flexible way for combining hybridity, collectiveness and adaptiveness of human-based and software-based services.

The rest of this paper is organized as follows: Section 2 discusses background, related work and our approach. Section 3 serves to describe programming elements covering units, relationships and non-functional parameters. In Section 4 we describe high-level programming constructs. Section 5 illustrates an example of how our approach works in practice. We conclude the paper and outline our future work in Section 6.

2 Background and Related Work

Several types of SBS, such as Infrastructure-as-a-Service (IaaS), Platform-as-a-Service (PaaS), Software-as-a-Service (SaaS), and Data-as-a-Service (DaaS), have been available and widely used in practice. Among these types of SBS, SaaS and IaaS are well conceptualized using service models and the developer can easily program and utilize SBS, their data and control flows, using APIs, such as, JClouds[1], Boto[2] and OpenStack[3]. On the other hand, HBS have been emerging and several work have devoted for virtualizing HBS and integrating them with SBS. Most systems support HBS in terms of providing specific platforms and plug-ins. Cloud APIs for interfacing to humans and on-demand accessing HBS have been proposed [4]. Although, such existing work has, to some extent, yet matured, there is an increasing demand for applications that use both HBS and SBS. However, existing programming languages and tools do not consider and exploit well the use of HBS and SBS together, in a flexible, on-demand, and pay-per-use manner. In the following, we discuss our main related work.

Software-Based Service Units Constructs: There exist several frameworks for engineering and executing cloud applications using different IaaS, PaaS and SaaS, such as Aneka [5], BOOM [6]. They abstract cloud resources and support different programming models, such as MapReduce and dataflows. But they do not consider hybrid services consisting of SBS and HBS and do not provide high level programming constructs for modelling the relationships among HBS and SBS. Most of them rely on traditional relationships among SBS, such as control and data dependencies, modeled in specific application structure descriptions, workflows and declarative programming languages.

[1] http://www.jclouds.org/

[2] http://docs.pythonboto.org/en/latest/index.html

[3] http://www.openstack.org/

Human Computation Programming Frameworks: There have been an increasing number of programming frameworks for human computation introduced in recent years. Most of existing work (e.g., Crowdforge [1], TurKit [2]) consider human workers as being homogeneous and interchangeable, which is useful in developing crowdsourcing solutions where scalability and availability are the main issues. Such frameworks, however, provide limited notion of identity, human skills, and social relationships which are important in developing an ecosystem of connected, heterogeneous people and software. The recent Jabberwocky framework [7] has addressed this issue to some extent by providing a programming environment for both human and machine computation. Jabberwocky also allows the programmer to specify types of people based on personal properties and expertise and route tasks based on social structure. However, Jabberwocky does not allow to explicitly model the relationships between people and machines. General-purpose programming languages for human computation, such as CrowdLang [8], do not rely on service models and do not consider quality, cost, benefits and elasticity as first-class entities in programming and constructing hybrid compute units.

High-Level Constructs for Hybrid Compute Units: Using several low level APIs for accessing SBS, like JClouds, Boto, and OpenStack, the developer can define SBS objects and establish data and control flows. Our previous work (e.g., [4]) has focused on providing well-defined APIs for provisioning HBS. However, there is a lack of support for programming different types of relationships among SBS and HBS. The developer has to do this on his/her own. As a result, he/she would find it difficult to code such relationships due to the lack of well-defined programming elements, in particular those related to cost, benefit, quality constraints and to mixed compositions of SBS and HBS. The use of generic "building blocks" abstracting patterns and providing them via APIs to simplify the developer task is well-known in SBS in clouds [9]. However, no high-level program constructs and code generation have been proposed for HBS and SBS in cloud environments.

Compared with existing work we are focusing on combining HBS and SBS for hybrid compute units using service computing and cloud computing models. Our approach supports unified framework for human and software, and provide high-level programming constructs for different types of services, relationships, and cost, quality, and benefits models.

3 Fundamental Elements for Hybrid Compute Units

3.1 Service-Based Compute Units

In our model, at the core of SBS and HBS there are "processing units", realized via either machine CPUs/cores or human brains. To program an application, the developer can exploit an SBS or HBS via an *abstract service unit*. Therefore, an application developed in our framework is abstractly viewed as consisting of a number of service-based compute units (see Figure 1) and their interactions. A *Unit* can perform a number functions (e.g., detecting a pattern in or enriching the quality of an image) with input and output data. A unit also has a number of cost, benefit, and quality properties (see Section 3.3 for more details). A unit can be either a *SBS* (Software-Based Service) or *HBS*

(Human-Based Service). We further divide HBS into *ICU* (Individual Compute Unit – representing a service offered by an individual) and *SCU* (Social Compute Unit – representing a service offered by a team). Both HBS and SBS units can potentially support elasticity in terms of capability (resource), cost and quality [10]. For example, a SBS for data analytics can increase its cost when being asked to provide higher analysis accuracy or a SCU can reduce its size and the cost when being asked to reduce the quality of the result. To support solving complex problems with elastic service units, we model elasticity capability (*ElasticityCapability*) and associate it with *Unit*.

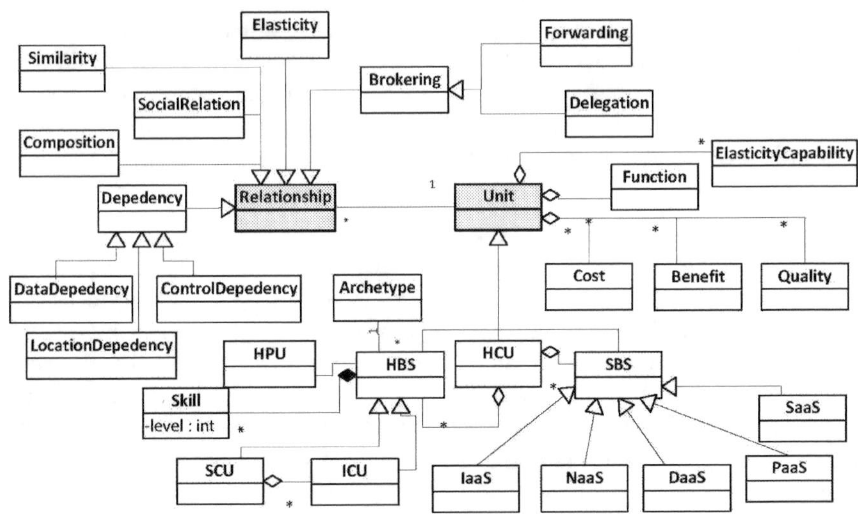

Fig. 1. A conceptual model for elements in programming hybrid compute units

A SBS unit can be in number of known software forms offered in cloud computing models, such as IaaS (e.g., Amazon EC), DaaS (e.g., Microsoft Azure Data Marketplace), PaaS (e.g., Google App Engine) or SaaS (e.g., Salesforce.com). Although many ongoing work is still being developed for SBS, SBS are already extensively explored in terms of service management, capabilities, and function modeling. Therefore, we rely on existing common models for representing SBS.

For HBS, their computing capability is specified in terms of human skills and skill levels. Therefore, in our model a HBS unit has a set of `Skills`, each of which is associated with a skill level. Those skills and skill levels can be defined consistently within a particular service provisioning platform (using evaluation techniques, benchmarking, or mapping skills from different sources into a common view for the whole platform). Therefore, we associate each HBS with a Human Power Unit (HPU) [4], a value defined by the HBS provisioning platform to describe the computing power of the HBS based on its skills and skill levels, which are always associated with specific `Archetypes` indicating the domain in which the skills are established.

By combining a set of HBS and SBS, we introduce *hybrid compute units* (HCUs). A HCU is a collective, hybrid service-based units among which there exist different types of relationships, covering human-specific, software-specific, as well as human-software specific ones. A *HCU*, as a collective unit, can be elastic: it can be expanded and reduced based on specific conditions.

3.2 Relationships between Service Units

Using cloud computing provisioning models in which SBS and HBS are abstractly represented under the same service unit model with pay-per-use and on-demand service usage, a range of programming elements reflecting relationships among different types of service units are important and useful in building complex applications. Table 1 describes different types of relationships between service units that we consider as important programming elements, each of which applies to HBS, SBS or HCU.

Table 1. Different types of relationships between services

Relationship Type	HBS	SBS	HCU	Description
Similarity	Yes	Yes	Yes	This traditional type of relationship indicates how similar a service is to another. In principle, similarity can be measured in terms of *functions*, *non-functional parameters* and *social contexts*.
Composition	Yes	Yes	Yes	This well-known type of service relationships indicates that a service is composed of several other services.
Data dependency	Yes	Yes	Yes	A service depends on another service if the former requires the latter for providing a certain data for one of its functions.
Control dependency	Yes	Yes	Yes	A service depends on another service if the outcome of latter determines whether former should be executed or not.
Location dependency	Yes	Yes	Yes	The locations of two service units are dependent, e.g., co-located in the same data center or country
Forwarding	Yes	Yes	Yes	This is a form of brokering/outsourcing in which a task is forwarded form one service to another.
Delegation	Yes	Yes	Yes	This is a form of brokering/outsourcing in which a service delegates a task to another service.
Social relation	Yes	No	Yes	This relationship describes different types of social relations (e.g. family or Linkedin connection) between two services.
Elasticity	Yes	Yes	Yes	This relationship describes how a service unit is formed by elasticizing another service unit, e.g. via resizing, replacing or (de)composing elements of the later to offer similar functions but different cost, benefit and quality at runtime.

Similarity. Given that certain tasks can be conducted by software or human, developers will need to compare HBS and SBS in order to select suitable ones for the tasks. We extend traditional similarity among SBS for HBS (e.g., simulation result analysis can be provided by two different research teams which are similar in terms of archetype and/or cost) or between HBS and SBS (e.g., specific image patterns can be detected by scientists or image processing software). From the programming perspective, similarity can be specified in applications in terms of cost and quality (for all unit types), archetype (between HBS units), capability (between SBS units) and function (between HBS and SBS units).

Composition. Composing HBS and SBS units for complex tasks are possible. Therefore, we extend traditional composition relationships to cover also composites of hybrid services, such as describing how ICU can be composed with SBS to establish human-based filter. Composition can be in different forms such as data or control decomposition, and can be structured in different ways (e.g., star vs. ring structure).

Dependency. We support the classical view of dependency between services in terms of data (a service requires data provided by another service) and control (a service requires an successful completion of another service). Data and control dependencies can be programmed for any types of SBS and HBS. In particular, data exchange between two units can be conducted via other service units (e.g., two HBS can exchange data via Dropbox – a SBS). Furthermore, we consider *location dependency* which is crucial in clouds due to not only performance but also compliance requirements. Developers can use the location dependency to control the co-location of services.

Brokering. We consider brokering relationships for work distribution among service units. Two types of brokering relationships are considered: *delegation* (a service manipulates a request/response and delegates the request/response to/from another services) and *forwarding* (a service just forwards request/result to/from another service). With hybrid services, such relationships can also be established between a SBS and a HBS, e.g., a SBS can decide where a SBS or an HBS will be used for evaluating the quality of data based on the type of the data.

Social Relation. When using HBS for certain tasks in complex applications, we may require specific social relations among HBS solving the tasks, for example, two scientists who have conducted a joint research before. To support this, social relations are considered as programming elements.

Elasticity. This emerging relationship is due to the elasticity capability of services at runtime [10]. To the consumer, elasticity means that the expected service function is unchanged but the cost, benefits and/or quality can be scaled up/down at runtime. To the service provider, to enable the elasticity of costs, benefits, and/or quality, at runtime service units can be replaced by different variants or similar units or (re)composed by adding/removing appropriate units, or new compositions are introduced.

3.3 Quality, Cost, and Benefits

SBS and HBS have common and distinguishable quality, cost and benefit properties. In order to allow programmers to specify these properties, we support the following programming elements:

- Quality: represents common quality metrics and models for processing units and data. Quality can be further classified into `Performance` for processing capabilities of service units and `QoD` (quality of data) for input/output of service units. `Performance` and `QoD` can have several other sub entities, such as ResponseTime, Availability, Accuracy, and Completeness.
- Cost: represents monetary pricing models, such as charging or rewarding models.
- Benefits: represents non-monetary benefits. It is classified into different entities, such as Return-on-Opportunity or Promotion.

We consider these properties as first-class programming elements since service units are constrained by various types of cost, benefit and quality models and the service provider wants to program her SBS/HBS/HCU to be able to scale in/out with expected quality under desirable cost and benefit at runtime. For example, in a situation with several real-time events signaling an emergency situation, an HCU might be programmed to reduce the accuracy of analytics in order to meet the response time to quickly react to the situation. On the other hand, in non-critical situations it could be programmed to utilize more (cheap) HBS to minimize the cost, maximize the accuracy, but accept an increasing response time as a trade-off. Therefore, treating these properties as first-class programming elements will allow the developer to explicitly specify, control, and enforce elastic constraints.

4 High-Level Constructs for Hybrid Compute Units

From our proposed fundamental elements, in order to assist the development of complex applications, we develop a number of high-level constructs for service units and the relationships between them that help establish interactions among units in a hybrid compute unit. Those constructs correspond to the conceptual model elements presented in Figure 1. Constructs for service units have a set of APIs that can be called upon the units. Constructs for a relationship have a set of (usage) patterns that can be used to establish the relationship. Constructs for cost, quality and benefits also have a set of APIs for specifying expected costs, quality and benefits. Using high-level programming constructs the developer can focus on the logic of the hybrid compute unit, instead of dealing with implementation-specific details of service units and complex algorithms for establishing relationships among units.

Table 2 presents main programming constructs for relationships, each of which is abstractly represented as a function which takes a number of arguments. There are two types of functions: one that takes grounded variables (denoted as capital letters) as arguments, and one that takes free variable (denoted as lower case letters) as arguments. The latter is denoted with the symbol "?" in the function name. In the following, we explain some possible algorithmic patterns for high-level constructs for relationships:

Similarity. The construct $similarity(U, V, criteria)$ represents a similarity relationship between units U and V with regard to a given $criteria$ (namely "Cost", "Quality",

Table 2. High-level constructs for relationships in hybrid compute units

Construct	Description
$similarity(U, V, criteria)$	true if U is similar to V w.r.t. $criteria$
$datadependency(U, D, [M,]V)$	U producing data D which is needed by V. The optional $medium$ is the location associated with a DaaS (e.g., a Dropbox URL) where the data will be placed and shared.
$controldependency(U, V)$	declares that V should execute only after U finishes.
locationdependency(U, V, ctx, path)	declares that U and V should be linked in a given location context (e.g., country or data center) with a path in that context (e.g., city or server rack)
$composition(structure, type, U_1, U_2, \cdots, U_n)$	construct a composition of $U_1, U_2, ..., U_n$ for a given structure model and type
$forward(U, t, V)$	U forwards task t to V.
$delegate(U, t, V)$	U delegates task t to V.
$socialrelation(U, V, ctx, path)$	returns a distance relation between U and V in a given social context.
$?elasticity(U, [Func,]NFPs, x)$	x is a new form of U or x provides function $Func$ to satisfy given cost/quality/benefit models specified in $NFPs$.

"Archetype", or "Function"). A variant of this construct is $?similarity(U, x, criteria)$ which returns a set of units similar to U with regard to a given $criteria$ and store them in a free variable x. Pseudo algorithmic for this construct usages is shown below.

```
if (criteria == "Cost") return simCost(U, V);
else if (criteria == "Quality") return simQuality(U, V);
else if (criteria == "Archetype" && U.type == HBS && V.type ==
    HBS)    return (U.Archetype == V.Archetype);
else if (criteria == "Function") return U.Function==V.Function;
return false;
```

Data Dependency. The construct $datadependency(U, D, M, V)$ states that V depends on U for data D and medium M where the data is stored. Variants of this construct include $?datadependency(x, D, M, V)$ (find unit x which provides data D needed by unit V), $?datadependency(U, D, M, x)$ (find unit x which needs data D), and $?datadependency(U, D, x[c], V)$ (find a medium x that can be used to share D between U and V satisfying a given constraint c). Pseudo algorithmic code for data dependency constructs are shown in the following:

```
datadependency(U, D, M, V) {
  Unit storageUnit = M;
  if (M==null) storageUnit = getDedaultMedium()
  request U stores D into storageUnit
  //get the URI indicating the location of the data
  URI uri = storageUnit.getURI(D)
  request V access D from uri
}
```

Location Dependency. The construct $locationdependency(U, V, ctx, path)$ establishes a location dependency between U and V based on a specific context ctx and a specific $path$ in cxt. Here ctx can represent human-specific location context, such as the cloud platform providing HBS (e.g., based on Amazon Mechanical Turk) or the country, or cloud data center locations hosting SBS (e.g., Amazon EC2 EU site). The $path$ can indicate further dependencies in ctx, such as the same city or the same server rack in a data center.

Brokering. Delegation and forwarding relations are simply represented by $delegate(U, task, V)$ and $forward(U, task, V)$ where $task$ is a given task that needs to be delegated or forwarded. A variant of the delegation construct is $?delegate(U, task, x)$ which finds a appropriate unit x that U can delegate task t to. Pseudo code generated for $delegate(U, task, x)$ are given as follows:

```
for u: listUnit()
    for f:u.listFunction()
        if ((f.input == task.in) && f.output == task.out) {
            u.execute(task);
            U.waitUntil(task.finished == true);
            U.addInput(task.out);
            return;
        }
```

Social Relations. The construct $socialrelation(U, V, ctx, path)$ returns a distance between U and V (HBS only) via social relations in a given social context, denoted by $(cxt, path)$. It can also be used to establish a social relation constraint between U and V. The context ctx is a social network (e.g., Linkedin) and $path$ is a specific group in that network (e.g., data scientist). A negative distance (e.g., -1) indicates that there is no social relation found between U and V, whilst a value of 0 indicates that they belongs to the same given social group (e.g., in data science group on Linkedin). On the other hand, a positive value indicates that they are related via some third parties who are directly related with them, e.g., A is a Linkedin colleague of B, B is a colleague of C, then the distance between A and C is 1. In order to find a HBS that is socially related to a given HBS within a specified distance, one can use the construct $?socialrelation(U, x, distance, ctx, path)$. The pseudo algorithmic code for $?socialrelation(U, x, distance, ctx, path)$ construct is as follows:

```
?socialrelation(U, x, distance, ctx, path) {
  for hbs:listHBS()
    //get the subgraph of the social network within a context
    Graph socialNet = getSocialNetwork(ctx);
    //find the distance
    int d = social.findDistance(U, hbs, path);
    if d <= distance
        x.addElement(hbs);
  return x;
}
```

Elasticity. Elasticity construct can be used for different purposes. In the simplest case, the construct $?elasticity(U, elasticityReq, x)$ returns a new unit x that offer similar functions as unit U does but guarantees the elasticity requirement $elasticityReq$:

```
for v:listUnit() {
    boolean result = similarity(U,v,''function'')
    if (result)
         ElasticityCapability elasCap = v.
             getElasticityCapability();
         result=result && (matches (elasCap, elasticityReq);
    if (result) return x ;
}
```

Elasticity construct $?elasticity(Func, elasticityReq, x)$ returns a (new) unit x that offers function $Func$ as long as the elasticity requirement is met.

5 Illustrating Examples and Comparison

5.1 Towards the Prototype Implementation

We are currently implementing our model of hybrid compute units and corresponding programming elements and constructs in our Vienna Elastic Computing Model (VieCOM)[4] using Java. Figure 2 depicts the general architecture of our prototype in which hybrid collective adaptive systems (hCAS) could be programmed using our programming elements and constructs.

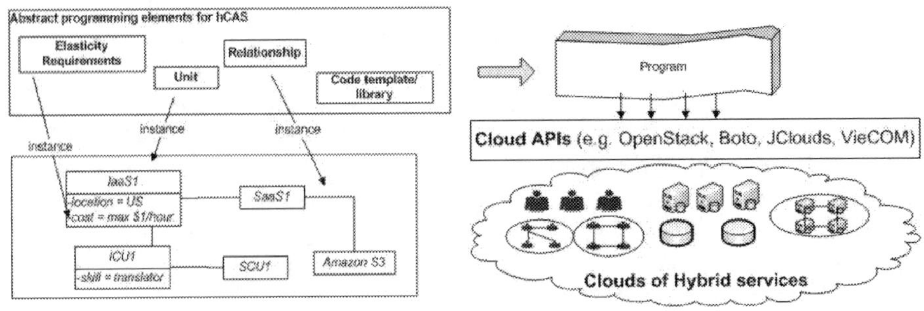

Fig. 2. The architecture of our approach

5.2 Illustrative Application

To illustrate the "expressiveness" of our programming models, we use an illustrative application which is based on a real-world simulation application. Consider a multi-scale simulation application that utilizes different software as simulation solvers and visualization services. Typically, the simulation application includes several components,

[4] dsg.tuwien.ac.at/research/viecom

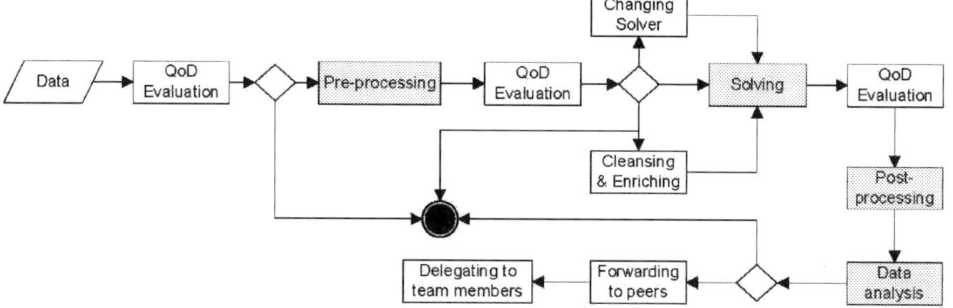

Fig. 3. Expected simulation components and their interactions using both SBS and HBS

each of which is a SBS unit performing a particular task. These components can be used to pre-process data, execute solver engines, post-process results and analyze final results. In such an application, the quality of input, and the intermediate and final resulting data is crucial. Therefore, several components for evaluating quality of data (QoD) can be introduced into the application. Currently, such QoD evaluation components are rarely designed in the application. When redesigning the simulation application with QoD evaluation components, we face a problem: evaluating QoD cannot be done fully by SBS and we need to augment the application with human-based services to carry out runtime quality evaluation [11]. Furthermore, whether the employment of software or human-based service units for QoD evaluation is dependent on runtime aspects. Based on this application, we present how our programming elements and high-level constructs can be useful for implementing complex tasks using cloud APIs for SBS and HBS units.

Figure 3 describes expected simulation components and control flows using both SBS and HBS. Typically, only four main components are described in the simulation, namely `pre-processing`, `solving`, `post-processing`, and `data analysis`. However, by employing QoD-aware activities, we can introduce several new components for evaluating QoD and utilizing QoD to control the simulation. In the following we will illustrate how our programming elements and constructs can simplify the development of such new components and their interactions. For the sake of simplicity, we will not show the whole applications but illustrate main parts.

QoD Evaluation. *QoDEvaluation* components can be implemented different: (i) only SBS is needed, for example, in the QoDEvaluation step before `pre-processing`, (ii) SBS or HBS is used interchangeably, for example, in the *QoDEvaluation* after `pre-processing`, or (iii) only HBS is used, e.g., in *QoDEvaluation* after `solving`.

Let `preprocessingUnit` be the SBS unit performing pre-processing activity. Let `qodEvalUnit` be the service unit required for *QoDEvaluation*. The following code excerpt shows how we can program two units to perform the QoD evaluation and `preprocessing`:

```
//create an instance of software unit
SBS preprocessingUnit =new SBS() ;
File data =new File(fileName);
//...
//create another unit for QoD evaluation
SBS qodEvalUnit = new SBS();
ArrayList paraType = new ArrayList();
paraType.add(File.class.getName());
//the unit must support qodEvaluate function which returns a
    value in [0,1]
qodEvalUnit.setFunction("qodEvaluate",paraType,Double.class.
    getName());
//...
ArrayList params = new ArrayList();
params.add(data);
//call qod evaluation unit
Double result =(Double)qodEvalUnit.execute("qodEvaluate",params)
    ;
Object preProcessedData = null;
//call preprocessing activity if QoD is satisfied
if (result > 0.9) {
        preProcessedData=preprocessingUnit.execute("
            preprocessing",params);
}
```

Specifying Location Dependency. Let `solverUnit` be the solver SBS unit. The following code excerpt shows how to make sure that the `preprocessingUnit` and `solvingUnit` should be colocated in the same data center in order to minimize the data transfer among them:

```
//create a new software unit for simulation solvers
SBS solverUnit = new SBS("solver");
//make sure the solver unit and the preprocessing unit are in
    the same data center
Relationship.locationDependency(preprocessingUnit,solverUnit,"
    AmazonEC2:Europe");
ArrayList params1 = new ArrayList();
params1.add(preProcessedData);
//execute solver unit with input data from preprocessing unit
Object solverResult= solverUnit.execute("solving",params1);
```

Programming Elasticity and Collectiveness in Solving Steps. Using different constructs, the programmer can invoke different types of units to deal with different situations. The following code excerpt shows examples of using ICU to check why the data is bad or to find solvers that can handle dirty data as long as they meet cost and quality requirements:

```
Double qodPreProcessedData =
    (Double)qodEvalUnit.execute("qodEvaluate", params1);
//get an ICU to check why data is bad
if (qodPreProcessedData < 0.5) {
//initiate a new unit
  ICU dataScientist = new ICU();
//create a dropbox place for sharing data
  DropboxAPI<WebAuthSession> scuDropbox = null;
  // ....
  DropboxAPI.DropboxLink link = scuDropbox.share("/hbscloud");
//ask the cloud of HBS to invoke the ICU
  VieCOMHBS vieCOMHBS = new VieCOMHBSImpl();
  vieCOMHBS.startHBS(dataScientist);
  HBSMessage msg = new HBSMessage();
  msg.setMsg("pls. use shared dropbox for communication " +link.
      url);
  vieCOMHBS.sendMessageToHBS(dataScientist, msg);
} else if (qodPreProcessedData < 0.7) {
//in this case, we just need a software to clean the data
     SBS dataCleansing = new SBS("datacleaner");
    //...
} else if (qodPreProcessedData < 0.9) {
  //specify some static properties of the solver
  SBS solverUnit2 = new SBS("solver");
  solverUnit2.capabilities.put("DIRTY_DATA", Boolean.valueOf(
      true));
  //specify expected cost and accuracy support
  CostModel costModel = new CostModel();
  costModel.price = 100; //max in EUR
  costModel.usageTime = 1000 * 60 * 60; //1 hour
  Quality quality = new Quality();
  quality.name = Quality.ACCURACY;
  quality.value = 0.95; // minimum value
  ArrayList nfps = new ArrayList();
  nfps.add(quality); nfps.add(costModel);
  //find solvers met quality and cost needs
  SBS elasticSolverUnit = (SBS)Relationship.elasticity(
      solverUnit2,nfps);          Object solverResult2 =
      elasticSolverUnit.execute("solving", params1);
} else {
      // ....
}
```

Forwarding and Delegating Analysis Request. After *post-processing*, in `data analysis`, an analyst can capture an unknown pattern which he/she can forward to his/her research connectors, who have a social relation to him/her in Linkedin.

A professor may receive this pattern and he/she delegates the analysis tasks to his/her SCU, a set of graduate students. The following code excerpt shows the above-mentioned illustrative tasks:

```
ICU dataScientist = new ICU();
// ....
ICU fUnit = new ICU();
Relationship.socialrelation(dataScientist, fUnit,1,"Linkedin:
    DataScienceGroup/TUWien");
Relationship.forward(data, fUnit);
// ...
SCU studentSCU = new SCU();
// ..
Relationship.delegate(data, studentSCU);
```

5.3 Comparison of Programming Models for Cloud Applications

We also conduct a comparison of our approach with other prominent programming frameworks for cloud applications. The set of features that are considered in this comparison is:

- *Proactive human service*: support for proactively invoking human-based service units through human's capabilities are utilized.
- *Elasticity*: support for adapting services against changing non-functional parameters.
- *Team interaction/collaborative patterns*: support for interactions and/or collaboration patterns among different services to establish teamwork.
- *Social structure/relations*: support to request services based on social structure and/or relations.
- *Unified framework for human and software*: allow the developer to naturally program software services and human-based services in similar ways.
- *Cross-platform*: work with any cloud platform that hooks into the framework and and can support execution across several platforms in the same program.

Programming Feature	Crowdforge	TurKit	Jabberwocky	JClouds	OpenStack	VieCOM
Proactive human service	N	N	Y	N	N	Y
Explicit cost/benefits/quality	N	N	N	N	N	Y
Elasticity	N	N	N	N	N	Y
Team interaction/collaborative patterns	N	N	N	N	N	Y
Social structure/relations	N	N	Y	N	N	Y
Unified framework for human and software	N	N	Y	N	N	Y
Cross-platform	N	N	Y	Y	Y	Y

Fig. 4. Comparison of different programming models for cloud applications

Figure 4 describes our comparison. It is not a strange result that, conceptually, our approach (VieCOM) supports several features, in particular, covering both SBS and HBS. The main reason is that currently existing frameworks focus either on SBS or HBS. While Jabberwocky also supports SBS and HBS, it does not support programming elements for defining costs, benefits and quality as well as elasticity relations.

6 Conclusions and Future Work

Emerging pay-per-use models, on-demand service acquisition, and advanced human-machine integration techniques enable the provisioning of human and machine capabilities under the same service model to support the development of complex applications. In this paper, we investigate high level programming supports for solving complex problems using software-based and human-based compute units. We have presented a range of possible fundamental programming elements abstracting software and people and several possible high-level constructs. As the paper mainly discusses about high-level models and constructs, our validation is limited to illustrating examples and comparisons. We believe that programming elements and high-level programming constructs presented in this paper can be foundations for the development of domain-specific languages and software engineering processes for hybrid compute units. Our future work involves further developing our prototype and tooling support for the proposed high-level programming constructs.

Acknowledgment. The work mentioned in this paper is partially supported by the EU FP7 SmartSociety.

References

1. Kittur, A., Smus, B., Khamkar, S., Kraut, R.E.: CrowdForge: crowdsourcing complex work. In: Proceedings of the 24th Annual ACM Symposium on User Interface Software and Technology, UIST 2011, pp. 43–52. ACM, New York (2011)
2. Little, G., Chilton, L.B., Goldman, M., Miller, R.C.: Turkit: tools for iterative tasks on mechanical turk. In: Proceedings of the ACM SIGKDD Workshop on Human Computation, HCOMP 2009, pp. 29–30. ACM, New York (2009)
3. Marcus, A., Wu, E., Karger, D., Madden, S., Miller, R.: Human-powered sorts and joins. Proc. VLDB Endow. 5, 13–24 (2011)
4. Truong, H.-L., Dustdar, S., Bhattacharya, K.: Programming hybrid services in the cloud. In: Liu, C., Ludwig, H., Toumani, F., Yu, Q. (eds.) ICSOC 2012. LNCS, vol. 7636, pp. 96–110. Springer, Heidelberg (2012)
5. Calheiros, R.N., Vecchiola, C., Karunamoorthy, D., Buyya, R.: The Aneka platform and qos-driven resource provisioning for elastic applications on hybrid clouds. Future Generation Comp. Syst. 28(6), 861–870 (2012)
6. Alvaro, P., Marczak, W.R., Conway, N., Hellerstein, J.M., Maier, D., Sears, R.: DEDALUS: Datalog in time and space. In: de Moor, O., Gottlob, G., Furche, T., Sellers, A. (eds.) Datalog 2010. LNCS, vol. 6702, pp. 262–281. Springer, Heidelberg (2011)
7. Ahmad, S., Battle, A., Malkani, Z., Kamvar, S.: The jabberwocky programming environment for structured social computing. In: Proceedings of the 24th Annual ACM Symposium on User Interface Software and Technology, UIST 2011, pp. 53–64. ACM, New York (2011)

8. Minder, P., Bernstein, A.: *crowdLang*: A programming language for the systematic exploration of human computation systems. In: Aberer, K., Flache, A., Jager, W., Liu, L., Tang, J., Guéret, C. (eds.) SocInfo 2012. LNCS, vol. 7710, pp. 124–137. Springer, Heidelberg (2012)
9. Fehling, C., Leymann, F., Ruetschlin, J., Schumm, D.: Pattern-based development and management of cloud applications. Future Internet 4(1), 110–141 (2012)
10. Dustdar, S., Guo, Y., Satzger, B., Truong, H.L.: Principles of elastic processes. IEEE Internet Computing 15(5), 66–71 (2011)
11. Reiter, M., Breitenbücher, U., Dustdar, S., Karastoyanova, D., Leymann, F., Truong, H.L.: A novel framework for monitoring and analyzing quality of data in simulation workflows. In: eScience, pp. 105–112. IEEE Computer Society (2011)

Towards Automating the Detection of Event Sources

Nico Herzberg, Oleh Khovalko, Anne Baumgrass, and Mathias Weske

Hasso Plattner Institute at the University of Potsdam
Prof.-Dr.-Helmert-Straße 2-3, 14482 Potsdam
{nico.herzberg,oleh.khovalko,anne.baumgrass,
mathias.weske}@hpi.uni-potsdam.de

Abstract. During business process execution, various systems and services produce a variety of data, messages, and events that are valuable for gaining insights about business processes, e.g., to ensure a business process is executed as expected. However, these data, messages, and events usually originate from different kinds of sources, each specified by different kinds of descriptions. This variety makes it difficult to automate the detection of relevant event sources for business process monitoring. In this paper, we present a course of actions to automatically associate different event sources to event object types required for business process monitoring. In particular, in a three-step approach we determine the similarity of event sources to event object types, rank those results, and derive a mapping between their attributes. Thus, relevant event sources and their bindings to specified event object types of business processes can be automatically identified. The approach is implemented and evaluated using schema matching techniques for a specific use case that is aligned with real-world energy processes, data, messages, and events.

1 Introduction

Service-Oriented Architecture (SOA) enables flexible operations by utilizing highly-distributed and loosely-coupled applications [1]. These applications use different functions encapsulated as services by information systems that are based on the SOA paradigm. These services interact with each other by the means of messages and events [2]. In parallel, these messages and events provide information required for operations (executed by services or humans) in an organization.

Nowadays, frequent changing markets and customer requirements force companies to quickly adapt their operations to stay competitive within their environment. That is why they strive to run their operations in a process-oriented way using tools and practices from Business Process Management (BPM) to achieve their goals. BPM comprises concepts, methods, and techniques to support the design, administration, configuration, enactment, and analysis of business processes [3].

One of the current research areas of BPM is Business Process Intelligence (BPI) that comprises process analysis, monitoring, and mining [4]. During the execution of business processes – run of the process instances – services and humans are utilized to fulfill certain tasks and at the same time events can occur which represent the real world happenings and the current process state. This information about process execution is

A.R. Lomuscio et al. (Eds.): ICSOC 2013 Workshops, LNCS 8377, pp. 111–122, 2014.
© Springer International Publishing Switzerland 2014

essential for analysis and improvement of business processes. It can be used for monitoring, to identify current and predict upcoming process steps by observing occurred events, and deriving process behavior from them [5,6]. However, processing events in distributed and heterogeneous environments in a semantically meaningful way requires explicit information about the structure and semantics of events. This is enabled by the framework presented by Herzberg et. al [7], but includes mostly manual steps to identify and connect the right event sources. These steps are subject for automation.

In this paper, we introduce a three-step approach that enables us to automatically identify an event source in a collection of event sources which matches a given Event Object Type (EOT) of a business process. It determines the similarity of event sources to event object types, ranks those results, and derives a mapping between their attributes. Thus, this technique establishes the basis for fine-grained business process monitoring by allowing the monitoring of an unlimited amount of events that originate from different kinds of sources and are specified by different kinds of descriptions.

The remainder of the paper is structured as follows. In Section 2, we introduce basic concepts and terms we build on, followed by the introduction of our use case from the utilities domain, in Section 3. In Section 4, we describe our approach of detecting event sources and detail the three main steps. The evaluation of the presented approach using schema matching techniques based on the introduced use case is explained in Section 5. In Section 6, related work is considered before we conclude our work in Section 7.

2 Preliminaries

In our work, we explicitly distinguish between real-world events and event objects. A *real-world event* happens in a particular *point in time* at a certain *place* in a certain *context* (cf. [8,9]). The context describes the situation in which the event has happened. Real-world events that are represented in information systems are called *event objects*. An event object is an object that represents, encodes, or records a real-world event, generally for the purpose of computer processing [10]. We embed our approach in the framework from Herzberg et. al [7] which is described below.

Real-world events are observed and published as machine-readable event objects via *event sources* (see Fig. 1). Typically, an event source publishes one specific type of event objects, e.g., the European Energy Exchange publishes the values of the European Electricity Index. The *event source description* defines the structure and semantics of event objects the event source provides.

The structure of event objects that need to be processed is described by an *EOT* (see Fig. 1). In particular, the EOT (i) defines the structure of the event content and (ii) provides the rules for mapping the information of real-world events into event objects, the so-called binding.

Definition 1 (Event Object Type (EOT))
An event object type $EOT = (cd, bind)$ consists of a specification of the event content structure cd and a binding $bind$ that describes the way how the information of a concrete event source needs to be utilized to form an event object. ◇

A binding is a function specifying the rules and methods to extract real-world event information from the event sources for an EOT. The implementation of the extraction

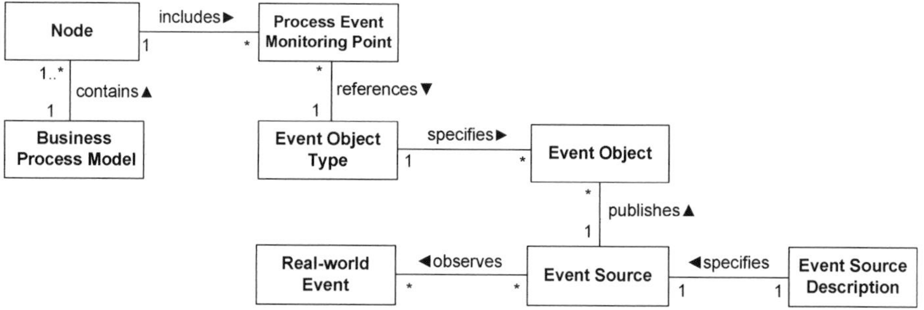

Fig. 1. The connection between a business process model and real-world events

of real-world event information can be established by applying techniques and methods from the domain of Complex Event Processing (CEP).

Event objects need to be assigned to specific points in the business process to enable BPI. Business processes are specified in business process models.

Definition 2 (Business Process Model)
A business process model $M = (N, F)$ consists of nodes N and flow relations $F \subseteq N \times N$ that connect nodes. Every node $n \in N$ has an assigned life cycle $C : N \rightarrow 2^S \times 2^T$ consisting of states S and state transitions $T \subseteq S \times S$. ◇

We utilize the concept of Process Event Monitoring Points (PEMPs) that define at which point in a process an event object is expected [7] (see Fig. 1). Therefore, a PEMP references an EOT. This connection is defined during design time in a process model. The points in the process model a PEMP can be assigned to are described by life cycles of the nodes, i.e., activities, gateways, and events. Assigning PEMPs on node life cycle level enables fine-grained BPI.

Definition 3 (Process Event Monitoring Point)
Let $M = (N, F)$ be a process model and $C(n) = (S', T')$ the node life cycle consisting of states $S' \in 2^S$ and state transitions $T' \in 2^T$ for a node $n \in N$. A *process event monitoring point* is a tuple $PEMP = (M, n, t, E)$, where M is the process model it is contained in, $n \in N$ is the node it is created for, $t \in T'$ is the state transition within the node life cycle of n, and E represents the set of references to its defined EOTs. ◇

3 Use Case

We introduce the approach of automating the event source detection along an example from the utilities domain. We consider the change of an energy supplier (COS) at the distribution organization from the request of a COS until all parties are informed about the COS or the rejection of the transactions. As a common technique to represent business processes, we illustrate the described process using a Business Process Model and Notation (BPMN) [11] process model shown in the upper part of Fig. 2. A customer requests a change of supplier at its new selected energy supplier. This request is then forwarded to the distributor by the new supplier and therewith, the change of supplier

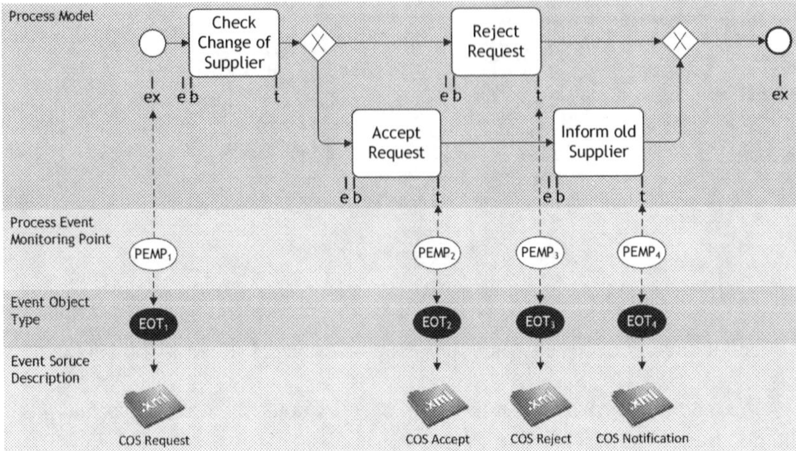

Fig. 2. Framework proposed by Herzberg et. al [7] applied to an use case from the utilities domain: business process model for handling the change of an energy supplier for a household from the distributor point of view, PEMPs associated to the node state transitions (e)nable, (b)egin, (t)erminate, or (ex)ecute, EOTs, and event sources

process at distributor site starts (start event). Afterwards the request is checked (*Check Change of Supplier*) for feasibility by the distributor and the corresponding acceptance or rejection is handled (*Accept Request* and *Reject Request*). In case the COS is accepted by the distributor a notification about the change of supplier is send to the old energy provider (*Inform old Supplier*). Afterwards, no further activities have to be performed by the client and the process ends (end event).

The data created during that process deliver valuable insights about the progress of each process instance. In our recent approach [7], we introduced a framework that allows to define PEMPs with which we are able to associate EOTs originating from different sources to business processes and enable BPI. Fig. 2 illustrates this association. Below the process model, the PEMPs are associated with state transitions of activities, start or end events, and thus contain the connection to a business process. To transform real-world events from different event sources to events relevant for the business process we define EOTs. We assume the association of an EOT to a PEMP is given and focus on identifying the binding between an EOT and an event source.

Examples for the use case are taken from real-world cases of the energy market. In particular, we used the data of the Association of Swiss Electricity Companies[1]. It provides 73 publicly available XML schema definitions (XSDs) which describe the message interchange format of Swiss electricity market[2] and represent our event sources. Their structure is rather complex, as they are interlinked with each other and contain a lot of complex element structure descriptions. For instance, the COS request schema definition (*RequestToMPA*) and its linked core component, shown in Listing 1.1,

[1] http://www.strom.ch/

[2] Schemas, descriptions, and examples are available at: http://www.strom.ch/de/dossiers/strommarkt/sdat.html

imports 30 other schemas, defines 22 elements and 62 complex types used for the structure definition. In Line 12 of Listing 1.1, we see the structure in which the switch date period of the COS request is indicated. This element is defined by a complex type, see Line 20, which refers to another simple type, see Line 26.

Furthermore, the systems used for message exchange, as well as the content of the COS-related messages may differ for each supplier that is communicating with the distribution organization in this process. Because of that numerous amount of structure information it is difficult to manually define the binding between the event sources and the defined EOTs. Therefore, an automatic approach is necessary.

Listing 1.1. An excerpt of a COS request schema definition (RequestToMPA)

```
1  <xsd:schema xmlns:rsm="http://www.strom.ch" ...>
2      <xsd:element name="RequestToMPA_10" type="rsm:RequestToMPAType_10"/>
3      <xsd:complexType name="RequestToMPAType_10">
4          <xsd:element name="MeteringPoint">
5              <xsd:complexType>
6                  <xsd:complexContent>
7                      <xsd:extension base="rsm:EnergyMeteringPointLocationType">
8                          <xsd:sequence>
9                              <xsd:element name="BalanceResponsible" type="rsm:EnergyPartyType"
                                   minOccurs="0"/>
10                             <xsd:element name="BalanceSupplier" type="rsm:EnergyPartyType" minOccurs="
                                   0"/>
11                             <xsd:element name="Consumer" type="rsm:ConsumerEnergyPartyType"
                                   minOccurs="0"/>
12                             <xsd:element name="SwitchDate" type="rsm:SwitchDatePeriodType"/>
13                         </xsd:sequence>
14                     </xsd:extension>
15                 </xsd:complexContent>
16             </xsd:complexType>
17         </xsd:element>
18         ...
19     </xsd:complexType>
20     <xsd:complexType name="SwitchDatePeriodType">
21         <xsd:choice>
22             <xsd:element name="StartDate" type="rsm:EnergyDateType"/>
23             <xsd:element name="EndDate" type="rsm:EnergyDateType"/>
24         </xsd:choice>
25     </xsd:complexType>
26     <xsd:simpleType name="EnergyDateType">
27         <xsd:restriction base="udt:DateType">
28             <xsd:pattern value=".{4}-.{2}-.{2}"/>
29         </xsd:restriction>
30     </xsd:simpleType>
31     ...
32 </xsd:schema>
```

To monitor the start of the process, we define an EOT indicating the execution of the start event, see Listing 1.2. Because of business needs, we are explicitly interested in information about a COS request (*MPA_Request*), consumer, switch date, and balance supplier.

Listing 1.2. The EOT definition to identify events for starting a change of supplier process

```
<?xml version="1.0" encoding="UTF-8"?>
<xs:schema xmlns:rsm="http://www.strom.ch" xmlns:xsd="http://www.w3.org/2001/XMLSchema"...>
    <xs:element name="MPA_Request" type="xs:string"></xs:element>
    <xs:element name="Consumer" type="xs:string"></xs:element>
    <xs:element name="Date" type="xs:date"></xs:element>
    <xs:element name="BalanceSupplier" type="xs:string"></xs:element>
</xs:schema>
```

Listing 1.3 shows an excerpt of a real-world event from the event source for the COS requests. To transform such an event to an event relevant for the given business process, we need to define a binding between EOT_1 and the event source structure RequestToMPA_10. Manually derived from the example, we can define a binding *bind* of EOT_1 including, for example, the switch date:
EOT_1.Date = *RequestToMPA_10.Switch.MeteringPoint.SwitchDate.StartDate*.

The other elements of EOT_1 can be mapped and the binding of the other EOTs can be defined accordingly. Establishing this bindings manually is time-consuming and error-prone, therefore, we present an approach establishing the bindings automatically.

Listing 1.3. Event of event source COS request

```
<rsm:RequestToMPA_10 xsi:schemaLocation="http://www.strom.ch RequestToMPA_1p0.xsd" xmlns:rsm="http://
      www.strom.ch" xmlns:xsi="http://www.w3.org/2001/XMLSchema-instance"> ...
  <rsm:Switch>
    <rsm:DocumentID>DID_Beispiel_3_2_1_x_LiefWec_10_11c</rsm:DocumentID>
    <rsm:MeteringPoint>
      <rsm:VSENationalID schemeID="VSE" schemeAgencyID="260">
            CH9999901234500000000000000000002</rsm:VSENationalID>
      <rsm:BalanceSupplier>
        <rsm:ID><rsm:EICID schemeAgencyID="305">12X-PARTY-A-000K</rsm:EICID></
              rsm:ID>
      </rsm:BalanceSupplier>
      <rsm:SwitchDate><rsm:StartDate>2008-06-30</rsm:StartDate></rsm:SwitchDate>
      ...
    </rsm:MeteringPoint>
  </rsm:Switch>
</rsm:RequestToMPA_10>
```

4 Approach to Detect Bindings between EOTs and Event Sources

As defined in Section 2, EOTs are defined in a PEMP for a process model. In this paper, we assume the EOTs for a business process are known and relevant event sources with its descriptions are available. Thus, we focus on the association of event sources to corresponding EOTs. We perform our approach in three steps (see Fig. 3), which are closely interrelated, but should be considered isolated as they can be implemented by different tools, algorithms, or means.

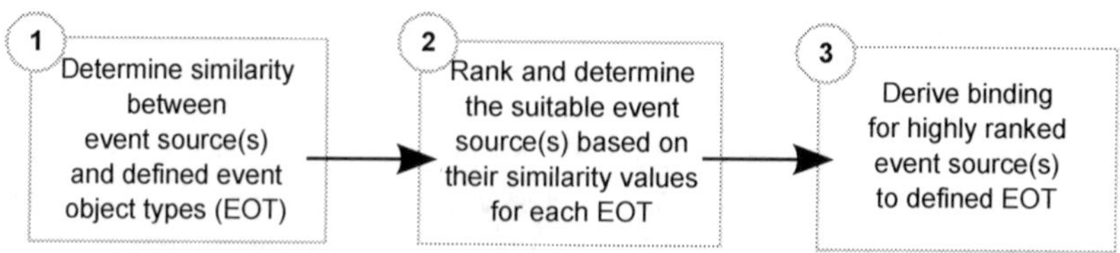

Fig. 3. Approach for the detection of suitable event sources for given EOTs

4.1 Step 1: Determine the Similarity between Event Sources and EOTs

In a collection of event sources, e.g., systems providing XML data, we aim at identifying those event sources that are similar and suitable to a defined EOT. This identification is conducted by comparing the elements of an EOT with every event source available and computing their similarity value.

A comparison requires the description and structural properties of the events originating from an event source and those that are expected for the EOT. The structural descriptions of event sources need to be stored in a repository, e.g., a database storing the descriptions as XSD files. The search of event sources in the repository can be utilized by matchers that compare the descriptions. As we cannot assume that each event source description is completely contained in an EOT and vice versa, element-level matchers are required that consider elements in isolation and ignore element's substructure and components. For instance, the fact that the elements *Date* defined in the EOT (see Listing 1.2) and the *SwitchDate* from the event source (see Listing 1.1) are likely to match (although contained in different sub-elements) can be derived by a name-based element-level matching without considering the hierarchical structure of the descriptions. As result of a comparison, we receive a matrix for each event source that includes the similarity values between the elements of the compared event source and the EOT.

Afterwards, the similarity values in each matrix need to be aggregated to receive a global similarity value for the EOT and the event source. It is likely to estimate the degree of the similarity is given by a normalized numeric value in the range 0 to 1, in order to identify the best matching event source. For example, in our scenario, the total amount of 73 event sources must be compared with the given EOT shown in 1.2 to calculate the overall similarity values.

4.2 Step 2: Rank and Determine Suitable Event Sources for an EOT

In this step, event sources that may deliver information for the requested EOT are ranked based on their overall similarity from highest to lowest. We use the computed similarity values of each comparison of an event source description with the EOT specification from the previous step. The assumption is that higher overall similarity values indicate the better suitability of the event sources to the EOT. However, note that these values do not contain an evaluation of how suitable the mappings of each attribute are. Therefore, it may be required that a domain expert looks into the set of event sources ranked at the first places to exactly evaluate their fitness. As we are aiming at automating the process of event detection, we use the event source ranked at the first place for further processing. According to our scenario, we rank all 73 event sources based on their similarity to the requested EOT shown in Listing 1.2. Such a ranking should indicate that the event source *RequestToMPA_10* will satisfy the given EOT most probably.

4.3 Step 3: Derive the Binding between an EOT and an Event Source

For the highly ranked event source(s) the binding is derived, so that for the requested elements or attributes in the EOT a corresponding counterpart from the event source(s) is assigned. The binding defines the rules and methods to extract raw event information from the data source within the information system landscape required for the events of the given EOT. To establish the binding the resulting similarity matrix from *step 1* can be reused. Same as for the global similarity, we assume that the higher similarity value are better suited and thus they are used for the matching of elements. Therefore, each required binding is produced by utilizing the element in the event source with the most promising similarity value. For example, it is likely to assume that the similarity value between the elements *Date* (of the EOT) and *SwitchDate* (of the event source) is higher then a value between *Date* and *Consumer*.

Based on the similarity matrix, we can obtain a binding of every element described by the EOT to an element in the determined event source. Using this technique, we can derive a binding between the EOT_1 requested in the scenario and the event source *RequestToMPA_10* describing that, for example, the content for filling *Date* can be found in *R2MPAType_10.Switch.MeteringPoint.SwitchDate*. This binding can then be used to generate CEP-queries and process events in a CEP engine or to generate XPath-like pattern and process XML documents using Extensible Stylesheet Language Transformation (XSLT), for instance. Both can be used to detect corresponding events and data coming from different sources but belonging to the specified EOT. In this context, the existing Event Processing Platform (EPP) [6,7][3] can be used as it is able to receive events from different kinds of sources, check the format of these events, associate them with an EOT, and then normalize, store, process, and forward them via the platform.

5 Evaluation Using Schema Matching

We show the applicability of our approach by using schema matching to implement the three steps and evaluate it for the use case described in Section 3. By automating the event source detection, we can decrease the efforts for enabling process monitoring and analysis in distributed and heterogeneous environments. In this evaluation, we did not investigate the quality of the matching results.

In general, schema matching techniques are used to identify an alignment that expresses the correspondence between elements and attributes belonging to different schemas or ontologies [12,13]. A schema can be, for example, an XSD, a database schema, an Electronic Data Interchange For Administration, Commerce and Transport (EDIFACT) message definition, or an event type definition. To apply schema matching, we assume that each event source as well as the EOT are represented by a schema, i.e., an XSD that describes the events produced by that event source as well as the expected events in a formal and standardized manner. This assumption is reasonable since XML is a common standardized data interchange format.

5.1 Evaluation Setup

For our experiment, we used a state-of-the-art schema matching tool called OntoBuilder[4] to implement the identification and matching of suitable event sources for EOTs. For the comparison in the OntoBuilder, we first defined an EOT in form of an XSD for each PEMP required by the use case in Section 3. The related XSDs of the event sources are taken from the data set provided by the Association of Swiss Electricity Companies (see Section 3). Second, each XSD was imported in the OntoBuilder and transformed to a generic ontology structure. Third, we conducted a schema matching for each pair of a target (EOT) and source schema (event source).

[3] Downloads, tutorials, and further information can be found at: `http://bpt.hpi.uni-potsdam.de/Public/EPP`

[4] See `http://ontobuilder.bitbucket.org/`

Table 1. Excerpt of results for matching of EOT_1 and event sources

#	Event source schema	Average similarity
1	RequestToMPA_1p0.xsd	0.78
2	ResponseFromMPA_Confirm_1p0.xsd	0.71
3	NotificationFromMPA_1p0.xsd	0.67

In the OntoBuilder, the schema matching is based on a sequence of two kinds of matchers: (1) first line matchers and (2) second line matchers. The first line matchers are applied to two schemas to determine their similarity using textual and structural heuristics. For each schema pair a first line matcher produces a similarity matrix which contains the similarity value for each attribute pair of those two schemas. In our use case each similarity value is calculated by comparing the names as well as the data types of the schema attributes. For this reason, we used the *OBTermMatch* algorithm for the name comparison and the *OBValueMatch* algorithm for the data type comparison. Then, a second line matcher is applied to the similarity matrix together with a set of constraints (e.g., allowing only 1:1 mappings of attributes) that returns for each attribute of the target schema a corresponding attribute of the source schema together with its computed similarity value. *OBStableMariage* was used as a second line matcher that implements the stable marriage algorithm for royal couples [14], extended for unequal sets of schema attributes.

Following this setup, our approach uses schema matching in the OntoBuilder as follows: for *step 1* the overall similarity of the EOT to an event source is calculated as the arithmetic mean of their similarity values, for *step 2* the overall similarity values of the event sources for each EOT are ranked, and for *step 3* the binding is derived from the matching between the attributes of event sources to attributes of the EOT.

5.2 Evaluation Results

The results presented in Table 1 show an excerpt of found event source descriptions that match the event type EOT_1 (see Listing 1.2) ordered by their computed overall similarity. The event source description *RequestToMPA_1p0.xsd*, which represents the event source *RequestToMPA_10* (see Listing 1.1), is ranked with the highest similarity of 0.78. It describes the supplier change request to a metering point administrator within Association of Swiss Electricity Companies and corresponds to the definition of the EOT_1 (see Listing 1.2).

Next, the matching of attributes were computed in the OntoBuilder. For example, using the *OBTermMatch* algorithm, which includes a set of weighted string comparison algorithms for similarity calculation, we receive a similarity between *Date* (EOT) and *SwitchDate* (event source) of 0.46, while the similarity between *Consumer* (EOT) and *Consumer* (event source) is 1. Table 2 shows the results of the mappings for each attribute of the EOT_1 to the attributes of the best matched event source description (*RequestToMPA_1p0.xsd*) and the similarity values for each mapping.

Table 2. Results for matching the attributes of EOT_1 and the best ranked event source description *RequestToMPA_1p0.xsd*

EOT_1 **attribute**	**RequestToMPA_1p0.xsd attribute**	**sim. value**
MPA_Request	RequestToMPA_10	0.65
Consumer	R2MPAType_10.Switch.MeteringPoint.Consumer	1.00
Date	R2MPAType_10.Switch.MeteringPoint.SwitchDate	0.46
BalanceSupplier	R2MPAType_10.Switch.MeteringPoint.BalanceSupplier	1.00

5.3 Evaluation Discussion

The produced results show that schema matching can be used for the identification of event sources in our introduced use case. The approach allows to identify heterogeneous event sources for a given EOT and to derive bindings for each of event sources. The derived bindings can, for example, be used to generate and run CEP-queries.

We argue that schema matching is a reasonable technique which can be used for an automated detection of event sources. However, the quality of the produced results may highly depend on the selected matching algorithms as well as on their configuration settings and may vary with the examined data set. Furthermore, the selection and adaption of first and second line matcher algorithms have a high impact on the outcome of the produced matching. Additional element-level matchings such as on type, description, and key property can be applied as well (see [12]).

In this paper, we focus on the binding of event sources to EOTs. Although the combination and association of several varying EOTs to one PEMP as well as the combination and association of several varying event sources to one EOT is possible. While illustrating our approach, we did not analyze these details, however, we plan to consider them in future work.

6 Related Work

Baier and Mendling introduce an approach to map events from event logs to activities in process models [15,16]. The mapping approach suggests relations between events and activities at type and instance level in an automated manner. These relations are derived from a comparison between the name of event types and activity's name and description. We complement this approach by considering all attributes of EOTs and of the event sources to identify a matching between these.

Other approaches in the area of complex event processing e.g., [17] address the problem of semantic decoupling of event subscriber and publisher in heterogeneous event-based systems. For instance, the approach of Hasan et al. includes an event model, a subscription model, and a matching model that leverage semantics of events and subscriptions (resp. EOT) to establish approximate matching.

Our work is also related to the area on automated or semi-automated techniques for schema matching, surveyed, for instance, in [12] and [18]. These techniques leverage textual and structural similarity measures, and apply different strategies to derive correspondences between concepts from such a similarity assessment [19]. While the results of schema matchers have been exceptional for distinguished settings, they are inherently uncertain due to the enormous ambiguity and heterogeneity of data description [20].

Several approaches were proposed to address the problem of service retrieval - a process of finding a set of service candidates for a given consumer request. The lack of an appropriate service description can be identified as one of the main challenges during the process of service retrieval [21]. Various approaches, e.g., [22], address these challenges using diverse information retrieval techniques. While these approaches allow the service consumer to reach high levels of recall, they remain to be prone to low precision [23].

A few works use schema matching techniques in service retrieval. In [24], the authors propose an approach to compute the similarity between web services under consideration of a tree edit distance. However, the introduced approach can be applied on the interface definition of web services only. It does not consider the exchanged data and their instances as it is needed for event source detection.

7 Conclusion

We automated the association of event sources to EOTs required by PEMPs in a business process and therewith enabled event source detection as basis for BPI. In particular, specified EOTs for business process monitoring are used to identify relevant event sources. The found event sources are ranked according their computed similarity to the requested EOT and a binding between the highest ranked event source and the EOT is generated. During business process execution, these bindings can be used to identify event objects for a business process in an event stream. We implemented the approach using schema matching and evaluated its applicability for an use case that is aligned with a real-world process from the utilities domain.

For future work, we plan to consider the combination and association of several varying EOTs to one PEMP as well as the combination and association of several varying event sources to one EOT. Furthermore, we aim to extend our evaluation using different kinds of configurations and combinations of matching algorithms and, thus, improve the quality of event source detection.

Acknowledgement. The research leading to these results has received funding from the European Union's Seventh Framework Programme (FP7/2007-2013) under grant agreement 318275 (GET Service) and from the German Research Association (DFG) under project number WE 1930/8-1.

References

1. Papazoglou, M.P., Heuvel, W.J.: Service oriented architectures: approaches, technologies and research issues. The VLDB Journal 16(3) (July 2007)
2. Levina, O., Stantchev, V.: Realizing Event-Driven SOA. In: 4th International Conference on Internet and Web Applications and Services, ICIW (2009)
3. Weske, M.: Business Process Management - Concepts, Languages, Architectures, 2nd edn. Springer (2012)

4. van der Aalst, W.: Process Mining: Overview and Opportunities. ACM Transactions on Management Information Systems (TMIS) 3(2) (July 2012)
5. Weidlich, M., Ziekow, H., Mendling, J., Günther, O., Weske, M., Desai, N.: Event-Based Monitoring of Process Execution Violations. In: Rinderle-Ma, S., Toumani, F., Wolf, K. (eds.) BPM 2011. LNCS, vol. 6896, pp. 182–198. Springer, Heidelberg (2011)
6. Bülow, S., Backmann, M., Herzberg, N., Hille, T., Meyer, A., Ulm, B., Wong, T.Y., Weske, M.: Monitoring of Business Processes with Complex Event Processing. In: BPM Workshops. Springer (2013) (accepted for publication)
7. Herzberg, N., Meyer, A., Weske, M.: An Event Processing Platform for Business Process Management. In: IEEE International EDOC Conference, Vancouver (2013)
8. Etzion, O., Niblett, P.: Event Processing in Action. Manning Publications Co (2011)
9. Luckham, D.: The Power of Events: An Introduction to Complex Event Processing in Distributed Enterprise Systems. Addison-Wesley (2002)
10. Luckham, D., Schulte, R.: Event Processing Glossary - Version 2.0 (July 2011), http://www.complexevents.com/wp-content/uploads/2011/08/EPTS_Event_Processing_Glossary_v2.pdf
11. OMG: Business Process Model and Notation (BPMN), Version 2.0 (2011), http://www.omg.org/spec/BPMN/2.0/
12. Rahm, E., Bernstein, P.A.: A survey of approaches to automatic schema matching. The VLDB Journal 10(4) (2001)
13. Euzenat, J., Shvaiko, P.: Ontology matching, vol. 18. Springer, Heidelberg (2007)
14. Marie, A., Gal, A.: On the Stable Marriage of Maximum Weight Royal Couples. In: AAAI Workshop on Information Integration on the Web (2007)
15. Baier, T., Mendling, J.: Bridging Abstraction Layers in Process Mining by Automated Matching of Events and Activities. In: Daniel, F., Wang, J., Weber, B. (eds.) BPM 2013. LNCS, vol. 8094, pp. 17–32. Springer, Heidelberg (2013)
16. Baier, T., Mendling, J.: Bridging Abstraction Layers in Process Mining: Event to Activity Mapping. In: Nurcan, S., Proper, H.A., Soffer, P., Krogstie, J., Schmidt, R., Halpin, T., Bider, I. (eds.) BPMDS 2013 and EMMSAD 2013. LNBIP, vol. 147, pp. 109–123. Springer, Heidelberg (2013)
17. Hasan, S., O'Riain, S., Curry, E.: Approximate semantic matching of heterogeneous events. In: 6th ACM International Conference on Distributed Event-Based Systems, DEBS (2012)
18. Bellahsene, Z., Bonifati, A., Rahm, E.: Schema Matching and Mapping. Springer (2011)
19. Gal, A., Sagi, T.: Tuning the ensemble selection process of schema matchers. Information Systems 35(8) (2010)
20. Gal, A.: Managing Uncertainty in Schema Matching with Top-K Schema Mappings. In: Spaccapietra, S., Aberer, K., Cudré-Mauroux, P. (eds.) Journal on Data Semantics VI. LNCS, vol. 4090, pp. 90–114. Springer, Heidelberg (2006)
21. Kuropka, D., Troeger, P., Staab, S., Weske, M.: Semantic Service Provisioning. Springer (2008)
22. Wang, Y., Stroulia, E.: Flexible Interface Matching for Web-Service Discovery. In: 4th Int. Conference on Web Information Systems Engineering (WISE). IEEE Computer Society (2003)
23. Klein, M., Bernstein, A.: Toward high-precision service retrieval. IEEE Internet Computing 8(1), 30–36 (2004)
24. Hao, Y., Zhang, Y.: Web services discovery based on schema matching. In: 13th Australasian Conference on Computer Science (ACSC), vol. 62, pp. 107–113. Australian Computer Society, Inc. (2007)

Discovering Pattern-Based Mediator Services from Communication Logs

Christian Gierds[1] and Dirk Fahland[2]

[1] Humboldt-Universität zu Berlin, Department of Computer Science, Germany
gierds@informatik.hu-berlin.de
[2] Technische Universiteit Eindhoven, The Netherlands
d.fahland@tue.nl

Abstract. Process discovery is a technique for deriving a conceptual high-level process model from the execution logs of a running implementation. The technique is particularly useful when no high-level model is available or in case of significant gaps between process documentation and implementation. The discovered model makes the implementation accessible to various kinds of analysis for functional and non-functional properties. In this paper we extend process discovery to mediator services (or adapters) which adapt the messaging protocols of 2 or more otherwise incompatible services. We propose a technique that takes as input logs of communication behaviors — one log for each service connected to the adapter — and a library of high-level data transformation rules relevant for the domain of the adapter, and then returns an operational adapter model describing the *control-flow* and the *data flow* of the adapter in terms of Coloured Petri Nets – if such model exists. We discuss benefits and limitations of this idea and evaluate it with a prototype implementation on industrial size models.

Keywords: Process Mining, Service Mining, Pattern Based Design, Coloured Petri nets, synthesis.

1 Introduction

The central idea of Service-oriented Computing (SoC) is to build complex distributed systems by connecting and integrating software components or services. Often a system integrates existing components that are not directly compatible with each other, but are made compatible through *mediator services* or adapters, also known as *middleware* [22]. Incompatibilities may arise due to incompatible service interfaces (available operations and message types), due to incompatible protocols of stateful services, or due to semantic mismatches between message contents. A mediator service sits between two or more other services and remedies these mismatches for instance through reordering messages sent by one service into a different protocol, or by processing, decomposing, and enriching messages to be compatible for the receiving service.

In larger systems, mediator services play a central role as they provide the flexibility to integrate existing key functionality in many different ways. This flexibility is key when designing new integrations for existing components or optimizing existing integrations. In both cases, the *existing* mediator services have to be considered to either

A.R. Lomuscio et al. (Eds.): ICSOC 2013 Workshops, LNCS 8377, pp. 123–134, 2014.
© Springer International Publishing Switzerland 2014

identify whether a particular mediator service already exists, or which properties this mediator service has. Ideally, one would analyze *high level conceptual* models of a mediator services, for instance using the abstract concepts provided by the *Enterprise Integration Patterns* (EIP) [10]. However, in many architectures in practice, e.g., *Enterprise Service Buses* (ESB) such as JBoss ESB [11], mediator services are implemented in software code only. The particular integration of two or more services may only arise from multiple software artifacts that are difficult to identify in the first place. In such situations, understanding and optimizing existing software-based integrations becomes a laborious, and error-prone task.

In this paper, we address the problem of *automatically* extracting a high-level conceptual model of a mediator service from the *communication logs* of an existing integration. The communication log of a service stores at which point in time the service sent or received a particular message. The implemented mediator service received and sent exactly the messages recorded in the event logs of the service to which it is connected. In this paper, we present a technique to *extract* from these event logs an operational model of a mediator service in terms of a *Coloured Petri Net* (CPN) [12]. This CPN describes the *message flow and message transformations* between the connected services that *fits* the communication behavior recorded in the logs.

We proceed as follows. In Section 2, we consider existing works on extracting models from event logs, and analyze the problem of extracting mediator services. Section 3 presents a conceptually simple formulation of our approach; Section 4 covers an experimental evaluation of our approach together with some thoughts of optimizing it. We discuss related work in Section 5 and conclude in Section 6.

2 Extracting Models from Event Logs

In this section, we discuss the problem of extracting behavioral models from logs that contain recorded events of previous executions. We first consider the "classical" problem of *process mining* [1] and available solutions, and then analyze the problem of extracting models of mediator services.

2.1 Classical Process Mining

Process mining comprises various techniques to analyze information recorded in event logs. The most prominent technique, *process discovery*, takes as input an event log L and returns a process model M that describes the behavior in L. [1]

An event e in an event log usually has a *type*, written $e.type$, indicating what kind of activity or operation happened, a *timestamp* ($e.time$) indicating *when* e happened, and possibly a number of attributes, e.g., describing the data that was involved in the occurrence of e. All events that occurred in the same *instance* of the process together form a *case*. Typically, the events of one case are recorded in a *trace* $t = e_1 e_2 \dots e_n$ where events are ordered by their timestamps; a *log* is a set $L = \{t_1, \dots, t_m\}$ of traces.

As our running example we consider a service providing beverages. The service offers tea (T) for costs of 1, and lemonade (L) for costs of 2; the choice for the beverage is made implicitly through the amount paid by the customer. Two possible traces of this service are $t_1 = (?m, time = 3, amt = 1), (!T, time = 6, bev = Tea)$ and

$t_2 = (?m, time = 7, amt = 2), (!L, time = 9, bev = Lem)$. In t_1, the service has received money ($?m$) worth of 1€ at time 3 and sent a tea ($!T$), at time 6; in t_2, 2€ were received at time 7 and the corresponding lemonade was sent at time 9 ($!L$).

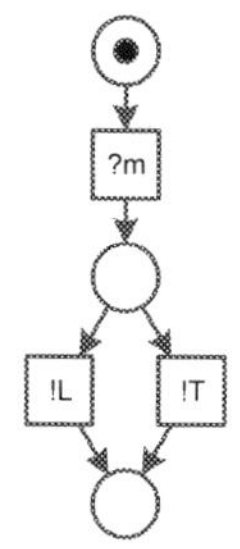

Fig. 1. Possible Result

A large number of process discovery algorithms exist to extract a process model M from an event log; see [1]. The α-algorithm, for instance, could extract from the log $L = \{t_1, t_2\}$ the model shown in Fig. 1. Most process discovery techniques create for each event type ($?m, !T, !L$) in L a separate activity, and then synthesize control-flow structures that "best" explain the behavior in L where "best" is measured in terms of different quality criteria: a model *fits* the log if it can reproduce any trace in the log; a model is *precise* wrt. the log if it does not allow for arbitrary more behavior than recorded in the log; finally, a model should be *simple*. The model in Fig. 1 can reproduce both traces t_1 and t_2, that is, it fits the log. Though, the model is *imprecise* because it ignores the data attribute *amt* of $?m$: it would also return a lemonade for the price of 1€. Generally, these quality criteria are competing: one often cannot find a fitting model that is precise and simple. [4]

2.2 The Problem of Discovering Mediator Services

In this paper, we consider a setting that is slightly different from classical process discovery. In our setting, we are considering an implementation $S_1 \oplus M \oplus S_2$ where two services S_1 and S_2 are integrated through a mediator service M.

For example, in addition to the beverage service S_1 of Fig. 1 we consider a customer S_2 that wants to order a hot beverage (H) or a cold beverage (C) from S_1. The customer can only pay in denominations of 1€: to order a hot beverage from the beverage service, the customer pays 1€ and then explicitly places the order ($!O$) and then receives the beverage; to order a cold beverage, the customer pays 2€, places the order, and receives the beverage. The mediator service M has to fulfill different tasks: the multiple payment by the customer have to be summed up into a single payment, and the type of beverage provided by the service has to be translated into the terminology of the customer (a hot tea vs. a cold lemonade).

All services S_1, S_2, and M are implemented, for instance in Java code, and running in a Service-Oriented Architecture [17] such as JBoss ESB [11]. The implementation recorded event logs L_1 and L_2 of invocations of the services S_1 and S_2, respectively.

Following the SOC paradigm of hiding implementation details behind an interface, the event logs L_1 and L_2 should only contain events related to interactions of S_1 and S_2 with their environment; events of activities not related to the interface do not have to be recorded. For example, $L_1 = \{t_1, t_2\}$ with $t_1 = (?m, time = 3, amt = 1)$, $(!T, time = 6, bev = Tea)$ and $t_2 = (?m, time = 8, amt = 2), (!L, time = 9, bev = Lem)$, and $L_2 = \{s_1, s_2\}$ with $s_1 = (!p, time = 1, amt = 1), (?ack, time = 2), (!o, time = 4), (?B, time = 7, temp = Hot)$ and $s_2 = (!p, time = 4, amt = 1), (?ack, time = 5), (!p, time = 7, amt = 1), (?ack, time = 8), (!o, time = 10), (?B, time = 13, temp = Cold)$.

In this setting, we want to discover from logs L_1 and L_2 a model of the mediator service M so that the following criteria hold:

1. *M fits* L_1 and L_2, that is, M describes how messages produced by S_1 or S_2 as described in the logs L_1 and L_2 are transformed, aggregated, and forwarded by M so that S_1 and S_2 can receive these messages as described in L_1 and L_2. For example, the two payment events $!p$ in s_2 describe that two payment messages p with contents $amt = 1$ are sent by S_2 at times 4 and 7. The model M has to aggregate these into a message m with contents $amt = 2$ that can be received by S_1 at time 8 (as recorded in t_2).
2. M is *precise*, that is M is *deterministic* wrt. transforming messages based on their contents. Unlike the model in Fig. 1, M shall have no ambiguous choice about how a particular message shall be treated. Otherwise M would describe an integration that could potentially deadlock.
3. M is *simple*, that is M contains as few message transformation activities as possible.

While the criteria for M are similar to classical process mining, our setting renders existing process mining techniques inapplicable. Here, we are not given a log L_M of the mediator service M, but only logs L_1 and L_2 of the connected services. The events recorded in L_1 and L_2 are not events of activities in M, but we have to discover activities of M. The cases in L_1 are independent from the cases in L_2; we do not have any information about cases of M, and how cases of M relate to cases of L_1 and of L_2. Altogether, this gives rise to the following challenges.

1. A technique to extract a model for M from logs L_1 and L_2 has to *infer* activities of M from events of the services S_1 and S_2 recorded in L_1 and L_2.
2. The technique has to correlate cases in L_1 to cases in L_2 to correctly describe event of S_1 sending a message lead to an event in S_2 receiving a (transformed) message.
3. The traces in L_1 and L_2 may not only concern communication between S_1 and S_2 only. Typically S_1 may be used in other service compositions. Thus, not every trace of L_1 has a corresponding trace in L_2, and vice versa. M has to distinguish correlated from non-correlated traces.
4. As S_1 and S_2 are incompatible, M has to describe how messages produced by S_1 are *transformed* into messages received by S_2 (and vice versa), in particular considering the *data values* exchanged between S_1 and S_2.

As in process mining we need to define a search space for the models to discover. Typically a technique cannot discover any arbitrary model, but is restricted by some underlying assumptions like discovering a sound or block-structured model.

In Section 3 we present a technique that overcomes these challenges and produces a *pattern-based* model of the mediator M that fits the logs, is simple, and precise through determinism. The resulting model will be a Coloured Petri Net, which we recall next.

2.3 Coloured Petri Nets

Coloured Petri Nets (CPN) [12] extend classical Petri nets with the notion of data; they are successfully applied in research and industry in modeling and analyzing distributed systems [20].

A Petri Net processes resources called *tokens*. *Places* hold these resources, and *transitions* process them. A *flow relation* connects places with transitions and vice versa.

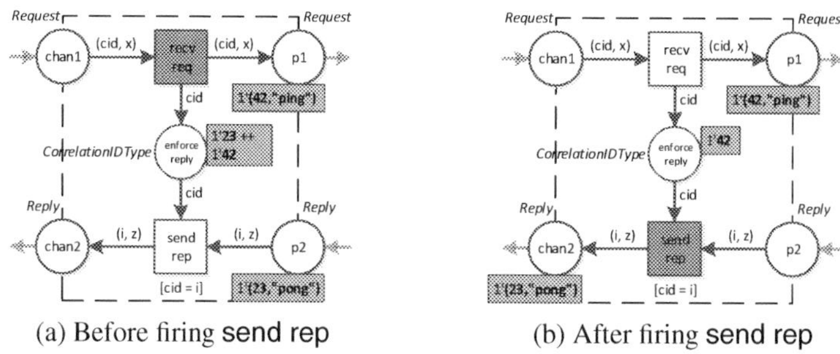

(a) Before firing send rep (b) After firing send rep

Fig. 2. Behavior of CPN: Effect of firing of and send rep

In CPN each token is a value (called *color*) of some type (called *colorset*). Each place is typed with a specific colorset and holds only tokens of that type. Each arc of the flow relation is labeled with either a variable, or a complex term such as function applications or complex data structures. The labels of arcs adjacent to a transition express which tokens the transition consumes and produces as explained below. In addition, a transition can have a guard to restrict consumption and production of tokens. The state of a CPN is a *marking* describing a distribution of tokens (colors) over places of the respective colorset.

Figure 2 shows an example for a CPN (we have chosen the Request-Reply pattern of the EIP as it shows all aspects of CPN); as usual, a circle depicts a place, a rectangle depicts a transition, and the arcs depict the flow relation. This basic structure already dictates that transition recv req has to consume a resource from place chan1 and that it produces new resources on places p1 and enforce reply. Places chan1 and p1 have type *Request*, enforce reply has type *CorrelationIDType*, and p2 and chan2 have type *Reply*. Identifiers like cid or x in the arc inscription are variables, (cid,x) then is a tuple. The transition send rep has the guard [cid = i], meaning it may only fire, if cid and i are equal. In Fig. 2a, we have the following marking: place p1 holds token (42,"ping") (a tuple of the colors 42 and "ping"), place enforce reply holds token 23 and 42, and place p2 holds token (23,"pong").

The behavior of a CPN is described by *firing* transitions, which consume and produce tokens. For that, the inscriptions of each incoming arc have to be bound to a token on the corresponding place. Only if we find a complete binding and do not violate a guard, a transition is allowed to fire.

In Fig. 2a transition send rep can fire for the binding i = 23, x = "pong", and cid = 23. The guard of send rep ensures that i and cid are bound to the same value. Firing means that the tokens bound to the inscription on the incoming arcs are removed, and a token corresponding to the inscription of each outgoing arc is produced on the appropriate place. The result of firing send rep is shown in Fig. 2b.

Please note, in the following we will omit the names for places, and instead write inside a place its type if needed.

3 Pattern-Based Mediator Discovery

This sections presents our main contribution. For logs L_1 and L_2 given for service S_1 and S_2 we want to discover a model of mediator service M acting between S_1 and S_2 and conforming to L_1 and L_2. We use CPN patterns to describe the fundamental building blocks of M, we describe the search space for M, and we check conformance of M based on replaying; that is, by comparing a model's run with the logs. The resulting model for M shall be fit and precise with respect to the logs.

We can compare our approach to solving a jigsaw puzzle, where the CPN patterns represent the single pieces that we try to arrange, and the replay checks whether the resulting picture of the puzzle makes sense.

3.1 Patterns as Building Blocks

A mediator transfers and transforms messages between services based on ontological description of message types. For discovering a model of a mediator we have at least to know its basic abilities; how it is able to relate events in S_1 and S_2. We advocate the idea to use *patterns* for describing relations between messages. A pattern does not only describe a *semantic relation* between messages, but also *control flow* to fulfill this relation.

Enterprise Integration Patterns (EIP) [10] are typical example for pattern-based design. This collection of patterns allows to specifically model single parts of a mediator. We have provided a translation to Coloured Petri Nets [6] in previous work. In the following we will only consider CPN patterns knowing that they are backed by EIP for modeling. Using patterns as building blocks allows us to look at a mediator in a more structured way. In our approach we exploit the idea of building pattern based mediators and use a set of patterns to describe our search space.

In order to make our approach feasible, we have to *define a search space*. Firstly, we assume only finitely many *different* patterns. Secondly, we restrict the number of times each pattern is allowed to be used. In general, there can be infinitely many combinations of patterns, if we are allowed to use them arbitrarily often. Allowing an unbounded number of candidates would render our approach semi-decidable. We could stop checking, if we find a conforming candidate, otherwise we would need to explore further combinations of patterns.

Although introducing a finite set of patterns may seem like a considerable *restriction* to the set of discoverable services, especially EIP show that such a set is suitable for describing a multitude of complex systems. As the patterns itself are simple, they can be provided by a domain user.

As running example we pick up the beverage vending machine. Figure 3 shows it on the left together with the customer service as described in Sec. 2.2 on the right. Figure 3b shows the patterns we want to use. Pattern P1 can accumulate € coins — each coin being acknowledged —, P2 forwards a lemonade as cold drink, P3 a tea as hot drink, and finally P4 allows to forward the one beverage sent by the vending machine to the customer. The mediator we want to discover should resemble the structure shown in Fig. 3b.

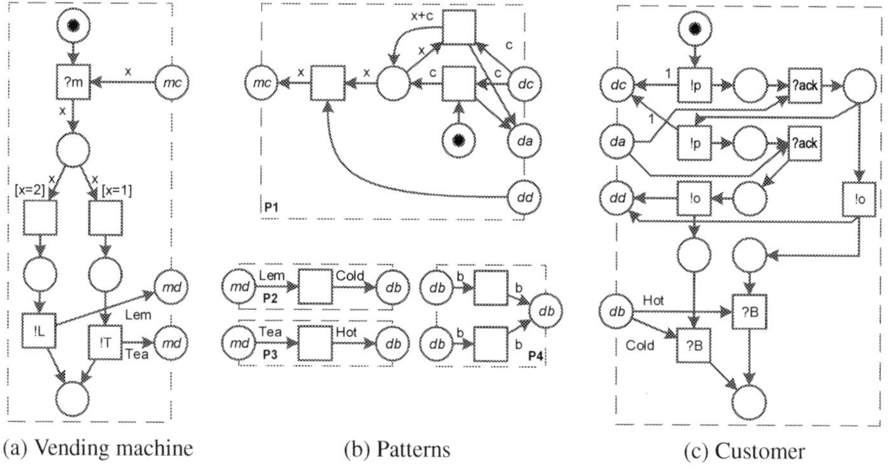

(a) Vending machine (b) Patterns (c) Customer

Fig. 3. Services and Patterns

3.2 Building Candidates

A *pattern* or *building block* P in our approach now is a small CPN with distinctive places that act as input and output places. The set $\mathcal{P}$ is the set of all building blocks. We are allowed to combine two building blocks $P_1, P_2 \in \mathcal{P}$ by merging an input place of P_1 with an output place of P_2, if they have the same type. Please note, that P_1 and P_2 can actually be the same building block used multiple times. A model is called $\mathcal{P}$*-based*, if and only if it can be built by combining building blocks from $\mathcal{P}$.

The first step is, that for each combination of building blocks, where each building block is used at most k times, we check for every type of places, if there is an equal number of input and output places.

Definition 1 (Type-Valid Combination). *Let $\mathcal{P}$ be a set of n building block patterns and k a given number restricting how often each pattern is allows to be used. Then the* combination *combo* $\in \{0, \ldots, k\}^n$ *is an n-dimensional vector over the numbers 0 to k indicating that pattern $P_i \in \mathcal{P}$ shall be used combo$[i]$ times.*

Such a combination combo is called type-valid *if and only if for each type used in the log interfaces and patterns the number of input and output places with this type equals.*

In our running example as seen in Fig. 3 using each pattern P1, ..., P4 once leads to a type-valid combination. The interface of the services also contribute to the counting as they represent the interfaces of the logs. The left service has 1 input place of type mc and 2 output places of type md. Using patterns P2 and P3 we have 2 output places of type db facing only 1 input place of the same type in the right service. Using pattern P4 equalizes the numbers. For the rest of the types we also have the same number input and output places. Using P2 twice, but P3 never would also result in a type-valid combination; however, not a suitable mediator.

For each of these combinations found in the first step, we then build pairs of input and output places of the same type. Every possible pair then is valid except for the case where we would pair an input and output place of the same pattern.

Definition 2 (Candidate). *A $\mathcal{P}$-based* candidate *is the result of a valid pairing of input and output places in a type-valid combination combo over $\mathcal{P}$ with at most k uses of each pattern $P \in \mathcal{P}$.*

In our running example, different pairings are for instance possible for the input places of P2 and P3 in the way how they are connected to the vending service. As they have the same type, any pairing with the lower two places with type md of the service is valid.

3.3 Replaying Logs

The replay does not only serve to check fitness for a pair of cases, but in our case also to find a correlation $\mathcal{C}$ between the given logs. Whenever a pair of cases can be completely replayed, we assume the two cases to be correlated; i.e., we assume that these two cases actually interacted with each other when they have been recorded. If we find two such correlated cases, we do not need to check them with other traces again. Since we consider deterministic behavior for the mediator, there cannot be any better correlation.

Definition 3 (Correlation by Replay). *For two logs L_1 and L_2 we define a correlation $\mathcal{C} \subset L_1 \times L_2$ between the single cases of L_1 and L_2. We correlate each case only once, and a pair of cases $(case_1, case_2) \in L_1 \times L_2$ is correlated, if the pair can be completely replayed for a candidate—meaning $(case_1, case_2) \in \mathcal{C}$.*

Please note, that although the choice of a pair is arbitrary, the number of correlated traces must be always the same. Otherwise, we could have cases $case_1, case_{1'} \in L_1$ and $case_2, case_{2'} \in L_2$ and the pair $(case_1, case_2) \in \mathcal{C}$ would hinder us to find the pairs $(case_1, case_{2'})$ and $(case_{1'}, case_2)$. With this assumption we know that we can completely replay $case_1$ with $case_2$ as well as $case_{2'}$. However, we assume determinism, such that the behavior implied by $case_1$ does not influence whether $case_2$ or $case_{2'}$ can occur. And neither can $case_{1'}$ influence this, such that the pair $(case_{1'}, case_{2'})$ must also be in $\mathcal{C}$.

In *replay*, we now have to replay events of a case in exactly the same order with exactly the values. We therefore translate a case into a sequence of CPN transitions ordered by places. Each transition then is connected with a corresponding interface place and sends/receives the value given in the log. For case t_1 we show an example in Fig. 4. As we can see, the structure on the right exactly follows the recorded case. The vending service's interface place that is not used in this case stays unconnected with rest of the case structure. This structure, however, is paired with a candidate as dictated by the pairing and then we simulate the whole system and check whether we can completely replay the chosen case pair.

By translating a case into a sequence of transitions in such a way, we impose the constraint that a candidate needs to send or receive a message in exactly the same order and with the same content as given in the log. The sequence of events in the case and the replay shall be identical.

We repeat this kind of replay for all possible pairs of cases. For each candidate we determine the number of correlated pairs and as result we choose a candidate with the best fitness.

$t_1 = (?m, time = 3, amt = 1), (!T, time = 6, bev = Tea)$

(a) Case t_1

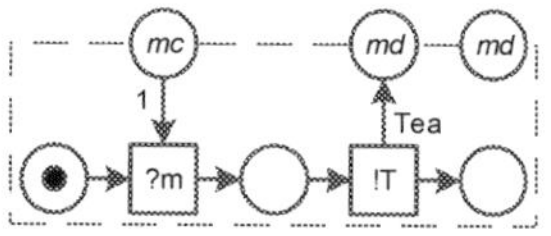

(b) Transition sequence for t_1

Fig. 4. Replay of a case

4 Evaluation

We have implemented a proof-of-concept prototype for checking our approach on examples of reasonable size. The prototype is implemented in Java and uses the Access/CPN [21] library which is a Coloured Petri Net simulator used in the replays. So far, the prototype is not publicly available, but we plan to integrate the technique as a plugin in the process mining framework ProM [19]. The following examples were done on a standard Linux PC.

4.1 Results

Running Example. For the running example we provided the interfaces and the patterns as described above. The generated logs contain each 101 cases totaling in 10201 possible pairs. However, after checking for overlapping timestamps only 101 pairs remain — when creating the logs only one instance was running at the same time. We allowed our tool to use each pattern at most twice which results in the 12 candidates. The overall time for the complete approach is 5.1 minutes, where building the 12 candidates took 1.5 seconds, and just running the replays took 7.6 seconds. The remaining time was spent for loading the simulator and syntax checking the candidates.

Industrial Example. As industrial example we use Google's Checkout Service and a self-designed webshop payment interface. We do not introduce the two service in detail here, but refer to our previous work on pattern-based design of mediator services [6]. Checkout [8] is a stateful payment back-end provided by Google. The webshop shall use this back-end, however in our design communication is only possible via a mediator service. With the help of Enterprise Integration Patterns [10] we modeled such a mediator and then translate it to Coloured Petri Nets.

For our check we created logs for Checkout and the webshop with 200 cases. A case has between 4 and 26 events using 6 different types of events, 2494 case pairs are possible when considering overlapping timestamps. We provide 9 different patterns, some of which need to be used up to 3 times. We find only 1 type-valid combination for these patterns (with a total of 12 patterns uses), however, 1728 possible candidates by pairing input and output places. After applying a heuristic (see below) 432 candidates need to be checked. Finally we can rediscover the original mediator with complete fitness. Many other candidates show partial fitness in various degrees. Running the experiments takes around 33 hours, where building the candidates takes 170 seconds and just running the replays without loading and syntax checking the candidates takes around 24 hours, or around 3 minutes per experiment. During each replay around 50,000 to 70,000 transitions were fired showing the slow performance when tokens remain after running an uncorrelated case pair.

4.2 Heuristics for Runtime Improvement

Our practical experiments show, that model candidates can be found in a reasonable time. However, the replay takes a considerable time. Due to the lack of alternatives to the used CPN library we have also implemented some heuristics to reduce the effort for replay.

Restricting Possible Case Pairs. Although the correlation of cases needs to be determined, we can exclude certain combinations. Looking at timestamps included for each event, we can safely assume, that correlated cases must have overlapping points of time during which there were executed. We can exclude every pair, where this is not given. If we have deeper domain knowledge, we may even exclude more pairs based on further event values or certain execution conditions.

Partial Replay. If a case pair is not related, then normally we can often recognize this already after the first exchange of a message, i.e., after a message has been routed from one service to the other. We check the candidate models structurally for corresponding messages, and then replay the logs only up to the point, when the first messages must have been exchanged. Many candidate models are structurally equal in this part, such that we can exclude whole sets of candidate, if the partial replay does not succeed.

Possible Further Improvements. Further work on this approach should focus on the problem of long replays. This can either be done by accelerating the actual replay, or by further restricting the possible candidates. As we consider data aspects, using semantic analysis of a candidate might help to exclude further candidates in a shorter amount of time.

5 Related Techniques

With respect to process mining there are no techniques that we can directly apply as we have the change of perspective in our approach. In process mining the discovered model shall contain the event classes used in the logs. In our setting the event classes are only used in checking conformance, because the logs just describe the interaction with the model we want to discover. To get an overview on process mining we refer to van der Aalst's book on Process Mining [1]. Similarly, service discovery (e.g., [7,9,13,15–17]) results in a service using the event classes of the log as activities neglecting service with rich internal or unobservable behavior, or using complex building blocks as in our approach.

A first solution for the problem described in this paper might be to discover the services S_1 and S_2 first, and then use existing techniques to synthesize a mediator services. However, in that case we cannot directly influence the fitness of the mediator service. Both S_1 and S_2 have individual fitness to the logs, but existing techniques do not allow to control the discovery with respect to message mediation. In the worst case, the discovered models are even not adaptable, such that no mediator service can be generated.

Our setting is closer related to *Service Composition* [18]. The idea there is to use existing services as building blocks and compose them in order to derive a complex composition that fulfills a given service specification. Often stateless atomic services are considered (e.g., [23]), only needing the services to build a certain structure and interaction is correct anyway; there cannot occur behavioral problems by interaction as opposed in our setting. Furthermore, we cannot define a target service as goal, such that we cannot apply such ideas in our setting.

In context of stateful service, service orchestration can be applied (e.g., [5]). A fixed set of stateful services is orchestrated; that is, a further service is generated that interacts with the given services, such that the interaction with an environment fulfills a certain specification. In our setting, however, we do not want to orchestrate the building blocks, but we actually want to compose them and let them interact directly. Furthermore we want to consider cases, where building blocks are used multiple times. There are also results on service composition that actually just compose a set of given services to meet a certain specification (e.g., [3]). Compared to our setting they can help us to build the candidates, but they do not check conformance to logs especially with respect to data values.

Correlation discovery [2, 9, 14] can help us in replay, but these approaches do not tackle the problem to find a model that is able to realize the found correlation.

Many of the existing publications can be used to further improve our approach, however, to the best of our knowledge, our approach of building pattern-based candidates and check their conformance is a new perspective in the area of service mining.

6 Conclusion and Outlook

We have presented an approach for discovering a mediator service. We use as input logs of the communication behavior of its interaction partner and a set patterns for structuring the search space. In order to make the discovery feasible at all, we introduced some restrictions, that allows us to discover a model not only in theory, but also in practice.

We consider our result a first step for tackling the problem and see much room for improvement. On the one hand, we may loosen the bounds on the number of patterns. Techniques for service composition allow to discover composition of basic services without necessarily restricting their number. We could use such techniques for finding candidates. On the other hand, the replay takes a considerable time so far, and an acceleration of the conformance checking is desirable. We see chances in further preprocessing the cases based on the values used, but also on semantic analysis of the patterns. In the second case we could exclude more candidate based on insufficient data transformation.

Last but not least, we may even introduce some form of non-determinism. We want to allow value-substitution acknowledging that some data seem to occur arbitrarily, but do not change during the run of a service instance. Although a case demands a different value, it can fit perfectly if we substitute that value.

References

1. van der Aalst, W.M.P.: Process Mining - Discovery, Conformance and Enhancement of Business Processes. Springer (2011)
2. Basu, S., Casati, F., Daniel, F.: Toward web service dependency discovery for SOA management. In: IEEE SCC (2), pp. 422–429 (2008)
3. Bertoli, P., Kazhamiakin, R., Paolucci, M., Pistore, M., Raik, H., Wagner, M.: Control flow requirements for automated service composition. In: ICWS, pp. 17–24 (2009)
4. Buijs, J.C.A.M., van Dongen, B.F., van der Aalst, W.M.P.: On the role of fitness, precision, generalization and simplicity in process discovery. In: Meersman, R., et al. (eds.) OTM 2012, Part I. LNCS, vol. 7565, pp. 305–322. Springer, Heidelberg (2012)
5. Calvanese, D., Giacomo, G.D., Lenzerini, M., Mecella, M., Patrizi, F.: Automatic service composition and synthesis: the roman model. IEEE Data Eng. Bull. 31(3), 18–22 (2008)
6. Fahland, D., Gierds, C.: Analyzing and Completing Middleware Designs for Enterprise Integration Using Coloured Petri Nets. In: Salinesi, C., Norrie, M.C., Pastor, Ó. (eds.) CAiSE 2013. LNCS, vol. 7908, pp. 400–416. Springer, Heidelberg (2013)
7. Gombotz, R., Dustdar, S.: On web services workflow mining. In: Bussler, C.J., Haller, A. (eds.) BPM 2005. LNCS, vol. 3812, pp. 216–228. Springer, Heidelberg (2006)
8. Google: Checkout, `https://checkout.google.com/` (retrieved June 10, 2013)
9. Guabtni, A., Motahari-Nezhad, H.R., Benatallah, B.: Using graph aggregation for service interaction message correlation. In: Mouratidis, H., Rolland, C. (eds.) CAiSE 2011. LNCS, vol. 6741, pp. 642–656. Springer, Heidelberg (2011)
10. Hohpe, G., Woolf, B.: Enterprise Integration Patterns: Designing, Building, and Deploying Messaging Solutions. Addison-Wesley Longman Publishing Co., Inc., Boston (2003)
11. JBoss: JBoss ESB, `http://labs.jboss.com/jbossesb/`
12. Jensen, K., Kristensen, L.M.: Coloured Petri Nets - Modelling and Validation of Concurrent Systems. Springer (2009)
13. Motahari Nezhad, H.R., Saint-Paul, R., Benatallah, B., Casati, F.: Deriving protocol models from imperfect service conversation logs. IEEE Trans. Knowl. Data Eng. 20(12), 1683–1698 (2008)
14. Motahari Nezhad, H.R., Saint-Paul, R., Casati, F., Benatallah, B.: Event correlation for process discovery from web service interaction logs. VLDB J. 20(3), 417–444 (2011)
15. Müller, R., van der Aalst, W.M.P., Stahl, C.: Conformance checking of services using the best matching private view. In: WS-FM, pp. 49–68 (2012)
16. Musaraj, K., Yoshida, T., Daniel, F., Hacid, M.S., Casati, F., Benatallah, B.: Message correlation and web service protocol mining from inaccurate logs. In: ICWS, pp. 259–266 (2010)
17. Papazoglou, M.P.: Web Services - Principles and Technology. Prentice Hall (2008)
18. Rao, J., Su, X.: A survey of automated web service composition methods. In: Cardoso, J., Sheth, A.P. (eds.) SWSWPC 2004. LNCS, vol. 3387, pp. 43–54. Springer, Heidelberg (2005)
19. TU/e, P.M.G.: ProM Tools, `http://www.promtools.org/` (retrieved June 10, 2013)
20. University of Aarhus - Department of Computer Science: CPnets - industrial use, `http://cs.au.dk/cpnets/industrial-use/` (retrieved June 10, 2013)
21. Westergaard, M., Kristensen, L.M.: The access/CPN framework: A tool for interacting with the CPN tools simulator. In: Franceschinis, G., Wolf, K. (eds.) PETRI NETS 2009. LNCS, vol. 5606, pp. 313–322. Springer, Heidelberg (2009)
22. Yellin, D.M., Strom, R.E.: Protocol specifications and component adaptors. ACM Trans. Program. Lang. Syst. 19(2), 292–333 (1997)
23. Zheng, G., Bouguettaya, A.: Service mining on the web. IEEE T. Services Computing 2(1), 65–78 (2009)

Cloud Service Brokerage - 2013: Methods and Mechanisms

Gregoris Mentzas[1], Anthony J.H. Simons[2], and Iraklis Paraskakis[3]

[1] Institute of Communication and Computer Systems,
National Technical University of Athens,
Iroon Polytechniou 9, 15773 Zografou, Greece
gmentzas@mail.ntua.gr
[2] Department of Computer Science, University of Sheffield,
Regent Court, 211 Portobello, Sheffield S1 4DP, United Kingdom
a.j.simons@sheffield.ac.uk
[3] South-East European Research Centre,
Proxenou Koromila 24, 54622 Thessaloniki, Greece
iparaskakis@seerc.org

Abstract. In the future, the Cloud will evolve into a rich ecosystem of service providers and consumers, each building upon the offerings of others. Cloud service brokers will play an important role, mediating between providers and consumers. As well as providing vertical integration and value-added aggregation of services, brokers will play an increased role in continuous quality assurance and optimization. This may range from setting common standards for service specification, providing mechanisms for lifecycle governance and service certification, to automatic arbitrage respecting consumer preferences, continuous optimization of service delivery, failure prevention and recovery at runtime. This workshop introduces some of these anticipated methods and investigates some of the mechanisms envisaged in future Cloud service brokerage.

Preface

This volume contains the proceedings of the 1st International Workshop on Cloud Service Brokerage (CSB-2013), which was held on 2 December 2013 in the historic city of Berlin, co-located with the 11th International Conference on Service Oriented Computing. The theme of this first workshop, which is sponsored by the EU FP7 Broker@Cloud project, is the investigation of methods and mechanisms to be deployed in future Cloud service brokerage.

It is an exciting time to be working in the area of Cloud computing. The world is waking up to the fact that in the future, we will be more likely to work in a location-independent way, with our personal and business-related information following us around as we go, accessed virtually in cyberspace. Large companies such as IBM have already realised the cost savings benefits of closing down under-utilized server rooms and migrating to a private Cloud, hosted on fewer, more efficiently operated

A.R. Lomuscio et al. (Eds.): ICSOC 2013 Workshops, LNCS 8377, pp. 135–136, 2014.
© Springer International Publishing Switzerland 2014

data centres. The market is growing rapidly for infrastructure, platform, and software service providers, such as Salesforce, Amazon, Microsoft, Oracle, Google, SAP, SoftLayer, Terremark, Rackspace, and NetSuite, who have reported turnovers in their Cloud-facing businesses ranging from \$1-3bn in 2013, demonstrating the increasing value in Cloud computing.

However, this is only the beginning. We are currently experiencing a highly competitive period, where the big vendors are seeking to establish their products in the marketplace. But we expect a more cooperative model to emerge as the market settles, with further vendors emerging, who are more open and build upon other vendors' offerings. This has already started, with the Heroku platform consuming Amazon infrastructure. Similarly, many bespoke CRM systems integrate already with Google Apps, providing mobile maps and calendars. In the future, Cloud Service Brokers will play a role in matching providers with consumers at each level in the Cloud stack. Industry analysts such as Gartner and Forrester have foreseen brokers playing the role of intermediaries, either integrating different partners, or aggregating their services, offering added value on brokered platforms.

The emergence of the Cloud Service Broker was the motivation behind the EU FP7 Broker@Cloud project, whose goal is to investigate methods and mechanisms for continuous quality assurance and optimization for Cloud service brokerage. This workshop reports some of the early findings from that project; but also presents an equal number of papers from outside the consortium. Three papers describe the birth of this new business model in cyberspace. Fowley, et al. look at different emerging models for Cloud service brokerage; while Kourtesis, et al. analyse the key requirements for delivering quality assurance and optimization in Cloud service brokerage. Duan et al. investigate value-driven business modelling, describing the incentives to brokers and others who operate in the Cloud. A further three papers look in detail at some of the technologies that will realize the goals described above. Bratanis and Kourtesis look at the whole notion of lifecycle governance in the Cloud, and the kinds of monitoring mechanisms needed for failure prevention and recovery. Kiran, et al. show how providing simple model-based specifications for services supports a powerful testing methodology to increase trust in the quality of service behaviour, and also acts as a powerful force for standardisation. Finally, Duan et al. offer a value-added modelling approach to describing the revenue increments earned by different players, including brokers, in the Cloud.

We, the workshop chairs, are grateful to our international and widely-experienced Programme Committee, who selected the most interesting six papers from twelve submissions. Altogether, the papers collected here represent a diverse range of analyses, ranging from the envisioning of the future, to the technical challenges and solutions and the measurement of economic benefits for Cloud Service Brokerage. We hope that you find these insights stimulating!

Acknowledgement. The research leading to these results has received funding from the European Union Seventh Framework Programme (FP7/2007-2013) under grant agreement no. 318392, the Broker@Cloud project (www.broker-cloud.eu).

A Comparison Framework and Review of Service Brokerage Solutions for Cloud Architectures

Frank Fowley[1], Claus Pahl[1], and Li Zhang[2]

[1] IC4, Dublin City University, Dublin 9, Ireland
[2] Northeastern University, Software College, Shenyang, China

Abstract. Cloud service brokerage has been identified as a key concern for future cloud technology development and research. We compare service brokerage solutions. A range of specific concerns like architecture, programming and quality will be looked at. We apply a 2-pronged classification and comparison framework. We will identify challenges and wider research objectives based on an identification of cloud broker architecture concerns and technical requirements for service brokerage solutions. We will discuss complex cloud architecture concerns such as commoditisation and federation of integrated, vertical cloud stacks.

Keywords: Cloud Broker, Service Brokerage, Architecture Patterns, Cloud Broker Comparison, State-of-the-art Review, Research Challenges.

1 Introduction

Several organisations active in the cloud technology area, such as Gartner and NIST [13,21], have identified cloud service brokerage as an important architectural challenge. Architecture and programming model concerns are key enabler of any service brokerage solution that mediates between different providers by integrating, aggregating and customising services from different providers. We compare cloud service management and brokerage solutions, i.e. we discuss a broader classification in terms of components and features of cloud service brokers, specifically looking at architecture, language and quality as technical aspects in a refined, more descriptive model. We address challenges based on an identification of cloud broker architecture patterns for service brokerage solutions. Our key contribution is a discussion of service broker solutions based on a 2-pronged comparison framework. Such a dedicated framework does not exist for cloud brokers and goes beyond existing service taxonomies such as [14].

The paper is organised as follows. Cloud service brokerage is introduced in Section 2. Section 3 discusses wider architectural concerns. In Section 4, we introduce and apply the comparison framework. These investigations lead into a broader research challenges discussion in Section 5.

2 Cloud Service Brokerage

Gartner and NIST define Cloud Service Brokerage [13,21]. They follow a similar three-pronged classification. They define a cloud broker as an entity that

A.R. Lomuscio et al. (Eds.): ICSOC 2013 Workshops, LNCS 8377, pp. 137–149, 2014.
© Springer International Publishing Switzerland 2014

manages the use, performance and delivery of cloud services and negotiates relationships between cloud providers and cloud consumers [12].

In this overview of key concepts, we follow Gartner. Aggregation is actually singled out by both organisations. NIST intermediation and Gartner customisation focus on enhancing existing service. NIST arbitration and Gartner integration have in common a flexible mediation and integration of different systems.

- Aggregation is about delivering two or more services to possibly many consumers, not necessarily providing new functionality, integration or customisation, but offering centralised management of SLAs and security.
- Customisation is about altering or adding capabilities, here to change or improve and enhance the service function, possibly combined with analytics.
- Integration addresses the challenges of making independent services work together as a combined offering, which is often integration of a vertical cloud stack or data/process integration within a layer. Classical techniques such as transformation, mediation and orchestration are the solutions.

We now look at the possible impact of the different cloud layers IaaS and PaaS on cloud service broker requirements. Brokers have to deal with various cloud layer-specific concerns [5], e.g. for IaaS these are:

- The key IaaS need is elasticity. With techniques such as replication, provisioned services can be scaled. Images can be replicated and moved to other, interoperable offerings and platforms to create a virtual layered environment.
- Problems that arise are that platform engines are often proprietary or do not replicate fully unless standards like OVF for VMs are used. Also, replicating an image with data needs bandwidth, which requires optimised solutions.
- Image and data handling aims to minimise replication and manage deletion, use segmentation for services, differentiate user-data and images/services to optimise and include intelligent data management such as map-reduce techniques. Horizontal scaling often requires the full dataset to be replicated. Vertical scaling can be based on data segmentation and distribution.

This indicates that automation is here of critical importance as the cloud elasticity need is the driver of these techniques. For the PaaS layer:

- Platforms need to facilitate composition and service mashups [11,4].
- For most applications, base image duplication can suffice, but too many users per application generally require full replication with customer-specific data/code. In case base images (e.g. for .NET) are available, we only need to replicate service instances, but not a full image.
- Further problems arise for composition as QoS is generally not compositional, e.g. the security of a composition is determined by its weakest link.

Automated management is a key concern. Standardisation in terms of OVF as an image format or OCCI as an interface for infrastructure-level resource management functionality are solutions. Interoperability can be achieved through standardisation – based on open and published standards or de-facto based on widely used open-source or proprietary systems. A problem is that even standards often do not succeed. Some proposals in the Web services stack (WS-*) are examples. Problems encountered are diversion of specifications, the slow process of standardisation and competing standardisation bodies – the latter is an obvious problem in the cloud domain, where organisations from different areas of IT and computing are active (SNIA, DMTF, OMG, W3C, OGF etc). While some mature standards exist for the services domain in the context of Web Services (W3C, OASIS etc), cloud services are not necessarily WS-compliant. Some solutions exist IaaS standards like OCCI and CIMI cover service lifecycle management, TOSCA addresses portability and CDMI is about data management. IaaS open-source systems supporting these standards are Openstack, which is a lifecycle management product in the line of CIMI and OCCI aims, or the mOSAIC API that supports composition and mashups at an infrastructure level [20]. PaaS systems include Cloudify, a management tool for vertical cloud stack integration, and Compatible One, a broker for horizontal integration [8,9].

3 Cloud Service Broker Architectures

Cloud brokerage solutions build up on existing virtualisation, cloud platform and IaaS/PaaS/SaaS offerings. We can single out three architecture patterns:

- Cloud Management: supports the design, deployment, provisioning and monitoring of cloud resources, e.g. through management portals. This is an extension of the core lifecycle management (LCM), adding monitoring features or graphical forms of interaction. Rudimentary features for the integration of compatible services can be provided.

  A management layer is often identified in cloud architecture to management that facilitate efficient and scalable provisioning in a number of the platforms reviewed below.
- Cloud Broker Platform: supports the broker activity types discussed earlier – aggregation, customisation, integration – which needs a specific language to describe services in a uniform way and to define the integration mechanism. The origin of this is the common broker pattern from software design patterns, applied to a cloud setting.
- Cloud Marketplace: builds up on broker platform to provide a marketplace to bring providers and customers together. Again, service description for core and integrated services plays a role for functionality and technical quality aspects. Trust is the second key element that needs to be facilitated.

  Marketplaces for apps are omnipresent and this marketplace pattern is a reflection of upcoming cloud-specific marketplaces (DT will be mentioned as a sample case below).

These layers can be put on top of the classical cloud architecture layers SaaS, PaaS and IaaS. The discussion below will show that a fine-grained characterisation of cloud brokerage solutions, even beyond these three is necessary to identify and distinguish specific challenges. We look into open-source solutions (or solutions provided by publicly funded projects) as these are well-documented.

3.1 Open-Source Solutions

Open-source solutions can thus be categorised based on the presented scheme:

- Open IaaS: OpenStack, for instance, is a basic IaaS cloud manager that transforms data-centres to become IaaS clouds [25].
- Open PaaS: OpenShift and CloudFoundry are open PaaS platforms assisting the cloud app developer by commoditising the software stack [7,24].

The Open IaaS/PaaS solutions can be differentiated from respective IaaS/PaaS brokers. In the following, we will try to point out the salient differences between some cloud brokers that go beyond IaaS/PaaS management solutions. Optimis and CompatibleOne are IaaS-oriented, and only 4CaaSt targets PaaS and to some extent also the SaaS domain. There is, however, SaaS broker activity in the commercial space.

An observation here is that the broker pattern receives attention and that reusable solutions are in development, starting with the IaaS layer, but including IaaS and PaaS over time. The existence of marketplaces, which are interesting for the diverse SaaS space, indicates the existence of broker solution. The AppDirect commercial broker is an example. However, a wider range of commoditised, ready-to-use broker platforms can be expected in the future – to service the different broker types defined, but also provide a fuller range of features as our discussion of the open-source solutions indicates.

4 Service Management and Brokerage Comparison

In this section, we compare cloud solutions using a dedicated 2-pronged framework, which we will introduce first.

- The first is a categorisation schema for a basic classification (Tables 1, 2).
- The second is a more detailed, descriptive classification (Tables 3 to 5).

We compare a number of selected solutions, essentially open-source solutions or publicly funded frameworks.

In Tables 1 and 2, we categorise a number of solutions [7,8,10,16,18,23,20,24,25,34,1,9]. We categorise languages in terms of the cloud layer support, but also specific features or functions each of them provides. We have defined a comparison framework to categorise solutions along the following concerns:

- System Type: Multi Cloud API Library, IaaS Fabric Controller, Open PaaS Solution, Open PaaS Provider.
- Distribution Model: Open Source (for all solutions considered).

Table 1. Open Source Clouds - System Category and Type

	CATEGORIES and TYPE					
Name	Category	Cloud Layer	Multi Cloud API Library	IaaS Fabric Controller	Open PaaS Solution	Open PaaS Provider
OpenNebula	CLOUD FABRIC CONTROLLER	IaaS		Y		
OpenStack	CLOUD FABRIC CONTROLLER	IaaS		Y		
libcloud	API LIBRARY	PaaS	Y			
jclouds	API LIBRARY	PaaS	Y			
simpleAPI	API LIBRARY	PaaS	Y			
DeltaCloud	API SERVER	PaaS	Y			
Cloudify	CLOUD DEVOPS & LCM	PaaS	Y		Y	
Mosaic	PAAS	PaaS	Y		Y	
Cloud Foundry	PAAS	PaaS	Y		Y	Y
OpenShift	PAAS	PaaS			Y	
CompatibleOne	IAAS BROKER	PaaS			Y	
4Caast	SERVICE BROKER	PaaS				
Optimis	IAAS BROKER	PaaS			Y	

Table 2. Open Source Clouds - Core Capabilities and Features/Components

	CORE CAPABILITES			CORE FEATURES						ADVANCED FEATURES		
Name	Multi IaaS Support	Multi Language / Multi Framework	Multi Stack	Service Description Language	Native Data store	Native Message Queue	Programming Model	Elasticity Scalability	QoS / SLA Monitoring	Service Discovery / Composition	Broker	Market-Place
OpenNebula												
OpenStack					Y							
libcloud	Y											
jclouds	Y											
simpleAPI	Y											
DeltaCloud	Y											
Cloudify	Y	Y	Y	Y			Y	Y	Y			
Mosaic	Y			Y	Y	Y	Y	Y		Y	Y	
Cloud Foundry	Y	Y	Y				Y					
OpenShift		Y	Y					Y				
CompatibleOne	Y			Y			Y	Y	Y	Y	Y	
4Caast				Y	Y	Y			Y	Y	Y	Y
Optimis				Y	Y		Y	Y	Y		Y	

- Core Capabilities: Multi-IaaS Support, Multi Language / Multi Framework Support, Multi Stack Support.
- Core Features/Components (development and deployment time): Service Description Language, Native Data Store, Native Message Queue, Programming Model, Elasticity & Scalability, QoS/SLA Monitoring.
- Advanced Features/Components: Service Discovery/Composition, Broker, Marketplace – towards broker and marketplace features.

We chose these concerns to, firstly, broadly categorise the solution in terms of is main function (the system type that indicates its target layer and central function in that layer) and whether it is proprietary or open-source. Secondly, a range of standard properties and individual components are singled out. Properties chosen here (the Core Capabilities) refer to necessary capabilities for brokers to integrate offerings. The two features categories organised a number of system components into common and more advanced ones.

In the following we review various solutions with respect to three facets: architecture & interoperability, languages & programming, and quality. This format allows us to drill down and compare using a more descriptive format. We will not

Table 3. Architecture and Interoperability

	Cloudify	*CloudFoundry*	*OpenShift*	*Compatible1*	*4Caast*
Architecture	- Console for platform commands. Web management console for monitoring. - Service Manager uses scripting (recipe) to cater for middleware stack - Cloud Controller is REST endpoint to manage app deployment & control; injects agent on VM to install & orchestrate app deploy/monitor/scale - Cloud Driver: VM templates for different IaaS clouds in configuration. Triggers host provisioning	- Console pushes app to cloud; deployment management / configuration through console - Controller runs as a cloud VM on the target IaaS; controls all Cloudify spawned cloud VMs. Does not manage IaaS layer functions. The IaaS provider must support Cloudify. Apps created using Cloudify are deployed to Cloudify VMs controlled by a cloud controller on Cloudify-compliant IaaS clouds.	- Divided into control plane (Broker) and messaging / application hosting infrastructure (Nodes). - Controller is command CLI shell, used to create apps. GIT for app management / deployment. - Gear is application container and a virtual server/node accessed via ssh. Cartridge service runs on a Gear. App LCM scripts allow for post-deployment action hooks to run on VMs.	- ACCORDS exposes features through REST API. - Parser validates Manifest against CORDS schema and maps elements to valid OCCI categories which are then instantiated. - Publisher provides which endpoint serves which categories. Parser runs and produces a plan of OCCI instances for resolution (instance can receive/send data). - Broker processes plan and invokes instances.	- Execution Container REC runs instances. - Deployment Manager maps deployment model (service template, QoS constraints) to OVF. Service Manager deploys images using Claudia. - REC includes an agent (application LCM, control) and a server (storage, config data). Deployment Server (Chef) talks to Service and REC Manager. OVF Manager creates extended OVFs from abstract resolved BluePrints.
Clouds Supported / Interoperability	Supports Azure, OpenStack, CloudStack, EC2, Rackspace, Terramark (buildable for any of the jclouds above)	Supports AWS, vSphere, Openstack, Rackspace. Is hosted as public PaaS on Cloudify. Private cloud is available.	Uses DeltaCloud; app runs on RedHat certified public cloud (needs deltacloud support).	OCCI provider interfaces (PROCCIs) for OpenStack, OpenNebula and Azure (also SlapOS and SlapGrid).	FlexiScale driver provided. OpenNebula supported. Generic IaaS Cloud API through Tcloud.

consider all 13 products initially compare, but only select the most advanced ones for each aspect. This second, deeper and more descriptive classification schema is based on three facets.

Architecture and Interoperability. The solution architecture is a key element in the definition of a broker. Of practical relevance are the existing, typically lower-layer solutions that the system supports. This is an interoperability concern. CompatibleOne is OCCI-compatible in its support for VM management. For instance, Mosaic assumes a Linux OS, which runs Mosaic App Components (called CloudLets). A number of common commercial cloud solutions are supported by Mosaic, including Amazon and Rackspace products.

In Table 3, a number of PaaS-level solutions are summarised in terms of these two aspects. Common are the utilisation of configuration management solutions, such as Chef or GIT. The deployment is managed through consoles or APIs, mapping PaaS-level requests down to IaaS operations. As often many IaaS solutions are supported, interoperability is a critical concern.

Languages and Programming. Service description plays a key role for interoperability [28]. For selected solutions, we look at the following three aspects:

- service language – the core notation, including the coverage of concerns vertically (PaaS/IaaS integration) and horizontally (full lifecycle management) and how this is manipulated (format and API).
- programming model – using the language to program brokerage solutions, linking to SOA principles and other development paradigms.
- service engineering – covering wider design and architecture concerns, including monitoring and mashups.

Cloudify, for instance, uses application recipes and resource node templates in the form of Groovy scripts as the programming model. A service recipe contains LCM scripts, monitoring probes and IaaS resources requirements. Mosaic uses an OWL ontology as the notation and a component-based application programming model for portability of apps across Mosaic-compliant clouds. More solutions are compared in Table 4. Patterns emerge as solutions to compose, connect and manage clouds in distributed contexts.

Quality. Scalability and elasticity are specific cloud concerns, and need to be addressed by the service description notation. Load balancers are typically used to control elasticity based on monitored key performance indicators (KPIs). Multi-tenancy, if available, can alleviate elasticity problems. Based on specifications, these are looked after by configuration management tools to set up probes and monitoring tools to collect and analyse data. Table 5 covers these concerns.

Summary. We can categorise the open-source solutions based on some of the central aspects. This summarises a selection of currently available solutions in terms of their support aims and allows us to identify trends. Developers are supported in three categories: a) API library: libcloud, Jcloud, deltacloud, b) Devops: Cloudify and c) Full PaaS: CloudFoundry, OpenShift. A trend goes from provider-oriented solutions to developer-oriented solutions to end user-oriented cloud management [3] – 4Caast being an example of the latter.

5 Challenges – Brokers, Markets and Federated Clouds

The need for interoperability becomes apparent in the context of cloud service brokerage, where independent actors in the ecosystem integrate, aggregate/compose and customise/adapt existing services [13,21]. End-to-end personalisation becomes achievable. Prosumers create mashups from existing services.

From the above comparison between various cloud solutions, we can note a difference between the needs of cloud brokerage and cloud marketplaces. We did already introduce them as different patterns above.

Table 4. Service Language, Programming Model and Service Engineering

	Reservoir	*Compatible One*	*4Caast*	*Optimis*
Service Language	Service Definition Manifest for metadata; software stack (OS, middleware, app, config, data) in a virtual image; has service descriptions for contracts between service provider SP and infrastructure provider IP. Manifests (OVF) relate abstract entities and LCM / operation of services. Feedback between SP and IP allows IP to scale and monitor.	Units of Service Manifest: Image & Infrastructure. Image: System (base OS) & Package (stack config); Infrastructure: Storage, Compute & Network. Image is description of manual app build. Image has agent that is embedded in VM & runs on startup. Agent is script to run required configuration, set up monitoring probes, or download components.	Resources and Services are described in a Blueprint BP, which is an abstract description of what needs to be resolved into infrastructure entities. BPs are stored and managed in a BP repository via a REST API. A BP is resolved when all requirements are fulfilled by another BP, via the Resolution Engine (is service orchestration feature).	Service Manifest includes sections per component per VM. Service Register has sections for SP requirements and IP capabilities, VM abstract description, TREC (trust, risk, eco-efficiency, cost), elasticity, data protection. Optimis also provides a cloud provider description schema for a SP to provide its capabilities in an XML Optimis-compliant format.
Programming Model	Elasticity is defined using ECA rules to scale infrastructure dynamically based on application KPI metrics. Rules in OCL.	PaaS4Dev: Java EE services (EE5/6 web profile) & Enterprise OSGi services (http, jndi, transaction) for development	Uses Active MQ, postgresql, jonas, ow2orchestra, apache serv bus. Ontology-based BP schema using Jena, SPARQL.	Java schemas, jaxb, xmlbeans, REST, monitor; also jax-ws, cxf, javagat. IDE is Eclipse with plugin for Optimis core classes.
Service Engineering	Service provisioning described in Deployment Descriptor. Service configuration automation based on Xen configuration. Service Elasticity is achieved through mapping Manifest KPIs with run-time metrics gathered by app monitoring agents.	- Nested manifests support service composition. - COSACS module embeds in VM image mechanisms to manage lifecycle actions, e.g. post-creation monitoring setup and appliance configuration, in conjunction with image production module.	- Request Language BRL & request patterns create Blueprint BP service specification - mapped to cloud operations and cloud mgmt API calls. Mashup for composition. - BP consists of BP images, contains functional, KPI & policy parameters.	Toolkit provides image mgmt, context manager injects context information to VMs and Elasticity Engine to add/remove resources. Service Deployment Optimiser optimises placement of services. Configuration using the Toolkit IDE.

– The *brokerage* needs to automate as far as possible the process of matching service requirements with resource capacity and capabilities [33]. The ideal would be a total commoditisation of IaaS so that any compute resource, be it from a private OpenStack cloud or a public EC2 instance, could be plugged into a user's compute capacity. Therefore, interoperability will remain of importance. In this regard, it is useful to look at new areas of compatibility that should be considered in matching that are not handled by brokers currently.

Table 5. Quality: Scalability/Elasticity and SLAs

	CloudFoundry	*OpenShift*	*Compatible1*	*4Caast*	*Optimis*
Elasticity / Scalability	Can add/remove instances for scalability and increase/ decrease CPU & memory limits on VMs	- Gears automatically added/removed as load changes - Multi-tenancy efficiency using multi-gears on same VM	Elasticity is provided by the load balancer module for the IaaS resources.	Not in current release.	The toolkit includes an Elasticity Engine to add / remove resources.
QoS / SLA Monitoring	There is only a basic logging facility with Cloud foundry but there are many third-party Cloud Foundry monitoring plugins can be used to provide application monitoring, such as Hyperic.	The application scaling, when automatic, is based on concurrent application request thresholds. The amount of resources consumed by an application can be monitored and viewed from the Console.	via COMONS Monitoring module.	Monitoring based on probe injection on PICs via REST. Modified JASMINe framework provides dynamic probe deployment & config. Chef recipe configs VM probes to be used by REC manager. Monitoring is based on collectd stats for forecasting.	Framework uses REST to get CPU/disk usage from monitoring. Monitors reside on logical/physical nodes and run as scripts to feed data to monitor store. SLA Manager built using WSAG4J is implementation of OGF WS-Agreement standard.

For example, none of the three open-source solutions that were assessed considered data integrity as a matching criterion; however, they all included performance in their criteria. Security policy is another aspect that has a technical nature, but is also abstract insofar as it can be implemented by a cloud provider. Data integrity and security policy enforcement, if considered as criteria when evaluating cloud interoperability, may need to be formalised using a language to describe common aspects, similar to the languages that have been created to model other cloud entities.

– The *marketplace* will need to additionally focus on the architecture of the applications as well as the cloud. The appstore model appears to be the de-facto model of choice for the marketplace, but this seems more an admission of the success of the Apple initiative rather than any research. There may be a potential to explore other forms of the online marketplace suitable to cloud apps and their composition [19,11]. This could also be pushed to an even more commodity-based scenario where all services could be registered on a wide-area multi-marketplace scale facilitating an even greater eco-system.

Commoditisation. The commoditisation of cloud services is an emerging need from the discussion above – specifically from the language and programming facet. A trend is to move from the lower IaaS layer to PaaS and onwards to encompass SaaS, aiming to integrate lower layers – 4CaaSt is an example. To make this work, services at all layers need to be available for a uniform way of processing in terms of selection, adaptation, integration and aggregation. Commoditisation is the concept to capture this need. Some concrete observations related to the reviewed three open-source solutions are: fully functional image and vertical stack building capabilities (CompatibleOne leadership), operational support of service composition (4CaaSt leadership) and graphical manipulation of service abstractions (Optimis leadership). Facilitated can commoditisation be through a uniform representation through description templates such as recipes, manifests or blueprints. These need to cover the architecture stack and meet the language and quality concerns discussed in Section 4. Commercial providers are equally working on the commoditisation of cloud services as described above.

Commoditisation is an enabler of marketplace functions that sit on top of a broker. Thus, additional challenges and requirements for marketplaces are:

- Data integration and security enforcement as non-functional requirements.
- Social network functions allow service ratings by the communities.
- SLA management to be integrated, e.g. in terms of monitoring results.

Commoditisation needs to be facilitated through an operational development and deployment model. It therefore acts as an enabler. Trust is an equally important concern that more difficult to facilitate technically than commoditisation. A mechanism is needed for not only vetting individual providers, but also to allow this to happen in layered, federated and brokered cloud solutions.

In another direction, there has not been a proliferation of cloud capacity clearing-houses that would operate similar to a spot market to allow clouds to buy and sell spare cloud capacity on a very short-term basis. It is not clear what new areas of research would be needed to facilitate such a movement in the cloud. It seems reasonable that, with the continued commoditisation of the cloud by brokers and marketplaces, such a trend could be seen eventually.

Federated Clouds. Federation is the second requirement for brokerage solutions [6], i.e. to work across independently managed and provided cloud offerings of often heterogeneous nature. Challenges and requirements in this context arising from the architecture and interoperability discussion (the first facet) are:

- Reference architectures – e.g. NIST cloud brokerage reference architecture.
- Scope of control – the management of configuration and deployment based on integrated and/or standards-based techniques [17].
- Federation and syndication – as forms of distributed cloud architectures [32].

6 Conclusions

We have introduced the main concepts of service brokerage for clouds, using some concrete systems and platforms to identify current trends and challenges and compare current, primarily open-source solutions. Brokerage relies on interoperability, quality-of-service and other architectural principles. Brokers and marketplaces will play a central role for new adopters migrating into the cloud or between cloud providers [15,29]. Brokers will act as first points of call.

A 2-pronged comparison framework is the first contribution where we provided a first categorisation scheme to characterise the solution in terms of type, common components and features. The second scheme is a more descriptive, layered taxonomy starting with architecture and interoperability, languages and programming, and quality as facets.

An observation of our comparison based on the framework is the emergence of cloud broker solutions on top of cloud management. A further separation of marketplaces, often in the form of appstores, is necessary. A number of activities work in this direction. Compatible One is a good example showing how OCCI is used as an infrastructure foundation and built upon to provider PaaS-level brokerage. 4CaaSt in a similar vein aims to integrate the layers and move toward a marketplace solution. Commercial solutions, such as DT and UShareSoft, show already existing brokerage and marketplace solutions ranging from images to software services, essentially commoditising the respective cloud resources.

Service description mechanisms discussed in [22,31,27] (in the form of manifests, recipes and blueprints) , but also in standards like TOSCA and CloudML, can serve to abstract, manipulate and compose cloud service offerings in an effort to commoditise the cloud. These description mechanisms, based on an abstract model serve two purposes: Firstly, to abstractly capture, present and manipulate cloud resources. Secondly, to serve as a starting point to link to configuration and other deployment concerns in federated clouds. Thus, commoditisation and federation emerge as challenges from our discussion.

Acknowledgments. This research has been supported by the Irish Centre for Cloud Computing and Commerce, an Irish national Technology Centre funded by Enterprise Ireland and the Irish Industrial Development Authority.

References

1. 4Caast. 4CaaSt PaaS Cloud Platform (2013), `http://4caast.morfeo-project.org/`
2. Barrett, R., Patcas, L.M., Pahl, C., Murphy, J.: Model Driven Distribution Pattern Design for Dynamic Web Service Compositions. In: International Conference on Web Engineering ICWE 2006, pp. 129–136. ACM Press, Palo Alto (2006)
3. Benson, T., Akella, A., Sahu, S., Shaikh, A.: Peeking into the Cloud: Toward User-Driven Cloud Management. In: CloudS 2010 Conference, Sydney, Australia (2010)
4. Benslimane, D., Dustdar, S., Sheth, A.: Services Mashups: The New Generation of Web Applications. Internet Computing 12(5), 13–15 (2008)
5. Bernstein, D., Ludvigson, E., Sankar, K., Diamond, S., Morrow, M.: Blueprint for the Inter-cloud: Protocols and Formats for Cloud Computing Interoperability. In: Intl. Conf. Internet and Web Appl. and Services (2009)
6. Buyya, R., Ranjan, R., Calheiros, R.N.: InterCloud: Utility-Oriented Federation of Cloud Computing Environments for Scaling of Application Services. In: Hsu, C.-H., Yang, L.T., Park, J.H., Yeo, S.-S. (eds.) ICA3PP 2010, Part I. LNCS, vol. 6081, pp. 13–31. Springer, Heidelberg (2010)

7. Cloud Foundry. Open Source PaaS Cloud Provider Interface (2013), http://www.cloudfoundry.org/
8. Cloudify. Cloudify Open PaaS Stack (2013), http://www.cloudifysource.org/
9. CompatibleOne. Open Source Cloud Broker (2013), http://www.compatibleone.org/
10. DeltaCloud. Deltacloud REST cloud abstraction API (2013), http://deltacloud.apache.org/
11. Fehling, C., Mietzner, R.: Composite as a Service: Cloud Application Structures, Provisioning, and Management. Information Technology 53(4), 188–194 (2011)
12. Forrester Research. Cloud Brokers Will Reshape The Cloud (2012), http://www.cordys.com/ufc/file2/ cordyscms_sites/download/09b57cd3eb6474f1fda1cfd62ddf094d/pu/
13. Gartner - Cloud Services Brokerage. Gartner Research (2013), http://www.gartner.com/it-glossary/cloud-services-brokerage-csb
14. Höfer, C.N., Karagiannis, G.: Cloud computing services: taxonomy and comparison. Journal of Internet Services and Applications 2(2), 81–94 (2011)
15. Jamshidi, P., Ahmad, A., Pahl, C.: Cloud Migration Research: A Systematic Review. IEEE Transactions on Cloud Computing (2013)
16. Jclouds. jclouds Java and Clojure Cloud API (2013), http://www.jclouds.org/
17. Konstantinou, A.V., Eilam, T., Kalantar, M., Totok, A.A., Arnold, W., Sniblel, E.: An Architecture for Virtual Solution Composition and Deployment in Infrastructure Clouds. Intl. Workshop on Virtualization Technologies in Distr. Computing (2009)
18. Libcloud. Apache Libcloud Python library (2013), http://libcloud.apache.org/
19. Mietzner, R., Leymann, F., Papazoglou, M.: Defining Composite Configurable SaaS Application Packages Using SCA, Variability Descriptors and Multi-tenancy Patterns. In: Intl. Conf. on Internet and Web Applications and Services (2008)
20. Mosaic. mOSAIC Multiple Cloud API (2013), http://www.mosaic-cloud.eu/
21. NIST. Cloud Computing Reference Architecture (2011), http://www.nist.gov/customcf/get_pdf.cfm?pub_id=909505
22. Nguyen, D.K., Lelli, F., Taher, Y., Parkin, M., Papazoglou, M.P., van den Heuvel, W.-J.: Blueprint Template Support for Engineering Cloud-Based Services. In: Abramowicz, W., Llorente, I.M., Surridge, M., Zisman, A., Vayssière, J. (eds.) ServiceWave 2011. LNCS, vol. 6994, pp. 26–37. Springer, Heidelberg (2011)
23. OpenNebula. OpenNebula - Open Source Data Center Virtualization (2013), http://opennebula.org/
24. OpenShift. Cloud computing platform (2013), https://openshift.redhat.com/
25. OpenStack. OpenStack Open Source Cloud Computing Software (2013), http://www.openstack.org/
26. Optimis. Optimis - Optimized Infrastructure Services (2013), http://www.optimis-project.eu/
27. Pahl, C.: Layered Ontological Modelling for Web Service-Oriented Model-Driven Architecture. In: Hartman, A., Kreische, D. (eds.) ECMDA-FA 2005. LNCS, vol. 3748, pp. 88–102. Springer, Heidelberg (2005)
28. Pahl, C., Giesecke, S., Hasselbring, W.: Ontology-based Modelling of Architectural Styles. Information and Software Technology (IST) 1(12), 1739–1749 (2009)
29. Pahl, C., Xiong, H.: Migration to PaaS Clouds - Migration Process and Architectural Concerns. IEEE 7th International Symposium on the Maintenance and Evolution of Service-Oriented and Cloud-Based Systems MESOCA 2013 (2013)

30. Pahl, C., Xiong, H., Walshe, R.: A Comparison of On-premise to Cloud Migration Approaches. In: Lau, K.-K., Lamersdorf, W., Pimentel, E. (eds.) ESOCC 2013. LNCS, vol. 8135, pp. 212–226. Springer, Heidelberg (2013)
31. Papazoglou, M.P., van den Heuvel, W.J.: Blueprinting the Cloud. IEEE Internet Computing (November 2011)
32. Paya, A., Marinescu, D.C.: Clustering Algorithms for Scale-free Networks and Applications to Cloud Resource Management (2013)
33. Rodero-Merino, L., Vaquero, L.M., Gil, V., Galn, F., Fontn, J., Montero, R.S., Llorente, I.M.: From Infrastructure Delivery to Service Management in Clouds. Future Generation Computer Systems 26, 226–1240 (2010)
34. simpleAPI. Simple API for XML (2013), http://en.wikipedia.org/wiki/Simple_API_for_XML
35. Sun, L., Dong, H., Ashraf, J.: Survey of Service Description Languages and Their Issues in Cloud Computing. In: Eighth International Conference on Semantics, Knowledge and Grids (SKG) 2012, pp. 128–135. IEEE (2012)

Brokerage for Quality Assurance and Optimisation of Cloud Services: An Analysis of Key Requirements

Dimitrios Kourtesis[1,2], Konstantinos Bratanis[1,2], Andreas Friesen[3], Yiannis Verginadis[4], Anthony J.H. Simons[2], Alessandro Rossini[5], Antonia Schwichtenberg[6], and Panagiotis Gouvas[7]

[1] South-East European Research Centre, International Faculty, The University of Sheffield, 24 Proxenou Koromila Street, Thessaloniki, 54622, Greece
{dkourtesis,kobratanis}@seerc.org
[2] Department of Computer Science, The University of Sheffield, Regent Court 211 Portobello Street, Sheffield, S1 4DP, United Kingdom
{d.kourtesis,k.bratanis,a.simons}@dcs.shef.ac.uk
[3] SAP AG, Vincenz-Priessnitz-Strasse 1, Karlsruhe, 76131, Germany
andreas.friesen@sap.com
[4] Institute of Communications and Computer Systems, National Technical University of Athens, Zografou, Athens, 15780, Greece
jverg@mail.ntua.gr
[5] SINTEF, P.O. Box 124 Blindern, 0314 Oslo, Norway
alessandro.rossini@sintef.no
[6] CAS Software AG, Wilhelm-Schickard-Str. 10-12, 76131 Karlsruhe, Germany
Antonia.Schwichtenberg@cas.de
[7] Singular Logic S.A., A. Panagouli & Siniosoglou Str., Nea Ionia, 14234 Athens, Greece
pgouvas@gmail.com

Abstract. As the number of cloud service providers grows and the requirements of cloud service consumers become more complex, the latter will come to depend more and more on the intermediation services of cloud service brokers. Continuous quality assurance and optimisation of services is becoming a mission-critical objective that many consumers will find difficult to address without help from cloud service intermediaries. The Broker@Cloud project envisages a software framework that will make it easier for cloud service intermediaries to address this need, and this paper provides an analysis of key requirements for this framework. We discuss the methodology that we followed to capture these requirements, which involved defining a conceptual service lifecycle model, carrying out a series of Design Thinking workshops, and formalising requirements based on an agile requirements information model. Then, we present the key requirements identified through this process in the form of summarised results.

Keywords: Cloud Service Brokerage, Cloud Service Broker, Requirements Analysis Methodology, Quality Assurance, Optimisation, Cloud Services.

A.R. Lomuscio et al. (Eds.): ICSOC 2013 Workshops, LNCS 8377, pp. 150–162, 2014.
© Springer International Publishing Switzerland 2014

1 Introduction

As the number of cloud service providers grows and the requirements of cloud service consumers become more complex, the need for third party entities to intermediate between consumers and providers of cloud services is becoming stronger. A number of cloud service intermediaries have already appeared on the market, helping enterprises to find and to compare cloud services (e.g. service marketplaces), to develop and to customise services (e.g. application Platform as a Service offerings), to integrate services (e.g. integration Platform as a Service offerings), and more [1]. What all these intermediation services have in common is that they offer a form of brokerage for cloud services. Cloud Service Brokerage (CSB)[1] is becoming increasingly recognised as a key component of the cloud computing value chain [2] with market analysts predicting that it will soon be the fastest growing segment of the cloud computing market [3].

Consumers of cloud services will come to depend more and more on the intermediation services of cloud service brokers, and as the needs of consumers evolve, so will the intermediation services offered by the brokers. A type of intermediation service with high added value to consumers, especially to those who rely on multiple external cloud service providers for their daily operations, will be brokerage for continuous quality assurance and optimisation of cloud services.

Broker@Cloud [4] is an EU-sponsored collaborative research project that was set up to investigate the challenges associated with introducing such capabilities into cloud service brokers. The project will deliver an extensible software framework allowing cloud service intermediaries to equip their platforms with advanced means for continuous quality assurance and optimisation of cloud services. The framework will comprise methods and mechanisms for platform-neutral description of enterprise cloud services; cloud service governance and quality control; cloud service failure prevention and recovery; and continuous optimisation of cloud services.

This paper reports on the methodology employed in the scope of Broker@Cloud to capture the high-level requirements for the envisaged framework, and presents the results obtained from this analysis. In Section 2 we set the context for this work by motivating the need for continuous quality assurance and optimisation brokerage for cloud services. In Section 3 we discuss the methodology that we followed to derive key requirements for the software framework. The methodology section comprises three parts: the cloud service lifecycle model that we used as conceptual framework to guide our thinking about cloud service brokerage requirements, the Design Thinking process that we followed to collect requirements, and the specification methodology that we followed to formalise the requirements. To the best of our knowledge there are not any similar requirements analysis efforts from the state-of-the-art that are focusing specifically to brokerage for quality assurance and optimisation of cloud

---

[1] There is an on-going debate on the definition of Cloud Service Brokerage, with disagreement over the characteristics that an intermediary should have in order to qualify as a Cloud Service Broker. The authors understand Cloud Service Brokerage as a business model, and we use the term Cloud Service Broker to denote an (IT) role of a business entity that creates value for consumers and providers of cloud services by acting as an intermediary.

services. In Section 4 we provide the actual requirements in the form of summarised results. For a full description of the results we refer the reader to [5], which covers the requirements analysis in full extent.

2 The Need for Cloud Service Brokers with Continuous Quality Assurance and Optimisation Capabilities

We are already witnessing a growing number of cloud service intermediaries that allow consumers to integrate, customise or aggregate cloud services [6]. In the future, however, service consumers will require much more sophisticated brokerage services, going far beyond the capabilities of today's cloud service brokers. One such type of brokerage services will be continuous quality assurance and optimisation [7].

As users come to depend on more and more cloud services, it will become increasingly more difficult to keep track of how these services evolve over time — through changes to their terms of provision, to their APIs, or variations in service performance and availability. Moreover, it will become increasingly more difficult to stay on top of all the implications that a change to a service can have, such as whether or not there is continuing compliance to different policies and regulations, continuing conformance to normative technical specifications or Service Level Agreements, and generally, continuous fulfilment of all the different kinds of functional and non-functional requirements surrounding a particular service's usage. The proliferation of increasing numbers of cloud services with similar functionality and comparable terms of provision will contribute to complexity, forcing users to invest more and more effort in identifying alternatives to the cloud services they are using.

For all these reasons, continuous quality assurance and optimisation of cloud services will become increasingly difficult for individual consumers to cope with by themselves, creating opportunities for a market of cloud service intermediaries addressing these needs. Brokerage services will step up to help consumers make sure that the cloud services they rely on meet quality standards on a continuous basis, and that they represent the optimal set of services to be using at any given time [1].

Much of the enabling technology that is needed to support continuous quality assurance and optimisation brokerage is certainly not new. Recent years have seen a proliferation of many relevant proprietary and open source tools that could provide building blocks for the implementation of such capabilities in brokers. Examples include tools for monitoring and managing applications, services and virtualised infrastructures, or tools for integrating heterogeneous data, processes and applications [1]. However, there exists no consolidated software design theory or set of best practices on how to engineer brokerage capabilities of this kind, and there is lack of dedicated software tools to build on [8].

Broker@Cloud aims to bridge this gap by delivering an extensible software framework which will allow cloud service intermediaries to equip their platforms with core capabilities for continuous quality assurance and optimisation of cloud services.

The framework will comprise methods and mechanisms for governance and quality control of cloud services, prevention and recovery of failures, as well as continuous optimisation, building on common means for platform-neutral description of cloud services.

3 The Requirements Derivation Process

In this section we describe the process that was followed in the scope of Broker@Cloud to derive the key requirements for the envisaged continuous quality assurance and optimisation brokerage framework. In Section 3.1 we present an abstract model of the cloud service lifecycle, the role of which was to frame our thinking about cloud service brokerage requirements. Then, in Section 3.2 we outline the Design Thinking process that was followed to organise the requirements analysis effort. Finally, in Section 3.3 we present the requirements information model that we adopted to formalise the requirements.

3.1 Service Lifecycle Model

To guide our requirements derivation process we started with defining a generic cloud service lifecycle model. The motivation behind defining this model as the first step in the requirements analysis process was to ensure that we have a consistent conceptualisation of the context in which the sought software brokerage framework is meant to operate. The model is generic as it covers phases and processes that are relevant in a variety of settings, with no grounding to a specific type of cloud service delivery platform or cloud service intermediary.

Our abstract lifecycle model comprises three plus one phases. The first three are *Service Engineering, Service Onboarding,* and *Service Operation.* The fourth, crosscutting phase is *Service Evolution.* The phases and processes under each phase are illustrated in Figure 1.

By analogy with software engineering, the service lifecycle starts with the *Service Engineering* phase. The *Service Engineering* phase consists of *Design, Development* and *Testing* processes, carried out by the cloud service provider.

Once a cloud service has been successfully developed and tested, and a "go to market" decision has been taken by the cloud service provider, the service enters the *Service Onboarding* phase. Processes under this phase include *Registration, Certification/Assessment*, and, once the service is successfully qualified, *Enrolment*, to make the service visible to potential consumers and make it available for subscription.

A service enters the *Service Operation* phase with the first Cloud Service Consumer deciding to use the service. The tasks performed during this phase can vary significantly from one setting to another, depending on the nature of the cloud service (e.g. if integration is required) and the conditions of its usage as agreed between the parties involved. Typical processes under this phase include *Service Management, Support* and *Assurance*, to manage relationships and meet agreed usage conditions.

Finally, there is a fourth, *Service Evolution* phase which cuts across the whole lifespan of a service. The prominent process here is *Change Management*. Ultimately, the service lifespan ends with the process of *Deprovisioning* the service.

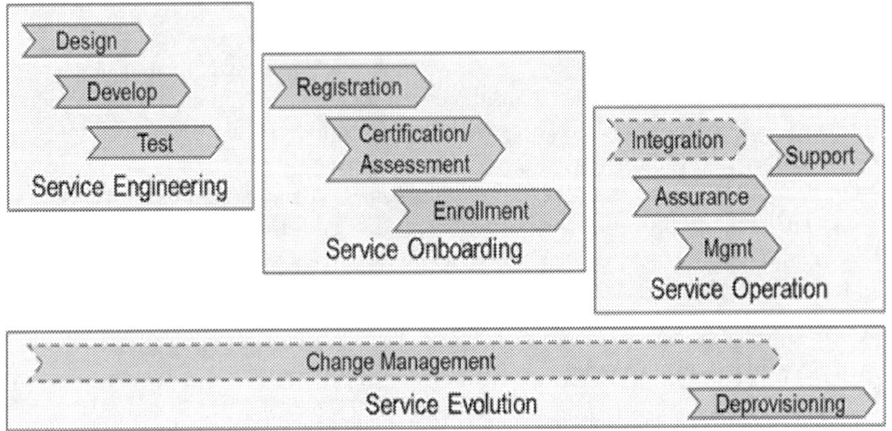

Fig. 1. Service Lifecycle Model

3.2 The Design Thinking Process for Deriving Requirements

To capture key requirements with respect to the framework developed by Broker@Cloud we carried out a series of Design Thinking workshops [9] with two companies that are active in the cloud computing market as cloud service providers and cloud service intermediaries. Both companies see potential in introducing capabilities for continuous quality assurance and optimisation into their cloud platforms and are presently considering a technology roadmap towards this direction.

We note that the Design Thinking is a methodology for collaborative analysis of the problem and solution space within a predefined timeframe. It takes into account requirements from different users and guides the design thinking team through the identification and prioritization of requirements profiles and corresponding solutions associated to different identified user types (personas). The scope and the approach of the Design Thinking methodology is very well fitting the challenge we are facing and is proved to be very helpful for derivation of requirements in our case, since our requirements analysis is based upon general state-of-the-art analysis and in-depth analysis of two industrial cloud platforms in the PaaS/SaaS area. Furthermore, it takes into consideration views of different stakeholders of the platform ecosystems.

Through Design Thinking workshops we gathered and analysed the requirements for the Broker@Cloud framework by mapping the existing and planned activities of the two pilot cloud platforms onto the phases and processes of our generic Service Lifecycle Model.

A Design Thinking process could have up to seven stages: *define, research, ideate, prototype, choose, implement,* and *learn*. Within these seven steps, problems can be framed, the right questions can be asked, more ideas can be created, and the best answers can be chosen. The steps are not linear; they can occur in parallel and can be repeated. For our requirements analysis we chose to apply a four stage Design Thinking process consisting of *research, synthesis, ideation,* and *prototyping*. The additional *synthesis* step was introduced to combine the results of separate investigations. In the *research* and *synthesis* steps we identified requirements. In the *ideation* and *prototyping* phases we focused on identification and prototyping of methods and mechanisms providing solutions to the chosen requirements.

For the *research phase* we relied on customer interviews. We developed a questionnaire guiding interviewers and interviewees from each company through different aspects of current and future usage of the cloud platform of each company, asking which processes they could imagine handing off to intermediaries, what kinds of optimisation they consider to be relevant, etc. The interviews were conducted with a number of employees from each cloud platform company who work in different positions and therefore have different perspectives on the theme of cloud service brokerage. The interviews were collated and analysed to extract information relevant to continuous quality assurance and optimisation. The information was classified and clustered by topic, and the interviewees were asked to prioritise the requirements for their usage scenarios. In the *ideation phase* we selected some requirements with high priority to develop solution ideas. This was performed through subsequent steps of brainstorming, clustering and selection. The selected solution ideas were taken into the *prototyping phase* to develop conceptual paper-based prototypes, in order to investigate the technical feasibility of the identified solutions and obtain feedback.

3.3 Requirements Specification Methodology

We used the results from the Design Thinking workshops as starting point for identifying, clustering and analysing requirements for cloud service brokerage, focusing on requirements for the continuous quality assurance and optimisation capabilities outlined earlier.

To formalise these requirements, we followed a methodology inspired by the agile requirements information model of Leffingwell and Aalto [10], who propose to think of requirements in terms of *Themes, Epics, Features* and *User Stories*. According to Leffingwell and Aalto, these four concepts represent different forms of expressing user need and implied benefit, but at different levels of abstraction [10]. Variants of this requirements analysis model have become very popular in agile software development, especially in connection with agile methodologies such as Scrum and Kanban [11]. Building on this information model, we organised requirements into *Themes, Epics, Capabilities* and *User Stories*. The four concepts are explained below and the logical relationships between them are illustrated in Figure 2.

Themes and Epics. A *Theme* is a strategic level objective of a software product. For instance, one of the strategic Themes for our proposed brokerage framework is 'Governance and Quality Control'. An *Epic*, on the other hand, is a high level expression of a customer need. Derived from the portfolio of strategic product *Themes*, *Epics* are units of software development work that are intended to deliver the value of a *Theme* and need to be prioritised, estimated and planned as part of the software development process [10]. In our methodology, every *Epic* is associated with exactly one *Theme*, whilst a *Theme* is associated with many *Epics*. For instance, one of the *Epics* for our software framework is 'Service Certification', and it maps to the *Theme* of 'Governance and Quality Control'. The *Theme* of 'Governance and Quality Control' is mapped to four *Epics* in total: 'Service Certification', 'SLA Enforcement', 'Policy Enforcement' and 'Service Lifecycle Management'.

Capabilities. A *Capability* is analogous to a *Feature* in the requirements information model of Leffingwell and Aalto. *Capabilities* can be understood as high level, complex (and possibly composite) services to be provided by a software system to fulfil a user need. As Leffingwell and Aalto put it, the purpose of this concept is to "bridge the gap from the problem domain (understanding user needs) to the solution domain (specific requirements intended to address the user needs)" [10]. In our methodology, a *Capability* may be mapped to more than one *Epic*. For example, 'Policy Evaluation' represents a *Capability* associated with two *Epics*: 'Service Certification' and 'Service Lifecycle Management'.

User Stories. A *User Story* is a brief statement of intent describing something the system needs to do for the user. A *User Story* often takes the following canonical form: "As a <role>, I want <goal/desire> so that <benefit>". *User Stories* should comply with "INVEST" properties, which means that they should be "Independent, Negotiable, Valuable, Estimatable, Small and Testable". In our methodology, each *User Story* maps to exactly one *Capability* and to exactly one *Epic*. For example, one *User Story* is the following: 'As a <broker>, I want to <check service descriptions against (broker's or consumers') policies> so that <I can recommend them with confidence>'. This *User Story* is associated with the 'Service Certification' *Epic*, and at the same time with the 'Policy Evaluation' *Capability*. The mapping of *User Stories* to *Epics* helps to capture the context in which a certain *Capability* is put into use, as exemplified by a *User Story*.

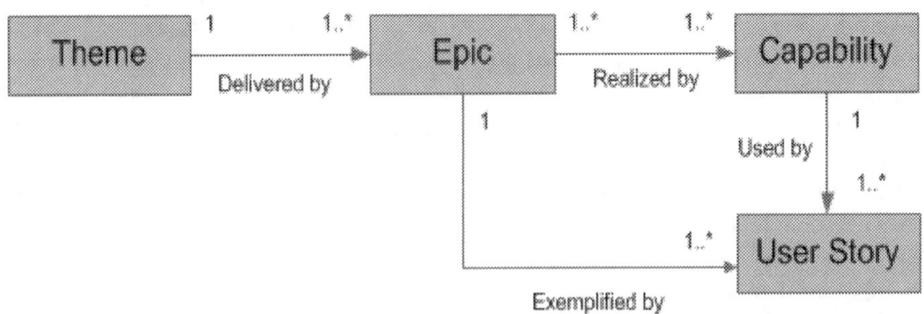

Fig. 2. Requirements information model adopted in Broker@Cloud

4 Key Requirements for a Software Framework Enabling Continuous Quality Assurance and Optimisation

In this section we summarise our requirements formalisation, by presenting the *Themes, Epics* and *Capabilities* that we identified. The results of our requirements analysis process include 4 *Themes*, 9 *Epics*, 15 *Capabilities* and 38 *User Stories*. Due to space limitations *User Stories* are not presented in this paper. For the complete list of *User Stories* that exemplify the *Epics* presented here we refer the reader to [5], which describes the requirements analysis results in full extent.

4.1 Themes and Epics

Governance and Quality Control. This *Theme* is concerned with managing the lifecycle of cloud services as they evolve; creating policies with respect to technical, business and legal aspects of service delivery and checking services for policy compliance; continuously monitoring services for conformance to Service Level Agreements; repetitively testing services to certify conformance to specifications or regulations and compatibility with expected behaviour. We have identified four *Epics* for the *Governance and Quality Control Theme*. The Epics are introduced in the table below (Table 1):

Table 1. Epics associated with the Governance and Quality Control Theme

No	Name	Description	Service Lifecycle
E1	Service certification	Service certification is a process that occurs during the onboarding and evolution of a cloud service. The process aims at certifying that a cloud service conforms to various requirements of the broker (e.g. pricing, fault-tolerance, correctness, etc.).	Onboarding, Evolution
E2	SLA enforcement	SLA enforcement is a process that aims at guaranteeing the expected service levels with respect to the agreements in place between a cloud service provider and a consumer.	Operation
E3	Policy enforcement	Policy enforcement is a process aiming at guaranteeing the conformance of the brokered cloud services to a variety of policies [12] – where policies may originate from different stakeholders.	Onboarding, Evolution
E4	Service lifecycle management	Service lifecycle management is a process that aims at controlling the evolution of different governed entities (e.g. providers, consumers, services, etc.) within the ecosystem of the broker.	Onboarding, Operation, Evolution

Failure Prevention and Recovery. This *Theme* is concerned with the reactive and proactive detection of cloud service failures; selection of suitable adaptation strategies to prevent or to recover from problematic situations as they surface; recommendation or (where possible) automated enactment of appropriate adaptation actions such as service substitution or renegotiation of service terms. We have identified two Epics for the Failure Prevention and Recovery *Theme*. They are introduced below (Table 2).

Table 2. Epics associated with the Failure Prevention and Recovery Theme

No	Name	Description	Service Lifecycle
E5	Failure identification	Failure identification is a process that aims at the detection of failures that have either occurred or are likely to happen in the near future, by monitoring and analysing runtime data, through a combination of different monitoring approaches [14].	Operation, Evolution
E6	Failure prevention & recovery decision making	Failure prevention & recovery decision making is a process that aims at the suggestion of actions to recover from a failure, or to prevent an impending failure, by analysing an identified failure in order to decide a corrective action.	Operation, Evolution

Service Optimisation. This *Theme* is concerned with continuously identifying opportunities to optimise the set of services consumed by an enterprise with respect to different goals such as cost, quality, or functionality; ranking of optimisation alternatives through multi-criteria decision making, based on precise and imprecise characteristics of services and their providers thus exploiting a large number of QoS attributes, such as accountability, agility, assurance of service, cost, performance, usability. We have identified three *Epics* for the Service Optimisation *Theme*. The Epics are summarised below (Table 3).

Table 3. Epics associated with the Service Optimisation Theme

No	Name	Description	Service Lifecycle
E7	Consumer preferences analysis	Consumer preferences analysis is a process that aims at the aggregation and processing of user preferences (e.g. regarding functionality, precise and imprecise criteria [13]) in a unified way. It involves the management of criteria values expressed as crisp numbers or linguistic terms, in order to enhance the optimisation mechanism.	Operation, Evolution
E8	Optimisation opportunity identification	Optimisation opportunity identification is a process that aims at identifying appropriate situations during which optimisation can be performed.	Onboarding, Operation, Evolution
E9	Optimisation decision making	Optimisation decision making is a process that aims at deciding the appropriate optimisation action and recommending that to relevant stakeholders.	Onboarding, Operation, Evolution

Platform-Neutral Cloud Service Description. The first three *Themes* described above are concerned with processes executed in different phases of the Service Lifecycle to achieve certain quality assurance and optimisation characteristics. This *Theme* is concerned with declarative descriptions of inputs/outputs consumed/ produced by the above processes. Hence, it is a cross-cutting concern that appears in the majority of the *Epics* presented so far. Platform-neutrality of descriptions is a precondition for addressing the above themes in the frame of an interoperable software framework. Many of the functional capabilities rely on the availability of certain kinds of suitable declarative descriptions defining the format of their inputs and outputs. The most of those descriptions can be specified as an integral part of a service or policy description. Therefore we define requirements on platform-neutral cloud service description by considering declarative descriptions such as service description and policy description to be capabilities as well.

4.2 Capabilities

To bridge the gap from the problem domain (understanding user needs) to the solution domain (specific requirements intended to address the user needs) we have identified 15 *Capabilities* as key requirements for our envisaged brokerage framework. The *Capabilities* are summarised in Table 4. For each *Capability* we provide a short description and the identifier of the *Epics* that it helps to realise.

Table 4. Capabilities and their association with Epics

No	Name	Description	Epics
C1	Functional testing (blackbox)	Functional testing is a capability that aims at validating the conformance of a cloud service to its behavioural specification, which is provided as part of the service description.	E1
C2	Policy evaluation (e.g. pricing model, security characteristics)	Policy evaluation is a capability that aims at checking if a process or an artefact complies with various policies established by different stakeholders (consumers, providers or broker).	E1, E4
C3	Code auditing (whitebox)	Code auditing is a capability that refers to the manual or automated inspection of the implementation of a cloud service with the intention to uncover faults, inconsistencies, security vulnerabilities and other issues.	E1
C4	Service description	Service description is a capability that aims at representing information about a cloud service in a form suitable to allow other capabilities in the same software framework to fulfil their goal.	E1
C5	Policy description	Policy description is a capability that aims at representing the policies of the various stakeholders (consumers, providers or broker), in order to enable policy evaluation.	E1
C6	Consumer optimisation preference description	Consumer optimisation preference is a capability that aims at representing the consumer preferences to be considered for the purposes of optimisation.	E7
C7	Consumer optimisation preference analysis	Consumer optimisation preference analysis is a capability that aims at handling and exploiting preferences expressed as crisp numbers or as linguistic terms in a unified way, in order to enhance optimisation.	E7

Table 4. (*Continued.*)

C8	Monitoring	Monitoring is a capability that aims at collecting, aggregating and correlating runtime and marketplace data, in order to facilitate several capabilities of the broker.	E2, E3, E5, E8
C9	Optimisation analysis	Optimisation analysis is a capability that aims at analysing optimisation opportunities, in order to identify optimisation actions.	E8, E9
C10	Optimisation recommendation	Optimisation recommendation is a capability that aims at reasoning about alternative optimisation actions, in order to recommend the best alternatives to the relevant stakeholders.	E9
C11	Optimisation validation	Optimisation validation is a capability that aims at collecting feedback about the recommended optimisation actions, in order to improve the optimisation process.	E9
C12	Failure recovery & prevention rules description	Failure recovery & prevention rules description is a capability that aims at representing the rules required for reasoning about potential failure recovery and prevention actions.	E6
C13	Failure analysis	Failure analysis is a capability that aims at identifying the cause of a failure which has already occurred or is impending, and to reason about the appropriate recovery or prevention actions.	E5, E6
C14	Failure recovery & prevention recommendation	Failure recovery & prevention recommendation is a capability that aims at recommending the best alternative recovery or prevention actions to the relevant stakeholders.	E6
C15	Failure prevention and recovery validation	Failure recovery & prevention validation is a capability that aims at collecting feedback about the recommended recovery or prevention actions, to improve the failure recovery and prevention process.	E6

5 Conclusions

As the number of cloud service providers grows and the requirements of cloud service consumers become more complex, the latter will come to depend more and more on the intermediation services of cloud service brokers. For many cloud service consumers, continuous quality assurance and optimisation of cloud services will become a mission-critical objective that they will find difficult to cope with by themselves, thus creating room for intermediaries to offer their services.

Broker@Cloud is a research project aiming to make it easier for cloud service intermediaries to address this emerging need. This is to be achieved by creating an extensible brokerage framework that allows cloud service intermediaries to equip their platforms with core capabilities for continuous quality assurance and optimisation of cloud services. The framework will comprise methods and mechanisms for governance and quality control of cloud services, prevention and recovery of failures, as well as continuous optimisation of cloud service usage, building on common means for platform-neutral description of cloud services.

In this paper we reported on the methodology followed to capture high-level requirements for the envisaged framework, and presented the results obtained from this first-level analysis. We presented the abstract cloud service lifecycle model which helped us to frame our requirements thinking, presented the Design Thinking process that was followed to derive initial requirements, and discussed our adopted information model for the formalisation of requirements. We then presented the key requirements identified through this process in the form of summarised results.

The Design Thinking process that was followed was rather effective in helping us to kick-start the requirements analysis process and to derive initial requirements from two companies that are already offering a number of cloud services on the market and are presently considering enhancing their platforms with capabilities for continuous quality assurance and optimisation of cloud services. This process served as groundwork for further internal discussion and reflection, and shed light on critical aspects to consider. The agile requirements capturing methodology that we followed was effective in helping us to ground these insights and to move forward, from analysis to specification. The resulting identified requirements are organised around 4 *Themes*, 9 *Epics*, 15 *Capabilities* and 38 *User Stories*. Next steps of this work include early prototypes to cover the core requirements discussed here. This will be the first step towards defining and implementing the architecture of a framework bringing capabilities for continuous quality assurance and optimisation brokerage closer to the reach of cloud service intermediaries.

Acknowledgments. The research leading to these results has received funding from the European Union Seventh Framework Programme (FP7/2007-2013) under grant agreement n°328392, the Broker@Cloud project (www.broker-cloud.eu).

References

1. Verginadis, Y., Patiniotakis, I., Mentzas, G., Kourtesis, D., Bratanis, K., Friesen, A., Simons, A.J.H., Kiran, M., Horn, G., Rossini, A., Schwichtenberg, A., Gouvas, P.: D2.1 State of the art and research baseline. Broker@Cloud Project deliverable (2013)
2. Liu, F., Tong, J., Mao, J., Bohn, R., Messina, J., Badger, L., Leaf, D.: Cloud Computing Reference Architecture, pp. 292–500. National Institute of Standards and Technology, USA (2011)
3. Plummer, D., Lheureux, B., Karamouzis, F.: Defining Cloud Service Brokerage: Taking Intermediation to the Next Level. Gartner (2010)
4. Broker@Cloud project website, `http://www.broker-cloud.eu/`
5. Kourtesis, D., Bratanis, K., Friesen, A., Simons, A., Kiran, M., Verginadis, Y., Rossini, A., Schwichtenberg, A., Gouvas, P.: D2.3 Requirements Analysis Report. Broker@Cloud Project deliverable (2013)
6. Cloud Services Brokerage Is Dominated by Three Primary Roles. Gartner (2011)
7. Bratanis, K., Kourtesis, D., Paraskakis, I., Verginadis, Y., Mentzas, G., Simons, A., Friesen, A., Braun, S.: A Research Roadmap for Bringing Continuous Quality Assurance and Optimization to Enterprise Cloud Service Brokers. eChallenges (2013)

8. Kourtesis, D., Bratanis, K.: Towards Continuous Quality Assurance in Future Enterprise Cloud Service Brokers. In: Proceedings of the 8th South East European Doctoral Student Conference, SEERC (2013)
9. Cross, N.: Design Thinking: Understanding How Designers Think and Work. Berg, Oxford UK and New York (2011)
10. Leffingwell, D., Aalto, J.: A Lean and Scalable Requirements Information Model for the Agile Enterprise. Leffingwell LLC(2009)
11. Kniberg, H., Skarin, M.: Kanban and Scrum - Making the Most of Both. LULU (2010)
12. Kourtesis, D.: Towards an Ontology-driven Governance Framework for Cloud Application Platforms. Tech. Rep. CS-11-11. Department of Computer Science, The University of Sheffield, Sheffield (2011)
13. Patiniotakis, I., Rizou, S., Verginadis, Y., Mentzas, G.: Managing Imprecise Criteria in Cloud Service Ranking with a Fuzzy Multi-criteria Decision Making Method. In: Lau, K.-K., Lamersdorf, W., Pimentel, E. (eds.) ESOCC 2013. LNCS, vol. 8135, pp. 34–48. Springer, Heidelberg (2013)
14. Bratanis, K.: Towards Engineering Multi-layer Monitoring and Adaptation of Service-based Applications. Tech. Rep. CS-12-04. Department of Computer Science, The University of Sheffield, Sheffield (2012)

Towards Value-Driven Business Modelling Based on Service Brokerage

Yucong Duan[1], Keman Huang[2], Ajay Kattepur[3], and Wencai Du[1]

[1] College of Information Science and Technology, Hainan University, China
duanyucong@hotmail.com, wencai@hainu.edu.cn
[2] Department of Automation, Tsinghua University, China
victoryhkm@gmail.com
[3] ARLES Group, INRIA Paris-Rocquencourt, France
ajay.kattepur@inria.fr

Abstract. Service engineering is an emerging interdisciplinary subject which crosscuts business modeling, knowledge management and economic analysis. To satisfy service providers' profiting goals, the service system modeling needs to take care of both the short and long run customer satisfaction. The ideology of value driven design fits well for this need. We propose to work towards value driven design by introducing a form of service design patterns, we call *service value broker*(SVB), with the aim to shorten the distance between economical analysis and IT implementation and increase the value added on all sides. SVB allow us to not only study the value added in terms of functional and business aspects, but also reason about the need for brokerage across various domains. In this paper, we model the basis of SVB and its network based organization architecture in the background of Cloud.

1 Introduction

Software design patterns [1] have been well studied with formal semantics and applications in multiple domains. In case of service oriented computing (SOC) applications, such design patterns[2] may yield a standard for composing services dependent on improvement in functional, Quality of Service (QoS) or business contractual aspects. Most existing work focuses on a specific functionality or quality property from a technical perspective which does not directly cater the core value of service applications where providers' side profitability and growth depend more directly on customer satisfaction[3] in short run and customer loyalty in long run[4]. "Value Driven Design"[5] promotes a movement that is using economic theory to transform the system engineering to better utilize optimization to improve complex design. Enlightened by this ideology, we work towards the foundation of integrating the IT implemenation, business modeling and economic analysis by introducing the *Service Value Broker* (SVB) [6] pattern. SVB has been already proposed for cloud service brokerage [7] which we foresee as an important characteristic of the optimization of the E-Service composition of [8] E-Service Economics. To the best of our knowledge, there is little work available

A.R. Lomuscio et al. (Eds.): ICSOC 2013 Workshops, LNCS 8377, pp. 163–176, 2014.
© Springer International Publishing Switzerland 2014

in this field. We show that at multiple domains , such patterns may be applied to improve services' performance. Emphasis is placed on situations where mismatch of customer requirements and provided services may occur.These are solved by introducing a SVB pattern to improve the resulting composite outputs. In cases where composite services may be improved, the $DSVB$ patterns are also introduced which can traverse the entire composition space to achieve improvements. A simulation is performed which shows improvements of multiple metrics based on the broker patterns introduced.

The rest of the paper is organized as follows: Section 2 presents related work of SVB. Section 3 models the knowledge foundation of SVB. Section 4 demonstrates SVB patterns in the Cloud architecture. Section 5 models a two-level E-contract based implementation framework. Section 6 explains the case for the service contract broker. Section 7 provides a simulation to demonstrate the SVB pattern in use. This is followed by conclusions with future directions.

2 Related Work

Cloud service brokerage [9] has been identified by many organizations as an key architectural challenge in the Cloud era. In general, most of existing broker research [10,11] focus on using brokers to discover, match, negotiate and select services [12] with best QoS in a service composition. Srikumar et al. [13] adopt brokers to enable grid resource searching and distribution where a broker works mostly as an autonomous agent [14]. D'Mello et al. [15] employ brokers to select qualified services in terms of QoS of SLA for service composition. Loreto et al. [16] use brokers to integrate telephone business and IT world by means of an intermediate layer. Rosenberg and Dustdar [17] use brokers to bridge the difference between heterogeneous business rules. Bichler et al. [18] promote to use brokers to enhance the application level interpretability of electronic commerce.

SVB distinguishes from these approach since it starts from the service contract which covers more issues than SLA. SVB is related to services not only on the technological level which covers all three layers of SaaS, PaaS and IaaS of a Cloud architecture, as most SLA based approaches [19], but also on the business level [17,20]. By integrating business services and technology services with value modeling, SVB identifies a bigger diagram where it can be successfully applied above QoS assurance [21].

3 Modeling the Foundation of *SVB*

In this section, we model the SVB pattern in terms of value, exchange, brokers and composition from the formal view of conceptualization [22].

3.1 Value

Combining the perspective of conceptualization [22] and multiple semantics [23], the concept of value is denoted as: $concept(value)$. In business modeling, an

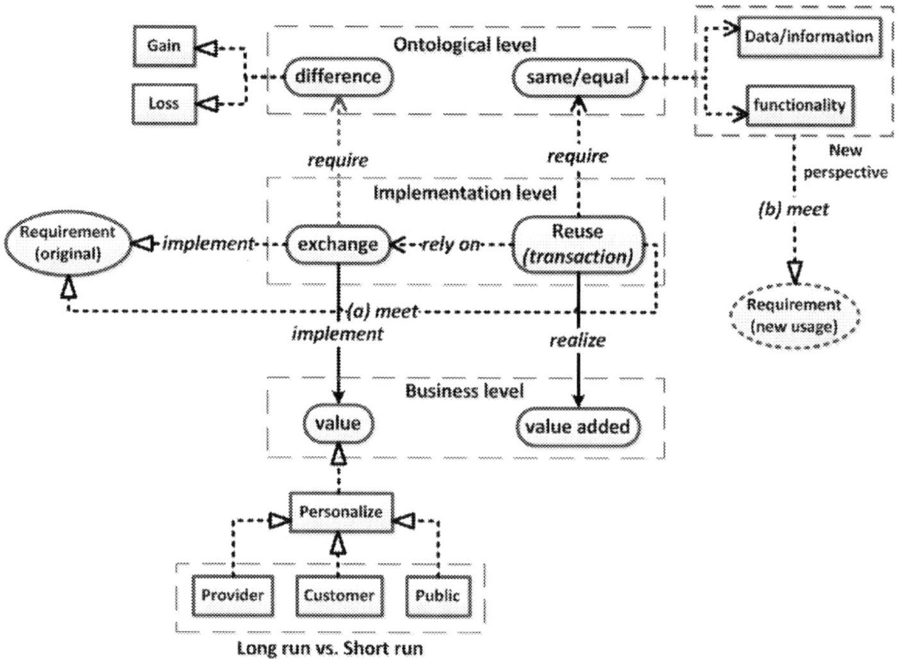

Fig. 1. Value vs. Value added

intuitive expression of value [24] can be found in Fig. 1. Value and value added are modeled along a conceptual route of "Ontological level → Implementation level → Business level". The Ontological level models the essential difference for cognition purpose as "difference vs. same/equal". The implementation level models the basic implementation relationship from "exchange" to "reuse" at transaction level which is distinguished for (a) original requirement and (b) newly identified usages. Newly identified usages demands a difference from existing requirements. The *concept*(*value*) bears several meanings which are denoted as *semantic*{*value*}.

semantic{value}= {difference (observation
(object(x))), existence(object(x))}

It means that a meaningful difference can be observed on an existing object in contrast to other objects. The positiveness of the observed difference motivates a business exchange. The observation can either be tangible or intangible.

3.2 Exchange

We improve the explanation from [6,24] as follows: value is realized by exchanging of goods which include information, data, activities, for the purpose of implementation of users' requirements. The existence of the difference of the goods is required for supporting difference in the value. In a business transaction, users' satisfaction concerning an exchange comes from the positive difference of the expected value of goods. An exchange/transaction should be motivated on both sides of roles of source(A) and target(B). This motivation can exist only when both sides observe a positive value, by subtracting the self evaluated value of the owned object from the self evaluated value of the target one.

3.3 Brokerage

We have introduced the concept of service value broker (SVB) in [6]. Here we give the following definitions:

- *Service Value Broker* (SVB): driven by a value based goal, when a direct service composition cannot meet some required constraints from the service contract [25] or service level agreement(SLA) such as response time, location, license area, available period, currency format. If the introduction of a intermediate service can help to solve these problems and enable a service composition to be qualified, the introduced intermediate service is a SVB.
- *Direct Service Value Broker* ($DSVB$): direct SVB is a special type of SVB resulting from a composition of services. This composition must bring more value to the stakeholder who introduces the $DSVB$. By value we mean not only monetary value but also non-monetary such as reputation and brand value, etc.

Normally a service transaction is driven by an economical goal marked with a service value scope (SVS) which is denoted as:
SVS = (FBV, OMV)
FBV is the fixed bottom value which is demanded as a profit threshold for a business transaction. OMV is the maximum value which is an open value in most business following the maximization of profit. The SVS is the result of a service composition $composition(x)$ where the involved services are denoted as x. In general, a SVS is denoted as follows:

$$SVS_{ins} = SVS(composition(x))$$

When the restriction $SVS_{ins} \leq FBV$ applies, an independent decision consists of canceling the service. However if other transactions rely on this transaction for constructing an integrated business value, or the transaction is viewed as contributing to accumulated value from a long run economical view [4], then the SVB is expected to enable a business transaction. Even those not qualified candidate services could be considered to be transformed into qualified candidates through the introduction of SVB.

When the restriction of $SVS_{ins} \geq FBV$ is met, the main goal is the maximization of the value of SVS_{ins}. DSVS can be introduced for this purpose.

Besides introducing new services to replace existing services in a composition, the adjustment of the order of existing services by means of DSVS might also change the value of SVS_{ins}.

3.4 Composition of SVB and $DSVB$

In basic situations SVB can be introduced to solve direct constraints which are faced in a service composition in the context of a service transaction. $DSVB$ is introduced for the optimization of a service system in terms of output value.

In Composed Situations. $DSVB$ is the exhaustive search pattern: it requires the traversing of all possible service compositions before a decision is made. SVB can function as a transformer which transforms previous not qualified services or service compositions into qualified candidate service compositions which should be considered by $DSVB$. In a real world engineering practice, we can not follow strictly the theoretical conclusion which is drawn here. We can follow a simple process aimed at scaling down the candidate services using matchmaking before a service composition and introduce SVB in case that very few candidates are available. $DSVB$ will include proactive SVB activities only when there is sufficient time left after an initial solution has been found and an optimization is planned.

4 Service Value Broker Patterns: Scenarios and Brokers in Cloud Architecture

When implementing SVB or $DSVB$, usually service contracts [25] are required for both locating the mismatching situations and identification of possible solutions. The driving force of applying SVB or $DSVB$ is to minimally realize expected functionality and optionally attain the highest added value.

We denote the contract on the source end of an exchange as CS, the contract on the target end of an exchange as CT, the input of $SVB/DSVB$ contract as $iSVB$ and the output of a $SVB/DSVB$ contract as $oSVB$. There is no requirement that the $iSVB$ and $oSVB$ belong to the same service since the integration of a parallel set of $SVB/DSVB$ is allowed. We propose to demonstrate the brokerage within Cloud based on the three-layer architecture of SaaS, PaaS, and IaaS. Fig. 2 demonstrates the brokers in relationship with the three layer Cloud architecture.

4.1 Brokers at the SaaS Layer

There are many kinds of SVB at the SaaS layer. One example is as follows:

Price ($PR \in \mathbb{D}_B$): the price for the service usage is set at "10-20 USD/ month for USA users" while the customers require "5-10 USD/ month for Asia user".
Problem: $PR|_{CS} > PR|_{CT}$
$SVS = (0, \delta(PR|_{CT}, PR|_{CS}))$

Price broker: the price broker is implemented with flexible strategies such as asking a location broker to convey the requests coming from USA to Asia. If the final price after subtracting the cost due to the introduction of the location broker is lower than the original price, the location broker actually implements the role of price broker. There will be other forms of price broker which depend on the specific constraints of the service contracts of both the request and the response sides.
Solution: $(PR|_{CS} = PR|_{iSVB})$ AND $(PR|_{oSVB} = PR|_{CT})$

4.2 Brokers at the PaaS Layer

There are many kinds of SVB at the PaaS layer. One example is as follows:

File/data format ($FF \in \mathbb{D}_B$): requested to provide files with "MS word format" while the provider supplies only files with "pdf or ps format".
Problem: $FF|_{CS}! = FF|_{CT}$
$SVS = (0, \delta(FF|_{CT}, FF|_{CS}))$
File/data format broker: a service which can convert file format from "pdf or ps format" to "MS word format" has the possibility of playing the broker.
Solution: $(FF|_{CS} = FF|_{iSVB}) AND (FF|_{oSVB} = FF|_{CT})$

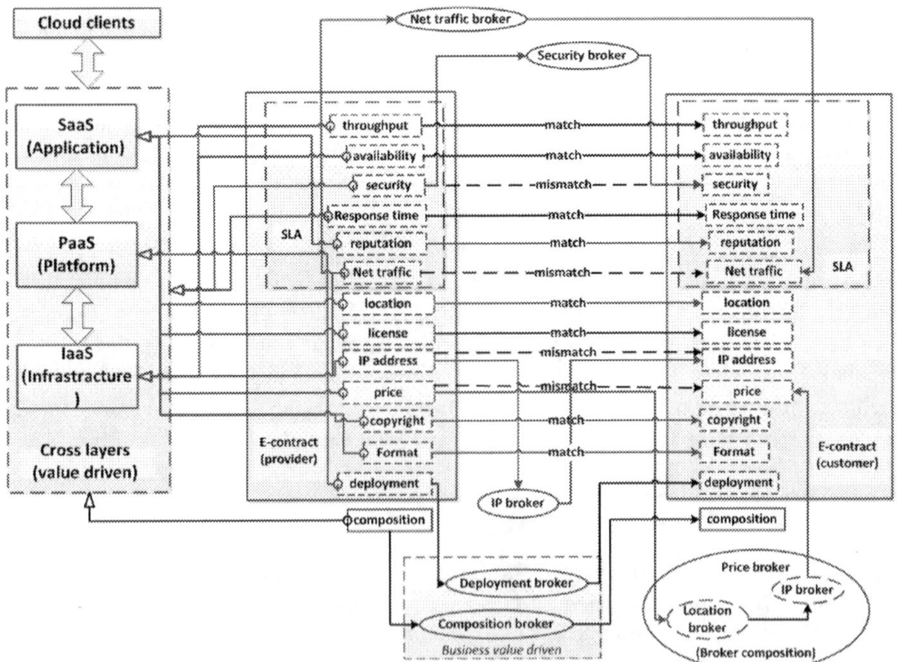

Fig. 2. *SVB* and *DSVB* in the context of Cloud

4.3 Brokers at the IaaS Layer

There are many kinds of SVB at the IaaS layer. One example is as follows:

Network traffic ($NT \in \mathbb{D}_Q$): requests are limited to "band width of 50 MB/ Minute" while customers require "100 MB/Minute".
Problem: $NT|_{CS} < NT|_{CT}$
$SVS = (0, \delta(NT|_{CT}, NT|_{CS}))$
Network traffic broker: a service which can firstly take the request from the customer side of "100MB/Minute", secondarily separate the request into two parallel tasks and finally distribute the two tasks for two services of "band width of 50 MB/Minute ", can play the broker.
Solution: $\sum(RA|_{CS} = RA|_{iSVB})$ AND $(RA|_{oSVB} >= RA|_{CT})$

4.4 The Brokerage Crossing Three Layers

There are also some kinds of SVB which cross different layers of IaaS, PaaS and IaaS. For example, security will crosscut all three layers:

Security limit ($SL \in \mathbb{D}_S$): there will be many security restrictions which might be difficult for a functional service to fulfill.
Problem: $SL|_{CS}! = SL|_{CT}$
$SVS = (0, \delta(SL|_{CT}, SL|_{CS}))$
Security broker: a distributed mode of public-private key architecture can be introduced to enhance the security level of the provided service while not breaking the integrity of the original service. For example, the introduction of audition service and a keying system, can help to avoid a denial-of-service attack (DoS) on the main service.
Solution: $(SL|_{CS} = SL|_{iSVB})$ AND $(SL|_{oSVB} = SL|_{CT})$

4.5 Value Broker

Value broker or $DSVB$ is a general form of price broker. It is different from previous brokers which are introduced to solve a mismatch in the conditions for composition, which is demanded rigidly by a service matchmaking process [25]. Value broker is introduced as a mean for the implementation of the optimization process leading to a better business profit for the stakeholder who employs the service based transaction. A glance of value broker enabled maximization of the business solution space is shown in Fig. 3 [24]. In theory, during the implementation of a $DSVB$, all possible service compositions should be considered, including those situations where service compositions are enabled by SVB through bridging the functionality mismatching among original services.

Fig. 2 demonstrates a scenario where mismatching situations of security, net traffic and IP between two services represented by E-Contracts are bridged by SVB: *Security broker*, *Network traffic broker* and *IP broker*; the optimization for deployment is fulfilled by the *Deployment broker* $DSVB$. It also shows that brokers can be composed for complex functionalities. For a service transaction comprising more than two parties, there will be the chance to introduce a *Composition broker* $DSVB$ to optimize the organization.

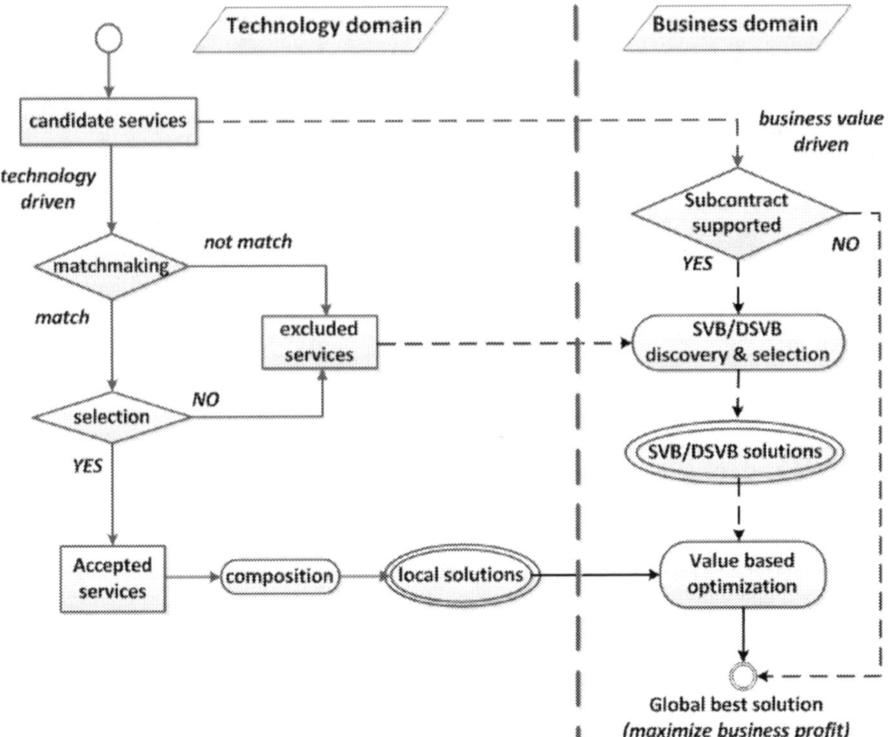

Fig. 3. DVBS enabled maximization of business solution space

5 Two-Level E-contract Based Implementation Framework

In the service ecosystem, due to the interface of the services and their correlation history, the services in the ecosystem will form the composable relation between each other which means that the two services can be used to form a composition to offer added-value for the consumers. As the number of services available for consumers is increasing rapidly, there are many services which offer the similar functionality. For examples,all of "Google Map", "Baidu Map", "Yahoo Map" and "Facebook Map" provide the map related services. These services with the similar functionality will form a specific domain. The service in the same domain can somehow replace each other with some adapters [26]. Furthermore, the providers will publish services into the ecosystem so that the consumers can use the services to fulfill their requirement. Some providers such as Google, Yahoo and Amazon will offer different services in different domains so that they may offer the complete solution for the consumers. Some others will provide a few specific services in the specific domain. Taking Twilio as an example, it focuses on telephony and only offers the Twilio service in the telephony domain for the consumers. As different providers perform well in different domain, the providers will assign the contract with the others to form a vertical alliance or horizontal alliance to guarantee their core competencies [27]: the providers who provide similar services may assign contracts with each other so that they can get the replace services to increase the fault-tolerance for the consumers; the providers who provide the composable services may assign contracts with each other that they can increase the Qos for the whole composition.

Thus we can get a two-level service contract framework in the service ecosystem which consists of two networks: the service composable network is a directed network in which each node refers to a service and each edge refers to the composability between two services, the direction of the edge refers that the output of the source service can be the input or part of the input for the target service. The provider contract network is an undirected network in which each node refers to a provider and each edge refers to the service contract assigned by two providers.

Fig. 4 demonstrates a two-level service contract network framework for the service ecosystem which consists two networks: the service composable network which refers to the composablity among services, and the provider contract network which refers to the contract relation among providers.

Example: For the illustration shown in Fig. 4 , providers Pa, Pb, Pc, Pd, Pe form the provider contract network based on their contract with each other. Provider Pa offers service S1 and S2, Provider Pb offers services S3, S4 and S5, etc. Service s1, s2, s3, s4, s5, s6, s7, s8 and s9 construct the service composable network and S1, s3, and s6 are similar in the functionality that they form a specific domain.

6 The Case for the Service Contract Broker

6.1 Service Contract Broker for Service Selection

The requirement of the consumer is becoming more complex. Sometime single services cannot fulfill the requirement that they need to select some services to form compositions. If the services are provided by different providers, the providers with a contract can help to guarantee the reputation of the composition. For example, Pd and Pc have a contract while it is not for Pd and Pb, the composition for s6 and s7 will gain a higher reputation than s6 and s5. In this case, the service contract broker will suggest services with higher reputation for the consumers. Even if the services are provided by the same provider, sometimes the QoS cannot meet the consumers' requirement. For example, s1 and s2 can fulfill the consumer's functionality requirement while the price is too high for the consumer. In this case, the service contract broker will help to find the services which are offered by the provider's contractors and then use the service to replace the similar service to fix the mismatch for the consumers. For example, suppose that s3 is much cheaper than s1 and then the broker will use s3 to replace s1 and offer s3 and s2 for the consumers.

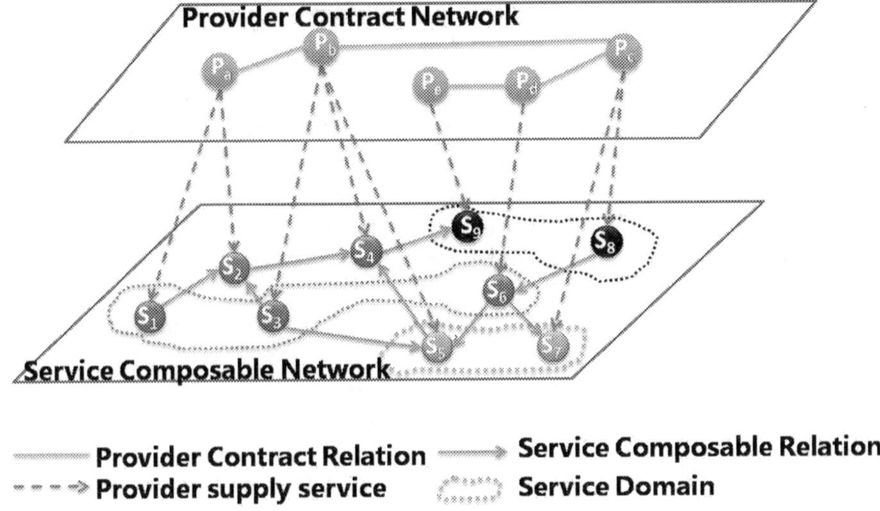

Fig. 4. Two-level service contract network framework

6.2 Service Contract Broker for Service Emerging

For the providers with a strong contract, if the services they offer are not composable, the providers will intend to build an adapter among their services so that their alliance can gain higher competitiveness in the ecosystem. For example, Pb offers service s4 which can be composed with s9 provided by Pe and there is no contract between these two providers. Also Pc offers service s8 which has a similar functionality as s9, however there is huge mismatch between s4 and s8. As Pb and Pc builds a strong contract relation with each other, they may modify the interface of their services to make them composable or create a new service together to bridge their services. In this case, the service contract broker will offer the suggestion for new services. Thus the service contract broker can promote the growth of the service ecosystem.

7 Simulating *SVB*

In order to simulate *SVB* patterns and their effect on customer value [28], we make use of the scenario provided in Fig. 5. While *Customer 1* accesses the sequence of services directly, *Customer 2* makes use of *SVB* brokers to aid in his response. This may come from multiple domains of values.

This scenario is simulated using Monte-Carlo simulations in MATLAB with distributions representing various domains of functional, QoS and business value aspects studied in Section 4. Values such as *response time* and *availability* are modeled as heavy tailed distributions [29]. *Request amount* and *Network Traffic* are modeled with exponential distributions; *Price*, *License Values* and *Security*

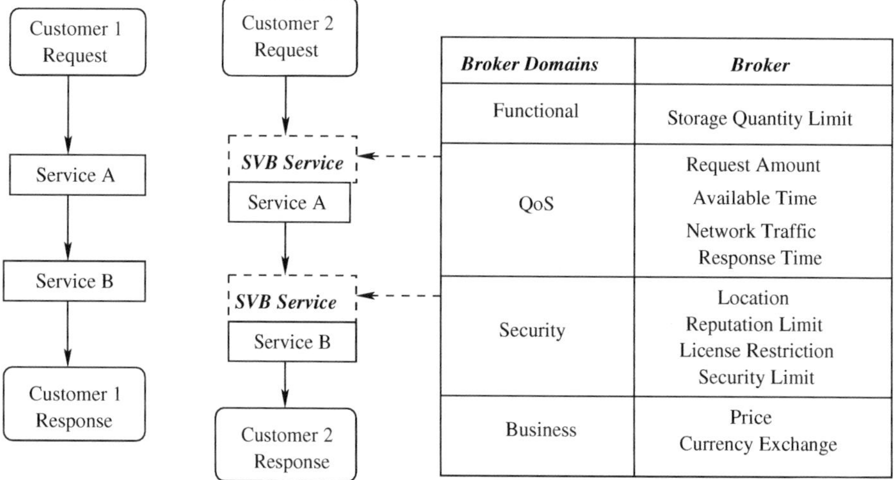

Fig. 5. Scenario comparing two customers

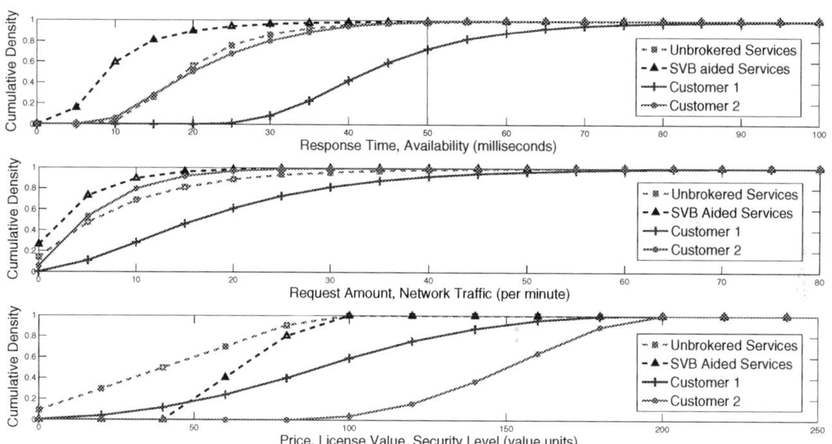

Fig. 6. Monte-Carlo runs of two customers' output behaviors

Levels are drawn from uniform distributions. Note that some brokers such as *Location* and *Reputation Limit* would require a real-world implementation over actual services and are exempted from this analysis. Such a probabilistic model for value is consistent with perspectives of function/QoS/business [29,30].

As observed in Fig. 6, the inclusion of an *SVB* broker improves multiple domains. The response time distribution and network traffic show *lower* values for customer 2. This is traded off with the necessity to pay higher cost values that can provide better security and license values. Though this is a representative example, it can be envisioned as being applicable to real world applications. The service broker can provide access to valuable upgrades in multiple domains that should be encouraged.

From a *business* perspective, the improved performance due to the introduction of a broker could provide better contractual agreements to a composition of these services. In spite of higher costing services, the tradeoffs can be improved in multiple contractual domains of QoS, security and composition efficiency. Aspects provided by the *DSVB* such as testing and advertisement provide further impetus to the adoption of brokers for business based services.

8 Conclusion and Future Work

This paper presents a value driven design approach that introduces service value brokers as a new form of service design patterns. With this approach, we try to leverage traditional design approaches [2] in order to cope also with business and economical aspects that affect service selection and composition from a value driven design perspective. We present our work towards building an architecture for service brokerage composition in Cloud.

Individually, *SVB*s can be viewed as plain service design patterns [2] when they are used for fulfilling the same functionalities or quality properties. However, from a process perspective, *SVB*s are firstly designed and deployed according to the highest level of economical consideration and profiting context; secondarily, they address specific functionalities and quality requirements. This is usually the reverse process that takes place for plain design patterns. The evaluation of plain design patterns is relatively independent from their combined deployment. However, the evaluation of a *SVB* depends on the integrated business value analysis of the whole project and with relationship to cooperating *SVB*. Moreover, the deployment of *SVB* is expected to be accompanying a value model [5]. In the next steps, we will continue with the labeling of *SVB* with economical properties.

In order to plan and assess a value based composition, we want to explore the constraint space and variability space of the value in *SVB* compositions. We will proceed to the analysis of usability and applicability aspects concerning the adoption of *SVB*s in E-Service contracts.

Acknowledgment. This paper was supported in part by CNSF grant 61162010 and 61363007 and by HNU Research program grant KYQD1242 and HDSF201310. We thank Prof. Zibin Zheng for precious advice.

References

1. Gamma, E., Helm, R., Johnson, R.E., Vlissides, J.M.: Design patterns: Abstraction and reuse of object-oriented design. In: Wang, J. (ed.) ECOOP 1993. LNCS, vol. 707, pp. 406–431. Springer, Heidelberg (1993)
2. Erl, T.: SOA Design Patterns, 1st edn. Prentice Hall PTR, Upper Saddle River (2009)

3. Heskett, J.L., Jones, T.O., Loveman, G.W., Sasser, W.E., Schlesinger, L.: Putting the Service-Profit Chain to Work. Harvard Business Review, 118–129 (July-August 2008)
4. Feldstein, M.: Domestic saving and international capital movements in the long run and the short run. Technical Report 947, National Bureau of Economic Research (1982)
5. Collopy, P., Hollingsworth, P.: Value-driven design. Journal of Aircraft 48(3), 749–759 (2011)
6. Duan, Y.: Modeling service value transfer beyond normalization. In: SNPD, pp. 811–816 (2012)
7. Plummer, D.: Cloud services brokerage: A must-have for most organizations. Gartner, Inc. (2012)
8. Kattepur, A., Benveniste, A., Jard, C.: Optimizing decisions in web services orchestrations. In: Kappel, G., Maamar, Z., Motahari-Nezhad, H.R. (eds.)ICSOC 2011, LNCS, vol. 7084, pp. 77–91. Springer, Heidelberg (2011)
9. Fowley, F., Pahl, C., Zhang, L.: A comparison framework and review of service brokerage solutions for cloud architectures. In: Service-Oriented Computing - ICSOC 2013 Workshops and Ph.D. Symposium (2013)
10. Pan, Z., Baik, J.: Qos broker-based trust model for effective web service selection. In: Proceedings of the 11th IASTED SEA2007, Anaheim, CA, USA, pp. 590–595 (2007)
11. Kumar, P.S.A., Mahadevan, G., Krishn, C.G.: Article: A qos towards dynamic web services recapitulation and selection. International. Journal of Computer Applications 54(4), 12–18 (2012)
12. Shi, C., Lin, D., Ishida, T.: User-centered qos computation for web service selection. In: ICWS, pp. 456–463 (2012)
13. Venugopal, S., Buyya, R., Winton, L.: A grid service broker for scheduling distributed data-oriented applications on global grids. In: Proceedings of the 2nd workshop on Middleware for grid computing, MGC 2004, 75–80 (2004)
14. Qian, Z., Lu, S., Xie, L.: Mobile-agent-based web service composition. In: 4th Intl. conf. on Grid and Cooperative Computing, pp. 35–46
15. D'Mello, D.A., Ananthanarayana, V.S., Thilagam, S.: A qos broker based architecture for dynamic web service selection. In: Proceedings of AMS 2008, pp. 101–106 (2008)
16. Loreto, S., Mecklin, T., Opsenica, M., Rissanen, H.M.: Service broker architecture: location business case and mashups. Comm. Mag. 47(4), 97–103 (2009)
17. Rosenberg, F., Dustdar, S.: Design and implementation of a service-oriented business rules broker. In: CECW, pp. 55–63 (2005)
18. Bichler, M., Segev, A., Beam, C.: An electronic broker for business-to-business electronic commerce on the internet. Int. J. Cooperative Inf. Syst. 7(4), 315–330 (1998)
19. Yu, T., Lin, K.J.: A broker-based framework for qos-aware web service composition. In: EEE, pp. 22–29 (2005)
20. Ferreira, J.E., Braghetto, K.R., Takai, O.K., Pu, C.: Transactional recovery support for robust exception handling in business process services. In: ICWS, pp. 303–310 (2012)
21. Kourtesis, D., Bratanis, K., Friesen, A., Verginadis, Y., Simons, A.J.H., Rossini, A., Schwichtenberg, A., Gouvas, P.: Brokerage for quality assurance and optimization of cloud services: an analysis of key requirements. In: Service-Oriented Computing - ICSOC 2013 Workshops and Ph.D. Symposium (2013)

22. Duan, Y., Cruz, C.: Formalizing semantic of natural language through conceptualization from existence. IJIMT 2(1), 37–42 (2011)
23. Duan, Y.: Semantics Computation: Towards Identifying Answers from Problem Expressions. In: SSNE, pp. 19–24 (2011)
24. Duan, Y.: Value Modeling and Calculation for Everything as a Service (XaaS) based on Reuse. In: Proceedings of SNPD 2012, 162–167 (2012)
25. Duan, Y.: Service Contracts: Current state and Future Directions. In: ICWS, pp. 664–665 (2012)
26. Tan, W., Zhou, M.: Business and Scientific Workflows: A Web Service-Oriented Approach. IEEE Press Series on Systems Science and Engineering. Wiley (2013)
27. Huang, K., Fan, Y., Tan, W., Qian, M.: Bsnet: a network-based framework for service-oriented business ecosystem management. Concurrency and Computation: Practice and Experience 25(13), 1861–1878 (2013)
28. Duan, Y., Kattepur, A., Zagarese, Q., Du, W.: Service value broker patterns: Integrating business modeling and economic analysis with knowledge management (short paper). In: SOCA, pp. 140–145 (2013)
29. Kattepur, A.: Importance sampling of probabilistic contracts in web services. In: Kappel, G., Maamar, Z., Motahari-Nezhad, H.R. (eds.) ICSOC 2011. LNCS, vol. 7084, pp. 557–565. Springer, Heidelberg (2011)
30. Kattepur, A., Benveniste, A., Jard, C.: Negotiation strategies for probabilistic contracts in web services orchestrations. In: ICWS, pp. 106–113 (2012)

Introducing Policy-Driven Governance and Service Level Failure Mitigation in Cloud Service Brokers: Challenges Ahead

Konstantinos Bratanis[1,2] and Dimitrios Kourtesis[1,2]

[1] South-East European Research Centre,
International Faculty, The University of Sheffield,
24 Proxenou Koromila Street, Thessaloniki, 54622, Greece
{kobratanis,dkourtesis}@seerc.org
[2] Department of Computer Science, The University of Sheffield,
Regent Court 211 Portobello Street, Sheffield, S1 4DP, United Kingdom
{k.bratanis,d.kourtesis}@dcs.shef.ac.uk

Abstract. Cloud service brokerage represents a novel operational model in the scope of cloud computing. A cloud broker acts as an intermediary between a service provider and a service consumer with the goal of adding as much value as possible to the service being provisioned and consumed. Continuous quality assurance is a type of brokerage capability having high value to both providers and consumers of cloud services. At the same time, it can be among the most challenging kinds of capability for cloud service brokers to realise. In this paper we focus on two specific themes within this scope. We present a motivating scenario and outline key research challenges associated with introducing policy-driven governance and service level failure mitigation capabilities in brokers.

Keywords: Cloud computing, cloud service brokerage, continuous quality assurance, policy-driven governance, service level failure mitigation.

1 Introduction

With the increasing adoption of cloud computing the enterprise IT environment is progressively transformed into a matrix of interwoven infrastructure, platform and application services, delivered from diverse providers. As the number of providers grows and the requirements of consumers become more complex, the need for entities to assume a role of intermediation between providers and consumers is becoming stronger. Cloud service intermediation is increasingly recognised as an indispensable component of the cloud computing value chain.

Examples of existing cloud service intermediation offerings include services helping enterprises to find and compare cloud services (e.g. marketplaces/stores), to develop and customise services (e.g. application platform as a service offerings), to integrate services (e.g. integration platform as a service), to monitor and manage services, and many more. Despite differences with respect to the capabilities such

A.R. Lomuscio et al. (Eds.): ICSOC 2013 Workshops, LNCS 8377, pp. 177–191, 2014.
© Springer International Publishing Switzerland 2014

cloud service intermediaries offer, or how these capabilities are combined, they have one thing in common: making it easier, safer and more productive for cloud computing adopters to navigate, integrate, consume, extend and maintain cloud services. According to Gartner, this is precisely the value proposition of a 'Cloud Services Brokerage', a term coined in 2010 to refer to the emerging role of brokers in the context of cloud computing [1].

In the future, enterprises will require brokerage capabilities that are much more sophisticated than what is on offer by cloud service intermediaries today. Continuous quality assurance of cloud services is one such type of brokerage capability; foreseen to be most valuable for service consumers, but at the same time rather challenging for future brokers to implement.

In this paper we are briefly introducing the concept of cloud service brokerage (CSB) and motivating the need for continuous quality assurance as an important intermediation capability of future enterprise cloud service brokers. We focus our attention on two specific forms of continuous quality assurance intermediation: (i) policy-driven cloud service governance and (ii) service level failure mitigation for cloud services. For each area we present key challenges and provide an overview of related work.

2 Cloud Service Brokerage

As an enterprise comes to rely on an increasing number of externally-sourced cloud services, it becomes more difficult for the enterprise to keep track of when and how these third-party services evolve. Service evolution may be the result of change that is intentional – such as when the provider makes changes to a service's terms of provision, changes to its implementation, or changes to its deployment environment, but also unintentional – such as when the provider suffers an unexpected failure or variation in service performance.

Because of the complexity inherent in consuming multiple services from different cloud service providers, it becomes increasingly more difficult for the service consumer to appreciate all the different kinds of impact that a change to a service can have. A change to a service may mean that the service is no longer conformant to the internal policies of the consumer or to regulations that the consumer is required to observe, or more generally, that the service no longer fulfils the consumer's objectives and needs to be replaced.

Cloud service brokerage represents a new type of service and emerging business model in the space of cloud computing which is aimed at helping enterprises to address such challenges and to mitigate the risks that ensue from the complexity in large-scale cloud service usage [1]. In an analogy to the way other kinds of intermediaries operate within different areas of traditional commerce, a cloud service broker is an entity that works on behalf of a consumer of cloud services to intermediate and to add value to the services being consumed.

Much of the enabling technology that is needed to support different cloud service brokerage capabilities is certainly not new. Recent years have seen a proliferation of many relevant proprietary and open source tools that can provide building blocks for the implementation of such services, such as tools for monitoring and managing applications and virtual infrastructures, or tools for integrating heterogeneous processes and applications. Companies such as SpotCloud[1], Vordel[2], Rightscale[3], JitterBit[4], or SnapLogic[5], who have already created offerings based on such enabling technologies, can be considered early examples of cloud service brokerages.

The kinds of intermediation capability offered by most of today's cloud service brokers relate to cloud service discovery, integration, customisation, or aggregation [2]. But as cloud service consumption grows and quality assurance becomes more of a problem to cloud service users, intermediation capabilities for continuous quality assurance of cloud services will become more and more prevalent.

Intermediation for continuous quality assurance of cloud services represents an open research topic which, to the best of our knowledge, is only now receiving attention by research communities working on related fields. At the time of this writing the theoretical and pragmatic challenges of introducing continuous quality assurance functions in brokers of cloud services remain largely unexplored.

3 Continuous Quality Assurance Intermediation Example

In this section we present an abstract usage scenario that exemplifies two new forms of continuous quality assurance intermediation: policy-driven governance and service level failure mitigation for cloud services.

We assume a setting where a cloud service broker operates an online platform, though which it offers continuous quality assurance intermediation for cloud services. The broker's customers are enterprises that make extensive use of third-party cloud services and prefer to outsource their continuous quality assurance functions to a specialised and trusted third-party entity – the broker. The broker allows service consumers to exercise fine grained control over the cloud services they rely on. This is achieved by allowing consumers to express their objectives about how cloud services should be delivered to them, in the form of policies. The brokerage platform then undertakes to ensure that the objectives in the policies are met. Service consumption objectives may relate to the pricing characteristics of a cloud service, its security features, its availability guarantees, and many other service attributes. The brokerage platform is capable of monitoring service delivery on a continuous basis, detecting violations of consumer policies, and proposing mitigation measures.

Providers of cloud services who are interested in making their services available to the customers that the broker is serving need to onboard their services to the brokerage platform. For this to be done, providers need to create descriptions of their cloud services. The broker maintains its own vocabulary for service description that providers have to use. This vocabulary can be understood as a kind of reference model for cloud service attributes that allows a service description to be reconcilable

[1] `http://www.spotcloud.com/`
[2] `http://www.vordel.com/`
[3] `http://www.rightscale.com`
[4] `http://www.jitterbit.com/`
[5] `http://www.snaplogic.com/`

with descriptions of other cloud services as well as with consumers' policies. The broker offers the same description vocabulary to consumers, in order for them to create their own custom policies about the services they consume through the broker. Once a cloud service is accepted for onboarding into the brokerage platform it is continuously monitored for quality assurance purposes. Intentional or unintentional changes to the service or to its associated descriptive artefacts will be detected and evaluated as soon as they occur, allowing the consumer to be notified early and to take appropriate mitigation measures to continue meeting their service consumption objectives.

Below we provide a step-by-step walkthrough of a usage scenario where the three roles (broker, provider and consumer) are interacting. To improve readability we have decomposed the scenario into four phases. The interactions between roles in each phase are illustrated with the help of a respective BPMN diagram.

Phase 1: Service Onboarding

1. The provider creates a description of the service to be onboarded based on the broker's vocabulary and submits the description to the broker. The description references a wide range of service characteristics, including the service's pricing, security features, and reliability guarantees.
2. The broker checks if the service description includes all necessary description elements. The provider is not obliged to describe a service with respect to all of the attributes listed in the broker's vocabulary but some service attributes are required. Service availability over a defined period of time is one such mandatory description element[6]. For the service in question the provider commits to availability of 99.92% on a monthly basis.
3. The broker determines that the service description includes all of the required description elements, onboards the service, and starts to monitor the service and its associated description artefacts for changes.

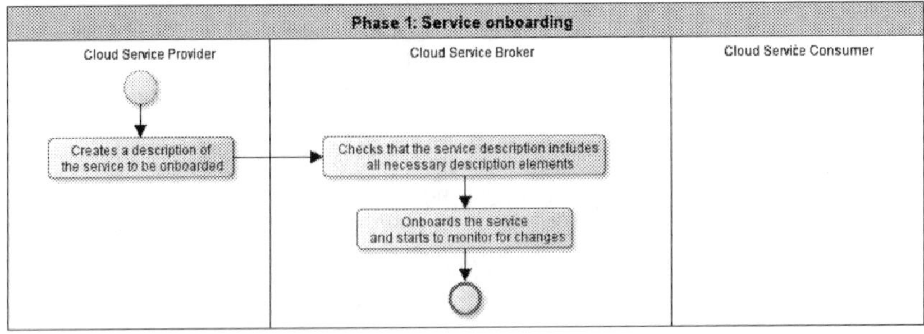

Fig. 1. The flow of service onboarding activities

[6] For example, the availability guarantees that Amazon offers for its EC2 and EBS services is a Monthly Uptime Percentage of at least 99.95% (as of June 2013). In the event that Amazon does not meet this commitment, consumers receive service credit as compensation.

Phase 2: Service Selection

4. The consumer discovers the service in the broker's service directory and subscribes to use it.
5. The consumer creates a policy governing how the service should be delivered. Based on the broker's vocabulary, the policy states that monthly service availability should be no less than 99.90%[7] and the time it takes for the service to recover from a failure should be no more than 30 minutes per outage. This is the recovery time objective (RTO) policy of the consumer.
6. The consumer submits the policy to the broker so that the latter can monitor the compliance of the selected service to the consumer's policy on a continuous basis.
7. The broker evaluates the consumer's policy against the description of the selected service and determines that the service description is conformant to the policy. The broker takes no further action.

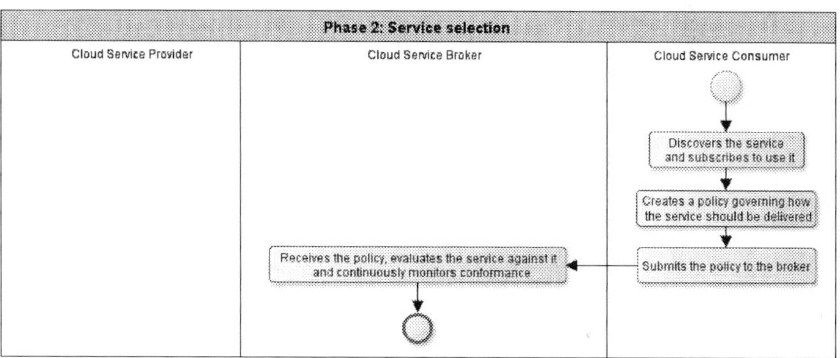

Fig. 2. The flow of policy conformance evaluation activities during service selection

Phase 3: Change to the Service's Terms of Provision

8. The provider updates the service description, changing the service availability commitment to 99.95%.
9. The broker detects the change in the service description artefact and carries out a conformance check to determine whether or not this creates a conflict with the consumer's policy. The change is not found to raise any conformance issues because the new availability commitment (99.95%) is higher than the consumer's monthly availability objective (99.90%). The broker takes no further action.[8]

[7] In a 24x7 setting, 99.90% availability translates to 43 min and 12 sec of downtime per month.

[8] In case the change to the service's terms of provision gave rise to a violation of the consumer's policy (e.g. if the new availability commitment was 99.85%) the broker would have alerted the consumer to take action. This could mean substituting the service or lowering the consumer's expectations in their RTO policy.

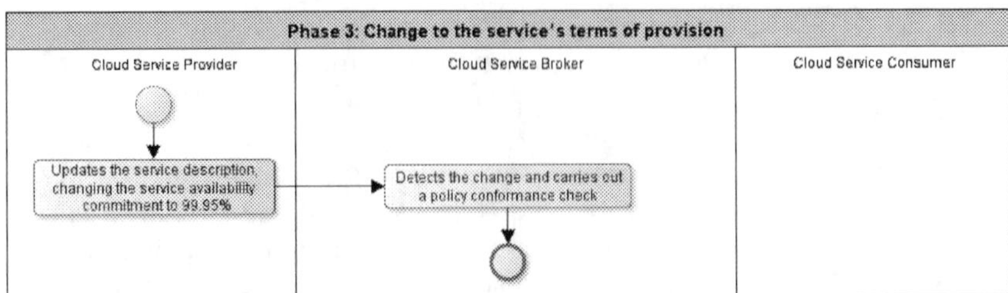

Fig. 3. The flow of policy conformance evaluation activities upon a change to the service caused by updating its terms of provision

Phase 4: Change to the Service's Availability

10. The service provider experiences an unexpected failure that causes service outage.
11. The broker detects a change in service availability (downtime).
12. The broker alerts both the consumer and the provider about the failure.
13. The broker starts a timer to track the service's downtime. At the same time, it proactively attempts to identify alternative services to potentially serve as substitutes for the failing service.
14. The broker predicts that the time it will take for the service to resume operation (time to recovery, or TTR) is 12 minutes. This is shorter than the objective of 30 minutes per outage as specified in the consumer's RTO policy. The broker concludes that the service is likely to recover within a time period that is tolerable for the consumer, and takes no further action.
15. The 12 minute period lapses and the service is still down, which means that the broker's predicted TTR was optimistic. The broker concludes that it is very likely that the provider will not be able to meet the consumer's RTO of 30 minutes[9], thus causing a major disruption to business continuity for the consumer.
16. The broker alerts the consumer to obtain approval to proactively substitute the service with one of the identified candidates before downtime exceeds the consumer's tolerable threshold. At the same time, it also alerts the provider.
17. The consumer approves the proactive substitution of the service. The broker has thus helped the consumer to mitigate the impact from a potential service level failure due to a sustained service outage and the consequent violation of the consumer's RTO. In doing so, the broker has helped the consumer to meet their objectives with respect to business continuity.

[9] In case the predicted TTR value was greater than the RTO specified in the consumer's policy (e.g. if the broker predicted a TTR of 31 minutes), the broker would have immediately alerted the consumer to obtain approval for proactive service substitution.

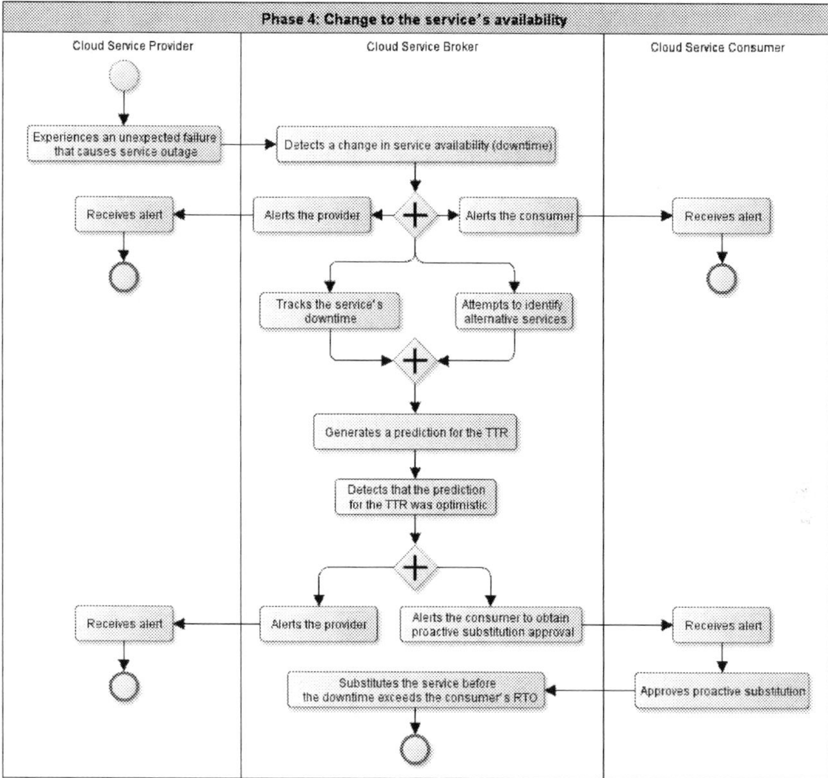

Fig. 4. The flow of service level failure mitigation activities upon a change to the service caused by an unexpected outage

For more example scenarios of continuous quality assurance intermediation we refer the interested reader to [3].

4 Challenges for Continuous Quality Assurance Intermediation

In this section we discuss the challenges associated with introducing capabilities for policy-driven service governance and service level failure mitigation in cloud service brokers. A research roadmap that considers other intermediation capabilities in the broader scope of continuous quality assurance and optimisation can be found in [4].

4.1 Challenges of Policy-Driven Governance for Cloud Services

Because of the fact that cloud service brokers intermediate between a consumer of cloud services and multiple service providers, they are uniquely positioned to address the need of the consumer to exercise as much control as possible over the external services on which it relies. This can be understood as a problem of cloud service governance. In this context we take governance to mean the enforcement of policies to manage the lifecycle of a cloud service as seen from the consumer's perspective, as well as to apply quality control over the service and its associated artefacts. These two concerns map onto two complementary forms of policy-driven governance: process governance and artefact governance.

Process governance refers to defining and enforcing policies to ensure that cloud services are selected, tested, used and retired in a structured and disciplined manner, with explicit conditions for transitioning from one service lifecycle phase to the next. Artefact governance, on the other hand, refers to defining and enforcing policies to ensure that artefacts associated with cloud services conform to certain technical or business constraints.

Some key challenges in the scope of supporting policy-driven governance inside a cloud service brokerage platform include:

- *How to achieve adequate separation of concerns in the design of the brokerage platform's governance support system?* In designing a governance support system we need to take into account the fact that there are three main roles at play in a policy-driven governance setting: (1) the role of providing the policies, (2) the role of providing data about the resources which are governed by the policies, and (3) the role of evaluating the governed resource data against the policies. In the scenario of Section 3 these roles are assumed by the service consumer, the service provider and the service broker, respectively. Each role has a different primary concern (i.e. maintaining governance policies, maintaining data about governed resources, and maintaining mechanisms to evaluate policies). The governance support system should be designed so as to facilitate all of them. As Baker puts it, "if we are attempting to separate concern A from concern B, then we are seeking a design that provides that variations in A do not induce or require a corresponding change in B (and usually, the converse)" [5]. For instance, in our context, this means that if the service consumer changes the way that a governance policy is represented this should not induce a change in how cloud service providers represent governed resource data, or how the broker evaluates service provider data against service consumer policies. The entities assuming the three roles should be allowed to evolve independently of each other.
- *How to effectively represent governance policies and governed resource data?* The means of policy representation determine the ease with which policies can be: (1) analysed in a systematic way for validation/troubleshooting and policy evaluation, (2) shared with other stakeholders in a cloud service ecosystem, (3) exchanged between different software systems, (4) cross-referenced to other policies so as to keep track of relationships between policies at different hierarchical levels and be able to know which policy needs to change when some other policy changes, (5) cross-referenced to classes of governed resources so as to keep track of which policies are relevant to each kind of governed resource. Likewise, the means of representing governed resource data determine the ease with which the data can be: (1) analysed in a systematic way for validation/troubleshooting and policy evaluation, (2) shared with other stakeholders in a cloud service ecosystem, (3) exchanged between different software systems, (4) cross-referenced to other governed resource

data so as to keep track of dependencies between cloud services and between cloud service artefacts, (5) cross-referenced to policies so as to keep track of which policies are applicable to each governed resource. Notably, the way in which this challenge is met in the design of a governance support system is highly relevant to how adequately the first challenge above can be addressed (separation of concerns).

4.2 Challenges of Service Level Failure Mitigation for Cloud Services

The service levels delivered by cloud services cannot be assumed to be static. Service performance may degrade over time, and infrastructure failures (i.e. failures of servers or network equipment) may result in outages. When service performance does not meet the service level objectives(s) that a consumer has specified this is called a service level failure. This means that a temporary failure to the service delivery infrastructure of a provider may not necessarily give rise to a service level failure for a particular consumer. Consumers need to monitor their service level objectives and to mitigate the impact of service level failures when these occur. This creates scope for a cloud service broker to offer highly valuable services as an intermediary.

The goal of service level failure mitigation is to assist the consumer to avoid or minimise the impact from a potential failure of the service to meet the consumer's targets. Mitigation of service level failures requires processes for monitoring various metrics about the operation of a cloud service and generating predictions about how the values of those metrics will evolve. Based on the predictions, the likelihood of the service to continue meeting the consumer's service level objectives can be assessed. If there is indication of an impending service level failure the broker can issue early warnings to consumers allowing them to take proactive mitigation measures.

Key challenges in the scope of developing intermediation mechanisms for service level failure mitigation for cloud services include the following:

- *Which metrics are relevant and useful for consumers and which of those should the broker collect data for?* The cloud service broker has to support metrics that are useful to consumers, by performing data collection for those metrics and predicting impending failures of the service providers to meet the consumer's objectives. For example, some useful metrics include availability, throughput, completion time, response time, mean downtime and others. However, there is no uniform standard for metrics used across cloud service providers, which makes it more challenging for the broker to monitor the same metric in different providers.
- *How to implement scalable monitoring for different types of metrics from a large number of cloud services, without overwhelming the cloud service broker, or introducing additional overhead to the cloud service?* The broker has to monitor metrics for a continuously increasing number of cloud services and analyse them in near real-time to identify impending failures of the provider to meet the consumers' objectives. The broker has to offer affordable means for service providers to publish data about the service for monitoring, because most service providers do not have appropriate interfaces in place. In addition, the broker has to minimise the overhead introduced to the cloud services as a result of the monitoring activity.

- *Which is the most appropriate prediction technique that the cloud service broker can employ for identifying impeding service level failures with acceptable accuracy?* The broker has to analyse the monitored data about the metrics by applying appropriate prediction techniques for determining future values of metrics, preferably in near real-time. The broker has to deal with the use and maintenance of different prediction models, depending on the type of the monitored data, and instantiate those models for making predictions in massive scale. The broker has to generate predictions for several metrics which concern many cloud services and several objectives of a large number of consumers who use those services.

5 Related Work

5.1 Related Work on Policy-Driven Cloud Service Governance

A look at different cloud service intermediaries, such as cloud application platform providers, reveals different approaches and tools for policy-driven governance over processes and artefacts. Development and deployment of cloud services on the Intuit Partner Platform[10] proceeds through four phases, each of which is called 'a line of development'. The phases are called development, quality assurance, staging, and publishing. Similarly, on Heroku[11], add-ons (i.e. third-party services) advance through the phases of development, alpha, private beta, beta, and general availability. In Force.com[12] the majority of quality checks on cloud service artefacts are associated with a particular phase towards the end of the development and deployment process, referred to as 'security review' – though the scope of the review carried out is actually much broader than security.

The industrial state of the art in policy-based governance follows closely on the evolution of tools supporting different aspects of service governance, such as artefact cataloguing and storage, service lifecycle management, dependency tracking, and policy enforcement. Those tools are typically integrated within some kind of registry and repository system [6], [7]. Vendors of today's governance registry and repository systems support different means by which policies can be encoded and enforced [8], [9], [10]. As shown by a recent survey of methods for policy management in contemporary open source registry and repository systems [11], a major weakness in the state of the art is the lack of proper separation of concerns with regard to defining rules for governance and acting upon them. Policy definition and policy enforcement are entangled in the implementation of a single software component – the policy evaluation engine. For the most part, the rules that a policy comprises are encoded in an imperative manner, in the same programming language that the registry and repository system has been implemented, and as part of the same code that checks the data for violations. This can be shown to create many negative side effects.

---

[10] `https://developer.intuit.com/`

[11] `https://www.heroku.com/`

[12] `http://www.force.com/`

To avoid the problems stemming from insufficient separation of concerns, recent works in the field of policy-based systems management stress the importance of designing software applications such that business rules are kept separate from the core program logic. It is best for such rules to be captured though policy-specification languages and to be consulted at run-time when user activity dictates to do so [12].

Several works motivated by similar objectives have focused on the enhancement of existing policy languages and tools with ontology-based methods of representation and processing. The most prominent early works along this line were KAoS [13], Ponder [14], and Rei [15]. Other, more recent works in a similar direction are those by Kolovski et al. [16] and Kolovski and Parsia [17].

Several recent research efforts and industrial pilot projects have been turning their attention to the benefits that the application of ontology-based modelling and reasoning can have with respect to different aspects of software engineering [18]. As Bergman points out [19], many of the benefits which are generally obtained by ontology-centric approaches to the development of information systems are attributed to the fact that the locus of effort is shifted from software development and maintenance to the creation and modification of knowledge structures. Uschold cites six important benefits which result from the increased level of abstraction and the use of formal structures and methods in ontology-driven information systems: reduced conceptual gap; increased automation; reduced development times; increased reliability; increased agility/flexibility; decreased maintenance costs [20].

The above benefits of ontology-centric approaches to information systems engineering, in combination with the Semantic Web standards and tools currently available [21] appear to provide a promising foundation for addressing the shortcomings of policy management in contemporary governance support systems [11]. Results from efforts with similar objectives are already being reported in the wider context of policy-driven systems management, such as the work by IBM on the transformation of sources of management data into Linked Data providers to allow for uniform logic-based queries over heterogeneous systems in a network [22].

5.2 Related Work on Service Level Failure Mitigation for Cloud Services

Over the past decade there has been an increasing interest in incorporating self-managing capabilities in software systems, motivated by high complexity involved in the everyday administration, as well as the detection, diagnosis, and resolution of failures in software systems. The research fields of Autonomic Computing [23] and Self-Adaptive Systems [24] continue to demonstrate fundamental advances towards understanding the challenges associated with the aforementioned research directions. Several approaches have been proposed for partially addressing the detection of failures, the diagnosis process to identify the cause of failure and, the automation of adaptation actions, as a solution to recovering from failures.

Recent research works on cloud service monitoring [25], [26] focus on the infrastructure level, and do not consider cloud services related to the platform and the application levels. The monitoring techniques found in the field of service-oriented computing can provide a useful inspiration for addressing those two levels.

Research in self-adaptive service-based systems outlined in Papazoglou et al. [27] can serve as the foundation for exploring novel mechanisms for service level failure mitigation in the context of cloud service brokerage, since cloud services, ranging from programmatically-accessible web APIs to complex software applications delivered as a service, present characteristics similar to those of services in the service-oriented architecture. Therefore, the research literature focusing on self-adaptive service-based systems is considered highly relevant.

Monitoring is well studied in self-adaptive service-based systems. Monitoring approaches follow either a push mode, where events or data are sent to a monitoring component, or a pull mode, where a monitoring component queries the subject of monitoring. Such approaches range from verification of service behaviour [28] and evaluating rules for detecting SLA violations [29] to dependency analysis for identifying causes offending some KPIs [30] and complex event processing for detecting situations based on the correlation of basic events [31], [32].

There exist approaches that attempt to proactively prevent failures from occurring by systematically testing services to uncover failures and deviations of quality of service from what is expected. Existing approaches for testing service-based systems mostly focus on testing during design-time, which is similar to testing of traditional software systems [33]. Others, like PROSA [34], exploit online testing [35] at run-time in order to proactively trigger adaptation. The focus of these approaches is to prevent QoS degradation of the service-based system.

A more relevant work is the PREvent framework [36], [37], which integrates event-based monitoring, prediction of SLA violations using machine learning, and runtime prevention of such violations at the provider-side by triggering adaptation actions in service compositions. There are also few other similar works [38], [39] concerned with prediction that make use of historical data regarding the execution of a business process to predict the performance of process instances.

The goal of the aforementioned works is to help the provider to prevent failures from occurring at the provider-side, whereas in our work we aim at helping a service consumer to avoid the impact of the provider's failure to meet the consumer's objectives. Furthermore, these approaches come from a different domain than cloud computing and they do not consider the intermediary's perspective, which aims at adding value to service consumers. Nevertheless, they offer inspiration for investigating prediction techniques for mitigation of service level failure realised by a cloud service broker. To the best of our knowledge, our work is the first that addresses service level failure mitigation in the context of cloud service brokerage.

6 Conclusion and Future Work

In this paper we have examined two facets of continuous quality assurance intermediation that we expect to become increasingly important in the scope of cloud service brokerage: policy-driven governance for cloud service and service level failure mitigation for cloud services. We presented an example scenario which demonstrates the utility of such types of continuous quality assurance intermediation capability. We attempted to introduce some basic concepts and key challenges, and to provide a glimpse of related work that one can build upon to develop solutions.

Our future work relative to policy-driven governance will focus on evaluating a new approach to the design of governance support systems that addresses the challenges discussed in section 4.1. This new approach overcomes many of the limitations in existing governance support systems and is natively suitable for use in a cloud service brokerage context. The solution builds on Linked Data principles and Semantic Web technologies [40] and comprises four major components: 1) a cloud service governance ontology serving as common vocabulary for describing governance policies and governed resources; 2) a methodology for encoding governance policies that facilitates better knowledge management about governance operations and enables automated semantic analysis of governance policies; 3) mechanisms to automatically generate semantic descriptions of governed resources by means of transformation from their native representation into Linked Data; and 4) a generic and reusable infrastructure to automatically evaluate descriptions of governed resources against applicable policies. Past research by Kourtesis et al. [11], [41] will serve as baseline to this work.

In the context of service level failure mitigation, our future work will focus on addressing the three challenges mentioned in section 4.2 through the development of a scalable approach for monitoring and prediction of metrics comprising three major components: 1) a set of metrics that are relevant to cloud service consumers; 2) a scalable software architecture for data collection based on the convergence of the "push" and "pull" communication paradigms and the use of Linked Data principles; 3) a study of failure prediction approaches using machine learning techniques appropriate for generating predictions for different kinds of metrics. We will use as baseline previous work on engineering of monitoring architectures for service-based systems [42], measuring many kinds of non-functional and functional properties of services [43] and the different metrics across the cloud stack [44].

References

1. Benoit, J., Lheureux, D., Plummer, C.: Cloud Services Brokerages: The Dawn of the Next Intermediation Age. Gartner (2010)
2. Verginadis, Y., Patiniotakis, I., Mentzas, G., Kourtesis, D., Bratanis, K., Friesen, A., Simons, A.J.H., Kiran, M., Horn, G., Rossini, A., Schwichtenberg, A., Gouvas, P.: D2.1 State of the art and research baseline. Broker@Cloud Project deliverable (2013)
3. Kourtesis, D., Bratanis, K., Friesen, A., Simons, A.J.H., Kiran, M., Verginadis, Y., Rossini, A., Schwichtenberg, A., Gouvas, P.: D2.3 Requirements Analysis Report. Broker@Cloud Project deliverable (2013)
4. Bratanis, K., Kourtesis, D., Paraskakis, I., Verginadis, Y., Mentzas, G., Simons, A.J.H., Friesen, A., Braun, S.: A Research Roadmap for Bringing Continuous Quality Assurance and Optimization to Enterprise Cloud Service Brokers. In: Proc. of eChallenges 2013, Dublin, Ireland (2013)
5. Baker, M.: The Lost Art of Separating Concerns.InfoQ (2006)
6. Marks, E.A.: Service-Oriented Architecture Governance for the Services Driven Enterprise. John Wiley & Sons, Hoboken (2008)
7. Zhang, L., Zhou, Q.: CCOA: Cloud Computing Open Architecture. In: Proc. 2009 IEEE Int. Conf. on Web Services (ICWS 2009), pp. 607–616. IEEE (2009)
8. WSO2 Governance Registry, `http://wso2.com/products/governance-registry/`

9. IBM WebSphere Service Registry and Repository, http://www.ibm.com/software/integration/wsrr/
10. Oracle Service Registry, http://www.oracle.com/us/products/middleware/soa/service-registry/overview/index.html
11. Kourtesis, D.: Towards an ontology-driven governance framework for cloud application platforms, Dept. Comp. Sci. Univ. Sheffield, UK. Tech. Rep. CS-11-11 (2011)
12. Fisler, K., Krishnamurthi, S., Dougherty, D.J.: Embracing policy engineering. In: Proc. of the FSE/SDP Workshop on Future of Software Engineering Research. ACM (2010)
13. Uszok, A., Bradshaw, J., Jeffers, R., Johnson, M., Tate, A., Dalton, J., Aitken, S.: KAoS Policy Management for Semantic Web Services. In: IEEE Intelligent Systems, vol. 19(4), pp. 32–41. IEEE (2004)
14. Damianou, N., Dulay, N., Lupu, E.C., Sloman, M.: The Ponder Policy Specification Language. In: Sloman, M., Lobo, J., Lupu, E.C. (eds.) POLICY 2001. LNCS, vol. 1995, pp. 18–38. Springer, Heidelberg (2001)
15. Kagal, L., Finin, T., Johshi, A.: A Policy Language for a Pervasive Computing Environment. In: Proc. of the 4th IEEE Int. Workshop on Policies for Distributed Systems and Networks, pp. 63–74. IEEE, Washington, DC (2003)
16. Kolovski, V., Parsia, B., Katz, Y., Hendler, J.: Representing Web Service Policies in OWL-DL. In: Gil, Y., Motta, E., Benjamins, V.R., Musen, M.A. (eds.) ISWC 2005. LNCS, vol. 3729, pp. 461–475. Springer, Heidelberg (2005)
17. Kolovski, V., Parsia, B.: WS-Policy and beyond: application of OWL defaults to Web service policies. In: Proc. of the 2nd Int. Semantic Web Policy Workshop, USA (2006)
18. Gasevic, D., Kaviani, N., Milanovic, M.: Ontologies and Software Engineering. In: Handbook on Ontologies, 2nd edn., pp. 593–615. Springer, Heidelberg (2009)
19. Bergman, M.: Ontology-Driven Apps Using Generic Applications, AI3 blog (2011)
20. Uschold, M.: Ontology-Driven Information Systems: Past, Present and Future. In: Eschenbach, C., Gruninger, M. (eds.) Proc. of the 5th Int. Conf. on Formal Ontology in Information Systems (FOIS 2008), pp. 3–18. IOS Press, The Netherlands (2008)
21. Hitzler, P., Krotzsch, M., Rudolph, S.: Foundations of Semantic Web Technologies. Chapman & HallCRC (2009)
22. Feridun, M., Tanner, A.: Using linked data for systems management. In: Proc. of the IEEE Network Operations and Management Symposium, NOMS (2010)
23. Huebscher, M.C., McCann, J.A.: A survey of autonomic computing—degrees, models, and applications. ACM Computing Surveys 40(3), 1–28 (2008)
24. Salehie, M., Tahvildari, L.: Self-adaptive software: Landscape and research challenges. ACM Transactions on Autonomous and Adaptive Systems 4, 1–42 (2009)
25. Bertolino, A., Calabro, A., Lonetti, F., Sabetta, A.: GLIMPSE: a generic and flexible monitoring infrastructure. In: Proceedings of the 13th European Workshop on Dependable Computing, New York, NY, USA, pp. 73–78 (2011)
26. Romano, L., De Mari, D., Jerzak, Z., Fetzer, C.: A Novel Approach to QoS Monitoring in the Cloud. In: Proceedings of the First International Conference on Data Compression, Communications and Processing (CCP), pp. 45–51 (2011)
27. Papazoglou, M., Pohl, K., Parkin, M., Metzger, A. (eds.): Service research challenges and solutions for the future internet: S-Cube - towards engineering, managing and adapting service-based systems. Springer, Berlin (2010)
28. Dranidis, D., Ramollari, E., Kourtesis, D.: Run-time Verification of Behavioural Conformance for Conversational Web Services. In: Proceedings of the 7th IEEE European Conference on Web Services, ECOWS (2009)

29. OriolHilari, M., Marco Gomez, J., Franch, X., Ameller, D.: Monitoring Adaptable SOA Systems using SALMon. In: Proceedings of the 1st Workshop on Monitoring, Adaptation and Beyond (MONA+), pp. 19–28 (2008)
30. Wetzstein, B., Leitner, P., Rosenberg, F., Dustdar, S., Leymann, F.: Identifying influential factors of business process performance using dependency analysis. Enterp. Inf. Syst. 5(1), 79–98 (2011)
31. Baresi, L., Caporuscio, M., Ghezzi, C., Guinea, S.: Model-Driven Management of Services. In: Proceedings of the 2010 IEEE 8th European Conference on Web Services (ECOWS), pp. 147–154 (2010)
32. Hermosillo, G., Seinturier, L., Duchien, L.: Using Complex Event Processing for Dynamic Business Process Adaptation. In: Proc. of the IEEE SCC 2010, pp. 466 (2010)
33. Gehlert, A., Metzger, A., Karastoyanova, D., Kazhamiakin, R., Pohl, K., Leymann, F., Pistore, M.: Integrating Perfective and Corrective Adaptation of Service-based Applications. In: Dustdar, S., Li, F. (eds.) Service Engineering: European Research Results Book, pp. 137–169. Springer (2011)
34. Hielscher, J., Kazhamiakin, R., Metzger, A., Pistore, M.: A framework for proactive self-adaptation of service-based applications based on online testing. In: Mähönen, P., Pohl, K., Priol, T. (eds.) ServiceWave 2008. LNCS, vol. 5377, pp. 122–133. Springer, Heidelberg (2008)
35. Dranidis, D., Metzger, A., Kourtesis, D.: Enabling Proactive Adaptation through Just-in-Time Testing of Conversational Services. In: Di Nitto, E., Yahyapour, R. (eds.) ServiceWave 2010. LNCS, vol. 6481, pp. 63–75. Springer, Heidelberg (2010)
36. Leitner, P., Wetzstein, B., Rosenberg, F., Michlmayr, A., Dustdar, S., Leymann, F.: Runtime prediction of service level agreement violations for composite services. In: Dan, A., Gittler, F., Toumani, F. (eds.) ICSOC/ServiceWave 2009. LNCS, vol. 6275, pp. 176–186. Springer, Heidelberg (2010)
37. Leitner, P., Michlmayr, A., Rosenberg, F., Dustdar, S.: Monitoring, Prediction and Prevention of SLA Violations in Composite Services. In: Proceedings of the 2010 IEEE International Conference on Web Services (ICWS 2010), pp. 369–376. IEEE (2010)
38. Sahai, A., Machiraju, V., Sayal, M., Van Moorsel, A., Casati, F.: Automated SLA monitoring for web services. In: Feridun, M., Kropf, P.G., Babin, G. (eds.) DSOM 2002. LNCS, vol. 2506, pp. 28–41. Springer, Heidelberg (2002)
39. Zeng, L., Lingenfelder, C., Lei, H., Chang, H.: Event-Driven Quality of Service Prediction. In: Bouguettaya, A., Krueger, I., Margaria, T. (eds.) ICSOC 2008. LNCS, vol. 5364, pp. 147–161. Springer, Heidelberg (2008)
40. Heath, T., Bizer, C.: Linked Data: Evolving the Web into a Global Data Space. In: Synthesis Lectures on the Semantic Web: Theory and Technology, vol. 1(1), pp. 1–136. Morgan and Claypool (2011)
41. Kourtesis, D., Paraskakis, I., Simons, A.J.H.: Policy-driven governance in cloud application platforms: an ontology-based approach. In: Proc. 4th. Int. Workshop on Ontology-Driven Information Systems Engineering (2012)
42. Bratanis, K.: Towards engineering multi-layer monitoring and adaptation of service-based applications, Dept. Comp. Sci. Univ. Sheffield, UK. Tech. Rep. CS-12-04 (2012)
43. Bratanis, K., Dranidis, D., Simons, A.J.H.: An Extensible Architecture for Run-time Monitoring of Conversational Web Services. In: Proc. of the 3rd International Workshop on Monitoring, Adaptation and Beyond / ECOWS 2010, pp. 9–16. ACM (2010)
44. Bratanis, K., Dranidis, D., Simons, A.J.H.: SLAs for cross-layer adaptation and monitoring of service-based applications: A case study. In: Proc. of the International Workshop on Quality Assurance for Service-Based Applications, p. 28. ACM (2011)

Model-Based Testing in Cloud Brokerage Scenarios

Mariam Kiran[1], Andreas Friesen[2], Anthony J.H. Simons[1], and Wolfgang K.R. Schwach[2]

[1] Department of Computer Science, University of Sheffield, Regent Court, 211 Portobello, Sheffield S1 4DP, United Kingdom
{M.Kiran,A.J.Simons}@sheffield.ac.uk
[2] SAP AG, Vincenz-Prießnitz-Str. 1, 76131 Karlsruhe, Germany
{Andreas.Friesen,Wolfgang.Karl.Rainer.Schwach}@sap.com

Abstract. In future Cloud ecosystems, brokers will mediate between service providers and consumers, playing an increased role in quality assurance, checking services for functional compliance to agreed standards, among other aspects. To date, most Software-as-a-Service (SaaS) testing has been performed manually, requiring duplicated effort at the development, certification and deployment stages of the service lifecycle. This paper presents a strategy for achieving automated testing for certification and re-certification of SaaS applications, based on the adoption of simple state-based and functional specifications. High-level test suites are generated from specifications, by algorithms that provide the necessary and sufficient coverage. The high-level tests must be grounded for each implementation technology, whether SOAP, REST or rich-client. Two examples of grounding are presented, one into SOAP for a traditional web service and the other into Selenium for a SAP HANA rich-client application. The results demonstrate good test coverage. Further work is required to fully automate the grounding.

Keywords: Model-based Testing, Cloud Service Brokerage, Cloud Broker, Web Service Testing, Lifecycle Governance.

1 Introduction

Business are shifting to Cloud computing as a new paradigm and a 5th utility service after water, electricity, gas and telephony [1] to save money on infrastructure maintenance and technical personnel. Increasingly complex Cloud ecosystems are arising, which offer various kinds of intermediation services that cater to the large number of consumers and service providers. Examples of such intermediation include finding services needed from a range of providers or marketplaces, integrating services with ERP systems, aggregating services for added-value, or monitoring and managing them. *Cloud brokerage* is the term given to explain this business model [2].

Cloud brokerage caters to a variety of capabilities supporting the needs of consumers and providers. In addition to integration and discovery, quality assurance (QA) is an important role for the broker as well. Mechanisms for QA may include such techniques as SLA monitoring, policy checks or service testing. Few examples

A.R. Lomuscio et al. (Eds.): ICSOC 2013 Workshops, LNCS 8377, pp. 192–208, 2014.
© Springer International Publishing Switzerland 2014

of such mechanisms have appeared in the Cloud so far, although CloudKick [3] provided monitoring, and Rightscale [4] provided load-balancing as services. This paper reports on some work conducted by the EU FP7 project *Broker@Cloud* that explicitly targets the functional testing of services in the Cloud, as part of a suite of quality assurance mechanisms. The paper presents a complete model-based testing methodology supporting automatic test generation for software services that are offered in Cloud brokerage scenarios.

In the rest of this paper, section 2 introduces the Cloud brokerage scenarios in which model-based testing is an enabling technology for functional QA. Section 3 presents the specification and test generation methodology. Section 4 illustrates two case studies, for which model-based tests were generated. Section 5 concludes with an analysis of the approach so far.

2 Functional Testing in Cloud Brokerage Scenarios

Previous research on service testing has come out of strategies for testing Service-Oriented Architectures (SOA) [5, 6, 7, 8]. The emphasis is on provider-based testing of services, using translations into agreed web standards [5]. For example, Bertolino et al. [6] translate category-partition testing to XML [6], Heckel et al. devise a graph-based approach [7] and a contract-based approach [8] to exercise service functional protocols in a black-box way. A few approaches [9, 10, 11] have developed finite state-based testing methods, recognizing the state-based nature of services, but find it necessary to augment web standards, which only describe service interfaces (WSDL[1]) and message formats (SOAP[2]), with additional semantic information, in order to capture how the services should behave. These research prototypes have yet to be taken up in industry, where provider-based service testing typically relies on writing manual tests to cover common usage scenarios.

In the future, functional testing may form a much stronger integral part of service development, certification and composition in Cloud ecosystems. Not only is there a need for a standard way to specify services for assuring compatibility, but testing will form part of the trust-building process at multiple stages in the service lifecycle:

- Providers will wish to offer comparable services that conform to agreed standards (in a competitive market).
- Brokers will publish these standards and offer a certification process for validating services as part of their onboarding onto a given platform.
- Consumers will want to verify their correct behaviour, before they use services, or compose applications around them.

We expect this to emerge in the same way as standards for certifying security, or for general software development. To provide such a level of assurance, it will be necessary to reduce the difficulty and cost of repeatedly recertifying services, where these are constantly evolving and being upgraded. Model-based testing is one enabling technology that may be exploited to support automatic test re-generation and

[1] Web Services Description Language.

[2] Simple Object Access Protocol.

re-testing when functional specifications are changed. Below, we describe the future business context for certifying services in the Cloud and investigate the potential benefits of model-based testing.

2.1 Cloud Brokerage and the Service Lifecycle Model

Service intermediation, or brokerage, is becoming increasingly recognized as a key component of the Cloud computing value chain [2]. We propose a Service Lifecycle Model (SLM) to describe systematically the relevant processes governing services in the context of Cloud brokerage. The SLM consists of four phases. The first three are related to the stages of service provision: *Service Engineering, Service Onboarding,* and *Service Operation*. The fourth is the on-going *Service Evolution* phase.

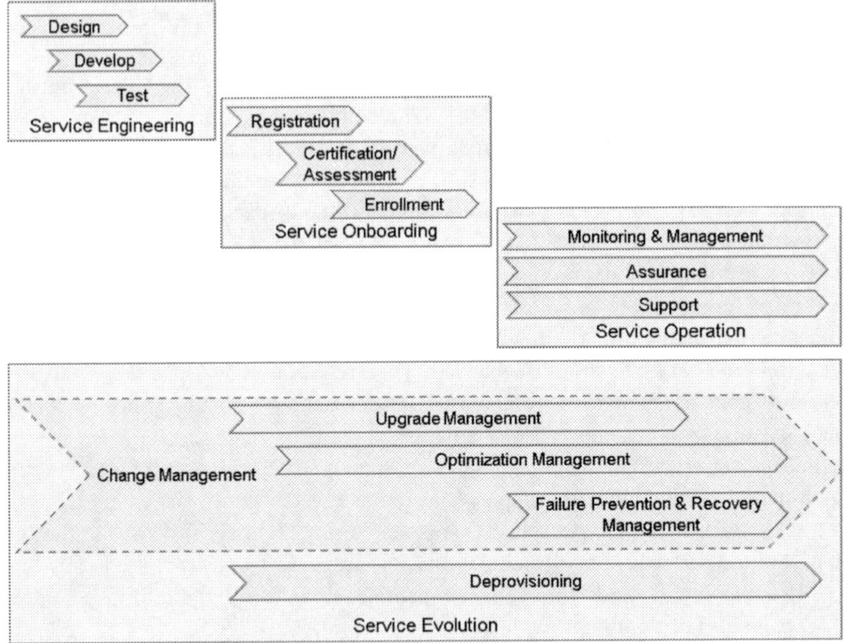

Fig. 1. The proposed Service Lifecycle Model

By analogy with software engineering, the service lifecycle starts with *Service Engineering*. The *Service Engineering* phase consists of *Design*, *Development* and *Testing* steps, carried out by the service provider. Once a Cloud service has been successfully developed and tested, and a "go to market" decision has been taken by the provider, the service enters the *Service Onboarding* phase. This phase consists of *Registration*, *Certification/Assessment* and, once the service is successfully qualified, *Enrolment*, to make the service visible to potential consumers and make it available for subscription. A service enters the *Service Operation* phase with the first consumer deciding to use the service. The most typical tasks are *Service Management* and

Assurance to manage relationships and meet agreed usage conditions. Finally, there is a fourth, *Service Evolution* phase which cuts across the whole lifespan of a service. The main task here is *Change Management*. Ultimately, the service lifespan ends with the *Deprovisioning* of the service.

It is clear that functional testing forms part of this lifecycle. Service testing currently relies on informal usage scenarios offered by the provider for certification purposes, which typically describe only part of the service's behaviour (SAP; CAS Software; SingularLogic)[3]. Testing determines whether the scenarios execute as specified, but tests are usually incomplete. While providers make use of test execution engines such as JUnit (for code) and Selenium (for web interfaces), tests are devised manually and this represents a large effort, duplicated at different stages of the lifecycle. Furthermore, there is no unified testing approach adopted by providers and brokers, since there is no shared formal specification of the service, so it is unclear whether the same QA has been applied across different service implementations, or across different host platforms. The need for commonality in service description and repeatable quality assurance after testing on multiple platforms is what distinguishes the current research from other work on service testing [5-11].

To address this, we propose a common model-based testing approach, offered as a service to providers, hosting platforms, brokers and consumers, as a means to close this interoperability gap and offer a shared level of QA. Brokers will publish common specifications and providers will agree to develop services up to these specifications. During the development stage, providers will test the services thoroughly. During the certification stage, brokers will validate the service up to the expected specification, using model-based testing. Testing may be repeated whenever a service is deployed to a different platform requiring a different implementation strategy (or *grounding*, see below), whether as a RESTful[4] web service, or a SOA-based web service using WSDL and SOAP, or even a rich-client application written in bespoke JavaScript. Internal improvements which do not change the interface may be validated by retesting. Service upgrades will need to offer a modified specification, from which all-new tests are generated. This will significantly help with the re-certification of comparable services, in a rapidly evolving Cloud ecosystem.

2.2 Model-Based Testing as an Enabling Technology

Model-based testing (MBT) is a methodology in which the designer supplies a specification, or model, that succinctly describes the behaviour of a software system, from which tests are eventually generated. The kinds of model or specification may include: a state-based specification, a functional specification, UML with OCL[5] pre- and postconditions, or a language grammar [12, 13]. The model serves as an oracle when generating tests for the system, linking specific test inputs with expected outputs [14, 5] deriving the correct results for the tests. The test generation algorithm

---

[3] Personal communication, Broker@Cloud industry partners.

[4] Representational State Transfer - standard HTTP running on TCP/IP.

[5] Object Constraint Language, part of the Unified Modelling Language.

also makes use of the model to determine the necessary and sufficient test coverage, up to some assumptions about the system-under-test [14].

Algorithm-driven test generation creates test-cases missed by developers (blind spots in their perceived behaviour of the system) and avoids duplicate tests that redundantly check a property more than once. The tests are then executed on the system, whose actual outputs are validated against the expected outputs. The advantages of MBT are the creation of a model, which can be internally verified for completeness and consistency, the automatic generation of test suites, the ability to determine the necessary system coverage and the automatic execution of the tests. The disadvantages are that the approach demands certain skills of testers in understanding the models, and that testing sometimes leads to state-space explosion [15].

The demands of software testing require that you drive an implementation through all of its states and transitions and observe that the implementation corresponds to the specification after each step. One of the first extended finite-state machine models to support this was Laycock's Stream X-machine (SXM) [16], which captures the behaviour of a software system in a fully-observable step-wise fashion. This work was extended by Holcombe and Ipate [14], who resolved the problem of the state explosion by abstraction into hierarchies of nested SXMs, which could be tested separately. Their proof of the equivalence of the nested machines to the expanded flat machine resulted in a tractable testing methodology that was guaranteed to find all faults in a system after testing [17].

Most work on testing software services has to date focused on Service-Oriented Architectures (SOA) rather than specifically on the Cloud [5], although the mechanisms are similar. SOA services are published using WSDL[6] interfaces that typically support testing only single operations. However, Ramollari et al. [9] presented an approach that leveraged extra semantic information attached to SAWSDL[7], in the form of production rules (RIF-PRD[8]), which supported the inference of a Stream X-Machine that was then used to generate complete functional tests. Ma et al. [10] also adopted Stream X-Machine based testing techniques to automatically generate test cases for BPEL[9] processes. Ramollari [11] used a similar approach to test SOA using explicit X-Machine specifications attached to SAWSDL service descriptions and using SOAP[10] communication. This work was the first to explore the symmetrical problems of *grounding* and *lifting*, the two-way translation between high-level abstract tests and low-level concrete tests for particular architectures.

Recent work [18, 19] has explored test generation for rich-client applications, where the application's state is maintained as a DOM[11]-tree, manipulated both by client-side user-interactions and via asynchronous AJAX callbacks from the server-side. These approaches rely on automatic inference of a state-based model of the application, from which suitable test sequences might be determined. Whereas one method [19] failed to use the model to determine full coverage, relying instead on

[6] Web Service Description Language.
[7] Semantic Annotations for WSDL and XML Schema.
[8] Rule Interchange Format-Production Rule Dialect.
[9] Business Process Execution Language.
[10] Simple Object Access Protocol.
[11] Document Object Model.

property-based testing, the other [18] converted all sequences into Selenium tests to drive the user interface, a useful approach to grounding tests for rich-client applications that we also explore in section 4 below.

3 Testing Methodology in Cloud Brokerage

We expect functional testing to be embedded into the relevant processes of the *Service Lifecycle Model.* Figure 2 illustrates the stages in the testing process. A specification (model) of a Cloud service is created and linked into its service description. This description is first published to a broker during the onboarding of the first service of its kind. Once a specification is available, high-level test sequences may be generated, offering a guaranteed level of state and transition coverage, linking expected inputs and outputs. Since these will be expressed in a platform-neutral way, it is necessary to translate the high-level tests into concrete tests, for a particular architecture, a process we call *grounding*. The concrete test suite may then be executed, to produce pass/fail test reports.

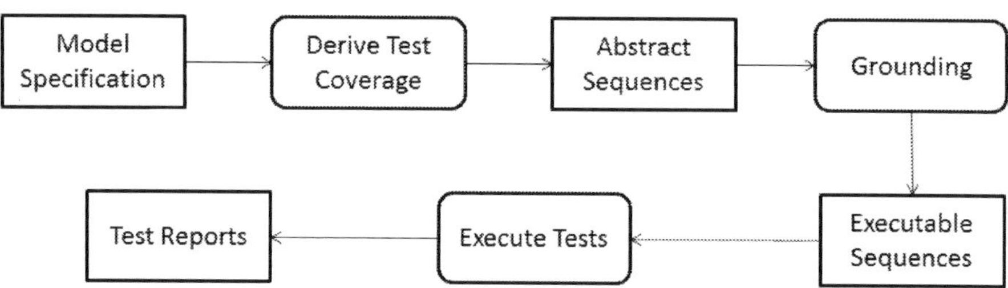

Fig. 2. Activity diagram illustrating the model-based testing methodology

This testing process may be offered at different stages of the service lifecycle. For example, a provider may use an existing service specification to generate tests for a new, replacement service in development; or a broker may perform functional testing prior to certifying a service for a particular platform. The functional testing capability may also be offered as-a-service, for the convenience of other service providers, or to consumers wishing to gain confidence in the service.

3.1 Design of the XML Specification Model

XML was chosen for the design of the common specification model, since both Cloud and SOA already make extensive use of XML. The specification of a service consists firstly of a functional part, which expresses the signatures of the service's operations and their inputs, outputs, branching conditions and state update effects on variables defined in memory. The second part consists of a finite-state machine specification, capturing the high-level control states of the service and its allowed transitions, where these are labelled with the names of distinct request/response (event/action) pairs taken from the operations. The specification language reported here is still a working prototype and is subject to revision.

The BNF for the main XML elements of the specification language is presented in figure 3, in which the notation *x ::=* <*y, z, …*> denotes a sequence of dependent children and *x ::= y / z /* denotes a set of alternative specializations. The set of XML attributes associated with each node are shown in set-braces.

```
Service{name} ::= <Memory, Protocol, Machine>
Memory ::= <Constant*, Variable*, Assignment*>
Protocol ::= <Operation+>
Operation{name} ::= <Request, Response+>
Message{name, type} ::= Request | Response
Request{name, type} ::= <Input*>
Response{name, type} ::= <Condition?, Output*, Effect?>
Machine{name} ::= <State+, Transition*>
State{name, initial?, final?} ::= <Transition*>
Transition{name, source, target}
Condition ::= <Predicate>
Predicate ::= Comparison | Proposition | Membership
Effect ::= <Assignment+>
Expression{name, type} ::= Parameter | Function
Parameter{name, type} ::= Constant | Variable | Input | Output
Function{name, type} ::= Assignment | Predicate | Arithmetic
  | Manipulation
Assignment{name, type} ::= <(Variable | Output), Expression>
Proposition{name, type} ::= <Predicate, Predicate>
Comparison{name, type} ::= <Expression, Expression>
Membership{name, type} ::= <Expression, Expression>
Arithmetic{name, type} ::= <Expression, Expression>
Manipulation{name, type} ::= <Expression, Expression, Expression?>
```

Fig. 3. BNF (Backus-Naur Form) of the service specification language

3.2 Procedure for Generating Complete Functional Tests

A version of the Stream X-Machine test generation algorithm [10, 7] was used to generate high-level test sequences from the specification. The algorithm determines the state cover by breadth-first search, then constructs languages of events, consisting of all possible interleaved sequences of length 1, 2, .., *k*, up to some chosen coverage criterion. These are concatenated onto the state cover to generate the high-level coverage sequences. For low values of $k = 2..4$, it is possible to ensure that:

- all specification states exist in the implementation;
- no unexpected states exist, such as ill-behaved clones of the expected states;
- all specified target states of transitions also exist in the implementation;
- no unexpected transitions exist in the implementation.

The sequences were then simulated in a model of the machine and protocol, to determine which sequences should be accepted or rejected. Attempting to traverse a missing transition should always be rejected, whereas traversing a present transition may be allowed conditionally, according to the guards governing each response. Where guards govern an input, more than one test case should be generated, to cover each input partition. The result is a tree of high-level tests, also expressed in XML, corresponding to positive sequences that should succeed, and negative sequences that should fail, when presented to the implementation.

The automatic algorithm ensured that every distinct case in the specification was covered by at least one test; and also that the tests were minimal (non-redundant) and exhaustive up to the assumptions in the specification. The algorithm determined the extent of testing needed to achieve the coverage goals, up to assumptions about redundancy in the implementation. The algorithmic nature of test generation means that it is possible to re-test, or generate new tests (after a service upgrade) to the same coverage levels, promoting a degree of uniformity in QA.

4 Analysis and Evaluation via Case Studies

Two case studies were developed to prototype the test grounding strategy. The first study was a traditional web service, implemented using Java, WSDL and SOAP. The second study was a rich-client application developed for the SAP HANA Platform-as-a-Service (PaaS), which currently offers independent software vendors (ISVs) a platform and a manual certification process for onboarding their third-party web services. Whereas the first study focused on the feasibility of translating high-level tests into SOAP, the second study also investigated ways of supplying grounding information for creating Selenium tests, as an additional part of the specification.

4.1 Case Study: A Shopping Cart Web Service

The first case study was created as a stand-alone web service, as though developed by a provider seeking to offer a SOA application, similar to others available in the Cloud. The provider was allowed to develop the service as they liked (c.f. the *Service Engineering* phase), and also provided the specification for it, indicating the service's expected behaviour using the XML specification language of figure 3.

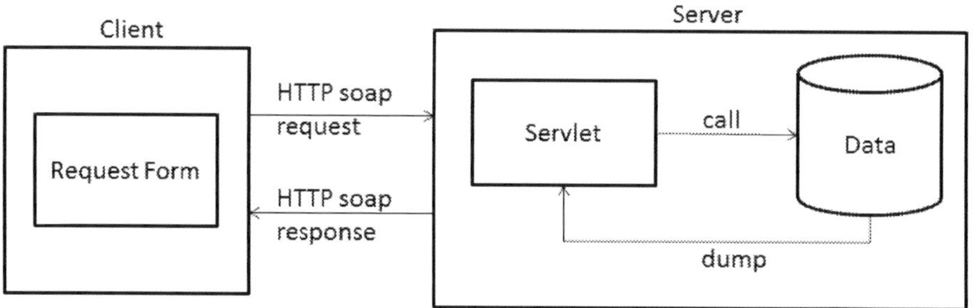

Fig. 4. Client-server architecture for a *Shopping Cart* web service

Figure 4 illustrates the client/server architecture of the *Shopping Cart* web service. The client's presentation logic offered a list of items to purchase, as shown in the screenshot of figure 5. A Java servlet modelled the control logic, whose high-level control states and transitions are illustrated by the diagram in figure 6.

Shopping Cart Example

Choose What to Buy?:

- tele
- dvdpr
- dvdprA
- dvdprB
- dvdprC
- dvdprD Proceed to CheckOut...

Fig. 5. The web form offered by the client-side of the *Shopping Cart*

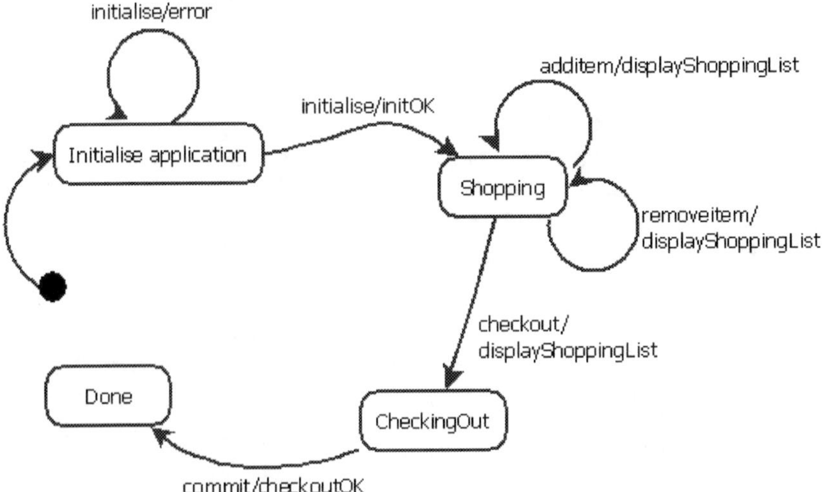

Fig. 6. The state machine for the server-side of the *Shopping Cart*

The memory-state of the application, which corresponded to the items currently ticked in the web-form, was stored in a database on the server-side. Communication between the client and server was via SOAP messages and WSDL interfaces. The client-side issued commands as SOAP requests, which were interpreted on the server-side. After responding and updating the data state, the server returned a SOAP response, indicating the action taken. The client-side used Java wrappers to issue SOAP messages and interpret the responses, which allowed comparison of actual and expected values.

Figure 6 shows the state machine representing the intended design of the *Shopping Cart* service. The states: *S = {InitialiseApplication, Shopping, CheckingOut, Done}* represent the control stages in the shopping lifecycle. The alphabet of the machine: A = {*initialise/error, initialize/initOK, additem/displayShoppingList, removeitem/displayShoppingList, checkout/displayShoppingList, commit/checkoutOK*} represents the complete set of operations. The state-transition logic shows when particular operations are allowed, for example, the client must connect successfully to the shopping service before adding items to the cart; and after checking out no further items may be added. The labels on the transitions correspond to event/action pairs that eventually correspond to SOAP request/response messages, in this implementation.

The state machine and abstract functional behaviour were encoded in the XML specification language, and then passed to an independent agent acting as a broker. From this, abstract coverage sequences were generated by algorithm, using the parameter setting *k=1*, yielding the transition cover (sufficient for an implementation with no redundant states). This test-set attempts to reach every single state and then fire every possible valid and invalid transition. The sequences were filtered by the machine to identify present/missing transitions, and then filtered by the functional specification, to identify the conditions guarding certain transitions.

```
<TestSuite id="0">
  <Sequence id="1" source="Init" target="Init"/>
  <Sequence id="2" source="Init" target="Shopping">
    <TestStep id="3" name="initialise/initOK">
      <Request id="4" name="initialise" type="Request">
        <Condition id="5">
          <Comparison id="6" name="equals" type="Boolean">
            <Variable id="7" name="isServerReady" type="Boolean"/>
            <Constant id="8" name="true" type="Boolean"/>
          </Comparison>
        </Condition>
      </Request>
      <Response id="9" name="initOK" type="Success"/>
    </TestStep>
  </Sequence>
  … <!-- omitted further Sequence elements -->
</TestSuite>
```

Fig. 7. Fragment of a high-level test suite for the *Shopping Cart*

Figure 7 illustrates a fragment of the resulting high-level test suite. The first empty sequence denotes a test to determine whether the application can be initialized. The second sequence shows the single step necessary to reach the *Shopping* state, with extra information about the memory-state of the server needed to satisfy the precondition guard. The response denotes a *positive* test step confirming expected behaviour; *negative* test steps were also synthesized for requests that should be ignored in certain states (corresponding to missing transitions in the model).

These high-level tests were given back to the provider, who then had the task of grounding these sequences as SOAP request/response pairs, where a request transmitted the input data, and a response showed which action had been triggered. In this first study, the grounding was performed by hand, following simple rules for converting the high-level tests. The purpose of this was to determine whether a mapping to SOAP was feasible, and whether testing could observe the properties required by the testing method [14, 16, 17]. For example, to achieve *output distinguishability*, it is necessary to identify uniquely which transition fires in response to each input.

```
<?xml version="1.0" encoding="UTF-8"?>
<S:Envelope xmlns:S="http://schemas.xmlsoap.org/soap/envelope/">
  <S:Header/>
  <S:Body>
    <ns2:getSelectedProduct xmlns:ns2="http://service.amazonian.org/">
      <pnames>tele</pnames>
    </ns2:getSelectedProduct>
  </S:Body>
</S:Envelope>
<?xml version="1.0" encoding="UTF-8"?>
<S:Envelope xmlns:S="http://schemas.xmlsoap.org/soap/envelope/">
  <S:Body>
    <ns2:getSelectedProductResponse
         xmlns:ns2="http://service.amazonian.org/">
      <return> * Good News, You have just bought: tele</return>
    </ns2:getSelectedProductResponse>
  </S:Body>
</S:Envelope>
```

Fig. 8. SOAP request and response for the *addItem*/*displayShoppingList* action

Figure 8 shows the SOAP request sent when the user checks the *tele* box on the client-side. The response indicates the success of the *addItem* request. Further SOAP responses were created for each action, including planned error-handling and an explicit null response for events that are ignored in the current state, corresponding to missing transitions in the state-transition diagram. A JUnit test driver was built on the client-side, driving a Java EE wrapper-class that issued the SOAP requests and unpacked the SOAP responses. During testing, it was found that the implemented service did not always signal explicitly when it had ignored a request, as required by the specification. This was considered a successful testing outcome.

4.2 Case Study: A SAP HANA Cloud Application

The second case study was created as a software service, designed to be deployed on an existing Cloud platform, SAP HANA. As above, the provider was allowed to develop the service, but designed this up to a specification, written in the XML specification language, that was regulated by an independent agent, acting as a broker. Unlike the previous case study, which used the open standards WSDL and SOAP, this study had a bespoke rich-client implementation, so would prove significantly more difficult to test, in the grounding phase.

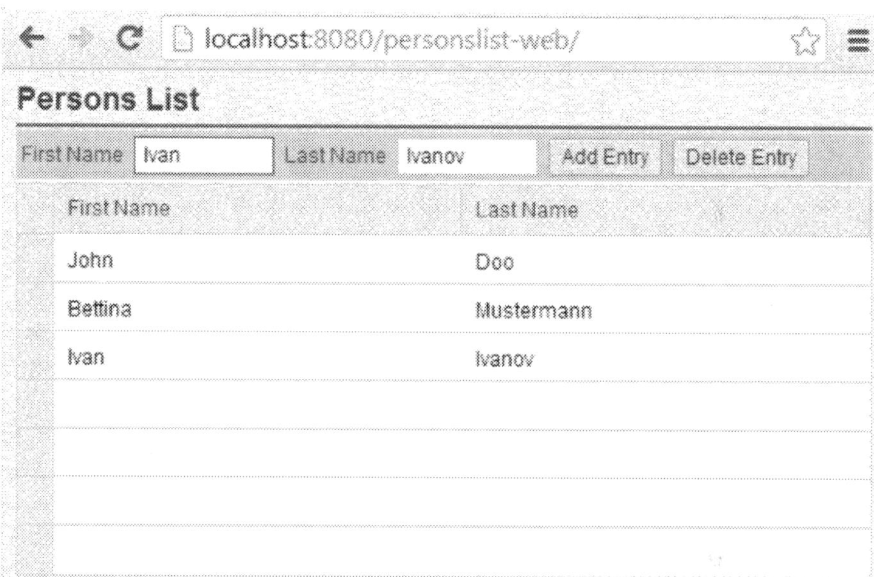

Fig. 9. Rich-client application for a *Contact List* built on the SAP HANA platform

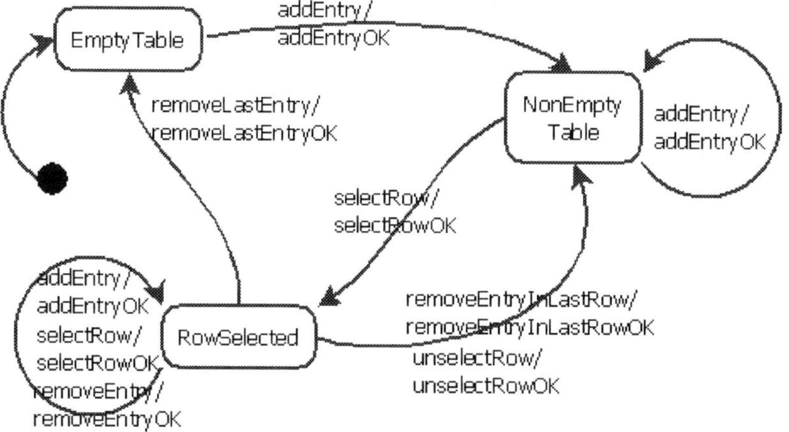

Fig. 10. The state machine for the SAP HANA *Contact List* application

Figure 9 shows a screenshot of the web service for maintaining a *Contact List*, deployed as a rich-client application on the SAP HANA Cloud PaaS. The application allows the user to add names, or remove selected names from a list of contacts. Figure 10 shows the corresponding control logic of the state machine specification. Only the successful cases of each operation were modelled explicitly, using guards on the responses. Thus, all errors were treated as missing transitions, which were later signalled using a pop-up dialog box in the grounding of the tests. In the case of failure, the state should not change. High-level test coverage sequences were generated from the model, in the same manner as described above.

In this second case study, we were particularly interested in providing broker support for testing a non-standard or unknown implementation. In such a situation, it is clearly the provider's responsibility to identify the route to grounding the high-level test suite. The provider decided that the best strategy was to treat the rich-client's web interface as the entry-point to the service, so suggested grounding the tests as generated Selenium code, to drive the client's browser in predetermined ways.

Selenium [20] is a tool that is conventionally used for recording user interactions in a web-browser, which can later be replayed as tests. Here, the provider wished to derive the concrete Selenium tests from the high-level test sequences, derived in turn from the broker's specification (see figure 2) and use them to drive client's browser, and hence the deployed SAP HANA Cloud service, through all of its states and transitions. The goal was to convert all abstract sequences into concrete Selenium tests, which, if executed without reporting errors, signify that the application has conformed to the specification.

```
<TestSuite id="0">
   <Sequence id="1" source="EmptyTable" target="EmptyTable"/>
   <Sequence id="2" source="EmptyTable" target="NonEmptyTable">
      <TestStep id="3" name="addEntry/addEntryOK">
         <Request id="4" name="addEntry">
            <Input id="5" name="forename" type="String"/>
            <Input id="6" name="surname" type="String"/>
         </Request>
         <Response id="7" name="addEntryOK" type="success"/>
      </TestStep>
   </Sequence>
  ... <!-- omitted further Sequence elements -->
</TestSuite>
```

Fig. 11. Fragment of generated high-level test suite for the *Contact List*

Figure 11 focuses on the abstract test sequence with *id=2*, showing the inputs required by the *addEntry* request that triggers the *addEntryOK* response. To support the grounding to Selenium, extra grounding information was added to the functional part of the specification of the *addEntry* operation, shown in figure 12.

```
<Operation name="addEntry">
   <Request name="addEntry">
      <Input name = "forename" type = "String">
         <Grounding>
            <Target>Selenium<Target/>
            <ElementType>TextField</ElementType>
            <ElementID>firstNameFieldId</ElementID>
            <TestValue>John</TestValue>
         </Grounding>
      </Input>
      <Input name="surname" type="String">
         <Grounding>
            <Target>Selenium<Target/>
            <ElementType>TextField</ElementType>
            <ElementID>lastNameFieldId</ElementID>
            <TestValue>Smith</TestValue>
         </Grounding>
      </Input>
      <Grounding>
         <Target>Selenium<Target/>
         <ElementType>Button</ElementType>
         <ElementID>addPersonButtonId</ElementID>
         <Action>click</Action>
      </Grounding>
   </Request>
   <Response name="addEntryOK" type="success">
      <Grounding>
         … <!-- omitted grounding info, to report success  -->
      </Grounding>
      … <!-- omitted Effect, for updating memory -->
   </Response>
</Operation>
```

Fig. 12. Fragment of the functional specification for *Contact List*, with grounding information

The new idea here is that an XML sub-language for grounding may be created to support the grounding of the high-level test suites in any particular technology. The Selenium engine is driven by a table of instructions provided in an XML DOM-tree[12], which also records the before- and after-states of each interaction. In figure 12, the *Grounding* nodes contain extra information about the Selenium DOM-tree elements to insert as part of the test input data, along with the Selenium button-click event that should be triggered to fire the *addEntry* request. This information was created by the service provider, in a similar format to the original functional specification. The bespoke grounding algorithm ensured that, whenever an *addEntry* request was listed

[12] Document Object Model - memory representation of an XML file.

in the high-level tests (see figure 11), this would be matched against the *addEntry* operation in the grounding information (see figure 12), which supplied the input and button-click data for generating the concrete Selenium test instructions. Code snippets from the DOM-tree generated for the Selenium driver are shown in figure 13:

```
<tr> <td>type</td> <td>id=firstNameFieldId</td> <td></td> </tr>
<tr> <td>sendKeys</td> <td>id=firstNameFieldId</td> <td>John</td> </tr>

<tr> <td>type</td> <td>id=lastNameFieldId</td> <td></td> </tr>
<tr> <td>sendKeys</td> <td>id=lastNameFieldId</td> <td>Smith</td> </tr>

<tr> <td>click</td> <td>id=addPersonButtonId</td> <td></td> </tr>
```

Fig. 13. Sample code generated for the Selenium test driver, for the *Contact List*

As above, the grounding algorithm was only partially automated; but enough was learned to see how a fully automated method might be developed, using translation strategies similar to the *Visitor Design Pattern* [21]. It seems likely that, whereas a broker may eventually be expected to provide standard groundings for SOAP and WSDL services, non-standard implementations will always require bespoke grounding strategies, supplied by the service provider.

During testing of this application, it was found that the implemented service did not exactly follow the state-based model, as required by the specification. After removing the last entry from the table, it was found that the implemented service remained in the state *RowSelected* instead of switching into the state *EmptyTable*. This was a successful testing outcome demonstrating the discovery of a (non-obvious) incorrect behavior.

5 Conclusions

This paper presents early results from the development of a standard method and a supporting mechanism for automated functional testing in the Cloud. The mechanism supports (at least) the certification phase of a Service Lifecycle Model, as operated by Cloud service brokers, and may also support providers during the service engineering phase, and consumers during the operation phase. Some service consumers may also be providers, seeking to compose larger services out of smaller ones, hence will be interested in validating component services in the Cloud.

Central to this effort is the development of a common service specification language. The XML specification language was able to model adequately the two case studies described, and is also fairly close in its syntax to other service description languages, such as Linked USDL[13] [22], so is likely to be acceptable in the community. Once a specification has been parsed, the resulting model also supports symbolic checking for the completeness of the specification (for missing transitions and exhaustiveness of the guards). This is essential if the mechanism is to be widely

[13] Unified Service Description Language.

adopted by developers who are not necessarily trained in formal methods. The fully automatic generation of high-level tests was successful in achieving levels of coverage not yet found in manual service testing in industry. This was borne out in the feedback from industry partners (SAP; CAS Software; SingularLogic) and also demonstrated in the detection of some non-obvious faults in the case studies.

The work on automated grounding is still incomplete, but a manually-assisted grounding strategy was shown, for the sake of demonstrating the general strategy and the fault-finding potential of the concrete tests. Future work will concentrate on building an improved model simulator and test oracle; and on developing automatic groundings for certain standard service implementation technologies. This may go some way towards the goal of providing Testing-as-a-Service in the Cloud [23].

Acknowledgment. The research leading to these results has received funding from the European Union Seventh Framework Programme (FP7/2007-2013) under grant agreement no. 328392, the Broker@Cloud project (www.broker-cloud.eu).

References

1. Buyya, R., Yeo, C.S., Venugopal, S., Broberg, J., Brandic, I.: Cloud Computing and Emerging IT Platforms: Vision, Hype, and Reality for Delivering Computing as the 5th Utility. Future Generation Computer Systems 25, 599–616 (2008)
2. Plummer, D.C., Lheureux, B.J., Karamouzis, F.: Defining Cloud Services Brokerage: Taking Intermediation to the Next Level. Report ID G00206187. Gartner, Inc. (2010)
3. Rao, L.: Using CloudKick to manage Amazon Webservices' EC2. TechCrunch, `http://techcrunch.com/2009/03/16/y-combinators-cloudkick-offers-simple-cloud-management-system/` (March 16, 2009)
4. Higginbotham, S.: Rightscale Makes Multiple Clouds Work. GigaOM, `http://gigaom.com/2008/09/17/rightscale-makes-multiple-clouds-work/` (September 17, 2008)
5. Bozkurt, M., Harman, M., Hassoun, Y.: Testing & Verification in Service-Oriented Architecture: A Survey. Software Testing, Verification and Reliability 32(4), 261–313 (2012)
6. Bertolino, A., Frantzen, L., Polini, A., Tretmans, J.: Audition of Web Services for Testing Conformance to Open Specified Protocols. In: Reussner, R., Stafford, J.A., Szyperski, C. (eds.) Architecting Systems. LNCS, vol. 3938, pp. 1–25. Springer, Heidelberg (2006)
7. Heckel, R., Mariani, L.: Automatic Conformance Testing of Web Services. In: Cerioli, M. (ed.) FASE 2005. LNCS, vol. 3442, pp. 34–48. Springer, Heidelberg (2005)
8. Heckel, R., Lohmann, M.: Towards Contract-based Testing of Web Services. In: Proc. Int. Workshop on Test and Analysis of Component Based Systems, Barcelona, Spain. ENTCS, vol. 116, pp. 145–156 (2004)
9. Ramollari, E., Kourtesis, D., Dranidis, D., Simons, A.J.H.: Leveraging Semantic Web Service Descriptions for Validation by Automated Functional Testing. In: Aroyo, L., et al. (eds.) ESWC 2009. LNCS, vol. 5554, pp. 593–607. Springer, Heidelberg (2009)
10. Ma, C., Wu, J., Zhang, T., Zhang, Y., Cai, X.: Testing BPEL with Stream X-Machine. In: Proceedings of the 2008 International Symposium on Information Science and Engineering, pp. 578–582. IEEE Computer Society, Shanghai (2008)

11. Ramollari, E.: Automated Verification and Testing of Third-Party Web Services. PhD Thesis, Dept. of Computer Science, University of Sheffield, UK (2012)
12. Utting, M., Legeard, B.: Practical Model-Based Testing: A Tools Approach. Morgan Kaufmann, Burlington (2007)
13. Pretschner, A., Philipps, J.: Methodological Issues in Model-Based Testing. In: Broy, M., Jonsson, B., Katoen, J.-P., Leucker, M., Pretschner, A. (eds.) Model-Based Testing of Reactive Systems. LNCS, vol. 3472, pp. 281–291. Springer, Heidelberg (2005)
14. Holcombe, W.M.L., Ipate, F.: Correct Systems - Building a Business Process Solution. Applied Computing Series. Springer, Berlin (1998)
15. El-Far, I.K., Whittaker, J.A.: Model-Based Software Testing. In: Marciniak, J.J. (ed.) Encyclopedia of Software Engineering. John Wiley & Sons, London (2002)
16. Laycock, G.: The Theory and Practice of Specification Based Software Testing. PhD Thesis. Dept. of Computer Science, University of Sheffield, UK (1993)
17. Ipate, F., Holcombe, W.M.L.: An integration testing method which is proved to find all faults. Int. J. Comp. Math. 63, 159–178 (1997)
18. Marchetto, A., Tonella, P., Ricca, F.: State-Based Testing of Ajax Web Applications. In: Proceedings of the 2008 International Conference on Software Testing, Verification, and Validation, pp. 121–130. IEEE Computer Society Press, Washington, DC (2008)
19. Mesbah, A., van Deursen, A., Roest, D.: Invariant-Based Automatic Testing of Modern Web Applications. IEEE Trans. Software. Eng. 38(1), 35–53 (2012)
20. Selenium, H.Q.: Browser Automation, `http://www.seleniumhq.org/`
21. Gamma, E., Helm, R., Johnson, R., Vlissides, J.: Design Patterns - Elements of Reusable Object-Oriented Software. Addison-Wesley (1996)
22. KMI and SAP Research: Linked USDL, `http://www.linked-usdl.org`
23. Yang, Y., Onita, C., Dhaliwal, J., Zhang, X.: TESTQUAL: conceptualizing software testing as a service. In: Proc. 15th Americas Conf. on Information Systems, USA, paper 608 (2009)

Value-Added Modelling and Analysis in Service Value Brokerage

Yucong Duan[1], Yongzhi Wang[2], Jinpeng Wei[2], Ajay Kattepur[3], and Wencai Du[1]

[1] College of Information Science and Technology, Hainan University, China
duanyucong@hotmail.com, wencai@hainu.edu.cn
[2] Florida International University, Miami, USA
{ywang032,weijp}@cis.fiu.edu
[3] ARLES Group, INRIA Paris-Rocquencourt, France
ajay.kattepur@inria.fr

Abstract. In our previous work, we have introduced various *Service Value Broker* (SVB) patterns which integrate business modeling, knowledge management and economic analysis. We have identified that value added is a main driving force for adoption and application of SVB by different stakeholders including providers, customers and public administrators. Based on an e-tourism platform, we analyze the sources of value added which could originate in SVB application from the perspective of various stakeholders. We model the situations of value added balancing and tradeoff in the background of long run and short run economical goals. Experiments and simulations are developed for demonstration purpose.

1 Introduction

Software design patterns [1] have been proved, proposed and verified successfully in the modeling processes of multiple technical domains. However for modeling service oriented computing (SOC) applications, design patterns have to be adapted according to value of Quality of Service (QoS) or business contractual aspects. We refer to this as the *Service Value Broker (*SVB*)* pattern [2]. Brokers have already been proposed for cloud service brokerage [3] which we foresee as an important characteristics of the optimization of E-Service Economics [4]. The related definitions are as follows [2]:

- *Service Value Broker* (*SVB*): driven by a value based goal, when a direct service composition cannot meet some required constraints from the service contract [5] or service level agreement(SLA) such as response time, location, license area, available period, currency format. If the introduction of a intermediate service can help to solve these problems and enable a service composition to be qualified, the introduced intermediate service is a *SVB*.
- *Direct Service Value Broker* (*DSVB*): direct *SVB* is a special type of *SVB* resulting from a composition of services. This composition must bring more

A.R. Lomuscio et al. (Eds.): ICSOC 2013 Workshops, LNCS 8377, pp. 209–222, 2014.
© Springer International Publishing Switzerland 2014

value to the stakeholder who introduces the *DSVB*. By value we mean not only monetary value but also non-monetary such as reputation and brand value, etc.

In this paper, we propose to use *SVB* as the base to integrate three important sides of a service ecosystem: service provider, service customer and public administration [6]. Each of these three sides maintains an independent interest or value system and at the same time relates to others as an element of an global value calculation system. SVB is expected to function as an important source of *value added* for optimizing the whole system under the comprehensive evaluation/measure in terms of increased business value added.

The rest of the paper is organized as follows: Section2 presents background knowledge and the general scenario. Section 3 presents the analysis of the sources of value added brought by introducing SVB. Section 4 presents the scenario of modeling and calculation of value added. This is followed by related work in Section 5 and conclusions with future directions in Section 6.

2 The Background and Scenario

2.1 Demonstration of SVB

We denote the service contract on the source end of an exchange as CS, the contract on the target end of an exchange as CT, the input of SVB/DSVB contract as iSVB and the output of a SVB/DSVB contract as oSVB.

- **Weather forecasting:** weather forecast is a costly and challenging task, however a lot of organizations might need this service with specific precision request.

  Weather forecasting broker: by subcontracting the weather forecasting to a professional service, it actually implement a reuse of resources including professional knowledge, etc. Similarly we can identify numerous application level brokers such as: vender broker, data cleaning broker, etc.

- **Information privacy:** during a transaction, some pieces of information which are not required or are not necessary for a transaction might be required or leaked without notice.

  Information privacy broker: a service which checks and restricts the usages of service information based on a necessary-only policy may play the broker.

There are various situations where SVBs are composed with different cardinalities of "1:1", "1:n", "m:n", and sequences. Figure 1 shows the state diagram of a E-Service in a SVB composition process. A traditional process is embedded as a comparison. During a traditional process, a service is firstly discovered and then it will go through a sequential process of "*matchmaking* → *selection* → *composition*". The result is a local solution which does not fully take advantage

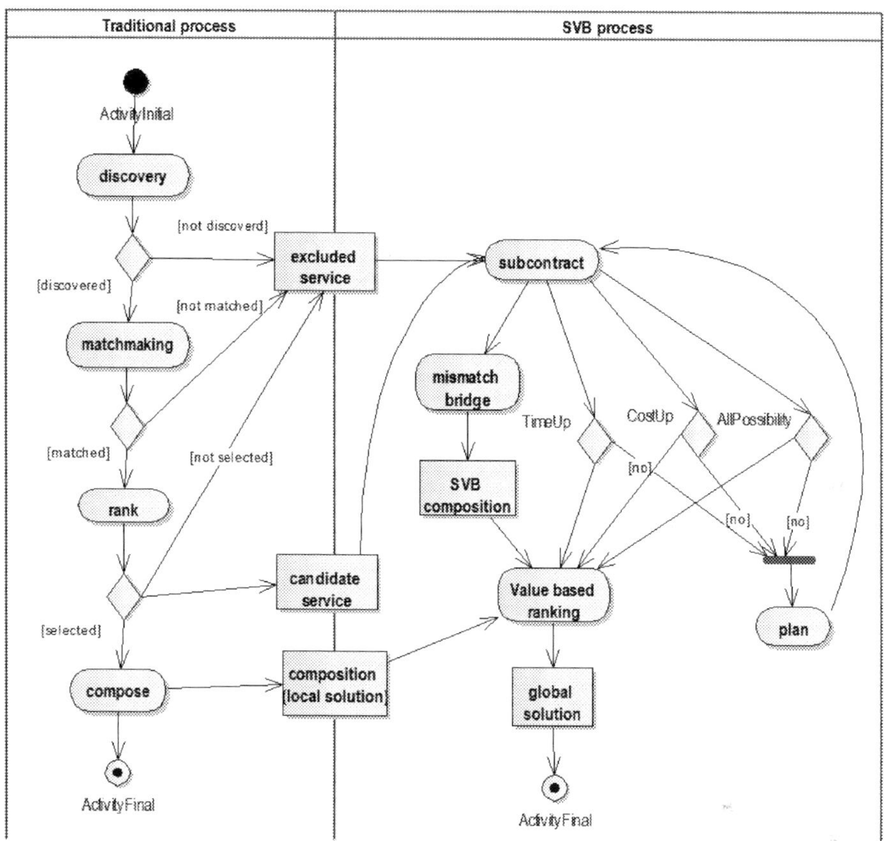

Fig. 1. The object flow

of the potential of the flexibility of E-Services in a scalable cloud environment. When the business value is given the highest priority, the subcontracting relationship implemented by SVB could bring potentially higher value. SVB based solution can fully explore the potential of the available resources, for the processing only when one of the conditions of: (a) the assigned search time is finished, (b) the cost reaches limit, and (c) all possible subcontract scenarios have been explored, has been met, the search will end. The result will be a global best value in terms of business gains on all parties.

2.2 The General Business Scenario

Figure 2 shows the general scenario of multiple service values from mainly three sources. We summarize them as follows:

1. *Provider value (PRV)* - At the service provider side, business value needs to be considered from the temporal dimension as short run vs. long run

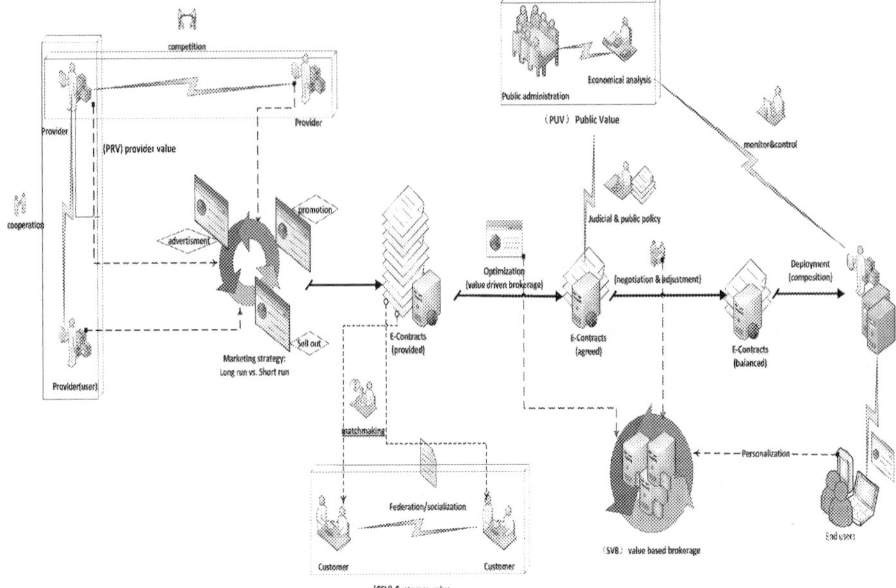

Fig. 2. Integrating value considerations from multiple stakeholder with value brokerage

target which will decide specific business strategies such as new product advertisement, promotion, sell out, etc. Among providers the value can be classified into two categories:

- *Negative competitive cost* - Negative competitive cost occurs when other business competitors who offer similar services bid for the same order or market.
- *Positive cooperative wins* - When service vendors who offer related or similar services agree on some fixed conditions such as market share, sells area, etc, they can build some cooperations to profit from the customer side such as lifting the price of services or charges of maintenance, etc.

2. *Customer value (CSV)* - Service customers in general have independent views on the value of the targeted services. However customers can socialize with other customers to query the quality of a service from others' experiences and comments. The experience information or news/advertisment propagated through social media among customers is playing an increasing role in promoting sales and adjusting commerce behavior. Customers can also build federations to protect their shared interests against malicious service providers with shared cost. Small scale of customer cooperation can cooperate to win promotion sale packages from providers in a win-win manner.
3. *Public value (PUV)* - The public administration is the third party which can play the juridical role for solving the argumentation. The public administration also has other critical responsibilities: (i) monitor the service market through economical analysis to avoid the competition between the provider

and customer side to enter an Zero-Sum game; (ii) employ public policies to intervene the strong cooperation against customer interests at the provider side, or collusive customers [7], etc.

2.3 Domain Knowledge Based Classification of SVB

From the domain of E-Tourism, we have identified many application areas which can be implemented with SVB in different categories[8] which is shown in Figure 3.

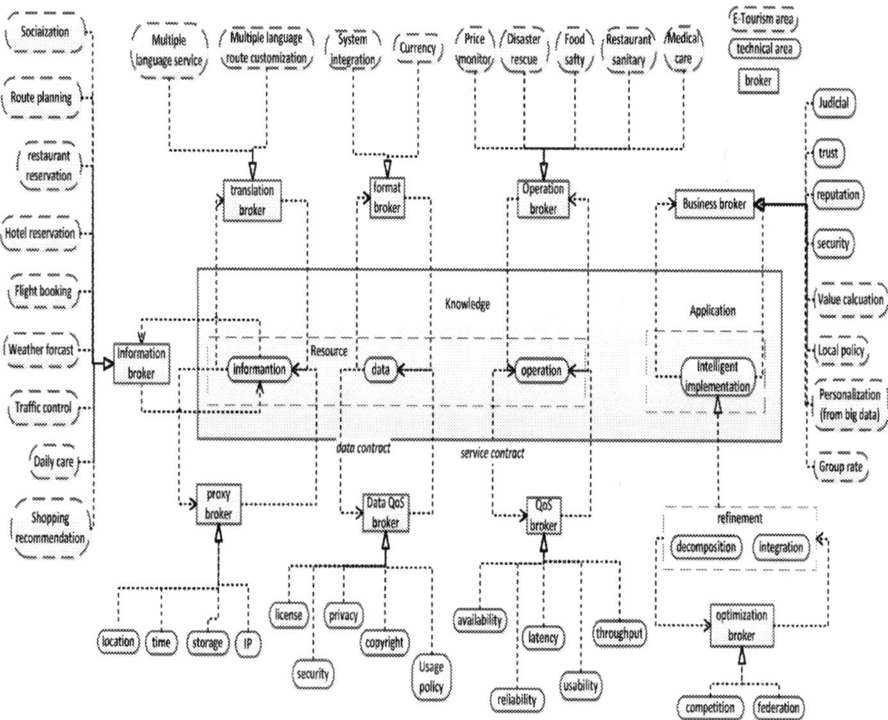

Fig. 3. Empirical SVB classification from a knowledge management perspective

3 The Analysis on *Value Added*

3.1 Sources of Value Added

Building an E-Tourism architecture on top of SVB are expected to have several possible advantages if well managed including the following basic situations:

- *Added value of PRV* - On the provider side, SVB can bring more business chances through relating otherwise not related business together such as creating an international language translation platform which can redistribute translation request to individual translation service providers. The added value $\triangle_{PRV}$ on a specific provider X_P can simplified as as the multiplying of the increased amount of request $\triangle_{req}$ with the difference of the price $\triangle_{price}$. In more detail, we assume the original price, request number and SB (service broker) cost as pri_0, req_0 and SB_0 respectively, and the new price and request number as $pri_0+\triangle_{pri}$, $req_0+\triangle_{req}$ and $SB_0+\triangle_{SB}$ respectively. The added value of provider is formulated as follows:

$$\triangle_{PRV}(X_P)$$
$$= (pri_0+\triangle_{pri} *(req_0+\triangle_{req}) - pri_0 * req_0 - ((SB_0+\triangle_{SB}) - SB_0)$$
$$=\triangle_{req} *pri_0 + (\triangle_{req} +req_0)* \triangle_{pri} - \triangle_{SB}$$

The cost on the broker provider X_{PSVB} can be assumed to be balanced to simply the calculation here for demonstration purpose. But in real situation, there can be added value on X_{PSVB} through reuse of information and operation, etc [9].

- *Added value of CSV* - On the customer side, SVB can bring more opportunities through sub-contract [2] relationships for customers to find expected services with the highest comprehensive value. The added value $\triangle_{CSV}$ on a specific customer X_C side can simplified as the sum of the gains from the saved cost on service payment $\triangle_{pay}$, the increased satisfaction $\triangle_{sat}$ and the cost for extra searching $\triangle_{cos}$. In more detail, we assume the original payment, satisfaction and extra search cost as pay_0, sat_0 and cos_0 respectively. We also assume the new price and request number as $pay_0+\triangle_{pay}$, $sat_0+\triangle_{sat}$ and $cos_0+\triangle_{cos}$ respectively. Here we regulate that satisfaction degree sat_0 and $sat_0+\triangle_{sat}$ ranges between -1.0 and 1.0. Negative value means a negative satisfaction. Positive value means a positive satisfaction. The added value of customer is :

$$\triangle_{CSV}(X_C)$$
$$= ((1+sat_0+\triangle_{sat})*(pay_0+\triangle_{pay})-(cos_0+\triangle_{cos}))-((1+sat_0)*pay_0-cos_0)$$
$$=\triangle_{sat} *pay_0 + (1+\triangle_{sat} +sat_0)* \triangle_{pay} - \triangle_{cos}$$

- *Added value of PUV* - On the public administrative side, SVB can be utilized for several important purposes which include the follows:

  - *Added value of $PUV_{competition}$*- play the judical role which can lower the cost of market adjustment in comparison with the free market situation where Zero-Sum game can hurt the gain of both CSV and PRV. The gains can be calculated as:

    $\triangle_{competition}= \Sigma avoid(loss(PRV)) - cost(interfere(PUV))$.
  - *Added value of $PUV_{cooperation}$*- SVB can also be used to interfere the forming of a dominating side in the provider side through collusive cooperation which will hurt the regular competition and the gain of CSV. The gains can be calculated as:

    $\triangle_{cooperation}= \Sigma avoid(malpractice) - cost(tradeoff(PUV))$.

- *Added value of $PUV_{security}$*- SVB can be employed to provide public qualified third party security services which will save the total spends from the individual cooperations. The gains can be calculated as:

  $\triangle_{security} = \Sigma increaseefficency(individual) - cost(security(PUV))$.
- *Added value of $PUV_{BigData}$*- SVB can be employed by the public administration to evaluate the technological innovations such as Big Data processing for both personalization and public intelligence, and harness their implementation to avoid their malpractice in terms of both business value and social effect. The gains can be calculated as:

  $\triangle_{BigData} = \Sigma avoid(malpractice) - cost(tradeoff(PUV))$.

The general added value brought from public side can be calculated as:

$\triangle_{PUV} = \Sigma \triangle_{competition} + \Sigma \triangle_{cooperation} + \Sigma \triangle_{security} + \Sigma \triangle_{BigData}$.

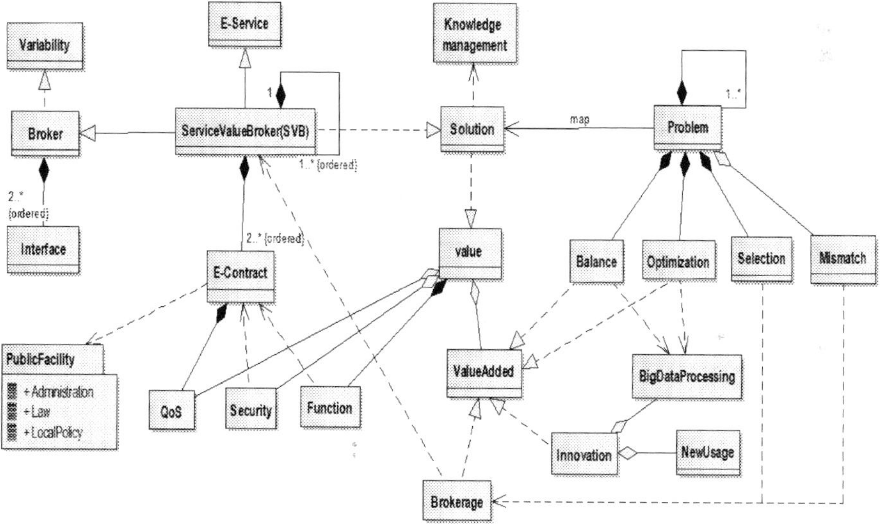

Fig. 4. The metamodel of the brokerage supported value added attaining

The metamodel of SVB is shown in Figure 4. It shows: (a) the inherent architecture of SVB with regard to well known concepts such as interface, broker, E-Service, E-Contract, SLA, and public facility[6] which includes law, local policy and administration; (b) the relationship with target problems including service mismatching processing, service selection, optimization and their composition; (c) the target solution in the form of SVB value including functional value, QoS value, security value and business value in general; (d) the sources of added value related to technological innovation related to Big Data processing, new usage discovery and SVB application. Different from traditional brokers which focus on functional value and QoS, the value which is implemented by SVB requires the composition of business value and functional value.

3.2 Tradeoff on Long Run vs. Short Run

Influence Factors. In classical economics, the profit mode of a business transaction will be distinguished as long run vs. short run [10]. In a long run, factors such as cost and price will be modeled as variables in contrast to being modeled as fixed amount in a short run. This difference will be reflected directly to value added accumulation towards profit-maximization. For a short run mode, the value added of $\triangle_{PRV}$ or $\triangle_{CSV}$ or $\triangle_{PUV}$ will be positive as long as the marginal cost is lower than the marginal revenue which represents the added profit corresponding to the increase of a unit of production. Similarly a production decrease strategy can be made. There are several variability which should be taken as knowledge rules to guide the attaining of the profit-maximization considering both long run and short run.

- *Cost/price adjustment* - by taking advantage of the timely processing of E-Contracts, SVB can realize timely adjusting price to balance the ratio of price/cost for a short run.
- *Marketing plan* - SVB can be composed to implement complex price strategies of a long run such as at the beginning of a business, the marginal cost is allowed to be greater than the marginal price to implement the marketing strategy of advertisement, the price can be increased since after to gain the main profit, and a sold out can be planned to recollect the money flow for an investment with higher reward business, etc. The general evaluation can be positive as long as the average profit in a long run is positive.
- *History based prediction* - the transaction history of customers/providers can be analyzed based on the added value calculation on the top of SVB to make decision on the adaptation of price and production.
- *Public policy implementation* - the public side can employ the power of Big Data processing to analyze added value from various sources covering both $\triangle_{PRV}$ and $\triangle_{CSV}$. Corresponding encouragement policies can be made when the
  $\sum(\triangle_{PRV} + \triangle_{CSV})$
  is decreasing or the acceleration of the increase of the
  $\triangle\sum(\triangle_{PRV} + \triangle_{CSV})/\triangle_{time}$
  is decreasing. Intervention can also be introduced to interfere the situation that the provider side dominates the price making against customer side through the monitoring of the ratio of
  $\sum(\triangle_{PRV})/\sum(\triangle_{CSV})$.

4 Experiment

We implement a prototype system to demonstrate the added value brought by introduction of *SVB*. We pick the personalization (right lower corner of Figure 2 as an example to show how *SVB* can improve the value of both the service provider and the customer sides. In the E-tourism, recommending suitable restaurants for tourists will increase the degree of their satisfaction. As a result, it will bring higher profit for both the restaurant and tourism company sides. With a *SVB*, both parties's attained values are added. Our system offers a value based brokerage service to make personalized restaurant recommendation based on the history rating record provided by previous customers. By delegating recommendation service to value based broker, our experiment shows that such a system could provide added value to both the service provider (tourism company) and the customer (tourist) sides. Specifically, the tourism company (TC) usually delegates the recommendation service to the service broker (SB). It authorizes the SB to access its history records regarding to customers' rating towards restaurants they have visited. TC expects the recommendation service provided by SB to bring added value to both TC and customers. In order to maximize the added value to both customer and TC, SB can sub-contract the recommendation service to multiple *analytic service providers* (ASP_S) in order to evaluation their recommendation service quality and find the best recommendation service. Suppose SB finds that ASP_i offers the best recommendation method, SB will only delegate TC's recommendation service to ASP_i in the future.

Our experiment uses "Restaurant & Consumer Data" dataset[1] from UC Irvine Machine Learning repository to show the above scenario and the effect of *SVB* in leveraging the added value. We only use the file *rating_final.csv*, which records 1161 ratings from 138 customers. Each record is a rating of a customer towards a restaurant. The possible rating values are 0, 1, 2. We preprocess the data set and feed the following format to SB: "*customerid | restaurantid | customer'srating*". We assume that each ASP uses Mahout Recommender[2] as an analytic tool to perform *item based recommender*. However, different ASP uses different similarity measurements. The similarity measurement which each ASP uses is shown in Table 1. The output of the Mahout Recommender is the top ten most recommended restaurants for each customer, along with the predicted rating. In order to test the accuracy of each ASP's recommendations. SB partitions TC's history data into two parts. The first partition consists of 80% of data. The second partition consists of the remaining 20%. For each ASP, SB first feeds it with the first partition so that ASP could learn the rating rule of customers and return the recommendation output. After that, SB will check the accuracy of the recommendation output against the ratings in the second partition. Using the second partition as the ground truth, SB determines the quality of each ASP. It computes the Mean Squared Error (MSE) between the ground truth and each ASP's recommendation output. If the ratings of a specific customer towards a specific restaurant appear in both the ground truth and the ASP output, the square of the rating difference is considered in MSE. Intuitively, a lower value of MSE which a ASP will generate means a higher recommendation quality. Different MSE generated from different ASP is shown in Table 1. (We will explain the Recommendation Accuracy later.) The figure indicates that

[1] `http://archive.ics.uci.edu/ml/index.html`

[2] `https://cwiki.apache.org/confluence/display/MAHOUT/Recommender+Documentation`

Table 1. Mean Squared Errors with different similarity measurements

ASP #	Similarity Measurement	MSE	Recommendation Accuracy
1	Co-occurrence	1.80	0.5
2	Log likelihood	1.80	0.5
3	Tanimoto coefficient	1.81	0.5
4	city block	1.80	0.5
5	cosine	1.79	0.5
6	Pearson correlation	1.45	0.8
7	Euclidean distance	1.80	0.5

ASP #6, which uses Pearson correlation similarity measurement, generates the lowest MSE. When SB finds the best ASP (ASP #6), it will delegate the future recommendation service only to such an ASP.

We model the added value of both the provider (TC) and the customer (tourist) with the employment of *SB*. According to Section 3, the added values of the provider and the customer are as follows:

- *Added value of PRV* - The added value of PRV involves the original price and requests (pri_0 and req_0), added number of customer satisfaction ($\triangle_{req}$), unit price increase ($\triangle_{pri}$),and the recommendation service fee charged by the SB ($\triangle_{SB}$). That is $\triangle_{PRV}$ (X_P) $=\triangle_{req} *pri_0+(\triangle_{req} +req_0)* \triangle_{pri} - \triangle_{SB}$
- *Added value of CSV* - The added value of CSV involves the original payment and the original degree of satisfaction (pay_0 and sat_0), payment increment for a meal ($\triangle_{pay}$), the degree of increased satisfaction ($\triangle_{sat}$), and the cost of extra search ($\triangle_{cos}$). That is

  $\triangle_{CSV}$ (X_C) $=\triangle_{sat} *pay_0 + (1+ \triangle_{sat} +sat_0)* \triangle_{pay} - \triangle_{cos}$

We assume the unit price of a meal on average is m_0, the recommendation service fee charged by the ASP is r per customer, the delegation fee charged by the service value broker is b. We also assume the total number of customers TC feeds to the SB for the recommendation evaluation is t. The number of customers TC feeds to the SB for the future recommendation is f. We define a recommendation is satisfactory if the customer's actual rating is no less than the recommendation rating by a tolerance threshold, marked as δ. We define the Recommendation Accuracy (RA) as the fraction of satisfactory recommendations in all the recommendations. That is

$$RA = \frac{\#of satisfactory recommendations}{\#of recommendations}$$

In our experiment case, we only consider the recommendation where the customer-restaurant pair appears in the ground truth. For those recommendations, if the rating of a customer towards a restaurant appears in both the ground truth and the ASP output, a recommendation of the ASP is satisfactory only if the ASP's rating is no less than the ground truth rating by δ. The RA is the ratio of satisfactory recommendation to the total recommendations. We set δ as 1.0 in the experiment. We get the RA of each ASP in the last column of

Table 1. Consistent with the MSE, ASP # 6 generates a better recommendation accuracy (0.8), compared to other ASP_S (0.5). We assume that the recommendation accuracy provided by SB is RA. The original recommendation accuracy without using SVB is RA_0. We list all the parameters for the added value model in Table 2. , along with the experiment value we choose. For simplicity, we assume that the meal price increases and the extra search cost as 0. We also assume the original customer satisfactory is 0, the SVB added satisfactory is 1.0, the original recommendation accuracy without using SVB is RA_0. If the customer will make a request only if a recommendation is satisfactory, the number of requests the f future customers will make with and without SVB will be $f * RA$ and $f * RA_0$ respectively. We set RA as 0.8 (according to Table 1), and RA_0 as 0.5, which is equal to the other ASP's recommendation. The number of customers for the training or testing is the number of customers in the recommendation evaluation, which is 138. The number of candidate ASP_S N_{ASP} are 7. The SVB service fee cost includes the broker fee b and the ASP service fee. The service fee charged by ASP is r per customer. At the recommendation evaluation, SB delegates the service to N_{ASP} ASP_S. So the service fee in this phase is $N_{ASP} \star t * r$. Later, SB delegates the service to only one ASP. The cost in this phase is $f * r$.

Table 2. Parameters of added value SVB Model

symbol	**name**	**experiment value**
pri_0, pay_0	original meal unit price	m_0
r	recommendation fee per customer	r
b	recommendation broker fee	b
RA	SVB recommendation accuracy	0.8
RA_0	Original recommendation accuracy	0.5
t	# of customers for training or testing	138
f	# of future customers	f
δ	tolerate threshold	1.0
N_{ASP}	# of candidate ASP	7
$\triangle_{pri}$	meal price increment	0
$\triangle_{req}$	request number increment	$f * (RA - RA_0) = 0.3 * f$
$\triangle_{SB}$	Service fee cost for SVB	$N_{ASP} * t * r + f * r + b =$ $(966 + f) * r + b$
$\triangle_{pay}$	meal price increment	0
$\triangle_{sat}$	satisfactory increment	1
$\triangle_{cos}$	extra search cost	0
sat_0	original satisfactory	0

We compute the added value with the values listed in Table 2. We have $\triangle_{PRV}$ $(X_P) = 0.3 * f * m_0 - (966 + f) * r - b$

$\triangle_{CSV}$ $(X_C) = m_0$

Since $m0 > 0$, the added value for the customer is positive. In order for the added value of provider to be positive, we have $0.3 * f * m_0 - (966 + f) * r - b > 0$

Solving the inequation by f, we have $f > \frac{b+966*r}{0.3*m_0-r}$

To give readers an intuitive understanding, we assume the meal price is \$10, the broker fee is \$1,000, and the recommendation service fee for each customer is \$0.1. We get $f > 378.1$. That is to say, TC will gain added value from the SVB when SB provides restaurant recommendation for more than 378 customers.

5 Related Work

Brokers are envisioned to be a key concern in cloud era, whether in the basic forms of storage brokerage and computation brokerage, or in the advanced form of solution brokerage [11]. Most of existing broker research [12,13,14,15,16,17] focus on using brokers to discover, match, negotiate and select services [18] with best QoS in a service composition. Yu and Li [19] utilize service brokers to meet SLAs in service lifecycle [20]. However, their solution supports only one QoS constraint and a single point of failure. Srikumar et al. [21] adopt brokers to enable grid resource searching and distribution where a broker works mostly as an autonomous agent [22]. D'Mello et al. [23] employ brokers to select qualified services in terms of QoS of SLA for service composition. Loreto et al. [24] use brokers to integrate telephone business and IT world by means of an intermediate layer. Rosenberg and Dustdar [25] use brokers to bridge the difference between heterogeneous business rules. Bichler et al. [26] promote to use brokers to enhance the application level interpretability of electronic commerce. *SVB* is a value oriented form of "design by unit" [27] which contributes to enable the elasticity of cloud computing. *SVB* distinguishes from these approach since it starts from the service contract which covers more issues than SLA. *SVB* is related to services not only on the technological level, as most SLA based approaches [19], but also on the business level [25,28]. By integrating business services and technology services with value modeling, *SVB* identifies a bigger diagram where it can be successfully applied.

6 Conclusion and Future Work

Service value broker (SVB) is a critical element for constructing a coming era of E-Service Economics since it coherently supports IT implementation of service system and integration of business strategies under the analysis of economical goals. We have empirically collected useful SVBs which can be reused directly by stakeholder in [8]. Value added is a main driven force for adoption and application of SVB by different stakeholder. In this paper, we have analyzed various sources of value added covering service including providers, customers and the public administrative sides. We modeled the value added calculation and analysis based on experimental data to demonstrate the advantage of applying SVB. In the future, we will improve the added value modeling modules on each parties and consider comprehensive business applications in the E-Tourism markets in Hainan province for further refinement and validations.

Acknowledgment. This paper was supported in part by CNSF grant 61162010 and 61363007 and by HNU Research program grant KYQD1242 and HDSF201310.

References

1. Gamma, E., Helm, R., Johnson, R.E., Vlissides, J.M.: Design patterns: Abstraction and reuse of object-oriented design. In: Wang, J. (ed.) ECOOP 1993. LNCS, vol. 707, pp. 406–431. Springer, Heidelberg (1993)
2. Duan, Y., Kattepur, A., Du, W.: Service value broker patterns: Integrating business modeling and economic analysis with knowledge management. In: IEEE ICWS, pp. 615–616 (June 2013)
3. Plummer, D.: Cloud services brokerage: A must-have for most organizations.
4. Kattepur, A., Benveniste, A., Jard, C.: Optimizing decisions in web services orchestrations. In: Kappel, G., Maamar, Z., Motahari-Nezhad, H.R. (eds.) ICSOC 2011, LNCS, vol. 7084, pp. 77–91. Springer, Heidelberg (2011)
5. Duan, Y.: Service Contracts: Current state and Future Directionsmeasure. In: ICWS, pp. 664–665 (2012)
6. Duan, Y.: A Survey on Service Contract. In: SNPD, pp. 805–810. IEEE Computer Society Press (2012)
7. Wang, Y., Wei, J.: Viaf: Verification-based integrity assurance framework for mapreduce. In: IEEE CLOUD, pp. 300–307 (2011)
8. Duan, Y., Kattepur, A., Zhou, H., Chang, Y., Huang, M., Du, W.: Service value broker patterns: An empirical collection. In: IEEE SNPD, pp. 675–682 (2013)
9. Duan, Y.: Value Modeling and Calculation for Everything as a Service (XaaS) based on Reuse. In: Proceedings of SNPD 2012. IEEE Computer Society (2012)
10. Feldstein, M.: Domestic saving and international capital movements in the long run and the short run. Technical Report 947, National Bureau of Economic Research (1982)
11. Fowley, F., Pahl, C., Zhang, L.: A comparison framework and review of service brokerage solutions for cloud architectures. In: Service-Oriented Computing - ICSOC 2013 Workshops and PhD Symposium (2013)
12. Pan, Z., Baik, J.: Qos broker-based trust model for effective web service selection. In: Proceedings of the 11th IASTED SEA2007, Anaheim, CA, USA, pp. 590–595 (2007)
13. Kumar, P.S.A., Mahadevan, G., Krishna, C.G.: Article: A qos towards dynamic web services recapitulation and selection. International Journal of Computer Applications 54(4), 12–18 (2012)
14. Ran, S.: A model for web services discovery with qos. SIGecom Exch. 4(1), 1–10 (2003)
15. Casati, F., Ilnicki, S., Jin, L., Krishnamoorthy, V., Shan, M.-C.: Adaptive and dynamic service composition in eFlow. In: Wangler, B., Bergman, L.D. (eds.) CAiSE 2000. LNCS, vol. 1789, pp. 13–31. Springer, Heidelberg (2000)
16. Moore, B., Mahmoud, Q.H.: A service broker and business model for saas applications. In: AICCSA, pp. 322–329 (2009)
17. Farmer, R., Raybone, A., Uddin, R., Odetayo, M., Chao, K.M.: Metadata discovery for a service-broker architecture. In: Proceedings of the 2008 IEEE International Conference on e-Business Engineering, pp. 173–178 (2008)

18. Shi, C., Lin, D., Ishida, T.: User-centered qos computation for web service selection. In: ICWS, pp. 456–463 (2012)
19. Yu, T., Lin, K.-J.: A broker-based framework for qos-aware web service composition. In: EEE, pp. 22–29 (2005)
20. Gkourtesis, D., Bratanis, K., Friesen, A., Verginadis, Y., Simons, A.J.H., Rossini, A., Schwichtenberg, A., Gouvas, P.: Brokerage for quality assurance and optimization of cloud services: an analysis of key requirements. In: Service-Oriented Computing - ICSOC 2013 Workshops and PhD Symposium (2013)
21. Venugopal, S., Buyya, R., Winton, L.: A grid service broker for scheduling distributed data-oriented applications on global grids. In: MGC, pp. 75–80 (2004)
22. Qian, Z., Lu, S., Xie, L.: Mobile-agent-based web service composition. In: Zhuge, H., Fox, G.C. (eds.) GCC 2005. LNCS, vol. 3795, pp. 35–46. Springer, Heidelberg (2005)
23. D'Mello, D.A., Ananthanarayana, V.S., Thilagam, S.: A qos broker based architecture for dynamic web service selection. In: Proceedings of AMS 2008, pp. 101–106 (2008)
24. Loreto, S., Mecklin, T., Opsenica, M., Rissanen, H.-M.: Service broker architecture: location business case and mashups. Comm. Mag. 47(4), 97–103 (2009)
25. Rosenberg, F., Dustdar, S.: Design and implementation of a service-oriented business rules broker. In: CECW, pp. 55–63 (2005)
26. Bichler, M., Segev, A., Beam, C.: An electronic broker for business-to-business electronic commerce on the internet. Int. J. Cooperative Inf. Syst. 7(4), 315–330 (1998)
27. Tai, S., Leitner, P., Dustdar, S.: Design by units: Abstractions for human and compute resources for elastic systems. IEEE Internet Computing 16(4), 84–88 (2012)
28. Ferreira, J.E., Braghetto, K.R., Takai, O.K., Pu, C.: Transactional recovery support for robust exception handling in business process services. In: ICWS, pp. 303–310 (2012)

Introduction to the Proceedings of the 9th International Workshop on Semantic Web Enabled Software Engineering (SWESE) 2013

Gerd Gröner[1], Jeff Z. Pan[2], Yuting Zhao[2], Elisa F. Kendall[3], and Ljiljana Stojanovic[4]

[1]Paluno – The Ruhr Institute for Software Technology
University of Duisburg-Essen, Germany
[2]University of Aberdeen
Aberdeen, UK
[3]Sandpiper Software Inc.
USA
[4]FZI, Forschungszentrum Informatik
Karlsruhe, Germany

Preface

The 9th international workshop on *Semantic Web Enabled Software Engineering (SWESE)* has been hold in conjunction with the 11th International Conference on Service Oriented Computing (ICSOC 2013) in Berlin, Germany. This workshop builds on prior events and have begun to explore and evaluate the potential of Semantic Web technologies in software, system and service engineering. Semantic Web technologies provide understandable modeling formalisms and tractable reasoning services with widely established tool support. In this workshop series, we are interested in applying Semantic Web technologies to support, improve and ease both the process and product of software and service development.

The advent of the World Wide Web has led many corporations to web-enable their business applications and to adopt web service standard in systems and platforms. However, as a next step, it is expected that technologies and methods from the Semantic Web research will provide various benefits to software and service engineering. Over the past years, there have been several attempts to bring together languages and tools, such as the Unified Modeling Language (UML), developed for software engineering, with Semantic Web languages such as RDF and OWL. The Semantic Web Best Practice and Deployment Working Group (SWBPD) in W3C included a Software Engineering Task Force (SETF) to investigate potential benefits.

The SWESE 2013 workshop has been a successful event in terms of high quality presentations, valuable and constructive discussions, and interesting and novel research papers. The workshop was started with a retrospection on related research and research questions that have been addressed in the European project MOST (Marrying Ontologies and Software Technologies), presented by the workshop organizers. Thereafter, novel research results on Semantic Web technologies in software and service engineering has been shown. Several papers addressed (Web) service discovery, composition and matchmaking. A new approach for Web service composition based on fluent calculus has been discussed. Another approach uses OWL-S in a multi-agent system for

A.R. Lomuscio et al. (Eds.): ICSOC 2013 Workshops, LNCS 8377, pp. 223–224, 2014.
© Springer International Publishing Switzerland 2014

service matchmaking and planning. Another area of the workshop was variability management in ontologies. Ontologies for data models, domain models and population of domain models has been extensively discusses and the presented research results outlined interesting solutions to contemporary software and service engineering problems.

We sincerely thank the program committee members of SWESE 2013 for their great support in the reviewing process. We would also like to thank the authors and workshop participants for their involvement.

The SWESE 2013 organizers

Management of Variability in Modular Ontology Development

Melanie Langermeier[1], Peter Rosina[1], Heiner Oberkampf[1,2], Thomas Driessen[1], and Bernhard Bauer[1]

[1] Software Methodologies for Distributed Systems, University Augsburg, Germany
[2] Siemens AG, Corporate Technology, Munich, Germany

Abstract. The field of variability management deals with the formalization of mandatory, alternative and optional domain concepts in product line engineering. Ontologies in turn, describe domain knowledge in form of predicates, subjects and constraints in various forms. Based on existing ontology mapping approaches, we developed a method to organize a set of modular ontologies using the concepts of variability management (MOVO). This ontology driven variability model can be stepwise adapted to the needs of a business driven one, resulting in a variability model that fits the needs of business and makes modular ontologies reusable in a simple manner. In order to avoid a technological break and to benefit from the opportunities that ontologies offer, the resulting variability model is expressed in an ontology itself. The approach is evaluated by one case study with enterprise architecture ontologies.

Keywords: Modular Ontology Management, Variability Management, Feature Models, Ontology Mapping.

1 Introduction

Knowledge management (KM) is a central aspect in organizations. KM tools mainly rely on knowledge models, specifying how knowledge is represented. In general, there is not one single knowledge model which could be used within all applications or tools. In contrast, the knowledge models used in KM tools are largely dependent on the application and/or the customer's/department's needs. Within one organization, different departments might need different models to describe their knowledge, even though parts of their models describe similar aspects. Since the creation of knowledge models is costly and error prone, it is desirable to reuse existing knowledge models which have proven to be useful and only customize them to specific needs. Modular developed knowledge models allow to reuse parts and ease the customization. Similar to software products, knowledge models have certain logical and functional dependencies. What we need, is a mechanism to make these dependencies between modules of knowledge models transparent in order to enable a flexible combination of them.

In classical software product lines, the variability management has proven to be useful. Thereby, commonalities and differences between domain concepts are made explicit and allow an effective management of the variability in the product development process. This systematical approach enables a consequent reuse of existing concepts and

A.R. Lomuscio et al. (Eds.): ICSOC 2013 Workshops, LNCS 8377, pp. 225–239, 2014.
© Springer International Publishing Switzerland 2014

makes possible combinations and dependencies transparent [7]. This general-purpose and reusable methodology is not only applicable to software products.

Ontologies, and in particular the Web Ontology Language OWL 2[1], have become very popular for the representation of knowledge. Ontologies offer a flexible and powerful way to represent a shared understanding of a conceptualization of some domain [15]. Efficient reuse of (parts of) ontologies is one of the main goals behind modular ontology development [24]. OWL offers some mechanisms, such as the `owl:import` relation, to combine and integrate ontologies. The use of logical axioms contained in different ontologies, however, restricts the possible combinations. A formalism representing these restrictions is needed.

The management of possible combinations of modular knowledge models is similar to the management of variabilities in software products. In this paper, we describe the use of variability management for the management of modular ontologies (MOVO), i.e., to describe the logical and functional dependencies between ontologies. Each possible variant is described through a set of features, that are linked to ontology modules. In our scenario, the knowledge engineer (KE) iteratively selects ontology modules from the ontology repository and creates the variability model (VM) using these ontology modules. In each iterative step, validations are run on the ontology to check the consistency of the VM. The resulting VMs are realized with feature models, formalized in OWL, and stored in a VM Repository. They are instantiated to create specific customized application ontologies. Formalizing feature models with OWL avoids a technology break and enables the use of reasoning capabilities to support the KE by detecting and dissolving inconsistencies in individual and aligned ontologies. We evaluate our approach with an enterprise architecture (EA) case study.

The remainder of the paper is organized as follows: in section 2 we describe the state of the art in modular ontology development and variability management, followed by an overview of related work in section 3. Based on this, we describe our proposed method in section 4 and their technical realization in section 5. The evaluation is done with the aid of our use case in section 6, before we conclude our work in section 7.

2 State of the Art

2.1 Modular Ontology Development

Large ontologies have certain disadvantages regarding reuse and performance. Modular ontology development tries to overcome these obstacles. The general idea is to keep ontologies small in creating ontology modules focusing on one particular aspect to enhance (partial) reuse and performance (e.g. more efficient reasoning), ease maintenance (smaller ontologies are easier to comprehend) and collaborative development as well as harmonization and interoperability (using common upper ontologies, it is easier to identify mappings). Details can be found in [24] and [25]. These modules themselves are again ontologies [12]. Application ontologies, which have to cover different topics, are created using several small ontologies (modules). A number of different promising approaches have already been investigated and evaluated [25]. In accord with [21], modularized ontologies cover two separate topics: (1) module extraction (i.e., modularization

[1] `http://www.w3.org/TR/owl2-overview/`

of existing large ontologies into smaller logically consistent modules) and (2) modular development (i.e., the creation of modular (non-redundant, orthogonal) ontologies). Our work targets the management of ontology modules and their composition into one application ontology. With OWL 2, we have a standardized vocabulary for the description of ontology meta data such as the ontology IRI, `owl:versionInfo`, or `owl:versionIRI` and relations between ontologies such as `owl:imports`, `owl:backwardCompatibleWith`, `owl:incompatibleWith` or `owl:priorVersion`. All relations between ontologies, except `owl:imports`, are annotation properties and have only a documentation purpose or describe functional dependencies.

Similarly, the Vocabulary of a Friend ontology[2] (VOAF) defines properties to express relations between RDFS vocabularies or OWL ontologies: for instance, `voaf:reliesOn`, `voaf:extends`, `voaf:specializes` or `voaf:generalizes` can be used to *indicate* how some ontology is related to others. Besides relations between ontologies, OWL also offers relations between concepts of different ontologies, e.g., stating equivalence between individuals and classes respectively. These relations are regarded by standard reasoners. With `owl:imports`, other ontologies can be included into an ontology through reference onto the other ontology's IRI. Critic concerning this approach has come up, because it is not possible to only import parts of another ontology, but only all the axioms of the other ontology. Therefore, if just a subset of another ontology is needed, a modularization can be helpful. Simply referencing single entities of another ontology, without using the `owl:imports` construct, does not transfer its semantics and context. Working with modules leads to ontology mappings to align different modules. According to [8] there are three types of mappings: *i.)* mapping between one integrated global ontology and various local ontologies; *ii.)* mapping between different local ontologies; and *iii.)* ontology merging and alignment. Since our work focuses on the management and composition of ontology modules, we mainly deal with the second and third type of mappings.

2.2 Variability Management

The discipline of variability management deals with the consequent and explicit documentation of the variability of software artifacts in product line engineering [7]. Variability is the "ability of a system or artifact to be extended, changed, customized, or configured for use in a specific context" [23]. Through a consequent and explicit representation of variabilities using variability modeling techniques, the software engineers are able to manage those and thus complexity in the development process can be reduced [23]. An overview of variability techniques can be found in [7] and [23]. One of the major benefits is the systematic reuse of existing artifacts [6,18,7]. The development of a product in product families is done in two steps: first, in the domain engineering, the commonalities and differences of the products are determined and a set of reusable artifacts like a product family architecture and a set of components is created. Second, during application engineering, the final products are build through configuration of the reusable artifacts [23,6].

Features are a widely used concept for the identification and documentation of variabilities. In the context of software product lines, they are defined as logical units of

[2] `http://purl.org/vocommons/voaf`

behavior that are visible to the end-user [13,3]. These features are encapsulated within components at the architectural level and thus enable an easy inclusion or exclusion of single components [18].

Kang et al. introduced in 1990 the Feature-Oriented Domain Analysis (FODA) with the first Feature Models. They replaced the formerly used sequence diagrams. The intent of the author was "to capture in a model the end-user's (and customer's) understanding of the general capabilities of applications in a domain" [17]. Figure 1 depicts the graphical notation of Kang's feature models. The different features of a domain are structured in Parent-Child-Relationships, which result in a feature tree. Depending on the connection between parent and child, the semantics between both is defined as follows:

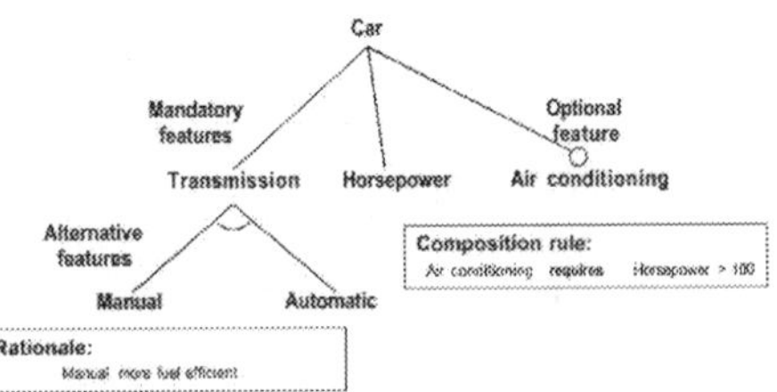

Fig. 1. Graphical notation of the FODA Feature model [17]

Optional Feature:	defined by a line with a circle at its end; can, but has not to be, chosen, if the parent feature is selected.	
Mandatory Feature:	defined by a line without an additional decoration; has to be selected, if the parent feature is selected.	
Alternate Feature:	defined by two or more lines, that are connected via an arc; exactly one of those has be chosen if the parent feature is selected.	
Composition Rule:	dependencies between features of different sub-trees, that can not be expressed in the hierarchical way of the feature tree.	
	Requires:	a feature has to be selected, based on the selection of another feature.
	Mutually exclusive with:	a feature must not be selected if another feature is already selected.

This kind of feature model is restricted to the analysis phase of a software project. Kang et al. extended his approach to the design phase of a project (Feature-oriented reuse method, FORM) [16]. In order to be able to reference possible implementations of a feature in code, Kang et al. introduced the concept of layers, explicit generalizations and an implemented-by reference. Czarnecki et al. extended the FODA Feature model with concepts for the assignment of cardinalities to features and feature groups, the assignment of data types to features and the definition of references from features to the root of another feature tree [10].

3 Related Work

The state of the art regarding modular ontologies, as well as mappings, are described in section 2.1. There, we also described existing vocabularies for relations between ontologies like, e.g., those provided by OWL or VOAF. In this section, we describe related work regarding the use of ontologies to represent feature models and to use established reasoning mechanisms to validate them. The expressiveness of feature models (FM) in comparison to ontologies is analyzed, for instance, in [11]. They identified, that basic feature models are less expressive than OWL ontologies. However, there exist several extensions of basic feature models enhancing the expressiveness, e.g., the addition of attributes, the cloning of entities or feature value constraints. [26] describe, which requirements should be fulfilled by a Semantic Web technology-based feature model: *automated inconsistency detection*, *reasoning efficiency*, *scalability*, *expressivity* and *debugging aids*. They state, that "OWL can be adopted to reason and check feature models effectively". OWL DL syntax is used to represent feature models, where feature nodes are represented as OWL classes. They demonstrate that all of the standard feature model relations (mandatory, optional, alternative, or) as well as simple constraints (excludes, requires) can be represented. Similarly, [27] use OWL DL to represent feature models, even though the modeling is significantly different to [26]. In [27], classes are used to represent features, compositions, feature attributes and feature relations. OWL properties are used to represent feature to feature constraints, attribute value constraints and compositional properties. The consistency is checked using an OWL DL reasoner and SWRL rules, e.g., the mutual exclusiveness of certain properties. In summary, the model presented by [27] is even more expressive than the one presented by [26]. Another approach of using ontologies for modeling variability in a product/service family domain is presented in [19]. In this approach not only the variability itself is captured in an ontology, but also the reasons that led to the respective variability point.

[20] use FMs and ontologies to support the selection of features in multi-cloud configurations. Their method proposes to create the FM first, then map a cloud (the domain) ontology's concepts to the FM's features until every connection is established. These procedures are performed manually by domain experts. Afterwards, they are validating their model. In contrast to our approach, they are using EMF meta models, resp. XMI models, that represent their FMs, as well as their ontologies and mapping models. This way, ontological (OWL) reasoning cannot be performed, but they propose using a SAT solver, for instance Sat4j [2], for checking the FM's configuration validity.

4 Method

In the following, we propose our method for the management of variability in modular ontology development (MOVO). This method aims to address the issues of modular ontology development described in section 3. Thereby, our method focuses on dealing with the complexity of mandatory and optional dependencies between the single modules as well as mandatory exclusions between them. Figure 2 shows the main concepts of MOVO as well as the two phases of the method. In the first step, the KE has to select the modular ontologies, which will be stored in the ontology

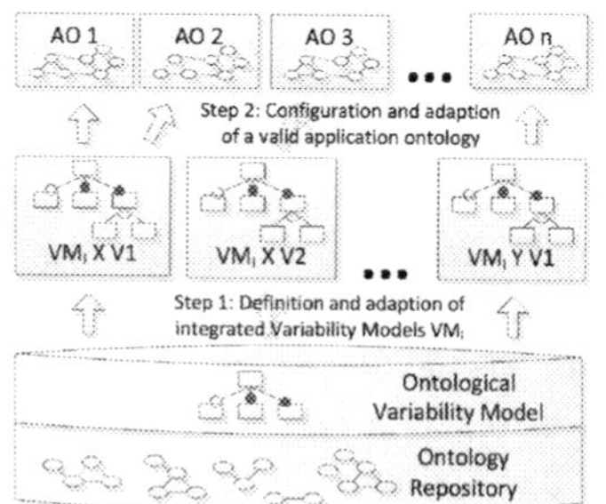

Fig. 2. Overview of the concepts in MOVO

repository. Based on those ontologies an ontological variability model VM_O is defined. VM_O formalizes the dependencies between the modular ontologies that are annotated in the ontologies. It defines allowed and not allowed variants of the application ontology. The variants are defined using features which could/should be (not) included. Each feature can, but has not to, be linked to one or more modular ontologies. Based on VM_O, the KE creates VM_I through selection of features and relationships and addition of stronger constraints according to specific domain requirements. This model formalizes the dependencies according to the requirements from the domain while considering the ontological restrictions. In other words, it formalizes which variants make sense and which not in combination with what is allowed and what is not allowed.

VM_O formalizes the dependencies annotated in the ontologies whereas VM_I customizes these constraints according to specific domain requirements. We differentiate between these models to be able to differentiate between ontological and domain specific requirements and therefore enable the creation of several VM_I for different domains upon one set of ontological modules. The method ensures that the created VM_I is consistent according to the `owl:import` and `owl:incompatibleWith` assertions, which can be made in the single ontological modules. After the creation of a consistent VM_I by the KE, the domain expert can easily create consistent configurations for his application ontology. Figure 3 illustrates the relationships between the concepts used in MOVO.

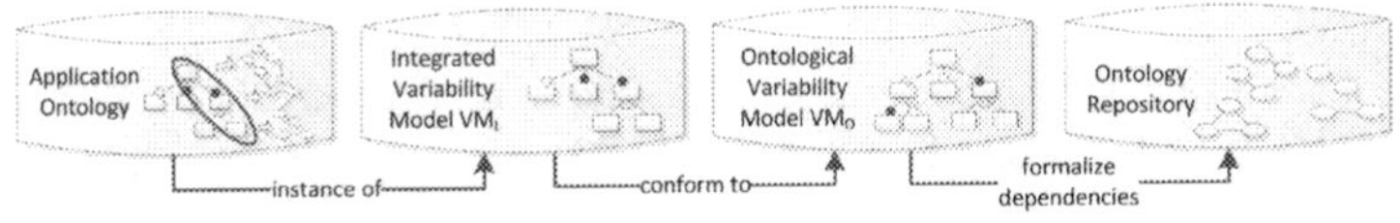

Fig. 3. Concepts and their relationships required for the definition of the VM

In the following, the definition of the ontological VM, along with the creation of the ontology repository, the definition of the integrated VM as well as the configuration of an application ontology, are described in more detail. The technical realization of those steps is described in section 5.

4.1 Define Ontological Variability Model VM_O

Before the ontological variability model VM_O can be determined, the KE has to fill the ontology repository. There are several sources for modular ontologies: reuse of existing ontologies, modularization of existing bigger ontologies or creation of new ontologies. Creating mappings between different vocabularies can either be done manually or with the assistance of automated methods. These methods for matching heterogeneous resource models with semantic technologies are introduced and explained in [22].

In the next step, the meta data and assertions of the modular ontologies in the repository are analyzed to determine the dependencies between them. For this work we decided to focus on the assertions that can be realized using OWL 2. These are the `owl:import` and the version informations. Whereas from the later one only the `owl:incompatibleWith` has effects for the definition of consistent variants. At the moment, OWL 2 does not offer an annotation property that expresses an inconsistency between two different ontologies. Therefore, we introduce an `movo:inconsistent` relationship, to be able to assert such an information. To create VM_O for each modular ontology, one feature will be created with a link to the corresponding ontology. The dependencies between the ontologies are then formalized in the ontological VM. This model is consistent in sense of allowed combinations of the modular ontologies, but it must not necessarily fulfill certain requirements of the domain. This newly created VM_O acts as the bootstrapping VM for the following creation of VM_I.

4.2 Define Integrated Variability Model VM_I

The integrated Variability Model VM_I can extend and restrict VM_O to be conform to specific requirements of the application domain. Thereby, new features or relations can be added and existing relations between features can be strengthened. For the creation of VM_I, the KE has to select a root feature(existing from VM_O or new one), and then repeats the following loop until all desired features are considered.

i.) Select a parent feature from VM_I or a new one
ii.) Select a child feature from VM_O or VM_I or a new one
iii.) Determination of valid relations that can be used to connect those features
iv.) Select the new features' type of relation
v.) Automatic addition of the features with their relations to VM_I
vi.) Optional: add further cross-tree constraints

Cross-tree constraints can be necessary, for example, when defining that a specific mapping ontology $OntA2OntB$ should be always used for two ontologies $OntA$ and $OntB$. In this case, the constraint $OntA \wedge OntB \rightarrow OntA2OntB$ is necessary to ensure that the mapping ontology $OntA2OntB$ is selected when $OntA$ and $OntB$ are selected. Finally the KE has an integrated VM which represents all allowed and useful variants of the application ontology.

4.3 Configuration of a Specific Knowledge Model

Preliminary for this step is the defined VM_I. The domain expert is then able to create a specific configuration which serves as an application ontology. Therefore, he selects those features from a list of selectable features he wants to have included in his configuration. After each feature he selects, a consistency check will take place. First, it will be checked, if there is any required feature that is not yet included in the final configuration. If so, then this feature will be included. Second, after the addition of a feature, all features that are excluded by this feature will be deleted from the list of selectable features. At the beginning, the list of selectable features SF includes all features that are in VM_I: $SF := \{f \mid f \in VM_I\}$. The list of selected features in the configuration C is empty at the beginning. If a feature f from SF should be inserted into C the insert function is defined as followed:

$$\begin{aligned}
&insert(f) := addToConfiguration(f) \wedge removeExludedFeatures(f) \wedge \\
&\qquad (\forall reqF.((reqF \in SF \wedge f \rightarrow reqF) \rightarrow insert(reqF)) \\
&\text{With } \; addToConfiguration(f) : C := C \cup \{f\} \\
&\qquad removeExludedFeatures(f) : SF := SF \backslash \{exclF \mid exclF \in SF \wedge f \rightarrow \neg exclF\}
\end{aligned}$$

SF ensures that only features can be selected that fit to the current state of the configuration. The last point ensures that no feature will be dismissed that is required by a selected feature in the configuration. After the domain experts has defined his configuration of features, the corresponding ontologies to the features have to be selected and composed to the resulting application ontology.

5 Technical Realization

Along with our method described in the previous chapter, we describe the technical realization of the two main steps: the creation of the ontological and integrated variability model (VM_O and VM_I) and the instantiation of VM_I. The technical realization is exemplary demonstrated using the FODA feature model from [17] described in section 3. In this context, we are using Protégé[3] to create our ontologies and a Fuseki Server[4] as a triple store for our prototype implementation.

5.1 Variability Model Ontology

The VM_O is specified using OWL 2 semantics. The central class of the VM_O is `movo:Feature`. An instance of `movo:Feature` represents a node of the VM and might be related to some ontology of the ontology repository using the object property `movo:isRealizedIn`. As described in section 3, OWL and especially OWL 2 specify several annotation properties for meta information of ontologies and relations between ontologies. Some of them are shown in figure 4. These annotation properties are not interpreted by reasoners, thus the idea is to translate these annotation properties (which describe the coherence between different ontologies) to object properties in VM_O. For instance, we defined the object properties `movo:excludes` (for `owl:incompatibleWith`) and `movo:requires` (for `owl:imports`). The property `movo:excludes` is a symmetric property and is mutual exclusive with `movo:requires` (using `owl:propertyDisjointWith`).

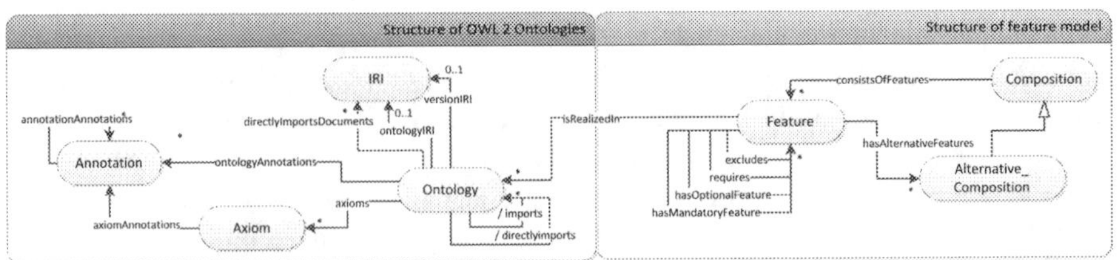

Fig. 4. The Variability Model Ontology combined with OWL 2 Ontology structure [4]

This is similar to ideas presented in [27] where "*Incompatible* and *Excludes* are defined as symmetric properties. Some are mutual exclusive: (*Requires*, *Excludes*), (*Requires*, *Incompatible*), (*Uses*, *Excludes*), (*Extends*, *Incompatible*)". Other OWL annotation properties like `owl:backwardCompatibleWith`, `owl:priorVersion`,

[3] `http://protege.stanford.edu/`; 11/09/2013

[4] `http://jena.apache.org/documentation/serving_data/`; 11/09/2013

owl:deprecated, etc. can be used or realized in VM_O as well and will be considered. In addition to the representation of OWL properties, VM_O has to capture feature model semantics presented in section 2 so that the KE can express further dependencies. For instance, we define properties for optional and mandatory properties, i.e., the relations movo:hasOptionalFeature and movo:hasMandatoryFeature. Again, these properties are mutually exclusive. In our prototype implementation we are using the movo:hasMandatoryFeature and movo:requires relations as logically equivalent properties, because the difference is only important for the graphically distinguished visualization as a feature model tree for the user.

Furthermore, we have a class movo:Composition with the subclass movo:Alternative_Composition to represent alternative compositions (AC). When the AC is created, the source feature is related to the movo:Alternative_Composition via the object property movo:hasAlternativeFeatures. Other compositions, for instance an *OR* composition can be added. Furthermore, enhancements can be made in order to consider the extensions of the FORM feature model, e.g., the cardinalities. The work of [27] demonstrates that OWL DL in combination with some rule language like, e.g., SWRL can be used to represent even more sophisticated feature model constraints.

5.2 Creation of VM_O with Mapping Semantic

Our prototype implementation is realized using a Apache Jena Fuseki triple store with two data sets, one for the ontology repository (ontrepo) and one for the Variability Model Ontology (vmo). We separate ontologies in our repository using named graphs and use the following procedure to create the ontological variability model VM_O: First, for all ontologies in the repository, instances of movo:Feature are created in the dataset vmo. Second, the dependencies between ontologies, such as *import* relations, are transferred to relations between features (see listing 1.1).

```
INSERT {
    ?feature a movo:Feature ;
    movo:isRealizedIn ?ont ;
    movo:requires ?req .
}
WHERE {
    SERVICE <http://localhost:3030/ontrepo/query> {
    SELECT ?feature ?ont ?req ?excl WHERE {
        ?x owl:ontologyIRI ?ont .
        OPTIONAL { ?ont owl:imports ?r .
            BIND (URI(CONCAT("http://www.ds-lab.org/↩
                ontologies/2013/7/variabilityOntology#", ↩
                strafter(str(?r), "http://www.ds-lab.org/↩
                movo/ea/"))) AS ?req) }
        BIND (URI(CONCAT("http://www.ds-lab.org/ontologies↩
            /2013/7/variabilityOntology#", strafter(str(?↩
            ont), "http://www.ds-lab.org/movo/ea/"))) AS ?↩
            feature)
}}}
```

Listing 1.1. Extract of SPARQL statement example for the creation of the ontological Variability Model VM_O

The feature is related to its source ontology by the `movo:isRealizedIn` property. Furthermore, the dependencies between different ontologies are extracted and interpreted, e.g., `owl:imports` to `movo:requires`, using the same SPARQL statement. For other dependencies, such as `owl:incompatibleWith` or `movo:inconsistent`, we have similar update queries. More precisely, for each relation between ontologies, a corresponding relation is added for the respective features. Since the *import* and *incompatible* relations only exist occasionally, we use the `OPTIONAL` statement for these object properties. In this context, we are substituting the resources' URI paths from the ontology repository's source ontologies' location with the new feature ontology's URI path. Thus, the dependencies between ontologies are transformed to the variability model ontology.

During the creation of VM_O, the OWL reasoner and additional SPARQL queries can be used to check the consistency of the created feature model [26]. For instance, it is checked that there are no features related with contradictory properties `movo:excludes` and `movo:requires` at the same time. We are also using SPARQL queries to receive all dependent features, i.e., the required features of the selected feature and thus can add them automatically to our VM_O. Following the principles of the Semantic Web Stack, it is generally advised to use the Rule Interchange Format (RIF) for expressing rules. For instance, RIF would be suitable for stating complex composition rules. Since up to now, RIF is still immature and tool support is hardly available, we use SPARQL in our implementation to insert relations between features.

5.3 Creation of VM_I

The creation of VM_I is done according to section 4.2. Thereby, the features created for VM_O can be reused, but it is also possible to add new features as place-holder features, that do not yet have a relation to an ontology of the ontology repository. For each new feature, a new instance of `movo:Feature` is created and stored in a named graph for the respective VM_I. To ensure that VM_I is conform to VM_O, the integrated variability model will be defined iteratively. In each step, only consistent constraints can be added to the model. The following pseudo code 1.2 represents this procedure.

```
select ROOT FEATURE root
insert(root)
LOOP
    select PARENT FEATURE p
    select CHILD FEATURE[S] c = {c1, .., cn}
    if (|c| = 1)
         then ask(required), ask(hasMandatoryFeature), ask↩
              (excludes)
         else ask(alternateComposition)
    select POSSIBLE RELATION relation
    for all (x in (c or p); x not in VMI)
         insert (x)
    insert(relation)
    OPT: if(ask(crossTreeConstraint))
                       then insert(crossTreeConstraint)
END LOOP
```

Listing 1.2. The procedure for creating VM_I

To ensure the consistency, the following SPARQL queries are defined:

insert(feature): adds an existing feature from VM_O to VM_I with all (transitively) required features

ask/insert(required|hasMandatoryFeature|excludes): asks if possible or inserts the respective relationship between a parent and one child

ask/insert(alternateComposition): asks if possible or inserts an alternate composition between a parent and a set of childs

ask/insert(crossTreeConstraint): asks if possible or inserts a specific cross tree constraint, typically in a manner like '$feature_1$ requires $feature_2$' or '$feature_1$ excludes $feature_2$'

For selecting a specific feature, the following constraints must be satisfied:

select ROOT FEATURE: root $\in VM_O$ or root is a new feature
select PARENT FEATURE: parent $\in VM_O \cup VM_I$ or parent is a new feature
select CHILD FEATURES: c = c_1, .., c_2 with $c_i \in \{VM_O \cup VM_I\}$ or c_i is a new feature

During the creation of object properties between the selected features, some constraints have to be fulfilled: for the sake of simplicity, we only allow the creation of relations between exactly two different features (an exception is the alternative composition(see below)). Additionally, there can only be exactly one or zero relations between two different features. These constraints will be checked using the *ask* queries. Only when these queries return true, the KE can fulfill an insert of the relationship. Adding the `movo:hasOptionalFeature` or the `movo:requires` relation is only valid if there is no `movo:excludes` between the source feature and an existing transitive `movo:requires` path to the target feature. Adding a `movo:excludes` relation is only valid if there is no transitive `movo:requires` or `movo:hasOptionalFeature` in VM_O or VM_I.

A precondition for the creation of the alternative composition (AC) is the non-existence of any relationship from the source feature to any of its target features. We also forbid a transitive `movo:requires` relation between any two features that are in the set of the AC. Besides, to keep it simple, another constraint is that we do not allow the creation of nested or overlapping ACs. This constraint could be relaxed in the future. When the AC is created, the source feature is related to the `movo:Alternative_Composition` via the object property `movo:hasAlternativeFeatures`. Simultaneously, we add `movo:excludes` relations between all members of the AC, since it represents an XOR selection. The AC is the only existing relation between more than two features. Once VM_I is finished, it is saved in a fresh data store.

5.4 Instantiation of VM_I

The instantiation of VM_I corresponds to the creation of the user configuration C (compare section 4). We create a new data set and add a property to each feature in VM_I that expresses its status: selectable, selected and not selectable. According to the rules already described earlier, we automatically select all required features by querying the transitive paths and disable the not selectable features in case of a `movo:excludes` resp. AC relation. The validation of our user configuration using OWL is not part of this paper, because there already exist some reliable approaches (see, e.g., [26] or [27]). Once the final configuration has been found, the qualified ontologies, including the mappings between them, are deployed as the compound application ontology .

6 Evaluation

The design and implementation of enterprise architecture (EA) methods and analyses are dependent on the meta model used in the organization. Typical for EA is, that each organization has its own meta model for EA. Typical for EA is also, that this meta model depends on already existing ones in the different organization units. For example, the process modelers have their model about processes, the IT administrator has its model about the infrastructure and the software development unit has its meta model about the application landscape. To increase the acceptance of the enterprise architecture in the organization, it should be built with respect to those existing models.

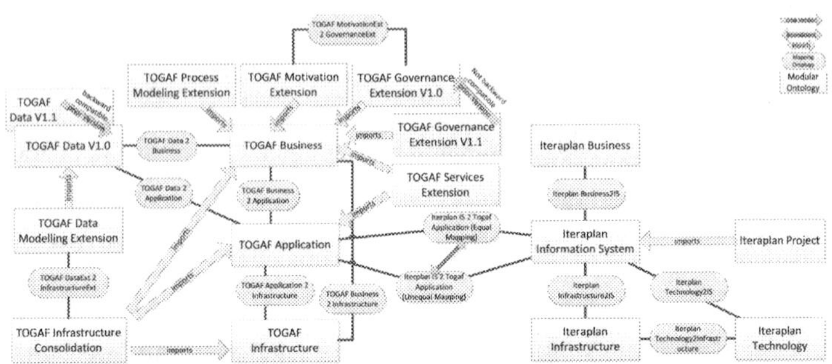

Fig. 5. Modules and their relationships in the EA Use Case

Especially for those providing tool support for EA, this issue is a challenge. On the one hand, the organizations want to rely on existing frameworks and meta models, but, on the other hand, they also want to adapt them to their specific needs. To illustrate this problem, we choose two meta models for enterprise architecture, modularize them, and establish a variant model, which allows a flexible combination of different parts of the meta model. This enables the tool provider, who plays the role of the KE, to establish methods, that support the enterprise architect, independently from the final meta model or with respect to a special selection. The enterprise architect, which will be the domain expert, can easily create his desired configuration which will act as his customized meta model.

For the case study we choose the TOGAF Core Content Metamodel[5], a standard from the Open Group, and the meta model behind the enterprise architecture tool iteraplan[6]. To get modular ontologies, we first divided the two meta models into smaller modules according to the architecture layers the frameworks present. The relationships between these layers are represented through import relationships and mapping ontologies. I.e. there exist two different mappings from Iterplan Information System to the TOGAF Application module, that cannot be used together. All determined modules with the mapping ontologies and imports are shown in figure 5. This set of modules represents the ontology repository. The generated VM_O formalizes the `owl:imports`

[5] `http://pubs.opengroup.org/architecture/togaf9-doc/arch/chap34.html`

[6] `http://www.iteraplan.de`

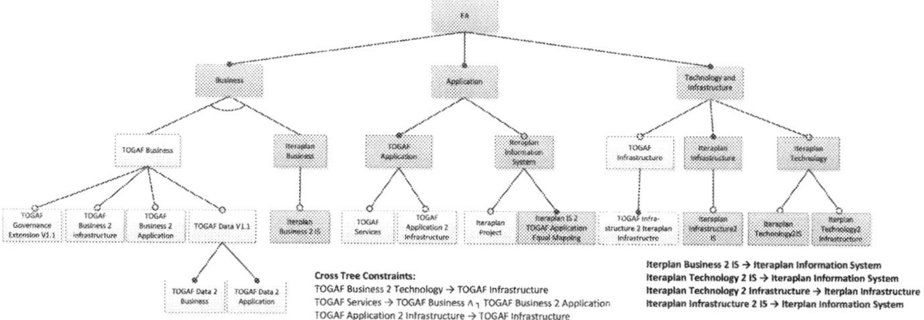

Fig. 6. Feature Model VM_I in the EA Use Case

and `owl:incompatibleWith` relationships. All relationships are correctly transformed into *required* and *exclude* relationships.

For the further evaluation, we define and establish an integrated variability model by selecting the desired features and adding further constraints. The shaded rectangles highlight a possible configuration. The integrated variability model with the configuration is shown in figure 6. VM_I is conform to VM_O and we are able to model all requirements from the domain. All *ask* queries enable us to insert the desired relationships. Additionally, every other required module, that we do not explicitly select, is inserted. To model the alternate choice between the iteraplan business and the TOGAF business module, we create a feature, that is not linked to any ontology. This enables the modeling of a choice between several features. We also introduce such empty features for the other architectural layers, since the resulting feature model is more comprehensive for a domain expert. These empty features are depicted by dashed lines surrounding the rectangles. Furthermore, we introduce one more feature that is not related to any ontology. This ontology has to be added if this feature is selected in a configuration.

Our test set for the evaluation, including the data sets, queries and a documentation, has been published at `http://megastore.uni-augsburg.de/get/HAth0VS7qw/`.

7 Conclusion

In this paper, we proposed a method for the management of modular ontological models. We especially addressed the problem that the dependencies between the single modules can not be specified using the standard OWL vocabulary. We use the concept of variability management in software product line engineering and adapted it to the domain of modular ontology management to be able to formalize possible combinations of the modules. Therefore, we defined a mapping from the OWL concepts `owl:imports` and `owl:incompatibleWith` as well as from `movo:inconsistent` to the concepts `movo:requires`, `movo:excludes`, `movo:hasMandatoryFeature` and `movo:Alternative_Composition` to determine an ontological variability model. Additionally, we provide a method to create an integrated variability model which is, on the one hand, conform to the ontological variability model, which specifies what is allowed and what not. On the other hand, it specifies what makes sense and what not in the resp. business domain. Based on the integrated variability model, a domain expert can easily create her application ontology through selection of those features she wants to have. The required set of ontologies to create the application ontology can then be retrieved from the variability model using existing feature model solver. To be able to use the reasoning techniques of ontologies we defined the variability model ontology to express the VMs in ontologies.

Our method enables the reuse and flexible combination of knowledge modules in several application ontologies. Thereby, it ensures that the resulting application ontology is conform to the annotations that are made in the ontology modules and also to the requirements that the KE specified. Our goal is to support KEs in assembling a customized ontology set by providing a modeling environment that applies semantic technologies.

Future work has to be done to explicitly provide methods to adapt the variability model when changes in the ontology or requirements for the features have taken place. In our prototype implementation, we are just using two annotations of the given OWL functionality for combining modular ontologies. In the future, we want to cover additional annotation possibilities in OWL, vocabularies like VOAF and also consider more expressive approaches for defining coherences between the ontologies. Alternative approaches, like $\mathcal{E}$-Connections [9], Package Based Description Logics (P-DL) [1], Distributed Description Logics (DLL) [5] or the Interface-based modular ontology Formalism (IBF) [14] are eligible alternatives and extensions for modular ontologies. These approaches offer similar functionalities: they offer bridge rules between multiple ontologies, a specific *point of views* interpretation for modular ontologies or the support for well-defined interfaces between the ontological modules. Therefore, we also want to extend the expressiveness of the method and the variability model ontology, e.g., with an OR composition or cardinalities.

References

1. Bao, J., Caragea, D., Honavar, V.G.: Modular ontologies - A formal investigation of semantics and expressivity. In: Mizoguchi, R., Shi, Z.-Z., Giunchiglia, F. (eds.) ASWC 2006. LNCS, vol. 4185, pp. 616–631. Springer, Heidelberg (2006)
2. Berre, D.L., Parrain, A.: The Sat4j library, release 2.2. JSAT 7(2-3), 6–59 (2010)
3. Beuche, D., Papajewski, H., Schrder-Preikschat, W.: Variability management with feature models. Science of Computer Programming 53(3) (December 2004)
4. Bock, C., Fokoue, A., Haase, P., Hoekstra, R., Horrocks, I., Ruttenberg, A., Sattler, U., Smith, M.: OWL 2 Web Ontology Language Structural Specification and Functional-Style Syntax. Tr, W3C (2009)
5. Borgida, A., Serafini, L.: Distributed Description Logics: Assimilating Information from Peer Sources. Journal on Data Semantics 1, 153–184 (2003)
6. Bosch, J., Florijn, G., Greefhorst, D., Kuusela, J., Obbink, J.H., Pohl, K.: Variability issues in software product lines. In: van der Linden, F. (ed.) PFE 2002. LNCS, vol. 2290, pp. 13–21. Springer, Heidelberg (2002)
7. Chen, L., Babar, M.A., Ali, N.: Variability management in software product lines: a systematic review. In: Proceedings of the 13th International Software Product Line Conference, SPLC 2009, pp. 81–90 (2009)
8. Choi, N., Song, I.-Y., Han, H.: A survey on ontology mapping. SIGMOD Rec. 35(3), 34–41 (2006)

9. Cuenca Grau, B., Parsia, B., Sirin, E.: Ontology integration using ε-connections. In: Stuckenschmidt, H., Parent, C., Spaccapietra, S. (eds.) Modular Ontologies. LNCS, vol. 5445, pp. 293–320. Springer, Heidelberg (2009)
10. Czarnecki, K., Helsen, S., Eisenecker, U.: Staged Configuration Using Feature Models. In: Nord, R.L. (ed.) SPLC 2004. LNCS, vol. 3154, pp. 266–283. Springer, Heidelberg (2004)
11. Czarnecki, K., Hwan, C., Kalleberg, K.T.: Feature Models are Views on Ontologies. In: Software Product Line Conference, vol. 1 (2006)
12. d'Aquin, M., Haase, P., Rudolph, S., Euzenat, J., Zimmermann, A., Dzbor, M., Iglesias, M., Jacques, Y., Caracciolo, C., Aranda, C.B., Gomez, J.M.: NeOn Formalisms for Modularization: Syntax, Semantics, Algebra. Deliverable 1.1.3, NeOn Integrated Project (2008)
13. de Oliveira Junior, E.A., Gimenes, I.M., Huzita, E.H.M., Maldonado, J.C.: A variability management process for software product lines. In: Proceedings of the 2005 Conference of the Centre for Advanced Studies on Collaborative Research, pp. 225–241 (2005)
14. Ensan, F.: Semantic Interface-Based Modular Ontology Framework. PhD thesis, University of New Brunswick (2010)
15. Gruber, T.R.: Toward Principles for the Design of Ontologies Used for Knowledge Sharing. International Journal Human-Computer Studies 43, 907–928 (1993)
16. Kang, K., Kim, S., Lee, J., Kim, K., Shin, E., Huh, M.: FORM: A feature-oriented reuse method with domain-specific reference architectures. Annals of Software Engineering 5(1), 143–168 (1998)
17. Kang, K.C., Cohen, S.G., Hess, J.A., Novak, W.E., Peterson, A.S.: Feature-Oriented Domain Analysis (FODA) Feasibility Study. Technical report. Carnegie-Mellon University Software Engineering Institute (1990)
18. Lee, J., Muthig, D.: Feature-oriented variability management in product line engineering. Communications of the ACM - Software Product Line 49(12) (December 2006)
19. Mohan, K., Ramesh, B.: Ontology-based support for variability management in product and families. In: Proceedings of the 36th Annual Hawaii International Conference on System Sciences, p. 9. IEEE (2003)
20. Quinton, C., Haderer, N., Rouvoy, R., Duchien, L.: Towards multi-cloud configurations using feature models and ontologies. In: Proceedings of the 2013 International Workshop on Multi-Cloud Applications and Federated Clouds, MultiCloud 2013, pp. 21–26. ACM, New York (2013)
21. Rector, A., Brandt, S., Drummond, N., Horridge, M., Pulestin, C., Stevens, R.: Engineering use cases for modular development of ontologies in OWL. Applied Ontology 7, 113–132 (2012)
22. Shvaiko, P., Euzenat, J.: Ontology Matching: State of the Art and Future Challenges. IEEE Transactions on Knowledge and Data Engineering 25(1), 158–176 (2013)
23. Sinnema, M., Deelstra, S.: Classifying variability modeling techniques. Journal of Information and Software Technology 49(7) (July 2007)
24. Spaccapietra, S., Menken, M., Stuckenschmidt, H., Wache, H., Serafini, L., Tamilin, A.: D2.1.3.1 - Report on Modularization of Ontologies (July 2005)
25. Stuckenschmidt, H., Parent, C., Spaccapietra, S. (eds.): Modular Ontologies. LNCS, vol. 5445. Springer, Berlin (2009)
26. Wang, H.H., Li, Y.F., Sun, J., Zhang, H., Pan, J.: Verifying feature models using OWL. Web Semantics: Science, Services and Agents on the World Wide Web 5(2), 117–129 (2007)
27. Zaid, L.A., Kleinermann, F., De Troyer, O.: Applying semantic web technology to feature modeling. In: Proceedings of the 2009 ACM Symposium on Applied Computing, SAC 2009. ACM, New York (2009)

Towards Automated Service Matchmaking and Planning for Multi-Agent Systems with OWL-S – Approach and Challenges

Johannes Fähndrich, Nils Masuch, Hilmi Yildirim, and Sahin Albayrak

DAI-Labor, TU Berlin
Ernst-Reuter-Platz 7, 10587 Berlin, Germany
forename.surname@dai-labor.de

Abstract. In the past, the demand for modular, distributed and dynamic computer systems has increased rapidly. In the field of multi-agent systems (MAS) many of the current approaches try to account for these requirements. In this paper we discuss the shortcomings of the semantic service selection component SeMa^2, propose improvements and describe an integration concept into a multi-agent framework. Further, we illustrate how this system can be extended by an automated service composition component using methods from the AI planning community.

Keywords: OWL-S, Automated Service Selection, Automated Service Composition, Planning, Multi-Agent Systems.

1 Introduction

Distributed systems based on the Service Oriented Architecture (SOA) paradigm have become more and more popular in recent years. One of its inherent strengths is the definition of a clear autonomy of each service, which means that it is represented as a separate module. Further, services are designed for enhancing the reusability as well as the interoperability which is one of the key issues for distributed systems. Especially when talking about huge computer systems with different providers and parties involved these attributes are essential.

In order to cope with dynamic aspects in huge systems, such as the immediate (dis-)appearance of services, solutions to adapt the process via an automated service selection and composition are desirable. As a first step, service matching techniques have been developed that enable the automated selection of services. However, this is not enough when the system has to deal with complex goals, where the involvement of different services is necessary. In this case, the system needs some form of automated service composition solution, which can also be interpreted as planning. In the area of multi-agent systems and AI in general there has been done research leading to approaches, such as hierarchical task networks (HTN) or STRIPS.

In this paper we propose to combine semantic service technologies of the SOA community with the planning techniques of the AI community. We do so by using our semantic service matchmaking component $SeMa^2$ [12] as a fundament and discuss the

A.R. Lomuscio et al. (Eds.): ICSOC 2013 Workshops, LNCS 8377, pp. 240–247, 2014.
© Springer International Publishing Switzerland 2014

adaptions necessary to set up an HTN planning component, which is capable of being integrated into a service-oriented multi-agent framework.

The remainder of the paper is structured as follows. In section 2 we will shortly present the current status of our service matching component $SeMa^2$ and provide new concepts for its improvement in detail. In section 3 we describe our concept of extending $SeMa^2$ by a planning component integrated into a multi-agent system. Section 4 presents the related work in automated service composition. Finally, we close with a conclusion.

2 Automated Service Matchmaking - The SeMa^2 Approach

The service matcher $SeMa^2$ follows a hybrid approach combining logic-based and non-logic-based matching techniques using OWL-S and SWRL. Figure 1 shows all relevant components, for example the *OWLS-ServiceAnalyzer* as the document parser/writer and the *MatcherController* which triggers all different matching techniques and aggregates them to a single result. As for the non-logic-based evaluation $SeMa^2$ processes syntactical comparison on service names (*ServiceName Matcher*) and service descriptions (*TextSimilarity Matcher*) based upon well-known lexicographic techniques, such as Jaccard index or Hamming distance. Further, three different approaches are used for logic-based matching, namely the *Taxonomy Matcher*, the *RuleStructure Matcher* and the *Rule Evaluator*.

All these results are combined via linear weighted aggregation, with no adaptability so far. At the S3 Contest 2012 $SeMa^2$ performed well regarding the precision coming with the best matching accuracy in graded relevance ranking. However, at the contest Rule Evaluation (due to missing ABox information) and RuleStructure Matching (due to syntactic incompatibility of the SWRL services) were not integrated. Internal tests with modified service descriptions have shown, that the integration of rule structure matching has even a minimal negative influence on the results lowering the average precision based on the nDCG-measure from 92,7% to 92,1%. Since there is no obvious reason for that and we consider rule matching as an important part for the matcher to be used in a planning component we decided to formalize our approach at first and then focus on improving the aggregation concept of the different matching techniques.

2.1 Scoring and Aggregation of Different Matching Techniques

Due to the best-first search we are aiming to use in our planning component, the results of the Precondition and Effect (PE) matching are crucial. The rule structure component has multiple matching layers and thus has many decision points on how to rate full, partial or other matches. A further challenge is the assignment of weights to the different matching results to achieve a single score for a service. Each scoring for the equivalence of two concepts can be seen as an expert opinion assigning a probability to the match. For example there could be an expert on *semantic distance based scoring* and one on *logic based scoring*. The resulting probability of equivalence is published to be used by an aggregation method. Doing so, the scorings of an expert will be formalized as $p_i(R,S) \in [0,1]$ with R,S being a request and a service and $i \in \{1,\dots,n\}$ representing

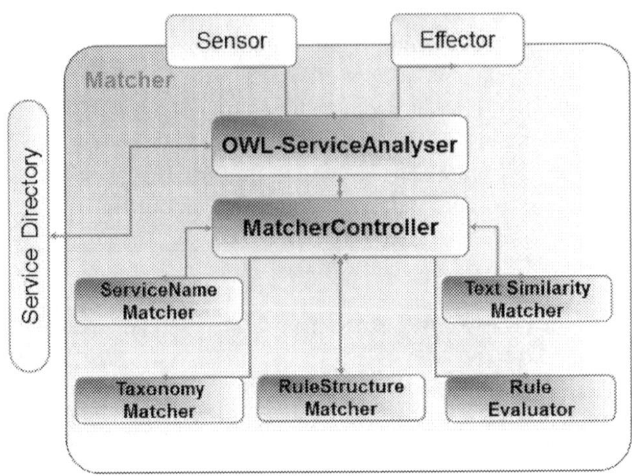

Fig. 1. The component architecture of SeMa^2

one of the n different expert opinions. Right now, each of the expert opinions are evaluated in a static way mapping a concrete result (e.g. full match, sub match, super match) to a fixed value.

In the following we propose different scoring methods to extend the PE matching and present one example in a probabilistic framework similar to [1,7]. Afterwards some aggregation methods taken from information fusion will be presented to create a probabilistic matching score. In SeMa^2 the comparison of concepts is reduced to the equivalence of the URI of ontology and concept. Here a collection of possible extensions is presented. *Semantic distance based scoring* [19] analyzes the embedded ontology of two concepts to find the shortest path from one concept to another. *WordNet based scoring* [1] can be used to find lexical similarity in used words. If two concepts out of different ontologies need to be matched a *bipartite matching score* is able to rate the similarity by i.e. the maximum cardinality match counting the edges between the different concepts. More sophisticated methods use ontology matching to find a semantic relation between concepts. Logic based scoring like proposed in *Approximated Logical Matching* [7] are further scoring methods using reasoning on formal features of the rules describing the preconditions and effects.

Probabilistic Model of Opinion. To formalize such different scoring methods we apply the results of *Morris* [13] and have modeled expert opinions as probabilities $p_i(R,S)$. The following section will detail this model. As an expert observes two concepts and elaborates their semantic distance we can abstract his opinion as $p_i(\Theta|d)$ where Θ is the subject of interest and d are the observations. An expert can then collect evidence for his opinion by conducting multiple observations d_i. Each observation might then be interpreted as evidence to strengthen his opinion. Following *Beyerer* [2] a Bayesian interpretation of the probability the conditional probability $p_i(\Theta|d)$ could be interpreted as a degree of confidence or better a degree of belief. With such an interpretation we can use this formalism to model the expert opinions as described in equation 1.

$$\underbrace{p(\Theta|d)}_{A-Posteriori} = \frac{p(d|\Theta)p(\Theta)}{p(d)} \propto \overbrace{p(d|\Theta)}^{Likelihood-Function} \underbrace{p(\Theta)}_{A-Priori} \quad (1)$$

Here the subject of interest is Θ e.g. equivalence of a Horn-clause. The observations or information used by the expert to assess its opinion is formalized in d. An example of this d could be the attached ontologies to the concept in order to calculate the semantic distance. The expert can update its opinion after observing another d using Bayesian fusion by calculating the product described in equation 1. If one concept for example is a hypernym of the other, $p(d|\Theta)$ could be proportional to the minimal distance between those two concepts [19]. Further, $p(\Theta)$ allows the expert to formalize a-priory knowledge about probability of Θ.

Opinion Aggregation. The opinions $p_i(\Theta|d)$ are collected and need to be fused to one score. Since the experts are not always equally important the possibility to prioritize the weightings of the different expert opinions is a requirement for the fusion method. With the probabilistic formalization of the expert opinions method like the *Dempster-Schafer theory of evidence* [16], fuzzy logic or artificial neuronal networks can be used for information fusion [3]. This work introduces a method of opinion aggregation called pooling method formalized in a function $K(p_1,\ldots,p_n)(\Theta)$. It is acquired by adapting a weighted mean to the aggregation of opinions. We choose a weighted arithmetic mean called linear opinion pool [18]. This arithmetic mean has been generalized by *Genest* [5] to be able to use weights in the interval $[-1,1]$ in a more general class of linear opinion pools (GenLinOP). This opinion pool has the form of equation 2.

$$K(p_1,\ldots,p_n)(\Theta) = \sum_{i=1}^{n} w_i p_i(\Theta) + \left[1 - \sum_{i=1}^{n} w_i\right] R(\Theta) \quad (2)$$

$w_1,\ldots,w_n \in [-1,1]$ are weights and R is an arbitrary probability function, with the restriction: $\forall J \subseteq \{1,\ldots,n\} : \left|\sum_{j\in J} w_j\right| \leq 1$.

The method shown in equation 2 has been chosen because of its theoretical sound standing. Other pooling methods have been and are continued to be evaluated which is subject to research. The GenLinOP has the possibility to include – besides the opinion of the group – an a-priori established probability which can be modeled as $R(\Theta)$.

Taking this theoretical framework as a basis we implement the different measures used in the service matching as experts returning a probability $p_i(\Theta)$ and aggregate them with a pooling method $K(p_1,\ldots,p_n)(\Theta)$. For an example we have adapted the comparison of the arguments of a predicate. The probability here is as follows:

$$p(\Theta) = \begin{cases} \frac{1}{dist(a_r,a_s)} & \text{, if } 1 \geq dist(a_r,a_s) > 0 \\ 1.0 & \text{, if } a_r.getURI() \equiv a_s.getURI() \\ 0 & \text{, else} \end{cases} \quad (3)$$

$dist(a_r, a_s)$ defines the distance between the two concepts as proposed above. In a similar manner all other fixed values will be turned into probabilistic expert opinions. With this change, we are able to distinguish partial argument matches. We want to emphasize the importance of such a partial match for planning tasks. Here multiple services can be used to fulfill the arguments of a predicate in a precondition. Thus on a higher level: we are able to use multiple services to fulfill the preconditions of a successor task or state. For planning, we do not only need the probability after defuzzification, but also the already matched elements with their matches. The extension from a binary to a probabilistic representation is one step towards this goal.

Selecting one service to satisfy a query assumes that this given query has been foreseen and a corresponding service has been implemented. Without loss of generality we assume that this is not always the case, making it necessary to compose multiple services to fulfill a task. Thus using the service matcher as part of a planning component rises the next challenge.

3 Automated Service Composition

Similar to *Klusch* [6] the approach of this paper aims at connecting the research area of the semantic web with the flexibility and adaptiveness of agent planning. Here we see services as actions and a plan as equivalent to a service composition. A goal state in agent planning is modeled with the fulfillment of a query in the semantic web community. With this mapping of terms, we aim at building a *Hierarchical Task Network* (HTN) planner, which uses web services to achieve a defined goal state. As basis for our approach, we use the multi-agent system *JIAC V* [10] in which the agents have the capability to publish their actions as web services including semantic service descriptions [11]. The published service can then be used, like all other services contained in the service directory. The agent provides the planning component with a goal description and its knowledge base. This is necessary so that the current state can be assessed by the planner.

3.1 Challenges

In the following we will have a look at some challenges which arise by service composition. First of all, the preconditions of a service need to be split up as fine granular as possible, enabling more services to fulfill a subset of them. This means to invert the *Lloyd-Topor Transformation* [9]. Another challenge is to narrow the search space of possible actions for each state. In the planning domain heuristics are used to choose via *best-first search*, in the semantic web research area semantic descriptions are used to decide if a service is useful for a given task. These semantic descriptions might allow sound heuristics and thus narrow the search space in the same way as in traditional planning. Services can be separated into two classes: *information gathering service* and *world altering service*. We postulate that the execution of information gathering services at plan time might be helpful for the planning process. The challenge here is how the adaption of an information gathering service (executed during plan time) is reflected in the knowledge base, how they are reverted if the planner comes to a backtracking point and which adaption is communicated back to the agent instead of adding the information gathering service to the plan and re-executing it at plan execution time. To be able to generalize a created plan as a non-primitive task in the HTN, the plan including the information gathering services would be needed at the agent side. A more technical design decision is the placement of the planner. To avoid a centralized solution which would rise privacy issues, every agent could have a planning component which would get the agent closer to the BDI paradigm. But in order to avoid the overhead every node should instead provide a planner for its agents. In an multi-agent system, a heterogeneous landscape of ontologies can be used among the agents, making ontology matching a challenge worth while facing.

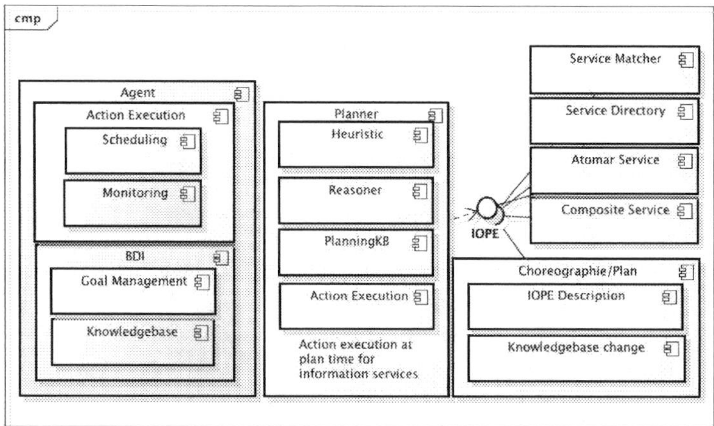

Fig. 2. Component diagram of the extended AI Planner

In more detail, we extend a Hierarchical Task Network (HTN) Planner as shown in Figure 2. The gray components are off-topic for this paper. During a planning process the retrieval of applicable services will be implemented by the SeMa^2 service matcher, searching for services in a *service directory* consisting of *atomic services* and *composite services*. The composite services are published plans or non-primitive tasks of the HTN planner. The *monitoring* component measures the quality of the plan/orchestration during execution and enables the heuristic to adapt to changes. Further plan execution failures can be detected to initiate re-planning. The *heuristic* component evaluates the matching results and creates a heuristic for the *search* component to guide its search. The search is implemented as a *best-first search*. The planner has a copy of the knowledge base of the agent which will be held in the *planning knowledge base* component, which is responsible to be able to revert changes and to keep the knowledge base consistent. The result of a planning process is a *plan* which consists of two parts. The first part are the descriptions of the used services containing their grounding information. The second part is the knowledge base needed by the agent to schedule and execute the plan.

4 Related Work

The literature provides a huge set of different service composition approaches and concepts. In this section we introduce some of these frameworks. One service composition approach is WSPlan, developed by *Peer* [15]. WSPlan uses a knowledge base and services described in WSDL extended by semantic annotations in a PDDL syntax. The knowledge base and the annotations of web services are transformed into PDDL documents. It uses an online planning method for service composition which means that the planning and execution is interleaved. Another service composition solution is OWLS-XPlan, developed by *Klusch* [6]. It transforms OWL-S descriptions of services into PDDLXML, an XML dialect for PDDL. For service composition it uses a combination of a Fast-Forward-planner and an HTN planner. There are other solutions which also transform service descriptions into another description language for service composition. The solution developed by *Okutan et al.* [14] transforms OWL-S descriptions of services into the Event Calculus framework in which actions and their effects are expressed, the solution by *Kuzu and Cicekli* [8] transforms OWL-S descriptions into PDDL and the solution by *Sirin et al.* [17] transforms OWL-S descriptions into the SHOP2 domain to use SHOP2 as an HTN planner. There are also service composition solutions which use multi-agent systems for load balancing. One approach which uses a multi-agent system is the approach by *El Falou et al.* [4]. There is one central agent which receives a request from a client which includes the initial and goal state. It forwards the request to service agents, each managing a group of web services. All service agents compute a local partial plan and send it back to the central agent. The central agent merges the partial plans together to obtain a global partial plan. Then it applies it on the initial state to obtain a new state and sends a new request based on the new state to the service agents. They in turn compute a new plan iterating until the goal state is reached. A simular approach is DPAWSC (Distributed Planning Algorithm for Web Service Composition) which also uses a multi-agent system for service composition.

The overview reveals that there exist different, mostly domain specific approaches for solving the task of service composition with AI planning. The planner proposed in this work will not transform service descriptions into a PDDL like description language. Instead, the planning is done directly on the results of the semantic service matcher and semantic service descriptions. This requires the creation of sound heuristics and backtracking from dead-ends in the planning process.

5 Conclusion

Within this paper we discussed how our automated service selection component approach $SeMa^2$ can be extended to fulfill needed requirements for service composition. We presented $SeMa^2$ shortly, specified the current shortcomings and proposed a formalism how to aggregate the partial results in an adaptive way. Further, we presented our initial concept of extending $SeMa^2$ by an automated service composition component using HTN planning on SWRL. Finally, we have shown how this work can fit into a comprehensive multi-agent framework.

References

1. Bener, A.B., Ozadali, V., Ilhan, E.S.: Semantic matchmaker with precondition and effect matching using SWRL. Expert Systems with Applications 36(5), 9371–9377 (2009)
2. Beyerer, J.: Verfahren zur quantitativen statistischen Bewertung von Zusatzwissen in der Messtechnik. VDI Fortschritt-Bericht, vol. 8. VDI/Verl. (1999)
3. Fähndrich, J.: Analyse von Verfahren zur Kombination von Expertenwissen in Form von Wahrscheinlichkeitsverteilungen im Hinblick auf die verteilte lokale Bayes'sche Fusion. Diploma thesis. Karlsruhe Institut of Technology (May 2010)
4. Falou, M.E., Bouzid, M., Mouaddib, A.-I., Vidal, T.: Automated Web Service Composition: A Decentralised Multi-agent Approach. In: IEEE/WIC/ACM International Joint Conferences on Web Intelligence and Intelligent Agent Technologies, vol. 1, pp. 387–394 (2009)
5. Genest, C.: Pooling operators with the marginalization property. The Canadian Journal of Statistics/La Revue Canadienne de Statistique 12(2), 153–163 (1984)
6. Klusch, M., Gerber, A., Schmidt, M.: Semantic Web Service Composition Planning with OWLS-Xplan. In: Proceedings of the 1st Int. AAAI Fall Symposium on Agents and the Semantic Web, pp. 55–62 (2005)
7. Klusch, M., Kapahnke, P.: The iSeM matchmaker: A flexible approach for adaptive hybrid semantic service selection. Web Semantics: Science, Services and Agents on the World Wide Web 15, 1–14 (2012)
8. Kuzu, M., Cicekli, N.K.: Dynamic planning approach to automated web service composition. Applied Intelligence 36(1), 1–28 (2012)
9. Leuschel, M., Craig, S.-J.: A Reconstruction of the Lloyd-Topor Transformation using Partial Evaluation. In: Pre-Proceedings of LOPSTR, 2005 (2005)
10. Lützenberger, M., Küster, T., Konnerth, T., Thiele, A., Masuch, N., Heßler, A., Burkhardt, M., Tonn, J., Kaiser, S., Keiser, J., Albayrak, S.: JIAC V — A MAS Framework for Industrial Applications (Extended Abstract). In: Proceedings of the AAMAS 2013, Saint Paul, MN, United States of America (2013)
11. Masuch, N., Brock, P.: Integration of semantic service description techniques into a multi-agent framework. In: Trends in Practical Applications of Agents and Multiagent Systems, pp. 155–162. Springer International Publishing (2013)
12. Masuch, N., Hirsch, B., Burkhardt, M., Heßler, A., Albayrak, S.: SeMa^2: A Hybrid Semantic Service Matching Approach. In: Semantic Web Services, pp. 35–47. Springer, Heidelberg (2012)
13. Morris, P.A.: Combining expert judgments: A Bayesian approach. Management Science 23(7), 679–693 (1977)
14. Okutan, C., Cicekli, N.K.: A monolithic approach to automated composition of semantic web services with the Event Calculus. Knowledge-Based Systems 23(5), 440–454 (2010)
15. Peer, J.: A PDDL Based Tool for Automatic Web Service Composition. In: Ohlbach, H.J., Schaffert, S. (eds.) PPSWR 2004. LNCS, vol. 3208, pp. 149–163. Springer, Heidelberg (2004)
16. Shafer, G.: A mathematical theory of evidence, vol. 1. Princeton University Press (1976)
17. Sirin, E., Parsia, B., Wu, D., Hendler, J., Nau, D.: HTN planning for Web Service composition using SHOP2. Web Semantics: Science, Services and Agents on the World Wide Web 1(4), 377 (2004)
18. Stone, M.: The opinion pool. The Annals of Mathematical Statistics 32(4), 1339–1342 (1961)
19. Wu, J., Wu, Z.: Similarity-based web service matchmaking. Services Computing (2005)

Re-engineering the ISO 15926 Data Model: A Multi-level Metamodel Perspective

Andreas Jordan, Matt Selway, Georg Grossmann,
Wolfgang Mayer, and Markus Stumptner

University of South Australia
School of Information Technology and Mathematical Sciences
Adelaide, Australia
{andreas.jordan,matt.selway}@mymail.unisa.edu.au
{georg.grossmann,wolfgang.mayer,markus.stumptner}@unisa.edu.au

Abstract. The ISO 15926 standard was developed to facilitate the integration of life-cycle data of process plants. The core of the standard is a highly generic and extensible data model trying to capture a holistic view of the world. We investigated the standard from a software modelling point of view and identified some challenges in terminology, circular definitions and inconsistencies in relationships during the mapping from concepts specified in the standard to an object-oriented model. This makes the standard difficult to understand and more challenging to implement. In this paper we look at mapping the ISO 15926 data model to a *multilevel* metamodel, and aim to formalise critical aspects of the data model which will simplify the model and ease the adoption process.

Keywords: Conceptual modelling, multilevel modelling, metamodel engineering.

1 Introduction

ISO 15926 was developed to capture information that is frequently exchanged by organisations in the process-driven industry. Organisations that share data across the life-cycle of assets spanning design, engineering, operations and maintenance require an infrastructure for interoperabiliy and hand-over of data in an automated fashion. At the heart of the ISO standard is a generic data model (ISO 15926-2) such that any organisation within the process-driven industry can adopt and use. Combined with a reference data library (ISO 15926-4) and a set of initial templates (ISO 15926-7) to facilitate intended use enables information exchange at the *semantic* level.

However, in an effort to make the data model sufficiently generic to be suitable for adoption by a diverse range of organisations across the process-driven industry, the model itself has become modelled in an unorthodox fashion from an ontology engineering perspective because the specification of concepts and their relations do not follow a formal ontology construction methodology [1,2].

The data model contains a number of significant issues from a software modelling point of view. Many of these issues stem from the lack of accountability

A.R. Lomuscio et al. (Eds.): ICSOC 2013 Workshops, LNCS 8377, pp. 248–255, 2014.
© Springer International Publishing Switzerland 2014

in the use of terms such as 'instance', 'entity', 'object' and 'represent' which are used differently by different communities [3]. Others are caused by a tendency to preemptively overspecialise parts of the data model. Moreover, despite the standard purporting to enable information exchange at the semantic level, its documentation illustrating its intended use places constraints on the various classes but these constraints are missing from the data model, which can result in modelling lifecycle information in a way not intended.

In this paper our objective is to map the data model of ISO 15926 into a *multilevel data model* which we refer to as *target model* in the paper. By enabling metalevels of representation we are able to better represent the intended meaning by simpler and consistent naming conventions, and adhering to conventional ontological theories of roles, representation and mereology. Through this re-engineering process we aim to simplify the mapping process for domain experts.

The presence of concept names including terms like *Class_of_Class*, *Class* and *Individual* intuitively suggests a minimum of three metalevels could be constructed. Therefore, the two levels of instantiation as made available by the Object Management Group's (OMG) Meta Object Facility (MOF) will not suffice as we need to support modelling "ontological" classification across more than one type/instance level. For this we employ the notion of multilevel metamodelling such as has been proposed by Atkinson et al [4].

In previous work we investigated the principal application of a multi-level modelling approach which revealed some of the challenges when applying an object-oriented modelling approach on ISO 15926 [5]. This paper goes beyond previous work and focuses on a more detailed discussion from an ontological perspective, in particular on the specifications of *representation*, *part-whole relationships* and *roles*.

Section 2 discusses related work, Section 3 discusses some key aspects of the ISO 15926 data model in more detail, Section 4 briefly discusses some of the key notions of multilevel metamodelling outlining our ideas for re-engineering the flat data model into a multilevel model followed by our conclusion and further work in Section 5.

2 Related Work

Our work on transforming the flat data model into a multilevel model is based on model-based transformation. We use rules to extract/derive a model that allows more than just the two metamodel levels offered by the MOF framework. This is motivated by the ISO 15926 data model which contains a number of terms such as *Class_of_X* and *Class_of_Class_of_X* which suggests the relationship between these classes represent *ontological instantiation*. In multilevel modelling terms, three ontological model levels would be needed to represent the ISO 15926 data model.

In [4], Atkinson et al introduces a model element termed "clabject" to represent the dual nature of model elements that possess properties of both a 'class' with respect to model elements in the model level below and an 'instance' with respect to model elements in the above model level. The work of De Lara et al in [6] aims to move beyond the limitations of two meta-modelling levels by introducing a framework called MetaDepth that similarly provides an implementable alternative to model-based transformations. Although using similar concepts as [4], the framework extends the *potency* concept to constraints. Additional related work also includes that of Gonzalez-Perez et al [7] whose use of so-called powertypes provide a mechanism to extend the influence of model elements to beyond their immediate model-level. While this approach adopts the concept of *clabject*, the approach differs from [4] and [6] in that the enabling factor for providing a level-agnostic modelling approach employs the powertype pattern as described by Odell in [8].

In addition to the multilevel modelling aspects of this work, we investigate alternative conceptual elements to construct an ontology which incorporates a more detailed ontological theory of roles, representation and mereology than what is currently defined in ISO 15926-2. This is motivated by the need to enable mapping at the semantic level between other standards in the process-driven industry (e.g. MIMOSA's OSA-EAI[1]) and ISO 15926.

In the area of computer science, research into roles began as early as 1977 with Bachman et al's paper (see [9]). The advent of the semantic web has also seen increased interest in developing a robust theory of roles of which a number of contributions have been made, e.g. see [10,11,12]. Mizoguchi's theory of roles introduces a number of additional concepts, namely "Role Holder"(also referred to as a qua-individual in [11]), "Role Concept" and "Role Player" where the Role Holder is a composition of the Role Concept and the Role Player.

3 Discussion on ISO 15926-2 Concepts

Part 2 of the ISO 15926 standard describes the data model comprising some 201 concepts and forms the core of the standard. It provides a generic data model for the representation of life-cycle information[5]. In this section we analyse a number of concepts from the data model, discuss their ontological nature and how an alternate representation can result in a more understandable ontology.

3.1 Modelling in 3D vs 4D

A conceptual model based on a 3D view of the world is fundamentally different to modelling in 4D. One of the most important distinctions is recognising what constitutes *identity* of an *object* [13]. Considered more in-line with a common-sense understanding of the world, the 3D view considers the three spatial dimensions separately from time, and recognises objects as having identity. In contrast, a 4D view treats time as a fourth dimension. The identity of an object is its trajectory through space-time. An example is a person changing as they age. In a

[1] `http://www.mimosa.org/`

3D world-view, we accept that the person changes but their identity does not. In a 4D world-view, the temporal part of a person at time t_1 is not the same as the temporal part of the person at time t_2. In this world-view the identity of the person would need to be determined by summing the temporal parts of the person, summarised by the expression that the person's identity is determined by its "spatio-temporal envelope". While elegant to express in abstract terms, this does not provide an effective way to compute or reference identity.

A challenge in this work is the fact that ISO 15926 is modelled on the 4D world view. While the 4D approach seems ideal for modelling the lifecycle of assets, in terms of implementation and practicality, it becomes challenging to minimize the complexity of queries relating to identity of objects. These types of queries would not be possible using OWL or formulated as a SPARQL query but would necessitate implementation in either a procedural or declarative language. Moreover it makes understanding, applying and modelling in ISO 15926 more complex, particularly when mapping 3D-based standards to it. Therefore, our target model is based on the 3D world view.

One of the ways this impacts on the 3D model, is the handling of the concept *Possible_Individual* and its subtypes. This concept is defined as "A "thing" that exists in space and time. This includes "things" which are *imaginary* or *possibly exist* in the past, present or future." [14]

The subtypes of *Possible_Individual* include *Physical_Object*, *Event*, *Period_-in_Time* and *Point_in_Time*. These subtypes are treated the same in ISO 15926 due to the 4D world view. However, in the 3D world view, *Physical Objects* and *Events* must be treated differently. Furthermore, in ISO 15926 a *Point_in_Time* is an *Event* and those "events that are not points in time are spatial parts of a *Point_in_Time*, defining the time of the event" [14].

An *Event* and a *Point_in_Time* are linked via a part-whole relationship where the *whole* is the *Point_in_Time* an *Event* occurs. By adopting a 3D world view in our multilevel model, we separate events and temporal concepts such that we can use the more intuitive notion of an event occurring at a certain point in time.

3.2 Representation of Concepts in the Real World

The specification of *representation* is particularly challenging because specifying the user's intention is not straight forward. Its definition in [14] is given as "A *representation_of_thing* is a relationship that indicates that a *possible_individual* is a sign for a *thing*.". To illustrate its meaning, it's accompanying example is as follows "The relationship between a *nameplate* with its *serial number* and other data, and a particular pressure vessel (*materialized_physical_object*) is an example of *representation_of_thing* that is an *identification*." [14]

According to Mizoguchi et al in [13] he states a representation is only embodied when it becomes a represented thing and consists of two parts, form and content. The previous example can be misleading in that it can be interpreted in different ways: For example, the nameplate itself could be the representation and then be used to identify a pressure vessel. However, the intention of the user might be to use the nameplate only as the medium which holds an identification number rather than representation of the pressure vessel. It is the symbols comprising the serial number that is the representation of the pressure vessel. In ISO 15926-2, *Identification* is defined as a subclass of *Representation_of_Thing*. The example is ambiguous in at least two senses, the first is whether the symbols comprising the serial number are the representation of the pressure vessel or the representation of the *identification* of the pressure vessel. Another ambiguity relates to the inclusion of the terms "other data" mentioned in the example. Does the "other data" form part of the representation of the *Identification* of the pressure vessel or part of the *representation* of the pressure vessel itself? "Other data" could refer to any property of the pressure vessel, e.g., max pressure rating, in which case, the "other data" does not form part of the representation of either the identification of the pressure vessel nor the pressure vessel itself. To disambiguate these types of issues ISO 15926-2 needs to be supplemented with a more formal notion of representation.

3.3 Mereology - Part/Whole Relations

In order to adequately represent the different interpretations of mereological relations, it is necessary to first distinguish between the different types that exist. Winston et al in [15] identifies six distinct kinds of part-whole relations:

- Component/Integral Object E.g./ handle-cup
- Member/Collection E.g. tree-forest
- Portion/Mass E.g. slice-pie
- Stuff/Object E.g. steel-bike
- Feature/Activity E.g. paying-shopping
- Place/Area E.g. oasis-desert

Three key characteristics are used to distinguish each type of part-whole relation. They are *functional* roles such as 'an impeller is part-of a pump', the *similarity* of the parts with respect to the whole such as 'a molecule of water is a part of water' and lastly whether the parts are *separable* from the whole. ISO 15926-2 also contains mereological relations and we apply the criteria outlined in [15] to determine which category ISO 15926's part-whole relations belong to.

Composition_of_Individual is the most abstract part-whole relation. We argue that it fits the "Member/Collection" relation type as no arrangement between its members is implied and therefore it does not satisfy the functional criteria. Since both part and whole attributes are of type *Possible_Individual*, dissimilar objects can be involved in this type of relation and by definition the *Possible_Individuals* involved in the part/whole relation are separable.

However, *Composition_of_Individual* is also a catchall for other types of part-whole relations. An example of *Composition_of_Individual* is that a grain of sand is part of a pile of sand, which is a portion/mass relationship. Therefore, when mapping a specific instance of *Composition_of_Individual* into the target model, the entities that constitute the part and whole must be reasoned over in order to determine the relationships correct classification.

Arrangement_of_Individual is a specialisation of the concept 'Composition_of_Individual' that restricts the range of the 'whole' to an *Arranged_Individual*, which is defined in [14] as "A possible_individual that has parts that play distinct roles with respect to the whole."

Therefore, we argue that *Arrangement_of_Individual* be classified as a component/integral object relationship. By classifying the way in which part/whole relationships are utilised in ISO 15926 we can better support the mapping of other standards to ISO 15926 through our target model.

Our target model involves representation in a 3D model with time and so does not consider temporal events to contribute to the identity of an object. Instead we employ Mizoguchi's approach by treating a continuant as a role in the context of a process[13].

3.4 Roles

A generally acceptable informal definition of a *role* is an entity that is played by another entity in some context. From a pragmatic perspective we believe the role theory of Mizoguchi is suitable to implement our domain ontology intended to be used to map to ISO 15926-2. When trying to define the characteristics of roles, the differing theories generally agree on a number of fundamental characteristics.

- Rigidity i.e. whether a role is essential/non-essential to all its instances.
- Externally founded i.e. roles require external concepts to define them
- Dynamicity i.e. entities can stop and start playing one or more roles

We suggest to adopt the theory of roles from Mizoguchi[13] and redefine the role-related concepts in ISO 15926 based on this theory. The goal of this change is to provide a more formal, robust and intuitive framework that appeals to a commonsense understanding of roles and remove confusing terminology such as *Class_Of_Possible_Role_And_Domain*. ISO 15926-2 contains a number of types that represent roles. These are given first-class status in the model where five are specialisations of the entity *Class* and the remainder are reified relationships. However ISO 15926 does not give detailed semantics for their intended use. Further to the issue of comprehensibility the term *role* is used interchangeably to refer to different *kinds* of roles whose semantics are quite different (see Table 1). ISO 15926-2's definition of role is loosely analogous to Mizoguchi's *role concept* in [10], however this is where the similarity ends. Although ISO 15926 provides documentation on intended use, the data model does not adequately contain the necessary semantics/constraints to properly enforce the use of roles. Therefore, we believe the data model would benefit by introducing a more robust theory of roles such as that by Mizoguchi in [10].

4 Multilevel Modelling

Research addressing a number of limitations to the UML began as early as 1997 and has continued through to the present day, e.g. see [16,4,6,7]. The major

Table 1. Role *Kinds* used in ISO 15926

Role Kind	Semantics
UML	Appear at either end of an association between two class objects
Description Logic	Binary relationships which are interpreted as sets of pairs of individuals and permit the establishment of role hierarchies
Mizoguchi	Defines roles as a composition of a role concept and a potential player of the role within a context.
Activity	Describes an ISO 15926 'Role_And_Domain' that occurs in the context of an activity

issues surround UML's instantiation mechanism when needing to model more than two model levels which restrict the ability of classes to influence the semantics of objects past a single model level[4]). Since UML's adoption by the Object Management Group (OMG) in 1997, it has become the standard modelling language. Although the UML has shown significant value in many areas particularly in the field of software engineering, despite its ubiquity a number of limitations have been identified along the way. A key limitation relates to the *instantiation* mechanism which can only carry information concerning attributes and associations across a single level[4]. Proposed frameworks for multilevel modelling supporting more than two instantiation levels have been around for more than a decade (e.g. see [16,6]).

While OWL-DL supports *punning*, it's semantics restrict its ability to enforce two key properties of multilevel modelling, i.e. 'potency' and 'level'. Moreover, its accompanying rule language, the Semantic Web Rule Language (SWRL) does not support rules between classes. For these reasons we are required to use a more expressive language with which to implement our multilevel metamodel.

Of the 201 concepts comprising the ISO 15926 data model, 81 of the concepts are prefixed with either class_of_X or class_of_class_of_X. This seems to imply that there exists a minimum of three *logical* levels of instantiation. The definitions of (most of) these 81 classes seem to also support this view, e.g. consider the three classes listed in Table 2.

Table 2. Logical/Ontological instantiation

Concept	Definition in ISO 15926-2 [14]
relationship	"something that one thing has to do with another"
class_of_relationship	"a class_of_abstract_object whose members are members of relationship"
class_of_class_of_relationship	"a class_of_class whose members are instances of class_of_relationship"

5 Conclusion and Future Work

In this paper we discussed a number of issues concerning the complexities and modelling idiosyncrasies of ISO 15926. We proposed the use of a number of alternative theories covering roles, parthood and representation based on a 3D world view intended to make the data model easier to understand and to implement through re-engineering into a multilevel metamodel. Future work consists of implementing additional rules to discriminate between concepts that represent linguistic classification through the use of structural information of the class hierarchy.

References

1. Guarino, N., Welty, C.A.: Evaluating ontological decisions with OntoClean. Commun. ACM 45(2), 61–65 (2002)
2. Mizoguchi, R.: Tutorial on Ontological Engineering: Part 2: Ontology Development, Tools and Languages. New Generation Comput. 22(1), 61–96 (2003)
3. Smith, B.: Against Idiosyncrasy in Ontology Development. In: Proc. of FOIS 2006, pp. 15–26. IOS Press (2006)
4. Atkinson, C., Kühne, T.: The Essence of Multilevel Metamodeling. In: Gogolla, M., Kobryn, C. (eds.) UML 2001. LNCS, vol. 2185, pp. 19–33. Springer, Heidelberg (2001)
5. Jordan, A., Grossmann, G., Mayer, W., Selway, M., Stumptner, M.: On the Application of Software Modelling Principles on ISO 15926. In: Proc. of MODELS Workshop on Modelling of the Physical World (MOTPW 2012). ACM (2012)
6. de Lara, J., Guerra, E.: Deep meta-modelling with METADEPTH. In: Vitek, J. (ed.) TOOLS 2010. LNCS, vol. 6141, pp. 1–20. Springer, Heidelberg (2010)
7. Gonzalez-Perez, C., Henderson-Sellers, B.: A powertype-based metamodelling framework. Software and System Modeling 5(1), 72–90 (2006)
8. Odell, J.J.: Power types. Journal of Object-Oriented Programming 7(2), 8 (1994)
9. Bachman, C.W., Daya, M.: The Role Concept in Data Models. In: Proc. of VLDB 1977, pp. 464–476. IEEE (1977)
10. Mizoguchi, R., Kozaki, K., Kitamura, Y.: Ontological Analyses of Roles. In: Proc. of FedCSIS 2012, pp. 489–496 (2012)
11. Masolo, C., Guizzardi, G., Vieu, L., Bottazzi, E., Ferrario, R.: Relational roles and qua-individuals. In: Proc. of AAAI Fall Symposium on Roles, an Interdisciplinary Perspective, pp. 103–112. AAAI Press (2005)
12. Loebe, F.: Abstract vs. social roles - towards a general theoretical account of roles. Applied Ontology 2(2), 127–158 (2007)
13. Mizoguchi, R.: Tutorial on Ontological Engineering: Part 3: Advanced Course of Ontological Engineering. New Generation Comput. 22(2), 193–220 (2004)
14. I.S.O.: ISO 15926- Part 2: Data Model (2003)
15. Winston, M.E., Chaffin, R., Herrmann, D.: A Taxonomy of Part-Whole Relations. Cognitive Science 11(4), 417–444 (1987)
16. Atkinson, C.: Meta-Modeling for Distributed Object Environments. In: Proc. of EDOC 1997. IEEE (1997)

Fluent Calculus-Based Semantic Web Service Composition and Verification Using WSSL

George Baryannis and Dimitris Plexousakis

Department of Computer Science, University of Crete, Heraklion, Greece
Institute of Computer Science, FORTH, Heraklion, Greece
{gmparg,dp}@csd.uoc.gr

Abstract. We propose a composition and verification framework for Semantic Web Services specified using WSSL, a novel service specification language based on the fluent calculus, that addresses issues related to the frame, ramification and qualification problems. These deal with the succinct and flexible representation of non-effects, indirect effects and preconditions, respectively. The framework exploits the unique features of WSSL, allowing, among others, for: compositions that take into account ramifications of services; determining the feasibility of a composition a priori; and considering exogenous qualifications during the verification process. The framework is implemented using FLUX-based planning, supporting compositions with fundamental control constructs, including nondeterministic ones such as conditionals and loops. Performance is evaluated with regard to termination and execution time for increasingly complex synthetic compositions.

Keywords: service composition, service verification, service specification, frame problem, ramification problem, qualification problem.

1 Introduction

Semantic Web Services technologies aim to enable automatic and dynamic interaction between software systems by combining the machine-interpretable features of the Semantic Web and the Internet-accessible interfaces of Web services [16]. The main discerning characteristic of Semantic Web Services involves describing what a Service-Based Application (SBA) actually does (and possibly how) in a way that is machine-interpretable, employing concepts that are modeled using formal and semantically rich representations, such as ontologies.

The incorporation of Semantic Web features in the service world benefits all phases of an SBA lifecycle, including service composition and verification. Service composition encompasses all methods for creating SBAs by employing the engineering principles of reusability and composability, with the aim of creating value-added services that achieve functionality otherwise unattainable by atomic services. Service verification, then, focuses on checking whether a service, atomic or composite, meets some properties or conforms to a given specification.

Both service composition and service verification benefit greatly when services are described using a formal, well-defined semantic specification language,

A.R. Lomuscio et al. (Eds.): ICSOC 2013 Workshops, LNCS 8377, pp. 256–270, 2014.
© Springer International Publishing Switzerland 2014

detailing service behavior in the form of inputs, outputs, preconditions and effects (collectively known as IOPEs), using concepts defined in ontologies. Such a specification language can assist in automatically deducing service composability according to given composition patterns, by detecting inconsistencies among service specifications; it is also indispensable in verification processes, since one cannot determine whether a service satisfies a property if no detailed specification of the service exists.

Service specifications usually include conditions that should hold before and after service execution. This makes them prone to a family of problems, known in the AI literature as the frame, ramification and qualification problems. The frame problem stems from the need to express in a (service) specification not only what is changed, but also what remains unchanged, as a safeguard against inconsistencies and erroneous formal proofs. The ramification problem is directly related, as it concerns itself with the ability to adequately represent and infer information about the knock-on and indirect effects that might accompany the direct effects of a service. Finally, the qualification problem deals with the inability to take into account every circumstance and condition that must be met prior to a service execution, especially in the case of qualifications that are outside the scope of our knowledge and result in observed behavior that is inconsistent with the specification.

In previous work [4], we defined the Web Service Specification Language (WSSL), designed with the explicit purpose of addressing these problems by exploiting existing solutions proposed for the fluent calculus formalism [20]. In this work, we propose a composition and verification framework for services, based on an extended version of WSSL that supports control and data flow specification.

The fundamental innovative feature of the proposed framework is that it relies on WSSL, the only service description language that supports solutions to the aforementioned problems. Two major novel aspects rise from that fact: the composition process takes advantage of complete behavioral specifications of services, which includes taking ramifications into account, while verification considers qualifications when attempting to provide explanations for unexpected observed behavior.

The second but equally important innovative feature is the fact that the framework supports semantics, while at the same time satisfying a series of desirable requirements: the framework offers an *automated* way of producing *dynamic* service compositions that support a multitude of control constructs including *non-deterministic* ones, are *QoS-aware*, even under *incomplete knowledge* of the initial state, while achieving *scalability*. As analyzed in Section 6, to the best of our knowledge, no Semantic Web Service composition and verification framework simultaneously satisfies all aforementioned requirements. The proposed framework is implemented as a FLUX [19] planner that attempts to achieve composition goals based on heuristic encodings of the planning problem, while also answering verification queries, given a planning problem solution. The framework is evaluated in order to investigate effectiveness and scalability issues.

The rest of this paper is organized as follows. Section 2 offers a motivating scenario illustrating the need for a composition framework that exploits the unique features of WSSL, while Sect. 3 provides an overview of the language. Section 4 extends WSSL to support control and data flow specification, followed by a detailed presentation of the proposed framework, which is then evaluated in Sect. 5. Section 6 offers a concise description of the most prominent related work and Sect. 7 concludes and points out topics for future work.

2 Motivating Scenario

In this section, we present an indicative scenario that illustrates the motivation behind employing an expressive specification language, such as WSSL, to facilitate service composition and verification. The scenario is inspired by HelpMeOut, a process for vehicle drivers to get assistance in case of an emergency, presented in [1]. In our scenario, a call center for road assistance can be reached by vehicle drivers in need of assistance in two ways, via call or via SMS. In order to effectively assist the driver, necessary information has to be collected, such as the driver's location and details about the problem encountered. Based on this information, a search for the most suitable repair center is conducted and they are dispatched to the driver's location. After resolving the issue, the payment process follows. Finally, a report is sent to the driver either electronically or through traditional mail, depending on the driver's choice.

Given a service repository containing services that implement the separate tasks described above, we would like to automatically create a composite process that realizes the complete HelpMeOut road assistance scenario, such as the one shown in Fig. 1. The following features are also required:

- take into account ramifications of services when attempting to create a composition schema, e.g. the payment process has the knock-on effect of credit card invalidation if a daily spending limit has been reached.
- verify the composability and correctness of a candidate composite process that realizes the HelpMeOut scenario
- determine the changes in the state of affairs that are brought upon by a successful execution of a HelpMeOut composite service
- determine the results of executing a HelpMeOut composition, even under incomplete information, e.g. without knowing in advance if the user will request electronic or mail delivery for the report.
- determine what went wrong when unexpected results occur, e.g. no report is delivered to the driver, when all preceding tasks were successful.

Supporting all these features requires that services participating in the composition are described using semantically rich specifications that take into account the frame, ramification and qualification problems. These problems have been largely ignored by every Semantic Web Service description language that has been proposed in recent years (SAWSDL [9], OWL-S [12] and WSML [22]) and were the main motivation behind the creation of the Web Service Specification Language (WSSL) [4], described in the following section.

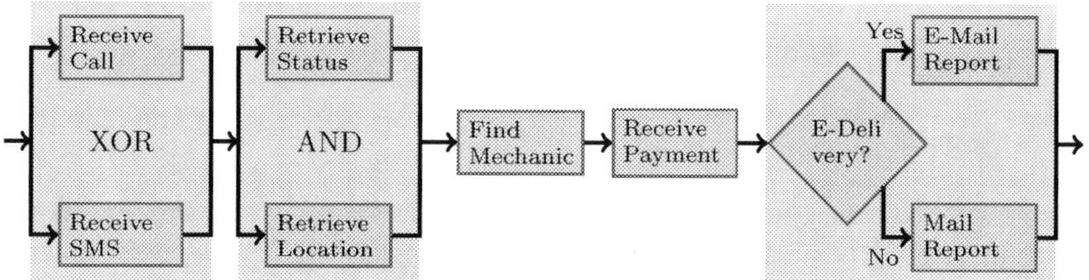

Fig. 1. Composite process of the motivating scenario

3 Web Service Specification Language

In this section, we offer a brief overview of WSSL and its fluent calculus foundations. A detailed definition and analysis of the language syntax and semantics, as well as the problems it addresses, can be found in [4].

3.1 Fluent Calculus Basics

The fundamental entity of the fluent calculus is the *fluent*, a single atomic property of the physical world which may change in the course of time. A *state* is a snapshot of the environment at a certain moment. A fluent is equivalent to a state where only this particular fluent holds. An *action* represents high-level actions. Finally, a *situation* is a history of action performances. Predefined function *Do* maps an action to the situation after performing it, while *State* maps situations to equivalent states. A fluent f is said to hold in a state z, if z can be decomposed into two states, one of which is f: $Holds(f, z)$.

While the fluent calculus was conceived for the field of autonomous robotics, its modeling of dynamic environments is perfectly suited for service specifications. Services (atomic or composite) can be represented by actions, while fluents can model the state of the world before and after executing a service operation. The execution of a service and its effects can be described using the fluent calculus definitions that follow. A ***state formula*** $\Delta(z)$ is a first-order formula where z is a free state variable, states occur exclusively in expressions of the form $Holds(f, z)$ and no actions or situations are allowed. A ***situation formula*** is defined accordingly. Given an action $A(x)$[1], a state variable z and a state formula $\Pi_A(z)$ (where z is free by definition and x may also be free), an ***action precondition axiom*** is a formula $Poss(A(x), z) \equiv \Pi_A(z)$, with the semantics that action A is possible at state z, if and only if Π_A is true.

A ***state update axiom*** is a formula $Poss(A(x), s) \rightarrow (\exists y)(\Delta(s) \wedge \wedge State(Do(A(x), s)) = State(s) + \theta^+ - \theta^-)$ stating that, if action A is possible at situation s, executing it results in a successor state derived from $State(s)$ if we add fluents that have been made true (*positive effects* θ^+) and subtract falsified ones (*negative effects* θ^-), under additional conditions $\Delta(s)$ (a situation formula containing variables x and y). Note that disjunction can be used to

[1] Note that actions may also have a vector variable as an argument $(A(\overrightarrow{x}))$

express multiple state updates with different $\Delta(s)$ formulas. As analyzed in [18], state update axioms are a provably correct solution to the frame problem.

3.2 Defining WSSL Specifications

Service preconditions and postconditions can be directly represented using action precondition axioms and state update axioms respectively. To represent service inputs and outputs, we introduced two unary predicate symbols corresponding to fluents, namely $HasInput$ and $HasOutput$. $HasInput$ denotes that the associated argument is available to the service as an input while $HasOutput$ denotes that the associated argument is produced as a service output.

Definition 1. An **input formula** in z is a state formula $I(z)$ with free state variable z, which is composed exclusively of $HasInput$ fluents. An **output formula** $O(z)$ is defined accordingly.

Apart from the frame problem, the fluent calculus offers a solution to the problem of representing ramifications as well, using causal relationships that link a ramification to the direct effect (or ramification) that brings it about (see Chap. 9 in [20]). A ***causal relationship*** is formally defined as a formula $(\forall)(\Gamma \rightarrow Causes(z, p, n, z', p', n', s)$ with the semantics that in situation s, under conditions expressed in Γ, the positive and negative effects p and n that have occurred cause an automatic update from state z to z', with effects p' and n'. A ***state update axiom with ramifications*** is a formula $Poss(A(x), s) \rightarrow (\exists y)(\Delta(s) \wedge Ramify(z, \theta^+, \theta^-, z', Do(A(x), s))$, where $Ramify$ stands for applying any matching causal relationships in state z, leading to z'.

Finally, the fluent calculus offers a way to represent qualifications outside the scope of our knowledge, solving the exogenous qualification problem (see Chap. 10 in [20]) by modeling any unforeseen situation that obstructs an action as an *accident*, represented by new predicate $Acc(c, s)$, with the semantics that accident c, which is a variable of new sort $ACCIDENT$, happened in situation s. In order to assume away accidents, default logic rules are employed, such as $\frac{:\neg Acc(c,s)}{\neg Acc(c,s)}$, which is essentially a universal default on the non-occurrence of all accidents. To express the case where no accident has taken place, the conjunct $(\forall c)\neg Acc(c, s)$ is included in the right-hand side of a state update axiom. Any other accident case is expressed as a separate state update using disjunction. Action precondition axioms are rewritten in the form $Poss(A(x), s) \equiv [(\forall c)\neg Acc(c, s) \rightarrow \Pi_A(x, s)]$ meaning that A is possible at s provided that no accidents have happened and the preconditions are true.

Using all of the above, we are able to formally define a WSSL specification:

Definition 2. A **WSSL specification** is a 6-tuple
$\mathcal{S} = \langle \mathbf{service}, \mathbf{input}, \mathbf{output}, \mathbf{pre}, \mathbf{post}, \mathbf{causal}, \mathbf{default} \rangle$ where:

- **service:** identifiers offering general information about the service (e.g. service or operation name, invocation information), or the symbol *nil*,
- **input:** the required input of the service, expressed as *input formulas*

- **output:** the expected output of the service, in the form of *output formulas*,
- **pre:** service preconditions, expressed as *action precondition axioms*,
- **post:** service postconditions, in the form of *state update axioms*,
- **causal:** causal relationships linking effects and ramifications,
- **default:** default qualifications formalized as default rules.

Table 1 offers a WSSL specification of indicative services for the tasks in the motivating scenario (omitting *Poss* and no-accident clauses). We also defined an XML syntax for WSSL, named WSSL/XML, in order to provide machine readability for WSSL documents and facilitate standard parsing processes. The XML Schema can be found online at www.csd.uoc.gr/˜gmparg/research.html.

Table 1. Example WSSL specifications

Service	**Inputs**
ReceiveSMS/Call	-
RetrieveLocation	$Holds(HasInput(request), ?z\_in)$
RetrieveDiag	$Holds(HasInput(request), ?z\_in)$
FindMech	$Holds(HasInput(status), ?z\_in) \wedge Holds(HasInput(loc), ?z\_in)$
ReceivePay	$Holds(HasInput(payform), ?z\_in) \wedge Holds(HasInput(loc), ?z\_in)$
EReport	$Holds(HasInput(invoice), ?z\_in)$
MReport	$Holds(HasInput(invoice), ?z\_in)$
Service	**Preconditions**
ReceiveSMS/Call	$Holds(CallCenterUp)$
RetrieveLocation	$Holds(GPSActive(user), ?z\_in)$
RetrieveDiag	$Holds(SystemActive(vehicle), ?z\_in)$
FindMech	$Holds(Rcvd(loc, ?user), ?z\_in) \wedge$ $Holds(Rcvd(status, vehicle), ?z\_in) \wedge \neg Holds(Solved(status, loc), ?z\_in)$
ReceivePay	$Holds(HasInput(credCard), ?z\_in) \wedge Holds(Solved(status, loc), ?z\_in)$
EReport	$Holds(PayCompleted(payform), ?z\_in) \wedge$ $Holds(Generated(mechlog), ?z\_in) \wedge \neg Holds(Emailed(report), ?z\_in)$
MReport	$Holds(PayCompleted(payform), ?z\_in) \wedge$ $Holds(Generated(mechlog), ?z\_in) \wedge \neg Holds(Delivered(report), ?z\_in)$
Service	**Outputs and Postconditions**
ReceiveSMS	$?z\_out = ?z\_in + HasOutput(request) + Rcvd(request, sms)$
ReceiveCall	$?z\_out = ?z\_in + HasOutput(request) + Rcvd(request, call)$
RetrieveLocation	$?z\_out = ?z\_in + HasOutput(loc) + Rcvd(loc, user) - HasInput(request)$
RetrieveDiag	$Ramify(?z\_in, HasOutput(status) + Rcvd(status, vehicle),$ $HasInput(request), ?z\_out)$
FindMech	$?z\_out = ?z\_in + HasOutput(payform) + HasOutput(credCard) +$ $Solved(status, loc) - HasInput(status) - HasInput(loc)$
ReceivePay	$?z\_out = ?z\_in + HasOutput(invoice) + PayCompleted(payform)$ $- HasInput(payform)$
EReport	$?z\_out = ?z\_in + HasOutput(report) + Emailed(report) - HasInp(invoice)$
MReport	$(\forall ?c)\neg Acc(?c, ?s)(?z\_out = ?z\_in + HasOutput(report) + Delivered(report)$ $- HasInput(invoice)) \vee (\exists deliv)(Acc(Failure(deliv, s) \wedge ?z\_out = ?z\_in)$
Causal Relationships	
$?p = HasOutput(status) + Rcvd(status, vehicle) \wedge ?n = HasInput(request) \Rightarrow$ $Causes(?z, ?p, ?n, ?z + Generated(mechlog), ?p + Generated(mechlog), ?n, ?s)$	
$DailyLimitReached(payform) \wedge ?p = HasOutput(invoice) + PayCompleted(payform) \Rightarrow$ $Causes(?z, ?p, ?n, ?z + Invalid(credCard), ?p + Invalid(credCard), ?n, ?s)$	

All fundamental entities of WSSL, from fluents to accidents, can be expressed using concepts defined in service ontologies. It is envisioned that existing OWL-S and WSMO descriptions can be ported to WSSL and then annotated to fill up information related to causal relationships and accident modeling, resulting in complete semantic service specifications that take into account the frame, ramification and qualification problems.

4 Composition and Verification of WSSL Services

In this section, we present a composition and verification framework for services specified using WSSL. First, we extend WSSL to support control and data flow of compositions, as well as planning and then analyze the composition and verification capabilities separately.

4.1 WSSL for Composition

The definition of WSSL in Sect. 3 allows for black-box specifications of services where only IOPEs are considered, disregarding any knowledge about its control and data flow. In order to be able to employ WSSL for composition, we need to extend it to include the definition of fundamental control constructs.

Definition 3. A tuple $S \cup \langle \epsilon, ;, If, \cdot, +, \oplus, Loop \rangle$ is an extended WSSL signature for composition if S is a WSSL signature and: $\epsilon : ACTION$ (empty action), *If:* $FLUENT \times ACTION \times ACTION \rightarrow ACTION$ (conditional execution), *Loop:* $FLUENT \times ACTION \rightarrow ACTION$ (iterative execution) and $;, \cdot, +, \oplus : ACTION \times ACTION \rightarrow ACTION$ (sequence, AND-Split/AND-Join, OR-Split/OR-Join and XOR-Split/XOR-Join, respectively).

It follows that the foundational axioms that govern the fluent calculus and WSSL, as expressed in [4], need to be extended in order to account for the newly introduced function symbols. The extension is based on the definition and analysis of control constructs conducted in previous work [2].

Definition 4. The foundational axioms for **preconditions** consist of:

1. $Poss(\epsilon, s) \equiv T$
2. $Poss(a_1; a_2, s) \equiv Poss(a_1, s) \wedge Poss(a_2, Do(a_1, s))$
3. $Poss(If(f, a_1, a_2), s) \equiv [Holds(f, s) \wedge Poss(a_1, s)] \vee [\neg Holds(f, s) \wedge Poss(a_2, s)]$
4. $Poss(a_1 \cdot a_2, s) \equiv Poss(a_1 + a_2, s) \equiv Poss(a_1 \oplus a_2, s) \equiv Poss(a_1, s) \wedge Poss(a_2, s)$
5. $Poss(Loop(f, a_1), s) \equiv [Holds(f, s) \Rightarrow Poss(a_1, s)] \wedge$ $[Holds(f, Do(a_1, s) \Rightarrow Poss(a_1, Do(a_1, s))] \wedge \ldots$

These foundational axioms allow for calculating preconditions for composite services, based on their composition schema. For instance, the precondition of the *RetrieveStatus/RetrieveLocation* composition can be calculated using axiom 4 of Definition 4 as the conjunction of the preconditions of the two services. Note that this axiom may appear too strong for OR and XOR cases, but it stems directly from the fact that, at design time, we do not know which branch is going to be executed; hence, we cannot disregard either precondition. If such knowledge is available at runtime, then the conditions may be adapted accordingly.

Definition 5. The foundational axioms for **postconditions** consist of:

1. $State(Do(\epsilon, s)) = State(s)$
2. $Poss(a_1; a_2, s) \Rightarrow State(Do(a_1; a_2, s)) = State(Do(a_2, Do(a_1, s)))$

3. $Poss(If(f, a_1, a_2), s) \Rightarrow [Holds(f, s) \wedge State(Do(If(f, a_1, a_2), s)) = State(Do(a_1, s))] \vee \neg[Holds(f, s) \wedge State(Do(If(f, a_1, a_2), s)) = State(Do(a_2, s))]$
4. $Poss(a_1 \cdot a_2, s) \Rightarrow State(Do(a_1 \cdot a_2, s)) = State(Do(a_2, s)) + \theta_1^+ - \theta_1^- = State(s) + \theta_2^+ - \theta_2^- + \theta_1^+ - \theta_1^-$
5. $Poss(a_1 + a_2, s) \Rightarrow [State(Do(a_1 + a_2, s)) = State(s) + \theta_1^+ - \theta_1^-] \vee [State(Do(a_1 + a_2, s)) = State(s) + \theta_2^+ - \theta_2^-]$
6. $Poss(a_1 \oplus a_2, s) \Rightarrow [State(Do(a_1 \oplus a_2, s)) = State(s) + \theta_1^+ - \theta_1^-] \oplus [State(Do(a_1 \oplus a_2, s)) = State(s) + \theta_2^+ - \theta_2^-]$
7. $Poss(Loop(f, a_1), s) \Rightarrow [\neg Holds(f, s) \Rightarrow (State(Do(Loop(f, a_1))), s) = State(s)] \wedge [Holds(f, s) \wedge \neg Holds(f, Do(a_1, s)) \Rightarrow (State(Do(Loop(f, a_1), s))) = State(s) + \theta_1^+ - \theta_1^-] \wedge ...$

These axioms complement the ones in Definition 4, resulting in a whole view of a composite service execution. For instance, by combining the third axioms in Definitions 4 and 5, we can express the fact that the conditional execution of *EReport* and *MReport* requires only one of the two services' preconditions to be true, depending on the truth value of the condition fluent, while a successful execution leads to a state change as a result of *EReport* or *MReport*.

Definitions 4 and 5 can be extended in a straightforward way for compositions of more than two services. As it will be discussed later on, the nature of loops leads to an infinite expression for the associated foundational axioms, which can only be made finite if the number of iterations is known or limited beforehand.

Apart from defining control flow for service composition, WSSL needs to account for data flow as well. The following axiom models the simplest case of routing between outputs and inputs of services:

Definition 6. The foundational axiom for **data flow** expresses the fact that any produced output can potentially be consumed as an input from that state onward and is written as $Holds(HasOutput(f), z) \Rightarrow Holds(HasInput(f), z)$.

QoS-Awareness. By definition, any WSSL term can be associated with concepts defined in a knowledge representation model, using IRI [8] sequences. For instance, expressions used in WSSL preconditions can refer to concepts of any origin, including ontology-based QoS models. We are investigating the integration of such a model, OWL-Q [11], with WSSL. OWL-Q is an OWL-S [12] extension that provides a semantic, rich and extensible model for describing QoS aspects, which can be used by service providers to model QoS attributes. Such models can be referenced in either WSSL specifications or queries, realizing in that way QoS-aware service description and composition, respectively.

4.2 Service Composition Planning

Based on planning in the fluent calculus with FLUX (see Chap. 6 in [20]), we define planning for service composition using WSSL.

Definition 7. A WSSL planning problem is defined as the problem of reaching a goal state defined by a state formula $\Gamma(z)$, starting from an initial state defined by a state formula $\Phi(z)$. A WSSL plan is a sequence $\alpha_1, ..., \alpha_n$ of service executions, with $n \geq 0$. The plan is a solution to the problem iff the following holds: $Poss([\alpha_1, ..., \alpha_n], \Phi(z)) \wedge \Gamma\{z/State(Do([\alpha_1, ..., \alpha_n], \Phi(z)))\}$

A planning problem is encoded in FLUX in a sound and complete way using the following two clauses: $P(z,p,z) \Leftarrow Goal(z), p = []$ and $P(z,[a|p],z_n \Leftarrow Poss(a,z), StateUpdate(z,a,z_1,[]), P(z_1,p,z_n)$, stating that if we are at the goal state, the solution is either the empty plan, or a sequence of actions constructed recursively until the goal state is reached. For the motivating scenario, a planning problem encoding is: $AssistPlan(z,p,z) \Leftarrow Holds(Solved(status, location), z)$, $Holds(PayCompleted(payform), z), Holds(HasOutput(report), z), p = []$ and $AssistPlan(z,[a|p],z_n) \Leftarrow Poss(a,z), StateUpdate(z,a,z_1,[]), P(z_1,p,z_n)$.

Encodings based on Definition 7 have two major drawbacks: they do not take into account the issues of termination and computational complexity and can produce only sequential compositions. The first step towards handling both issues is introducing heuristics, further specifying the planning encoding.

Definition 8. A heuristic encoding of a WSSL planning problem is defined as a FLUX program P_{plan} defining a predicate $P(z,p,z_n)$ that describes the problem of reaching a goal state $\Gamma(z)$, starting from an initial state $\Phi(z)$. The encoding is sound iff the following holds: for every computed answer θ to the FLUX query $\Leftarrow \Phi(z) \wedge P(z,p,z_n)$, $p\theta$ is a solution to the planning problem and $Poss(p\theta, \Phi(z)) \wedge \Gamma\{z/State(Do(p\theta, \Phi(z)))\}$.

In order to consider plans more complex than sequences of services, heuristic encodings need to include control construct definitions. Based on Definitions 4, 5 and 6, we extend the FLUX Prolog kernel with clauses that support fundamental control constructs and data flow between inputs and outputs. For instance, plans that contain looped executions are considered based on the following rules:

```
poss_loop(F,K,A,Z) :- K\==0, (holds(F,Z)->poss(A,Z)),update(Z,A,Z_PR),poss_loop(F,K-1,A,Z_PR).
state_update_loop(Z,F,K,A,Z_PR) :- not_holds(F,Z)->Z_PR=Z ; K\==0,(holds(F,Z),update(Z,A,Z_1),
            not_holds(F,Z_1)) -> state_update(Z,A,Z_1), state_update_loop(Z_1,F,K-1,A,Z_PR).
```

The iterative nature of loops is expressed using Prolog rules that refer to themselves. As already mentioned, it is necessary to impose an upper bound K on the number of iterations, to avoid non-terminating executions. The complete extended kernel can be found online at www.csd.uoc.gr/~gmparg/research.html. One possible heuristic encoding for the problem of the motivating scenario is:

```
assist_plan(Z,[A|P],Z_PR) :- A1=receivesms, A2=receivecall, A=xor(A1,A2),
    poss_xor(A1,A2,Z), state_update_xor(Z,A1,A2, Z_1), assist_plan1(Z_1,P,Z_PR).
assist_plan1(Z,[A|P],Z_PR) :- A1=retrievelocation, A2=retrievediagnostics,
    A=and(A1, A2), poss_and(A1,A2,Z),state_update_and(Z,A1,A2,Z_1),assist_plan2(Z_1,P,Z_PR).
assist_plan2(Z,[A|P],Z_PR) :- A=findmech, poss(A,Z),
                              state_update(Z,A,Z_1), assist_plan3(Z_1,P,Z_PR).
assist_plan3(Z,[A|P],Z_PR) :- A=receivepay, poss(A,Z),
                              state_update(Z,A,Z_1), assist_plan4(Z_1,P,Z_PR).
assist_plan4(Z,A,Z_PR) :- F=req_deliv, A1=ereport,A2=mreport, A=if(F,A1,A2),
                              poss_if(F,A1,A2,Z), state_update_if(Z,F,A1,A2,Z_PR).
```

Executing the FLUX query `assist_plan([callcenterup, gpsactive(user1), systemactive(vehicle1), req_deliv], P, Z_PR).` will yield a plan corresponding to the composite process of Fig. 1. FLUX is also able to handle incomplete initial states thanks to embedded constraint handling rules. For instance, we may exclude `req_deliv` (which corresponds to the user wanting the report e-mailed to him) from the definition of the initial state and the planner will still produce plans that assume either case, with or without that fluent.

4.3 Verification

Given a generated plan that solves a planning problem, service verification aims to check that the composite service that corresponds to the plan meets some properties. The verification process in our framework focuses mainly on answering questions about the behavior of the composition. Examples of the properties that can be verified are the following:

- *Composability* of a set of services: given a composition goal, the nature of the composition process yields results about whether this particular set can lead to a valid composition.
- *Liveness* and *safety* properties that check whether the composition plan realizes the desired behavior.
- *Conformance* of an observed composite service behavior to the corresponding plan specification and, in case conformance fails, possible *explanations* for the conflict in order to perform troubleshooting actions.

For example, a liveness property in our motivating scenario would be to verify whether the composition plan leads to the final report being delivered (either by mail or electronically), by proving $Emailed(report, z) \vee Delivered(report, z)$, where z is the final state, while a safety property would be to make sure that payment is performed for the correct payment form $(HasInput(payform, z_{in}) \wedge \neg PayCompleted(payform2, z))$. Verification queries of the third type can be answered due to WSSL's solution to the qualification problem. For instance, after executing the composite process of Fig. 1, we observe its behavior in the form of WSSL state descriptions and pose the query: in the final state z, is the goal `holds(solved(status, location), z), holds(paycompleted(form), z), holds(hasoutput(report), z)` satisfied? If the answer is no and no accidental qualifications have been expressed, then the observed behavior is deemed inconsistent with the composition specification. However, given the specification shown in Table 1, the framework deduces that an accident has occurred, namely `failure(deliv)`. Such explanations are valuable for determining follow-up actions to unexpected situations, such as re-executing services that failed or adapting the composition in order to replace them.

4.4 Complexity, Decidability and Planning Efficiency

As discussed in [4], decidability results for WSSL are directly related to its foundations in the fluent calculus, as well as default logic. Decidability is guaranteed for the fragment that is equivalent to the two-variable situation calculus with counting, and for default theories without prerequisites. Such results also hold for the extended version that supports control and data flow, provided that an upper bound on iterations is imposed for all loops.

In general, the planning problem is considered undecidable. Even in the case of decidable planning problems, the complexity of finding a solution is directly analogous to the number of choice points, since each choice point splits the search tree into two branches. Heuristic encodings based on problem-specific knowledge can improve efficiency by trimming parts of the search tree that do not conform to the heuristics definition. However, even then scalability is not guaranteed, because increasing the problem size linearly may lead to a non-linear increase in the number of choice points. In Sect. 5, we investigate scalability issues for our framework, while a complexity and decidability analysis for heuristics-based WSSL planning is part of ongoing research we are currently conducting.

For a given planning problem, there may be more than one solution. For instance, in the motivating scenario, the goal of delivering the report can be satisfied by two different tasks, *EReport* and *MReport*. The planner can either return the first solution found, or generate all possible solutions and rank them according to a ranking function. FLUX supports ranking based on cost.

4.5 Other Features

The fluent calculus foundations of WSSL imbue our framework with several other interesting features. First of all, the fluent calculus has been extended to support knowledge (or belief) states (see Chap. 5 in [20]), a generalization of expressing incomplete initial states (supported by our framework) in the direction of defining which states are possible at a given situation, based on how complete our knowledge is. Knowledge states, combined with non-determinism and qualifications, allow for comprehensive modeling of partially observable behavior.

An especially desirable feature in the case of services is supporting asynchronous execution, i.e. services that do not wait for a response after being invoked. Asynchronous services can be easily modeled as a pair of distinct WSSL services, similarly to the invoke/receive combination of WS-BPEL [13], thanks to the definition of states in WSSL: the first service has no postconditions, since it simply invokes the operation, while the second has no preconditions, since they have already been checked on invocation. Thus, the state after invoking the service is decoupled from the state after receiving the reply.

Finally, WSSL compositions can be translated to executable processes based on the included definition of control and data flow. For instance, plans comprising of WSSL services that do not contain invocation information can be translated to abstract BPEL processes, which can then be concretized via suitable service discovery mechanisms. If WSSL specifications are linked to specific service endpoints, then they directly lead to executable BPEL processes.

5 Experimental Evaluation

In order to evaluate the proposed composition framework, we run a series of experiments, calculating the time needed for the planner to produce a valid service composition plan, given a set of services, an initial state and a goal state. To investigate scalability, we varied the complexity of the planning problem in two ways: by increasing the size of the service repository and by allowing for more elaborate plans. The service specifications are synthetically generated in FLUX, each one consisting of one or two sets of IOPEs. The computation time values are an average of 10 runs in the ECL^iPS^e constraint programming system. The evaluation was performed on an Intel® Core™ i7-740QM processor running at 1.73GHz, with 6 GB RAM.

In the first two experiments, we examined the scalability of our approach given simple composition schemas, considering only sequential composition in the first and only parallel composition (AND-Split/Join) in the second. In both cases, we increased linearly the number of services that need to be considered in order to find an executable one at a given state. As shown in Fig. 2, even for a repository of 1000 services, computation time is around 1 second, which is rather efficient considering the fact that choice points increase from 1 in the initial state to 1000 in the penultimate state.

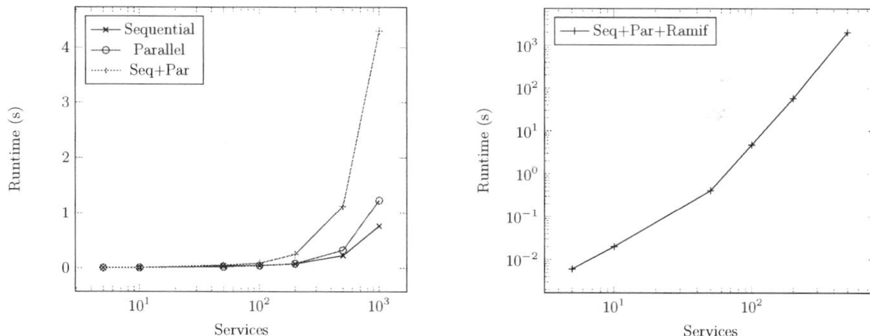

Fig. 2. Scalability results for compositions of varying complexity

For the third experiment, we combine the first two, creating a composition schema of alternating sequential and parallel executions. Fig. 2 shows that there is a reasonable increase to around 4 seconds for the case of 1000 services. Note that other composition schemas such as OR and XOR Split/Join, conditionals and loops are not included in our experiments, since their use is expected to be dictated explicitly in heuristic encodings, as in the motivating scenario; in our test sets, AND Split/Join schemas are always the first to evaluate to true.

In the final experiment, we investigate the effect of including ramifications in service specifications. Each postcondition in our test set is associated with a ramification through the inclusion of a causal rule (a 50% increase in the size of specifications). Once again, we increase linearly the number of causal rules that are considered until a matching one is found. As we can see in Fig. 2 on the right, there is a significant increase in computation time, up to 2000 seconds for 500 services. These results are expected, considering that the planner has to examine around 500 causal rules one by one at the final states of the composition. Note that real-world problems are expected to be much simpler than the ones generated synthetically for our evaluation, since only some postconditions are usually associated with ramifications.

6 Related Work

Employing fluent calculus in order to solve the service composition problem has been attempted in [7] and [6]. In both approaches, Semantic Web Services are translated to fluent calculus theories and forward chaining composition algorithms implemented using FLUX are proposed, with [6] considering QoS thresholds as well. However, neither takes into account the fluent calculus extensions that solve the ramification and qualification problems, resulting in frameworks that ignore their effects and fail to capitalize on the benefits of their solutions, such as expressing ramifications or explaining non-conforming behavior. Moreover, both planners produce at best sequences of parallel executions, disregarding any other control constructs, such as the ones supported by our framework. Finally, their choice to model inputs and outputs using the $KnowsVal$ macro is invalid since, by definition, it was introduced to represent a subset of fluent-related variables that is true in all possible states, and not the semantics of a service input, which is a fluent that holds at the state before service execution.

Extensive literature exists that employs AI planning techniques to realize automated service composition. Klusch and Gerber [10] propose OWLS-XPlan, a framework that combines the benefits of graph-based planning with HTN planning for service composition, while also employing re-planning techniques to adjust outdated plans during execution time. However, the framework does not support non-deterministic control constructs or planning with incomplete state descriptions, while the authors do not consider QoS-awareness or the ramification and qualification problems. The work of Peer [14] translates semantic Web services to PDDL descriptions which are then fed to a VHPOP planner framework that supports re-planning as well as non-determinism in the sense of considering failure in service executions. Looped execution, ramifications, QoS-awareness and incomplete states are again not supported.

Arguably the most prominent realization of service composition using planning techniques is the WS-SYNT mechanism included in the ASTRO framework. As analyzed in [5], WS-BPEL processes are translated into state transition systems (STSs), which are then combined to construct an STS that represents all possible behaviors and afterwards this STS is searched in order to find subsystems of it that satisfy the composition goal. The solutions are then translated back to executable WS-BPEL processes. This work realizes two features, namely support for asynchronous services and translation to executable processes, that are currently not supported by our framework but can be easily integrated, as indicated in Section 4.5. Unlike our framework, however, WS-SYNT does not support Semantic Web services (although one of the earliest works [21] in the authors' research line did), is not QoS-aware and, more importantly, does not consider the frame, ramification and qualification problems and their effects.

[17] and [15] share similar logic foundations with our approach. [15] is based on GOLOG, a logic programming language based on the situation calculus in the same way that FLUX is based on the fluent calculus. The authors integrate user preferences in a GOLOG-based planner, modeling them using a first-order logic language. Employing preferences drastically limits the search space for

the planner, resulting in significantly less computation time. [17] proposes the representation of service I/O schemas and behavioral constraints as Horn clauses and realizes service composition through logical inference as well as structural analysis of Petri nets that model the Horn clause set and the goal. The resulting compositions, however, are restricted to sequences of parallel executions, while behavioral constraints in both approaches ignore knock-on or indirect effects and accidental qualifications, which are supported in our framework.

7 Conclusions and Future Work

In this paper, we proposed a service composition and verification framework using WSSL, a novel semantics-aware service specification language based on the fluent calculus. The framework satisfies significant requirements such as automation, dynamicity, nondeterminism and incomplete state knowledge, in addition to supporting semantics and exploiting WSSL's solutions to the frame, ramification and qualification problems. Experimental evaluation shows that efficiency is achieved even in the presence of ramifications. The framework is an effective demonstration of the benefits of rich semantic behavior specifications in the context of service science and an indicative example of how such benefits can be reaped for the purposes of service verification and composition.

Future work includes further concretizing the link between WSSL and OWL-Q [11], exploring QoS-aware matchmaking and selection mechanisms and identifying ways to improve efficiency by limiting the search space before the planning process, as well as exploring graph-based rule optimization. Additionally, we plan to build upon the discussion in Sect. 4.5 in order to support knowledge states, asynchronous service interactions and derivation of executable composite processes. Moreover, we intend to integrate the ideas of formal behavior specifications in the lifecycle of Cloud-based services deployed on multiple Cloud providers, as initially explored in [3].

Acknowledgments. The research leading to these results has received funding from the European Community's Seventh Framework Programme FP7/2007-2013 under grant agreement 317715 (PaaSage), as well as the Special Account for Research Grants, University of Crete (Grant No. 3742).

References

1. Ali, S.A., Roop, P.S., Warren, I., Bhatti, Z.E.: Unified Management of Control Flow and Data Mismatches in Web Service Composition. In: Gao, J.Z., Lu, X., Younas, M., Zhu, H. (eds.) SOSE, pp. 93–101. IEEE (2011)
2. Baryannis, G., Carro, M., Plexousakis, D.: Deriving Specifications for Composite Web Services. In: COMPSAC, pp. 432–437 (2012)
3. Baryannis, G., Garefalakis, P., Kritikos, K., Magoutis, K., Papaioannou, A., Plexousakis, D., Zeginis, C.: Lifecycle Management of Service-based Applications on Multi-Clouds: A Research Roadmap. In: Proceedings of the International workshop on Multi-Cloud Applications and Federated Clouds, pp. 13–20. ACM (2013)

4. Baryannis, G., Plexousakis, D.: WSSL: A Fluent Calculus-Based Language for Web Service Specifications. In: Salinesi, C., Norrie, M.C., Pastor, Ó. (eds.) CAiSE 2013. LNCS, vol. 7908, pp. 256–271. Springer, Heidelberg (2013)
5. Bertoli, P., Pistore, M., Traverso, P.: Automated composition of Web services via planning in asynchronous domains. Artif. Intell. 174(3-4), 316–361 (2010)
6. Bhuvaneswari, A., Karpagam, G.R.: Applying Fluent Calculus for Automated and Dynamic Semantic Web Service Composition. In: Proceedings of the 1st International Conference on Intelligent Semantic Web-Services and Applications (2010)
7. Chifu, V.R., Salomie, I., Harsa, I., Gherga, M.: Semantic Web Service Composition Method Based on Fluent Calculus.. In: Watt, S.M., Negru, V., Ida, T., Jebelean, T., Petcu, D. (eds.) SYNASC, pp. 325–332. IEEE Computer Society (2009)
8. Duerst, M., Suignard, M.: Internationalized Resource Identifiers (IRIs). RFC 3987 (2005)
9. Farrell, J., Lausen, H.: Semantic Annotations for WSDL and XML Schema. World Wide Web Consortium, Recommendation REC-sawsdl-20070828 (August 2007)
10. Klusch, M., Gerber, A.: Semantic Web Service Composition Planning with OWLS-Xplan. In: Proceedings of the 1st Int. AAAI Fall Symposium on Agents and the Semantic Web, pp. 55–62 (2005)
11. Kritikos, K., Plexousakis, D.: Requirements for QoS-based web service description and discovery. IEEE T. Services Computing 2(4), 320–337 (2009)
12. Martin, D., Burstein, M., Hobbs, J., Lassila, O., McDermott, D., McIlraith, S., Narayanan, S., Paolucci, M., Parsia, B., Payne, T., Sirin, E., Srinivasan, N., Sycara, K.: OWL-S: Semantic Markup for Web Services (2004)
13. OASIS: Web Services Business Process Execution Language Version 2.0. Specification (April 2007)
14. Peer, J.: A POP-Based Replanning Agent for Automatic Web Service Composition. In: Gómez-Pérez, A., Euzenat, J. (eds.) ESWC 2005. LNCS, vol. 3532, pp. 47–61. Springer, Heidelberg (2005)
15. Sohrabi, S., Prokoshyna, N., McIlraith, S.A.: Web Service Composition via the Customization of Golog Programs with User Preferences. In: Borgida, A.T., Chaudhri, V.K., Giorgini, P., Yu, E.S. (eds.) Mylopoulos Festschrift. LNCS, vol. 5600, pp. 319–334. Springer, Heidelberg (2009)
16. Studer, R., Grimm, S., Abecker, A. (eds.): Semantic Web Services. Springer, Berlin (2007), `http://www.springerlink.com/content/kj5458/`
17. Tang, X., Jiang, C., Zhou, M.: Automatic Web service composition based on Horn clauses and Petri nets. Expert Syst. Appl. 38(10), 13024–13031 (2011)
18. Thielscher, M.: The Fluent Calculus. Tech. Rep. CL-2000-01. Dresden University of Technology (2000)
19. Thielscher, M.: FLUX: A Logic Programming Method for Reasoning Agents. CoRR cs.AI/0408044 (2004)
20. Thielscher, M.: Reasoning Robots. Applied Logic Series, vol. 33. Springer, Netherlands (2005)
21. Traverso, P., Pistore, M.: Automated Composition of Semantic Web Services into Executable Processes. In: McIlraith, S.A., Plexousakis, D., van Harmelen, F. (eds.) ISWC 2004. LNCS, vol. 3298, pp. 380–394. Springer, Heidelberg (2004)
22. WSML Working Group: The Web Service Modeling Language WSML (2008), `http://www.wsmo.org/wsml/wsml-syntax`

Template-Based Ontology Population for Smart Environments Configuration

Sebastián Aced López, Dario Bonino, and Fulvio Corno

Dipartimento di Automatica ed Informatica
Politecnico di Torino
Torino, Italy
{sebastian.acedlopez,dario.bonino,fulvio.corno}@polito.it

Abstract. Smart Environments is one of several domains in which Semantic Web technologies are applied nowadays. Ontologies, in particular, are used as core modeling languages for representing devices, systems and environments. Developing such ontologies, that typically involve several device descriptions (individuals) and related information, i.e., individuals of classes contributing to the device model, is often done by a manual, time consuming, and error-prone approach.

This paper presents a template based approach, which increases accuracy, ease of use, and time-effectiveness of the ontology population process by reducing the amount of user-given information of about an order of magnitude, with respect to the fully manual approach. User-required information only pertains device features (e.g., name, location, etc.) and never implies knowledge of Semantic Web technologies, thus enabling end-user configuration of smart homes and buildings. Experimental results with a prototypical implementation confirm the viability of the approach on a real-world use case.

1 Introduction

Semantic Web technologies have allowed cities, workplaces and homes to become *smarter* over the years by supporting explicit context representation, expressive context querying, and flexible context reasoning [9]. Ontologies can be used to model agents, contexts and behaviors, while SPARQL querying helps to easily retrieve data from them, and reasoners can use these data to infer relations and describe complex scenarios, enriching the model capabilities.

Modeling Smart Environments (SmEs) by means of ontologies enables the creation of a layer of abstraction, in which reality is represented in terms of classes, properties and instances, and allows developers to work with conceptualizations of real entities instead of dealing with low-level representations of them.

Adding new instances into the ontology is known as populating (or instantiating) the ontology, and it is an essential part of almost every ontology based application, especially in the SmE field, because the only way of configuring a specific SmE, such as *my-particular-room*, is by creating specific instances, such as *my-particular-floor* or *my-particular-lamp*. However, as it will be explained

A.R. Lomuscio et al. (Eds.): ICSOC 2013 Workshops, LNCS 8377, pp. 271–278, 2014.
© Springer International Publishing Switzerland 2014

later, most of the available methods to populate ontologies are error prone and time consuming.

This paper proposes an OWL-template based approach that allows accurate, fast and semi-automatic population of ontologies that can be used in general, but specifically helps in the configuration of SmEs.

2 Related Works

Even if many ontologies have been created and are actually being used in a variety of fields such as SmE modeling, better methods to populate them are still object of research due to the challenging nature of the task. However, like for the content and the structure, population techniques (listed in [7]) change a lot from one type of ontology to another. The approaches for ontology population found in literature can be divided into two types depending on how the information to generate the individuals is gathered: either through *Information extraction* or *User-given* data.

Information extraction approaches assume that the needed information is already available somewhere, it could be on text documents, Internet pages, databases etc., so they extract and process it to identify pieces that fit as instances of some reference ontology[1]. This is the case of the Artequakt system [1], which automatically extracts biographical information from the web to instantiate a reference ontology and generate artists biographies.

Approaches based on user-given data, on the converse, gather the information needed for instantiation directly from the user, as proposed in [6] and in [4]. This is the case in SmE context, since the needed information is specific for each particular environment configuration and cannot be mined elsewhere. However, few of the approaches that gather information from the user, focus on the generation of new individuals. Instead, they aim to support the design and creation of new concept classes. See [5].

On the other hand, this paper presents an approach to enhance the creation process of new individuals from already defined classes, exploiting different techniques (inherited from the software engineering) based on automatic code generation and template modeling, which have already been proven appropriate for working with ontologies [8].

3 Background

In this paper, examples and experimentation exploit a publicly available ontology for smart environments named DogOnt[2] [2]. It is organized in 5 main hierarchies of concepts:

[1] The term *Reference ontology* refers to an ontology containing the classes from which the instances are going to be created.

[2] `http://elite.polito.it/ontologies/dogont`

- Building Environment (BE): The concepts below this hierarchy are used to describe the architectural spaces of built environments (Garage, Flat, Room, etc.)
- Building Thing (BT): The concepts below this hierarchy are used to describe the controllable (i.e., devices) and uncontrollable objects (e.g., furniture) of a given environment.
- State: The concepts below this hierarchy are used to describe the working configurations (observable status) that controllable BT objects can assume.
- Functionality: The concepts below this hierarchy are used to describe the controllable BT objects capabilities.
- Network Component: The concepts below this hierarchy are used to describe the technology-specific information needed for describing real-world devices.

Users configure specific SmEs by instantiating BE and BT concepts and by connecting them according to the ontology-defined domain semantics.

4 Problem Statement

The population process, as stated previously, is time-consuming and error-prone [7], mainly because of two challenging tasks it encompasses: *instance properties determination* and *implicitly derived instantiation*. Figure 1 presents a DogOnt fragment example to help to illustrate those concepts.

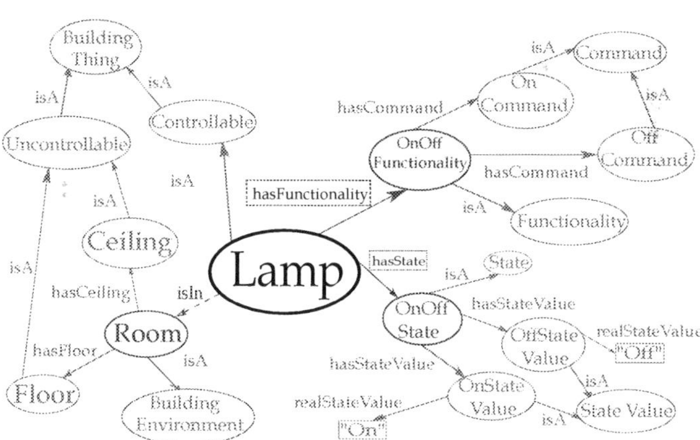

Fig. 1. Ontology fragment showing a DogOnt Lamp class

Instance Properties Determination

When a class is instantiated, it is not easy to identify which properties must be included in the new instance description, for it to be valid and logically consistent, and which properties can, instead, be omitted. The former type of properties, namely *Mandatory properties* need to be created for the model to be valid (under a logic and semantics standpoint) whereas the latter properties (*Optional properties*) are not strictly required from a formal standpoint but might be crucial for the model to be usable in the real world (e.g., the location of a given device).

Classifying the properties of a class as mandatory or optional, helps to determine which of them *must* and which of them *may* be part of a new instance description. More in detail:

- *Mandatory properties*: A property is mandatory if, in the class definition of a given individual, its Cardinality Constraint is at least one. In other words, the class mandatory properties are those that an individual must include in its description, to be considered a valid instance of such class. Figure 1 shows the mandatory properties of Lamp class: *hasState* and *hasFunctionality.*

- *Optional properties*: Optional properties may be included in an individual description but are not required for it to be a valid instance of any class. The user decides whether to include optional properties in a particular instance description. In the example of Figure 1, the optional property *isIn* is represented by a dashed arrow.

Implicitly Derived Instantiation

Assuming that the properties of a new individual have been established somehow and it has been determined which of them can be automatically generated, the *implicitly derived instantiation* problem has to be solved. Implicitly derived instantiation refers to the fact that sometimes the *explicit* creation of a new instance, *implicitly* leads to the generation of additional individuals. This happens when an explicitly created instance is described by *object properties*, because they describe instances by associating them with other URI resources (classes or individuals), that also need to be created in order to produce valid associations and valid descriptions. This is illustrated better by Figure 1: when an instance is created explicitly, for example a Lamp instance, and it has an *object property*, such as *hasState*, implicitly another instance has to be created, in this case a new *OnOffState* individual.

Implicitly derived instantiation becomes a problem in large and highly interrelated ontologies because the creation of one instance can start a chain reaction of instantiations, making of the population task a long and complex process.

5 Proposed Solution

In order to improve the ontology population process, and in particular to tackle the inherent complexity of the tasks discussed in the previous section, a two stage approach is proposed which aims at reducing the cardinality of information needed from the user and at hiding ontology formalisms by only requiring actually needed data (e.g., device types and names instead of device instance definitions). The two stages exploit different techniques based on automatic code generation and template modeling, respectively.

The information cardinality reduction is based on the identification of which objects/properties require external information to be created. For example, in DogOnt, to describe a room instance, the Room class property *hasFloor* must be filled with a *Floor* individual manually defined by the user (two rooms can share the same floor). Instead, other classes, e.g., OnOffStateValue, are completely specified and individuals creation can be automatically carried. Moreover, if a given class has mandatory properties that refer to fully specified classes, individuals of such a class can also be generated automatically, by implementing a suitable recursive mechanism. In this way the amount of instances that need manual creation can be greatly reduced, depending on the ontology branching and the adopted modeling approach: highly specified models experience greater improvements with respect to loosely specified ones. SmE ontologies typically fall in the former typology.

Formalism hiding, instead, is obtained through a template-based mechanism which models repetitive syntactical structures in OWL, (e.g., type definitions) and replaces information that must be given by users with suitable placeholders to be filled at configuration time. In such a way, the actual data that users are required to fill decreases (contributing to an additional cardinality reduction) and ontology constructs are completely hidden and exposed as free parameters to be filled.

In such a way, this approach helps to populate ontologies more quickly (due to cardinality reduction) and more accurately (templates are validated once and ensure syntactical correctness) than in the current state of the art. More in detail, the overall approach is divided in the following three phases, and is illustrated in Figure 2:

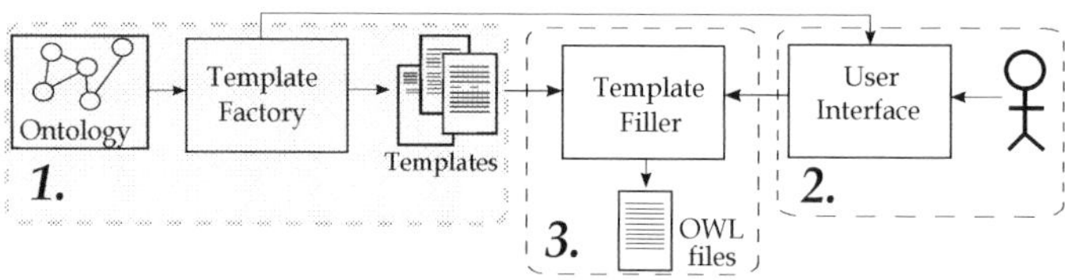

Fig. 2. Block diagram of the proposed approach

5.1 Template Generation

The template generation phase, which is executed offline only once (unless the reference ontology itself changes) by the Template Factory, aims to create a template for each target class.

Templates are divided into two parts: a *main block* and a *secondary block*. The main block contains the description of the target class instance (*the main instance*) for whom the template is created. The secondary block contains the descriptions of all the *implicitly* derived instances (*secondary instances*).

In order to obtain a template, two steps have to be followed: *reference ontology exploration*, to determine and classify the properties used in the instance descriptions and *the template writing* in which those instance descriptions are structured and written in a template body.

Reference Ontology Exploration. To create a template of a target class, the reference ontology is recursively explored to find all the classes and properties "connected" to such a class, identifying which information shall be filled by the user and which one can be generated by an unsupervised process. Such an exploration is based on SPARQL querying. The query process retrieves the properties that can be used to describe target classes, and the information needed to classify those properties as mandatory or optional.

Exploration queries should be designed to exploit the specific characteristics of each reference ontology. As an example, in the DogOnt ontology used throughout this paper for illustrating the proposed approach, mandatory properties do not have free parameters, whereas the optional object properties always have them. Consequently, its particular exploration query only returns the necessary information to classify properties in the following groups:

- *Mandatory object properties*
- *Mandatory datatype properties*
- *Optional object properties*

Template Writing. Once the template information is gathered and the class properties properly classified, the template can be written. As stated before a template is structured in blocks (main and secondary), each one describing an instance. In general, such blocks contain:

- *Namespace* and *main instance name* placeholders.
- Static OWL statements: Corresponding to the mandatory properties with no free parameters.
- Parametrized OWL statements: Corresponding to the mandatory properties with free parameters, i.e., placeholders.
- Optional Statements: Corresponding to IF statements enclosing the optional properties.
- A `rdf:type` property stating the class of the instance described in the block.

5.2 User Input Information

After the template generation phase, information from the user is required to resolve the Optional Statements and to assign proper values to the template placeholders. Such information could be gathered through any user interaction mechanisms, e.g. through a graphical user interface (GUI). Figure 2 shows an arrow that goes from the Template Factory to the UI block, to indicate that the former must supply information, such as the placeholder labels, to configure the latter.

5.3 Ontology Consolidation

The last phase of the overall process, consists in merging the template-encoded information with the data entered by the user. The latter, in particular, replaces all the template placeholders providing a valid and fully consistent OWL instance definition. The steps to consolidate it are very simple:

1. Replace all the *namespace* and *main instance name* placeholders.
2. Resolve the IF statements (if present) to determine which optional properties to include in the instance description.
3. Replace the rest of the template placeholders.
4. Write the output OWL file.

6 Experimental Results

The template based approach exposed along this document has been initially tested in a real world case of ontology-based smart environment configuration. More precisely, experiments were carried to populate a specific SmE: the *Simple Home* [3] which is based on the DogOnt ontology (1835 classes) and describes a flat with several (114) domotic devices modeled by 1408 concept instances.

The prototype tool developed for experimentation uses the Jena framework to manage the ontologies and the ARQ engine to issue SPARQL queries at the template generation phase. User information is collected through a dynamically generated JavaFX application which also drives the consolidation process. User given information, is mapped to a set of automatically generated Java Beans accompanying each template and providing the additional information to check the correctness of filled data, e.g., the allowed placeholder filler classes. This set of beans, is then used in the ontology consolidation phase by a Velocity Template Engine to fill the templates.

Experimental results confirm that by following the approach presented in this document, the effort and time that users spent manually populating such a large ontology was significantly reduced by using templates: the entire population process took, in fact, less than one day (vs. over a week in the fully manual case) and only required to fill free parameters for the 114 devices (roughly 300 parameters) instead of manually describing the 1408 required instances (amounting to about 7000 triples), with a cardinality reduction of over one order of magnitude.

7 Conclusions

This paper discussed a general template-based approach for effective ontology population, with a particular focus on the smart environment domain. While the general problem of implicitly derived instantiation affecting current tools (e.g., general editors as Protégé) cannot be fully solved as ontology modeling implies the creation of related instances, with a complexity that depends on the ontology branching factor, template-based solutions, as the one presented, allow to greatly reduce the cardinality of user-given information and, at the same time hide ontology-specific formalisms from the end users.

Preliminary experimental results, confirmed the viability of the proposed solution with over an order of magnitude reduction in the cardinality of information required to users: about 300 parameters vs over 7000 triples.

Future works will involve extensive experimentation with users, by exploiting different ontology models for SmEs and a thoroughly study of user interfaces for filling free parameters.

References

1. Alani, H., Kim, S., Millard, D.E., Weal, M.J., Hall, W., Lewis, P.H., Shadbolt, N.: Using protege for automatic ontology instantiation. In: 7th International Protégé Conference, Event Dates: July 6-9 (2004), http://eprints.soton.ac.uk/259479/
2. Bonino, D., Corno, F.: DogOnt - ontology modeling for intelligent domotic environments. In: Sheth, A.P., Staab, S., Dean, M., Paolucci, M., Maynard, D., Finin, T., Thirunarayan, K. (eds.) ISWC 2008. LNCS, vol. 5318, pp. 790–803. Springer, Heidelberg (2008), http://dblp.uni-trier.de/db/conf/semweb/iswc2008.html#BoninoC08
3. Bonino, D., Corno, F.: Dogsim: A state chart simulator for domotic environments. In: PerCom Workshops, pp. 208–213. IEEE (2010), http://dblp.uni-trier.de/db/conf/percom/percomw2010.html#BoninoC10
4. Doherty, L., Kumar, V., Winne, P.: Assisted ontology instantiation: a learningkit perspective. In: Seventh IEEE International Conference on Advanced Learning Technologies, ICALT 2007, pp. 265–267 (2007)
5. Jupp, S., Horridge, M., Iannone, L., Klein, J., Owen, S., Schanstra, J., Stevens, R., Wolstencroft, K.: Populous: A tool for populating templates for owl ontologies. In: Burger, A., Marshall, M.S., 0001, P.R., Paschke, A., Splendiani, A. (eds.) SWAT4LS. CEUR Workshop Proceedings, vol. 698. CEUR-WS.org (2010), http://dblp.uni-trier.de/db/conf/swat4ls/swat4ls2010.html#JuppHIKOSSW10
6. Kawamoto, K., Kitamura, Y., Tijerino, Y.: Kawawiki: A semantic wiki based on rdf templates. In: WI-IATW 2006: Proceedings of the 2006 IEEE/WIC/ACM International Conference on Web Intelligence and Intelligent Agent Technology, pp. 425–432. IEEE Computer Society, Washington, DC (2006), http://portal.acm.org/citation.cfm?id=1194764
7. Maleshkova, M., Martínez, I.: Ontology instantiation state of the art report. Tech. rep. (2008)
8. Parreiras, F.S., Gröner, G., Walter, T., Staab, S.: A model-driven approach for using templates in OWL ontologies. In: Cimiano, P., Pinto, H.S. (eds.) EKAW 2010. LNCS, vol. 6317, pp. 350–359. Springer, Heidelberg (2010), http://dx.doi.org/10.1007/978-3-642-16438-5_25
9. Wang, X., Dong, J.S., Chin, C., Hettiarachchi, S., Zhang, D.: Semantic space: An infrastructure for smart spaces. IEEE Pervasive Computing 3(3), 32–39 (2004)

Introduction to the 3rd International Workshop on Cloud Computing and Scientific Applications (CCSA'13)

Suraj Pandey[1] and Surya Nepal[2]

[1] IBM Research Australia
suraj.pandey@au.ibm.com
[2] CSIRO Computational Informatics
surya.nepal@csiro.au

CCSA workshop has been formed to promote research and development activities focused on enabling and scaling scientific applications using distributed computing paradigms, such as cluster, Grid, and Cloud Computing. With the rapid emergence of virtualized environments for accessing software systems and solutions, the volume of users and their data are growing exponentially. According to the IDC, by 2020, when the ICT industry reaches $5 billion - $1.7 billion larger than it is today - at least 80% of the industry's growth will driven by 3rd platform technologies, such as cloud services and big data analytics. Existing computing infrastructure, software system designs, and use cases will have to take into account the enormity in volume of requests, size of data, computing load, locality and type of users, and every growing needs of all applications. Cloud computing promises reliable services delivered through next-generation data centers that are built on compute and storage virtualization technologies. Users will be able to access applications and data from a Cloud anywhere in the world on demand. In other words, the Cloud appears to be a single point of access for all the computing needs of users. The users are assured that the Cloud infrastructure is robust and will always be available at any time. To address the growing needs of both applications and Cloud computing paradigm, CCSA brings together researchers and practitioners from around the world to share their experiences, to focus on modeling, executing, and monitoring scientific applications on Clouds. In this workshop, there were 20 submissions. The committee decided to accept 7 papers. The program also includes 1 invited talk as a keynote.

Summary of Papers Presented in the Workshop

The paper titled "SLA-Aware Load Balancing in a Web-Based Cloud System over OpenStack" presents an architecture that enables load balancing of web-application by distributing the load across virtual machines, while preserving the service-level-agreement. The paper maintains the SLA by expanding the computing capacity dynamically to avoid system overload by adding additional VMs when experiencing sudden increases in the number of users and requests in system.

The paper titled "Are Public Clouds Elastic Enough for Scientific Computing?" presents a review of solutions proposed by public cloud providers and points the open

A.R. Lomuscio et al. (Eds.): ICSOC 2013 Workshops, LNCS 8377, pp. 279–280, 2014.
© Springer International Publishing Switzerland 2014

issues and challenges in providing elasticity for scientific applications. It also describes initiatives that are being developed in that space.

The paper titled "A light-weight framework for bridge-building from desktop to cloud" describes a light-weight framework based on cloud and REST to address (i) the heavy weight and diversity of infrastructures that inhibits sharing and collaboration between services, (ii) the relatively complicated processes associated with deployment and management of web services for non-disciplinary specialists, and (iii) the relative technical difficulty in packaging the legacy software that encapsulates key discipline knowledge for web-service environments.

The paper titled "Planning and Scheduling Data Processing Workflows in the Cloud with Quality-of-Data Constraints" introduces a new scheduling criterion, Quality-of-Data (QoD), that specifically focuses on continuous data processing workflows, where the scheduler does not perform any reasoning about the impact new input data may have in the workflow final output. The authors have illustrated the viability of their research by developing a WaaS (Workflow-as-a-Service), a workflow coordinator system for the Cloud where data is shared among tasks via cloud-based columnar databases.

The paper titled "Galaxy + Hadoop: Toward a Collaborative and Scalable Image Processing Toolbox in Cloud" presents a cloud-based image processing tool- box by integrating Galaxy, Hadoop and CSIRO's proprietary image processing tools. The paper provides the integration architecture and technical details about the whole system. In particular, it investigates the use of Hadoop to handle massive image processing jobs.

The paper titled "SciLightning - a Cloud Provenance-based Event Notification for Parallel Workflows" presents a workflow event notification mechanism based on runtime monitoring of provenance data produced by parallel scientific workflow systems in clouds. The paper also evaluated their proposed mechanism by monitoring SciPhy, a large-scale parallel execution of a bioinformatics phylogenetic analysis workflow.

The paper titled "Energy Savings on a Cloud-based Opportunistic Infrastructure" presents the problem of virtual machines consolidation on the opportunistic cloud computing resources. It investigates four workload packing algorithms that place a set of virtual machines on the least number of physical machines to increase resource utilization and to transition parts of the unused resources into a lower power states or switching off. In addition, it empirically evaluates these heuristics on real workload traces collected from our experimental opportunistic cloud, called UnaCloud.

Acknowledgement. We would like to thank Dr Shiping Chen for chairing the event. We also thank EasyChair.org for providing the conference management system.

SLA-Aware Load Balancing in a Web-Based Cloud System over OpenStack

Jordi Vilaplana, Francesc Solsona, Jordi Mateo, and Ivan Teixido

Dept. of Computer Science and INSPIRES, University of Lleida,
Jaume II 69, E-25001 Lleida, Spain
{jordi,francesc,jmateo,iteixido}@diei.udl.cat
http://gcd.udl.cat

Abstract. This paper focuses on the scalability problem in cloud-based systems when changing the computing requirements, this is, when there is a high degree of requesting service variability in cloud-computing environments. We study a specific scenario for web-based application deployed in a cloud system, where the number of requests can change with time. This paper deals with guaranteeing the SLA (Service-Level Agreement) in scalable clouds with web-based load variability.

We present an architecture able to balance the load (mainly web-browser applications) between different computing virtual machines. This is accomplished by monitoring the system in order to determine when to create or terminate virtual machines. A novel scheduling policy to manage the requested cloud services based on the presented architecture is also proposed.

The good results obtained by implementing the proposed architecture in a real cloud framework prove the applicability of our proposal for guaranteeing SLA.

1 Introduction

Cloud computing offers a wide range of benefits by moving the computing infrastructure to the Internet, reducing the costs for the maintenance and management of hardware and software resources [2]. In cloud computing, hardware and software services are more efficiently handled than in other High-Performance Computing (HPC) infrastructure, as they can be added and released dynamically [4]. In our case, Virtual Machines (VM) will be the basic computing infrastructures to be managed. Cloud computing has gained worldwide attention from many researchers, but only a few have addressed the performance problem [6].

A Service-Level Agreement (SLA) is an agreement between a service provider and a consumer, where the provider agrees to deliver a service to the consumer under specific terms, such as time or performance. In order to comply with the SLA, the service provider must closely monitor the QoS (Quality of Service) through such parameters as throughput or response time [1]. In this scenario, the SLA contract usually states that the consumer only pays for the resources and services used according to negotiated QoS requirements at a given price [3].

A.R. Lomuscio et al. (Eds.): ICSOC 2013 Workshops, LNCS 8377, pp. 281–293, 2014.
© Springer International Publishing Switzerland 2014

To study and determine SLA-related issues is a big challenge mainly due to the complex nature of cloud computing and especially to its high variability [8]. We do not focus on SLA cloud interface, specification or similar issues, such as the SLAng project, a language for specifying Service-Level Agreements within the ASP language [16].

We focus our research on designing a cloud-computing framework providing QoS and high performance for a given SLA and number of HPC users. We have based this on the response time as the QoS performance metric. Response time is defined as the time spent by a request to be processed and a response to be sent back to the client. Job response time is perhaps the most important QoS metric in a cloud-computing context [3]. For this reason, it is also the QoS parameter chosen in this work. This paper also deals with problems of variability [8] and reliability [12], leaving aside such other cloud-computing issues as security capabilities [9], cloud availability [10] and power-aware energy consumption [11].

As stated in [5], most current cloud-computing infrastructures consist of services that are offered and delivered through a service center that can be accessed from a web browser anywhere in the world. Thus, the cloud has a single access point, accessed through a web browser. In addition, for the same reason, we also consider that the main workload, the applications being executed in the cloud, will be of the web-browser kind. As was pointed out in [7], user requests are sent by users and redirected by the scheduler to the web servers (located at the virtual machines) running a service application, which has an associated SLA.

The main contribution of this paper consists of a cloud-based architecture capable of monitoring and managing cloud-computing resources, i.e. virtual machines (VMs). In other words, it takes into account the variability of cloud systems. In this model, the main component of this architecture is the scheduler (acting as a load balancer), which will initialize or terminate VMs depending on the current state of the system in order to comply with the SLA. We based this on Ming [15], who presented a programming mechanism to automatically scale computing resources on a cloud-based system based on workload information and performance desire. It was based on the load activity by starting and shutting down VM instances. The mechanism enables cloud applications to finish submitted jobs within the deadline by controlling the amount of instances, and reduces user costs by choosing appropriate instance types. As web-browser applications require a high response time performance, we have replaced a deadline on the response time as the QoS metric.

We also apply and modify the ideas presented in [13,14], but applied to cloud computing managing mainly web-browsing applications. In [13], a mechanism for managing SLAs in a cloud computing environment using the Web Service Level Agree- ment (WSLA) framework was proposed. In [14], Buyya presented the main challenges and architectural elements of SLA-oriented resource management.

The proposed architecture was implemented using *OpenStack*[1], which is an open-source software that provides facilities for dynamically managing VMs.

[1] `http://www.openstack.org` *OpenStak.* `http://www.openstack.org`

This adds additional value to the paper because the tests were performed on a real platform.

The remainder of the paper is organized as follows. In Section 2 the architecture and implementation of our cloud proposal are presented. Section 3 is focused in the main component, the scheduler. The experimentation showing the good behavior of our cloud framework is presented in Section 4, where representative workloads are tested and analyzed. Finally, Section 5 outlines the main conclusions and possible research lines to explore in the near future.

2 Architecture and Implementation

The proposed architecture is schematically presented in Figure 1. It has been designed to provide a certain degree of scalability and variability-aware and reliability. Therefore, the architecture is divided between different physical sites, which will host the different components of the system. In our case, it is composed of two different sites: *Site 1* and *Site 2*. Both sites are mode up of a single physical machine. *OpenStack* is deployed on top of *Site 1* and *Site 2*. *Site 2* adds redundancy, hence increasing the fault tolerance and reliability of the system and to provide scalability. Note that additional sites could be added without major changes to the underlying architecture.

Site 1 hosts the VM where the *Load Balancer* or simply the *Scheduler* is located. The *Scheduler* acts as the entry point to the system. The *Scheduler* was implemented using the *Apache HTTP Server v2.2*[2] with the *mod_proxy_balancer* module. The *mod_proxy_balancer* is governed by the scheduling policy presented in the next section (Section 3).

As we designed the cloud to operate as a web server, users will access the system using a web browser. Thus, web-based applications are executed inside and are deployed over the cloud computing components. That being said, *HTTP* requests from different users enter the system through the *Scheduler* VM, which decides which *Computing VM* (or simply *VM*) the request will be sent to. Once a VM has been selected, the request is forwarded to it. The VMs are deployed on top of the Apache Tomcat web server.

The communication between the *Scheduler* and the computing VM nodes follows a master-worker paradigm. All computing VMs are configured with the *AJP*[3] protocol enabled, which is used by the scheduler to communicate with the VMs. The AJP protocol enables inbound requests from a web server like Apache HTTP server to be proxied to an application server like Apache Tomcat. It also allows the web server to perform a basic monitoring of the applications being executed in the cloud to determine their status and to know if the applications are operative or not.

---

[2] `http://httpd.apache.org` *Apache HTTP Server.* `http://httpd.apache.org`

[3] `http://tomcat.apache.org/connectors-doc/ajp/ajpv13a.html`
AJP. Apache Tomcat Connector - Apache JServ Protocol

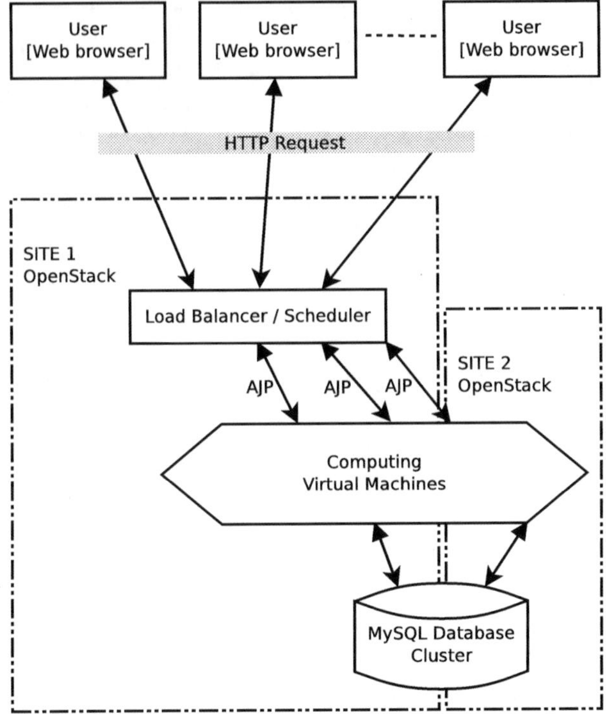

Fig. 1. System architecture

Each computing instance is created from a unique snapshot instance. A snapshot is an image created from a running VM. In OpenStack, a new snapshot can be created using the following command:

```
$ nova image-create <uuid> <snapshot\_name>,
```

where *nova* is a client of the *OpenStack Nova API*[4], *image-create* is a command to create a new image by taking a snapshot of a running server, *uuid* is the unique universal identifier of the VM running and *snapshot name* is the name assigned to the newly created snapshot. Once this process is complete, the snapshot is available for booting into a new VM instance.

The use of snapshots allows the VMs to be updated to newer versions of web application very easily. Therefore, future upgrading processes or configuration changes can be easily done and extended to the whole system without having to update each node manually. This way, required changes can be done in a single VM and then a snapshot of it created to be used to instantiate in other location.

Although this work is not focused on data-intensive architectures, the database has been implemented using *MySQL Cluster v7.3*[5], a widely used open-source

[4] `http://api.openstack.org` *OpenStack Nova API.* `http://api.openstack.org`

[5] `http://dev.mysql.com/downloads/cluster/` *MySQL Cluster v7.3.* `http://dev.mysql.com/downloads/cluster/`

SQL database. By doing so, we achieve a higher degree of robustness and availability in the cloud framework. The MySQL Cluster is distributed between the two sites, and can be implemented with the desired number of VMs in each site. Having multiple computing and data VMs ensures a higher degree of load scalability and reliability.

3 SLA-Aware Scheduling

First of all, we present the scheduling policy, named *Pending Request Policy* (PRP). This policy assigns an incoming request to the VM with the lowest number of active requests at that moment. Therefore, when a new request arrives, it is assigned to the VM that is currently processing the fewest requests. This policy performs very accurate balancing among the VMs when all requests have a similar difficulty to be served. When some requests could need a lot of computing resources and others may not, this policy would not be a good option. However, web-based requests are usually evenly balanced, so it was the chosen scheduling policy.

Next, PRP is defined formally. A normalized score is assigned to each VM. This determines the number of requests that the scheduler will send to such a VM. The normalized score is obtained as follows. Assuming that the scores of the computing VMs (VM_i, where $i = 1..n$, n being the actual number of computing VMs) are S_{VM_i}, the normalized score of VM_i, namely N_{VM_i}, is obtained as follows:

$$N_{VM_i} = \frac{S_{VM_i}}{\sum_k S_{VM_k}} \tag{1}$$

Therefore, the closer the normalized score is to one, the more requests will be mapped to such a VM. This policy is based on the computing capacity of the VMs, and allows us to decide which ones will process more requests.

Additional functionality is implemented through Python scripts and *OpenStack*.

Algorithm 1 describes in detail how the main script manages the creation and termination of OpenStack instances (VMs). See Fig. 2 for additional explanation. The script is responsible for guaranteeing the negotiated SLA for the overall users. T_{max} corresponds to the response time above which new VMs will be launched in order to try to lower it. Therefore, T_{max} should be close to, but no higher than, the maximum user response time negotiated in the SLA agreement. This is because new VMs become operational after an *Initialization* period of time (see Fig. 2). T_{min} corresponds to the response time below which additional VMs will be terminated. Hence, T_{min} should be below, an also close to, the minimum user-negotiated response time.

The current response time of the system is calculated through the $loadTest()$ function (explained in Algorithm 3). It performs various HTTP requests and calculates its average. Afterwards, if the average response time is above T_{max}, a new OpenStack instance is launched using the $newInstance()$ function (described in detail in Algorithm 2). If there is any error during the initialization of

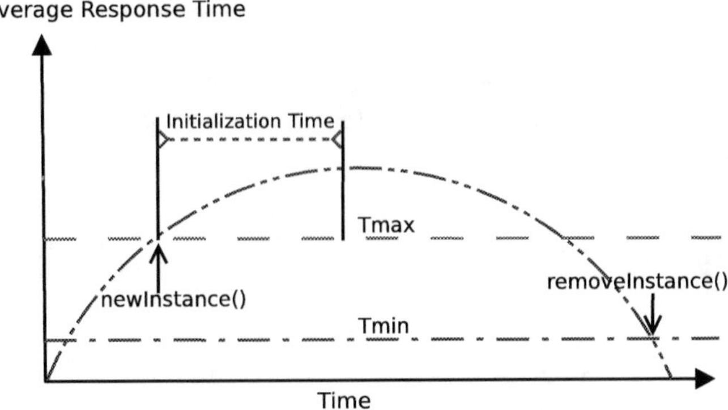

Fig. 2. Scheduling diagram

Algorithm 1. main()

Require: $maxTime = T_{max}$
Require: $minTime = T_{min}$
Ensure: $T_{max} > T_{min}$

```
avgTime = loadTest()
if avgTime ≥ maxTime then
   instance ⇐ newInstance()
   if instance == error then
      sendAlert()
   end if
   addInstance(instance)
   reloadConfig()
else if avgTime < minTime then
   instance ⇐ terminateInstance()
   removeInstance(instance)
   reloadConfig()
end if
```

---

the new instance, an alert is sent using the *sendAlert*() function. This function sends an email to a predefined email address to alert the system operator, as human intervention is likely to be needed. Once the new VM is running, it is added to the Apache HTTP Server configuration file, so that future incoming requests are also mapped to this instance. Finally, the configuration is reloaded through the *reloadConfig*() function to apply the previous modifications to the Apache HTTP Server configuration file. This is done by performing a system call to the *Apache HTTP Server* with the *reload* command. Note that by doing so, the server is not restarted and, hence, there is no time penalties from resetting the system.

Algorithm 2 describes the process of launching a new VM (namely *newInstance*()). The *openstack.newInstance*() function uses the *OpenStack API v2* to communicate with the OpenStack framework. Internally, this func-

Algorithm 2. newInstance()

```
instance = openstack.newInstance()
retries = 0
while not openstack.isActive(instance) do
   retries = retries + 1
   if retires > MAX_RETRIES then
      return error
   end if
   time.sleep(1)
end while
floatingIP = openstack.getFloatingIP()
openstack.addFloatingIP(instance, floatingIP)
return instance
```

Algorithm 3. loadTest()

```
url = TEST_URL
avgTime = 0
errors = False
for i = 0; i < 10; i++ do
   start = time.time()
   code = urllib.urlopen(url).getcode()
   end = time.time()
   if code == 200 then
      avgTime+ = (end − start) ∗ 1000)
   else
      errors = True
      break
   end if
end for
if errors then
   return loadTest()
else
   returnavgTime/10
end if
```

tion creates a new VM based on a snapshot instance. A maximum number of retires ($MAX\_RETRIES$) is allowed. A snapshot is an image created from a running VM. All the computing VMs are created using a snapshot, so when the instance is booted, it is already prepared and configured to execute the desired web-based application.

Algorithm 3 shows how the $loadTest()$ function works. It performs 10 consecutive requests to the $TEST\_URL$ web address. This parameter can be set to any valid address, hence it is able to perform the requests against any application endpoint. In our case, this parameter was set to the Internet address of the http server of our cloud framework.

The *start* time is stored before each request. Then, the request is made and the *HTTP status code* is stored in the *code* variable. The *HTTP status code* is a numeric code associated with each response. In our case, we are interested in the *200 OK* status code, which is the standard response for a successful *HTTP* request. Therefore, a *200* status code means that the request has been served successfully. Thus, once the request has been processed, the *end* time is stored. Then, if the request is successful, the time spent processing the request is added to the *avgTime* variable (in milliseconds). On the other hand, if the request is not successful, the algorithm will restart the entire load test. If there are no errors during the process, the average time is calculated and returned to the *main*() function described in Algorithm 1.

The creation of a new VM is not instantaneous, therefore Algorithm 2 checks the status of the new VM through the *openstack.isActive*(*instance*) function and waits until its status becomes active. Note that a maximum number of retries can be set by means of the *MAX_RETRIES* variable. This avoids situations where a new VM is never ready due to an unexpected error. Once active, it assigns a floating (public) IP to that instance. Finally, the function returns the newly-created instance.

The functions *addInstance*() and *removeInstance*() modify the Apache HTTP Server configuration file (*httpd.conf*) by adding or removing lines representing VMs.

Algorithm 4. bashScript.sh

```
#!/bin/bash
while true do
  /var/main.sh
  sleep5
end while
```

Algorithm 4 describes the work of an additional script responsible for executing the *main.sh* script every 5 seconds. This way, every 5 seconds the system will be tested in order to know its current average response time. Note that the 5-second interval could be made longer or shorter depending on the type of system and its characteristics.

4 Experimental Results

This section presents the experimental results obtained using the *Apache JMeter* [17] tool. This tool allows a series of load tests to be performed by sending HTTP requests to the system. This way, parametrized performance tests can be automatically performed.

Site 1 hosts two computing VMs and one VM from the MySQL Database cluster. *Site 2* allocates one computing VM and one VM from the MySQL Database

Cluster. Each VM has 4GB RAM and 2 VCPU (Virtual CPU). A VCPU corresponds to one core of an AMD Opteron 6,100 processor running at 2.1 GHz. The Scheduler was deployed on a VM with 512MB RAM and 1 VCPU in *Site 1*, as mentioned above.

The test plan was configured to simulate 600 different users. Each user performed a total of 200 requests, with a 100-millisecond delay between each request. A ramp-up period of 60 seconds was set. That means that all 600 users were launched within 60 seconds.

4.1 Response Time

Figure 3 shows the average response time (in milliseconds) of the system when using two computing VMs. The *Scheduler* was configured not to launch any additional VM during the duration of this test. Therefore, the scheduling algorithm described in Section 3 was not operative.

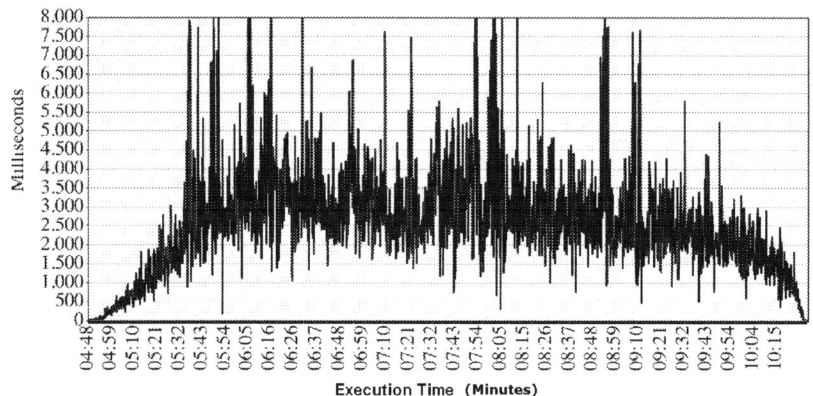

Fig. 3. Response time evolution without initializing additional VMs

It can be seen how response time increases sharply. Then it remains at between 2,000 and 4,000 milliseconds until the end of the test, when response time decreases as users are finishing and the number of requests is dropping. This test shows a severe saturation of the system, which leads to high response times. In the last interval of time, the average response time decreases due to users stopping sending requests and hence, the system load lowers.

The same test, with the same characteristics as described above was repeated (see Fig. 4). This time, the scheduling algorithm was configured to initialize two additional computing VMs (*newInstance()* and *removeInstance()* were executed twice) when the average response time exceeded 500 milliseconds. This is T_{max} was set to 500.

From Figure 4 we can see how average response time increases sharply at the beginning, like before, but stabilizes quickly and decreases continuously with new

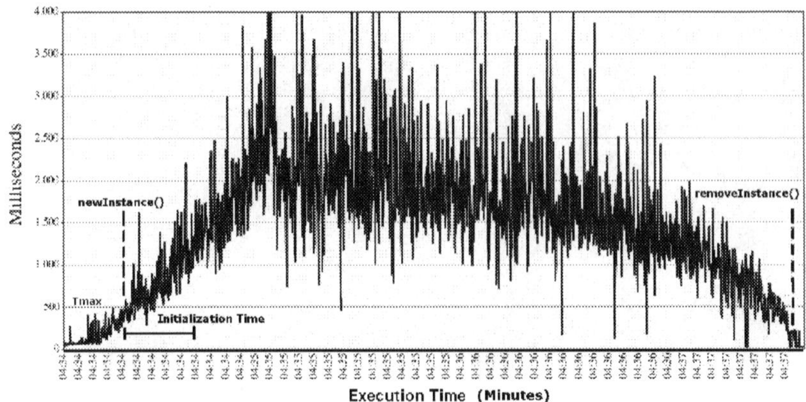

Fig. 4. Response time evolution when initializing additional VMs

VMs added. Note that there is a significant interval of time between the instant when the average response time exceeds 500 milliseconds and when it stops growing. This is due to the fact that the new VMs are not activated instantly, but rather take around 20 seconds to become operational (the Initialization Time). We obviated testing the system when T_{min} was underpassed because no stress information about the cloud behavior is added at all.

4.2 Additional Performance Measurements

Further tests were done in order to measure additional performance metrics. These metrics are the average response time, the median response time, the 90% line and the throughput. The 90% line (also called the 90th percentile) is the response time below which 90% of the request response times fall. In other words, a 90% line value of X means that 90% of the requests have been processed in X time or less. Consequently, 10% of the requests will be above and 90%, below X time. The median is equivalent to the 50th percentile. The throughput metric indicates the number of requests served per second. This metric can be useful for determining the performance of the system and detecting when it has reached its maximum capacity and become overloaded.

Fig. 5 shows the evolution of all these metrics (average, median, 90% line and throughput) when performing tests with different loads using the two additional computing nodes. The test plan was configured to simulate from 100 to 900 different users. Each user performed a total of 100 requests, with a 100-millisecond delay between each request. A ramp-up period of 60 seconds was set for all tests.

The 90% line was added as percentiles are commonly used in service-level agreements. It is a helpful complementary metric together with the median and average values in terms of SLA. As we do not have complete control over the Internet network, there can be momentary fluctuations that can greatly affect results in terms of the maximum time required to process a request through a test. For this reason, having a metric that takes most of the samples into account can offer a more reliable estimation of the performance of the system. This can be appreciated in Fig. 5. It can be seen how the average, median and 90% line start increasing rapidly over 400,000 requests. However, system throughput keeps steady until 800,000 requests, where it starts to drop. The median and average do not increase as rapidly as the 90% line, thus giving more SLA information about system behavior.

In Figure 6, the same tests were performed without additional VMs. It can be seen how the system throughput starts decreasing when performing more than 600,000 requests and how the 90% line is significantly higher than in Figure 5.

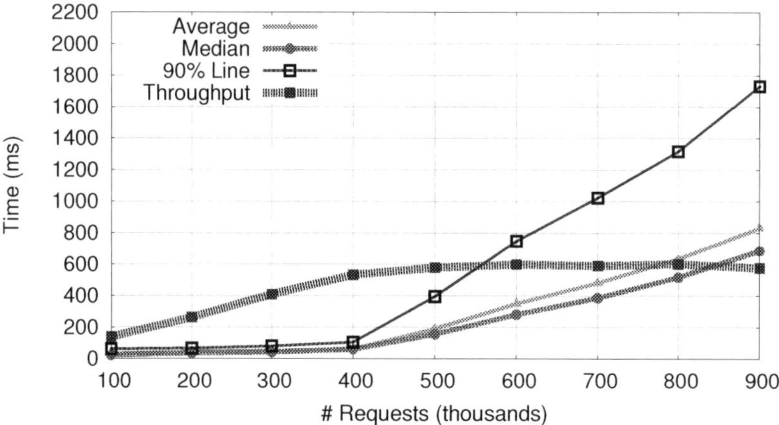

Fig. 5. Evolution of multiple QoS metrics (average, median, 90% Line and throughput) when using additional nodes

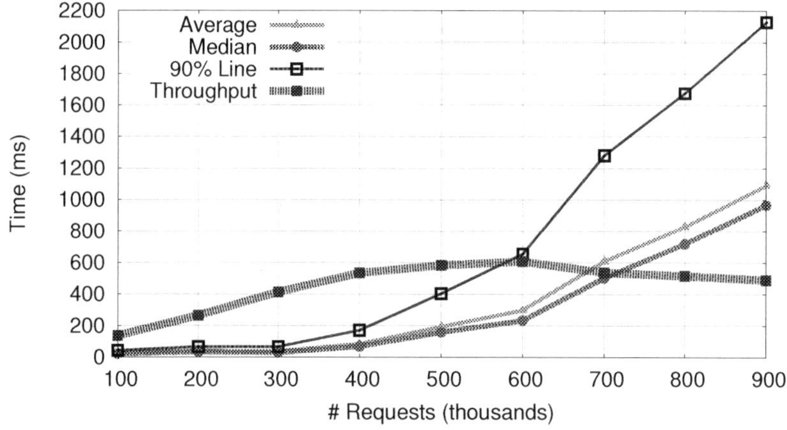

Fig. 6. Evolution of multiple QoS metrics (average, median, 90% Line and throughput) without additional nodes

It can be seen how, in this case, the average, median and 90% line start increasing over the 300,000 requests. System throughput starts decreasing over 600,000 requests. Compared to the previous results (of Figure 5), we can state that a significant increase in the overall performance of the system is obtained by adding two additional computing VMs.

Note also on comparing both tests, that the 90% line can give much better information about guaranteeing SLA. While the average, median and throughput metrics do not give much information about response time, the 90% clearly inform us that some action must be taken to reduce it (i.e. adding more computing VMs).

5 Conclusions and Future Work

This paper presents a cloud-based system architecture able to successfully respond to a high degree of variability complying with SLA agreements. We developed and implemented a cloud framework capable of detecting high response times, initializing new VMs and configuring the *Scheduler* to detect them on the fly. As our cloud mainly applies to web-based applications, response time was used. Moreover, the architecture and implementation design are flexible enough to allow dynamic changes to adapt to different requirements in terms of maximum allowed response time (i.e. the negotiated user SLA agreement). Experimental results show that it is possible to expand the computing capacity dynamically to avoid system overload by adding additional VMs when experiencing abrupt increases in the number of users and requests in system. This proves the good behavior of the system for correcting the problem of variability.

We still want to expand the architecture further by adding multiple schedulers to avoid having a single point of failure and hence, increasing the fault tolerance of the overall system. This could be achieved by using DNS Load Balancing.

We also plan to perform further experimentation with power-aware VM-placement scheduling and VM-migration policies. In this regard, previous research has been done with OpenStack with the OpenStack Neat project [18], which is a framework for dynamic consolidation of VMs within OpenStack. Also, further experimentation and testing with more complex load-balancing software is planned in order to achieve a higher degree of complexity in the scheduler. We have seen that instantiating and initializing a new VM is not instant, and there is a significant delay between the moment when the new instance is required and when the new instance is up and ready. For this reason, we plan to develop and incorporate traffic prediction models in the scheduler.

Acknowledgment. This work was supported by the MEyC under contract TIN2011-28689-C02-02. The authors are members of the research group 2009-SGR145, funded by Generalitat de Catalunya.

References

1. Keller, A., Ludwig, H.: The WSLA Framework: Specifying and Monitoring Service Level Agreements for Web Services. J. Netw. Syst. Manage. 11(1), 57–81 (2003)
2. Vaquero, L.M., Rodero-Merino, L., Caceres, J., Lindner, M.: A Break in the Clouds: Towards a Cloud Definition. ACM SIGCOMM Computer Comm. Rev. 39, 50–55 (2008)
3. Aversa, R., Di Martino, B., Rak, M., Venticinque, S., Villano, U.: Performance Prediction for HPC on Clouds. Cloud Computing: Principles and Paradigms (2011)
4. Armbrust, M., Fox, A., Griffith, R., Joseph, A.D., Katz, R., Konwinski, A., Lee, G., Patterson, D., Rabkin, A., Stoica, I., Zaharia, M.: A view of cloud computing. Commun. ACM 53(4), 50–58 (2010)
5. Xiong, K., Perros, H.: Service Performance and Analysis in Cloud Computing. In: Proc. IEEE World Conf. Services, pp. 693–700 (2009)
6. Khazaei, H., Misic, J., Misic, V.: Performance Analysis of Cloud Computing Centers Using M/G/m/m+r.Queuing Systems. IEEE Transactions on parallel and distributed systems, vol 23(5) (2012)
7. Martin, J., Nilsson, A.: On service level agreements for IP networks. In: Proceedings of the IEEE INFOCOM (2002)
8. Iosup, A., Yigitbasi, N., Epema, D.: On the Performance Variability of Production Cloud Services. In: 11th IEEE/ACM International Symposium on Cluster, Cloud and Grid Computing (CCGrid 2011), pp. 104–113 (2011)
9. Varia, J.: Architection for the Cloud: Best Practices. Amazon Web Services (2010)
10. Martinello, M., Kaâniche, M., Kanoun, K.: Web service availability: Impact of error recovery and traffic model. Journal of Reliability Engineering and System Safety 89(1), 6–16 (2005)
11. Beloglazov, A., Buyya, R.: Optimal online deterministic algorithms and adaptive heuristics for energy and performance efficient dynamic consolidation of virtual machines in Cloud data centers. Concurrency and Computation: Practice and Experiency 24(13), 1397–1420 (2012)
12. Vishwanath, K.V., Nagappan, N.: Characterizing cloud computing hardware reliability. In: Proceedings of the 1st ACM Symposium on Cloud Computing (SoCC 2010), pp. 193–204 (2010)
13. Patel, P., Ranabahu, A., Sheth, A.: Service Level Agreement in Cloud Computing. In: Cloud Workshops at OOPSLA 2009 (2009), `http://knoesis.wright.edu/aboutus/visitors/summer2009/PatelReport.pdf`
14. Buyya, R., Garg, S.K., Calheiros, R.N.: SLA-oriented resource provisioning for cloud computing: Challenges, architecture, and solutions. In: Proceedings of the International Conference on Cloud and Service Computing (CSC 2011), pp. 1–10 (2011)
15. Mao, M., Li, J., Humphrey, M.: Cloud Auto-scaling with Deadline and Budget Constraints. In: Proceedings of the 11th IEEE/ACM International Conference on GRID, pp. 41–48 (2010)
16. Lamanna, D.D., Skene, J., Emmerich, W.: Slang: A language for defining service level agreements, pp. 100–106 (2003)
17. Apache JMeter website. Date of access: (July 19, 2013), `http://jmeter.apache.org/`
18. Beloglazov, A., Buyya, R.: OpenStack Neat: A Framework for Dynamic Consolidation of Virtual Machines in OpenStack Clouds - A Blueprint. Cloud Computing and Distributed Systems (CLOUDS) Laboratory (2012)

Are Public Clouds Elastic Enough for Scientific Computing?

Guilherme Galante[1], Luis Carlos Erpen De Bona[1], Antonio Roberto Mury[2], and Bruno Schulze[2]

[1] Department of Informatics – Federal University of Paraná - UFPR
Curitiba, PR – Brazil
{ggalante,bona}@inf.ufpr
[2] National Laboratory for Scientific Computing - LNCC
Petrpolis, RJ – Brazil
{aroberto,schulze}@lncc.br

Abstract. Elasticity can be seen as the ability of a system to increase or decrease the computing resources allocated in a dynamic and on demand way. It is an important feature provided by cloud computing, that has been widely used in web applications and is also gaining attention in the scientific community. Considering the possibilities of using elasticity in this context, a question arises: "Are the available public cloud solutions suitable to support elastic scientific applications?" To answer the question, we present a review of some solutions proposed by public cloud providers and point the open issues and challenges in providing elasticity for scientific applications. We also present some initiatives that are being developed in order to overcome the current problems. In our opinion, current computational clouds have not yet reached the necessary maturity level to meet all scientific applications elasticity requirements.

Keywords: Cloud computing, elasticity, scientific applications.

1 Introduction

Recently, cloud computing has emerged as an alternative for solving scientific computing problems, with the promise of provisioning virtually infinite resources. According to Simmhan et al. [1], the use of cloud computing environment can be attractive to the scientific community in many ways, benefiting users that own small applications, but also those who perform their experiments in supercomputing centers. In fact, several authors in the technical literature share this opinion and present advantages and benefits of using cloud computing to perform scientific experiments [2].

Cloud computing offers to end users a variety of resources from the hardware to the application level, by charging them on a pay-per-use basis, allowing immediate access to required resources without the need to purchase additional infrastructure. In addition, an important characteristic, not available on traditional architectures (e. g., clusters and grids), emerged on cloud computing: *elasticity*. Elasticity can

A.R. Lomuscio et al. (Eds.): ICSOC 2013 Workshops, LNCS 8377, pp. 294–307, 2014.
© Springer International Publishing Switzerland 2014

be seen as the ability of a system to increase or decrease the computing resources allocated in a dynamic and on demand way. Ideally, to the consumer, the capabilities available for provisioning often appear to be unlimited and can be purchased in any quantity at any time [3]. There are two elasticity types: vertical and horizontal. In vertical elasticity resources, such as processing, memory and storage resources can be added/removed from a running virtual instance. Horizontal elasticity is the ability of the cloud to vary the number of VM's allocated to a service according to demand.

Traditionally, cloud elasticity has been used for scaling traditional web applications in order to handle unpredictable workloads, and enabling companies to avoid the downfalls involved with the fixed provisioning (over and under-provisioning) [4]. In scientific scenario, the use of cloud computing is discussed in several studies [5][6], but the use of elasticity in scientific applications is a subject that is starting to receive attention from research groups [7].

This interest is related to the benefits it can provide, including, improvements in applications performance and cost reduction. Improvements in the performance of applications can be achieved through dynamic allocation of additional processing, memory, network and storage resources. Examples are the addition of nodes in a master-slave application in order to reduce the execution time, and the dynamic storage space allocation when data exceeds the capacity allocated for the hosted environment in the cloud.

The cost reduction is relevant when using resources from public clouds, since resources could be allocated on demand, instead allocating all of them at the beginning of execution, avoiding over-provisioning. It could be used, for example, in applications that use the MapReduce paradigm, where is possible to increase the number of working nodes during the mapping and to scale back resources during the reduction phase. Elastic applications can also increase computational capabilities when cheaper resources became available. An example is the allocation of Amazon Spot Instances, when the price becomes advantageous [8].

Thus, considering the possibilities of using elasticity in the scientific context, a question arises: *are the available public cloud solutions suitable to support elastic scientific applications?* To answer this question, this paper presents a survey covering the elasticity mechanisms offered by major public cloud providers and analyses the limitations of the solutions in providing elasticity for scientific applications. We also present some initiatives that are being developed in order to overcome the current challenges.

1.1 Public Cloud Elasticity Mechanisms

In this section we present nine elasticity solutions proposed by major IaaS and PaaS public providers. In general, most public cloud providers offer some elasticity feature, from the most basic, to more elaborate automatic solutions.

Amazon Web Services [9], offers a mechanism called Auto-Scaling, as part of the EC2 service. The solution is based on the concept of Auto Scaling Group (ASG), which consists of a set of instances that can be used for an application.

Amazon Auto-Scaling uses an reactive approach, in which, for each ASG there is a set of rules that defines the number of VM's to be added or released. The metric values are provided by CloudWatch monitoring service, and include CPU usage, network traffic, disk reads and writes. The solution also includes an API and a command-line interface for manually access the scaling features.

Rackspace [10] also implements horizontal elasticity, but unlike Amazon, it does not have a native automatic elasticity service. The provider offers an interface and an API to control the amount of resources allocated, leaving to the user the implementation of more elaborate automated mechanisms.

Similarly, GoGrid [11] has not built in elasticity capabilities, although it provides an API for remote control of the hosted virtual machines (VM's). Thus, the user is responsible for monitoring the service and taking the scaling decisions. The creation and removal of resources is done through calls to the API. Besides VM's replication, GoGrid also support vertical elasticity for memory.

The solution provided by Joyent [12] is also based VM replication accessed via API. However, the provider include an automatic feature called CPU bursting, which temporarily increase the CPU capability of up to 400% in order to handle workload spikes.

A more comprehensive elasticity solution is provided by Profitbriks [13]. According to its documentation, it is possible to use horizontal and vertical elasticity, allowing changes in virtual environments manually (via interface) or using an API. It allows an user to build a virtual server with the exact number of cores it decides is right for the job (up to 62). This approach is different from the adopted by other providers, such as, Rackspace, GoGrid and Amazon, that offer pre-packaged machines configurations.

To overcome the lack of automated mechanisms of some cloud providers, tools such as RightScale [14] has been developed. RightScale is a management platform that provides control and elasticity capabilities for different public cloud providers (Amazon, Rackspace, GoGrid, and others) and also for private cloud solutions (CloudStack, Eucalyptus and OpenStack). The solution provides an reactive mechanisms based on an Elasticity Daemon whose function is to monitor the input queues, and to launch worker instances to process jobs in the queue. Different scaling metrics (from hardware and applications) can be used to determine the number of worker instances to launch and when to launch these instances.

In order to take full advantage of the elasticity provided by clouds, it is necessary more than just an elastic infrastructure. It is also necessary that the applications have the ability to dynamically adapt itself according to changes in its requirements. In general, applications developed in Platform-as-a-Service (PaaS) clouds have implicit elasticity. These PaaS clouds provide execution environments, called containers, in which users can execute their applications without having to worry about which resources will be used. In this case, the cloud manages automatically the resource allocation, so developers do not have to constantly monitor the service status or interact to request more resources [15].

An example of PaaS platform with elasticity support is Manjrasoft Aneka [16]. Aneka is a .NET-based application development platform, which offers a runtime environment and a set of API's that enable developers to build applications by using multiple programming models such as Task Programming, Thread Programming and MapReduce Programming, which can leverage the compute resources on either public or private Clouds. In Aneka, when an application needs more resources, new container instances are executed to handle the demand, using local or public cloud resources.

Other example is the Google AppEngine [17], a platform for developing scalable web applications (Java, Python, and JRuby) that run on top of server infrastructure of Google. These applications are executed within a sandbox and AppEngine take care of automatically scaling when needed.

Azure [18] is the solution provided by Microsoft for developing scalable applications for the Cloud using .NET framework. Despite offering platform services, Azure does not provide an transparent elasticity control. The scaling of resources (VM's) is based on rules that the user defines specifically for an application.

Other cloud providers also provide elasticity mechanisms but the features offered are not substantially distinct from presented above. Basically, the current elasticity solutions offer a VM replication mechanism, accessed using an API or via interfaces, and in some cases the resources allocation is managed automatically by a reactive controller, based in a set of rules. Vertical elasticity is not fully addressed by most cloud providers. Other feature implemented in IaaS and PaaS clouds is the load balancing. Load balancers are used to distribute the workload among all available VM instances [19].

The solutions presented in this section and their characteristics are summarized in Table 1.

Table 1. Elasticity Solutions Characteristics

System	Service	Mode	Elasticity
Amazon [9]	IaaS	Automatic/API	Horizontal
Rackspace [10]	IaaS	Manual/API	Horizontal
GoGrid [11]	IaaS	Manual/API	Horizontal Vertical (memory)
Joyent [12]	IaaS	Automatic/ Manual/API	Horizontal
Profitbricks [13]	IaaS	Manual/API	Horizontal Vertical
RightScale [14]	IaaS (service)	Automatic	Horizontal
Aneka [16]	PaaS	Automatic	Horizontal (container)
AppEngine [17]	PaaS	Automatic	Horizontal
Azure [18]	PaaS	Automatic/ Manual/API	Horizontal

2 Challenges and Open Issues

Although many elasticity solutions has been developed by cloud providers, there are some issues that must be addressed to enable the wide use of elasticity in scientific applications.

2.1 Inappropriate Elasticity Mechanisms

Most of the elasticity solutions implemented by public providers were originally developed for dynamic scaling server-based applications, such as http, e-mail and databases. Most of these mechanisms are based on controlling the number of virtual machines that host the applications server components and in the use of load balancers to divide the workload among the many VM instances. The control is carried out by an elasticity controller that employs data from a monitoring system to decide when instances must be added or removed. The decisions are based on a set of rules that specify the conditions to trigger some actions over the underlying cloud. Every condition is composed of a series of metrics which are compared against a threshold to trigger actions over the underlying cloud. These metrics include the number of connections, number of requests and resources usage such as CPU, memory and I/O.

An example is presented in Figure 1, where it is possible to observe the allocation of VM's in function of the connected clients. The elasticity controller uses the number of clients to dynamically allocate or deallocate VM's, enabling application to be ready to handle the load variations [20].

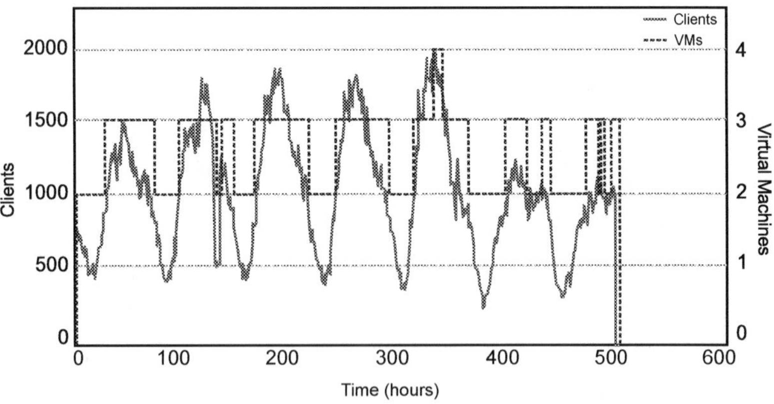

Fig. 1. Use of elasticity in a web application. Adapted from [20].

Although these solutions are successfully employed in server-based applications, scientific applications cannot benefit from the use of these mechanisms. Scientific applications have almost always been designed to use a fixed number of resources, and cannot explore elasticity without appropriate support [21]. The simple addition of instances and the use of load balancers has no effect in these applications since they are not able to detect and use these resources.

Most of scientific applications are executed in batch mode and their workloads are defined by input files containing the data to be processed [22]. Besides, scientific jobs tend to be resource-greedy, using intensively all provided resources. Figure 2 illustrates this behavior in the execution of a scientific experiment (multithreaded 2D heat transfer). Note that all processing capabilities are constantly used, independently from the number of threads/CPUs employed. The absence of external requests and the constant and intense use of resources make ineffective the use of traditional elasticity mechanisms based in monitoring data.

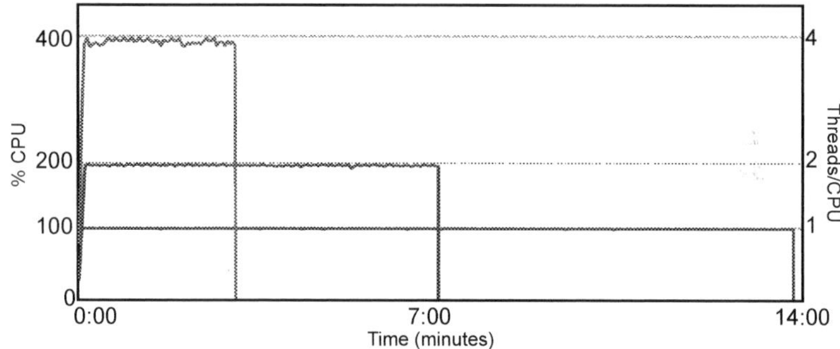

Fig. 2. Scientific application CPU usage with different number of threads

Using a elasticity mechanism such as offered by cloud providers, the high CPU usage could indicate the need for additional resources, causing the allocation of new virtual machines or new CPUs. However, the allocation of new resources has no effect in the CPU usage, since application is not designed to use the extra VM or CPU, and thus, more and more resources would be allocated indefinitely. Likewise, the use of manual approach neither is applicable, since is not possible to estimate the application state and if more resources are needed.

2.2 Resources Availability

Considering the available cloud platforms, none of them are able to accept the instantiation of a system with thousands of virtual machines for the period of time required to run a large scale scientific applications [23]. It happens because the elasticity of a cloud computing provider is limited by its capacity, and consequently, have to impose strict limits on the amount of resources that a single user can acquire in each instant of time, neglecting the infinite resources promise [24]. For instance, each Amazon EC2 regular customer has a limit of 20 reserved instances and 100 spot instances per availability zone that they can purchase each month; in Rackspace, all accounts have a preconfigured limit of 65 GB of total memory or approximately 130 individual 512 MB servers per region.

In fact, for the vast majority of users, the quota allowed is sufficient for their applications (generally, web applications). But, considering the applications characteristics, most of science-related users may want to receive from the cloud a high number of machines that could resemble a high-performance computing cluster. As resource-intensive applications begin effectively to use cloud computing, they will easily reach the scaling limits imposed by resources availability.

A possible solution to the resources availability problem is the use of multiple clouds to ensure the required amount of resources. Some academic works [25][26] have addressed this issue combining local and public clouds resources, however, the combined use of different public clouds remains challenging.

The reason for the current poor portability and limited interoperability between clouds is the lack of standardized API's, and consequently, each cloud provider has its own way on how cloud clients/applications/users interact with the cloud. As a consequence the interaction and migration of virtual machines and applications between clouds is a hard, if not impossible, task. This lack impacts on the development of mechanisms to provide large scale elastic computing models, able to scale resources among different cloud providers.

2.3 Limited Resources Granularity

Ideally, resources should be available at any granularity, allowing users to dynamically allocate from a single CPU to a complete virtual cluster, enabling different levels of elasticity [27]. However, in most IaaS clouds, clients acquire resources as a fixed set of compute, memory, and I/O resources (*instance types* in Amazon and *server sizes* in GoGrid and Rackspace). Renting a fixed combination of cloud resources does not reflect the applications demands [28].

There are a second point to be observed: Most of the cloud providers does not support vertical elasticity, i. e., it is impossible add a single CPU, memory, or I/O devices to a running VM. Changing the VM (or instance) type without rebooting is not also addressed. This limitations restrict the use of elasticity by diverse scientific applications, e. g., the ones that employ multithreaded parallelism or have phases with distinct demands of memory and I/O.

2.4 Spin-Up and Spin-Down Time

The great advantage of the elasticity is the ability to dynamically provide resources in response to a demand. However, one important fact in this dynamic process is that though cloud users can make their acquisition requests at any time, it may take some time for the acquired resources to be ready to use. This time period is called *spin-up time*.

In a perfectly elastic cloud, resourcing is instantaneous, i. e., there is no time delay between detecting load changes and changing resourcing levels [29]. However, in real world clouds, the startup time can vary (ranging from 1 to 10 minutes), depending on a number of factors including: type of cloud platform;

operating system type; number, size, or speed of resources requested; the availability of spare resources in the requested region and the demand on the cloud platform from other users. Thus, the resources provisioning could be slower than expected, affecting the efficacy and efficiency of actual elasticity mechanisms in handling highly dynamic workloads. Table 2 show the average VM spin-up time on Amazon EC2 (m1.small), Azure (Small) and Rackspace (Type IV) instances [30].

Table 2. Average VM spin-up time. Adapted from [30].

Cloud	**OS Image**	**Avg. Spin-up Time**
EC2	Linux(Fedora) ami-48aa4921	96.9 secs.
EC2	Windows (Win Server 2008) ami-fbf93092	810.2 secs.
Azure	WebRole default	374.8 secs.
Azure	WorkerRole default	406.2 secs.
Azure	VMRole - Win Server 2008R2	356.6 secs.
Rackspace	Linux (Fedora) flavor 71	44.2 secs.
Rackspace	Windows (Win Server 2008R2) flavor 28	429.2 secs.

In turn, *spin-down time* is the interval between no longer requiring a resource and no longer paying for it [27], and is directly related to the costs of using the cloud services. In Amazon, each partial instance-hour consumed will be billed as a full hour, i. e. the spin-down time is up to 1 hour. In Azure, instance hours are billed as full hours for each clock hour an instance is deployed. For example, if you deploy an instance at 10:50 AM and delete the deployment at 11:10 AM, you will be billed for two hours [18].

3 Towards Scientific Elastic Applications

Evaluating the challenges previously exposed, in this section we point some possibilities of using the elasticity in scientific applications, and describe some solutions that are being developed to overcome the challenges.

To address the problems related to *inappropriate mechanisms* we must consider two situations: (1) the development of new applications for the cloud, and (2) the execution of legacy applications in this environment type.

In new projects of scientific applications for the cloud, the applications must be reduced to frameworks that can successfully exploit the cloud resources. One possible approach is the use of building-blocks provided by PaaS clouds. In this case, the elasticity should be included in the modules and components provided, being managed transparently to the user. Generally, PaaS-based applications use execution environments called containers, which could automatically adapt their capabilities to satisfy the demands of the applications.

Another interesting approach, is the use of the MapReduce paradigm [31], that has gained popularity as a cloud computing framework on which to perform automatically scalable distributed applications. This application model can scale incrementally in the number of computing nodes. An user not only can launch a number of servers at the beginning, but can also launch additional servers in the middle of computation [8] [32]. The new servers can automatically figure out the current job progress and poll the queues for work to process. Previous work [33] has shown that MapReduce is well suited for simple, often embarrassingly parallel problems, but shown significant problems with iterative algorithms, like conjugate gradient, fast Fourier transform and block tridiagonal linear system solvers [34].

In case of legacy applications, scientific workflows is an example of approach that can benefit with cloud elasticity [35]. They can use the cloud capability to increase or reduce the pool of resources according to the needs of the workflow at any given time of processing [36]. Platforms and frameworks for executing scientific workflows in the cloud are being developed in academy. Examples of workflow system include Polyphony [37], Pegasus [38] and ClowdFlows [39].

Other legacy scientific applications (e. g. MPI, multithreaded) rely on IaaS cloud services and solely utilize static execution modes, in which an instance of VM is perceived as a cluster node [40]. To efficiently support elastic execution across cloud infrastructures, tools and frameworks, with support to scientific languages (C/C++, Fortran) and libraries are still required. Trying address this issue, a couple of academic researches have developed solutions to enable the development of elastic scientific applications. Some examples are the works of Raveendran et al. [21], addressing MPI applications, Rajan et al. [41], focusing on master-slave applications, and Galante and Bona [42] that present a platform for development of elastic applications based on the use of elasticity primitives.

The second problem addressed is the *resources availability*. It is closely related to the providers policies, but we believe that as demand grows, these limitations will be overcomed gradually. The potential of cloud resources are enormous and it became evident when a cluster composed by 1064 cc2.8xlarge instances (17024 cores) cluster was able to achieve 240.09 TeraFLOPS for the High Performance Linpack benchmark, placing the cluster at 127th position in the June 2013 Top500 list.

As we said before, a possible solution to resources availability problem is the use of multiple clouds, but there is a lack of standards that enable *interoperability*. In this sense, some initiatives are attempting to create cloud standards. The Cloud Computing Interoperability Forum [43], are working on the creation an open and standardized cloud interface for the unification of various cloud API's. The IEEE [44] also has a project (P2301) on cloud portability and interoperability.

Other (future) perspective is based on the cloud federation. A federated cloud is the deployment and management of multiple external and internal cloud computing services to match business needs [45]. In this scenario, the exceeding demands of a cloud are fulfilled by leasing available computational and storage capabilities from other cloud service providers. Some architectures for cloud federation has been proposed [46] [47], but practical results are still preliminary. Development of fundamental techniques and software systems that integrate distributed clouds in a federated fashion is critical to enabling composition and deployment of elastic application services.

The *resources granularity* issue is starting to be solved with the emergence of providers like Profitbricks (see Section 1.1) that enable users to combine different amounts of compute, memory, and I/O resources, i. e., offering vertical and horizontal scaling. This feature is very valuable for real elasticity, since resources can be allocated more efficiently.

Ben-Yehuda et al. [28] describe a perfect scenario, where compute, memory, and I/O resources could be rented and charged for dynamic amounts and not in fixed bundles. Clients rent VM's with some minimal amount of resources, and other resources needed are continuously rented in a fine-grained fashion. The resources available for rent include processing, memory, and I/O resources, as well as emerging resources such as accelerators, such as, FPGAs and GPUs. Processing capacity is sold on a hardware-thread basis, or as number of cycles per unit of time; memory is sold on the basis of frames; I/O is sold on the basis of I/O devices with bandwidth and latency guarantees.

The last issue, *spin-up and spin-down times*, will be overcomed with the use of new virtualization techniques and changing providers billing policy, respectively. Some works [48] [49] [50] present techniques to speed up the virtual provisioning process, but so far, these techniques have not yet been implemented by mainstream providers. In turn, the spin-down problem could be solved by changing the way providers charge by the use of resources. According to Brebner [29], even though it is unlikely that any cloud platform are perfectly elastic, it is possible to model it by assuming an extremely fine-grained cost model which only charges for resources that are actually consumed: the byte transmitted, the byte stored, and the millisecond of processing time.

To summarize, the challenges and perspectives of elasticity for scientific applications are presented in Table 3.

4 Final Remarks

Based on the analysis and studies made so far, from the point of view of providing elasticity, we argue that the use of cloud computing in supporting scientific applications may be an advantageous tool. Nevertheless, some care must be taken when using legacy applications, most of them will no fit to the current cloud model, and specific developments must be made when designed new scientific applications for this environment, to be able to use it in all its capability.

However, there are already scientific applications models (e. g. MapReduce and workflows) that can immediately benefit and with appropriate adjustments even more. Applications characterized by having data locality, loosely coupled, high throughput and fault tolerant, are more appropriate for the current cloud model.

Table 3. Elasticity: challenges and possibilities

Challenge	Possibilities	Related Works
Inappropriate elasticity mechanisms	– Use of PaaS and MapReduce for new applications – Workflows can be ported to clouds and adapted to use the cloud elasticity; – Development of new tools and frameworks	[40] [31] [33] [34] [35] [37] [38] [39] [21] [41]
Resources availability and Cloud interoperability	– Creation standards for cloud interoperability – Cloud Federation	[43] [44] [45] [46] [47]
Limited resources granularity	– Offering of replication and resizing of cloud resources for processing, memory, storage and networking	[13]
Spin-up and spin-down time	– Use of new virtualization techniques to speed up the virtual resources provisioning process – Changing providers billing policy in order to use a fine-grained cost model which only charges for resources actually consumed	[29] [48] [49] [50]

According to the presented in this paper, the answer to the question "*are the available cloud solutions suitable to support elastic scientific applications?*" is that the current computational clouds have not yet reached the necessary maturity level to meet all scientific applications requirements. We expect that in the coming years, significant advances in virtualization and in cloud management, allow the improvement of the elasticity solutions in scientific context.

Acknowledgment. This work is partially supported by CAPES and INCT-MACC (CNPq grant nr. 573710/2008-2).

References

1. Simmhan, Y., van Ingen, C., Subramanian, G., Li, J.: Bridging the gap between desktop and the cloud for escience applications. In: Proceedings of the 3rd Intl. Conference on Cloud Computing, CLOUD 2010, pp. 474–481. IEEE (2010)
2. Srirama, S.N., Willmore, C., Ivanitev, V., Jakovits, P.: Desktop to Cloud Migration of Scientific Experiments. In: 2nd International Workshop on Cloud Computing and Scientific Applications, CCSA 2012. IEEE/ACM (2012)
3. Badger, L., Patt-Corner, R., Voas, J.: Draft cloud computing synopsis and recommendations recommendations of the national institute of standards and technology. Nist Special Publication 146, 84 (2011)

4. Armbrust, M., Fox, A., Griffith, R., Joseph, A.D., Katz, A., Konwinski, A., Lee, G., Patterson, D., Rabkin, A., Stoica, L., Ionaharia, M.: A View of Cloud Computing. Commun. ACM 53(4) (April 2010)
5. Wang, L., Zhan, J., Shi, W., Liang, Y.: In cloud, can scientific communities benefit from the economies of scale? IEEE Transactions on Parallel and Distributed Systems 23(2), 296–303 (2012)
6. Oliveira, D., Baiao, F.A., Mattoso, M.: Migrating Scientific Experiments to the Cloud. HPC in the Cloud
7. Galante, G., Bona, L.C.E.: A survey on cloud computing elasticity. In: Proceedings of the Intl. Workshop on Clouds and eScience Applications Management, CloudAM 2012. IEEE/ACM (2012)
8. Chohan, N., Castillo, C., Spreitzer, M., Steinder, M., Tantawi, A., Krintz, C.: See Spot Run: Using Spot Instances for Mapreduce Workflows. In: Proceedings of the 2nd USENIX Conference on Hot Topics in Cloud Computing, HotCloud 2010. USENIX Association (2010)
9. Amazon Web Services, `http://aws.amazon.com/`
10. Rackspace, `http://www.rackspace.com/`
11. GoGrid, `http://www.gogrid.com/`
12. Joyent, `http://joyent.com/`
13. Profitbricks, `https://www.profitbricks.com/`
14. RightScale, `http://www.rightscale.com/`
15. Caron, E., Rodero-Merino, L.: F. Desprez, A.M.: Auto-scaling, load balancing and monitoring in commercial and open-source clouds. Technical Report 7857. INRIA (2012)
16. Calheiros, R.N., Vecchiola, C., Karunamoorthy, D., Buyya, R.: The aneka platform and qos-driven resource provisioning for elastic applications on hybrid clouds. Future Generation Computer Systems 28(6), 861–870 (2011)
17. Google App. Engine, `http://code.google.com/appengine`
18. Microsoft Azure, `http://www.windowsazure.com/`
19. Vaquero, L.M., Rodero-Merino, L., Buyya, R.: Dynamically scaling applications in the cloud. SIGCOMM Comput. Commun. Rev. 41, 45–52 (2011)
20. Roy, N., Dubey, A., Gokhale, A.: Efficient autoscaling in the cloud using predictive models for workload forecasting. In: Proceedings of the 4th Intl. Conference on Cloud Computing, CLOUD 2011, pp. 500–507. IEEE (2011)
21. Raveendran, A., Bicer, T., Agrawal, G.: A framework for elastic execution of existing mpi programs. In: Proceedings of the Intl. Symposium on Parallel and Distributed Processing Workshops and PhD Forum, IPDPSW 2011, pp. 940–947. IEEE (2011)
22. Wang, L., Zhan, J., Shi, W., Liang, Y.: In cloud, can scientific communities benefit from the economies of scale? IEEE Trans. Parallel Distrib. Syst. 23(2), 296–303 (2012)
23. Costa, R., Brasileiro, F., de Souza Filho, G.L., Sousa, D.M.: Just in Time Clouds: Enabling Highly-Elastic Public Clouds over Low Scale Amortized Resources. Technical report, Federal University of Campina Grande (2010)
24. Costa, R.,, F.B.: On the amplitude of the elasticity offered by public cloud computing providers. Technical report, Federal University of Campina Grande (2011)
25. Fitó, J.O., Presa, I.G., Fernández, J.G.: Sla-driven elastic cloud hosting provider. In: Proceedings of the 18th Euromicro Conference on Parallel, Distributed and Network-based Processing, PDP 2010, pp. 111–118. IEEE (2010)

26. Marshall, P., Keahey, K., Freeman, T.: Elastic site: Using clouds to elastically extend site resources. In: Proceedings of the 10th Intl. Conference on Cluster, Cloud and Grid Computing, pp. 43–52. IEEE (2010)
27. Islam, S., Lee, K., Fekete, A., Liu, A.: How a consumer can measure elasticity for cloud platforms. Technical Report 680, School of Information Technologies, University of Sydney (2011)
28. Ben-Yehuda, O.A., Ben-Yehuda, M., Schuster, A., Tsafrir, D.: The Resource-as-a-Service (RaaS) cloud. In: 4th USENIX Workshop on Hot Topics in Cloud Computing, HotCloud 2011 (2012)
29. Brebner, P.: Is your cloud elastic enough?: performance modelling the elasticity of infrastructure as a service (iaas) cloud applications. In: Proceedings of the Third Joint WOSP/SIPEW Intl. Conference on Performance Engineering, ICPE 2012, pp. 263–266. ACM (2012)
30. Mao, M., Humphrey, M.: A performance study on the vm startup time in the cloud. In: Proceedings of the IEEE Fifth Intl. Conference on Cloud Computing, CLOUD 2012, pp. 423–430. IEEE (2012)
31. Srirama, S.N., Jakovits, P., Vainikko, E.: Adapting scientific computing problems to clouds using mapreduce. Future Generation Computer Systems 28(1), 184–192 (2012)
32. Iordache, A., Morin, C., Parlavantzas, N., Riteau, P.: Resilin: Elastic MapReduce over Multiple Clouds. Rapport de recherche RR-8081, INRIA (October 2012)
33. Dean, J., Ghemawat, S.: Mapreduce: simplified data processing on large clusters. Commun. ACM 51(1), 107–113 (2008)
34. Bunch, C., Drawert, B., Norman, M.: MapScale: A Cloud Environment for Scientific Computing. Technical report, University of California (June 2009)
35. Pandey, S., Karunamoorthy, D., Buyya, R.: Workflow Engine for Clouds. In: Buyya, R., Broberg, J., Goscinski, A.M. (eds.) Cloud Computing: Principles and Paradigms, pp. 321–342. John Wiley & Sons, Inc. (March 2011)
36. Byun, E.K., Kee, Y.S., Kim, J.S., Maeng, S.: Cost Optimized Provisioning of Elastic Resources for Application Workflows. Future Gener. Comput. Syst. 27(8), 1011–1026 (2011)
37. Shams, K.S., Powell, M.W., Crockett, T.M., Norris, J.S., Rossi, R., Soderstrom, T.: Polyphony: A workflow orchestration framework for cloud computing. In: Proceedings of the 10th IEEE/ACM Intl. Conference on Cluster, Cloud and Grid Computing, CCGRID 2010, pp. 606–611. IEEE (2010)
38. Vöckler, J., Juve, G., Deelman, E., Rynge, M., Berriman, B.: Experiences using cloud computing for a scientific workflow application. In: Proceedings of the 2nd Intl. Workshop on Scientific Cloud Computing, ScienceCloud 2011, pp. 15–24. ACM (2011)
39. Kranjc, J., Podpečan, V., Lavrač, N.: ClowdFlows: A cloud based scientific workflow platform. In: Flach, P.A., De Bie, T., Cristianini, N. (eds.) ECML PKDD 2012, Part II. LNCS, vol. 7524, pp. 816–819. Springer, Heidelberg (2012)
40. Jha, S., Katz, D.S., Luckow, A., Merzky, A., Stamou, K.: Understanding Scientific Applications for Cloud Environments. In: Buyya, R., Broberg, J., Goscinski, A.M. (eds.) Cloud Computing: Principles and Paradigms, pp. 345–371. John Wiley & Sons, Inc. (March 2011)
41. Rajan, D., Canino, A., Izaguirre, J.A., Thain, D.: Converting a high performance application to an elastic cloud application. In: Proceedings of the 3rd Intl. Conference on Cloud Computing Technology and Science, CLOUDCOM 2011, pp. 383–390. IEEE (2011)

42. Galante, G., Bona, L.C.E.: Constructing elastic scientific applications using elasticity primitives. In: Murgante, B., Misra, S., Carlini, M., Torre, C.M., Nguyen, H.-Q., Taniar, D., Apduhan, B.O., Gervasi, O. (eds.) ICCSA 2013, Part V. LNCS, vol. 7975, pp. 281–294. Springer, Heidelberg (2013)
43. CCIF: The Cloud Computing Interoperability Forum, `http://www.cloudforum.org/`
44. IEEE: Cloud Profiles Working Group, `http://standards.ieee.org/develop/project/2301.html`
45. Celesti, A., Tusa, F., Villari, M., Puliafito, A.: Three-phase cross-cloud federation model: The cloud sso authentication. In: Proceedings of Second Intl. Conference on Advances in Future Internet, pp. 94–101 (2010)
46. Buyya, R., Ranjan, R., Calheiros, R.N.: InterCloud: Utility-oriented federation of cloud computing environments for scaling of application services. In: Hsu, C.-H., Yang, L.T., Park, J.H., Yeo, S.-S. (eds.) ICA3PP 2010, Part I. LNCS, vol. 6081, pp. 13–31. Springer, Heidelberg (2010)
47. Villegas, D., Bobroff, N., Rodero, I., Delgado, J., Liu, Y., Devarakonda, A., Fong, L., Sadjadi, S.M., Parashar, M.: Cloud federation in a layered service model. J. Comput. Syst. Sci. 78(5), 1330–1344 (2012)
48. Zhu, J., Jiang, Z., Xiao, Z.: Twinkle: A fast resource provisioning mechanism for internet services. In: Proceedings of the 30th IEEE Intl. Conference on Computer Communications, INFOCOM 2011, pp. 802–810. IEEE (2011)
49. Tang, C.: Fvd: a high-performance virtual machine image format for cloud. In: Proceedings of the 2011 USENIX technical conference, USENIX 2011, p. 18. USENIX Association (2011)
50. De, P., Gupta, M., Soni, M., Thatte, A.: Caching VM instances for fast VM provisioning: A comparative evaluation. In: Kaklamanis, C., Papatheodorou, T., Spirakis, P.G. (eds.) Euro-Par 2012. LNCS, vol. 7484, pp. 325–336. Springer, Heidelberg (2012)

A Light-Weight Framework for Bridge-Building from Desktop to Cloud

Kewei Duan[1,*], Julian Padget[1], and H. Alicia Kim[2]

[1] Department of Computer Science, University of Bath
{k.duan,j.a.padget}@bath.ac.uk
[2] Department of Mechanical Engineering, University of Bath
h.a.kim@bath.ac.uk

Abstract. A significant trend in science research for at least the past decade has been the increasing uptake of computational techniques (modelling) for in-silico experimentation, which is trickling down from the grand challenges that require capability computing to smaller-scale problems suited to capacity computing. Such virtual experiments also establish an opportunity for collaboration at a distance. At the same time, the development of web service and cloud technology, is providing a potential platform to support these activities. The problem on which we focus is the technical hurdles for users without detailed knowledge of such mechanisms – in a word, 'accessibility' – specifically: (i) the heavy weight and diversity of infrastructures that inhibits shareability and collaboration between services, (ii) the relatively complicated processes associated with deployment and management of web services for non-disciplinary specialists, and (iii) the relative technical difficulty in packaging the legacy software that encapsulates key discipline knowledge for web-service environments. In this paper, we describe a light-weight framework based on cloud and REST to address the above issues. The framework provides a model that allows users to deploy REST services from the desktop on to computing infrastructure without modification or recompilation, utilizing legacy applications developed for the command-line. A behind-the-scenes facility provides asynchronous distributed staging of data (built directly on HTTP and REST). We describe the framework, comprising the service factory, data staging services and the desktop file manager overlay for service deployment, and present experimental results regarding: (i) the improvement in turnaround time from the data staging service, and (ii) the evaluation of usefulness and usability of the framework through case studies in image processing and in multi-disciplinary optimization.

1 Introduction

With the increasing uptake of computational techniques for in-silico experimentation, scientists seek capacity computing power along with the means to collaborate at a distance.

Web services in principle provide a convenient means to publish and share computational representations of domain-specific knowledge, while grid computing has

* Student author.

A.R. Lomuscio et al. (Eds.): ICSOC 2013 Workshops, LNCS 8377, pp. 308–323, 2014.
© Springer International Publishing Switzerland 2014

delivered the infrastructure for capability scientific computing[1–3]. More recently, cloud computing, which can be seen as an evolution of the latter, offers a more accessible and flexible provisioning of capacity computing, that renders the usability issues around complex infrastructure largely invisible to end users. It also shows benefits for scientific applications in a wide range of domains[4–6]. However, there are still hurdles for scientists who have limited technical knowledge of cloud computing infrastructure and of the use of new technology in scientific applications. We identify them as: (i) the heavy weight and diversity of infrastructures that inhibits shareability and collaboration among distributed services, (ii) the relatively complicated processes associated with deployment and management of web services for non-discipline specialists, (iii) the relative technical difficulty in packaging the legacy software that encapsulates key discipline knowledge for web-service environments.

The aforementioned hurdles are determined by the nature of the end-user-scientist and the resources that need to be deployed in the cloud. Most scientists who have limited knowledge of web services or cloud infrastructure may need to face the need to learn new programming languages or system administrative skills for the purpose to build scientific applications in the cloud or as web services. For example, an engineer normally has the skill to develop desktop applications based on Fortran or Matlab, but rarely has knowledge of or experience of web application development based on languages like Java or Python. On the other hand, with years of development, numerous legacy codes and programs in which real domain-specific knowledge resides, may face the predicament that a new round of coding and translating work is needed or they simply lose the ability to be re-developed because of the lack of source codes, documents or language support[1].

Our REST based light-weight framework lowers the barriers by providing a set of GUI based client tools and a set of REST web services which serve as both portal for service deployment and service execution by following the PaaS service model[7]. In recent years, the REST architectural style[8] and REST-compliant Web services have emerged and the approach has rapidly gained popularity due to its flexibility and simplicity. Our framework is able to deploy legacy codes and command-line programs as RESTful services, which can support a wide range of languages and tools, such as C/C++, Fortran, Matlab, Python, Unix shell, JAVA, and some engineering design optimization frameworks, specifically OpenMDAO[9] and Dakota[10]. Furthermore, because the framework follows RESTful principles, it can be directly accessed from a wide range of programming languages (such as a command line scripts/applications) or a generic workflow management system (such as Taverna[11], see section 4) without any additional library support or tools. The services are made into as web applications, based on easily obtainable, free, open-source tools, such as Apache-Tomcat and MySQL. Embedded within the framework is a distributed data-flow mechanism, that can enhance data-staging performance in the execution of composite services. Through the desktop GUI tool, inexperienced users can learn about, create and use web services. We demonstrate the framework operating both in the context of a private server and the Amazon EC2 service, in order to show compatibility with both private and public cloud

[1] In the worst case, only a binary of the program may exist, which happens to be executable due to backwards hardware compatibility.

provisioning. Hence, we believe it should be readily deployable on top of other IaaS services with little change.

The primary technical contributions of the paper are: (i) the design of a RESTful framework for the deployment of legacy codes through a *service factory* facility, (ii) an architecture for the execution of those services, in which data services are supplied by an asynchronous data-flow mechanism providing *Data as a Service* and control can be provided by existing workflow engines, such as Taverna, and (iii) a *desktop GUI* and file system overlay to provide the interface for service management. Complementary to these is the social contribution, of providing access to web service functions, cloud computing infrastructure and user-controlled means for sharing the scientific knowledge embedded in computational resources (software). These aspects have been evaluated, using recognized HCI practices[12, 13] on the one hand through participatory exercises and surveys (usability) and on the other through two case studies (usefulness).

The rest of the paper is structured as follows. In Section 2, we discuss the challenges of migrating scientific applications to cloud and related work. Section 3 introduces our framework and the solutions proposed to meet those challenges. Section 4 evaluates the framework in respect of three issues: (i) performance, (ii) user-based experiments, and (iii) (two) case studies. Lastly, Section 5 presents conclusions and future work.

2 Related Work

Cloud computing is commonly categorized into three service models[7] known as {Infrastructure, Platform, Software} as a Service (IaaS, PaaS and SaaS, respectively), of which PaaS is the service model that provides the consumer with the capability to deploy consumer-created or acquired applications onto infrastructure, thus creating an instance of a service. Our aim is to provide access to cloud services so that regular users can deploy their own (command-line) applications as services, share them with others and utilise them in service workflows. We do this through the provision of a platform that provides: (i) deployment services, and (ii) data storage and transfer services.

This paper focuses on the use of cloud platform for science and engineering applications, in which the platform enables applications to appear as web services, creating a SaaS for public invocation. Our aim to provide a platform for users without sophisticated programming skills to be able deploy web services. There are several generic PaaS platforms like Google APP Engine [14] and Heroku [15], both of which provide the means for users to deploy web applications on the providers' public cloud infrastructure. However, both of them work via programming language APIs. For the purpose of deploying an application into their infrastructures, users must either write applications in specific languages or modify original codes in those languages. Other potential platforms – providing command-line interfaces – are: (i) CloudFoundry [16], which provides an open-source mechanism for application deployment, however it uses its own API – implemented for a range of popular languages – for service interaction, rather than the standardised (REST) mechanisms that we adopt, and (ii) Openshift [17], which aims to provide a platform for running web applications using cloud resources. It too needs quite sophisticated skills to write applications in supported languages by using the command-line administration tools specifically designed for this platform.

The Generic Worker framework [18] has similar goals to our framework: it provides PaaS service based on Microsoft's Azure Cloud platform. Services can be deployed by the client using command-line tools. They also adopt a distributed data transfer mechanism for performance enhancement. However, their services are tightly connected to Azure service elements, such as Azure's REST web service API and the Azure blob store.

Additionally, toolkits such as Soaplab[19], Opal[20] and Generic Factory Service (GFac)[2] wrap command-line applications for service deployment. Users can use them to describe the command-line and parameters to create services. These too differ from our framework in several ways:

1. We adopt a cloud infrastructure to provide the function of service deployment as web service, which allows hot-plug style program uploading and deployment. The above assume programs have been installed on the server and work as local tools on a server that needs to be set up and configured every time a new service is deployed.
2. We consider the deployment of web service in a broader context, assuming services will be composed, consequently a data staging mechanism is provided to assist in the effective composition of services. The above tools do not consider data communication as part of their concern, which can in the worst case result in centralized data transfer, when deployed as web services.
3. We provide a desktop GUI tool for clients to deploy web services based on command-line programs. This avoids the need to learn and use the description languages adopted in these tools ("Ajax Command Definition" in Soaplab, "serviceMap" in GFac and "Metadata" in Opal), as well as the overheads involved in authoring, debugging and maintaining such descriptions in parallel with the application.

Our framework should be deployable in any private cloud or any popular public cloud based as it is on a set of open-source tools and standard protocols. The data can also reside in any form of cloud computing storage, such as Dropbox, Ubuntu one, OwnCloud or SpiderOak, for example. We also note that data elements in our framework are transferred and stored without additional mark-up. To facilitate the delivery of the right data at the right time in the right place, we have developed a data-flow style Data-as-a-Service (DaaS) mechanism, called Datapool, that keeps all the data in their original format (ie., no encoding, no wrapping) and provides for asynchronous data transfer between services (described in detail in Section 3).

3 A Cloud-Based Framework for Scientific Applications

In this section, we describe our framework and how we believe it addresses the issues raised by the hurdles we identified earlier. We approach these issues from three perspectives: (i) service deployment, (ii) service invocation and execution, (iii) data staging.

3.1 Service Deployment

Scientific applications must be uploaded and registered with the framework before they are available for invocation and execution in the cloud. There are three tasks at this

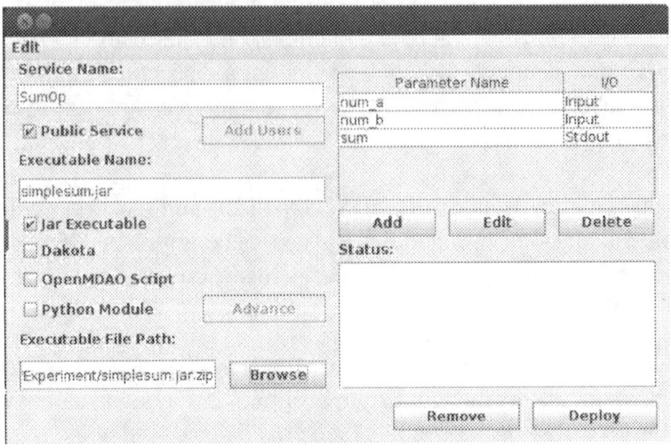

(a) The main window of GUI tool

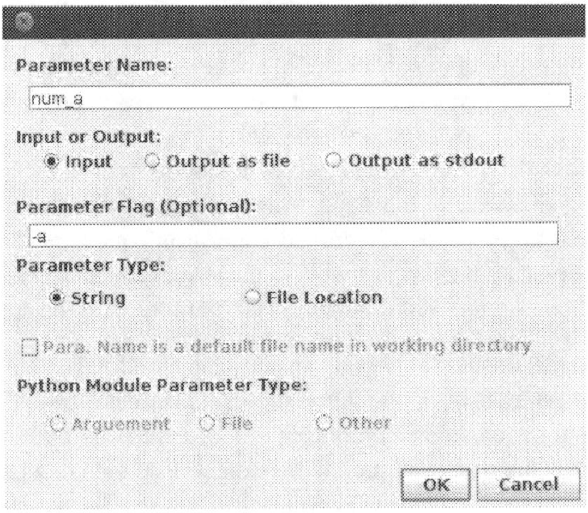

(b) The parameter window of GUI tool

Fig. 1. Windows of GUI tool

stage: (i) to upload and store the application and its dependencies in the cloud repository, (ii) to write and upload the description of the application to cloud for subsequent configuration and deployment, (iii) the configuration of authorization information that controls who may access the service once deployed. These tasks are all performed through the client GUI tool.

To illustrate the features of the deployment service, we use the screenshots shown in Figure 1, where Figure 1(a) shows the main window of the GUI tool. Our aim here is to make deployment tasks fit within the familiar range of operations of a desktop window manager. The GUI tool is set up to connect with the delpoyment service in the cloud through a URI with user authentication information. For the application uploading task, the user packs the binary and dependencies into a self-contained folder as a compressed

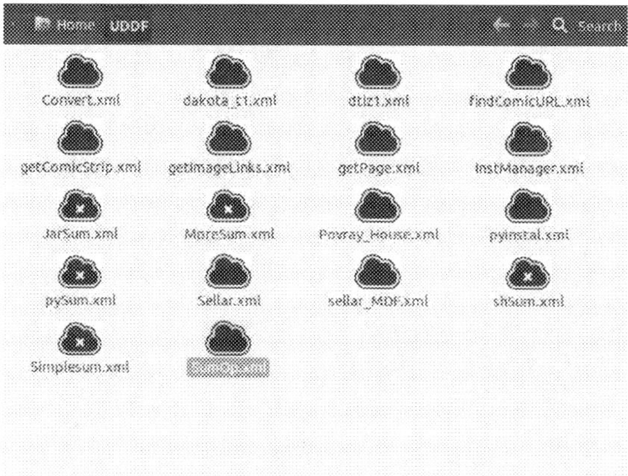

Fig. 2. Local folder for service description

Table 1. URIs of Datapool and Application Services

	Methods	URIs
Datapool Services	PUT	http://.../datapool/{Datapool_Name}/{Data_Object_Name}
	PUT	http://.../datapool/{Datapool_Name}?DO_URI={Data_Object_URI}
	GET	http://.../datapool/{Datapool_Name}/{Data_Object_Name}
	GET	http://.../datapool/{Datapool_Name}
	DELETE	http://.../datapool/{Datapool_Name}/{Data_Object_Name}
	DELETE	http://.../datapool/{Datapool_Name}
Application Services	PUT	http://.../APP_service/{Service_Name}
	GET	http://.../APP_service/{Service_Name}?DP_URI={Datapool_URI}
	DELETE	http://.../APP_service/{Service_Name}
	GET	http://.../APP_service/Service_Info/{Service_Name}

file and uploads it cloud side through the deployment service. The uploader can be started from the menu when the user right-clicks on the compressed file[2]. In this case, a Java executable which has two inputs and one output is uploaded. The Java runtime is a special case that can be specified by ticking "Jar executable". One another notable feature shown in Figure 1(a) is the access permission setting. The user can choose whether a service can be accessed by all users as a *public service* or by selected users. Permitted users can be added in a separate window by the service owner clicking the *Add Users* button. Figure 1(b) shows the parameter window of the GUI tool. In the deployment process of Web service, the framework needs the information for mapping each command-line argument into a parameter for the web service. At the same, the framework also needs to generate a command-line for the invocation of the program. Therefore, this window allows the description of a wide range of command-line I/O types, such as argument flag, file path, standard I/O stream, etc. The framework identifies the binary file type through the extension name of file name entered here as well.

[2] Thanks to integration with the file manager. Although, in this case, the integration is with the Nautilus file manager on Ubuntu, such overlays are common interface extensions on other operating systems, so we view this as a generic technique.

Lastly, users also need functions to remove, modify or redeploy the service, which requires the service description. During the deployment process, the description – represented as a XML file – is uploaded as a cloud resource. At the same time, a copy is stored in a designated local folder. Figure 2 shows the folder contains all the descriptions. Users can operate on them by starting the GUI tool from the right-click menu, to access operations for remove, modify and redeploy. The description of any service that is removed is kept in the folder, identified by a cloud icon with a cross, for possible future redeployment.

3.2 Service Invocation and Execution

Table 1 shows all the URIs of the two types of services. Datapool services are the services for I/O data item manipulation (uploading, retrieval, etc.). Application services include the services for application service deployment and execution. Uniform methods based on the HTTP protocol are allocated to each URI for each specific operation. For example, the first and third service in the application services list have the same URI, which denotes one application resource. The PUT method denotes a service deployment operation, while DELETE denotes a service removal operation. These services also support a role-based authorization system so that only an authenticated and authorized user can access those services. Authentication is carried out over HTTP and communication can be further encrypted and secured by HTTPS through the Transport Layer Security (TLS) protocol. In Section 3.1, we describe the means to specify the authorization permissions for a given service.

Of particular note are the datapool resources: each denotes a collection of data items, addressable through an unique URI. Multiple Datapool instances can be generated and customized through the Datapool service by the user. Each data item inside a Datapool is also given an unique URI. Only the creator of each Datapool and the creator's services can access the content, which is ensured by the role-based authorization mechanism. There are two advantages to organizing data in this way. First, because all the data items and the data collection are directly associated with URIs, they are all web resources that can be accessed over HTTP at any time rather than merely a data stream in the form of extra layer of XML or other structure. Therefore, each data item can also be transferred and kept in their original textual or binary format. Second, in the execution of an application service, the URI of one Datapool that contains all the input data is provided to the service. The application will pull the necessary data automatically from the provided local or remote Datapool. In this way, the interfaces are unified for different application services in the form of a URI, of which the Datapool URI is a constituent as a query string. The second URI in the application services list in Table 1 illustrates the unified format.

Figure 3 shows an example deployment using the framework. It contains one client and two servers. Each server is composed of a pair of a Datapool and an Application service, both of whose implementation is based on Apache-Tomcat. All the components communicate with each other through REST services invocations. The execution of application service depends on the data provided by its local Datapool, which are fed through a file system. Figure 4 shows more details about the execution sequence in an example workflow based on the framework in Figure 3. In this example, Application

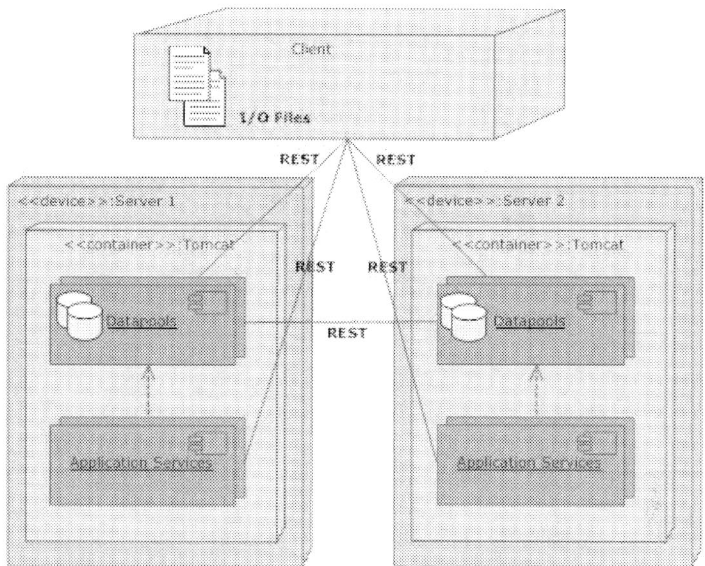

Fig. 3. The UML Deployment Diagram of the Framework Deployment Example

Service 1a(AS1a) consumes input D1. AS2a needs D2 and D3, which is the output generated by AS1a, as inputs. As depicted, client's duties are simplified to initializing input data and dispatching control signals to Datapool and Application Services. There are two essential features, which we emphasize here, namely: (i) inputs are uploaded to Datapool separately and in advance, so that Step 1 and Step 2 are able to execute concurrently (ii) DP2a can retrieve the input directly for AS2a in Step 12 and 13 from the other Datapool service without data needing to pass via the client.

3.3 The Data Staging Mechanism

Data staging and how to control it are not new problems. Already in 1997 [21], adopted the idea of distributed data-flows in a service composition framework to improve data transfer performance, as did also [22] some years later. Similar ideas are embodied in some distributed program execution engines, such as [23, 24], to overcome the bottleneck of data transfers. Meanwhile, several workflow management systems took up a peer-to-peer style mechanism for intermediate data movement[25–27]. Although there are differences in detail between the various aforementioned solutions, there is one common aspect, namely the use of a private – by which we mean internal, or closed – mechanism (functions are exposed by a set of developer defined specific interfaces and operations) to handle data transfer. A further point in common is the need for addressability: in each case the data objects are assigned some unique label that allows them to be accessed from any location on the network that is participating in the enactment process. These works inspired our data staging mechanism based on cloud resources and REST.

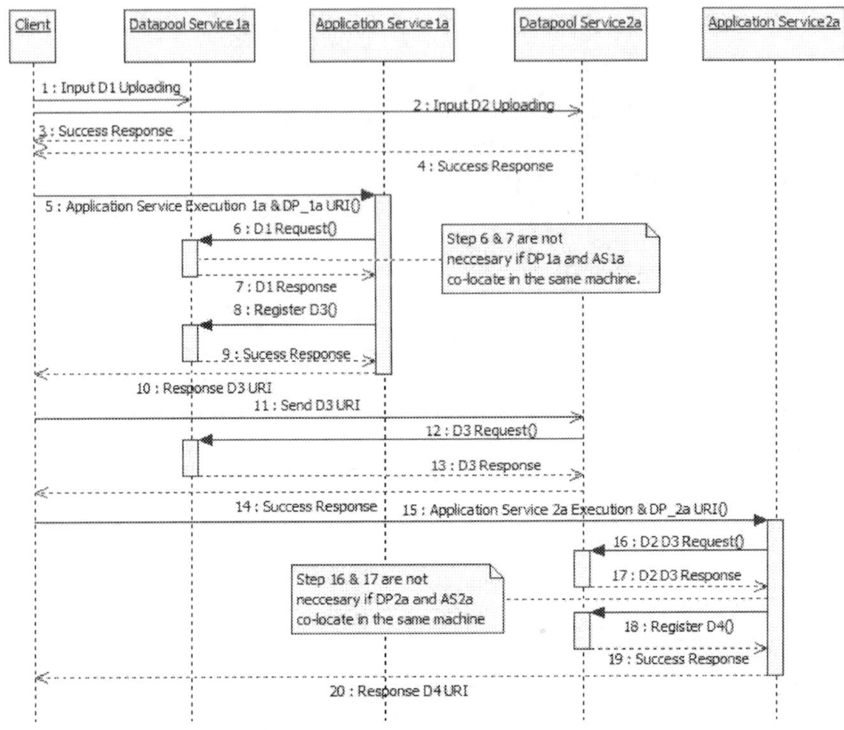

Fig. 4. The UML Sequence Diagram of the Execution of Workflow Example

We can make two quite obvious remarks about dataflows between several services: (i) for a given service invocation, the dataflow rarely involves the client or central controller, which means that dataflows can (normally) be distributed (point-to-point), and (ii) it is not uncommon that the necessary data objects (inputs) may come from different sources, suggesting that data transfers can be initiated asynchronously before the actual execution of a service. These constitute the properties our data staging mechanism needs to satisfy.

Distributed Data Transfer. Figures 5 and 6 illustrate the essential difference between a centralized and a distributed mechanism for data transfer. Figure 5 shows that both control-flow and data-flow are centrally coordinated for each Web service invocation. There is a high risk that the client or central controller becomes a bottleneck for data communication among computation components. In Figure 6, the data-flows are distributed among Web services directly rather than passing through a central controller, which also allows for the concurrent transfer of data items from different resources. This process is also demonstrated in the example of Section 3.2. The client can also obtain the complete set of data objects whenever it is desired. Hence, each service provider takes care of the task of data storage instead of the client. Furthermore, each data

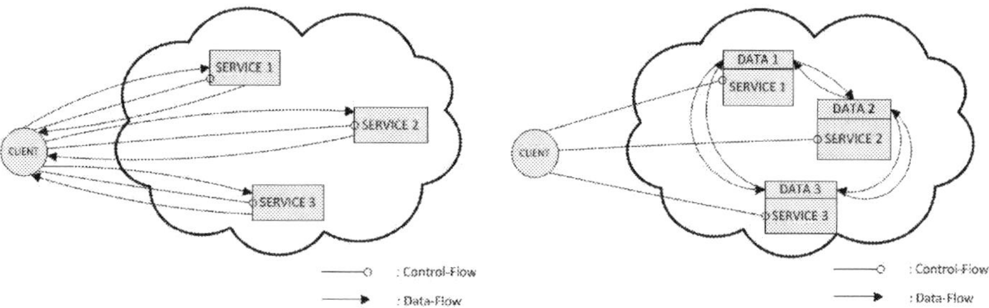

Fig. 5. Centralized Data-Flows in Web Services Compostion

Fig. 6. Distributed Data-Flows in Web Services Composition

object has the capability to be identified and accessed universally through the Internet by means of its URI.

Asynchronous Data Transfer. Under synchronous data transfer, because the data references are controlled through the client, data transfer only starts when the last service finishes and the next service invocation happens. However, with an asynchronous method, the transfers start as and when each preceding service finishes. The transfers are not synchronized with the invocation of the next service, rather data elements are transferred and stored in the 'next' Datapool in advance, the benefits of which are analysed in [28].

4 Evaluation

4.1 Experiment on Usefulness and Usability

A formal experiment with an after-experiment survey is carried out to collect evidence for the usefulness of the GUI tool-based service management mechanism. The objective here is assess usage of the tool for users who do not have any experience of building or deploying web services. A secondary aim is to collect evidence for the usability of the GUI. In this experiment, four programs are provided to the evaluators. Three of them have two inputs and one output, and are written in Java, Python and Unix shell, respectively. The other has three inputs and two outputs and is written in Python. The experiment has four stages: (i) a 3–5 minute training stage, which includes a tutorial video and question time, (ii) three simple programs are provided to participants to deploy in an order that they decide, while the time to complete the operation is recorded, (iii) a more complicated program for which deployment time is also recorded, and (iv) completing the survey.

Figure 7 shows the average time and full time range for deployment operations based on data collected from 9 participants. We note that none of the subjects claimed any prior experience of building or deploying web services.

In a question about their subjective views on simplicity with 5-point scales from very easy (1) to very difficult (5), 2 out 9 said very easy (1), and the rest said easy (2). All the

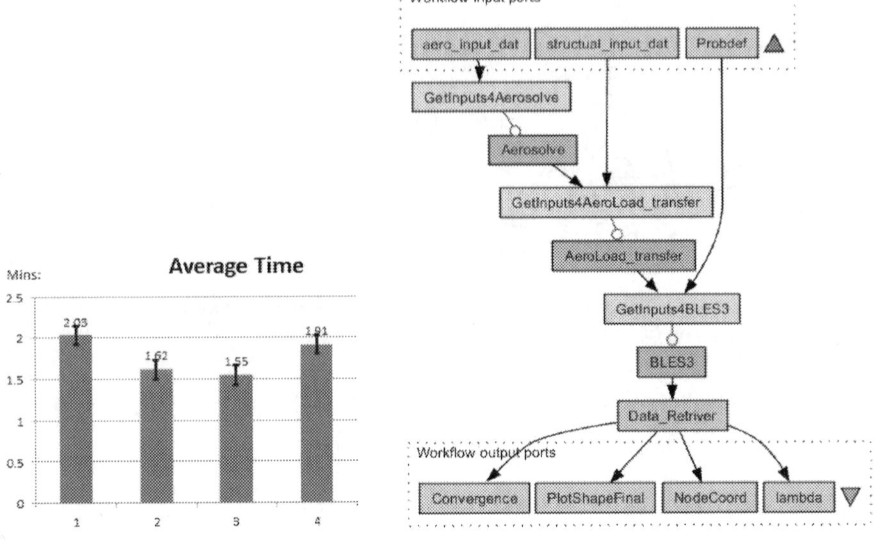

Fig. 7. The average time of deployment operations

Fig. 8. The wing structure optimization process built in Taverna

participants successfully deployed web services in around 2 minutes. In the randomly ordered simpler cases, it can be noticed that there is a significant fall in the time taken. It also can be noticed that after three test cases, the time taken for the more difficult case is less than the first of the simple ones. The objective evidence obtained from this experiment is that the GUI based mechanism is easy to learn and use for single service deployment.

4.2 Case Studies

Image Processing Workflow. In this workflow, the binaries for PovRay[29] and ImageMagick[30] are installed on the cloud-side of the framework. PovRay is a ray tracing program to draw 3-D image from scene description that is written in the POV description language. ImageMagick is a software suite to create, edit, compose, or convert images. In this case, we create a workflow to output a 3-D image in `png` format starting from a POV description as input, and then convert it to `jpg` format using ImageMagick. Both of their execution processes are written as Unix shell scripts. The uploaded package also includes related PovRay include files that serve as libraries for 3-D image generation. They are all deployed through the GUI tool as web services. In the deployment process, PovRay dependency files in the format of `inc` are compressed and uploaded to build the web service. The workflow contains two Datapool services and two Application services. They are invoked from the client-side by an executable script written in Python, which supports the invocation of RESTful web services. The `png` file is an intermediate data object, which is not transferred back to the client. The

Datapool service for ImageMagick receives this image as a URI reference (step 6 in Figure 4).

This case study serves to demonstrate how the binary versions of two command-line programs with libraries can be turned into web services and then invoked from a command-line program written in Python.

Multi-Disciplinary Optimization (MDO) Workflow. Multi-disciplinary design optimization (MDO) is a field of engineering that uses (multi-objective) optimization methods to solve design problems combining a number of disciplines. For the purpose of demonstrating multi-disciplinary design optimization process as a web services composition, we use the Taverna workflow management system [11] to carry out the tasks of composition, execution and monitoring, as in our previous work [28, 31]. The composition of services expressed as a workflow, is also able to operate in conjunction with the distributed data staging mechanism of our framework, even though the intermediate data movement in Taverna is centralized in style. Figure 8 shows a screenshot of the service composition design example, which serves to optimize the internal stiffness distribution of a typical aircraft wing under coupled aerodynamics and structural considerations. In Figure 8, the boxes *Aerosolve, AeroLoad_transfer, BLES3* are services deployed based on three command line programs, written in Fortran and C. The boxes *GetInputs4Aerosolve, GetInputs4AeroLoad_transfer, GetInputsBLES3* are the Datapool services. The input ports built into Taverna are located at the top of Figure 8, and the output ports are at the bottom. One local service, *Data_Retriever*, retrieves the data based on the URIs returned by the last application service.

Our framework can also deploy legacy MDO workflows based on existing MDO frameworks like OpenMDAO[9] and Dakota[10]. OpenMDAO is based on Python and a workflow is expressed as an executable python script. With the support of the OpenMDAO runtime installed in a server (ie. cloud side), the deployment process can be achieved as easily as for any other command-line program. Dakota has a different execution approach in that the workflow is defined as a input file, which is then executed by the Dakota runtime. With the Dakota runtime installed in server, the workflow can be executed as a web service by simply uploading the input file through the Datapool service.

This case study primarily serves to show how a popular workflow engine can enact a workflow whose services are the result of our deployment mechanism, thus enabling composition at a programmatic level and sharing of the discipline knowledge that is embedded in software.

4.3 Comparison of Data Staging Performance

In order to evaluate the performance of services deployed using our new framework, we have run the wing optimization process from Section 4.2 in two network-based configurations: (i) with all the programs deployed as SOAP services and controlled through a centralized client, including all the data transfers, constituting in effect a worst case scenario for data overheads, and (ii) with the programs deployed as REST services, using a centralized client for control, but the universal distributed flows framework for

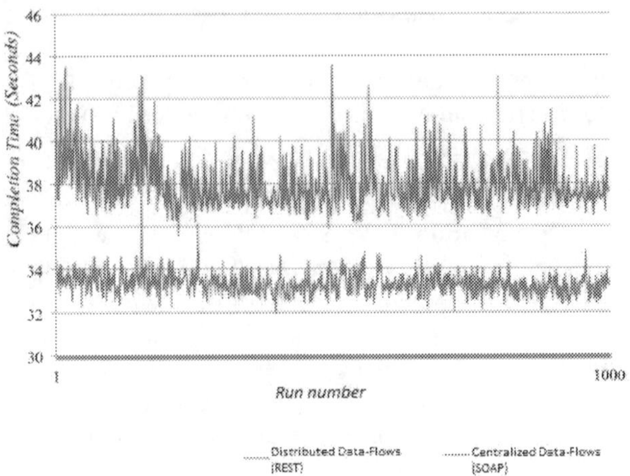

Fig. 9. Comparison of 1000 continuous executions

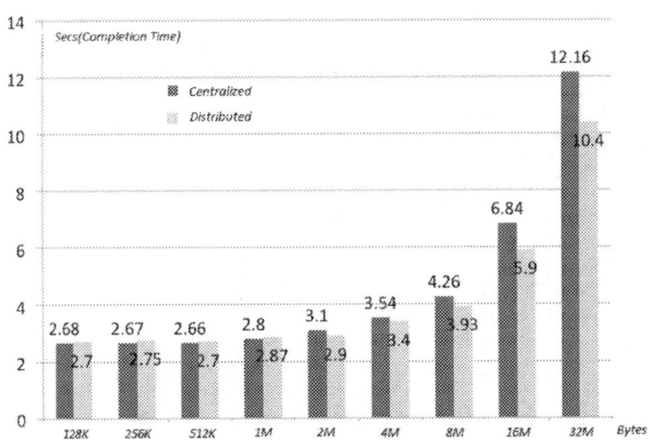

Fig. 10. Results of simple workflows with centralized and distributed data-flows

data. We first compare these two modes, where the programs or services are executed in the same machine environment and the network environment is also the same.

To provide preliminary evidence that the REST web services with distributed data-flows performs better than the centralized approach, we ran an experiment of 1000 consecutive executions for both processes in the same environment. The result is presented in Figure 9[3]. We can observe some spikes because of a changing network situation, but the figure shows that the REST workflow is faster by a clear margin and also demon-

[3] The x-axis only denotes the number of the run: it does not signify concurrent execution of the two modes. The data from the two sets of runs is overlaid to facilitate comparison of the execution times.

strates lower variation. In order to asses data transfer costs, we wrote a workflow that just moves data from client to one service, on to another, then back to the client. These two services are deployed in two different VMs on the same LAN as the client. Client and servers access each other by URIs. We set up two scenarios both using RESTful services, but while one uses centralized transfer, the other uses the distributed method. In the first scenario, the data transferred from the first service to the second is included in the HTTP body, while in the second just the URIs are transferred and data is transferred in the background by the Datapool service. The results are shown in Figure 10. Each workflow was run 10 times for the two scenarios and different data sizes to obtain the mean value. The results suggest the expected trend, in that gains increase with the size of data to be transferred. Crossover, in the test environment, occurs between and 1 and 2Mb, but clearly this will be different for different network environments.

5 Conclusion and Future Work

In this paper, we have presented evidence for the benefits arising from our light-weight framework for the deployment and execution of scientific application in the cloud. With our GUI based deployment mechanism, the technical barriers are lowered for non-specialist usage of web services and cloud resources. The framework reduces the effort for users to turn legacy codes and programs into web services and hence collaborate with each other. The distributed and asynchronous data staging mechanism helps reduce end-to-end times by hiding the costs of data staging between services as well as between client and service. This paper also evaluates the usefulness and usability of the framework through a simple user study and case studies, showing how different types of legacy programs and tools can cooperate seamlessly in workflow with the support of our framework.

In future work, we need to address support for the construction and deployment of composite services: one approach we have explored as proof-of-concept, is to treat a Taverna workflow as a service to be executed, where the workflow description is the data and the program is the enactment engine. Similar functionality should also be achievable with Kepler [25]. A more serious issue however, is the dependence on specific services, meaning there is a reliance on a service provided at a specific URL, as against a specification of a service by, say, its profile (in OWL-S terminology), and the late binding identification of suitable available candidate services close to enactment time. A preliminary effort in this direction appears in [32], based on a matchmaker that assumes WSDL format service descriptions, but a fresh approach that takes advantage of REST seems desirable when this is revisited. Hence, we hope this framework will allow more users to build their own services, and take advantage of the power offered by service composition to enable collaboration. Finally, we propose to take advantage of the availability of capacity computing facilities to support speculative enactment of services, following the design set out in [33].

Acknowledgements. We thank Lizzie Gabe-Thomas for advice on experiment design in user trials of the deployment tools and the participants for their help.

References

1. Gannon, D., Ananthakrishnan, R., Krishnan, S., Govindaraju, M., Ramakrishnan, L., Slominski, A.: Grid Web Services and Application Factories. In: Grid Web Services and Application Factories, pp. 251–264. John Wiley & Sons, Ltd. (2003)
2. Kandaswamy, G., Fang, L., Huang, Y., Shirasuna, S., Marru, S., Gannon, D.: Building web services for scientific grid applications. IBM Journal of Research and Development 50(2.3), 249–260 (2006)
3. Sneed, H.M.: Integrating legacy software into a service oriented architecture. In: Proceedings of the 10th European Conference on Software Maintenance and Reengineering, CSMR 2006, p. 11. IEEE, Bari (2006)
4. Gorder, P.F.: Coming soon: Research in a cloud. Computing in Science and Engineering 10(6), 6–10 (2008)
5. Sullivan, F.: Guest editors introduction: Cloud computing for the sciences. Computing in Science & Engineering 11, 10 (2009)
6. Rehr, J.J., Vila, F.D., Gardner, J.P., Svec, L., Prange, M.: Scientific computing in the cloud. Computing in Science & Engineering 12(3), 34–43 (2010)
7. Mell, P., Grance, T.: The nist definition of cloud computing (draft). NIST special publication 800(145), 7 (2011)
8. Fielding, R.T.: Architectural Styles and the Design of Network-based Software Architectures. PhD thesis, University of California, Irvine (2000)
9. NASA Glenn Research Center: OpenMDAO, `http://openmdao.org/` (accessed January 15, 2014)
10. Sandia National Laboratories: The DAKOTA Project, `http://dakota.sandia.gov/` (accessed January 15, 2014)
11. School of Computer Science, University of Manchester: Taverna, `http://www.taverna.org.uk/` (accessed January 15, 2014)
12. Kitchenham, B.A.: Evaluating software engineering methods and tool part 1: The evaluation context and evaluation methods. ACM SIGSOFT Software Engineering Notes 21(1), 11–14 (1996)
13. Moody, D.L.: Theoretical and practical issues in evaluating the quality of conceptual models: current state and future directions. Data & Knowledge Engineering 55(3), 243–276 (2005)
14. Google: Google App Engine, `http://developers.google.com/appengine/` (accessed January 15, 2014)
15. Lindenbaum, J., Wiggins, A., Henry, O.: Heroku (2008),`http://www.heroku.com` (accessed January 15, 2014)
16. GoPivotal, Inc.: Cloud Foundry, `http://www.cloudfoundry.com/` (accessed Augest 24, 2014)
17. Red Hat, Inc.: Openshift, `https://www.openshift.com/` (accessed January 15, 2014)
18. Simmhan, Y., van Ingen, C., Subramanian, G., Li, J.: Bridging the gap between desktop and the cloud for escience applications. In: IEEE 3rd International Conference on Cloud Computing (CLOUD), pp. 474–481. IEEE, Chengdu (2010)
19. Senger, M., Rice, P., Bleasby, A., Oinn, T., Uludag, M.: Soaplab2: more reliable Sesame door to bioinformatics programs (2008)
20. Krishnan, S., Clementi, L., Ren, J., Papadopoulos, P., Li, W.: Design and evaluation of opal2: A toolkit for scientific software as a service. In: 2009 World Conference on Services - I, pp. 709–716. IEEE, Los Angeles (2009)
21. Alonso, G., Reinwald, B., Mohan, C.: Distributed data management in workflow environments. In: Proceedings of the Seventh International Workshop on Research Issues in Data Engineering, pp. 82–90 (April 1997)

22. Liu, D., Peng, J., Wiederhold, G., Sriram, R.D., Aruthor, C., Law, K.H., Law, K.H.: Composition of engineering web services with distributed data flows and computations (2005)
23. Murray, D.G., Schwarzkopf, M., Smowton, C., Smith, S., Madhavapeddy, A., Hand, S.: CIEL: a universal execution engine for distributed data-flow computing. In: Proceedings of the 8th USENIX Conference on Networked Systems Design and Implementation, NSDI 2011, p. 9. USENIX Association, Berkeley (2011)
24. Isard, M., Budiu, M., Yu, Y., Birrell, A., Fetterly, D.: Dryad: distributed data-parallel programs from sequential building blocks. In: Proceedings of the 2nd ACM SIGOPS/EuroSys European Conference on Computer Systems 2007, EuroSys 2007, pp. 59–72. ACM, New York (2007)
25. Davis, U.C., Santa Barbara, U.C., San Diego, U.C.: Kepler project, `https://kepler-project.org/` (accessed: January 15, 2014)
26. Cardiff University: Triana project, `http://www.trianacode.org/` (accessed May 08, 2013)
27. Cao, J., Jarvis, S., Saini, S., Nudd, G.: Gridflow: workflow management for grid computing. In: Proceedings of the CCGrid 3rd IEEE/ACM International Symposium on Cluster Computing and the Grid, 2003, pp. 198–205 (May 2003)
28. Duan, K., Padget, J., Kim, H.A., Hosobe, H.: Composition of engineering web services with universal distributed data-flows framework based on roa. In: Proceedings of the Third International Workshop on RESTful Design, pp. 41–48. ACM, Lyon (2012)
29. Persistence of Vision Raytracer Pty. Ltd.: Povray, `http://www.povray.org/` (accessed Januray 15, 2013)
30. ImageMagick Studio: Imagemagick, `http://www.imagemagick.org` (accessed January 15, 2014)
31. Duan, K., Seowy, Y.V., Kim, H.A., Padget, J.: A Resource-Oriented Architecture for MDO Framework. In: Proceeding of 8th AIAA Multidisciplinary Design Optimization Specialist Conference, AIAA, Honolulu (2012)
32. Chapman, N., Ludwig, S., Naylor, W., Padget, J., Rana, O.: Matchmaking support for dynamic workflow composition. In: Proceedings of 3rd IEEE International Conference on eScience and Grid Computing, pp. 371–378. IEEE, Bangalore (2007), doi:10.1109/E-SCIENCE.2007.48
33. Fukuta, N., Satoh, K., Yamaguchi, T.: Towards "Kiga-kiku" services on speculative computation. In: Yamaguchi, T. (ed.) PAKM 2008. LNCS (LNAI), vol. 5345, pp. 256–267. Springer, Heidelberg (2008)

Planning and Scheduling Data Processing Workflows in the Cloud with Quality-of-Data Constraints*

Sérgio Esteves and Luís Veiga

Instituto Superior Técnico - ULisboa
INESC-ID Lisboa, Distributed Systems Group, Portugal
sesteves@gsd.inesc-id.pt, luis.veiga@inesc-id.pt

Abstract. Data-intensive and long-lasting applications running in the form of workflows are being increasingly more dispatched to cloud computing systems. Current scheduling approaches for graphs of dependencies fail to deliver high resource efficiency while keeping computation costs low, especially for continuous data processing workflows, where the scheduler does not perform any reasoning about the impact new input data may have in the workflow final output. To face such stark challenge, we introduce a new scheduling criterion, Quality-of-Data (QoD), which describes the requirements about the data that worth the triggering of tasks in workflows. Based on the QoD notion, we propose a novel service-oriented scheduler planner, for continuous data processing workflows, that is capable of enforcing QoD constraints and guide the scheduling to attain resource efficiency, overall controlled performance, and task prioritization. To contrast the advantages of our scheduling model against others, we developed WaaS (Workflow-as-a-Service), a workflow coordinator system for the Cloud where data is shared among tasks via cloud columnar database.

1 Introduction

Data-intensive applications generally comprehend several distinct and interconnected processing steps that can be expressed through a directed acyclic graph (DAG) and viewed as a workflow applying various transformations on the data. Such applications have been used in a large number of fields, e.g., assessing the level of pollution in a given city [17], detecting gravitational-waves [3], weather forecasting [12], predicting earthquakes [7], among others. The computation of such applications are being increasingly more dispatched to the Cloud, taking advantage of the utility computing paradigm. In this environment, scheduling plays a crucial role on delivering high performance, resource utilization and efficiency, while still meeting budget constraints.

* This work was partially supported by national funds through FCT - Fundação para a Ciência e a Tecnologia, under projects PEst-OE/EEI/LA0021/2013, PTDC/EIA-EIA/113613/2009.

A.R. Lomuscio et al. (Eds.): ICSOC 2013 Workshops, LNCS 8377, pp. 324–338, 2014.
© Springer International Publishing Switzerland 2014

Scheduling algorithms for workflows in the Cloud usually try either to minimize the overall completion time (or makespan) given a fixed budget, or to minimize the cost given a deadline. In workflows for continuous processing, resources are often wasted due to the small impact that data given as new input might have. This happens specially in monitoring activities, e.g., fire risk, air pollution, observing near-earth objects. Moreover, Workflow Management Systems (WMSs) typically disregard any semantics with respect to the output data, that could be used to reason about the amount of re-executions needed for a given data to be processed. As data may not always have the same impact and significance, we introduce a new scheduling constraint, named Quality-of-Data.

Quality-of-Data (QoD)[1] describes the minimum impact that new input data needs to have in order to trigger processing steps in a workflow. This impact is measured in terms of data size, magnitude of values, and update frequency. Having the QoD notion, we are thus able to change the workflow triggering semantics to be guided by the volume and importance that data communicated between processing steps might have on causing significant and meaningful changes in the values of final output steps. QoD can also be seen as a metric of triggering relaxation.

From the user (or consumer) point of view, reducing costs while meeting a deadline is what matters most. In turn, cloud providers are interested in having low prices and making resource utilization as efficient as possible. This volition on both sides gains a special importance for long-running tasks, where intelligent SLAs may come into place. These SLAs can be seen as QoD constraints that allow cloud providers to give lower costs in exchange of some relaxation.

By allowing QoD-based relaxation, cloud services providing workflow execution (on a pay-per-execution basis) can define different service-level agreements (SLA) with lower prices. With cloud consumers specifying QoD constraints for each task, a WMS would be able to offer reduced prices due to resource savings, and still give the best possible quality within the QoD to normal-execution range.

Having the current outlook, we propose the use of a novel workflow model and introduce a new scheduling algorithm for the Cloud that is guided by QoD, budget, and time constraints. We also present the design of WaaS (Workflow-as-a-Service), a WMS platform that portrays our vision of a Cloud service offered at the PaaS level, on top of of virtualization technology and the HBase [10] noSQL storage, bridging the gap between traditional WMS and utility computing. Results show that we are able to reduce costs by the use of our QoD model.

The remainder of this paper is structured as follows. In the next section we present our scheduling planner. The design and implementation of our framework follow in Section 3, and its experimental evaluation goes in Section 4. Related work is discussed in Section 5, and the paper concludes in Section 6.

[1] *Quality-of-Data* is akin to Quality-of-Service, and should not be confused with issues such as internal data correctness, semantic coherence, data adherence to real-life sources, or data appropriateness for managerial and business decisions.

2 Scheduling Planner

Scheduling, whether it is located at the IaaS or PaaS level, is a core activity in cloud computing that impacts the overall system performance and utilization. Due to the inherent dependencies between computation and data, scheduling workflow tasks is generally more difficult than scheduling embarrassingly-parallel jobs. As stated before, most Cloud scheduling approaches for workflows aim at single-shot workflow executions and only take into account simple constraints on time and costs. The model we propose, which targets data-intensive workflows for continuous and incremental processing, also enforces constraints over the data communicated between tasks, while still fitting the utility paradigm. Our model implies that data must be shared via NoSQL database, which achieves better performance, scalability, and availability. We first describe our QoD model, and then the scheduling planner which coordinates it.

2.1 Workflow Model with Quality-of-Data

Workflow tasks, with typical WMSs, usually communicate data via intermediate files that are sent from a node to another, or using a distributed file system. Sharing data through a NoSQL database, like in this work, allows us to reduce bandwidth and increase reliability in the presence of failing nodes.

Our workflow model [9] is differentiated from the other typical models by the following: the end of execution of a task A does not immediately trigger its successor tasks; instead, they should only be triggered when A has generated output with sufficient impact in relation to the terminal task (outcome) of the workflow (which can cause a node being executed multiple times with the successor nodes being triggered only once). For example, a workflow that is constantly processing data coming from a network of temperature sensors, to detect fires in forests, would not need to be always computing tasks (e.g., calculating hotspots, updating the risk level) whose output would not change significantly in the presence of small jitters in temperature. The workflow will only issue a displacement order to a fire department if more than a certain number of sensors have detected a steep increase in temperature. This way, tasks would only need to specify the minimum impact that their input data needs to have that is worth their execution towards final outcomes.

The level of data changes necessary to trigger a task, denoted by QoD bound κ, is specified through multi-dimensional vectors that associate QoD constraints with data containers, such as a column or group of columns in a table of a given column-oriented database. κ bounds the maximum level of changes through numeric scalar vectors defined for each of the following orthogonal dimensions: time (θ), sequence (σ), and value (ν).

Time. Specifies the maximum time a task can be on hold (without being triggered) since its last execution occurred. Considering $\theta(o)$ provides the time (e.g., seconds) passed since the last execution of a task that is dependent on the availability of data in the object container o, this time constraint κ_θ enforces that $\theta(o) < \kappa_\theta$ at any given time.

Sequence. Specifies the maximum number of updates that can be applied to an object container o without triggering a task that depends on o. Considering $\sigma(o)$ indicates the number of applied updates over o, this sequence constraint κ_σ enforces that $\sigma(o) < \kappa_\sigma$ at any given time.

Value. Specifies the maximum relative divergence between the updated state of an object container o and its initial state, or against a constant (e.g., top value), since the last execution of a task dependent on o. Considering $\nu(o)$ provides that difference (e.g., in percentage), this value constraint κ_ν enforces that $\nu(o) < \kappa_\nu$ at any given time. It captures the impact or importance of updates in the last state.

A QoD bound can be regarded as an SLA (Service-level agreement), defining the minimum performance required for a workflow application that is agreed between consumers and providers.

2.2 Abstract Scheduling Planner

Generally, scheduling workflow tasks is a NP-complete problem. Therefore, we provide here an approximation heuristic that attempts to minimize the costs based on local optimal solutions. The QoD bounds are involved in this process to offer price flexibility, which is very important for continuous processing.

We state the problem as a coordinator node attempting to map a workflow graph G to available worker nodes in a way that minimizes costs and yet respects time and QoD constraints. A single execution of each workflow graph must be completed until a specified time limit L (e.g., in minutes). A task T has a specification in terms of its complexity and tolerated relaxation QoD. This complexity represents the computational cost a task has for being executed in relation to a standard task in a standard machine (this section abstracts from such details, they are given in Section 3). Tolerated relaxation consists in the QoD constraints that are associated with the input data fed to each task.

Worker machines have a specification in terms of their current capability and reference price. This capability is the power of the machine with its current load availability (capability calculation is given in Section 3). Reference price is a standard value that is then adjusted for current availability and load usage of each worker.

The scheduling planning can be divided in two phases. First, tasks are organized into branches (e.g., Figure 1): connected tasks where each has exactly one predecessor and one successor, except from the last task which can have multiple successors (i.e., pipeline). Branches are ordered by their summed complexity. Tasks that do not fit in the pipeline, are still treated as a pipeline, albeit with a single task within. This means that such tasks will be simply allocated to workers offering the best cost for them.

Second, inner branch scheduling is performed by starting from the most complex branch to the least complex one. To schedule tasks inside a branch in an optimal manner, we decompose the problem into a Markov Decision Process (MDP) [16], since it is a common and proven effective technique for sequential decision problems (e.g., [23]).

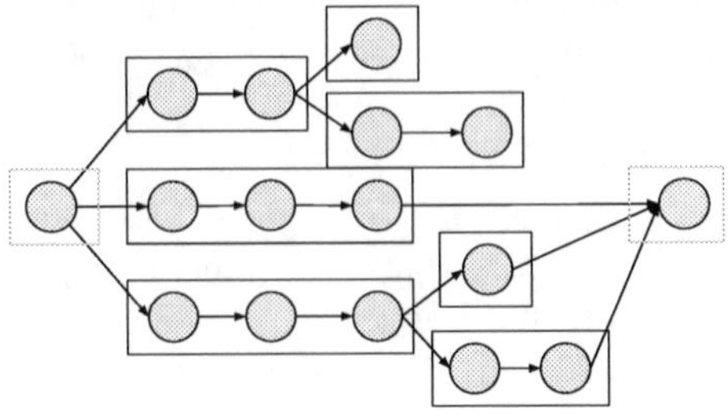

Fig. 1. Branches in a workflow

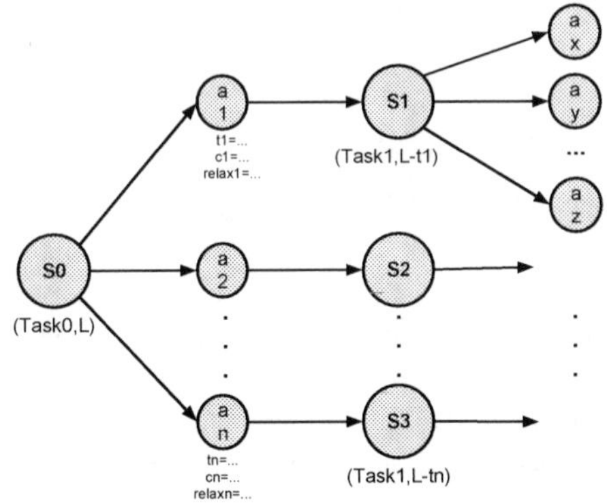

Fig. 2. Markov Decision Process diagram

Briefly, a MDP consists of a set of possible states S, a set of possible actions A, a reward function $R(S,a)$, and a transition model $Tr(S,a,S')$ describing each action's effects in each state. Since R values are guaranteed in our problem, we use deterministic actions instead of stochastic actions, i.e., for each state and action we specify a new state ($Tr : S \times A \rightarrow S'$). The core problem of MDP is to find an optimal policy $\pi(S)$ that specifies which action to take for every state S.

Figure 2, depicts a diagram representing the decomposition of the problem. Each state S in the model corresponds to a task and a time limit to the workflow makespan. Actions represent the allocation of tasks to VM slots in workers. When an action is taken, an immediate reward is given, i.e., 3 variables specifying the time taken for 1 execution, the reference cost per hour, and the minimum relaxation of data freshness, within specified QoD limits, that assures the lowest price.

Finding the optimal policy π for each state S (i.e., choosing the right action a to take when on state S) consists of minimizing the cumulative cost of the rewards obtained when transitioning from S to a terminal state. Hence, we only know the reward $R(S,a)$ after following all possible transitions from state S', such that $S \times a \rightarrow S'$, to a final state. Nonetheless, the processing time, retrieved from the immediate reward of an action a, is discounted from the time limit L when transitioning from S to S' through a. If L is zero or lower in a state S, all paths going through S are cut and it is necessary to find other paths. If there is no other path, it means that it is not possible to compute all tasks in the specified time limit.

To solve this optimization problem and optimally allocate tasks to workers (i.e., with overall lowest cost and yet respecting time and QoD constraints), we developed a dynamic programming algorithm, listed as follows.

```
1 def min_cost(tasks, workers, totalTime, timeLimit):
2   if not tasks:
3     return 0, 0, []
4   t = tasks[0]
5   minCost, minCostTime, minCostPath = float('inf'), None, []
6   for w in workers:
7     if not w.slots:
8       continue
9     time = calculate_time(t, w)
10    if(totalTime + time > timeLimit):
11      continue
12    w.slots -= 1
13    v1, v2, v3 = min_cost(tasks[1:], workers, totalTime + time,
        timeLimit)
14    w.slots += 1
15    if v2 == None | totalTime + time + v2 > timeLimit:
16      continue
17    totalCost = calculate_cost(t, w) + v1
18    if totalCost < minCost:
19      minCost = totalCost
20      minCostTime = time + v2
21      minCostPath = [w.name] + v3
22  return minCost, minCostTime, minCostPath
```

Lines 1-5: contain the stop condition, when there are no more tasks/states to follow; lines 6-13: contain the transition of states, thereby exploring all actions of a current state (which is represented by *task* and *totalTime*); lines 10-11, 15-16: check for whether the time limit was violated or not, causing the algorithm to explore other actions at the same level; lines 18-21: store the minimum cost found for the current state. Additionally, when a slot is locked (line 12) it can no longer be used by successor tasks.

This algorithm runs in $\mathcal{O}(w^t)$, where w is the number of workers and t the number of tasks. Some optimizations were performed, namely caching the rewards of states, obtained by roaming the sub-graphs until the terminal state in the MDP model (they were omitted from the algorithm above due to space constraints). The whole process of planning and scheduling is synthesized in the following:

1. Discover available workers and request cost and expected completion time for every task. These values should be guaranteed for a certain time frame, which should be higher than the time taken to perform the planning and allocate tasks.
2. Divide the workflow in pipelines.

3. Divide the overall time limit L per each pipeline and weighted by their summed complexity.
4. Generate scheduling plans for each pipeline, starting from the most complex and ending with the least complex.
5. Allocate tasks to workers according to the generated plans.
6. Start workflow execution and repeat steps 1, 4, and 5 if any worker fails.

3 WaaS Design and Implementation

In this section, we describe our proposed prototypical middleware framework that embodies the vision of a WMS at the PaaS level, that we call Workflow-as-a-Service (or WaaS). We approach its main design choices and the more relevant implementation details. We address: i) workflow description and WMS integration, ii) the cost model, and iii) how resource allocation is enforced.

We envision a WaaS distributed network architecture in the Cloud, where workflows are set up to be executed upon a cluster of worker machines connected through a local, typically high-speed, network. A designated coordinator machine, running the WaaS server VM instance, is in charge of allocating workflow tasks to available worker nodes (according to a scheduling algorithm), and collect monitoring information regarding node load and capacity.

The input/output data is shared among tasks via a shared columnar noSQL data store. Each worker node executes the workflow tasks scheduled to it as guest VM instances, using Xen or QEMU/KVM[1] images, and in particular, a Xen (or QEMU/KBM) virtual appliance with Linux OS, a JVM and a QoD-enabled middleware for cloud noSQL storage.

The WaaS middleware carries out three major steps in its operation. First, according to the workflow descriptions, WaaS performs the planning by exploring scheduling alternatives for the workflow tasks and branches, carrying out the algorithm described in Section 2. Then, according to the schedule calculated, it performs the allocation of resources at nodes, by assigning the corresponding VMs for tasks at nodes, according to their cost and available capacity. The workflow is then started, and tasks continually re-executed according the QoD parameters defined as new input becomes available and considered.

Additionally, all nodes inform the coordinator only of relevant changes in their available capacity, so that the coordinator can adjust and fine-tune scheduling and allocation decisions, since the coordinator makes use of declarative information stating resource requirements for tasks. When new nodes are added to the cluster or become unavailable, the scheduling must also be recalculated.

3.1 Workflow Description and WMS Integration

Workflow specification schemas need to be enhanced to include declarative information requiring for the scheduling. This is currently defined with special comments in the workflow descriptions in DAGMan [6] files, that are parsed by the WaaS framework. They should contain the description of the workflow graph where each processing step (to be executed as a task) is annotated specifying explicitly the underlying data containers in the noSQL storage (e.g., tables, columns, rows by ID or predicate, or combinations of any of these) it depends on for its input.

This approach is used throughout as it preserves transparency and compatibility where workflows are deployed in other, non-enhanced WMS. Additionally, in particular for the last processing step, it is necessary to specify the desired significance factor: the percentage of variation in the output tabular data that comprises a minimum semantically level of meaning to the workflow users, e.g., 5%. The scheduling is repeated after a predefined parameter of N workflow executions.

Regarding failure handling and cluster membership, if a node fails or every time a node enters or parts, the scheduling is recalculated. Note that all data is saved in the distributed storage (HBase cluster) and WMS can easily restart tasks.

3.2 Cost Model

The cost model of WaaS is based on considering task complexity and dynamic price definition. Assessing task complexity regarding processing and memory requirements has been explored in previous works [20,19,5]. Regarding CPU and memory requirements, the base approach is inspired in CloudSim and uses declarative definitions of MIs (millions of instructions) and MBs of memory required. Additionally, we leverage previous executions of tasks in a machine (e.g. one of the nodes) against the requirements from a reference workload, a unitary cost task, e.g., Linpack benchmark (as used in [20]), that can also be used to rank the relative capacity of different worker nodes against a reference one.

Regardless of the approach employed, we can determine an estimate on how long each task will take to complete with a given capacity awarded in the node (i.e., time = task complexity/worker capacity). More than one task may share a node resources for execution, but while ensuring resource and performance isolation as described in the next subsection.

In the general case where the infrastructure is shared by many users and workflows, the price of executing each task is calculated depending on the resources required pondered with the overall system load.

There is price elasticity: when resources are scarce or there are many users, unitary prices increase, otherwise, when resources are overabundant, prices decrease, with a reference price, as previously addressed in P2P Grids [15].

Usually, the cost of executing a workflow for the first time, will be the sum of the cost of executing its tasks. In the continuous execution model of WaaS, although input is being updated or new input being provided (e.g., sensory data), tasks are only re-executed when QoD parameters are reached. Therefore, the saved executions (i.e. task executions that are avoided until QoD is reached) will imply a lower total cost for a given number of workflow executions.

Additionally, since the interval between consecutive executions of a given task can be significant, there is no point in paying (regardless of real money or some form of credits) according to the common cloud cost model of VM hours of execution, as these may be idle the majority of time. Therefore, we implement a service where task executions are incurred only for the time of execution, plus a *tax* of 10% to account for the overhead of reusing resources by switching among guest VM instances that execute different tasks, possibly from different workflows.

3.3 Resource Allocation and Isolation

As already said, resources at nodes are engaged as virtual machine instances, in particular with images derived from virtual appliances described above. Thus, when the scheduling decides to allocate a virtual machine based on a task requirements and price constrains, it essentially aims at two things: i) allocate enough resources for the task, and ii) ensure that those resources and their availability are not hindered by the scheduling of other tasks in the same node. We make extensive use of virtualization technology to allow such fine-grained allocation and acceptable performance isolation guarantees.

The VM instances can be preconfigured and prelaunched, ready to execute a given workload, and by means of the WaaS component installed, can later execute the workload of another task, without the need of being shutdown and rebooted, easing resource sharing and reducing the amount of wasted resources. Therefore, we configure the hypervisor in Xen to cap the percentage of physical CPU(s) and physical memory awarded to a given VM according to the scheduling decided. This can be repeated until the node capacity is fully allocated, with a 10% safety quota for middleware own operation. This can also be achieved, albeit with less flexibility by parameterizing QEMU/KVM. This ensures that when a task is scheduled to a node, the resources it is expected to make use of, are not in contention with the resources required by other tasks executing at the same time. Any degradation will be graceful and only when contention is very high.

Recall that worker top capacity is established assessing the performance of a reference workload against the performance of the same workload against a reference machine. Regarding instantaneous available capacity at a node, in order to fine-tune the information driving the scheduling (that is aware of VM allocations at each node) we resort to the SIGAR[2] library that has enough precision and is actually platform-independent.

4 Experimental Evaluation

This sections presents experimental evaluation that was carried out to show the benefits of our approach. In particular, if our model can effectively reduce costs, complying with deadlines, and use relaxation (corresponding to the percentage of saved executions with the enforcement of QoD constraints).

[2] `http://support.hyperic.com/display/SIGAR/Home`

All tests were conducted using 6 machines with an Intel Core i7-2600K CPU at 3.40GHz, 11926MB of available RAM memory, and HDD 7200RPM SATA 6Gb/s 32MB cache, connected by 1 Gigabit LAN.

We compared three different approaches with our algorithm: Greedy-time, Greedy-cost, and Random. Greedy-time selects for each task the worker that offers the minimum processing time at that moment. Similarly, Greedy-cost selects at each step the worker that offers the minimum processing cost. And Random selects a random worker for each task.

We conducted a simulation, built in Python, to compare our model with different approaches. Note that this simulation corresponds to the isolation of the coordinator machine, so that it can be properly evaluated without the interference (delays) of worker machines (i.e., tasks complexity and workers capacity are synthetic). We generated hundreds of pipelines with 5, 10, and 15 tasks, corresponding to workloads A, B, and C respectively. Note that the payload of the intrinsic tasks were dummy content (i.e., we were only interested in the task meta-data for the coordinator scheduling). Inside each workload, results were averaged to reduce noise.

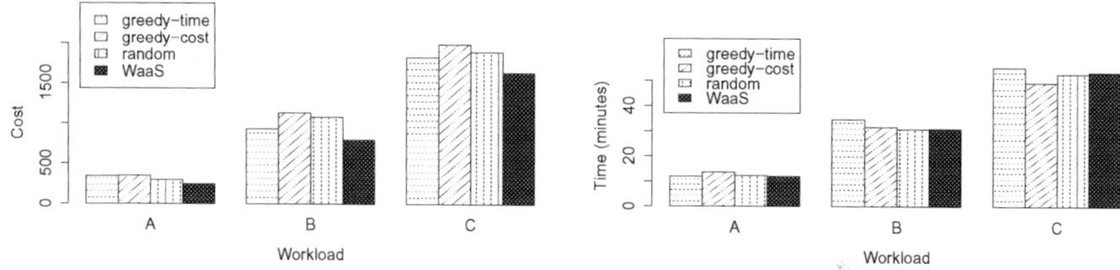

Fig. 3. Cost per hour (left) and time taken for pipeline execution (right)

Figure 3 (left) shows that our model, WaaS, can effectively reduce costs. The gains are higher when there is more variance in the worker's cost. The costs achieved by our model, represent the critical path of the MDP model, and, since no time limit was imposed, they are undoubtedly the minimum possible costs for the considered workloads.

Figure 3 (right) shows that the time obtained with WaaS for a single pipeline execution is not much different from the remaining approaches. Lower costs often mean that workers with lower capabilities were used, and therefore the makespan was higher.

Figure 4 illustrates the correlation observed between time (makespan) and cost for 1000 samples of different pipelines with 10 tasks and in diverse worker settings. Each sample, consisting of a different set of tasks and workers, was executed for the 4 different algorithms, and we can observe that the cost increases with the time. Unsurprisingly, this happens due to the cost and time functions being directly proportional with the task complexity. WaaS appears always at the bottom (blue points) with lower costs, as expected.

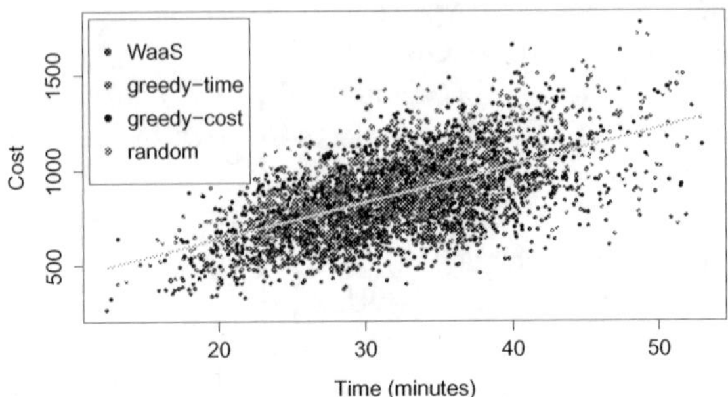

Fig. 4. Time cost correlation for 1000 samples

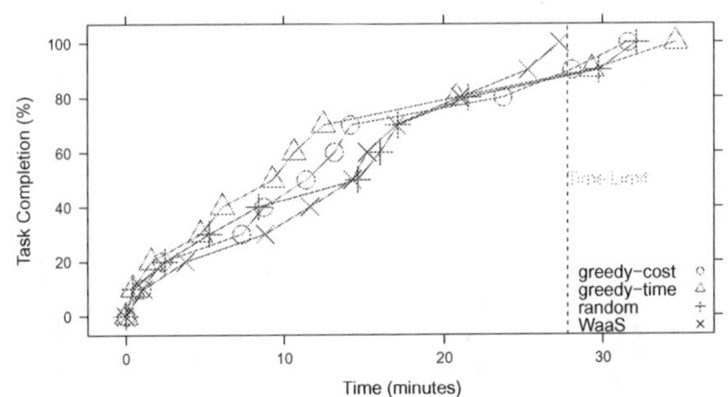

Fig. 5. Task completion over time

Through Figure 5 we may observe that our algorithm with WaaS exhibits the highest task completion rate and is able to meet time limits, while others fail to process the complete workflow inside specified time frames (i.e., roughly the last 20% of tasks are processed outside of the deadline). However, there is a price to pay when such time frames are shrunk, as shown in the next figure.

Figure 6 depicts how costs vary with the imposed time limits L_1, L_2, and L_3. We can see that costs decrease with the expansion of time limits. There is a point from which expanding more the deadline does not reduce the costs, which corresponds to the time taken to go through the critical path, the one that provides the lowest cost, in the MDP graph. Also, when the time limit is lower than the MDP path with the minimum time, it is not possible to complete the whole pipeline tasks inside the limit. Thus, there is an interval of time within which users can adjust the limits.

Figure 7 shows the time evolution for planning with pipelines with different number of tasks and workers (for simplicity, the number of workers is the same as the number of tasks). Although we performed optimizations with the MDP-based algorithm, we may see that time follows an exponential tendency with the number of tasks, like stated in Section 2.2. For less than 15 pipeline tasks

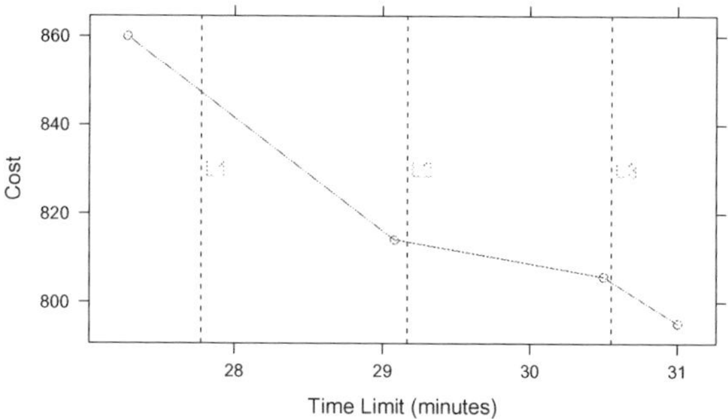

Fig. 6. Cost variation for different time limits

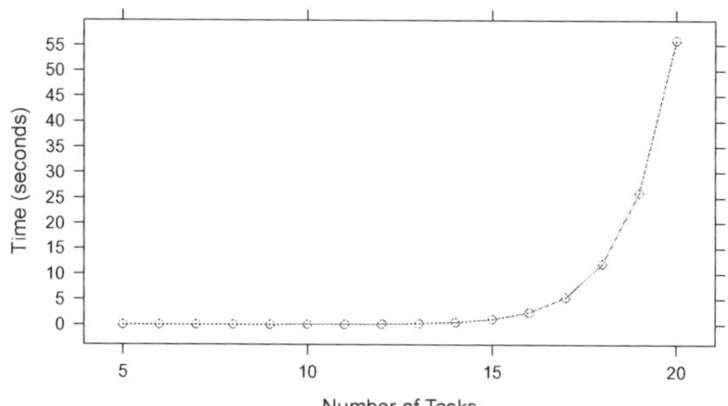

Fig. 7. Time taken for planning

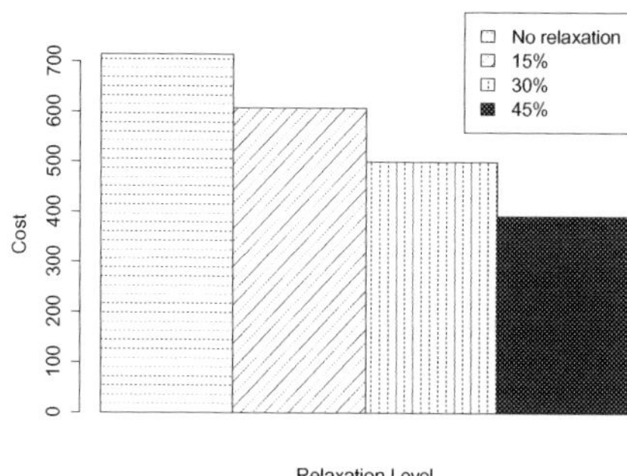

Fig. 8. Cost versus relaxation

the times obtained are negligible, and for more than 17 tasks the times start to increase drastically (above 10 seconds). However, workflows containing more than 10 tasks in pipeline are not common.[3] Furthermore, there is still space for optimization and parallelization on our MDP-based algorithm.

[3] `https://confluence.pegasus.isi.edu/display/pegasus/WorkflowGenerator`

We can see in Figure 8 how the cost varies with the level of relaxation for a pipeline with 10 tasks where each was set to have levels of relaxation of 0 (no relaxation), 15, 30, and 45%. The cost decreased down to 233 units with 45% of relaxation.

5 Related Work

Many work has been done regarding scheduling of tasks in grid and cloud settings. A subset of this work targets the scheduling of workflows in particular. For example, [21,4,13] for Grid computing. Our model inherits from and extends the traditional workflow model [24]. Next, we describe some solutions that are closer and more related with our Quality-of-Data model.

In [25], it is proposed a cost-based workflow scheduling algorithm that is capable of minimizing costs and meeting deadlines for result delivery. A MDP is also used to perform the scheduling, however over different constraints (e.g., tasks can request different services from certain providers). The impact of data in the results and workflow execution relaxation is not taken into account, unlike in our model. Nonetheless, it has been a common approach to impose time limits, instead of minimizing execution times [8].

In [18], authors claim that proposed heuristics for scheduling on heterogeneous systems fail by not considering processors with different capabilities. Our model also takes into account processors with different capabilities for scheduling, since the times and relaxation are calculated based on that within the WaaS environment, however, data impact is also not taken into account in their solution. Also, [13] presented a novel binding scheme to deal with heterogeneity presented in grid and cloud environments, and improve performance by attending to such different characteristics.

In [2], different task scheduling strategies for workflow-based applications are explored. Authors claim that many existing systems for the Grid use matchmaking strategies that do not consider overall efficiency for the set of (dependent) tasks to be run. They compare typical task-based greedy algorithms with workflow-based algorithms, that search for the entire workflow. Results show that workflow-based approaches have a potential to work better on data-intensive scenarios even when task estimates are inaccurate. This comes to strengthen our work, as most scheduling done, which is task-based, does not work well for workflows.

In [14], authors claim that most auto-scaling scheduling mechanism only consider simple resource utilization indicators and do not consider both user performance requirements and budgets constraints. They present an approach where the basic computing elements are virtual machines (VMs) of various sizes/costs, and, by dynamically allocating/deallocating VMs and scheduling tasks on the most cost-efficient instances, they are able to reduce costs. This task-to-VM optimization was also tasked in [22], where a hierarchical scheduling strategy was proposed. Furthermore, advantages of running in a virtual environment, even remotely, over local environment are highlighted here [11]. We also provide a resource utilization metric representing not only the capacity of a worker machine, but also its current load usage. In addition to this mechanism we also combined data relaxation which conveys in good cost savings.

6 Conclusion

This paper makes use of a novel workflow model for continuous data-intensive computing proposing a new Cloud scheduling planner, capable of relaxing prices and respecting time constraints, is proposed. This platform gains a special importance in e-science where long-lasting workflows are executed many times without any new significant and meaningful results (many times only getting noise), wasting monetary funds.

Evaluation results show that our approach is able to reduce costs while respecting time constraints. This cost reduction is higher for larger QoD contraints (which result in larger relaxation). However, larger QoD values can cause higher result deviations, but that problem is out of the scope of this paper.

To the best of our knowledge, no work in the cloud scheduling literature has ever before tried to reason about the data impact on processing steps that cause significant changes on the final workflow outcome for continuous and autonomic processing. Therefore, we believe we have a compelling advancement over the state-of-the-art.

References

1. Bartholomew, D.: Qemu: a multihost, multitarget emulator. Linux J. 2006(145), 3 (2006)
2. Blythe, J., Jain, S., Deelman, E., Gil, Y., Vahi, K., Mandal, A., Kennedy, K.: Task scheduling strategies for workflow-based applications in grids. In: Proceedings of the Fifth IEEE International Symposium on Cluster Computing and the Grid (CCGRID 2005), pp. 759–767. IEEE Computer Society, Washington, DC (2005)
3. Brown, D.A., Brady, P.R., Dietz, A., Cao, J., Johnson, B., McNabb, J.: A case study on the use of workflow technologies for scientific analysis: Gravitational wave data analysis. In: Taylor, I.J., Deelman, E., Gannon, D.B., Shields, M. (eds.) Workflows for e-Science. Springer, London (2007)
4. Chen, W.-N., Zhang, J.: An ant colony optimization approach to a grid workflow scheduling problem with various qos requirements. IEEE Transactions on Systems, Man, and Cybernetics, Part C: Applications and Reviews 39(1), 29–43 (2009)
5. Costa, F., Silva, J.N., Veiga, L., Ferreira, P.: Large-scale volunteer computing over the internet. J. Internet Services and Applications 3(3), 329–346 (2012)
6. Couvares, P., Kosar, T., Roy, A., Weber, J., Wenger, K.: Workflow management in condor. In: Taylor, I.J., Deelman, E., Gannon, D.B., Shields, M. (eds.) Workflows for e-Science, pp. 357–375. Springer, Heidelberg (2007)
7. Deelman, E., et al.: Managing large-scale workflow execution from resource provisioning to provenance tracking: The cybershake example. In: Proceedings of the Second IEEE International Conference on e-Science and Grid Computing, E-SCIENCE 2006, p. 14. IEEE Computer Society, Washington, DC (2006)
8. Eder, J., Panagos, E., Rabinovich, M.: Time constraints in workflow systems. In: Jarke, M., Oberweis, A. (eds.) CAiSE 1999. LNCS, vol. 1626, pp. 286–300. Springer, Heidelberg (1999)

9. Esteves, S., Silva, J.N., Veiga, L.: Fluchi: a quality-driven dataflow model for data intensive computing. Journal of Internet Services and Applications 4(1), 12 (2013)
10. George, L.: HBase: The Definitive Guide, 1st edn. O'Reilly Media (2011)
11. Hoffa, C., Mehta, G., Freeman, T., Deelman, E., Keahey, K., Berriman, B., Good, J.: On the use of cloud computing for scientific workflows. In: EEE Fourth International Conference on eScience, 2008, pp. 640–645 (2008)
12. Li, X., Plale, B., Vijayakumar, N., Ramachandran, R., Graves, S., Conover, H.: Real-time storm detection and weather forecast activation through data mining and events processing. Earth Science Informatics
13. Mandal, A., Kennedy, K., Koelbel, C., Marin, G., Mellor-Crummey, J., Liu, B., Johnsson, L.: Scheduling strategies for mapping application workflows onto the grid. In: Proceedings of the 14th IEEE International Symposium on High Performance Distributed Computing, HPDC-2014, pp. 125–134 (2005)
14. Mao, M., Humphrey, M.: Auto-scaling to minimize cost and meet application deadlines in cloud workflows. In: 2011 International Conference for High Performance Computing, Networking, Storage and Analysis (SC), pp. 1–12 (2011)
15. Oliveira, P., Ferreira, P., Veiga, L.: Gridlet economics: Resource management models and policies for cycle-sharing systems. In: Riekki, J., Ylianttila, M., Guo, M. (eds.) GPC 2011. LNCS, vol. 6646, pp. 72–83. Springer, Heidelberg (2011)
16. Puterman, M.L.: Markov Decision Processes: Discrete Stochastic Dynamic Programming, 1st edn. John Wiley & Sons, Inc., New York (1994)
17. Richards, M., Ghanem, M., Osmond, M., Guo, Y., Hassard, J.: Grid-based analysis of air pollution data. Ecological Modelling 194(1-3), 274–286 (2006)
18. Shi, Z., Dongarra, J.J.: Scheduling workflow applications on processors with different capabilities. Future Gener. Comput. Syst. 22(6), 665–675 (2006)
19. Simão, J., Veiga, L.: Qoe-jvm: An adaptive and resource-aware java runtime for cloud computing. In: OTM Conferences, vol. 2, pp. 566–583 (2012)
20. Veiga, L., Rodrigues, R., Ferreira, P.: Gigi: An ocean of gridlets on a "grid-for-the-masses". In: CCGRID, pp. 783–788. IEEE Computer Society (2007)
21. Wieczorek, M., Prodan, R., Fahringer, T.: Scheduling of scientific workflows in the askalon grid environment. SIGMOD Rec. 34(3), 56–62 (2005)
22. Wu, Z., Liu, X., Ni, Z., Yuan, D., Yang, Y.: A market-oriented hierarchical scheduling strategy in cloud workflow systems. The Journal of Supercomputing 63, 256–293 (2013)
23. Yih, Y., Thesen, A.: Semi-Markov Decision Models for Real-time Scheduling. Research memorandum. School of Industrial Engineering, Purdue University (1991)
24. Yu, J., Buyya, R.: A taxonomy of scientific workflow systems for grid computing. SIGMOD Rec. 34(3), 44–49 (2005)
25. Yu, J., Buyya, R., Tham, C.K.: Cost-based scheduling of scientific workflow application on utility grids. In: Proceedings of the First International Conference on e-Science and Grid Computing, E-SCIENCE 2005, pp. 140–147. IEEE Computer Society, Washington, DC (2005)

Galaxy + Hadoop: Toward a Collaborative and Scalable Image Processing Toolbox in Cloud

Shiping Chen, Tomasz Bednarz, Piotr Szul, Dadong Wang, Yulia Arzhaeva, Neil Burdett, Alex Khassapov, John Zic, Surya Nepal, Tim Gurevey, and John Taylor

CSIRO Computational Informatics (CCI), Australia
P.O. Box 76, Epping, NSW 1017, Australia
{Firstname.Lastname}@csiro.au

Abstract. With emergence and adoption of cloud computing, cloud has become an effective collaboration platform for integrating various software tools to deliver as services. In this paper, we present a cloud-based image processing toolbox by integrating Galaxy, Hadoop and our proprietary image processing tools. This toolbox allows users to easily design and execute complex image processing tasks by sharing various advanced image processing tools and scalable cloud computation capacity. The paper provides the integration architecture and technical details about the whole system. In particular, we present our investigations to use Hadoop to handle massive image processing jobs in the system. A number of real image processing examples are used to demonstrate the usefulness and scalability of this class of data-intensive applications.

Keywords: Galaxy, Hadoop, Image Processing, Workflow, Scalability, Data-Intensive Computation.

1 Introduction

The concept of cloud computing has been widely adopted by both industry and research community. As a result, a number of cloud providers came up to provide various computing resources in business model of *infrastructure as a service* (IaaS), such as Amazon S3 for storage service [1] and EC² for processing service [2]. Furthermore, various software systems are developed and deployed onto to these public/private cloud infrastructures in form of *platform as a service* (PaaS), e.g., Window Azure [3] and Microsoft's Google App Engine [4], or *software as a service* (SaaS), e.g., Saleforce's cloud-based CRM/ERP [5] and Apple's iCloud [6].

Due to its scalable computing resources, low total ownership of cost (TOC), and pay-as-go flexible cost model, Cloud has become an attract platform to start up business and support research. For example, Dropbox founded in 2008 provides file storage and sharing services by using cloud storage infrastructures [7]. Boxee, an Israel-based start-up company, developed both software and hardware to allow users to view, rate, recommend, and upload/download living media contends to/from clouds [8]. On the other hand, research communities are leveraging clouds to facilitate various researches, ranging from genome bank [9] to big data analysis [10].

A.R. Lomuscio et al. (Eds.): ICSOC 2013 Workshops, LNCS 8377, pp. 339–351, 2014.
© Springer International Publishing Switzerland 2014

One trend within research communities is to establish a virtual environment, called *virtual laboratory* (VL), by integrating and deploying various advanced proprietary tools onto clouds [13]. This powerful concept allows researchers distributed in different institutes to share and reuse these mature and advanced scientific tools to conduct big and complicated research tasks, which used to be impossible in the past. However, it is not an easy to build a VL. Facilitating a VL for a specific research community needs a good understand to the domain and the real requirements from the community. It also requires a well system design and implementation to provide a generic platform for unifying and integrating the heterogeneous tools that may be developed in different languages and have different requirements for the underlying operation systems and 3rd part software. In addition, scalability is another challenge as the loads (the number of current users and/or data to be processed) increase.

In this paper, we present a cloud-based image process toolbox as one of key facilities of Australian National Cloud Virtual Laboratory. The current implementation of this toolbox integrates three advanced image processing tools developed by CSIRO, which allows researchers to conduct complicated image processing analysis anytime and anywhere. This paper introduces the system design and implementation of the toolbox, including how to unify and integrate the image processing tools. Real science images are used to demonstrate the features and usefulness of the cloud-based toolkit. We also present our study of scaling the toolbox capability for processing massive big images using Hadoop in cloud.

2 System Design and Implementation

2.1 Key Requirements

The aim of this work is to build a collaborative platform/toolbox for research communities to share and reuse the advanced image processing algorithms and tools, which otherwise are distributed alone in different organizations. Such an image processing toolbox should meet the following key requirements:

- **Web-scope sharing:** Since the potential users can be very dynamic in terms of organizations and domains, it would be proper to support browsers-based user interface (UI) so that the services provided by the toolbox can be widely accessed via Web.
- **Workflow enabling:** Usually, each algorithm/tool is designed for a specific processing/analysis. As a result, there is a need for constructing workflows by composing multiple tools together for a complicated image processing analysis. The composed workflow can be packaged and published as a new tool for further reuse and composition.
- **Capability scaling:** Due to the dynamic nature of this platform (dynamic load) and image processing (dynamic image sizes and amounts), it requires the system should have a scalable mechanism to handling potential large amount of concurrent users and very big data in terms of image sizes and amounts.

2.2 System Architecture

Based on the above requirements, we designed and implemented a cloud-based image processing toolbox system to integrate various advanced image processing tools, whose overall software architecture is shown in Fig. 1.

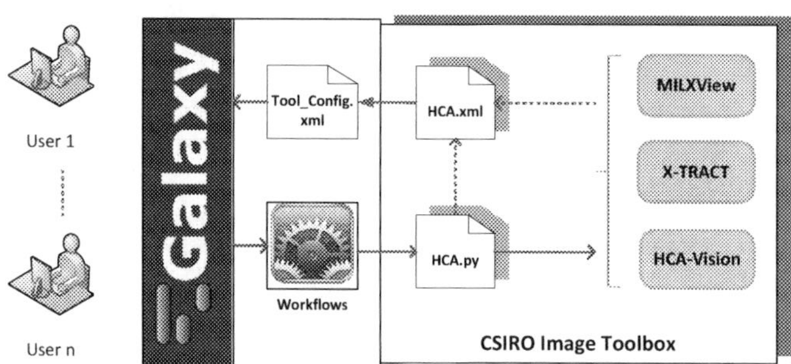

Fig. 1. Software Architecture of CSIRO Image Toolbox

As seen in the above software architecture, the toolbox system consists of two tiers: (1) Galaxy-based front-end; and (2) A set of image processing tools integrated with Galaxy as back-end.

Galaxy [11] is an open source web-based platform for integrating scientific tools to support research. It started up from bi-informatics domain, but has been widely adopted by many research communities. The key reasons for us to adopt Galaxy are: (a) it supports web browser user interface that makes our toolbox reachable by a large range of research communities; (b) it supports workflows, which enables our users (researchers) to conduct big and complex image processing analysis by composing these shared tools in form of workflow; (c) it is widely supported by a range of cloud infrastructures, such as Amazon EC²; and (d) it provides a simple and clean solution to integrating 3rd-party tools onto the web platform. Galaxy and its technical details are available at [14].

2.3 Image Processing Tools as Services

The purpose of this work is to deliver various image processing tools as services to research communities. Through the Galaxy web portal, the following three advanced image processing tools have been integrated into the collaboration platform:

- **HCA-Vision** (High Content Analysis) is software developed for automatically identify the cell features in microscopy images. The technology can be used to detect and locate proteomics, neurobiology and microbiology in cells, which allows researchers to accurately measure cell changes and improve their understanding of biological systems and processes [15].

- **X-TRACT** implements a large number of conventional and advanced algorithms for 2D and 3D X-ray image analysis and simulation. It provides tools for reconstruction and simulation of X-ray phase-contrast CT, including phase retrieval, parallel filtered back projection (FBP), cone beam Feldkamp Davis Kress (FDK) algorithms etc. [16].

- **MILXView** is a 3D medical imaging analysis and visualization platform for clinical applications. MILXView includes standard imaging functions, such as windowing, histogram inspection, panning, slicing, zooming, metadata inspection etc, as well as a large number of analysis functions and complex image processing pipelines. This tool allows rapid and accurate interpretations of 2D & 3D medical images [17].

2.4 Tools Integration

Galaxy provides a unify way to integrate new tools via a configuration file in xml, i.e. the tool_config.xml as shown in Fig. 2. In this configuration file provides a list of file names that refers to the actual configuration files (also in xml) for each tool, e.g., HCA.xml for the HCA-Vision tool. A tool configuration file specifies all information required for the tool, including inputs, output and the scripts/commands to execute the tool, e.g., HCA.py – a python script to call one or more HCA-Vision functions according to the input at runtime. Fig. 2 illustrates the skeleton of the two configuration files and their relationship with the executable scripts.

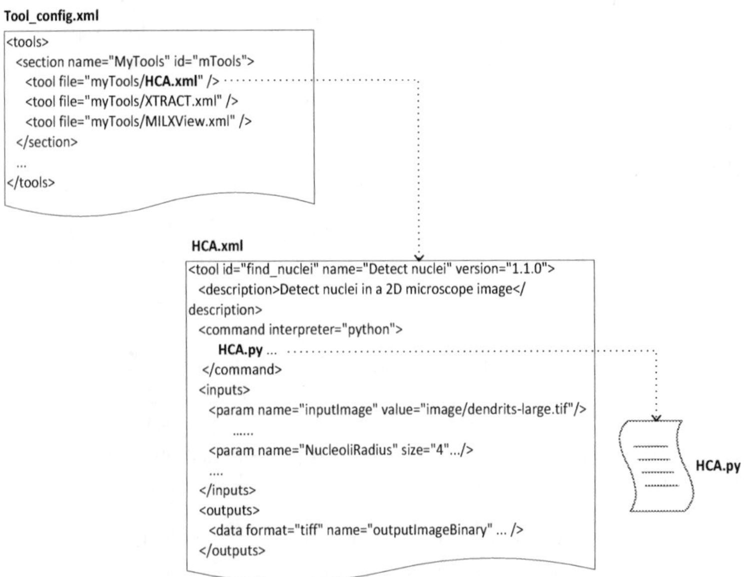

Fig. 2. How to integrate tools to Galaxy

With the above configurations, the three image processing tools become visible and ready to be used via Galaxy web application as shown in Fig. 3.

2.5 Compose Functionalities to Form a Workflow

Galaxy has a built-in support for scientific workflows. It simply records each step as a user is conducting analysis using the integrated tools by selecting a function from the left-hand tools menu, specifying the inputs and the output for the function invocation and executing the function on the left-hand menu. For example, to identify and mark nuclear of cells in a microscopy image, we need the following three steps:

1. Select *'get data'* from the tools menu to upload an image to the toolbox as shown in Fig. 3 (a)
2. Select *'detect nuclear'* from the functions of *Cellular Imaging*, specify its inputs, and execute the function. The output image of the processing is obtained as shown in Fig. 3 (b)
3. Select *'detect nuclear'* from the functions of *Cellular Imaging*, specify the outcomes of Step 1 and Sept 2 as its inputs and execute. The output image of the processing is displayed as shown in Fig. 3 (c)

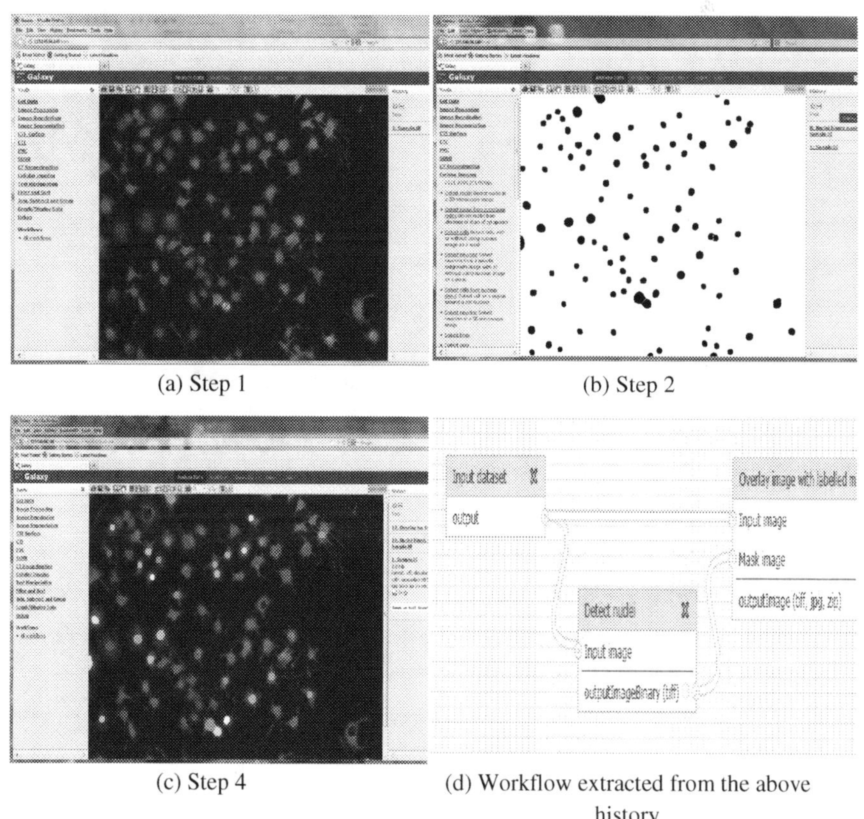

(a) Step 1

(b) Step 2

(c) Step 4

(d) Workflow extracted from the above history

Fig. 3. The user interface of the image processing toolbox

```
{
    "a_galaxy_workflow": "true",
    "annotation": "",
    "format-version": "0.1",
    "name": "Workflow1",
    "steps": {
        "0": {
            "annotation": "",
            "id": 0,
            "input_connections": {},
            "inputs": [
                {
                    "description": "",
                    "name": "Input Dataset"
                }
            ],
            "name": "Input dataset",
            "outputs": [],
            "position": {
                "left": 212,
                "top": 240
            },

        },
        "1": {
                ...
        },
        "2": {
                ...
            },
        }
    }
}
```

Fig. 4. Internal representation of a galaxy workflow

The collection of the recorded steps (also called history) for a particular data analysis task constructs a chain of operations, which can be extracted to form a workflow as shown in Fig. 3 (d). The workflow can be edited using Galaxy graphic user interface (GUI) within a browser. Galaxy use JSON as its workflow internal representation (IR) as shown in Fig. 4, which can be exported and imported across Galaxy platforms.

3 Scale Out Galaxy Using Hadoop

3.1 Requirements for Scalability

The above Galaxy-based image processing toolbox has been deployed onto a single virtual machine of our private cloud for internal testing. However, as deploying onto a public cloud for a large amount of users from different domains, there will be requirements for scalability of the system. The scalability requirements can come from the following sources:

R1. A large number of concurrent users: The image processing toolbox is supposed to be deployed onto a public cloud and shared among a wide range of research communities, such as medical, biologics, and bioinformatics. Potentially, there can be a large number of users to access and use the system at the same time, which requires the system is able to scale its capability to handle the increasing number of concurrent users.

R2. Computation-intensive image processing: Some applications need to conduct complicated processing on very large images, such as Synthetic-Aperture Radar (SAR) images [18]. This kind of image processing usually takes a lot of CPU cycles and a long execution time. In this case, the image should be partitioned into a set of small images that can be processed on multiple cloud *Virtual Machines* (VMs) in parallel.

R3. Data-intensive image processing: Some users may apply a specific identical processing function on a large number of images, e.g. microscope images and CT images. In this case, the system needs a solution to hosting and processing the large amount of images efficiently.

3.2 Using Hadoop for Data-Intensive Image Process

Scalability is a classic problem of software systems and has been well studied in literature [19]. Different scalability requirements need different technical solutions. For example, while R1 can be addressed by scaling out Galaxy with CloudMan [20], MPI-style parallel technology can be used for computation-intensive image processing (R2) [21]. In this paper, we address R3 by exploring and evaluating using Hadoop for data-intensive image processing, because of its elegant architecture and capability of hosting and processing big data in parallel [22]. Fig. 5 shows the basic software architecture of the Hadoop-based scale-out solution.

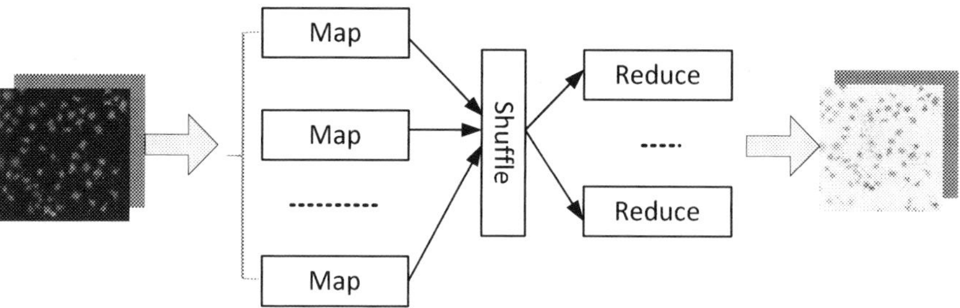

Fig. 5. Using Hadoop for parallel image process

3.3 Feed Hadoop with a Large Amount of Images

Hadoop was originally developed for text-based data processing. As a result, the whole design and implementation are based on the abstraction of a set of pairs of <key, value> computed and exchanged between map and reduce processes, where the key and value usually refer to a text string and its unique attributes. It is straightforward for people to adopt Hadoop software-harnesses and examples for text-mining based data mining applications. However, in our case, our inputs are a large amount of images.

There are a few technologies and research work on feeding Hadoop with images (binary data), such as Hadoop Sequence File (HSF) [23], Apache Avro [24] and HIPI (Hadoop Image Processing Interface) [25]. While the above three technologies are slightly different in their functionalities and features, they share the same design principal, i.e. compress and package multiple images into a big file to feed Hadoop. As a result, they all need to pack the big files in advance. The corresponding data reader/writer also needs to be provided to Hardoop for accessing to the specific formatted file.

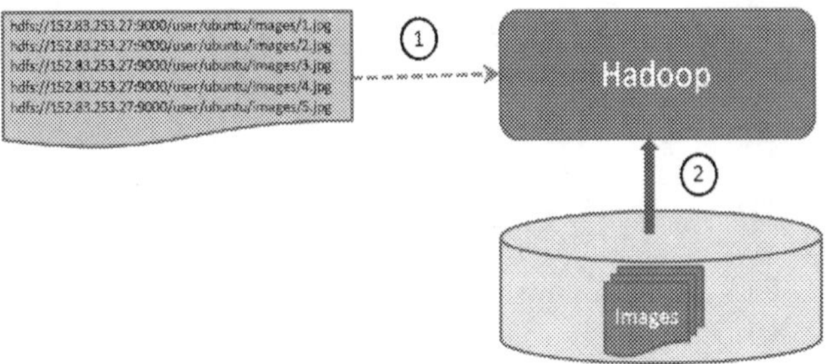

Fig. 6. Feed Hadoop with a list of image HDFS references

In this paper, we propose another way to feed Hadoop with a large amount of images as shown in Fig. 6. Instead of feeding Hadoop with data contents directly, we can simply feed Hadoop a file, where lists all files' URI as v of <k, v>. Each mapper uses the assigned <k, v> to load the corresponding data contents (e.g. images) from the source that each URI refers. In this way, we introduce an abstract layer between Hadoop and its input data. This allows us to feed Hadoop with different data sources, rather than the files from HDFS only. A simple comparison between the two solutions is summarized in Table 1.

Table 1. Big File vs. URI Reference

	Pros.	Cons.
Big File: -SF, -AVRO -HIPI	• Directly feed with data contents as *<k,v>* pair • Can benefit from Hadoop data-location-based schedule	• Need pack before processing • Tightly tired with HDFS
URI Reference	• Indirectly feed the data with uri references • Add another lay between Hadoop and data • Flexible to feed Hadoop with data from different sources	• Need coding in map to get data from the data sources • Cannot benefit from Hadoop data-location-based schedule

3.4 Integrate Hadoop with Non-Java Software

Almost of all Hadoop was implemented in java, except for some underlying native components for performance purpose. As a result, it is nature and straightforward to develop map/reduce in java and integrate with Hadoop. However, there are many scientific software (such as our image processing tools) were implemented in C/C++, and even FORTRAN. Therefore, integrating Hadoop with the non-java software is a important software reuse requirement for using Hadoop to preserve the previous software investments.

Basically, there are three ways to integrate non-java software with Hadoop: (a) Hadoop Pipes; (b) Hadoop Stream; and (c) JNI (Java Native Interface). While Hadoop pipes uses sockets for communication between Hadoop and non-java map/reduce processes, Hadoop Stream uses standard I/O [22]. As a result, neither of the two technologies is suitable for binary images, due to performance and binary encoding considerations. In our image toolbox system, we use JNI to integrate Hadoop with these non-java image processing tools (libraries). We report our preliminary performance testing results in next section.

4 Performance Evaluation

4.1 Performance Testing Environment

We conducted a set of tests to evaluate the performance of the software architecture and the corresponding technologies that we adopted for the imaging process toolbox. The testing environment is specified in Table 2.

Table 2. Testing environment specification

	Hardware/VM	Software
Cloud Server	• 1 VCPU (Small) • 2GB RAM • 10GB Disk	• Ubuntu 12.0.4 64bit • Galaxy v2.5 • Hadoop 1.1.2 • Oracle JDK 7.0.25
Client	• Dell Latitude Laptop • Intel 2.6GHz CPU • 4GB RAM • 232GB Disk	• Window 7 SP1 32bit • Firefox 23.0.1 • GridFTP 5.0 • WinSCP 5.1.0

4.2 Performance of Uploading Images to Cloud

The 1st step of using our toolbox to process images is to upload these images onto the cloud where the Galaxy and Hadoop are deployed. When Galaxy provides browser-based GUI for data uploading, Galaxy suggests using the 3rd-party tools to upload a large amount of data. We tested using ftp and SCP to upload 1MB~1GB data from my laptop to our private cloud. The test results are shown in Fig. 7.

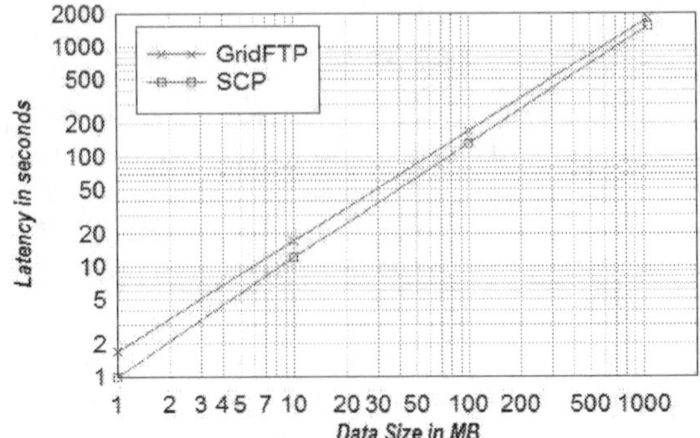

Fig. 7. Performance of uploading images to cloud

As shown in Fig. 7, both FTP and SCP are capable of transferring considerable big (1GB) data over the WAN within a reasonable time (25~30 minutes). Note that our tests are based on the default settings of FTP and SCP with no multiple port configuration and performance tuning.

4.3 Performance of Packing Images for Hadoop

To feed Hadoop with multiple images, we need to pack the images into a sequence file using Hadoop I/O APIs. In our tests, we pack 67 CT images for breast cancer study, whose sizes are between 5~10MB. A few examples of these images are provided as follows:

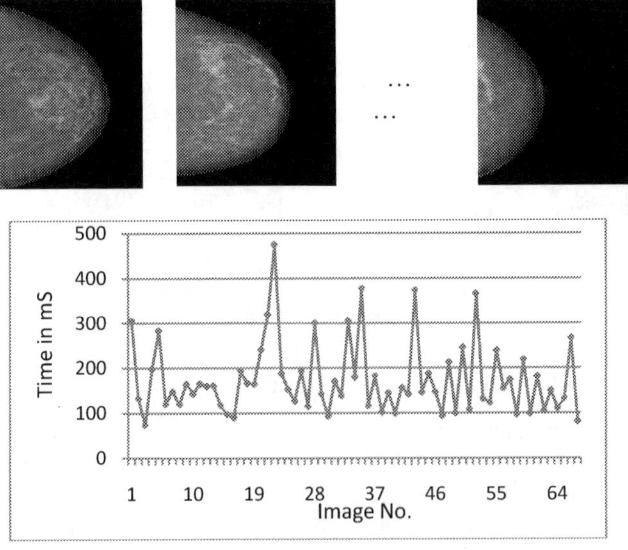

Fig. 8. Performance of packing images for Hadoop

Fig. 8 shows the testing results of packing the 67 CT images on a single VM as specified in Table 2. As we can see from the above results, it takes about 12 seconds to pack 67 images (~415MB) on the testing platform, i.e. 174 ms for each (image) file on average. The performance can be further improved by applying MapReduce to generate sequence files in parallel for even more and/or bigger images.

4.4 Performance of Processing Images with Hadoop

We use the above sequence file as input to test the scalability of processing the images with Hadoop. Each image is filtered with multiple Gaussian-based filters at different scales. Then the histograms are computed in each filtered image over the breast area. The output image is constructed as a matrix of histogram images: columns represent filters. We conducted the above image processing with Hadoop using 1, 2 and 4 VM, respectively. The performance results are shown in Fig. 9. As we can see, Hadoop scales well for processing multiple images in parallel as increasing numbers of VMs.

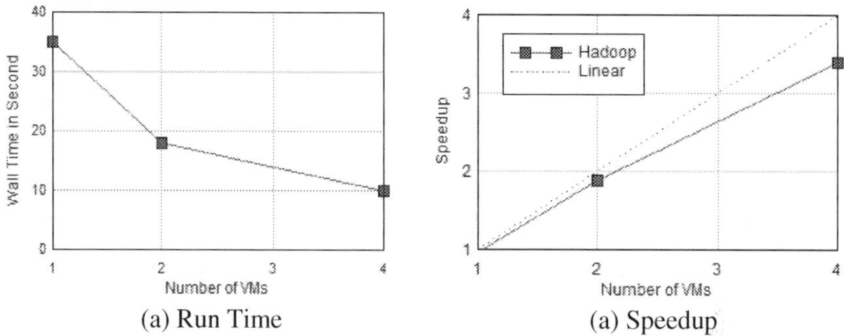

(a) Run Time (a) Speedup

Fig. 9. Performance of parallel images processing with Hadoop

5 Related Work

Galaxy, as an open collaborative platform, has been widely used in the genomics community. For examples, Ravi K. Madduri et al. used Galaxy for building an advanced sequencing analysis service [26]. Bo Liu et al. developed and deployed a high performance scientific workflow platform in cloud by extending Galaxy with Globus [27]. The work presented in this paper extends the application domain of Galaxy to image processing by leveraging its web-based UI and simple tool integration architecture. We also enhance Galaxy by adding new common functionalities and operations, such as upload and manage multiple images (files), which we will publish in another paper.

Hadoop is a promising technology for distributed data storage (HDFS) and parallel data processing (Map/Reduce) [22], and have been widely used for data-intensive processing and analysis, such as page ranking [28], network traffic analysis [29] and senior data management [30]. In fact, our work is strongly related to [31], i.e. both aims to enhance the scalability of (Galaxy vs. Kapler) workflow platforms. However, our approach is different from each other. While they tightly integrate Kapler with Hadoop at code level, our enhancement is loosely coupling. As a result, Hadoop is transparent from Galaxy each other in our architecture, which provides more flexibility to plug-in and other parallel solutions.

6 Conclusion

In this paper, we present a cloud-based collaborative and scalable image processing toolbox. Our toolbox offers an open and web-wide collaboration platform for image processing by leveraging the user friendly interfaces and simple integration software architecture of Galaxy. We also explored technologies and software architecture study of using Hadoop for data-intensive image processing. We evaluated the performance of technologies and operations for applying Hadoop for processing real CT images on real cloud environment. Our testing results show that Hadoop is a feasible and scalable solution to processing a large amount of images in cloud. We plan to extend this work by exploring and evaluating more Hadoop applications with more VMs and bigger (images) data.

References

1. http://aws.amazon.com/s3/
2. http://aws.amazon.com/ec2/
3. http://www.windowsazure.com/en-us/
4. https://cloud.google.com/products/
5. https://www.salesforce.com
6. https://www.icloud.com/
7. https://www.dropbox.com/
8. http://www.boxee.tv/
9. http://www.genecloud.org/
10. Agrawal, D., Das, S., Abbadi, A.E.: Big data and cloud computing: current state and future opportunities. In: The 14th International Conference on Extending Database Technology (EDBT/ICDT 2011), pp. 530–533 (2011)
11. Goecks, J., Nekrutenko, A.: James Taylorcorresponding and The Galaxy Team team: Galaxy: a comprehensive approach for supporting accessible, reproducible, and transparent computational research in the life sciences, Genome Biol. 11(8) (2010), http://www.ncbi.nlm.nih.gov/pmc/articles/PMC2945788/
12. Singh, R.P., Keshav, S.: Tim Brecht: A cloud-based consumer-centric architecture for energy data analytics. e-Energy, 63–74 (2013)
13. Roth, B., Hecht, R., Volz, B., Jablonski, S.: Towards a Generic Cloud-Based Virtual Research Environment. COMPSAC Workshops 2011, 267–272 (2011)
14. https://main.g2.bx.psu.edu/
15. Wang, D., Lagerstrom, R., Sun, C., Bischof, L., Vallotton, P., Götte, M.: HCA-Vision: Automated Neurite Outgrowth Analysis. Journal of Biomolecular Screening 15(9), 1165–1170 (2010)

16. Gureyev, T.E., Nesterets, Y., Ternovski, D.: Toolbox for advanced x-ray image processing. In: Proc. SPIE 8141, Advances in Computational Methods for X-Ray Optics II, 81410B
17. Chandra, S., Dowling, J., Shen, K., et al.: Patient specific prostate segmentation in 3-D magnetic resonance images. IEEE Transactions on Medical Imaging 31(10), 1955–1964 (2012)
18. Goller, A.: Parallel Processing Strategies for Large SAR Image Data Sets in a Distributed Environment. Computing 62(4), 277–291 (1999)
19. Rosenblum, D.S.: Software System Scalability: Concepts and Technologies, Keynote talk at ISEC (2009)
20. Afgan, E., Baker, D., Coraor, N., Chapman, B., Nekrutenko, A., Taylor, J.: Galaxy CloudMan: Delivering Cloud Compute Clusters. BMC Bioinformatics 11(12) (2010)
21. Warfield, S.K., Jolesz, F.A., Kikinis, R.: A High Performance Computing Approach to the Registration of Medical Imaging Data. Parallel Computing 24(9-10), 1345–1368 (1998)
22. Apache Hadoop: `http://hadoop.apache.org/`
23. `http://wiki.apache.org/hadoop/SequenceFile`
24. `http://avro.apache.org/`
25. Sweeney, C.: HIPI: A Hadoop Image Processing Interface for Image-Based MapReduce Tasks, B.S. Thesis. University of Virginia, Department of Computer Science (2011)
26. Madduri, R.K., Dave, P., Sulakhe, D., Lacinski, L., Liu, B., Foster, I.T.: Experiences in building a next-generation sequencing analysis service using galaxy, globus online and Amazon web service. ACM XSEDE 2013, Article 34
27. Liu, B., Sotomayor, B., Madduri, R., Chard, K., Foster, I.: Deploying Bioinformatics Workflows on Clouds with Galaxy and Globus Provision. In: SCC 2012, pp. 1087–1095 (2012)
28. Choi, H., Um, J., Yoon, H., Lee, M., Choi, Y., Lee, W., Song, S., Jung, H.: A partitioning technique for improving the performance of PageRank on Hadoop. In: ICCCT 2012, 458–461 (2012)
29. Lee, Y., Lee, Y.: Toward scalable internet traffic measurement and analysis with Hadoop. SIGCOMM Comput. Commun. Rev. 43(1), 5–13 (2012)
30. Bao, Y., Ren, L., Zhang, L., Zhang, X., Luo, Y.: Massive sensor data management framework in Cloud manufacturing based on Hadoop. Industrial Informatics (INDIN), 397–401
31. Wang, J., Crawl, D., Altintas, I.: Kepler + Hadoop: a general architecture facilitating data-intensive applications in scientific workflow systems. ACM WORKS 2009, Article 12 (2009)

SciLightning: A Cloud Provenance-Based Event Notification for Parallel Workflows

Julliano Trindade Pintas[1], Daniel de Oliveira[2], Kary A.C.S. Ocaña[1], Eduardo Ogasawara[3], and Marta Mattoso[1]

[1] COPPE - Federal University of Rio de Janeiro, Brazil
[2] IC/UFF - Fluminense Federal University, Brazil
[3] Federal Center of Technological Education (CEFET/RJ), Brazil
{julliano,kary,marta}@cos.ufrj.br, danielcmo@ic.uff.br, eogasawara@cefet-rj.br

Abstract. Conducting scientific experiments modeled as workflows is a challenging task due to the complex management of several (often inter-related) computer-based simulations. Many of these scientific workflows are compute intensive and demand High Performance Computing environments to run, such as virtual parallel machines in a cloud computing environment. These workflows commonly present long-term "black-box" executions (*i.e.* several days or weeks), thus making it very difficult for scientists to monitor its execution course. We present a workflow event notification mechanism based on runtime monitoring of provenance data produced by parallel scientific workflow systems in clouds. This mechanism queries provenance data generated at runtime for identifying preconfigured events and notifying scientists using technologies such as Android devices and message services in social networks such as Twitter. The proposed mechanism, named SciLightning, was evaluated by monitoring SciPhy, a large-scale parallel execution of a bioinformatics phylogenetic analysis workflow. SciPhy took six days to complete its execution in Amazon AWS cloud environment using a cloud parallel workflow engine called SciCumulus. The evaluation showed that the proposed approach is effective with respect to monitoring and notifying preconfigured events.

1 Introduction

Notification can be defined as the ability to perceive and to be conscious of events that have happened in a specific context [1]. Depending on the scenario, the lack of event notification can result in several different problems such as conflicts, duplicated results or unnecessary computations that may lead to unnecessary financial cost and time spent. In the context of large-scale scientific experiments, modeled as scientific workflows [2], notification mechanisms are in fact essential [1,3]. Many scientific workflows are executed 100,000 times or more using parallel Scientific Workflow Management Systems (SWfMS) such as Turbine [4] , Pegasus [5], Tavaxy [6],

A.R. Lomuscio et al. (Eds.): ICSOC 2013 Workshops, LNCS 8377, pp. 352–365, 2014.
© Springer International Publishing Switzerland 2014

Askalon [7], Chiron [8] and SciCumulus [9] and varying its input parameter values, thus consuming and producing a large volume of data. Although these workflow systems execute on large amounts of High Performance Computing (HPC) resources, as the workflow becomes increasingly complex (in terms of the number of times that their activities are executed or as the volume of processed data increases), they tend to execute for weeks or even months. This way, it is critical for scientists to be aware of the execution status in order to analyze if the current execution complies with scientists' quality and performance criteria (*e.g.* total execution time, maximum financial cost, reliability) or if scientists have to interfere in the execution (also known as steering [10]). SWfMS have to monitor the workflow execution to provide the necessary level of notification for scientists. Monitoring allows for performing debugging, partial results analysis or failures at predetermined points in the workflow structure. We have experienced the lack of monitoring while supporting workflow execution in different domains from engineering [11,12] to biology [13–16].

However, it is not trivial to monitor the parallel execution of scientific workflows in distributed environments [10]. For example, in the cloud, the same workflow can be executed in several different HPC virtual machines, each one storing different portions of data or executing different applications that are part of the workflow. Many SWfMS already implement monitoring mechanisms for providing some kind of notification features [17–19]. Each SWfMS usually designs and implements its specific monitoring component [20], or provides *log* messages after the completion of the workflow (*i.e. post mortem* analysis [21]). For workflows that are executed in the cloud, the cloud environment providers also dispose tools that monitor the performance of your hosted applications at runtime. There are also approaches that are SWfMS-independent [20,22] that monitor workflow execution decoupled from SWfMS. All of these approaches only consider performance analysis of the environment (*i.e.* cloud monitors) or the workflow execution using traditional monitoring packages such as NetLogger [23]. However, scientists need more than cloud and workflow performance metrics to analyze or to interfere in a workflow execution. In several cases, they need to access and analyze the contents of specific resultant files (such as DNA sequences or a finite element mesh [24–26]) produced by specific workflow executions. This way, the monitoring has to associate performance metrics with produced domain-specific results to improve steering for scientists.

This type of analysis, that associates performance metrics and domain-specific results, can be conducted by scientists using enriched workflow provenance data [27]. In provenance repositories scientists can find execution times, performance information and domain-specific information to support their steering decisions. This way, the monitoring mechanism could use the provenance data to identify important events for the scientists and notify them, thus providing subsidies to take important actions. However, this type of monitoring is not yet a reality in existing SWfMS. In SWfMS such as Swift, Tavaxy or Pegasus, runtime workflow data is only available after the execution finishes. It is not possible to query data provenance at runtime making it difficult to implement workflow monitoring mechanisms that consider not only performance but also domain-specific content. Other approaches such as SciCumulus and Chiron already provide provenance data to be queried at runtime;

however, they do not present monitoring mechanisms. Currently, in these systems, the scientist needs to perform periodic SQL queries to the provenance repository through Database Management Systems (DBMS) or using *log* messages to be aware of the scientific workflow executions steps, which is not desirable since this manual process does not scale, it is tedious and error-prone.

This paper proposes SciLightning, an event notification mechanism based on the monitoring of scientific workflows runtime provenance data. SciLightning is designed to be coupled to different existing SWfMS with low effort. SciLightning queries provenance data generated at runtime and notifies scientists about specific events that are important (*i.e.* preconfigured events) using Android devices and message mechanisms in social networks such as Twitter. This way, scientists can be aware of the execution status of their workflows, since they are able to perform partial results analysis or perform workflow steering actions. To evaluate SciLightning, we monitored the parallel execution of SciPhy workflow [14] for phylogenetic analysis in Amazon AWS cloud environment using SciCumulus workflow engine. The evaluation showed that SciLightning is effective with respect to monitoring and notifying preconfigured events thus improving scientists' awareness.

Besides this introduction, this paper is organized as follows. Section 2 discusses important issues of notification in scientific workflows. Section 3 describes SciLightning with its conceptual architecture and the provenance model used. Section 4 presents the experimental results while Section 5 discusses related work. Finally Section 6 concludes this paper and points to future work.

2 Monitoring in Scientific Workflows

A monitoring component for scientific workflows has to produce awareness information about events that happen or have happened, in a one or a set, of scientific workflow executions, reporting this information to scientists in a research group, in order to improve the interaction between the research group members and allowing them to interfere in the workflow execution to perform a fine-tuning in parameters or explore different input data, *i.e.* steering.

In general, the awareness information (*i.e.* notification) is associated with the research group (Who are the research group participants?), the group objectives (What are the activities that should be executed within a scientific experiment? What are the expected outcomes? Are the outcomes complying with quality and performance criteria?), and the workflow activities execution and coordination (What activities have finished? Is there any execution errors?). Workflow event notification mechanisms have to be implemented within a SWfMS or coupled to a SWfMS to support the generation of awareness information by monitoring parallel executions of the workflow and the distribution of that information to research group members. Using event information, participants of a research group can interfere in their own workflows and can also coordinate interferences in workflow executions of other participants, discovering and solving problems such as active failures and low quality data produced. The participant role in a research group is important to determine the kind of notification information he/she is interested in.

SciLightning considers three main roles: *Executors*, *Coordinators* and *Analysts*. *Executors* are those computer science specialists who specify, model and execute the workflow in the cloud using a shared workspace, typically distributed storages such as Amazon S3. They are interested in performance information about the workflow execution, and activity failures, *i.e.* computer scientists or technical support team. Most existing monitoring mechanisms proposed in the technical literature are designed to help this kind of user (*e.g.* Stampede [20,22]). *Coordinators* are users who are responsible for the research group and can grant access to other scientists. They usually need summarized and aggregated information about planned and executed activities to identify situations where their interference is necessary. *Analysts* are researchers who are responsible for analyzing the overall provenance data (including file content) to discover if the scientific hypothesis was confirmed or refuted. High level analysis queries might be "What are the produced phylogenetic trees in the workflow execution ID number 451?" or "Is the DNA sequence 'CCCATTGTTCTC' part of any phylogenetic tree?" It is not simple to answer these types of queries using existing monitoring mechanisms. The specific objective of SciLightning is to support the gathering and distribution of awareness information (*i.e.* notification) related to asynchronous interaction for executors, coordinators and analysts.

3 The SciLightning Event Notification Mechanism

SciLightning is designed to provide monitoring information and to be a non-intrusive approach regarding existing SWfMS. No change in the SWfMS is required as long as provenance data is provided at runtime for querying. It is based on event notification. Events are discovered using a specific interface (*i.e.* it can be SQL queries or a provenance graph transversing). In addition, traditional monitoring mechanisms, characterized by a central entity that polls individual workflows, are not adequate for today's large-scale scientific experiments. SciLightning components are distributed in the cloud (in several virtual machines) to monitor different scientific workflows on demand. Following we describe SciLightning architecture and its provenance model.

Architecture and Implementation

The architecture of SciLightning (Figure 1) is composed by five components: (i) *Rule Database* (*i.e.* Rule DB): in this local database the coordinator configures which types of events are captured and which type of notification information is delivered to scientists; (ii) *SciLightning Cartridge*: it implements a cartridge [28] to interface SciLightning and the SWfMS provenance repository. It accesses the notification rules used to identify events by querying provenance data in the repository, (iii) *SciLightning Monitor*: it monitors and analyzes provenance data provided at runtime by the SWfMS through cartridges; (iv) *SciLightning Social*: it publishes notification messages on social networks; and (v) *SciLightning Mobile*: sends notifications to Android-based devices.

SciLightning needs to be aware of the provenance database schema to extract required data, such as produced files, file content or activity and workflow execution times. Thus, SciLightning has to implement and access a different type of cartridge for each provenance repository. The implemented cartridge varies depending on how provenance is stored. For example, if provenance data is stored in a relational database, the cartridge has to implement a database view with a predefined signature that returns the notification information to be delivered to scientists according to rules stored in the Rule DB.

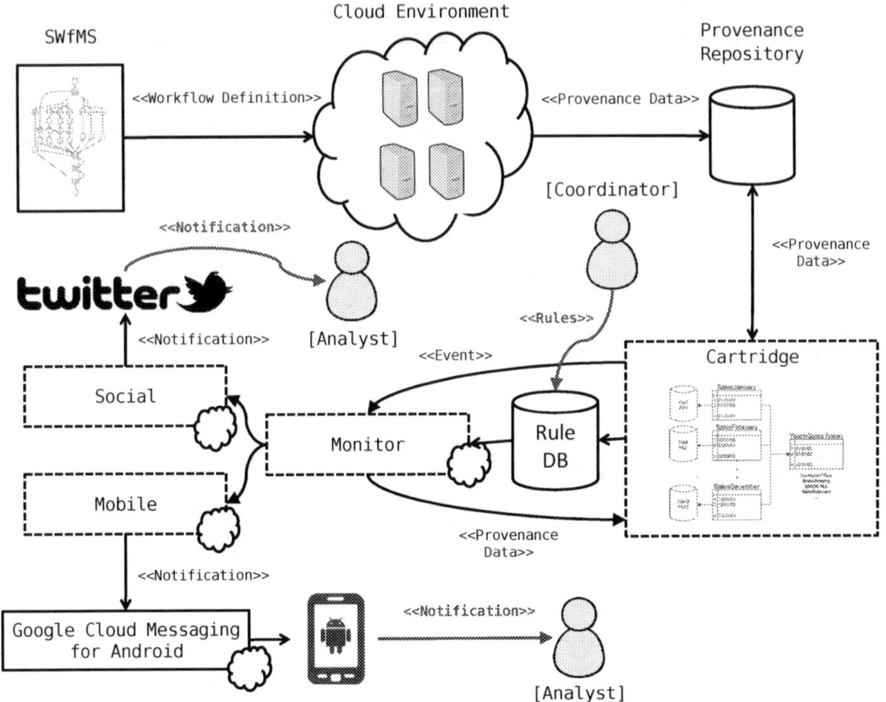

Fig. 1. Architecture of SciLightning

Rules are specified using an OCL-like [29] structure that is related to the tables in the provenance repository. For example, if scientists want to be notified when a specific set of biological sequences was aligned, they can configure a rule as presented in Figure 2.

```
context Alignment /* context can be a table, a graph or a log file */
inv: self. owner. Consensus_Alignment = "CCCATTGTTCTC"
```

Fig. 2. Example of Notification Rule

All rules stored in the Rule DB have to be associated with the entities provided by the cartridge. This way, any modification in these notification rules can be performed without the need for adaptation of other components of SciLightning. The coordinator configures the notification rules in SciLightning. These rules and also the specific workflow's monitoring parameters need to be informed/configured by the coordinator through a simple Web interface. Moreover, since SciLightning is based on event notification, the scientist defines the types of events that SciLightning needs to reacts. Six types of events were identified: (i) *Error in the Activity Execution* - every execution error of the monitored workflow activities are notified; (ii) *Workflow Termination* - notification of workflow execution termination; (iii) *Milestone* - a milestone can be of two types: Activity Start or Activity Termination. When each defined milestone is reached, notification information is sent to scientists specifying the milestone and time that it has been achieved; (iv) *Generated File* - one or more regular expressions (*i.e.* regex) can be defined for monitoring the generated files. For each file generated by the monitored scientific workflow that complies with at least one of the defined regex notification, information is sent; (v) *Activity with an Atypical Duration* - a query identifies activities with the execution time out of the threshold (*i.e.* atypical durations), which are considered outliers. The default range threshold execution time is 2.698 standard deviations when compared to the average [30], but the coordinator can adjust it before each execution. To calculate this value, the average and standard deviation of the execution time of each activity are estimated using the provenance database; then the distance between the average and current duration for each activity in execution is calculated; and (vi) *Configurable Event* - This event is configured by the coordinator using the OCL-like rules such as the one presented in Figure 2.

The SciLightning Monitor performs regular monitoring of the workflow executions through queries to the provenance database (using SciLightning cartridge). The monitoring frequency, *i.e.* the time between queries is configurable, with default value of 2.0 minutes. Besides this main functionality, the SciLightning Monitor allows for the registration of mobile devices and sends a notification to be handled by the SciLightning Social and SciLightning Mobile components. The SciLightning Monitor stores the identification token of each mobile device registered. Each identification token is related to just one scientist and every scientist may have multiple devices registered. When an event complies with the rules defined in the Rule DB, notification information is sent to all mobile devices registered for this scientist. Upon receiving the notification, a message is created in the status bar of the mobile device in a specific Android app (in its current version). If the scientist needs to obtain details of the notification, he/she can select the message in the status bar to open the SciLightning Mobile application screen and list all notification received. The SciLightning Mobile is an Android[1] application that receives, stores and organizes notification information sent by SciLightning Monitor. The Android platform was chosen, among other technology options for mobile devices, as it is an open source solution with free development tools. Also, it is used in a wide range of devices (mobile phones, tablets and netbooks) from various manufacturers. To register the SciLightning Mobile application, scientists need only to create an account and a password in the Rule DB.

[1] http://www.android.com/

Internally, the SciLightning Mobile registers the same account and password in the Google's Cloud to Device Message Service (C2DM)[2] to send messages to Android devices. SciLightning Mobile uses C2DM to dispatch notification to various Android-based devices that are registered in the SciLightning. The SciLightning Social is a component that acts as an interface between SciLightning and message features in social networks. SciLightning Social accesses the social network API to publish the monitoring results as messages in specific scientists' accounts. The main idea here is not to create a scientific social network but to benefit from a message service already used by scientists (since many scientists have a Twitter or Facebook account). For example, in the case of Twitter, SciLightning Social is associated with a specific account (@SciLightning) configured to send notifications to scientists about the workflows execution using direct messaging service (note that it does not send workflow results, just the notification of events). To receive notifications, scientists have only to follow the user @SciLightning. The coordinator can configure in the Rule DB that a scientist can receive both Android and Social network notifications.

Provenance Model

SciLightning is a non-intrusive approach, which has its own local provenance model. Besides monitoring and notifying scientists, SciLightning also stores data provenance related to this monitoring process (*i.e.* when it identified an event and the notification was received). This way changes performed using SciLightning do not impact the SWfMS provenance database (*e.g.* the SciCumulus provenance database). SciLightning entities are associated with the SWfMS using reference values. In this paper we coupled SciLightning to SciCumulus using the value of the field ID (which is a primary key). The model presented in Figure 3 shows the association between SciLightning and SciCumulus provenance models. The SciLightning provenance model allows for the definition and monitoring of parameters, the registration of the SciLightning Mobile application and the control of scientists and research groups while SciCumulus provenance model is responsible for storing prospective and retrospective provenance [27,31]. Since explaining SciLightning entities is the focus of this subsection, SciCumulus' entities were also presented in white and without attributes for not polluting the diagram (Figure 3).

The entity *monitorWorkflow* stores which workflows are monitored and which users or groups are notified. Notification parameters can be defined for each monitoring to configure, *e.g.*, to send a notification when the workflow generates a particular file or when the workflow reaches a certain milestone. These two monitoring parameters are respectively represented by the entities *monitorFile* and *monitorMilestone*. Scientists' information, such as login and password (that are used for registering the SciLightning Mobile application) and the Twitter account (used to send notifications) are stored in the table user. This table *user* has an associated type (*userExecutor*, *userCoordinator* and *userAnalyst*) and can be organized into research groups through the entities group and the associative entity *userGroup*, which allows

[2] C2DM is deprecated since June 26, 2012. Currently SciLightning is being adapted for using Google Cloud Messaging for Android (GCM).

for notifications for all members of the group. The registration tokens of the SciLightning Mobile application could not be stored in the entity *user*, since there may exist several devices registered to the same user. For this reason, the entity *userDevice* was created. The *monitorLast* is an auxiliary entity that stores the date of the last monitoring performed, which aims to optimize provenance queries. Finally, the *monitorError* is a domain entity that stores error codes and their respective associated messages, which are used to format the error notifications to the scientist.

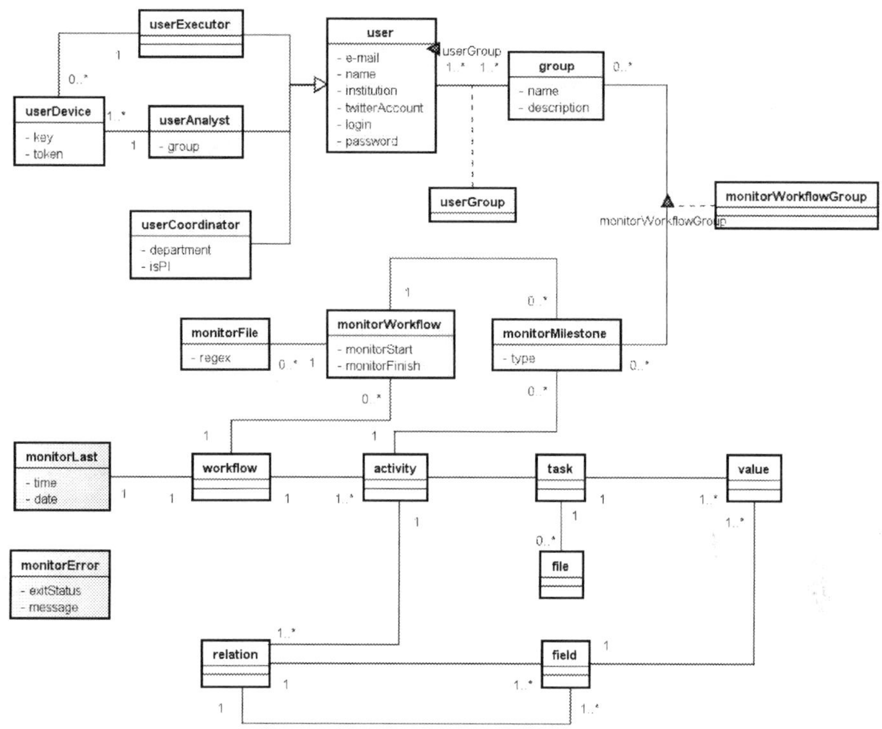

Fig. 3. The SciLightning provenance model coupled to SciCumulus

4 Experimental Evaluation

In this section, we analyze how SciLightning reacts to events when executing the SciPhy workflow with the SciCumulus workflow engine. Following we detail Sciphy workflow and presents experimental results.

SciPhy Workflow

Phylogenetic workflows aim at producing phylogenetic trees to support the evolutionary relationships between organisms that are used by biologists to infer a phylogeny (*e.g.*, ancestral relationships among species of organisms). SciPhy [14] is a phylogenetic analysis workflow which aims to processing a large collection of multi-fasta files (each containing multiple biological sequences from different organisms) to construct phylogenetic trees. It assists biologists to explore phylogeny and determine the evolutionary life of genes or genomes of these organisms. The SciPhy workflow consists of four main activities: (i) The construction of the multiple sequence alignment (MSA), (ii) the conversion of the alignment format, (iii) the election of the best evolutionary model, and (iv) the construction of the phylogenetic tree. These activities respectively execute the following bioinformatics programs (*i.e.*, applications): MSA programs (allowing the scientist to choose between MAFFT, Kalign, ClustalW, Muscle, or ProbCons), ReadSeq, ModelGenerator, and RAxML. SciPhy was designed to be executed in parallel, where each multi-fasta file is processed independently in different virtual machines and due to the performance fluctuations in the cloud environment, a typical execution of SciPhy presents from 2% to 9% activities execution failure, which requires the biologist to follow the execution to be aware of its state. This experience [13] motivated the design of SciLightning.

SciCumulus Cloud Workflow Engine

SciCumulus, proposed by Oliveira *et al.* [9], aims at scheduling, monitoring and load balancing the parallel execution of scientific workflows dispatched from a common workstation to the cloud such as Amazon AWS. SciCumulus orchestrates workflow execution in a set of virtual machines that form a virtual cluster in the cloud, providing resources dimensioning during the course of the workflow execution [26,32]. SciCumulus provides computational support for parallelism in workflows with runtime provenance, enabling queries to the performed at runtime by SciLightning Monitor. However, SciCumulus, as well as other approaches, does not provide more advanced mechanisms for monitoring and notification information that assist the scientist to be aware of the execution status without needing to be physically at a terminal. Currently, the monitoring mechanism in SciCumulus is based on SQL queries (conducted by scientist) to the provenance relational database.

Experimental Results

For executing the experiments presented in this paper we coupled SciLightning to SciCumulus engine executing in Amazon AWS environment. 16 amazon's large virtual machines (7.5 GB RAM, 850 GB storage, 2 virtual cores) were used in this experiment. Each instantiated virtual machine is based on a 64-bit Linux Cent OS 5.5. The experiment executed SciPhy consuming a dataset of 250 multi-fasta files containing protein sequences, as detailed by Ocaña *et al.* [14]. Each execution generated approximately 5,000 parallel activities. The entire execution of SciPhy was monitored using SciLightning by approximately 6.3 days.

Among all SciLightning monitoring options the following events were chosen by the scientist to monitor SciPhy: (i) Errors in activity executions; (ii) Workflow Termination; (iii) Start and Termination of ModelGenerator activity; (iv) Generation of files whose name complies the regular expression *^[A-Z]*.mafft*; (v) Activities with an atypical duration; and (vi) Generation of files whose content contains the biological sequence "ACGTAGTCC". To evaluate the results, we used metrics of Positive Predictive Value (PPV) and True Positive Rate (TPR) [33] to verify the success degree of each of the six types of events that are notified. For classification, we used the terms true positives (*tp*), true negatives (*tn*), false positives (*fp*), and false negatives (*fn*) [33]. Thus PPV and TPR can be calculated as presented by (1) and (2). Table 1 presents the achieved results.

$$PPV = \frac{tp}{tp+fp} \tag{1}$$

$$TPR = \frac{tp}{tp+fn}. \tag{2}$$

Table 1. Experimental Results

Event	*tp*	*fp*	*fn*	*tn*	*PPV*	*TPR*
i	73	2	0	0	0.97	1
ii	1	0	0	0	1	1
iii	1	0	0	0	1	1
iv	1,701	0	0	0	1	1
v	38	11	0	0	0.77	1
vi	21	0	0	0	1	1

For each of the six types of events, SciLightning presented a TPR value of 1 (*i.e.* 100%), which means that it was able to retrieve only relevant events and send notification information based on data provenance generated at runtime. However, when we analyze the PPV value we can note that for two events (i - Failed Activities and ii - Atypical Duration) the PPV value was 0.97 and 0.77 respectively. In the case of failure detection it depends on the exit status of the activity execution provided by the operational system to the workflow engine. This exit status is captured and stored in the provenance repository. However, in two executions the activity executed properly and the exit status was 1 (*i.e.* error). SciLightning provided a failure notification when there was an absence of failure. In the case of atypical duration, an activity is classified as with an atypical execution if its execution time exceeds 2.698 standard deviations (as suggested by Juristo and Moreno [34]) compared with the average execution times already stored in the provenance repository. There was not provenance data previously registered in the repository in the beginning of the execution, which makes SciLightning consider all first executions of activities as outliers. As new executions were computed, this atypical behavior ceased.

The second experiment analyzed the number of events and the number of notifications on the course of workflow execution (Figure 4) during the first 840 seconds. Figure 4 presents the number of events in a certain period of time and the number of notification information that were received at the mobile device or social network message service. We can note that after a peak of identified events (*i.e.* black line) there were also small peaks of received notifications (*i.e.* dashed line). Although SciLightning sends a notification as soon as an event is identified, there is a delay for this message to be received at the mobile device or at a social network message service. In the mobile device this is even more critical since SciLightning is susceptible to network traffic (*i.e.* internet connection since we are using a cloud service) and the delay in C2DM service. In general, SciLightning presents an acceptable communication delay for each notification presenting average delay of $\mu = 88.7$ seconds with standard deviation of $\sigma = 25.3$. A demonstration video (interface in English, but explanations in Portuguese) is available at: http://sites.google.com/site/scilightning/.

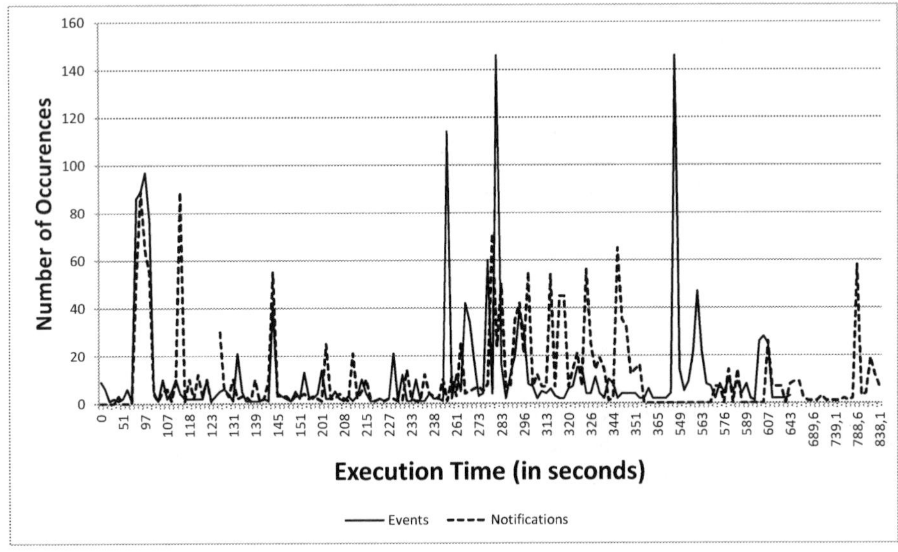

Fig. 4. Number of events and notifications during execution

5 Related Work

There are some studies in the literature that address the issue of monitoring scientific workflows executed in parallel. Balis *et al.* [35] and Gil *et al.* [10] present a set of monitoring and reporting requirements for scientific workflows. However, these requirements are generic and could be applied in several of different systems. Stampede [20,22] is one of the most prominent approaches that focus on monitoring workflows. Stampede is a monitoring framework, which captures performance metrics from workflows executed in a variety of environments. It captures information at the OS level and uses execution logs. Similarly to SciLightning, Stampede monitors the workflow at runtime; however, its monitoring only considers performance issues such as execution times and network bottlenecks. Using Stampede we were not able to build personalized events that are domain-specific to the scientific workflow. Tudruj *et al.* [36] also provide monitoring mechanisms by using user-defined control-dedicated processes called synchronizers. These synchronizers collect information about the state of the application execution, but it cannot identify events such as atypical execution times and domain-specific events.

6 Final Remarks

Large-scale scientific experiments involve several executions of compute intensive scientific workflows. These workflows need to be executed in parallel in HPC environments, such as clouds. However, the workflow execution may involve 100,000 activities executions or more, and even using HPC, it may last for days or weeks to complete. It is not acceptable that scientists monitor this execution on-line in a terminal without steering tools. Monitoring a workflow execution is essential to guarantee the reliability in the execution and check that it is going on the right track [37]. To allow for scientists to interfere in a workflow execution, they must be aware of what is happening in the execution using workflow steering mechanisms. In this paper, we present an approach for monitoring and notifying of events in parallel executions of scientific workflows, named SciLightning. Our approach uses provenance data generated at runtime and events configured by scientists. Using provenance data, SciLightning is able to identify and report events during the workflow execution such as semantic errors in activities and inconsistent file production workflow termination.

Our experimental evaluation showed that SciLightning is able to identify and report all events defined by scientists. With the exception of the notification of the atypical execution time and activity failure, all notifications presented 100% of Positive Predictive Value, which showed that SciLightning is effective in identifying and reporting events. SciLightning is designed to have a service-based architecture that is generic and can be coupled to existing SWfMS such as SciCumulus or Swift, since the provenance data is provided at runtime. Improving scientists' awareness by notifying workflow events at runtime is an essential requirement to allow interference in the workflow execution from an abort execution until runtime fine-tuning of parameters, or even the workflow adaptation during the execution [37].

Acknowledgments. This work was partially sponsored by CNPq, FAPERJ and CAPES.

References

[1] Kirsch-Pinheiro, M., de Lima, J.V., Borges, M.: A framework for awareness support in groupware systems. In: The 7th International Conference on Computer Supported Cooperative Work in Design, pp. 13–18 (2002)
[2] Deelman, E., Gannon, D., Shields, M., Taylor, I.: Workflows and e-Science: An overview of workflow system features and capabilities. Future Generation Computer Systems 25(5), 528–540 (2009)
[3] Sohlenkamp, M., Prinz, W., Fuchs, L.: PoliawaC: Design and evaluation of an awareness-enhanced groupware client. AI & SOCIETY 14(1), 31–47 (2000)
[4] Wozniak, J., Armstrong, T., Maheshwari, K., Lusk, E., Katz, D., Wilde, M., Foster, I.: Turbine: A distributed-memory dataflow engine for extreme-scale many-task applications. In: Proceeding of 1st International Workshop on Scalable Workflow Enactment Engines and Technologies (2012)

[5] Chen, W., Silva, R., Deelman, E., Sakellariou, R.: Balanced Task Clustering in Scientific Workflows. In: Proc. of 9th IEEE International Conference on e-Science (2013)
[6] Abouelhoda, M., Issa, S., Ghanem, M.: Tavaxy: Integrating Taverna and Galaxy workflows with cloud computing support. BMC Bioinformatics 13, 77 (2012)
[7] Fahringer, T., Prodan, R., Duan, R., Nerieri, F., Podlipnig, S., Qin, J., Siddiqui, M., Truong, H.-L., Villazon, A., et al.: ASKALON: a Grid application development and computing environment. In: 6th IEEE/ACM International Workshop on Grid Computing, pp. 122–131 (2005)
[8] Ogasawara, E., Dias, J., Silva, V., Chirigati, F., Oliveira, D., Porto, F., Valduriez, P., Mattoso, M.: Chiron: A Parallel Engine for Algebraic Scientific Workflows. In: Concurrency and Computation (2013)
[9] Oliveira, D., Ogasawara, E., Baião, F., Mattoso, M.: SciCumulus: A Lightweight Cloud Middleware to Explore Many Task Computing Paradigm in Scientific Workflows. In: 3rd International Conference on Cloud Computing, pp. 378–385 (2010)
[10] Gil, Y., Deelman, E., Ellisman, M., Fahringer, T., Fox, G., Gannon, D., Goble, C., Livny, M., Moreau, L., et al.: Examining the Challenges of Scientific Workflows. Computer 40(12), 24–32 (2007)
[11] Guerra, G., Rochinha, F., Elias, R., Oliveira, D., Ogasawara, E., Dias, J., Mattoso, M., Coutinho, A.L.G.A.: Uncertainty Quantification in Computational Predictive Models for Fluid Dynamics Using Workflow Management Engine. International Journal for Uncertainty Quantification 2(1), 53–71 (2012)
[12] Guerra, G., Rochinha, F., Elias, R., Coutinho, A., Braganholo, V., de Oliveira, D., Ogasawara, E., Chirigati, F., Mattoso, M.: Scientific Workflow Management System Applied to Uncertainty Quantification in Large Eddy Simulation. In: Congresso Ibero Americano de Métodos Computacionais em Engenharia, pp. 1–13 (2009)
[13] Ocaña, K.A.C.S., Oliveira, D., Dias, J., Ogasawara, E., Mattoso, M.: Optimizing Phylogenetic Analysis Using SciHmm Cloud-based Scientific Workflow. In: 2011 IEEE Seventh International Conference on e-Science (e-Science), pp. 190–197 (2011)
[14] Ocaña, K.A.C.S., de Oliveira, D., Ogasawara, E., Dávila, A.M.R., Lima, A.A.B., Mattoso, M.: SciPhy: A Cloud-Based Workflow for Phylogenetic Analysis of Drug Targets in Protozoan Genomes. In: Norberto de Souza, O., Telles, G.P., Palakal, M. (eds.) BSB 2011. LNCS, vol. 6832, pp. 66–70. Springer, Heidelberg (2011)
[15] Dudley, J.T., Pouliot, Y., Chen, R., Morgan, A.A., Butte, A.J.: Translational bioinformatics in the cloud: an affordable alternative. Genome Medicine 2(8), 51 (2010)
[16] Addis, M., Ferris, J., Greenwood, M., Li, P., Marvin, D., Oinn, T., Wipat, A.: Experiences with e-Science workflow specification and enactment in bioinformatics. In: Proceedings of UK e-Science All Hands Meeting, pp. 459–467 (2003)
[17] Deelman, E., Mehta, G., Singh, G., Su, M.-H., Vahi, K.: Pegasus: Mapping Large-Scale Workflows to Distributed Resources. In: Workflows for e-Science, pp. 376–394. Springer, Heidelberg (2007)
[18] Taylor, I., Shields, M., Wang, I., Harrison, A.: The Triana Workflow Environment: Architecture and Applications. In: Workflows for e-Science, pp. 320–339. Springer (2007)
[19] Zhao, Y., Hategan, M., Clifford, B., Foster, I., von Laszewski, G., Nefedova, V., Raicu, I., Stef-Praun, T., Wilde, M.: Swift: Fast, Reliable, Loosely Coupled Parallel Computation. In: 3rd IEEE World Congress on Services, p. 206, 199 (2007)
[20] Gunter, D., Deelman, E., Samak, T., Brooks, C.H., Goode, M., Juve, G., Mehta, G., Moraes, P., Silva, F., et al.: Online workflow management and performance analysis with Stampede. In: 2011 7th International Conference on Network and Service Management (CNSM), pp. 1–10 (2011)

[21] Missier, P., Embury, S.M., Greenwood, M., Preece, A., Jin, B.: Managing information quality in e-science: the qurator workbench. In: Proceedings of the 2007 ACM SIGMOD international conference on Management of Data, pp. 1150–1152 (2007)
[22] Vahi, K., Harvey, I., Samak, T., Gunter, D., Evans, K., Rogers, D., Taylor, I., Goode, M., Silva, F., et al.: A General Approach to Real-Time Workflow Monitoring. In: 2012 SC Companion High Performance Computing, Networking, Storage and Analysis (SCC), pp. 108–118 (2012)
[23] Tierney, B., Johnston, W., Crowley, B., Hoo, G., Brooks, C., Gunter, D.: The NetLogger Methodology for High Performance Distributed Systems Performance Analysis. In: Proceedings of the 7th IEEE International Symposium on High Performance Distributed Computing, p. 260 (1998)
[24] Elias, R.N., Paraizo, P.L.B., Coutinho, A.L.G.A.: Stabilized edge-based finite element computation of gravity currents in lock-exchange configurations. International Journal for Numerical Methods in Fluids 57, 1137–1152 (2008)
[25] Ocaña, K.A.C.S., de Oliveira, D., Horta, F., Dias, J., Ogasawara, E., Mattoso, M.: Exploring molecular evolution reconstruction using a parallel cloud based scientific workflow. In: de Souto, M.C.P., Kann, M.G. (eds.) BSB 2012. LNCS, vol. 7409, pp. 179–191. Springer, Heidelberg (2012)
[26] Oliveira, D., Ocaña, K.A.C.S., Ogasawara, E., Dias, J., Gonçalves, J., Baião, F., Mattoso, M.: Performance evaluation of parallel strategies in public clouds: A study with phylogenomic workflows. Future Generation Computer Systems 29(7), 1816–1825 (2013)
[27] Freire, J., Koop, D., Santos, E., Silva, C.T.: Provenance for Computational Tasks: A Survey. Computing in Science and Engineering 10(3), 11–21 (2008)
[28] Birsan, D.: On plug-ins and extensible architectures. Queue 3(2), 40–46 (2005)
[29] Warmer, J.B., Kleppe, A.G.: The object constraint language: getting your models ready for MDA. Addison-Wesley, Boston (2003)
[30] Freedman, D., Pisani, R., Purves, R.: Statistics, 4th edn. W. W. Norton (2007)
[31] Davidson, S.B., Freire, J.: Provenance and scientific workflows: challenges and opportunities. In: ACM SIGMOD International Conference on Management of Data, pp. 1345–1350 (2008)
[32] Oliveira, D., Viana, V., Ogasawara, E., Ocana, K., Mattoso, M.: Dimensioning the virtual cluster for parallel scientific workflows in clouds. In: Proceedings of the 4th ACM Workshop on Scientific Cloud Computing, pp. 5–12 (2013)
[33] Baeza-Yates, R., Ribeiro-Neto, B.: Modern Information Retrieval: The Concepts and Technology behind Search, 2nd edn. Addison-Wesley Professional (2011)
[34] Juristo, N., Moreno, A.M.: Basics of Software Engineering Experimentation, 1st edn. Springer Publishing Company, Incorporated (2010)
[35] Balis, B., Bubak, M., Łabno, B.: Monitoring of Grid scientific workflows. Sci. Program. 16(2-3), 205–216 (2008)
[36] Tudruj, M., Kopanski, D., Borkowski, J.: Dynamic Workflow Control with Global States Monitoring, p. 44 (2007)
[37] Dias, J., Ogasawara, E., Oliveira, D., Porto, F., Coutinho, A., Mattoso, M.: Supporting Dynamic Parameter Sweep in Adaptive and User-Steered Workflow. In: 6th Workshop on Workflows in Support of Large-Scale Science, pp. 31–36 (2011)

Energy Savings on a Cloud-Based Opportunistic Infrastructure

Johnatan E. Pecero[1], Cesar O. Diaz[1], Harold Castro[2], Mario Villamizar[2], Germán Sotelo[2], and Pascal Bouvry[1]

[1] University of Luxembourg, L-1359 Luxembourg-Kirchberg, Luxembourg
{firstname.lastname}@uni.lu,
[2] Universidad de los Andes, Bogotá D.C., Colombia
{hcastro,mj.villamizar24,ga.sotelo69}@uniandes.edu.co

Abstract. In this paper, we address energy savings on a Cloud-based opportunistic infrastructure. The infrastructure implements opportunistic design concepts to provide basic services, such as virtual CPUs, RAM and Disk while profiting from unused capabilities of desktop computer laboratories in a non-intrusive way.

We consider the problem of virtual machines consolidation on the opportunistic cloud computing resources. We investigate four workload packing algorithms that place a set of virtual machines on the least number of physical machines to increase resource utilization and to transition parts of the unused resources into a lower power states or switching off. We empirically evaluate these heuristics on real workload traces collected from our experimental opportunistic cloud, called UnaCloud. The final aim is to implement the best strategy on UnaCoud. The results show that a consolidation algorithm implementing a policy taking into account features and constraints of the opportunistic cloud saves energy more than 40% than related consolidation heuristics, over the percentage earned by the opportunistic environment.

Keywords: cloud computing, green computing, performance of system.

1 Introduction

In this paper, we consider a Cloud-based opportunistic infrastructure called UnaCloud [1]. UnaCloud implements an Infrastructure as a Service cloud model oriented to the provision of computing resources for the development of scientific projects and to support related activities (i.e., to execute applications such as BLAST, Hmmer or Gromacs). It uses a commodity underlying infrastructure implementing opportunistic design concepts to provide computational resources such as CPU, RAM and Disk, while profiting from the unused capabilities of desktop computer laboratories in a non-intrusive manner offering some of the most important advantages of cloud computing, as for example up-front investment elimination and the appearance of infinite resources available on demand. UnaCloud is composed of (almost) homogeneous computing resources of computer laboratories. This may not be the case for other opportunistic platforms

A.R. Lomuscio et al. (Eds.): ICSOC 2013 Workshops, LNCS 8377, pp. 366–378, 2014.
© Springer International Publishing Switzerland 2014

or community-based Cloud, in which private computer owners donate a portion of their idle computing resources to be used by anyone inside a community for supporting a specific project.

We aim to investigate energy savings on UnaCloud that can serve as a basis for related opportunistic cloud models. Although UnaCloud offers the performance capability of deploying Virtual Machines (VMs) in a sustainable way by using idle resources opportunistically, it lacks of energy saving consideration during the placement of the VMs. UnaCloud implements a random placement of VMs to the idle resources of the Physical Machines (PMs).

Techniques such as Dynamic Voltage and Frequency Scaling and Dynamic Power Management have been extensively studied and deployed to make the Cloud infrastructure components power efficient [2,3]. The consolidation of VMs to reduce the number of underutilized computing resources, and shutting down the unused resources or to transition parts into a lower power state is another efficient energy saving strategy. Therefore, in this paper we investigate four consolidation algorithms to minimize the Energy Consumption Rate (ECR) of UnaCloud. Three of the heuristics rely on classical bin-packing algorithms, and one is an ad hoc (opportunistic) consolidation algorithm proposed in [4], that places the VMs first on PMs already in use by a physical user. We empirically evaluate these heuristics on real workload traces. We use cloud workloads based on real production traces collected from the archives of UnaCloud. The traces have been collected during one year. Real UnaCloud scenarios provide a realistic VMs stream for performance evaluation based on simulations of VMs consolidation algorithms. We present results obtained by simulations, while the ultimate goal is to implement the best strategy on UnaCloud. The main reason is that UnaCloud is a production cloud infrastructure already in use making it difficult the implementation for testing the algorithms. However, based on the generated results a work in progress is considering the implementation on UnaCloud.

Although Unacloud may aggregate desktops from independent individuals it is meant to work with machines within a computer laboratory, each laboratory is managed by a single administrator. It gives UnaCloud several advantages in terms of homogeneity, control and risk of failures. In our tests, a computer laboratory with 35 machines presents a maximum of two failures a day. Besides, UnaCloud has been used to run Bag of Tasks applications, with many short-lived jobs, making unnecessary to deal with checkpoints and fault tolerance issues [5].

This paper is organized as follows: Section 2 presents related work. Section 3 describes the energy consumption behavior on an opportunistic cloud infrastructure, and details the energy model. The evaluated consolidation algorithms are described in Section 4. Section 5 presents the simulation results. Section 6 concludes the paper.

2 Related Work

The problem of VM allocation can be divided in two: the first part is admission of new requests for VM provisioning and placing the VMs on hosts, whereas the second part is optimization of current allocation of VMs. In this work we focus on the first part of the VM allocation problem. This problem can be modeled as a bin packing problem with variable bin sizes.

The problem in its single-objective variant is an NP-hard problem, and thus is expensive to compute with increasing numbers of PMs and VMs. Different heuristics and linear programming based solutions are used for getting a near optimal solution. Several proposed power-aware packing algorithms use a variant of First Fit Decreasing (FFD) heuristic to reduce resource fragmentation. Static consolidation considers that resource utilization does not change during execution and the number of reconfigurations depends solely of creation and deletion of VMs, one example is Entropy [6]. Dynamic VM management assumes that resource needs change over time, and thus VMs can be moved during their execution in order to improve the optimality placement, one framework that considers dynamic management of VMs is Snooze [7].

Verma et al. [8] modeled the VM workload placement as an instance of the one dimensional bin-packing problem and extended FFD to perform the placement. Li et al. [9] proposed the EnaCloud framework and a modified version of the Best-Fit algorithm is implemented. Buyya et al. [10] presented simulation-driven results for a workload consolidation algorithm based on a modified version of the Best Fit Decreasing algorithm. The algorithm sorts all the VMs in decreasing order of current utilization and allocate each VM to a host that provides the least increase of power consumption due to this allocation. This allows leveraging heterogeneity of the nodes by choosing the most power-efficient ones. Feller et al. [11] dealt with the workload consolidation problem and model it as an instance of the multi-dimensional bin-packing problem. The authors proposed a nature-inspired workload consolidation algorithm based on the Ant Colony Optimization framework. The proposed algorithm outperforms FFD, however, at greater complexity. Beloglazow and Buyya [12] proposed a resource management policy for virtualized cloud data centers. The objective is to consolidate VMs leveraging live migration and switch off idle nodes to minimize power consumption, while providing required Quality of Service.

Most of the related consolidation algorithms consider a pool of dedicated computing resources, however the work in this paper differs from related state of the art since we deal with an opportunistic cloud-based infrastructure.

3 Energy in an Opportunistic Cloud Environment

In this section we present the energy model. First, we present the energy function of a desktop machine, then the energy model is described.

3.1 Parameter Tunning

In opportunistic cloud solutions there are some desktops computers which are donned by users of the same or different institutions to aggregate processing capabilities of the system. Those desktop computers can be modeled as a Set of

Physical Machines (SPMs) each one with some hardware specifications including CPU cores, RAM memory, hard disk and networking. Researchers require the execution of a Set of Virtual Machines (SVMs) each one requiring a minimum hardware specification. Due to opportunistic environment, we assume that there are two states (idle and busy) of a PM to be selected to deploy a VM, and according to its state the ECR and the estimated execution time of a VM executing a CPU-intensive task can change. To analyze the relation between the CPU usage and the ECR consumed by a PM, experimental tests of a previous and recent work [5] show that the CPU usage and ECR are not directly proportional. Figure 1 shows the function $f(x)$ (based on a regression calculated on experimental tests) that allows to estimate the ECR of a PM according to its CPU usage. Here we present CPU usage as the percentage provided by the operating system which is in aggregation of the utilization across all cores of the CPU.

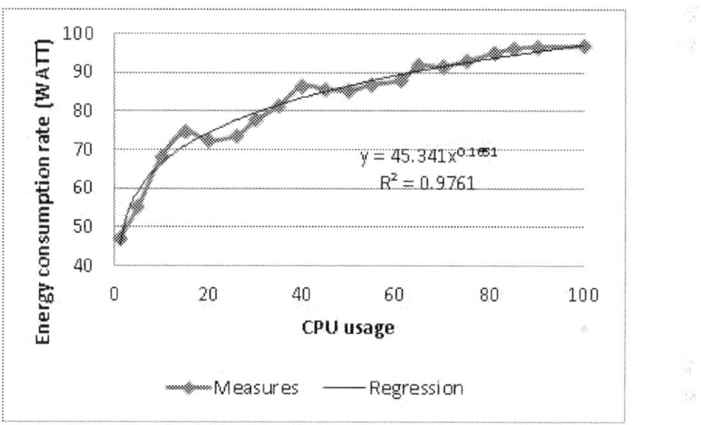

Fig. 1. Desktop Computer energy consumption. $f(x) = y(x) = 45.341x^{0.1651}$

Table 1 provides the ECRs required to execute a VM according to the state of the PM. We assume that a VM will execute a CPU-intensive task during a τ time. While the VM is in execution the ECR of the PM will increase to $f(x)$, where $f(x)$ is a real function that returns the ECR of a PM given its CPU usage percentage. The idle state represents a turned on PM without a user (a student, administrative, etc.) using it while the VM is in execution. The busy state represents a turned on PM with a user using it and a VM in execution.

When the physical machine is in idle state, the ECR consumed by the VMs is equal to the difference between $f(x)$ and $f(0)$, where $f(0)$ is the ECR consumed by the PM while is in idle state and $f(x)$ is the ECR when a virtual machine is in execution (by number of cores required from VMs determining the CPU usage). In the busy state, the ECR consumed by the VMs is equal to the difference among $f(x) + ECR_{MON}$, and ECR_{user}, where ECR_{MON} is the ECR of the monitor when there is a user using the PM, and ECR_{user} is the mean ECR of a physical machine when there is a user using it and there is not a VM in execution. In busy state the execution time of the VM takes more time because there is an user consuming computational resources (and competing by the resources required by the VM), therefore the execution time of the VM can be calculated as $100/L_{free} \times \tau$, where L_{free} is the percentage of CPU dedicated to the virtual machine and τ is the estimated running time (provided on demand when a VM is requested) of the VM. We assume that the execution time of an opportunistic CPU intensive task is linearly proportional to the amount of processor used in the PM that is running it. To estimate the percentage of CPU used by users of the PMs, during daylight working hours we executed different tests that show that the CPU utilization does not exceed 10% on average [13]. That is $L_{free} = 90\%$.

To estimate the ECR on different states, the results of Table 1 can be completed with the function $f(x)$ depicted in Figure 1. Additional parameters such as ECR_{MON} and ECR_{USER} were calculated using specific tests. In tests using a commodity desktop computer, the ECR_{MON} was equal to 20W and the ECR_{USER} was equal to 87W [13].

Table 1. ECR used by a VM executing a CPU-intensive task

Computer state	**Execution with VM**	**ECR for an intensive CPU Task (ECR with VM - without VM)**
1 (idle)	τ	$f(x) - f(0)$
2 (busy)	$\frac{100}{L_{free}} \times \tau$	$f(x) + ECR_{MON} - ECR_{user}$

τ is the sum of τ_{user} and τ_{free} if τ_{user} is less than τ. τ_{user} is given by the time of the PM with an user when it is executing VMs and τ_{free} is the rest of the time to finish the VM, Eq 1 shows the relation of the execution time of the VM when there is an user in the PM.

$$\begin{aligned} \tau &= \frac{100}{L_{free}} \tau_{user} + \tau_{free} = \frac{10}{9} \tau_{user} + \tau_{free} \\ 1.1 \times \tau_{user} + \tau - \tau_{user} &= 0.1 \times \tau_{user} + \tau \end{aligned} \tag{1}$$

Table 2 shows that from the energy consumption point of view, the best desktop PMs to deploy a VM are those in a busy state.

Table 2. Experimental results of energy consumption

Computer state	**Execution time**	**Mean ECR (W)**
1 (idle)	τ	$f(x) - 47$
2 (busy)	$0.1 \times \tau_{user} + \tau$	$f(x) + 20 - 87$

3.2 Energy Model

In this section we show a mathematical description to calculate the ECR required for executing a SVM on an opportunistic cloud infrastructure.

Once the consolidation process has finished, the program calculates the power consumption. $P_i^{core}(t)$ is the power of a core i at time t that belongs to a PM. Eq 2 shows how is defined this power.

$$P_i^{core}(t) = s_i(t) \cdot \left((1 - y_i(t))\, P_i^{idleC} + y_i(t) P_i^{workC} \right) \tag{2}$$

where P_i^{idleC} and P_i^{workC} are power consumed in idle and work state of the core. $s_i(t)$ denotes if the core is on or not at time t as $s_i(t) = 1$ and $s_i(t) = 0$ respectively. $y_i(t)$ denotes if the core is working or not at time t. When a core is on, without working, consumes P_i^{idleC} but if the core is on and working, it consume P_i^{workC}. The model assumes that power consumption of all system components is essentially constant regardless of the machine activity.

The power consumption of a PM is denoted by $P_j^{mach}(t)$ as Eq. 3 shows.

$$P_j^{mach}(t) = z_j(t) \cdot \left((1 - w_j(t))\, P_j^{idleM} + w_j(t) P_j^{workM}(t) \right) \tag{3}$$

where P_j^{idleM} and P_j^{workM} are power consumed in idle and busy states of the PM. $z_j(t)$ denotes different states of the PM as Eq. 4 shows. The value of $z_j(t) = 1.1$ refers to the extra power consumption because of competing by the resources required as aforementioned. $w_i(t)$ denotes if the core is working or not at time t. Hence, power consumed by machine have direct relation to power consumed by core.

$$z_j(t) = \begin{cases} 1 & if\ mach\ is\ on \\ 1.1 & if\ mach\ is\ on\ and\ user \\ 0 & otherwise \end{cases} \tag{4}$$

We assume that P_j^{idleM} is the sum of P_i^{idleC} of all cores belong to machine j and is the same when machine is in idle state. P_j^{workM} is calculated from the equation resulted from Figure 1 as Eq. 5 shows.

$$P_j^{workM}(t) = V_{j_{ini}} x_j(t)^{\left(\log_{10} \frac{V_{j_{max}}}{V_{j_{ini}}}\right)/2} \tag{5}$$

where $x_j(t)$ is taken from Figure 1 as Eq. 6 shows. We have specific homogeneous machines with a behavior as it shows in Figure 1 and related with Eq.5, we can deduce $V_{j_{ini}} = 45.341$ and if $V_{j_{max}} = 97$ we have $P_j^{workM}(t) = 45.341 x_j(t)^{0.1651}$.

$$x_j(t) = \frac{T\_u\_c}{T\_c} \times 100 \tag{6}$$

Where T_u_c refers to Total used cores and T_c refers to Total cores. As we assumed for P_j^{idleM}, we assume the power when a PM j is at full charge, it is when all the cores are working, therefore we can deduce:

$$\begin{gathered} P_j^{idleM} = \sum_i^{T\_c} P_i^{idleC} \\ P_j^{mach}(t_{max}) = P_j^{workM}(t_{max}) = P_i^{workC} \times T\_c \\ P_j^{workM}(t) = P_i^{core} \cdot T\_u\_c \end{gathered} \tag{7}$$

Now, from equations 5 and 7 we can conclude:

$$P_j^{idleM} = V_{j_{ini}} \quad P_{j_{max}}^{mach} = V_{j_{max}} \tag{8}$$

To calculate the energy consumed by a PM, once the placement process has finished, we sort all the VMs assigned to each machine by execution time (et) in descending order:

$$\tau_1 > \tau_2 \tag{9}$$

where τ_1 denotes the biggest execution time of VM in the machine assigned and τ_2 the next execution time in descending order. Using equation 10 we can calculate the energy consumed by a PM

$$E_j = \sum_{k=1}^{T\_v-1} P_j^{mach}(\tau_k) \cdot (\tau_k - \tau_{k+1}) + P_j^{mach}(\tau_{T\_v}) \cdot (\tau_{T\_v}) \tag{10}$$

where T_v refers to total of VMs assigned to a PM j. The total energy consumed by the system is denoted as E_{total} (see Eq. 11)

$$E_{total} = \sum_{j}^{T\_m} E_j \tag{11}$$

where T_m refers to the total PMs in the system.

4 Evaluated Consolidation Strategies for UnaCloud

UnaCloud usually executes VMs to run CPU-intensive applications. Therefore, we consider that the VMs consolidation problem is constrained by a single resource, in this case all the VMs are CPU bound, then the problem corresponds to the one dimensional bin packing problem with different bin capacity (i.e., different number of cores per PM).

The most popular and used heuristics to deal with the one dimensional bin packing problem are First-Fit, First-Fit Decreasing and Best-Fit algorithms [14]. These heuristics use a greedy weight function applied to the items such that every item is assigned a single value. In case of First-Fit Decreasing and Best-Fit algorithms the items are sorted and then placed sequentially into a decreasing order. The heuristics, specially First-Fit Decreasing, are best known to be very effective both in theory with performance guarantees and in practice. Several systems have implemented variants of the three heuristics. Therefore, we consider them to be evaluated in the context of UnaCloud.

To minimize the ECR rate used by the opportunistic cloud, the consolidation strategies should try to place the VMs first on a PM in a busy state (i.e., with a VM already assigned on it or with a physical user) that satisfies the VM requirements, instead of placing the VM on a PM in a different state. In [4] we proposed a packing algorithm that prioritizes the deployment of VMs on PMs already in use. The algorithm, called Sorting in [4], is a variant of First-Fit Decreasing. The algorithm starts by sorting the set of VMs and PMs. VMs are sorted in decreasing order of required cores and estimated running time. PMs are sorted by three attributes: (1) PMs that already have virtual machines running on them, (2) PMs in busy state (a user is using them), and (3) PMs with more available CPU cores. Then, VMs are placed on the PMs in a First-Fit policy. After a VM is placed on a PM the ordered list of the PMs is sorted again. The attributes used to sort PMs allow that PMs with a VM already assigned or in a busy state have priority over the others, hence reducing the ECR rate as described in Section 3.

Next section presents the evaluation comparison of First-Fit, First-Fit Decreasing, Best-Fit, and Sorting using UnaCloud scenarios.

5 Experimental Results

This section presents the empirical evaluation of the investigated consolidation algorithms. The aim is to gain a first insight into the performance of the algorithms on different real scenarios before implementing the best one on UnaCloud.

UnaCloud currently has access to three computer labs with 109 desktop computers, whose aggregated capabilities may deliver up to 592 processing cores (70 PMs have four cores each and 39 PMs with eight cores), 572 GB of RAM, 8 TB of storage and 1TB of shared storage in a Network Attached Storage (NAS).

5.1 Workload

In order to provide performance comparison, we use workloads based on real VMs production traces. Real UnaCloud scenarios provide a realistic VMs stream for performance evaluation based on simulations of VMs allocation algorithms. In this paper, traces from the archives of UnaCloud are used. The traces have been collected during one year. The total number of VMs in the workload requested during the year is up to 9800 each one requiring either 1, 2, 3, 4, 6, or 8 cores, 1, 2, 3, 4, 6, or 8 GB of RAM, and 20 GB of storage.

In order to estimate the energy consumed by a given placement, we use the information provided in Section 3. The VMs are also characterized by different time periods from 45 minutes up to 43200 minutes ($\approx$ 720 h), the time requested by users on demand to execute VMs. The ECR rate values represent the power drawn by the PMs at the utilization given by the placement over the execution time. We assume that when a PM does not have a VM assigned to it and a user is not working on it the PM can be turned off. Hence, no energy is consumed by the PM and is not included in the computation of the total ECR rate.

5.2 Experimental Scenarios

Different scenarios have been generated as follows. We consider that a given percentage of PMs has a user working on it. To simulate the scenarios and generate the instances used by the consolidation algorithms, we vary the percentage from 0% up to 50% with the increment 10%. We randomly assign a user to a PM and we generate 30 instances for each scenario. The number of VMs to be placed on the PMs varies from 40 up to 130 with the increment 10. We generate 30 instances at random for each size from the real traces and we used them as workloads for all the simulations discussed below. The maximum number of cores on each size is up to the total available physical cores in order to support the worst packing scenario, in which all the PMs run at least one VM. We assume that a physical user utilizes a PM during 60 minutes up to 240 minutes. We randomly assign the time of the physical user working on the PM (uniformly in the interval [60, 240]).

5.3 Algorithms Comparison

We measured the amount of provisioned PMs, and the ECR rate of the placement for every algorithm. We report average results. We only report results for scenarios assuming 0% and 50% of PMs with a user. The objective is to explore the behavior of the investigated heuristics and the gain of the opportunistic environment.

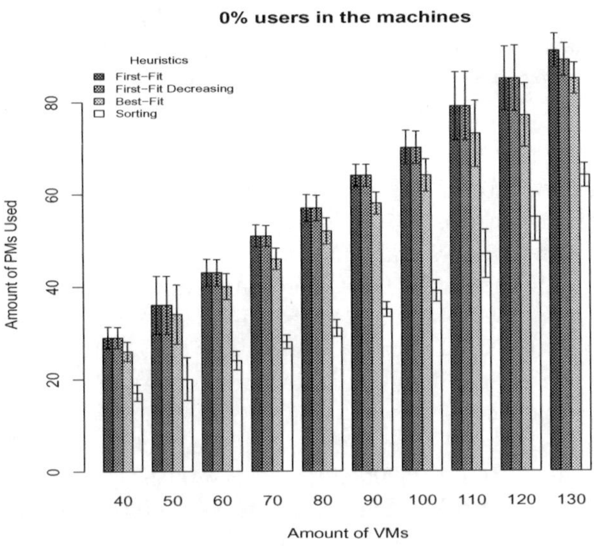

Fig. 2. Number of PMs to place the VMs when there are no users in PMs

Figures 2 and 3 show the number of PMs used by each of the heuristics to place all the VMs when there are no physical users using the PMs and when 50% of the machines already have a physical user, respectively. Figures 4 and 5 present the ECR rate for the considered scenarios without users and with 50% of machines with a user, respectively.

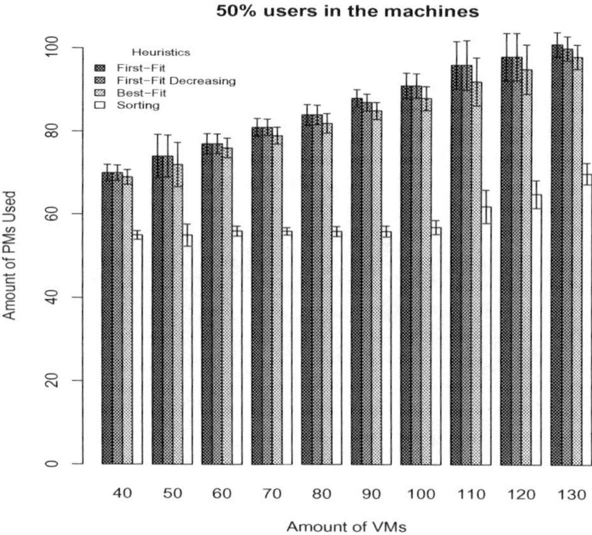

Fig. 3. Number of PMs to place the VMs when 50% of PMs have a physical user

As we can see the Sorting heuristic utilizes important lower amount of PMs yielding to superior average PM optimization and significant ECR lower consumption. The heuristic optimizes up to 41% more than First-Fit and First-Fit decreasing, and 36% more than Best-Fit when there are no physical users in the PMs. When 50% of the PMs are in an busy state Sorting requires 30% on average less PMs than the related heuristics. The main reason that Sorting needs more PMs in the second scenario is that it places the VMs to a maximum number of PMs in a busy state.

We can observe that Sorting gains significant energy saving (i.e. low ECR) regarding the related heuristics. The average gain of ECR by Sorting when no users are assigned to PMs is up to 38% regarding First-Fit, up to 34% concerning First-Fit Decreasing, and up to 35% with respect to Best-Fit. For the second scenario whit 50% of busy PMs all the investigated heuristics gain more energy than in the first scenario with all the PMs in an idle state. These results highlight the benefits and advantages of an opportunistic cloud, in this case UnaCloud, as a sustainable infrastructure.

The average ECR gain of Sorting is more important regarding related heuristics than in the first scenario. Sorting optimizes 48% more energy than First-Fit, it can gain up to 45% regarding First-Fit Decreasing, and up to 46% more than Best-Fit. The results highlight that prioritizing busy PMs to place the VMS is a good saving energy option to consolidate VMs.

It can be observed that First-Fit utilizes more PMs (approx. 4%) in the opportunistic environment to consolidate the VMs than Best-Fit in almost all the scenarios, however the ECR rate is lower than Best-Fit. We consider that it is

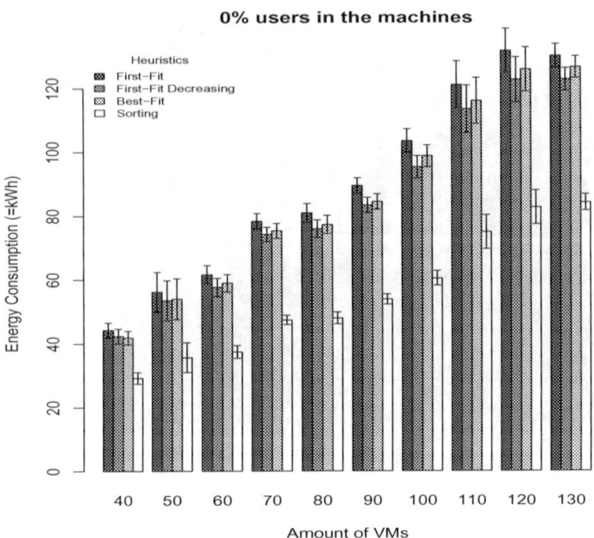

Fig. 4. Total ECR consumed when there are no users in PMs

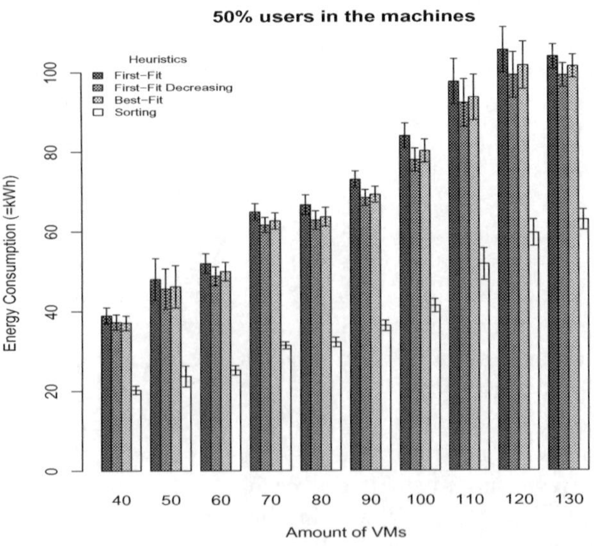

Fig. 5. Total ECR consumed when 50% of PMs have a physical user

due to the fact that First-Fit uses more PMs in an idle state than Best-Fit, nevertheless for a shorter time of period than Best-Fit, hence the ECR rate is less than Best-Fit.

6 Conclusions and Future Work

In this paper, we addressed energy savings on an opportunistic infrastructure, specially for UnaCloud. We investigated and empirically evaluated four state of the art consolidation algorithms. We focused on the optimization of the ECR rate. We have simulated different scenarios using real workload traces. The results showed that the opportunistic infrastructure seems to be a good option as a sustainable computing on demand infrastructure. The results also highlight that a consolidation algorithm implementing a policy that prioritizes the placement of VMs onto busy PMs can reduce the energy-consumption more than 40% against related heuristics, over the percentage earned by the opportunistic environment.

A work in progress is the implementation of Sorting on UnaCloud. However, we are adapting the heuristic by considering free-knowledge information (i.e., without assuming the estimated running time of VMs), and the dynamic feature of the infrastructure. We also plan to consider more than one resource during the placement of VMs, the problem can be modeled as a multi-dimensional packing problem.

Acknowledgment. This work was completed with the support of the FNR INTER/CNRS/11/03 Green@Cloud Project.

References

1. Rosales, E., Castro, H., Villamizar, M.: Unacloud: Opportunistic cloud computing infrastructure as a service. In: Cloud Computing 2011, pp. 187–194. IARIA (2011)
2. Wang, L., Khan, S.U., Chen, D., Koodziej, J., Ranjan, R., Zhong Xu, C., Zomaya, A.: Energy-aware parallel task scheduling in a cluster. Future Generation Computer Systems 29(7), 1661–1670 (2013)
3. Bilal, K., Khan, S., Madani, S., Hayat, K., Khan, M., Min-Allah, N., Kolodziej, J., Wang, L., Zeadally, S., Chen, D.: A survey on green communications using adaptive link rate. Cluster Computing 16(3), 575–589 (2013)
4. Diaz, C., Castro, H., Villamizar, M., Pecero, J., Bouvry, P.: Energy-aware vm allocation on an opportunistic cloud infrastructure. In: Proceedings of the 2013 13th IEEE/ACM Int. Symposium CCGRID, pp. 663–670. IEEE Computer Society (2013)
5. Castro, H., Villamizar, M., Sotelo, G., Diaz, C., Pecero, J.E., Bouvry, P.: Green flexible opportunistic computing with task consolidation and virtualization. Cluster Computing, 1–13 (2012)
6. Hermenier, F., Lorca, X., Menaud, J.M., Muller, G., Lawall, J.: Entropy: a consolidation manager for clusters. In: Proceedings of the 2009 ACM SIGPLAN/SIGOPS International Conference on Virtual Execution Environments, VEE 2009, pp. 41–50. ACM, New York (2009)

7. Feller, E., Rilling, L., Morin, C.: Snooze: A scalable and autonomic virtual machine management framework for private clouds. In: Proceedings of the 2012 12th IEEE/ACM Int. Symposium CCGRID, pp. 482–489. IEEE Computer Society, Washington, DC (2012)
8. Verma, A., Ahuja, P., Neogi, A.: pMapper: Power and migration cost aware application placement in virtualized systems. In: Issarny, V., Schantz, R. (eds.) Middleware 2008. LNCS, vol. 5346, pp. 243–264. Springer, Heidelberg (2008)
9. Li, B., Li, J., Huai, J., Wo, T., Li, Q., Zhong, L.: Enacloud: An energy-saving application live placement approach for cloud computing environments. In: IEEE CLOUD, pp. 17–24. IEEE (2009)
10. Buyya, R., Beloglazov, A., Abawajy, J.H.: Energy-efficient management of data center resources for cloud computing: A vision, architectural elements, and open challenges. In: Arabnia, H.R., Chiu, S.C., Gravvanis, G.A., Ito, M., Joe, K., Nishikawa, H., Solo, A.M.G. (eds.) PDPTA, pp. 6–20. CSREA Press (2010)
11. Feller, E., Rilling, L., Morin, C.: Energy-aware ant colony based workload placement in clouds. In: Proceedings of the 2011 IEEE/ACM 12th Int. GRID, pp. 26–33. IEEE Computer Society, Washington, DC (2011)
12. Beloglazov, A., Buyya, R.: Energy efficient allocation of virtual machines in cloud data centers. In: Proceedings of the 2010 10th IEEE/ACM Int. Conference CCGRID, pp. 577–578 (2010)
13. Castro, H., Villamizar, M., Sotelo, G., Diaz, C.O., Pecero, J.E., Bouvry, P., Khan, S.U.: Gfog: Green and flexible opportunistic grids. In: Khan, S.U., Wang, L., Zomaya, A.Y. (eds.) Scalable Computing and Communications, Theory and Practice. Wiley&Sons (forthcomming)
14. Panigrahy, R., Talwar, K., Uyeda, L., Wieder, U.: Heuristics for vector bin packing (2011), http://research.microsoft.com/pubs/147927/VBPackingESA11.pdf (accessed July 20, 2013)

Introduction to the Proceedings of the Workshop on Pervasive Analytical Service Clouds for the Enterprise and Beyond (PASCEB) 2013

A. Norta[1], Weishan Zhang[2], C.M. Chituc[3], and R. Vaculin[4]

[1] Department of Informatics, Tallinn University of Technology, 12618 Tallinn, Estonia
alex.norta@gmail.com
[2] Department of Software Engineering, China University of Petroleum, No. 66 Changjiang West Road, Qingdao, China
zhangws@upc.edu.cn
[3] TU-Eindhoven, PAV D.07, P.O. Box 513, 5600 MB Eindhoven, The Netherlands
c.m.chituc@tue.nl
[4] Thomas J. Watson Research Center, Yorktown Heights, NY USA
vaculinatus.ibm.com

1 Introduction

The First Workshop on Pervasive Analytical Service Clouds for the Enterprise and Beyond (PASCEB) 2013 was held in conjunction with the ICSOC'13 conference in Berlin, Germany. The workshop focused on an emerging area addressing the gap of how to design socio-technical, dependable and secure cloud-service ecosystems for commercial collaboration use. To establish separation of concerns, the addressed gap has different aspects in terms of concepts, frameworks, technologies that facilitate the management and coordination of large Internet of Things (IoT), -Services (IoS) and -People (IoP) that comprise a service-ecosystem for collaborating towards a common goal for which we envision a lifecycle. Integral is the analysis of large volumes of heterogeneous, high-speed data sets, i.e., big data. With the latter, the quality of socio-technical collaboration can evolve in a better way.

The PASCEB 2013 keynote of Prof. Schahram Dustar from the Distributed Systems Group of TU-Vienna focused on elasticity in cloud-ecosystems from a socio-technical perspective that examined how to integrate people, software services, and things into one composite system, which can be modelled, programmed, and deployed on a large scale in an elastic way. Furthermore, the thirteen full PASCEB-workshop papers were selected after a thorough peer-review by the Workshop Program Committee Members and fell into four categories of related topics. Following is a brief overview of the contributions.

The first paper category takes a collaboration perspective of socio-technical service clouds and comprises three papers. The paper 'Enabling Semantic Complex Event Processing in the Domain of Logistics' by authors T. Metzke, A. Rogge-Solti, A. Baumgrass, J. Mendling, and M. Weske shows the benefits of semantic complex event processing (SCEP) along a specific use case of tracking and tracing goods and processing related events. The second paper titled 'Towards Self-Adaptation Planning for Complex

A.R. Lomuscio et al. (Eds.): ICSOC 2013 Workshops, LNCS 8377, pp. 379–380, 2014.
© Springer International Publishing Switzerland 2014

Service-based Systems' by A. Ismail and V. Cardellini proposes a multi-layer adaptation planning with local- and global adaptation managers. Finally, the paper 'Towards an Integration Platform for Bioinformatics Services' by authors G. Llambias, L. Gonzalez, and R. Ruggia proposes enterprise middleware to integrate Bioinformatics services based on a multi-level reference architecture with focus on mechanisms to provide asynchronous communications, event-based interactions and data transformation capabilities.

The second PASCEB paper category on performance assessment and auditing in service computing has one paper with the title 'Model-driven Event Query Generation for Business Process Monitoring' by authors M. Backmann, A. Baumgrass, N. Herzberg, A. Meyer, and M. Weske that investigates where business process execution information can be found, how this information can be extracted, and to which point in the process it belongs to.

The third PASCEB paper category of analytics services on the clouds looks into making use of big data and comprises two papers. The first one with the title 'An Optimized Strategy for Data Service Response with Template-Based Caching and Compression' by Z. Peng, X. Kefu, L. Yan, and G. Li uses a specific compression algorithm to decrease the volume of data transmitted from a message template to extract application-relevant values from SOAP messages. The second paper with the title 'Towards a Formal Model for Cloud Computing' by Z. Benzadri, F. Belala, and C. Bouanaka focus on modelling interactions between cloud services and customers based on Bigraphical Reactive Systems.

The final fourth category of the workshop is on self-managing pervasive service systems in which the first paper has the title 'Towards Structure-Based Quality Awareness in Software Ecosystem Use' authored by K.M. Hansen and W. Zhang. This paper explores to which extent composition of components from a software ecosystem influences software quality. The second paper with the title 'Hybrid Emotion Recognition Using Semantic Similarity' by Z. Zhang, X. Meng, P. Zhang, W. Zhang, and Q. Lu adds semantic similarity to emotional keywords recognition to calculate the similarity between the keywords in a talk of the user and the words in a knowledge base. The third paper with the title 'Dynamic Adaptation of Business Process Based on Context Changes: A Rule-Oriented Approach' by G. Hu, B. Wu, and J. Chen describes the relationship between services and their context as rules used to generate a solution with a mapping mechanism. The paper with the title 'Component Migration in an OSGi based Pervasive Cloud Infrastructure' by W. Zhang, L. Chen, Q. Lu, P. Zhang, and S. Yang evaluate component migration in different scenarios in terms of performance and power consumption. The paper titled 'An Adaptive Enterprise Service Bus Infrastructure for Service Based Systems' by L. Gonzalez, J.L. Laborde, M. Galnares, M. Fenoglio, and R. Ruggia presents a JBossESB-based implementation demonstration. Lastly, the paper 'Requirements to Pervasive System Continuous Deployment' by C. Escoffier, O. Guenalp, and P. Lalanda focuses on deployment challenges of pervasive applications in reaction to unknown and fluctuating environments that makes traditional approaches unsuitable.

We sincerely thank the Program Committee Members of the PASCEB 2013 workshop for their time and support throughout the reviewing period.

Alex Norta, Claudia-Melania Chituc, Roman Vaculin, Weishan Zhang
PASCEB 2013 Workshop Chairs

Towards a Formal Model for Cloud Computing

Zakaria Benzadri, Faiza Belala, and Chafia Bouanaka

LIRE Laboratory
Department of Software and Information Systems Technology
University of Constantine 2, Constantine, Algeria
benzadri@gmail.com, belalafaiza@hotmail.com,
c.bouanaka@umc.edu.dz

Abstract. The use of formal methods is an effective means to improve complex systems reliability and quality. In this context, we adopt one of these methods to formalize cloud computing concepts. We focus on modeling interactions between cloud services and customers. Based on Bigraphical Reactive Systems, the formalization process is realized via the definition of a Cloud General Bigraph (CGB) obtained by associating; primarily, a CCB (Cloud Customers Bigraph) to cloud customers. Then, a Cloud Services Bigraph (CSB) is proposed to formally specify cloud services structure. Finally, juxtaposing these two bigraphs (CSB and CCB) gives rise to the suited CGB. In addition, a natural specification of cloud deployment models is specified. This paper also addresses cloud service dynamics by defining a set of reaction rules on bigraphs in a way that is amenable to reconfigure the designed cloud system.

Keywords: Cloud Computing, Bigraphical Reactive Systems, Formal Methods, Cloud Model, Cloud General Bigraph, Cloud Customers Bigraph, Cloud Services Bigraph.

1 Introduction

Software reusability has permanently triggered researchers and practitioners of software engineering. From the notion of modules defined by Djikstra to the well-known web services, we are still aiming on maximizing software reusability and thus reducing development cost. Based on service oriented paradigm and service oriented architectures and putting forward reduction of not only software development cost but also deployment effort, cloud computing [1] generalizes service reuse to all computer resources. The main principle behind this model is offering computing, storage, and software "as a service". It implies dynamic provisioning with on demand shared computing resources, and provides computing resources as services in an attempt to reduce IT capital and operating costs. Nevertheless, cloud computing is actually changing software design and development practices and involves revisiting and redefining some fundamentals and concepts. Much as service-oriented architecture (SOA), cloud architecture must be defined, governed, and managed independently [2].

A.R. Lomuscio et al. (Eds.): ICSOC 2013 Workshops, LNCS 8377, pp. 381–393, 2014.
© Springer International Publishing Switzerland 2014

Since it has emerged from the industry, a hard work of formalization is still needed to overcome one of cloud computing main obstacles; namely bugs in Large-Scale Distributed Systems – "*one of the difficult challenges in cloud computing is removing errors in these very large scale distributed systems*" [3]. The main issue that still needs to be addressed is the crucial absence of an appropriate model for cloud computing. This model might be able to support major cloud computing concepts specification and allows formal modeling of high level services provided over the cloud computing architecture.

In this work, we adopt Bigraphical Reactive Systems (BRS) proposed by Milner et al. [4] to formally specify cloud services and customers and their interaction schemes. The formalization process is realized via the definition of a Cloud General Bigraph (CGB); obtained by primarily associating a CCB (Cloud Customers Bigraph) to cloud customers. We enrich bigraphs signature with new controls (kinds of node) EU and ISV representing respectively End User and Independent Software Vendor. Then, we associate a Cloud Services Bigraph (CSB) to cloud services that also needs an enrichment of bigraphs signature to support all service types; IaaS, PaaS and SaaS. Finally, the juxtaposition of these two bigraphs (CSB and CCB) gives rise to the suited CGB. Besides, the model allows a natural specification of cloud deployment models. Cloud systems dynamics is specified via a set of reaction rules on both CSB and CCB bigraphs.

This paper is presented in a coordinated and integrated manner, starting with some fundamentals recall followed by presenting necessary definitions and rules that constitute the Cloud General Bigraph. It is organized as follows. In section 2, we present related work. A brief description of Bigraphical Reactive Systems and their essential concepts is introduced in section 3. In section 4, our cloud computing model is presented. Section 5 illustrates the proposed cloud formalization approach through a well-known case study of the Cloud-Health system. Finally, conclusion and future work are addressed in section 6.

2 Related Work

Nowadays researches on cloud computing are mainly focused on technical aspects, yet a modest attention is devoted to the formalization of cloud computing fundamental concepts.

H. Dong et al. [5]. and T. Grandison et al. [6], gave some discussion and exploration on establishing relationships between virtualization and Cloud Computing. Throughout their work, they attempt to give out a formal definition of cloud computing from a virtualization viewpoint using its theoretical basic concepts. S.-X. LUO et al. [7], propose an access control model to achieve a fine-grained data confidentiality and scalability via a formal definition of the HABAC model (Hierarchy Attribute-Based Access Control). A. Adamov and V. Hahanov [8] define a security model for individual cyberspace (ICS) protection as a means to ensure a secured user's virtual environment. They establish an analysis of security issues related to ICS and propose a conceptual model for modern security environments. L Freitas et al. [9], present an abstract formalization of federated cloud workflows using the Z notation. They define various rule based properties to restrict valid options with respect to: security and cost constraints. T. Binz et al. [10], propose Enterprise Topology Graphs (ETG) as a formal model to describe an enterprise topology. Based on the established graph theory, ETG is used to both formalize and verify cloud systems. Besides, authors have shown how ETG can improve the environmental impact of IT enterprise. R. He et al. [11], propose a trust model to specify trustworthiness and uncertainty of trust relationships between peers, namely cloud-model. Their model is strange and unspecified; it cannot be directly applied to model trust, and needs to be extended.

Up to now, however, cloud computing paradigm lacks a standard and formal definition of its basic concepts; service and deployment models, only some technological attempts are realized; for virtualization as it has been done in [5] and [6], for security as in [7], [8] and [9], or for IT enterprise as in [10].

Albeit, various models were adopted (Petri Nets [12] and [13], Semantic Technology [14], MDA [15], Agent-Based [16], or Component Model [17]), they do not show an efficient adequacy to cloud computing. Particularly, they deal with only one problem at a time. In this paper, BRS [4] will be adopted for two reasons. On the one hand, the model emphasizes on both locality and connectivity that can be used to specify cloud entities location and interconnection. On the other hand, bigraphical reaction rules are very useful to formalize cloud services elasticity providing them the ability to reconfigure themselves.

3 Bigraphical Reactive Systems

A bigraph as an ordinary graph is composed of nodes and edges, unlike nodes in a bigraph can be nested giving rise to hierarchical and larger bigraphs. Additionally, a bigraph is the result of composing a link graph; representing interconnection between nodes, and a place graph; expressing physical locations of theses nodes, hence the prefix 'bi' in bigraph.

3.1 Concrete Place Graph

The place graph consists of a forest of trees; each with its own root and servers to model locality or containment of entities. The formal definition of a place graph is:

Definition 1 (Place Graph [4]).
A place graph is a 3-tuple (V, ctrl, prnt): m→n having an inner interface m and an outer interface n, both are finite ordinals, used to index place graph sites and roots respectively. Where: V is a finite set of nodes, ctrl:V →S is a control map assigning controls to nodes. Each node has a control, which is an identifier belonging to a set that is called a signature (usually denoted as *S*). Each control indicates how many ports the node has, which controls are *atomic* (empty node), and which of the non-atomic controls are *active* (node permitting reaction inside) or *passive*. Finally, prnt: m⊎V→V⊎n is a parent map indicating the parent of each node.

3.2 Concrete Link Graph

The link graph models system connectivity or assembly and is composed of a set of nodes and a set of hyper-edges; meaning that each edge has multiple tentacles to connect different nodes; tentacles are called ports. Formal definition of a link graph is as follows:

Definition 2 (Link Graph [4]).
A link graph is a quadruple (V, E, ctrl, link): X →Y having an inner interface *X* and outer interface *Y*; called respectively the inner and outer names of the link graph. Where: *V* and *E* are sets of nodes and edges respectively, ctrl: V→S is a control map, and link: X ⊎ P →E ⊎ Y is a link map with *P* a set of ports. We shall call X ⊎ P the link graph points, and E ⊎ Y its links.

3.3 Concrete Bigraph

Having defined the place and link graph independently, we combine them to obtain a bigraph formal definition:

Definition 3 (Bigraph [4]).
A bigraph is a 5-tuple (V, E, ctrl, prnt, link): (m, X) → (n, Y), also written <GP, GL>, consisting of a concrete place graph GP = (V, ctrl, prnt):m→n and a concrete link graph GL = (V, E, ctrl, link): X →Y.

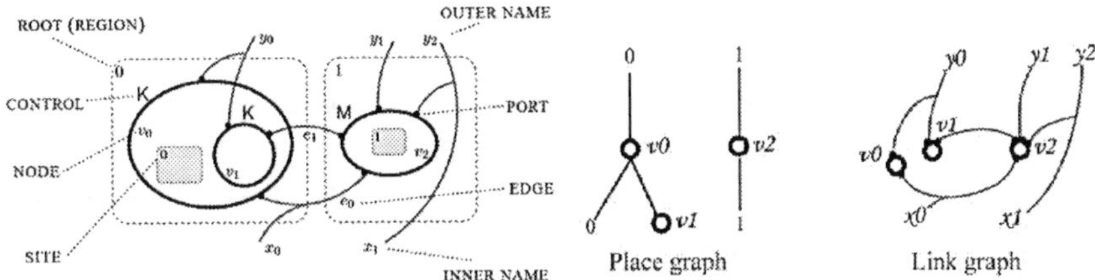

Fig. 1. Anatomy of bigraphs (Source: [4])

These definitions make precise the bigraph anatomy illustrated in Figure 1.

Additionally to graph theory based definitions that are insufficient to formally reason on bigraphs, an algebraic representation is also proposed offering various forms of bigraphs composition.

The language is summarized in Table 1:

Table 1. Terms language for bigraphs

Term	Meaning
U.V	Nesting. U contains V
$U \mid V$	Prime product
A⊗B	Juxtaposition
A∘B	Composition.

While nesting a bigraph within another bigraph is realized via the composition operation, placing them side-by-side is achieved using the juxtaposition operation which is a useful way for combining bigraphs.

3.4 Bigraphical Reactive Systems

Once bigraph structure presented, its dynamics will be defined through a BRS, consisting of a category of bigraphs and a set of reaction rules to be applied on them and describing bigraphs structural dynamics.

Definition 4 (Reaction Rule [4]).
A reaction rule takes the form (R, R', O) where R: m→J is a bigraph called redex (the pattern to be changed), R': m'→J is also a bigraph called reactum (the changed pattern), and O: m'→m is a map of ordinals establishing the correspondence between inner interfaces of R and R'.

BRS basic concepts introduced here will be exploited to formalize both cloud structure and dynamics in the following sections.

4 A Model for Cloud Computing

A bigraph represents orthogonal notions of locality and connectivity through the use of two separate graph structures (place graph and link graph), so it is an elegant solution and formal approach to describe cloud computing actors and their relationships. Cloud computing organization can be divided into two essential parts: the front-end and the back-end; usually connected via internet. The Front-end encloses customer's computer and necessary interface to access the cloud and the back-end contains the cloud services. In the present work, we adapt bigraphs to specify customers, services and their deployment models, and eventual interactions between them. Such formalization defines a precise semantics to the considered concepts. Our cloud model is called CGB (Cloud General Bigraph) which is a juxtaposition of two independent bigraphs: the Cloud Services Bigraph (CSB) defining the back-end part and the Cloud Customers Bigraph (CCB) modeling the front-end part. Additionally, a set of reaction rules is defined to formalize dynamics of the cloud computing architecture.

4.1 Cloud Customers Bigraph

We propose a formal definition of a Cloud Customers Bigraph that captures essential concepts identifying both, End users accessing only to SaaS and ISV (Independent Software Vendor) accessing to IaaS and PaaS types of customers. We model cloud customers as nodes equipped with specific controls to distinguish the two types of cloud customers; End user and ISV. Both are atomic nodes and have many ports to send their requests. We use the notation "*a: (x, act)*" where '*a*' is a control with arity (number of ports) 'x' and activity 'act'. We also use the ar(-) map to identify the arity of a given control, and we suggest a suitable graphical representation for each control (see table 2).

Definition 6 (Cloud Customers Bigraph).
The Cloud Customers Bigraph formalizing customers model takes the form (V_{CCB}, E_{CCB}, $ctrl_{CCB}$, GP_{CCB}, GL_{CCB}): $<m_{CCB},X_{CCB}>\rightarrow<n_{CCB},Y_{CCB}>$, with V_{CCB} representing all cloud customer nodes, E_{CCB} is a finite set of edges, $ctrl_{CCB}$: $V_{CCB}\rightarrow S_{CCB}$ is a control map that assigns a control to each cloud customer. The signature S_{CCB} is defined by $S_{CCB}=\{EU, ISV\}$. The map ar: $S_{CCB}\rightarrow N$ assigns an arity to each control, where ar(EU)= ar(ISV)=x and x>0. X_{CCB} is the inner face and Y_{CCB} is the outer face. GP_{CCB} represents the corresponding place graph and GL_{CCB} represents the link graph. Therefore, the link map $link_{CCB}$:$X_{CCB}\uplus P_{CCB}\rightarrow E_{CCB}\uplus Y_{CCB}$, with a set of ports $P_{CCB}=\{(v,i) \mid i \in ar(ctrl_{CCB}(v))\}$, i.e., a port is represented as a pair consisting of a node (from V) and an index.

In this definition, the signature of CCB is $S_{CCB}=\{EU: (x, atomic), ISV: (x, atomic)\}$. A suitable graphical representation of each control type is presented in table 2.

Table 2. Cloud Customers Signature

Control	Activity	G. Representation
EU (End User)	Atomic	
ISV(Independent Software Vendor)	Atomic	

4.2 Cloud Services Bigraph

Three different service models are deployed within a cloud architecture, to ensure front end requests: Infrastructure as a Service (IaaS), Platform as a Service (PaaS), and Software as a Service (SaaS). Albeit, all available cloud services are modeled by nodes in the Cloud Services Bigraph, controls attached to each nodes allow us to distinguish between the three categories of cloud services (see table 3). Additionally, services stack is naturally modeled via the hierarchy of nodes within the place graph (as shown in Figure 2) with respect to cloud services constraints. A node of control IaaS (infrastructure) can only contain nodes of control PaaS (platform). Also, a node of control PaaS can only contain nodes of control SaaS (software). Finally, a node of control SaaS does not contain any node. Consequently, nodes of control IaaS and PaaS are active, while nodes of control SaaS are atomic. Besides, we suggest a suitable graphical representation to each control (see table 3).

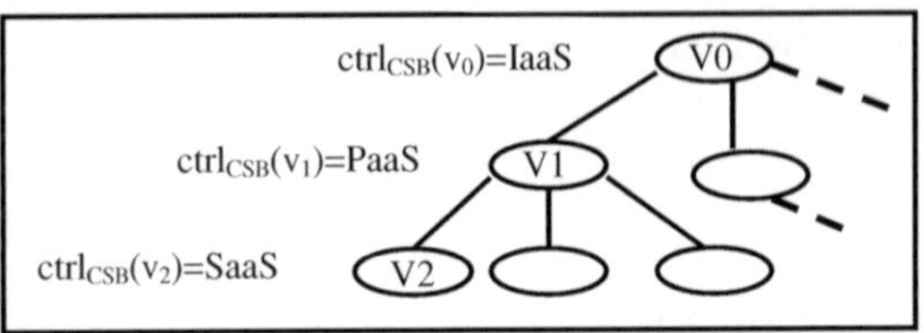

Fig. 2. Cloud Services Place Graph

To offer several access modes to cloud services, we propose that each cloud service (node) gets three different ports: Public (blue color in table 3), Private (red color in table 3), and Community (green color in table 3). As with Cloud Customers Bigraph, we now give a formal definition of the Cloud Services Bigraph enriched with a new map tp_{CSB} (-) assigning a type to each node port.

Definition 7 (Cloud Services Bigraph).
A Cloud Services Bigraph is associated to cloud service models and takes the form **CSB** = (V_{CSB}, E_{CSB}, $ctrl_{CSB}$, GP_{CSB}, GL_{CSB}, tp_{CSB}): $<m_{CSB},X_{CSB}>\rightarrow<n_{CSB},Y_{CSB}>$. Where V_{CSB} represents all cloud service nodes, E_{CSB} is a finite set of edges, $ctrl_{CSB}$: $V_{CSB}\rightarrow S_{CSB}$ is a control map that assigns a control to each cloud service. Controls range over the signature S_{CSB}= {IaaS, PaaS, SaaS} with a map ar: $S_{CSB}\rightarrow N$ assigning an arity to each control. Since each cloud service has three types of ports, ar(IaaS)=ar(PaaS)=ar(SaaS)=**3.** X_{CSB} is the inner face and Y_{CSB} is the outer face. GP_{CSB} represents its place graph and GL_{CSB} represents a link graph, such that, $link_{CSB}$: $X_{CSB} \uplus P_{CSB} \rightarrow E_{CSB} \uplus Y_{CSB}$, is a link map, with P_{CSB}= $\{(v,i) \mid i \in ar(ctrl_{CSB}(v))\}$ is the set of ports. Also, we define a new map assigning a type $t\in PT_{CSB}$={PbP, CmP, PrP}, to each node port $p \in P_{CSB}$, tp_{CSB}: $P_{CSB} \rightarrow PT_{CSB}$. So: tp_{CSB} (p)=PbP if p is Public Port, tp_{CSB} (p)=CmP if p is Community Port, tp_{CSB} (p)=PrP if p is Private Port.

In this definition, we summarize a suitable signature for CSB as follows: S_{CSB}={IaaS: (3, active), PaaS: (3, active), SaaS: (3, atomic)}.

Table 3. Cloud Services Signature

Control	Activity	G. representation	Conditions
IaaS	Active		∀ U, N in V_{CSB}, (U.N ∧ $ctrl_{CSB}$(U)=IaaS) => $ctrl_{CSB}$(N)=PaaS.
PaaS	Active		∀ U, N in V_{CSB}, (U.N ∧$ctrl_{CSB}$(U)=PaaS) => $ctrl_{CSB}$(N)=SaaS.
SaaS	Atomic		∀ U in V_{CSB}, $ctrl_{CSB}$(U)=SaaS => {v in V_{CSB} ∣ U.N} = ∅.

4.3 Cloud General Bigraph

Once structural concepts of both cloud services and customers bigraphs have been separately defined, their juxtaposition defines the cloud general bigraph. Its place graph formally expresses cloud services and customers location. Its link graph formally expresses interconnections, in terms of service request/response relationship, between cloud services and cloud customers. Formally, we have the following definition.

Definition 8 (Cloud General Bigraph).
A Cloud General Bigraph formalizing cloud computing, takes the form $CGB=CSB\otimes CCB: I_{CSB}\otimes I_{CCB}\rightarrow J_{CSB}\otimes J_{CCB}$, where:
CSB⊗CCB $=\langle GP_{CSB}\otimes GP_{CCB}, GL_{CSB}\otimes GL_{CCB}\rangle$, with:

- $GP_{CSB}\otimes GP_{CCB}: m_{CSB}+m_{CCB}\rightarrow n_{CSB}+n_{CCB}$ is defined by

$GP_{CSB}\otimes GP_{CCB} = (V_{CSB}\uplus V_{CCB}, ctrl_{CSB}\uplus ctrl_{CCB}, prnt_{CSB}\uplus prnt_{CCB})$.

- $GL_{CSB}\otimes GL_{CCB}: X_{CSB}\uplus X_{CCB}\rightarrow Y_{CSB}\uplus Y_{CCB}$ is defined by

$GL_{CSB}\otimes GL_{CCB} = (V_{CSB}\uplus V_{CCB}, E_{CSB}\uplus E_{CCB}, ctrl_{CSB}\uplus ctrl_{CCB}, link_{CSB}\uplus link_{CCB})$.

4.4 Cloud Deployment Models

Four cloud deployment models are identified in cloud computing. DM= {Public, Private, Community, Hybrid}. To take in charge such models, a formal description is done thanks to a meaningful interpretation of Cloud Services Bigraph. To identify service deployment models, we propose a function depm: $V_{CSB}\rightarrow DM$, where V_{CSB} represents cloud services. Since interconnections between cloud services and cloud customers are well defined via the link graph ($GL_{CSB}\otimes GL_{CCB}$), whenever a cloud service is connected to a cloud customer via a unique port, then service deployment model corresponds to the type of the port being used. Otherwise, if a cloud service is connected to cloud customers via various ports, then the cloud service is deployed as a hybrid cloud. Figure 3 represents cloud deployment models, using a link graph that is independent from locality, with C1, C2, C3 being Cloud customers and S1, S2, S3, S4 Cloud services. For instance, the cloud customer C2 is relied to S1 cloud service via its community port (CmP), so S1 is deployed as a community cloud (green color). Also the cloud customers C1 and C3 are relied to the cloud service S4, the first one with a public port (blue color) and the second one with a private port (red color), then S4 is deployed as a hybrid cloud (orange color).

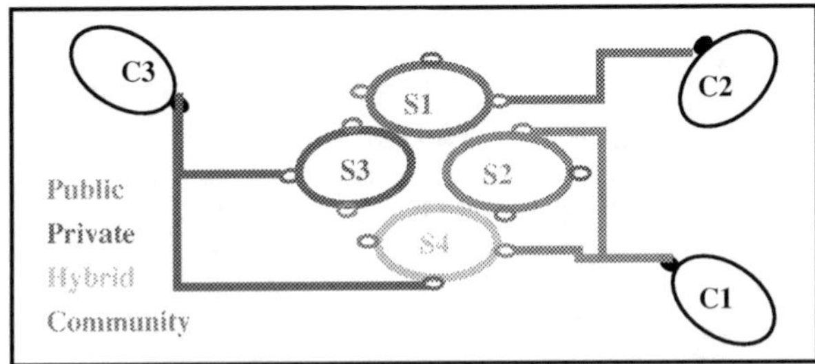

Fig. 3. Cloud Deployment Models Link Graph

Formally, $\forall$ s $\in V_{CSB}$, Ps={(s,i) | i ∈ ar($ctrl_{CSB}$(s))} represents the set of ports of s and ∃ pb, pr, cm ∈ Ps, such that: tp(pb)=PbP, tp(pr)=PrP, and tp(cm)=CmP. ∃ e ∈ E, ∃ c ∈ V_{CCB} and Pc={(c,i) | i ∈ ar($ctrl_{CCB}$(c))} represents the set of ports of c and p ∈ Pc. Such that:

- `link(s,`**`pb`**`)=e and link(c,p)=e → depm(s)=` **`Public.`**
- `link(s,`**`pr`**`)=e and link(c,p)=e → depm(s)=` **`Private.`**

- `link(s,`**`cm`**`)=e and link(c,p)=e →  depm(s)=` **`Community.`**
- `(depm(s) = Public and (depm(s) = Private or depm(s) = Community)) OR (depm(s) = Private and (depm(s) = Public or depm(s) = Community)) OR (depm(s) = Community and (depm(s) = Private or depm(s) = Public)) → depm(s) =` **`Hybrid`**`.`

4.5 Cloud Reaction Rules

We have now defined a Cloud General Bigraph in terms of its static structure, and being, expressive enough to model cloud services and customers connectivity and locality. To be moreover able to specify cloud system dynamics, CGB will be equipped with a set of reaction rules.

Locality reconfiguration is effected by shifting a cloud service from a parent cloud service to another one of the same control. Thereby, we propose two reaction rules defining the dynamics of bigraphs in this context.

- Rule PLR (PaaS Locality Reconfiguration). It expresses the fact that a platform may migrate from one infrastructure to another one. It changes the placing; a PaaS (P1) inside an IaaS (I1) shifts to another IaaS (I2), so we write: [I1.P1|I2 --> I1|I2.P1].
- Rule SLR (SaaS Locality Reconfiguration). Instead of migrating a platform to another infrastructure, rule SLR changes the placing of a service from one platform to another. A SaaS (S1) inside a PaaS (P1) shifts to another PaaS (P2), so we write: [P1.S1|P2-->P1|P2.S1].

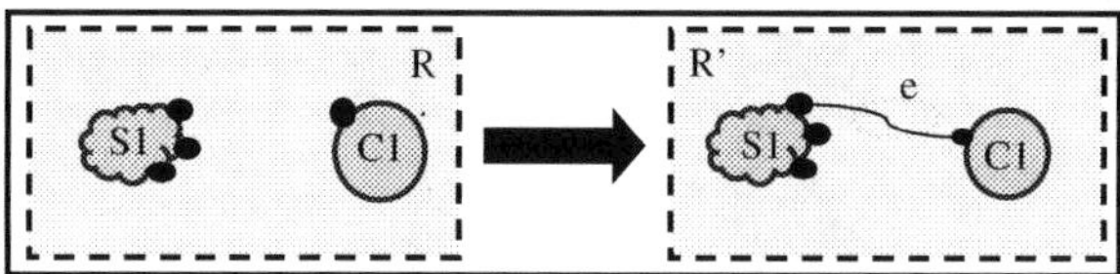

Fig. 4. Allocation Cloud Service Reaction Rule

Fig. 5. Liberation Cloud Service Reaction Rule

Connectivity reconfiguration changes only the linking—not the placing—in a bigraph. We suggest that the redex (R) —the left-hand pattern—can match any cloud service control (IaaS, PaaS, and SaaS), and we propose two reaction rules, defining the dynamics of bigraphs in terms of service allocation. While, figure 4 bellow shows a cloud customer (C1) allocating a cloud service (S1), figure 5 represents a cloud customer (C2) liberating a cloud service (S2).

5 Case Study

Cloud-Health is a cloud system, allowing doctors to exchange information concerning their patients. We present this example in order to illustrate how the Cloud General Bigraph model is able to capture and formally represent all cloud computing aspects.

Let's suppose that we have the following cloud services: three SaaS (S1, S2, S3) in two PaaS (P1, P2) within only one IaaS (I1), see figure 6 for more details.

- S1 allows consulting doctors directories by supplying multiple information (name, address, telephone, specialty), that can be used by everyone.
- S2 allows supplying administrative or medical information of every patient. It can be used by doctors. Only a private access is allowed to patients in order to modify their administrative information.
- S3 allows every doctor to manage his medical office. This service is only used by the concerned doctor.

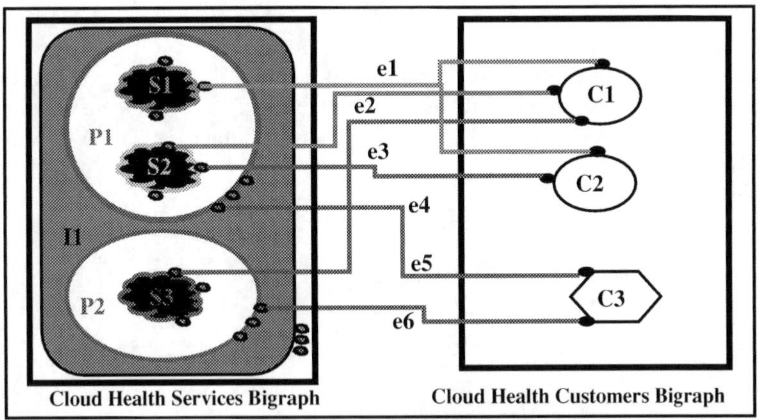

Fig. 6. Cloud Health General Bigraph

The cloud-health administrator ensures a smooth running of these three applications by supplying a private access to both PaaS (P1) and (P2).

According to our formalization approach, we can identify the CGB entities as follows (see figure 6):

- S1, S2, S3, P1, P2, I1 $\in V_{CSB}$, where: $ctrl_{CSB}$(S1)= $ctrl_{CSB}$(S2)= $ctrl_{CSB}$(S3)= SaaS, $ctrl_{CSB}$(P1)= $ctrl_{CSB}$(P2)= PaaS, and $ctrl_{CSB}$(I1)= IaaS.
- C1, C2, C3 $\in V_{CCB}$, where: $ctrl_{CCB}$(C1)= $ctrl_{CCB}$(C2)= EU (represents respectively a doctor and a patient), and $ctrl_{CCB}$(C3)= ISV (represents the administrator).

- The associated place graph in this case is represented in figure 7:

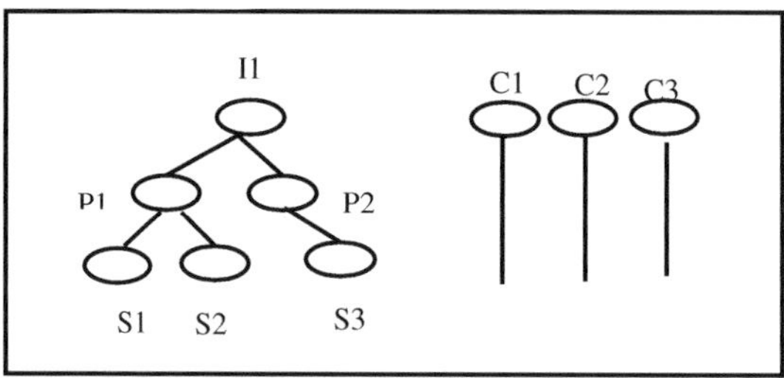

Fig. 7. Place graph of Cloud Health

- e1, e2, e3, e4, e5, e6 $\in E_{CGB}$, with each edge representing a connection between cloud customers and cloud services.
- The associated link graph, in this case, models cloud system connectivity (see figure 8):

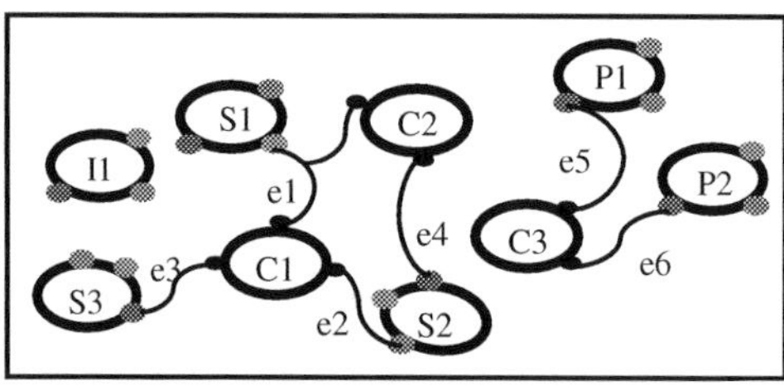

Fig. 8. Link graph of Cloud Health

Obviously, depm(-) function; defined in section 4.4, returns in our case the following values: depm(S1)=Public (edge e1 in figures 6 and 8), depm(S2)=Hybrid (edge e2 and e4 in figures 6 and 8), depm(S3)=Private (edge e3 in figure 6 and 8), depm(P1)=Private (edge e5 in figures 6 and 8), and depm(P2)=Private (edge e6 in figures 6 and 8).

Whenever a PaaS (P1) becomes unavailable for maintenance reasons, reconfiguring S1 service can be applied in order to migrate S1 to P2 using the SLR reaction rule (defined in section 4.5) which is denoted as follows:

`[I1.(P1.(S1|S2)|P2.S3)→I1.(P1.S2|P2.(S1|S3))]`

6 Conclusion

Bigraphical Reactive Systems (BRS) have been adopted as a formal model for cloud computing architecture specification. Two different bigraphs have been associated to both cloud services and customers, by enriching them with new sorts of nodes and ports. Their juxtaposition (CSB and CCB) gives rise to Cloud General Bigraph. The defined bigraphs allow developers to correctly reason about all cloud computing features, including modeling, composition, scheduling, monitoring and reconfiguration.

Particularly, we have shown how this model provides a flexible conceptual framework where cloud deployment models can be naturally defined. A nice consequence is that relationships between cloud services and cloud customers have been exploited to formally define cloud architecture reconfiguration via a set of reaction rules. Our ongoing work will focus on validating the proposed model by verifying some cloud computing inherent properties. BigMC, a Bigraphical Model Checker [18] designed to operate on Bigraphical Reactive Systems (BRS), will be used to formally model check the chosen properties.

References

1. Mell, P., Grance, T.: The nist definition of cloud computing. Technical Report 800-145, National Institute of Standards and Technology (NIST), Gaithersburg, MD (2011)
2. Marks, E.A., Lozano, B.: Executive's Guide to Cloud Computing. John Wiley and Sons Inc., Hoboken (2010)
3. Armbrust, M., Fox, A., Grith, R., Joseph, A.D., Katz, R.H., Konwinski, A., Lee, G., Patterson, D.A., Rabkin, A., Stoica, I., Zaharia, M.: Above the clouds: A berkeley view of cloud computing. Technical Report UCB/EECS-2009-28, EECS Department, University of California, Berkeley (2009)
4. Milner, R.: The Space and Motion of Communicating Agents. Cambridge University Press (2009)
5. Dong, H., Hao, Q., Zhang, T., Zhang, B.: Formal discussion on relationship between virtualization and cloud computing. In: 2010 International Conference on Parallel and Distributed Computing, Applications and Technologies (PDCAT), pp. 448–453 (2010)
6. Grandison, T., Maximilien, E., Thorpe, S., Alba, A.: Towards a formal definition of a computing cloud. In: 2010 6th World Congress on Services (SERVICES-1), pp. 191–192 (2010)
7. Luo, S.X., Liu, F.M., Ren, C.L.: A hierarchy attribute-based access control model for cloud storage. In: 2011 International Conference on Machine Learning and Cybernetics (ICMLC), vol. 3, pp. 1146–1150 (2011)
8. Adamov, A., Hahanov, V.: A security model of individual cyberspace. In: 2011 9th East-West Design Test Symposium (EWDTS), pp. 169–172 (2011)
9. Freitas, L., Watson, P.: Formalising workflows partitioning over federated clouds: Multi-level security and costs. In: 2012 IEEE Eighth World Congress on Services (SERVICES), pp. 219–226 (2012)
10. Binz, T., Fehling, C., Leymann, F., Nowak, A., Schumm, D.: Formalizing the cloud through enterprise topology graphs. In: 2012 IEEE 5th International Conference on Cloud Computing (CLOUD), pp. 742–749 (2012)
11. He, R., Niu, J., Hu, K.: A novel approach to evaluate trustworthiness and uncertainty of trust relationships in peer-to-peer computing. In: The Fifth International Conference on Computer and Information Technology, CIT 2005, pp. 382–388 (2005)
12. Fitch, D.F., Xu, H.: A petri net model for secure and fault-tolerant cloud-based information storage. In: SEKE, Knowledge Systems Institute Graduate School, pp. 333–339 (2012)
13. Fang, X., Wang, M., Wu, S.: A method for security evaluation in cloud computing based on petri behavioral profiles. In: Yin, Z., Pan, L., Fang, X. (eds.) Proceedings of The Eighth International Conference on Bio-Inspired Computing: Theories and Applications (BIC-TA). AISC, vol. 212, pp. 587–593. Springer, Heidelberg (2013)

14. Hu, L., Ying, S., Jia, X., Zhao, K.: Towards an Approach of Semantic Access Control for Cloud Computing. In: Jaatun, M.G., Zhao, G., Rong, C. (eds.) Cloud Computing. LNCS, vol. 5931, pp. 145–156. Springer, Heidelberg (2009)
15. Howard, F., George, S.: Formal methods in model-driven development for service oriented and cloud computing (2010)
16. Sim, K.M.: Agent-based cloud computing. IEEE Transactions on Services Computing 5, 564–577 (2012)
17. Di Cosmo, R., Zacchiroli, S., Zavattaro, G.: Towards a Formal Component Model for the Cloud. In: Eleftherakis, G., Hinchey, M., Holcombe, M. (eds.) SEFM 2012. LNCS, vol. 7504, pp. 156–171. Springer, Heidelberg (2012)
18. Perrone, G., Debois, S., Hildebrandt, T.T.: A model checker for bigraphs. In: Ossowski, S., Lecca, P. (eds.) SAC, pp. 1320–1325. ACM (2012)

An Optimized Strategy for Data Service Response with Template-Based Caching and Compression

Zhang Peng[1,2], Xu Kefu[1,2,*], Li Yan[3], and Guo Li[1,2]

[1] Institute of Information Engineering, Chinese Academy of Sciences, Beijing, China
[2] National Engineering Laboratory for Information Security Technologies, Beijing, China
[3] National Computer Network Emergency Response Technical Team, Beijing, China
zhangpeng@software.ict.ac.cn, xukefu@iie.ac.cn

Abstract. Data service is a specialization of Web service, and end-users can synthesize cross-organizational data by composing data services. As composite schemes overlap each other, some primitive data services could be called repeatedly by composite data services, so that the response delay and server load are aggravated. In this paper, an optimized strategy for data service response with template-based caching and compression is proposed. Firstly, the strategy uses the message template to extract the application-relevant values from SOAP messages. Secondly, the strategy holds the objects from application-relevant values rather than XML representations to decrease the overhead of SOAP message parsing. Thirdly, the strategy uses the XMill compression algorithm to decrease the volume of data transmitted. Extensive experiments based on Spring-WS-Test benchmark demonstrate the strategy is an effective approach to reduce response latency and server load compared to non-caching tehcnniques.

Keywords: data integration, message template, data caching, data compression, SOAP, data service.

1 Introduction

Data services are software components that providing rich metadata, expressive languages, and APIs for service consumers to use to send queries and receive data from service providers [1,2]. Data service hides the complexity of the multi-source and heterogeneous data sources, and helps the implementation of user-steering data integration. Compared to the traditional data integration techniques, data service separates the data access interface from the information system, which not only achieves loose coupling between integrated schemes and data sources, but also has good scalability. More importantly, data services have the same data schema, so that the user could directly integrate data souces without middleware schema. Through data service composition, the scattered data from the organizations can be integrated seamlessly to respond to transient business needs [3,4]. Nonetheless, as a specialization of Web services, the very feature that makes data service universally usable for structured and

[*] Corresponding author.

A.R. Lomuscio et al. (Eds.): ICSOC 2013 Workshops, LNCS 8377, pp. 394–405, 2014.
© Springer International Publishing Switzerland 2014

semi-structured data sources, namely the adoption of the ubiquitous XML standard, makes it difficult to reach the performance level required by large-scale data access. A major performance bottleneck resides in widespread SOAP message processing. The reason for SOAP message processing performance criticality is twofold:

1. On one hand, SOAP communication produces considerable network traffic, and causes high latency.
2. On the other hand, and perhaps more importantly, the generation and parsing of SOAP message, and their conversion to and from in memory application data can be computationally expensive.

In addition, there are special features for data service as shown in Table 1 to differentiate the effect providing service to make the SOAP processing performance become more criticality.

Table 1. Data Providing Service vs Effect Providing Service

Aspects	Data Providing Service	Effect Providing Service
Core Function	Data Query	Business Process
Transfer Type	Information Data	Effect Data
Data Volumn	Large-scale	Small-scale
Intertal Logic	Data Access Logic	Business Logic

We found that most SOAP messages have similar byte representations. SOAP messages created by the same implementation have the same message structure. In addition, the number of SOAP implementations is relatively small. Therefore it seems that the number of message patterns with which data service processor has to deal should be very small. This is especially more likely in enterprise data integration, where the message patterns are very limited and might be known to the server beforehand. In such cases, it is inefficient to repeatedly parse the almost-same messages each time.

```
<? xml version="1.0" encoding="UTF-8" ?>
<SOAP-ENV:Envelope xmlns:xsd="..."
xmlns:SOAP-ENV="..."
xmlns:xsi="...">
<SOAP-ENV:Body>
<nsl:getReport xmlns:nsl="...">
<nsl:eventReport>XXX</nsl:eventReport>
</nsl:getReport>
</SOAP-ENV:Body>
</SOAP-ENV:Envelope>
```

```
<? xml version="1.0" encoding="UTF-8" ?>
<soap-Envelope xmlns:xsi="..."
xmlns:xsd ="..."
xmlns:soap="...">
<soap-Body>
<getReport xmlns="...">
<eventReport>XXX</eventReport>
</getReport>
</soap-Body>
</soap-Envelope>
```

Fig. 1. SOAP messages created with Apache Axis and .NET

We also found that the application has far less interest in the literal message structure than the application-defined data structure. Figure 1 show the SOAP message examples emitted by Apache Axis and .NET respectively. For both messages, the application focuses on the string "XXX" rather than on the associated namespace prefixes, etc. In other words, what is important for the application is returning the event information corresponding to the symbol XXX, but not the parsing of the entire SOAP envelope.

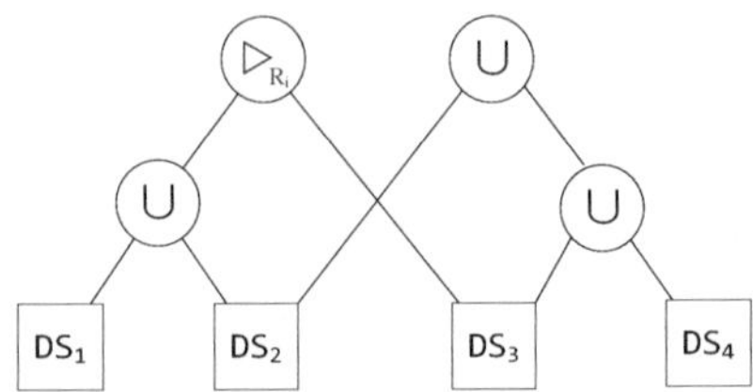

Fig. 2. The data services are called repeatedly

In addition, as composite schemes overlap each other, some primitive data services usually are called repeatedly by different composite data services [2]. For example, one client creates two composite data services denoted by (DS1∪DS2) ▷ Ri DS3 and (DS2∪DS3)∪DS4 as shown in Figure 2, where DS1, DS2, DS3 and DS4 are primitive data services, ∪ is union operation and ▷ Ri is join operation with respect to attribute Ri. When the two composite data services are executed, the DS2 and DS3 will be called repeatedly, and the SOAP transfer involves the some results. So how to optimize the data service communication based on above facts is our goal.

In this paper, a middleware Data Service Accelerator (DSA) is designed. The middleware takes into account the caching data structure and reduces the volume of data transmitted through the combined use of caching of recent responses and data compression techniques. We keep caching and data compression transparent and add a proxy layer that intercepts exchange messages. The paper is organized as follows: Section 2 introduces some related works. Section 3 introduces the DSA with the template-based caching and compression in details. Section 4 is experiment and discussion. Section 5 sums up with several concluding remarks.

2 Related Works

In Data Service environments, SOAP provides interoperability between the clients and the service. However, as the client and the hosted services are connected by a network and communicate through XML-encoded messages, substantial overhead is induced due to (de)serialization. Special care must hence be taken to reduce the response latency for data service invocations, and thus improve service throughput. In this paper, we adopt template-based caching and data compression techniques to address this performance issue of data services invocations.

A. Template-based

As mentioned previously, SOAP processing performance enhancement has been widely researched [5, 6, 7]. Many approaches build on the simple observation that SOAP message exchange usually involves a number of highly similar messages. Several proposals addressing SOAP performance enhancement exploit the differential SOAP parsing, in order to gain in performance, e.g., reducing execution time, increasing throughput, and saving on network traffic. The main idea is to identify the common parts of SOAP messages, to be processed once, regardless of the number of messages. The main approaches to differential SOAP parsing include Template-based [5], Multiple Templates [6] and Detecting Repeatable Structures [7].

B. Response Caching

Research on remote object caching for distributed systems [8] has caught substantial attention, including efforts that target CORBA, SOAP objects, and Java RMI. An efficient response cache mechanism appropriate for the Web Services architecture is proposed by Takase et al [9]. This mechanism reduces the overhead of XML processing and application object copying by optimized data representation. We extend on this approach and add two additional techniques to further improve performance, textual data compression and optimized data representation of cached entries.

C. XML Compression

XML, the foundation of the SOAP protocol, is a self descriptive textual format for structured data. XML provides a good basis for interoperability and facilitates the adaptation of services, but it is also renowned to be verbose. This verbosity, mainly due to the excessive use of markup and metadata, can cause problems due to communication and processing overhead in resource-constrained environments such as small wireless devices and in environments with network limitations. Fortunately, the impact of this verbosity can be alleviated through the use of text compression techniques. According to a summary [10], three categories of compression algorithms can be used to reduce the verbosity of XML: general-purpose compression agnostic of XML, algorithms based on the general knowledge that the data is XML-based, and techniques that take advantage of the schema used for the particular XML documents to be compressed. DSA does not depend on any specific compression algorithm. While we currently use XMill [11], a general-purpose compression algorithm for textual data, replacing this with another compression algorithm is straight-forward.

One can realize that the above techniques are not mutually exclusive, but are rather complementary. Unfortunately, interference and synergy between different techniques is not yet completely understood, and less works make some preliminary research about combing these techniques. In this context, this paper makes efforts toward combining these techniques, and gains some benefits.

3 Template-Based Caching and Compression

Based on the observations above, we implemented a middleware Data Service Accelerator to execute three tasks. The first is to use the message template to extract the application-relevant values from the SOAP messages. The second is to hold the objects from the values rather than XML representations to decrease the overhead of XML parsing. The third is to uses the XMill compression algorithm to decrease the volume of XML transmitted. Here we describe its design and implementation.

3.1 Template-Based Extraction

Figure 3 shows an overview of our template-based processor, where the solid and dotted lines denote the processing flow and the data flow respectively.

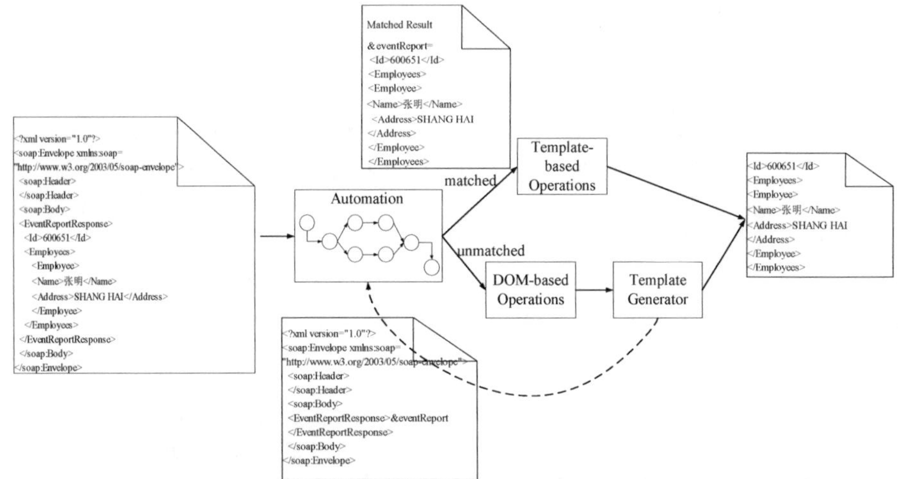

Fig. 3. The application-relevant values extraction based on message template

First, the incoming message is matched against the automaton that contains multiple message templates in a merged form. If the message matches any template, the application-relevant values are extracted using the template and DOM processing is done based on the extracted values. Otherwise, the processing is performed by an ordinary DOM-based processor and a new template corresponding to the unmatched message is generated. The new template is merged into the automaton, and thereafter any messages having the same message structure can be matched against the template. The resulting messages are same in both cases. The message template describes the byte-level structure of SOAP messages. It consists of a few kinds of message fragments: constant fragments corresponding to the unchanging parts in the messages and variable fragments corresponding to the variable parts. All the application-relevant values are regarded as variable parts. In Figure 3 the variable fragments are denoted as "${variable_name}" and printed in bold italic. Since the template-based processor initially has no information about the XML tree structure without help from DOM-based processor, message templates are generated in cooperation with the DOM-based processor. In order to tell where the application-relevant values start and end, we implemented a specialized XML parser that can record the offset and length information for each XML node. Using the DOM created by the specialized parser, the DOM-based processor can select all of the application-relevant nodes and specify them as the variable fragments with the offset and length information. Finally, the message parts that were not selected in the previous process are consolidated as a constant fragment, and a message template is generated from these fragments. Note that DOM-based operations are performed only when a message with a new structure arrives. Based on our observations, most messages match the existing templates and the frequency of creating templates is low.

Let's introduce the automaton. The automaton provides two interfaces, one for matching the incoming messages and one for learning the new message templates. If the incoming message matches any of the existing message templates, the matching result returned is a map object that contains pairs of variable names and the corresponding actual variable values. In Figure 3, for example, the incoming message is matched against the message template and a map of {eventReport, <id>600651</id> <Empolyees>…</Empolyees>} and so on is returned. The DOM operations are done based on the extracted values. However, if the matching failed, the processor would have had to create a new message template and make the automaton learn that template, in preparation for the later incoming messages for which the new template will be applied. Learning message templates means updating the state diagram in the automaton. All of the templates inside the automaton are stored in a merged form and can be represented as a state diagram.

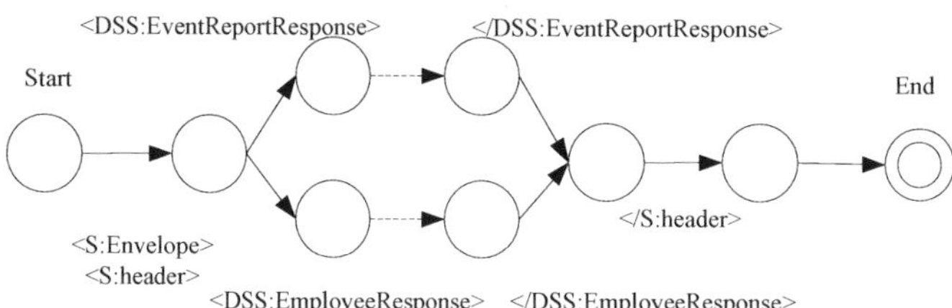

Fig. 4. The message template

Figure 4 shows a simple example of a state diagram which has been created from two message templates, where a solid line and a dotted line denote an actual state transition and one or more transitions (intermediate states might be omitted), respectively. Concretely in this example, this means two message templates have already been learned. Since "<S: Envelope><S: Header>" and "</S: Header> ..." are common to both messages, their paths are merged. As seen in the figure, one XML node (or tag) does not necessarily correspond to one state.

After the application-relevant values have been extracted from the message, there are no substantial differences in the operations themselves between the template-based processor and the DOM-based one. They differ in the way they retrieve the values from the message. The template-based processor uses template matching while the DOM-based one traverses DOM tree. The next step is how to transfer the extracted values over the network. For this purpose, the caching and compression techniques in DSA are given in following sections.

3.2 Proxy-Based Caching

In the context of Web services, data representation requires the transformation of application data into internal representations in the form of XML Infosets[1]. For data services, this means that the internal XML Infoset representation is serialized into an XML document before it is transferred over the network. As data services are platform neutral and thus cannot depend on a specific wire protocol. This leaves us with only one opportunity for communication performance improvements, namely data representation. For this purpose, a caching layer is added to the data service framework. This layer is provided through interface techniques instead of hard-coded implementations in the data service engine. The DSA Client shown in Figure 5 is a lightweight component that mediates communication between the data services client and the remote DSA Proxy. It forwards requests from the data services client, buffers the entire results, and responses to the data services client to acquire the results. The DSA Client provides the ability to retrieve results from hash-based descriptions (digest) sent by the proxy by maintaining an in-memory cache of recently received results.

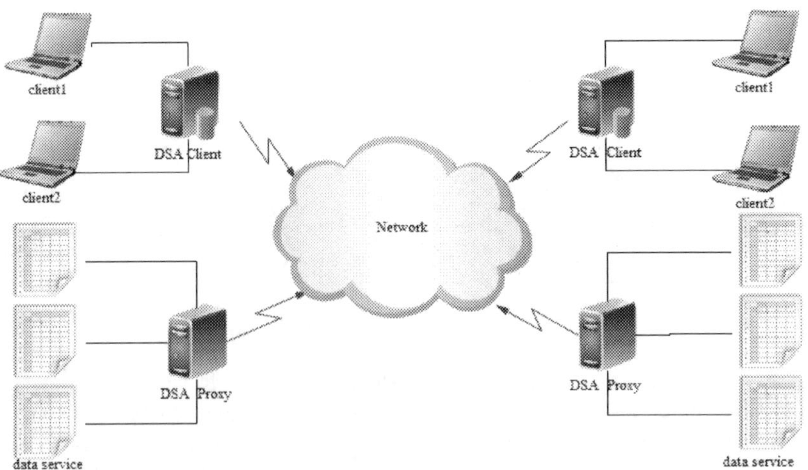

Fig. 5. Conceptual overview of the DSA architecture

[1] http://www.w3.org/TR/xml-infoset/

The DSA Proxy shown in Figure 5 does not examine any request messages received from the DSA Client but directly forwards them to the Data Service. Instead, the proxy is responsible for inspecting response results received from the Data Service provider. The proxy rapidly generates hash-based encodings of the results and caches these encodings. If the results are similar to previous ones, only the hash digests are sent to DSA. Note that the proxy does not need to keep the actual response messages but only the digests. This enables the proxy to scale well also when many clients are using the same service.

3.3 Data Handling at Service and Client Side

Figure 6(a) shows the dataflow for results handling at the DSA Proxy side. The DSA Proxy first receives response results from the Data Services provider, and then checks the size of the result. If the size of the result is less than a threshold value, the proxy does not generate a hash digest of that result, but forwards it directly to DSA Client. Otherwise, the proxy generates a digest of the result. DSA does not depend on any specific hash function. Modern hash functions computes hash digests very fast. The size of the digest depends on the hash function used, but is in general much smaller than the size of the original response. In our prototype, we currently use SHA-1[12] as the hash function and the size of each hashed result is thus 160 bits. The next step is to check whether the hashed result already is stored in the cache. If so, the client has requested this result before and the proxy only needs to transmit the hashed result. Otherwise, the hashed result is new and the DSA Proxy stores it in the cache. The proxy also compresses the original response message to a compact one before finally transmitting it to the client side. This way, large messages are always compressed and the amount of data transmitted over the network is reduced even if cache misses occur.

Figure 6(b) shows the overall dataflow in the DSA Client. The first step in the client is to inspect the type of a result received from the DSA Proxy. If the result message is a hash digest, DSA retrieves the stored response result from cache through the use of the received hash digest as key. Otherwise, DSA checks whether the result is compressed and if so, the result is decompressed to the original one. Next, the response result is stored in cache with the hash digest as key before it is passed to the DSA client.

At the client side, the data representation for cached data is made efficient by de-serializing responses only once and storing the resulting objects in the cache. This way, upon a cache-hit, the client can immediately fetch the object from cache without any parsing or de-serialization process, and the response latency is further reduced. In detail, before delivering a response message to the client, the response result is converted to an object in advance. This process is fulfilled by an XML parser, which can be based either on DOM or SAX. If it is a DOM parser, a DOM tree object, as the post-parsing representation, is created from the XML message. If the parser is a SAX parser, the SAX parser reads the XML documents and notifies the de-serializer of the SAX events sequentially. The de-serializer constructs the objects from the DOM tree object or the SAX events sequence. As the parsing and de-serialization of XML messages constitutes a large part of the Data Services overhead, caching of objects instead of XML objects can significantly improve the performance of service response caching.

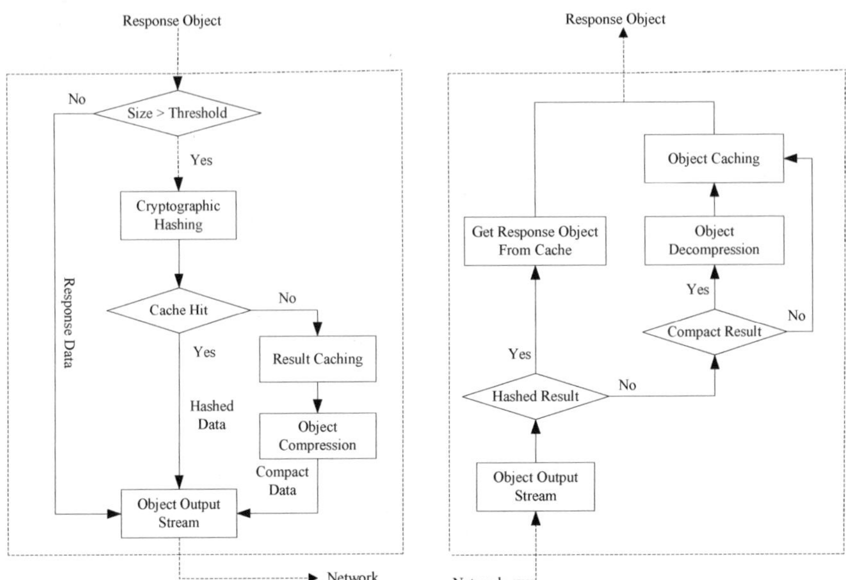

(a). Dataflow for data handling at the DSA Proxy side.

(b). Dataflow for data handling at DSA Client side.

Fig. 6. Dataflow for data handling

Experiment and Analysis

3.4 Benchmarking

We test the performance through industry standard benchmarks from Spring-WS-Test[2]. Spring-WS-Test consists of a multi-threaded application that could performs multiple data service calls in parallel in order to simulate a real life scenario with multiple clients that access the services. Spring-WS-Test measures the throughput of a system handling multiple types of data service invocations.

3.5 Experimental Setup

The experimental setup consists of a client side extended with a DSA Client module. This client has five threads, one for each benchmark. The other part in the setup is the server side that implements the data services. The server side is extended with a DSA

[2] http://javacrumbs.net/spring-ws-test/

Proxy module. The two sides have identical system configurations, of which CPU Intel Core i5, 3.09 GHz, Main Memory 4 GB, Operating System Win XP Professional Edition, Application Server Apache Tomcat, version 6.0.14. The client side and the server side are connected by a network router that allows us to control the bandwidth and latency settings on the network. We focus our evaluation on three network configurations; 5 Mb/s, representative for severely constrained network paths, 20 Mb/s, representative for moderately constrained network paths, and 100 Mb/s, representative for unconstrained networks. The last setup is used to investigate any potential overhead of DSA in situations where bandwidth is not a limiting factor. Each client submits a mix of invocations, with 20 % of the calls for each of the five benchmarks. The number of invocations executed and the response time is accumulated during a steady state period of 600 seconds and is reported at the end of the execution. Moreover, invocations during each execution have a certain repetition rate. For repeating invocations the same request parameters are used and the response results from the server are thus the same. Steering this repetition rate, i.e., the cache-hit ratio, enables us to study the performance impact of caching in the DSA system. Using this setup, we measured results for various combinations of number of clients, cache-hit ratio, and network bandwidth for the following two configurations:

- The Native configuration, corresponding to Figure 5 where DSA layer is not used.
- The DSA configuration, corresponding to Figure 5 where the DSA layer is used. For a given number of client threads and a certain network bandwidth, comparing these results to the corresponding Native ones investigates the potential performance improvements.

3.6 Performance Analysis

When the cache-hit ratio is increased to 8 %, we observe in Figure 7 that the benefits of caching balances out the overhead induced DSA and the performance Native and DSA is almost identical for the EchoVoid, EchoStruct, and EchoSynthetic

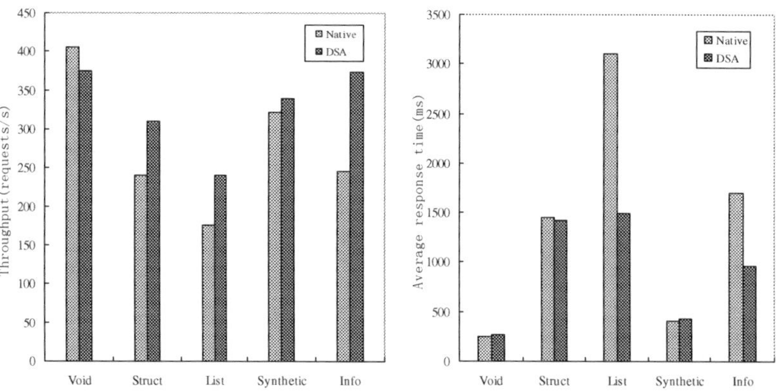

Fig. 7. Throughput and response time with 8 % cache-hit ratio and a bandwidth of 5 Mb/s

benchmarks. Furthermore, for this configuration, DSA gives around half the response time of Native for EchoList and EchoInfo. We observe in Figure 8 that for 8 % cache-hit ratio and a 20 Mb/s network, the response times of Native are similar to those of DSA, except for the EchoList benchmark, where DSA performs substantially better. As caching and data compression are more beneficial for slower networks, we note that the performance improvement of using DSA is much higher for 5 Mb/s networks than for 20 Mb/s ones.

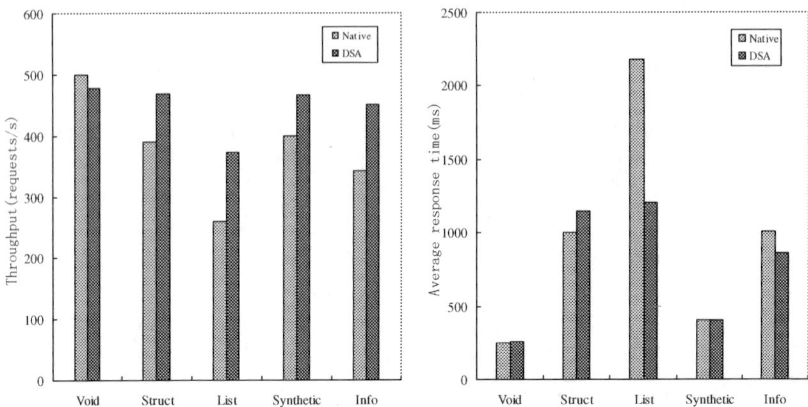

Fig. 8. Throughput and response time with 8 % cache-hit ratio and a bandwidth of 20 Mb/s

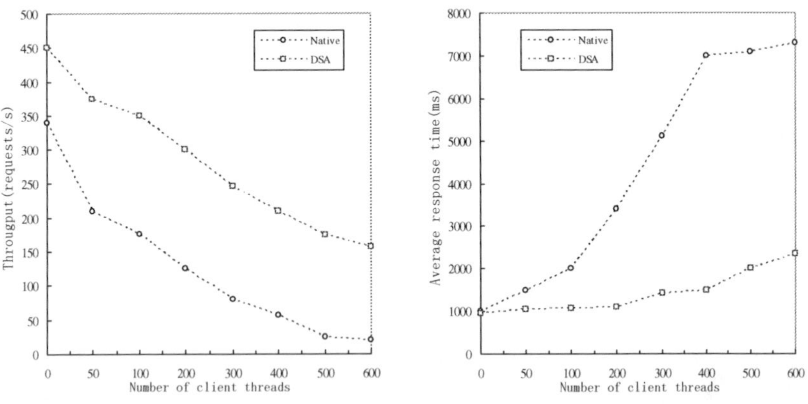

Fig. 9. Throughput and response time with 8 % cache-hit ratio and a bandwidth of 20 Mb/s and different number of concurrent client threads

Figure 9 illustrates, for a varying number of client's threads, the performance of Native and DSA for a 20 Mb/s network and a cache-hit ratio of 8 %. We note that the performance improvement of DSA over Native increases with the number of client threads. This suggests that DSA is a scalable solution that can improve both response time and throughput for highly loaded data services.

4 Conclusion

Data Services have received substantial attention and there is a great deal of industry excitement around the opportunities they provide. Most of the attention today has focused on data service modeling and composition, leaving the performance problem of data services somewhat ignored. In this paper, we focus on the response latency issue that arises in data services invocations. Our solution demonstrates that the impact of low network performance can be substantially reduced through caching and compression.

Acknowledgements. The research work is supported by Supported by the National High Technology Research and Development Program 863 under Grant No.2011AA010703; the Strategic Priority Research Program of the Chinese Academy of Sciences under Grant No.XDA06030602; the China Postdoctoral Science Foundation under Grant No. 2013M541076.

References

1. Carey, M.J., Onose, N., Petropoulos, M.: Data Services. Communication of ACM 55(6), 86–97 (2012)
2. Zhang, P., Wang, G., Ji, G., Liu, C.: Optimization Update for Data Composition View Based on Data Service. Chinese Journal of Computers 34(12), 2344–2354 (2011)
3. Han, Y., Wang, G., Ji, G., Zhang, P.: Situational data integration with data services and nested table. In: Service Oriented Computing and Application, pp. 1–22 (2012)
4. Lin, H., Zhang, C., Zhang, P.: An optimization strategy for mashups performance based on relational algebra. In: Sheng, Q.Z., Wang, G., Jensen, C.S., Xu, G. (eds.) APWeb 2012. LNCS, vol. 7235, pp. 366–375. Springer, Heidelberg (2012)
5. Takeuchi, Y., Okamoto, T., Yokoyama, K., Matsuda, S.: A Differential-Analysis Approach for Improving SOAP Processing Performance. In: Proceedings of the IEEE International Conference on e-Technology, e-Commerce and e-Service (EEE 2005), pp. 472–479 (2005)
6. Makino, S., Tatsubori, M., Tamura, K., Nakamura, Y.: Improving WS Security Performance with a Template Based Approach. In: ICWS 2005, pp. 581–588 (2005)
7. Teraguchi, M., Makino, S., Ueno, K., Chung, H.-V.: Optimized Web Services Security Performance with Differential Parsing. In: Dan, A., Lamersdorf, W. (eds.) ICSOC 2006. LNCS, vol. 4294, pp. 277–288. Springer, Heidelberg (2006)
8. Bal, H.E., Bhoedjang, R., Hofman, R., et al.: Performance evaluation of the Orca shared-object system. ACM Trans. Comput. Syst. 16(1), 1–40 (1998)
9. Takase, T., Tatsubori, M.: Efficient Web Services response caching by selecting optimal data representation. In: Proceedings of the 24th International Conference on Distributed Computing Systems (ICDCS 2004), pp. 188–197. IEEE Computer Society (2004)
10. Ericsson, M.: The effects of XML compression on SOAP performance. WWW Journal 10(3), 279–307 (2007)
11. Liefke, H., Suciu, D.: XMill: an efficient compressor for XML data. ACM SIGMOD Record, 153–164 (2000)
12. National Institute of Standards and Technology. Secure hash standard (May 2010), `http://csrc.nist.gov/publications/fips/fips180-2/fips180-2withchangenotice.pdf`

Model-Driven Event Query Generation for Business Process Monitoring*

Michael Backmann, Anne Baumgrass, Nico Herzberg,
Andreas Meyer, and Mathias Weske

Hasso Plattner Institute at the University of Potsdam
Prof.-Dr.-Helmert-Str. 2–3, D-14482 Potsdam, Germany
Michael.Backmann@student.hpi.uni-potsdam.de
{Anne.Baumgrass,Nico.Herzberg,Andreas.Meyer,
Mathias.Weske}@hpi.uni-potsdam.de

Abstract. While executing business processes, a variety of events is produced that is valuable for getting insights about the process execution. Specifically, these events can be processed by Complex Event Processing (CEP) engines to deliver a base for business process monitoring. Mobile, flexible, and distributed business processes challenge existing process monitoring techniques, especially if process execution is partially done manually. Thus, it is not trivial to decide where the required business process execution information can be found, how this information can be extracted, and to which point in the process it belongs to. Tackling these challenges, we present a model-driven approach to support the automated creation of CEP queries for process monitoring. For this purpose, we decompose a process model that includes monitoring information into its structural components. Those are transformed to CEP queries to monitor business process execution based on events. For illustration, we show an implementation for Business Process Model and Notation (BPMN) and describe possible applications.

Keywords: Business Process Management, Complex Event Processing, Business Process Monitoring, Event Pattern Language Query Generation.

1 Introduction

During business process execution, various systems and services produce a variety of data, messages, and events that are valuable for gaining insights about business process execution [13]. This data enables business process monitoring, e.g., to ensure a business process is executed as expected. However, nowadays, business processes are executed in different places, times, and by a variety of people or devices leading to more mobile, flexible, and distributed business processes. In a business process, activities are executed automatically and manually, where manual execution may be supported by information systems. In this environment, the different systems used to execute business processes generate a large amount of events (e.g., Global Positioning System (GPS) signals of driving trucks) that can be used to enable the monitoring of business processes across enterprise boundaries [6, 11, 15].

* The research leading to these results has received funding from the European Union's Seventh Framework Programme (FP7/2007-2013) under grant agreement 318275 (GET Service).

A.R. Lomuscio et al. (Eds.): ICSOC 2013 Workshops, LNCS 8377, pp. 406–418, 2014.
© Springer International Publishing Switzerland 2014

The detection and processing of events originating from different systems can be handled by Complex Event Processing (CEP) engines [9,13]. In contrast, the orchestration and enactment of business processes is in the control of Business Process Management (BPM) systems [16,19] in semi-automated environments. Existing works argues that the incorporation of modeling process logic and describing complex event patterns is essential to capture the overall process context [2]. Thus, there is the need to complement the modeling and execution of business processes in semi-automated execution environments with CEP capabilities.

In this paper, we demonstrate the combination of BPM with CEP for monitoring business process execution in semi-automated environments. We utilize the Refined Process Structure Tree (RPST) [17] to decompose process models into their structural components. Subsequently, these components are automatically transformed into CEP queries using an Event Pattern Language (EPL). For process modeling, we use Business Process Model and Notation (BPMN) [14] enriched with process event monitoring points (PEMPs) [11] that specify where which events are expected during execution. The corresponding CEP queries derived from the BPMN model are represented by Esper EPL [3, 8]. Although we use BPMN and Esper, the general approach presented in this paper is not restricted to a certain process modeling notation nor an EPL. The concept of PEMPs allows to exactly specify which parts of a process model shall be monitored, while existing approaches aim at monitoring each construct of the process model. This may lead to unexpectedly incomplete event logs resulting in severe issues with respect to CEP. In summary, the query generation presented in this paper can be conducted without the need to learn a specific syntax of an EPL and helps if either only parts of a process are of interest or some parts are not observable due to missing sensors, for instance.

The remainder of this paper is structured as follows. Section 2 introduces the set of basic notations that we use throughout the paper. Next, Section 3 describes the scenario including its process model which is used in this paper to demonstrate our approach. Our automation of the query generation from process models is given in Section 4. It includes the three necessary steps to generate CEP queries and the description of their implementation. Afterwards, the application areas of our approach are shown in Section 5 followed by the comparison of our approach with related work in Section 6. Finally, Section 7 concludes this paper.

2 Preliminaries

Working with CEP requires a profound understanding of events and their utilization. An event is a real-world happening occurring in a particular point in time at a certain place in a certain context [13]. Capturing an event in an information system requires the transformation of an event into an event object, each being classified by an event object type [11]. In the process context, we define both concepts as follows.

Definition 1 (Event object). An *event object* $\mathcal{E} = (type, id, P, timestamp, \mathcal{C})$ refers to an event object *type* $\mathcal{ET}$, has a unique identifier *id*, refers to a set P of *process instances* being affected by the event object, has a *timestamp* indicating the occurrence time, and contains an additional *event content* $\mathcal{C}$. $\diamond$

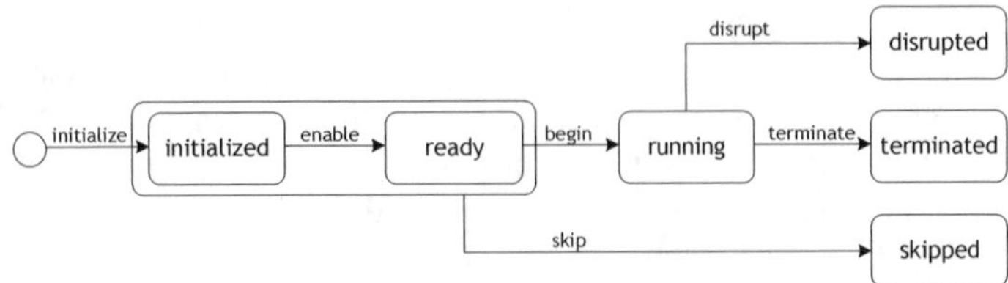

Fig. 1. Activity life cycle (cf. [19])

Definition 2 (Event object type). An *event object type* $\mathcal{ET} = (name, cd)$ refers to a unique *name* indicating the object type identifier and has a *content description cd* of a particular event being of this event type. ◇

As indicated in Definition 1, event objects affect one or several process instances by indicating, for instance, process state changes. Each process instance refers to exactly one process model, which we define as follows.

Definition 3 (Process model). A *process model* $M = (N, F, \eta, \mu, \psi)$ contains of a finite non-empty set $N \subseteq A \cup E \cup G$ of flow nodes being *activities* A, *events* E, and *gateways* G. Events $E \subseteq E^S \cup E^I \cup E^E$ are distinguished into start events E^S, intermediate events E^I, and end events E^E. $F \subseteq N \times N$ represents the *control flow relation* which constraints the partial order of nodes. Functions $\eta : E^S \cup E^E \rightarrow \{plain, message\}$ and $\mu : E^I \rightarrow \{message, time, cancel, error\}$ assign a type to each event. Function $\psi : G \rightarrow \{xor, and\}$ assigns a type to each gateway. ◇

We require each process model to be structural sound and block-structured[1]. Process monitoring deals with capturing events based on node execution; but monitoring on node level may be too coarse-grained. Assuming, there exist waiting times between the execution of two activities, the termination of the first activity does not indicate the start of the second one such that multiple measures are needed. Therefore, we utilize the concept of life cycles for nodes of a process model [19] and attach PEMPs to the state transitions of the node life cycles [11]. Formally, we define a node life cycle as follows.

Definition 4 (Node life cycle). A *node life cycle* $L = (S, T, \varphi)$ contains of a finite non-empty set S of states and a finite set $T \subseteq S \times S$ of state transitions. Let $\mathcal{L}$ be the set of all node life cycles defined for the nodes N of process model M. Then, there exists a function $\varphi : N \rightarrow \mathcal{L}$ assigning a node life cycle to each node $n \in N$ of M. ◇

Fig. 1 depicts the life cycle L_A for activities consisting of states *initialized*, *ready*, *running*, *terminated*, *disrupted*, and *skipped* connected by transitions *(i)nitialize*, *(e)nable*, *(b)egin*, *(t)erminate*, *(d)isrupt*, and *(s)kip*. For events and gateways, we utilize a subset of these states removing states *running* and *disrupted* and the transitions leading to

[1] The process model contains exactly one start and one end event and each node is on a path from that start event to the end event. Each activity has exactly one incoming and one outgoing edge, each start event has one outgoing and no incoming edges, each end event has one incoming and no outgoing edges, each gateway has at least three edges with either exactly one incoming or exactly one outgoing edge, and for each merging gateway there exists a splitting one.

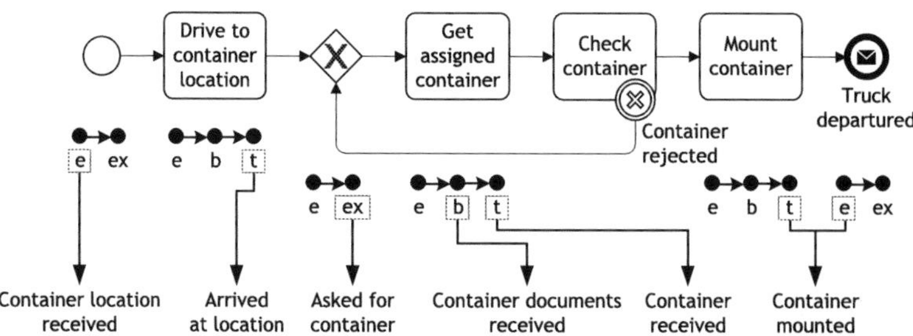

Fig. 2. Business process model of a container pick-up process modeled in BPMN with associated node life cycles and event object types

them. Further, the states *ready* and *terminate* are connected via transition *(ex)ecute*. We distinguish state transitions into the ones observable by occurring events and the ones requiring the context of the process instance to deduce their triggering. For a given node of a process model, each state transition belongs to either group. Utilizing PEMPs for process monitoring is independent from the process instance execution. Thus, a PEMP can only be attached to state transitions being directly observable.

Definition 5 (Process event monitoring point). Let M be a process model, L a node life cycle, and $O_L \subseteq T_L$ the set of state transitions not requiring process instance information. Then, a *process event monitoring point* is a tuple $PEMP = (M, n, t, et)$, where M is the process model it is contained in, $n \in N$ is the node of the process model it is created for, $t \in O_L$ is a state transition within the node life cycle L it is created for, and $et \in \mathcal{ET}$ is an event object type specifying the event object to be recognized. $\diamond$

3 Scenario

Next, a business process from the logistics domain is used as scenario to discuss the approach presented in this paper (see Fig. 2). Assume, a terminal stores containers from different companies and provides them to truck drivers as requested by the owners of the container. First, the truck driver needs to drive to the pick-up location of the terminal. Arrived there, the driver gets the container assigned to her regarding the company the driver is executing the transport for. Second, the driver checks the container she received for several aspects like, for instance, sufficient capacity, special capabilities as cooling means if required, tidiness, and intactness. While the first two mentioned checks are rather guaranteed aspects due to the booking in advance of containers, the two latter aspects are very critical. If any of the checks leads to a negative result, the task `Check container` gets canceled and the corresponding intermediate event is raised. As next step, the driver gets another container, which she checks again. If all checks succeed, the driver can mount the container to her truck and depart from the pick-up location.

To each task, event, and gateway of the process model shown in Fig. 2, a life cycle is assigned that consists of the states and transitions introduced above. For activities, the state transitions *enable*, *begin*, and *terminate* are potentially observable by occurring events. For gateways and events, such state transitions are *enable* and *execute*. In contrast, the disruption of an activity by an attached intermediate event or the skip of an activity due to exclusiveness cannot be observed directly. For instance, the triggering of state transition *disrupt* can only be deduced by observing the execution of that attached event. Potentially, each of these observable transitions is connected to a PEMP [10] used for process observation. However, this does not mean that each observable transition is actually monitored during process execution. Transitions may be excluded from monitoring due to unavailable capturing mechanisms for corresponding event data or due to the stakeholders' interests. For instance, the start of the process is observable when the driver receives the location where she should pick up the container. For activity `Drive to container location`, we receive GPS coordinates that we aggregate to identify when the truck arrived at its destination; i.e., activity termination takes place. In contrast, activity `Check container` cannot be observed, because it is a manual task without any system interaction. Likewise, the intermediate cancellation event cannot be captured, because it is a manual interaction between the driver and the pick-up location worker. However, indirectly, the happening of both can be derived whenever another container is requested. Altogether, we are able to observe at least one state transition for the tasks `Drive to container location`, `Get assigned container`, and `Mount container`, the start and end events as well as the gateway by recognizing events of the event object types specified in the lower part of Fig. 2. Task `Check container` and the attached intermediate cancellation event cannot be observed.

4 Query Generation

Monitoring the execution of a process instance requires CEP queries to recognize state transitions of its given process model. Next, we introduce the algorithm enabling the automatic generation of such queries from a process model with attached Process Event Monitoring Points (PEMPs) as introduced above. This algorithm comprises three main steps which will be explained in detail in the following sections. First, a RPST is created from a given process model (see Section 4.1). The RPST is based on the edges of a process model, but for the actual query generation, we require the nodes. Therefore, in a second step, we transform the RPST into a *component tree* representing the structure of the process model based on nodes (see Section 4.2). Finally, we utilize this component tree and automatically create the CEP queries for the given process model (see Section 4.3).

Fig. 3 illustrates the first two steps of this algorithm for the process model introduced in Section 3 and again shown in Fig. 3a. Fig. 3b depicts its graph used to construct the RPST given in Fig. 3c. The resulting component tree is presented in Fig. 3d and its transformation (resp. step three) to CEP queries in Section 4.3. The implementation for this particular case is given in Section 4.4.

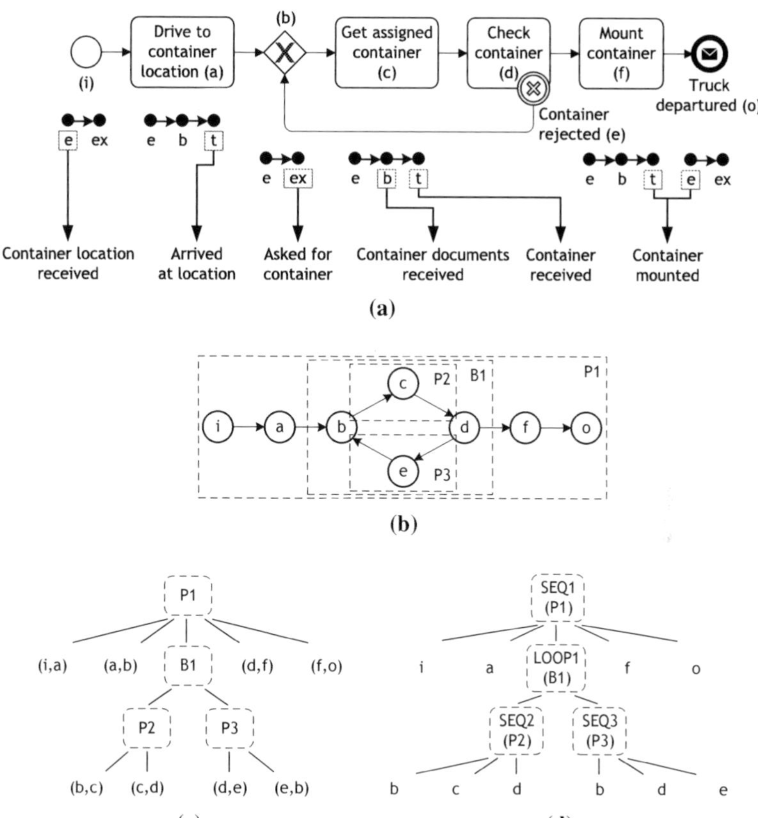

Fig. 3. Scenario as (a) BPMN model, (b) graph, (c) RPST, and (d) component tree

4.1 Creation of the RPST

In order to generate queries from a process model, it is necessary to split the model into smaller parts (sub-graphs). In particular, we use the RPST that decomposes a model respectively the graph into a hierarchy of single-entry / single-exit (SESE) blocks. These SESE blocks have special characteristics as they are canonical fragments. A fragment is canonical if its contained nodes do not overlap with the nodes of another fragment, i.e., the nodes of canonical fragments can either interleave or be disjoint. A formal definition is provided in [17]. Thus, the RPST is a tree which contains the canonical fragments of a graph as tree nodes and the edges between nodes of the graph as tree leaves (see Fig. 3c). Additionally, this decomposition provides special characteristics for the canonical fragments which are derived from the so called triconnected components. Note that each canonical fragment is also a triconnected component each of which being either a bond, a polygon, or a rigid (see [17]).

4.2 Transformation of a RPST to a Component Tree

In the second step, the RPST is transformed into a node-oriented tree, the so called **component tree**. This tree contains a component for every canonical fragment and its leaves are build from the edges of this fragment. For example, Fig. 3d shows that for every canonical fragment (P1, B1, P2 and P3) from the RPST shown in Fig. 3c a component is created in the component tree. The edges of a graph contained in the RPST such as (b, c) and (c, d) for the P2-fragment are then split up into its contained notes b, c and d. These nodes represent the XOR-gateway as well as the `Get assigned container` and the `check container` activity.

Afterwards, we assign a type to every component of the tree. The component types characterize the behavior of the component and are distinguished into *AND*, *XOR*, *Sequence*, *Loop* and *SubProcess*. The assumption of block-structuredness enables an easy mapping of polygons to sequences and bonds to the other mentioned component types. AND, XOR, Sequence, and Loop represent the control flow structure with AND- or XOR-Gateways, while SubProcess indicates an entire subprocess as component. Corresponding to that, the scenario process model contains three components of type Sequence (SEQ1, SEQ2, SEQ3) and one component of type Loop (LOOP1) (see Fig. 3d).

4.3 Query Generation from the Component Tree

Finally, we generate event processing queries from component trees to monitor the execution of a process model. A query is generated for every node in the component tree. Depending on the component types, we generate different types of queries. In addition, we consider the PEMPs of a process model to create queries for state transitions. These *state transition queries* allow to monitor the life cycles of observable process nodes.

A CEP query can be written in any EPL, e.g., Esper [3]. Using an EPL allows to query an *event stream* and use patterns as part of the query to define particular ordering relations among the events and its event types respectively. For demonstration, we used the *Esper Query Language*. The CEP query pattern for the component types and state transitions of BPMN in Esper are summarized in Table 4.3, where $et_1..et_{11} \in \mathcal{ET}$ are the event types that are expected. These event types can be defined in a PEMP. As a subprocess is a specific type of an activity that can contain several other flow nodes and control flows, it is transformed to CEP queries as complement of the other patterns. For example, the process shown in Fig. 2 could be seen as subprocess part of a complete transportation chain including planning and invoicing.

All the queries are ordered and nested according to the fact that they can depend on each other. The triggering of one query can expedite the progress of other queries which are on a higher hierarchy level. While the sequence in which the queries are called is derived from the process-flow, the hierarchy is derived from structure of the component tree. For instance, in Fig. 3d the query for LOOP1 depends on SEQ2 that itself depends on the state transition query for node c. Examples for the implementation of these queries is given in Section 4.4.

Table 1. Esper patterns for query generation

BPMN pattern	Esper pattern
Loop	FROM PATTERN [(EVERY S4=et_1) UNTIL EVERY S5=et_2]
Sequence	FROM PATTERN [(EVERY S0=et_3 $\rightarrow$ EVERY S1=et_4)]
XOR	FROM PATTERN [(EVERY S0=et_5 OR EVERY S1=et_6)]
AND	FROM PATTERN [(EVERY S0=et_7 AND EVERY S1=et_8)]
State transition	FROM PATTERN [(EVERY S0=et_9 $\rightarrow$ EVERY S1=et_{10} $\rightarrow$ EVERY S2=et_{11})][2]

In addition, we support intermediate timer events and intermediate cancel events. An intermediate timer event has a duration from which we generate a *timer query* that waits for the specified time and signals the expiration of the timer duration. Intermediate cancel events are attached to activities and subprocesses. The cancel events can indicate the abortion of the node the cancel event is attached to. Thereby, it is possible to monitor models with expected runtime exceptions.

4.4 Implementation

A process can be monitored based on its process model. We have implemented a service in our Event Processing Platform (EPP) [4, 11][3] which generates the component tree from a process model that includes PEMPs. We provide two combinations for importing process models and defining its PEMPs. First, the business user may import BPMN-specific models and directly adapt the PEMP definitions for specific nodes in the user interface of the EPP. Second, we defined an BPMN extension[4] with which life cycles and PEMPs can be attached to a node in a BPMN model used to derive CEP queries. Thus, process models used in the EPP are specified in the BPMN-conform XML format and include the representation of state transitions of activities, gateways, and events using PEMPs. Finally, we take these annotated models and generate the CEP queries.

In our EPP, each query must be written and registered before the events can be captured and processed. The EPP registers each CEP query in Esper [3] via listeners. These listeners get informed if the query matches observed events with the specified conditions defined by the query. Based on the patterns given in Table 4.3, Listing 1.1 shows the four queries in the Esper query language for our scenario process model in Section 3. These queries are derived from the component tree as described in Sections 4.2 and 4.3. As not every activity is observable the derived queries are restricted to those events that are observable.

---

2 This query depends on the transitions that are observable for a node. In our case, only enable, begin, and terminate are observable.

3 Downloads, tutorials, and further information can be found at: `http://bpt.hpi.uni-potsdam.de/Public/EPP`

4 Due to page limitations, we could not include this definition in the paper but provide it on our website at `http://bpt.hpi.uni-potsdam.de/Public/EPP#BPMN_Extension`

Listing 1.1. Monitoring queries using Esper

```
St1:
SELECT *
FROM PATTERN [(EVERY S0=ContainerDocsReceived -> EVERY S1=ContainerReceived)]
WHERE SetUtils.isIntersectionNotEmpty({S0.ProcessInstances, S1.
      ProcessInstances})

Seq2:
SELECT *
FROM PATTERN [(EVERY S2=AskedForContainer -> EVERY S3=St1)]
WHERE SetUtils.isIntersectionNotEmpty({S2.ProcessInstances, S3.
      ProcessInstances})

Loop1:
SELECT *
FROM PATTERN [(EVERY S4=Seq2) UNTIL EVERY S5=MountContainer]
WHERE SetUtils.isIntersectionNotEmpty({S4.ProcessInstances, S5.
      ProcessInstances})

Seq1:
SELECT *
FROM PATTERN [(EVERY S6=ContainerLocReceived -> EVERY S7=ArrivedAtLocation ->
      EVERY S8=Loop1)]
WHERE SetUtils.isIntersectionNotEmpty({S6.ProcessInstances, S7.ProcessInstances
      , S8.ProcessInstances})
```

At first, the *St1* query monitors the sequence of two monitoring points with the event types of the `Get assigned container` activity. While the definition of the sequential ordering of the events for this query is enclosed in `PATTERN[...]` in the `FROM`-clause, the `WHERE` clause checks whether the events from both event types have occurred for the same process instance. In the *Seq2* query monitors whether the gateway event is followed by the previously defined query (resp. `Get assigned container` activity). Since activity `Check container` as well as the intermediate event `Container rejected` are not observable, the *Loop1* query can only check if *Seq2* is followed by events belonging to the *Mount container* activity. Finally, we can use the *Seq1* to check occurrences of events for process instances executing the process shown in Fig. 2.

It is possible to decouple the query creation from the monitoring part into a separate service module. In this vein, it is possible to generate queries that are independent from a specific EPL. Depending on the EPL used, it might require adaptations. In all cases, it is required to represent the dependencies between the queries and enable the checking of events through the graph of queries. For example, the termination of the *Loop1* query is required for the complete observation of the *Seq1* query and thus the whole process execution.

5 Application

In this section, we exemplarily address three areas of BPM the presented approach can be applied to: (i) monitoring of business process progress, (ii) monitoring of process model deviations, and (iii) calculation of Key Performance Indicators (KPIs).

(i) Through the usage of our approach, it is possible to correlate events in a CEP engine to the nodes of a process model. Therewith, the monitoring of a single process execution can be established. As per the introduced framework, the life cycles for single process nodes and for the components of the process model are observable. Thus, a very detailed status of the execution progress for process instances can be presented. Recognizing an event at a PEMP will predict the actual state of a process execution and its performed activities. For example, when we see the events *Container location received* and *Arrived at location*, we can infer that the activity `Drive to container location` was fully performed.

(ii) Further, based on this monitoring information, deviations from the process model during runtime can be determined. In comparison to the approaches of [18] or [1], we do not create queries to detect deviations, but search for deviations on the basis of the execution status of a process instance. The usage of the component tree allows to determine order relations between the process nodes, which are similar to the order relations defined in [18]. Every time a query is triggered in our approach, a special monitoring component looks for execution deviations. By doing so, it is possible to detect nodes which should be exclusive but were observed together in the same process instance, nodes which should be in a strict sequential order but were monitored deviant to this order, nodes which should be present but were absent during runtime of the process instance, nodes which should occur only once but happened more often, and all execution deviations for nodes which are contained in a loop.

However, the detection of execution deviations for nodes that are part of a loop is limited, because exclusiveness, order, missing, or duplicate violations cannot be distinguished with certainty. For example, assuming activity `Check container` is observable allows to monitor both activities contained in the loop. In case, the trace *A,B,C,D,E,G,G,F*[5] is observed, a loop-deviation is detected. The deviation is monitored, because event *F*, indicating the container was mounted, was monitored only once, whereas the event *G*, indicating the performance of `Check container`, was observed twice. Thus, it is possible that the events *C,D,E* for the XOR join and the activity `Get assigned container` are missing for the second loop iteration or that the second `Check container` activity instance represented by the second event *G* is a duplicate.

(iii) Besides the application of our approach for process monitoring, we can utilize the events relating to a particular PEMP to measure KPIs. We refer to the definition of a KPI as stated in [19]. A KPI is linked to a business goal it is contributing to and has a name and a data type. The KPI definition includes an algorithm that describes how to measure the KPI, a target value, and upper and lower target margins. For KPI measurement, the particular PEMPs can be used in the corresponding algorithm. As described in Section 3, the terminal operator has the business goal to ensure a certain customer satisfaction that is influenced by the duration the drivers need to spend at the terminal to mount a container, for instance. Therefore, a KPI is defined that measures the time between the truck driver getting the information about the location of the assigned container to be mounted (start point of KPI measure) and the truck departure (end point of KPI measure).

---

[5] In accordance to Fig. 2: A is an event of the Event Object Type (EOT) *Container location received*, B is an event of EOT *Arrived at location*, C is an event of EOT *Asked for container*, D is an event of EOT *Container documents received*, E is an event of EOT *Container received*, F is an event of EOT *Container mounted*, and G is the newly introduced event of EOT *Container checked* for monitoring `Check container`.

Referring to the scenario described in Section 3, one can see that the KPI may be influenced by the loop. In case a container is rejected, because of an identified damage for instance, the start point of the KPI measure is passed again. This challenges the measurement of the KPI, because it has to be decided whether the KPI measurement is still valid (start point of the KPI measure is still the first occurrence of the event captured at the beginning of activity `Get assigned container`) or the start point of the KPI measure needs to be reset. This constellation is not trivial to handle, as we cannot observe the entrance into the loop cycle explicitly, because the activity `Check container` nor the event of rejecting the container can be observed. Thus, we cannot differentiate whether the loop was intended as described in the process model and the KPI measure needs to be reset, because the assignment of the container is not in the responsibility of the terminal, or there was another execution of activity `Get assigned container` by mistake or any other reason and the KPI measurement needs to be kept.

6 Related Work

Barros et al. [2] present a set of patterns describing relations and dependencies of events in business processes that have to be captured in process models to observe the overall process context. Their assessment of the modeling languages BPMN and Business Process Execution Language (BPEL) resulted in their language proposal called Business Event Modeling Notation (BEMN) [7], a graphical language for modeling composite events in business processes. BEMN allows to define event rules, e.g., specific combinations of events, that are to be used in stand-alone diagrams or as integration into BPMN. Similarly, Kunz et al. [12] introduce an approach to enhance the creation of CEP queries. In particular, the approach presents how EPL statements can graphically be represented by BPMN elements. In this way, the authors provide a means to model CEP queries with a better usability for business users. Both modeling approaches, in [7] and [12], focus on the representation of CEP in business processes. Complementary, our approach includes a standard-conform extension of BPMN with which we are able to automatically derive CEP queries from process models and not only check the process-flow but also life cycle transitions of nodes via events.

In [1], the authors introduce techniques to automatically generate Esper queries by taking a choreography model as a formalization of the process, however, without including the life cycles of nodes or basing the approach on a specific modeling language. Similar, Weidlich et al. [18] take BPMN models as basis to create EPL statements to monitor process violations only. Both approaches presume complete and structured event logs. Thus, they are not suited for processes that include non-observable events. In our approach the process model must be annotated with PEMPs that bind events to state transitions of BPMN elements as described in [11] first.

In the context of BPM, Dahanayake et al. [5] give an overview of Business Activity Monitoring (BAM) and introduce a four class-categorization of BAM systems all basing on events. Therefore, the approach presented in this paper can be applied to enable BAM techniques and methods to provide valuable monitoring results by using the produced extracted events as input.

7 Conclusion

We combined BPM with CEP to allow model-driven monitoring of business process executions in semi-automated environments. In essence, we can decompose a process model via a graph representation into a RPST, which we then transform into a component tree, which in turn is the basis to derive CEP queries determining the status of an execution. The constructs of a process model being considered for query generation are specified by the stakeholder by attaching PEMPs to nodes of the process model. This allows to specify the activities, events, and decisions to be observed in a process model to especially receive information about happenings the stakeholder is interested in and lowers the effort for creating those perticular queries manually. Further, the specification of PEMPs to nodes of a process model is implemented in an EPP allowing business users to do so without the need to know the technical specialties. In future work, we will apply this approach to process monitoring and analysis tasks in general, e.g., runtime or process cost analysis. Analyzing process event occurrences is another application area the approach can contribute to.

References

1. Baouab, A., Perrin, O., Godart, C.: An Optimized Derivation of Event Queries to Monitor Choreography Violations. In: Liu, C., Ludwig, H., Toumani, F., Yu, Q. (eds.) ICSOC 2012. LNCS, vol. 7636, pp. 222–236. Springer, Heidelberg (2012)
2. Barros, A., Decker, G., Grosskopf, A.: Complex events in business processes. In: Abramowicz, W. (ed.) BIS 2007. LNCS, vol. 4439, pp. 29–40. Springer, Heidelberg (2007)
3. Bernhardt, T., Vasseur, A.: Esper: Event stream processing and correlation. O'Reilly Media (2007), published at `http://onjava.com/`
4. Bülow, S., Backmann, M., Herzberg, N., Hille, T., Meyer, A., Ulm, B., Wong, T.Y., Weske, M.: Monitoring of Business Processes with Complex Event Processing. In: BPM Workshops. Springer (2013) (accepted for publication)
5. Dahanayake, A., Welke, R., Cavalheiro, G.: Improving the Understanding of BAM Technology for Real-time Decision Support. IJBIS 7(1), 1–26 (2011)
6. Daum, M., Götz, M., Domaschka, J.: Integrating CEP and BPM: how CEP realizes functional requirements of BPM applications (industry article). In: DEBS, pp. 157–166 (2012)
7. Decker, G., Grosskopf, A., Barros, A.: A graphical notation for modeling complex events in business processes. In: EDOC, pp. 27–36. IEEE (2007)
8. EsperTech: Esper - Complex Event Processing, `http://esper.codehaus.org` (as of May 2013)
9. Etzion, O., Niblett, P.: Event Processing in Action. Manning Publications Co. (2011)
10. Herzberg, N., Kunze, M., Rogge-Solti, A.: Towards Process Evaluation in Non-automated Process Execution Environments. In: Services and Their Composition, ZEUS (2012)
11. Herzberg, N., Meyer, A., Weske, M.: An Event Processing Platform for Business Process Management. In: EDOC. IEEE (2013) (accepted for publication)
12. Kunz, S., Fickinger, T., Prescher, J., Spengler, K.: Managing Complex Event Processes with Business Process Modeling Notation. In: Mendling, J., Weidlich, M., Weske, M. (eds.) BPMN 2010. LNBIP, vol. 67, pp. 78–90. Springer, Heidelberg (2010)
13. Luckham, D.: The Power of Events: An Introduction to Complex Event Processing in Distributed Enterprise Systems. Addison-Wesley (2002)
14. OMG: Business Process Model and Notation (BPMN), Version 2.0 (2011)

15. Rozsnyai, S., Lakshmanan, G.T., Muthusamy, V., Khalaf, R., Duftler, M.J.: Business Process Insight: An Approach and Platform for the Discovery and Analysis of End-to-End Business Processes. In: 2012 Annual of the SRII Global Conference (SRII), pp. 80–89. IEEE (2012)
16. van der Aalst, W.M.P., ter Hofstede, A.H.M., Weske, M.: Business process management: A survey. In: van der Aalst, W.M.P., ter Hofstede, A.H.M., Weske, M. (eds.) BPM 2003. LNCS, vol. 2678, pp. 1–12. Springer, Heidelberg (2003)
17. Vanhatalo, J., Völzer, H., Koehler, J.: The Refined Process Structure Tree. Data & Knowledge Engineering 68(9), 793–818 (2009)
18. Weidlich, M., Ziekow, H., Mendling, J., Günther, O., Weske, M., Desai, N.: Event-Based Monitoring of Process Execution Violations. In: Rinderle-Ma, S., Toumani, F., Wolf, K. (eds.) BPM 2011. LNCS, vol. 6896, pp. 182–198. Springer, Heidelberg (2011)
19. Weske, M.: Business Process Management: Concepts, Languages, Architectures, 2nd edn. Springer (2012)

Enabling Semantic Complex Event Processing in the Domain of Logistics*

Tobias Metzke[1], Andreas Rogge-Solti[1], Anne Baumgrass[1], Jan Mendling[2], and Mathias Weske[1]

[1] Hasso Plattner Institute at the University of Potsdam, Germany
tobias.metzke@student.hpi.uni-potsdam.de
{firstname.lastname}@hpi.uni-potsdam.de
[2] Institute for Information Business at Vienna University of Economics and Business, Austria
jan.mendling@wu.ac.at

Abstract. During the execution of business processes, companies generate vast amounts of events, which makes it hard to detect meaningful process information that could be used for process analysis and improvement. Complex event processing (CEP) can help in this matter by providing techniques for continuous analysis of events. The consideration of domain knowledge can increase the performance of reasoning tasks but it is different for each domain and depends on the requirements of these domains. In this paper, an existing approach of combining CEP and ontological knowledge is applied to the domain of logistics. We show the benefits of semantic complex event processing (SCEP) for logistics processes along the specific use case of tracking and tracing goods and processing related events. In particular, we provide a novel domain-specific function that allows to detect meaningful events for a transportation route. For the demonstration, a prototypical implementation of a system enabling SCEP queries is introduced and analyzed in an experiment.

1 Introduction

The enterprise system landscape has significantly changed in the last decade. Sensors are increasingly used to track objects via Global Positioning System (GPS), measure temperature, energy consumption and other types of data. Sensors provide this data in event streams. An event, in general, is something that happens or occurs and might change the current state of a system [1].

For the detection of complex and meaningful patterns in event streams, users can rely on different event operators and temporal relationships that are provided by *Complex Event Processing (CEP)* technology [1]. The enrichment of event streams with high-level knowledge is required for handling the context in which the stream data is interpreted and analyzed [2]. At present, research in this area

* The research leading to these results has received funding from the European Union's Seventh Framework Programme (FP7/2007-2013) under grant agreement 318275 (GET Service).

A.R. Lomuscio et al. (Eds.): ICSOC 2013 Workshops, LNCS 8377, pp. 419–431, 2014.
© Springer International Publishing Switzerland 2014

has formed the term of *Semantic Complex Event Processing (SCEP)* [2,3,4]. There are prototypes combining ontological knowledge with CEP techniques, dealing with specific domains like smart grids, advanced facility management and stock markets. The domain of logistics, however, has not been covered by these considerations yet. In logistics, considerable amounts of event-based data are produced, e.g. traffic and weather information [5]. These data are relevant for logistics processes to ensure timely transport of goods [5,6]. Besides the events that occur directly on the planned routes, also events in geographical proximity of planned routes can affect logistics processes. For example, you might want to circumnavigate congestions, flooded areas, or other dangerous regions in safe distance.

In this paper, we address the need for domain-specific event operators to serve logistics scenarios. Thereby, this paper makes the following contributions. First, the usage of domain-specific knowledge in form of an ontology for CEP is shown for the logistics domain. To use the DBpedia as a top-level ontology[1] only minor extensions where necessary. Second, we use SCEP to implement a novel logistics-specific built-in function. This function is able to consider geo-spatial distance and, thus, support the special requirements of logistics processes for CEP query creation. In this way, our contribution can serve as a basis for a convenient routing, re-routing and transportation of goods in the domain of logistics. To demonstrate the applicability of the approach, we implemented a lightweight SCEP prototype. This prototype is used in an evaluative experiment to illustrate the effectiveness of the proposed concepts.

The remainder of this paper is structured as follows: Section 2 provides an overview of the characteristics of CEP in the domain of logistics and introduces several use cases. Section 3 outlines the general approach taken for the inclusion of ontological knowledge in CEP and explains the mechanisms that allow for semantic querying in logistics. Based on the SCEP concepts, Section 4 presents the logistic-specific adaption for identifying transportation-related events. Following, Section 5 depicts the details of the prototypical implementation of the approach before Section 6 evaluates the general benefits and shortcomings of it. Section 7 then summarizes research related to the presented approach. This work concludes with Section 8, summarizing the work done and providing an outlook on future steps.

2 Usage of SCEP in Logistics

An important use case in the logistics domain is *track and trace* [5,6]. Logistics service providers (LSPs) monitor their means of transportation like trucks, ships, and containers on their respective routes worldwide. LSPs depend on the detection of relevant complex events from numerous data sources. In particular, events from external sources need to be correlated to the respective routes and transportation means.

[1] See `http://dbpedia.org/About`

Weather events like floods and storms as well as road blockages can have an impact on transporation routes. Therefore, events located near these routes can affect the schedule of a transportation plan. Thus, LSPs need to detect those events to be able to react appropriately and timely. The more information an LSP gains on such events, the more precise its reaction can be. To this end, complex event queries can be constructed to listen to event streams. Without external knowledge, however, it is inconvenient to construct queries that capture the necessary information for such scenarios. More specifically, query designers would need to know the characteristics of all the routes that the LSP's trucks, ships, or containers are on. These specifics could include knowledge about the waypoints on the routes, the overall lengths of the routes as well as the time needed to complete them. This hampers convenient and efficient query creation for this and more complex use cases. Therefore, CEP engines that are used in logistics should make use of background knowledge.

SCEP engines [3,7,8] provide knowledge to query designers in a convenient way, by abstracting from domain-specific complexities. Furthermore, semantic technologies enable automatic normalization of event stream sources by semantic annotation. With ontological background knowledge, a query designer can conveniently create high-level queries that capture relevant information, instead of having to cope with stream source specifics. Section 3 provides further information on how semantically rich CEP queries can be written and how they are evaluated.

3 Querying Semantic Events

Semantic CEP querying on event streams allows for the combination of CEP and semantic web technologies. The user defines queries, in this case *semantic queries*, which are registered in a *semantic CEP engine*. Incoming event streams are monitored by this engine and evaluated against the defined user queries with the help of *ontological background knowledge* and CEP capabilities. The results of these evaluations are gathered and the user is informed about the matching queries. The model of semantic events is introduced in Section 3.1. In Section 3.2, the structure of SCEP queries and their difference to CEP queries is given. Afterwards, the process of *semantic querying* is explained in Section 3.3.

3.1 Semantic Event Model

In order to integrate semantics in CEP queries, Zhou et al. [9] propose a *semantic event model* that captures event attributes, their semantics, domain entities and the relations between them. This model describes how event attributes are matched to semantic entities and linked to external knowledge bases in order to enrich the information of the events. In the end, incoming *raw events* (e.g. lightweight data tuples) are transformed into *semantic events* (graph-based data, see Fig. 1) that point into existing ontologies. Such ontologies comprise entities, literals and links between them. The resulting graph structure

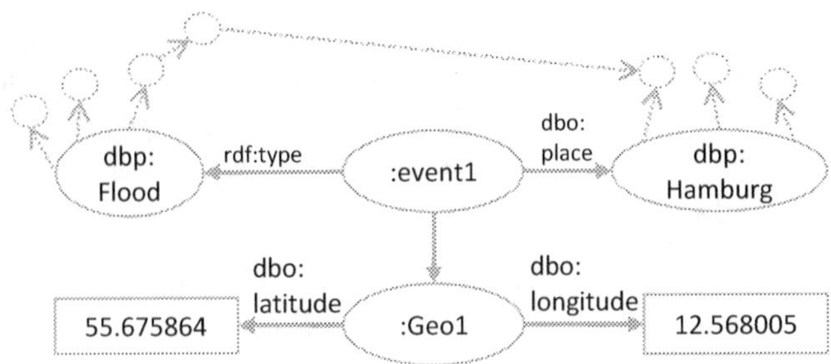

Fig. 1. A semantic event dynamically created from the raw event in Listing 1.1

allows for graph-specific queries and algorithms to be applied on the information stored. There have been several approaches to introduce a common logistics domain-ontology [10,11]. However, common knowledge ontologies (or top-level ontologies) like the DBpedia include most of the transportation-related entities already. Minor extensions to this knowledge base are provided in the paper where necessary.

With the help of semantic events, semantic queries can be defined that make use of knowledge in ontologies events are linked to. For example, the *raw event* shown in Listing 1.1 is a flood warning for Hamburg, a city in Germany. Such an event can be dynamically annotated either with the help of semantic annotation techniques [12] or static mapping files that are maintained for specific event streams [3]. The resulting *semantic event* is shown in Fig. 1. It references entities from the underlying DBpedia ontology like *dbp:Flood* and *dbp:Hamburg*. The *dbo* namespace describes all DBpedia ontology predicates and some basic classes while the *dbp* namespace primarily describes entities that have a Wikipedia website. Thus, the event is linked to all the knowledge available for these two entities in that ontology, indicated by the dotted circles and arrows. SCEP queries can then use these connections and work with knowledge the event itself does not provide but it is linked to.

Listing 1.1. An incoming raw event with a list of string-based key-value pairs

```
[ ('type', 'FloodWarning'), ('city', 'Hamburg'), ('location','52.181701 11.600692')]
```

3.2 Semantic Event Queries

Based on the semantic event model, a basic structure for semantic queries can be introduced. These SCEP queries start with a traditional CEP pattern and can further be specified by a semantic part as shown in Listing 1.2.

Listing 1.2. Structure of a semantic query

```
SCEP Query ::=
  [PREFIX <namespace>]
  [CEP Subpattern ::=
   SELECT <event*, attribute*, aggregation*>
    FROM <input stream AS event>*
    (WHERE <relational constraints>)?
    (SEQ <event, event, ...>)?
    (WINDOW <window specifications>)?]
  [Semantic Subpattern ::=
    {(<subject URI> <predicate URI> <object URI|Literal>.)*}]
```

First, the *CEP subpattern* specifies the temporal and relational constraints of events based on their attributes. The CEP subpattern consists of the traditional *SELECT* and *FROM* statements specifying the data stream and the projection of attributes and aggregations the query returns. The *event* specified in this pattern will be passed on to the semantic subpattern upon evaluation process of an incoming event. The *where*, *sequence* and *window* selectors are optional and help to further specify the query. The CEP subpattern does not directly correspond to one existing CEP language definition but rather generalizes common features of several ones [8,13].

Second, the *semantic subpattern* places semantic constraints over events and their associated domain entities [3]. Semantic patterns are written in SPARQL[2] triple notation. The pattern is a list of statements that comprise a subject, a predicate, and an object. While the subject and predicate have to be given by an uniform resource identifier (URI), the object can be either defined by an URI or a literal (e.g. a *string*, an *integer*, or any other data type) (see Listing 1.2).

Following the example use case of Section 2 and the event described in Listing 1.1 and Fig. 1, a query following the SCEP pattern is shown in Listing 1.3. This specific query asks for the given event type and its geographical location, if it contains information about the city of *Hamburg* in Germany and warns about a flood.

Listing 1.3. An example for a SCEP query

```
PREFIX dbo: <http://dbpedia.org/ontology/>
PREFIX dbp: <http://dbpedia.org/resource/>
SELECT type, location
FROM WorldWeatherStream as $event
{$event dbo:place ?city.
$event rdf:type dbp:Flood.
filter(?city = dbp:Hamburg)}
```

[2] See http://www.w3.org/TR/sparql11-query/

The query in Listing 1.3 basically works with information that is present in the event itself and has simply been transferred into an ontology. Furthermore, a SCEP query can work with data that is not provided by the event directly. For example, the population of a city the event happens at could be taken into account, although it is not provided by the event itself (see Listing 1.4).

3.3 Semantic CEP Querying

In order to semantically evaluate incoming events, they have to be transformed into semantic events (see Section 3.1) and evaluated with the help of registered semantic queries (see Section 3.2). More specifically, the semantic subpatterns of the semantic queries are used for the semantic evaluation. Therefore, the semantic part is transformed into a SPARQL ASK query[3], as shown in Listing 1.4.

Listing 1.4. An example ASK query

```
PREFIX dbo: <http://dbpedia.org/ontology/>
ASK {$event dbo:place ?city.
?city dbo:populationTotal ?population.
filter(?population > 1500000)}
```

In general, these queries return either *True* or *False* upon evaluation. The evaluation workflow of the given query displayed in Listing 1.4 for the event shown in Fig. 1 would be the following:

1. *Hamburg* is saved into the variable *?city*
2. The related total population (*1,796,077*) of this *?city* is read from the knowledge base, here DBpedia, and is saved into the variable *?population*
3. The value of the *?population* is compared to the specified *1.5 million*
4. The *?population* is higher than 1.5 million that is why the query returns *True*, otherwise it would have returned *False*. If the *?city* would not have a *population* value in the DBpedia ontology, the *?population* variable would be empty and the query would return *False*.

As the semantic subpattern query for the example event in Listing 1.1 returns *True*, it passes the event to a CEP evaluation module. In this module, the CEP subpattern is evaluated for the event in the traditional CEP manner. If the criteria of the CEP subpattern are fulfilled, the user is informed of a match with his SCEP query. Details on how this is prototypically implemented are described in Section 5.

4 Identifying Transportation-Related Events via SCEP

In the domain of logistics, the locality of events and their distance to transportation routes are of special interest, as these events might be relevant to the

[3] See `http://www.w3.org/TR/sparql11-query/#ask`

transportation plan and its execution (e.g., a flood event in a nearby location could affect the transportation plan). We assume that a transportation route is stored in an ontology consisting of route segments that have a start and an end point, which in turn are places with geographical coordinates (in latitude and longitude format). We want to determine, whether an event is in a given distance to a route (i.e., whether it is relevant for transportation). Each route segment can be checked independently. An event is transportation-relevant, if it is nearby at least one segment. Fig. 2 shows three methods that determine whether an event is relevant for a route. These methods were selected due to the simplicity of their calculation and are described as follows.

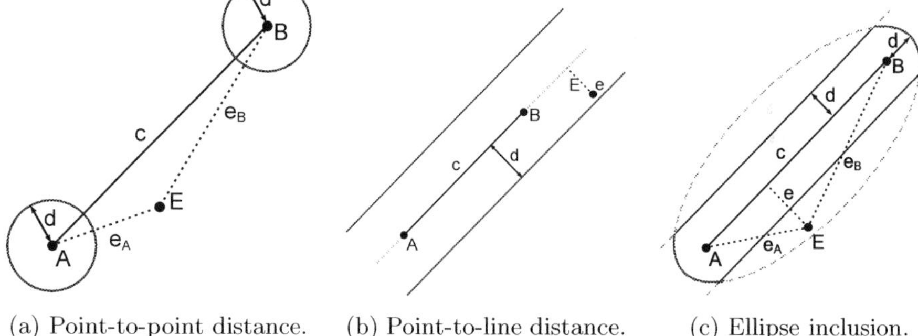

(a) Point-to-point distance. (b) Point-to-line distance. (c) Ellipse inclusion.

Fig. 2. Three different ways of finding nearby events (E) to a route (A, B). (a) Distance between two points. (b) Distance of a point to a line. (c) Ellipse inclusion and distance of a point to a line.

Distance between two points. The event is considered transportation-related, if the location of the event is closer to any of the points on the route than a defined distance d. Assuming that the geographical points on the route are dense, the error introduced by this simple solution can be acceptable. However, as Fig. 2a shows, if the distance between the points on the route is high compared to d, a relevant event E lying between two route points might not be detected.

Distance of a point to a line. The event is considered transportation-related, if the location of the event is closer to the line between two consecutive points on a route than distance d. However, as Fig. 2b highlights, events that are close enough to the line between two points are marked as relevant even if the events are too far away from the two points on that line.

Ellipse inclusion. An event is considered transportation-related, if it lies within the ellipse spanned by the two points and the defined distance d with the formula $a + b < c + 2 * d$, and if the distance of the event's location to the line between the two route points is less than distance d (cf. previous method). The addition of the ellipse constraint ensures that we do not include events far from the route segments.

With current CEP querying, the task to find transportation-related events to a route would require the query designer to know all the relevant transportation plans, the geographical points on these plans and their order on the route. He could then compute the distance according to the before mentioned methods. Although the approach introduced by Zhou et al. [3] provides the knowledge about transportation plans and their segments in a convenient way, a user would still have to manually create a query that computes the distance of an event to any of the segments in the transportation plans.

Therefore, the presented approach can be extended by a convenient built-in function that serves exactly this purpose. A query example with the built-in function is shown in Listing 1.5. As displayed, users can filter for specific event types like *floods* and define, at what distance to the route they are to be included. The example sets a distance threshold of 50km for floods nearby the transportation route of plan *LSP_1*. In practice, domain experts need to determine distance thresholds for the inclusion of events.

Listing 1.5. Usage of the built-in function `nearby` provided by the prototype

```
PREFIX dbo: <http://dbpedia.org/ontology/>
PREFIX dbp: <http://dbpedia.org/resource/>
PREFIX logistics: <http://example.org/logistics#>
SELECT type, location
FROM WorldWeatherStream as $event
{$event rdf:type dbp:Flood.
$event dbo:place ?location.
logistics:LSP_1 dbo:plan ?plan.
filter($nearby(?location, ?plan, 50))}
```

On query registration, the query is automatically translated to a more complex query including the necessary distance calculations[4]. Note that the rewritten query comprises more than forty additional lines of SPARQL code in that example. A query designer without the proposed method based on SCEP would have to manually write that amount of additional code to enable the search of nearby events for transportation plans. Our generated queries are less error-prone, as they are generated from a shorter – and therefore, more understandable – query. Furthermore, queries are also less error-prone, since the code is generated automatically and individual mistakes can be avoided. Besides, once the improved calculation of nearby search is implemented with the built-in method `nearby`, all queries using the method benefit from that improvement automatically.

5 Implementation/Architecture

The concepts introduced in the previous sections were implemented in a prototype[5] based on *Python*[6] for server-side implementation and *JavaScript* on the

[4] The rewritten query stub can be found at `http://bpt.hpi.uni-potsdam.de/pub/Public/EPP/nearby_function.txt`

[5] Instructions and downloads are available at: `http://bpt.hpi.uni-potsdam.de/Public/EPP#Semantic_Extension`

[6] See `http://www.python.org/`

client side. The prototype , depicted in Fig. 3, provides a client-server architecture, serving a web interface that can be accessed through a common web browser. In Fig. 3, the web interface is marked in gray, denoting that it has been exchanged or added compared to the initial architecture, provided by Zhou et al. [3]. This holds for all other components that are depicted in out architecture as well. The SCEP engine includes an Resource Description Framework (RDF) Server, namely *Virtuoso RDF Triple Store*[7] which holds the ontologies necessary for the use cases of the logistics domain mentioned before. It allows for querying these ontologies through a web interface as well as programmatically. The semantic engine is build around an existing CEP engine further described by Herzberg et al. [14]. The CEP engine supports simple filtering, sequence and aggregation patterns over event streams. It also allows for sliding time window aggregations. It offers a web interface as well, allowing for the registration of queries as well as the sending of events. The prototype we developed in this paper provides additional semantic filtering functionality around the CEP engine in order to enable SCEP querying on incoming event streams. These additional modules, shown in Fig. 3, serve the following purposes:

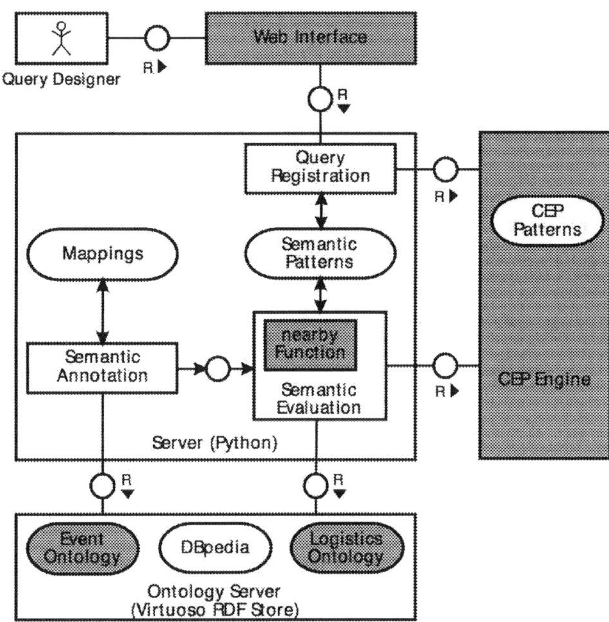

Fig. 3. Architectural Component Overview

The Query Registration module processes the user queries entered through the web interface of the SCEP engine. They are split into their semantic and their CEP pattern, the latter of them is registered in the CEP engine for

[7] See `http://virtuoso.openlinksw.com/dataspace/doc/dav/wiki/Main/VOSTriple`

CEP evaluation later on. The semantic subpattern is stored in the server, shown in the interface and evaluated on incoming event streams that match the defined stream source in the CEP subpattern part.

The Ontological Library holds the defined knowledge bases in OWL[8] format. They capture the relations between semantic entities and rules defined for them. Events are linked into these ontologies by pointing to any of their entities. The *Event Ontology* reflects the *semantic event model* mentioned before.

The Semantic Annotation module materializes semantic events from incoming raw events arriving on a registered event stream source. Mapping files describe the correlation between input event attributes and the semantic event properties and entities. These mapping files can be static, direct mappings or dynamic mapping files that use semantic annotation techniques in order to find the best matching semantic properties and entities for incoming event attributes. For the prototype, the direct mappings are implemented.

The Semantic Evaluation module processes incoming semantic events and evaluates them according to the workflow shown in Section 3.3. Therefore, the registered semantic subpatterns that match the stream source of the incoming event are evaluated for it with the help of the RDF Server. If a semantic subpattern evaluates to *True* , the raw event associated to the semantic event is passed on to the CEP Engine where the event is evaluated with the corresponding CEP pattern of the semantic subpattern.

Finally, the CEP engine evaluates the passed raw events and performs the actions registered in the CEP pattern when identifying a pattern match. For performance reasons, if no registered semantic subpatterns associated to the event's stream exist, the raw events are not semantically annotated but passed on to the CEP engine directly.

6 Experiment

The prototype presented in this paper basically relies on the concepts introduced by Zhou et al. [3] and would therefore yield no new insights concerning event throughput performance. However, the built-in function for nearby search serving as a logistics specific extension may introduce new computational complexity.

Therefore, the median response time of a query similar to the one depicted in Listing 1.5 was measured with the help of the prototype introduced in Section 5. The evaluation routes where given by a list of real-world transportation routes containing different numbers of geographical points describing them. The different routes contain 4, 8, 36, 187, 201, 388, 744, 1520, 3040, 6080, 12160, 24320, 48640, and 97280 points, where 97280 points can describe a route of approximately 16,000 kilometers with a GPS coordinate for every 170 meters. All routes were stored in the Virtuoso Server in RDF triple format. For every route,

[8] See `http://www.w3.org/2004/OWL/`

a query evaluating incoming events against the route was registered in the prototype. Only one query was registered at a time in the system in order to avoid dependencies between the response times of the queries. Each query was then evaluated three times with a set of 400 randomly created events which were fed into the system sequentially. The average of the measured response times builds the final value for every query.

Fig. 4 displays the behavior of a query containing a nearby search. The response times themselves are rather high compared to the prototype build by Zhou et al. [3] due to the client-server architecture of the prototype (see Section 5). The nearby search query however indicates a linear relationship between points on the route and the response time of the query. When doubling the number of points on the transportation route from 48,640 to 97,280, the response time grows by a factor of approximately 1.6. Thus, the overhead produced by a nearby search can be well estimated and stays in a feasible range when increasing the accuracy by introducing more points along a route. Further work on decreasing the complexity while preserving the accuracy of the nearby search could yield better results concerning computational overhead in the future.

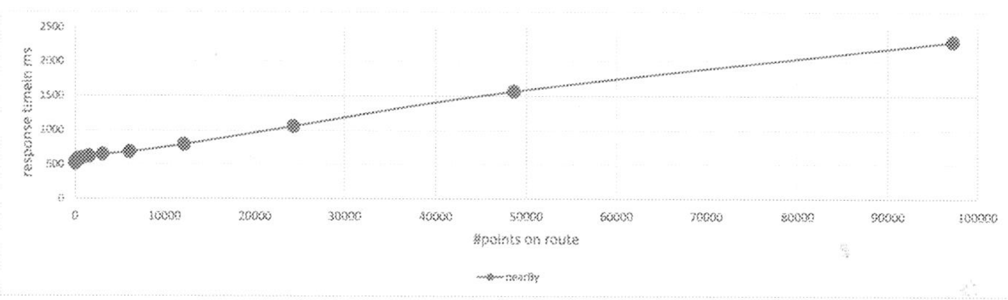

Fig. 4. Response time of a query containing the *nearBy* function for different numbers of points on a transportation route

7 Related Work

Recently, the fusion of complex event processing with semantic background knowledge as presented in this paper has been widely researched [2,3,8,15,16]. Anicic et al. [17] proposed EP-SPARQL, an extension of the SPARQL language that allows to process streams of data that are temporally related. They introduced new language constructs that allow for queries not only on stored background knowledge but also the time relations between incoming events. With ETALIS, Anicic et al. [8] provided a rule-based deductive system that acts as a semantic event processing engine and uses EP-SPARQL. Event queries are written in SPARQL and enriched by the temporal operators introduced in EP-SPARQL. All background knowledge and event queries are transformed into Prolog rules and executed in a Prolog engine. While this approach is independent from existing, traditional CEP engines, the approach presented in this paper leverages their expressibility and performance.

Teymourian et al. [7] proposed a modular ontology model and architectural vision for SCEP. In their architecture, the semantic knowledge base includes ontologies and inferencing rules. They use a rule-based engine in order to process the incoming event data and to evaluate the user queries. However, they do not leverage existing CEP engines and their expertise and performance in the field of event processing. Zhou et al. [3] built on the architectural model shown in [7], employing a state of the art CEP engine instead of a rule-based engine and extending the approach by the ability to evaluate historical event data as well. They enable semantic event queries that can evaluate past, present, and future event data. The approach presented in this paper builds on the proposed architecture, event model, and query definitions. It explores the applicability of the given approach for the domain of logistics, uses a recently build CEP engine and extends the given approach by logistics specific ontologies and a built-in function.

The need for special functionality in the domain of logistics originates in the typical use cases of this domain like *tracking and tracing*. It has been introduced by van Dorp [5] and Shamsuzzoha et al. [6], highlighting the benefits and possibilities of real-time monitoring of transportations for the domain of logistics. The presented approach employs an example from the tracking and tracing use cases and outlines the effectiveness and expressibility of semantic CEP queries in this domain.

In order to work on semantic background knowledge, it has to be provided in the form of ontological knowledge. Approaches by Lian et al. [10] and Hoxha et al. [11] have introduced how such ontologies can be established and which concepts are relevant in the domain of logistics. The work presented in this paper bases on concepts introduced in the DBpedia ontology like companies, means of transportation, and geographical regions. The necessary extension points for this ontology to work in the domain of logistics are minimal, this is why no logistics specific ontology was used in the presented approach. However, more complex use cases may imply the use of a specific ontology rather than a top-level ontology like the DBpedia.

8 Conclusion

In this paper, the applicability of SCEP for the domain of logistics is evaluated. The presented approach clearly shows that the use of domain-specific knowledge in logistics can lead to expressive and convenient CEP query creations. As shown, typical logistics use cases can benefit from the capabilities provided by semantic web technologies with only a few adaption when it comes to semantic event processing. The paper also introduces a prototype that leverages the advantages of an existing CEP engine. Furthermore, the work outlines a novel built-in functionality for logistics based on event query rewriting which can easily be integrated in any similar SCEP approach. Nonetheless, the use of domain-specific knowledge also introduces computational overhead compared to state of the art CEP which has to be tackled by efficient implementations and caching mechanisms. Future work will focus on further logistics use cases and their characteristics and needs in terms of CEP. Beyond that, the applicability of other approaches to the logistics domain needs to be evaluated.

References

1. Luckham, D.C.: The Power of Events. Addison-Wesley (2002)
2. Teymourian, K., Rohde, M., Paschke, A.: Fusion of Background Knowledge and Streams of Events. In: Proc. of the 6th ACM International Conference on Distributed Event-Based Systems (DEBS), pp. 302–313 (2012)
3. Zhou, Q., Simmhan, Y., Prasanna, V.: SCEPter: Semantic Complex Event Processing over End-to-end Data Flows. Technical report, Technical Report 12-926. Computer Science Department, University of Southern California (2012)
4. Walavalkar, O.B.: Streaming Knowledge Bases. ProQuest (2007)
5. Van Dorp, K.J.: Tracking and Tracing: A Structure for Development and Contemporary Practices. Logistics Information Management 15(1), 24–33 (2002)
6. Shamsuzzoha, A., Helo, P.T.: Real-time Tracking and Tracing System: Potentials for the Logistics Network. In: Proceedings of the 2011 International Conference on Industrial Engineering and Operations Management, pp. 22–24 (2011)
7. Teymourian, K., Paschke, A.: Enabling Knowledge-based Complex Event Processing. In: Proc. of the 2010 EDBT/ICDT Workshops, vol. 37, pp. 1–37. ACM (2010)
8. Anicic, D., Rudolph, S., Fodor, P., Stojanovic, N.: Stream Reasoning and Complex Event Processing in ETALIS. Semantic Web 3(4), 397–407 (2012)
9. Zhou, Q., Simmhan, Y., Prasanna, V.: Towards an Inexact Semantic Complex Event Processing Framework. In: Proc. of the 5th ACM International Conference on Distributed Event-based Systems (DEBS), pp. 401–402 (2011)
10. Lian, P., Park, D.W., Kwon, H.C.: Design of Logistics Ontology for Semantic Representing of Situation in Logistics. In: Proc. of the 2nd Workshop on Digital Media and its Application in Museum & Heritages, pp. 432–437. IEEE (2007)
11. Hoxha, J., Scheuermann, A., Bloehdorn, S.: An Approach to Formal and Semantic Representation of Logistics Services. In: Proc. of the Workshop on Artificial Intelligence and Logistics (AILog), pp. 73–78 (2010)
12. Kiryakov, A., Popov, B., Terziev, I., Manov, D., Ognyanoff, D.: Semantic Annotation, Indexing, and Retrieval. Web Semantics: Science, Services and Agents on the World Wide Web 2(1) (2011)
13. Demers, A., Gehrke, J., Panda, B., Riedewald, M., Sharma, V., White, W.M., et al.: Cayuga: A General Purpose Event Monitoring System. In: CIDR (2007)
14. Herzberg, N., Meyer, A., Weske, M.: An Event Processing Platform for Business Process Management. In: Proc. of the 17th IEEE International EDOC Conference (2013)
15. Crapo, A., Wang, X., Lizzi, J., Larson, R.: The Semantically Enabled Smart Grid. In: Proc. of the Grid-Interop Forum, vol. 2009, pp. 177–185 (2009)
16. Barbieri, D.F., Braga, D., Ceri, S., Grossniklaus, M.: An Execution Environment for C-SPARQL Queries. In: Proc. of the 13th International Conference on Extending Database Technology, pp. 441–452. ACM (2010)
17. Anicic, D., Fodor, P., Rudolph, S., Stojanovic, N.: EP-SPARQL: A Unified Language for Event Processing and Stream Reasoning. In: Proc. of the 20th International Conference on World Wide Web, pp. 635–644. ACM (2011)

Towards Self-adaptation Planning for Complex Service-Based Systems

Azlan Ismail[1] and Valeria Cardellini[2]

[1] Faculty of Computer and Mathematical Sciences
Universiti Teknologi MARA (UiTM), Malaysia
azlanismail@tmsk.uitm.edu.my

[2] Department of Civil Engineering and Computer Science Engineering
University of Roma Tor Vergata, Italy
cardellini@ing.uniroma2.it

Abstract. A complex service-based system (CSBS), which comprises a multi-layer structure possibly spanning multiple organizations, operates in a highly dynamic and heterogeneous environment. At run time the quality of service provided by a CSBS may suddenly change, so that violations of the Service Level Agreements (SLAs) established within and across the boundaries of organizations can occur. Hence, a key management choice is to design the CSBS as a self-adaptive system, so that it can properly plan adaptation decisions to maintain the overall quality defined in the SLAs. However, the challenge in planning the CSBS adaptation is the uncertainty effect of adaptation actions that can variously affect the multiple layers of the CSBS. In a dynamic and constantly evolving environment, there is no guarantee that the adaptation action taken at a given layer can have an overall positive effect. Furthermore, the complexity of the cross-layer interactions makes the decision making process a non-trivial task. In this paper, we address the problem by proposing a multi-layer adaptation planning with local and global adaptation managers. The local manager is associated with a single planning model, while the global manager is associated with a multiple planning model. Both planning models are based on Markov Decision Processes (MDPs) that provide a suitable technique to model decisions under uncertainty. We present an example of scenario to show the practicality of the proposed approach.

Keywords: Self-adaptation, Adaptation planning, Cross-layer services, Markov Decision Process.

1 Introduction

Service-based systems are becoming increasingly complex (also called CSBS) due to their multi-layer structure and the heterogeneous and dynamic execution environment in which they operate [14]. The multi-layer structure of CSBS is referred to the application, platform, and infrastructure layers. The application layer consists of the composite software services to fulfill the business process

A.R. Lomuscio et al. (Eds.): ICSOC 2013 Workshops, LNCS 8377, pp. 432–444, 2014.
© Springer International Publishing Switzerland 2014

activities. The platform layer provides the computing platforms to execute and manage services, while the infrastructure service layer provides the resources (computing, storage, network) to provision software services. These layers are inter-related to fulfill the CSBS's goals. The complexity of CSBS imposes challenges in managing its lifecycle in a multi-cloud environment [2], where multiple Clouds can be used in a concomitant way to offer the service and each of the CSBS layers may be deployed by different Cloud providers.

Self-adaptation in autonomic computing [13] is the prominent paradigm to manage and maintain the quality of service (QoS) of CSBS. The key idea of self-adaptation is to introduce the IBM's MAPE (Monitor, Analyze, Plan, Execute) loop into the system. The self-adaptation goal is to alleviate the software management efforts in managing highly changing and evolving environments. During run-time, the monitoring component observes the CSBS behavior and detects or predicts any problematic situation such as failures and SLA violations [22]. If a problematic condition is detected, the analysis component analyzes the situation to discover more information such as the impact, or the cause of the failure. Then, the planning component decides the appropriate adaptation strategies to be undertaken by the execution component.

The Quality of Service (QoS) of CSBS needs to be maintained during runtime. The QoS characteristics are specified in an agreement known as Service Level Agreement (SLA), which contains the contractual service levels to be met by the services of each layer. The self-adaptation framework can utilize the multiple SLA information [7] to maintain the QoS of CSBS. The monitoring component can use the contractual information to observe, detect, and predict any SLA violation. The analysis component can use the contractual and the observed information to discover new information, such as the impact region [10]. The planning component can use the discovered information to decide about appropriate adaptation strategies, such as which layer to be adapted and what kind of adaptation action to be executed.

Planning and deciding the appropriate adaptation actions are challenging research problems. There are two core factors, namely, the complexity of CSBS and the uncertainty effect, which need to be taken into consideration at the same time. In general, there are several sources of uncertainty, such as those discussed in the context of service delivery [20] and self-adaptive software systems [8]. Herein, the uncertainty effect refers to the CSBS state as a result of executing the adaptation actions. Meanwhile, the complexity refers to the multi-layer interactions among services and the CSBS dynamism. These factors demand a robust adaptation planning and failing to consider these factors may cause a failure in maintaining the overall QoS of CSBS.

This paper contributes to twofolds. First, a conceptual framework of multi-layer self-adaptive service-based system. The uniqueness of the framework is the decentralized adaptation managers to support the multi-layer planning. Second, a planning model based on Markov Decision Processes (MDPs) to appropriately select the adaptation action for the respective service layer. This model can complement the existing decision making proposals in selecting the adaptation strategy.

The remainder of this paper is organized as follows. We present a decentralized self-adaptation architecture for multi-layer services in Section 2. Then, we elaborate the model and the method for solving the adaptation planning problem in Section 3. We discuss a motivating example to illustrate the practicality of the approach in Section 4. In Section 5, we analyze the related work. Finally, we summarize and highlight future work in Section 6.

2 Self-adaptation Framework for CSBS

The key idea to enable self-adaptation in service-based systems is to adopt the IBM's MAPE reference framework [13]. It consists of four components (Monitor, Analyze, Plan, and Execute) that interact in a feedback control loop. The Monitor is responsible to observe the system behavior and to detect or predict any problematic situation, e.g., a SLA violation. The Analyze component is responsible to gain more information about the identified problem and to decide whether it occurs to trigger an adaptation. The Plan component is responsible to produce a policy or a plan to support the adaptation. The generated plan can contain which service layer(s) to be adapted and what adaptation action(s) to be executed. Finally, the Execute component is responsible to execute the planned adaptation actions.

A single MAPE has been argued as to be insufficient to adapt a CSBS due to its multi-layer architecture. The main challenge of a multi-layer architecture is the complexity of the system in dealing with changes and evolution. The complexity is attributed to the vertical and horizontal dependencies among the services in the CSBS. Thus, in this paper, we propose a self-adaptation framework for CSBS with multiple MAPE loops as illustrated in Figure 1.

The framework consists of the adaptation managers and the CSBS. The adaptation manager is classified into two types of managers, namely the *global adaptation manager* (GAM) and the *local adaptation managers* (LAMs), on which we focus below. The proposed framework follows the hierarchical control pattern as discussed in [21]. This pattern is suitable to manage the complexity of self-adaptation by providing a hierarchy of MAPE loops. The higher-level MAPE loop concerns with the global adaptation, while the lower-level MAPE loops concern with the local adaptation. In the case of demanding the local adaptation only, this pattern can potentially reduce the adaptation time. Its drawback is the possibility of not being able to achieve a global adaptation due to conflict of interests from the lower level. Furthermore, the global MAPE loop might be dealing with a considerable workload of adaptation requests triggered by the lower MAPE loops. We will investigate in future work the evaluation of the effectiveness and efficiency of the hierarchical control pattern.

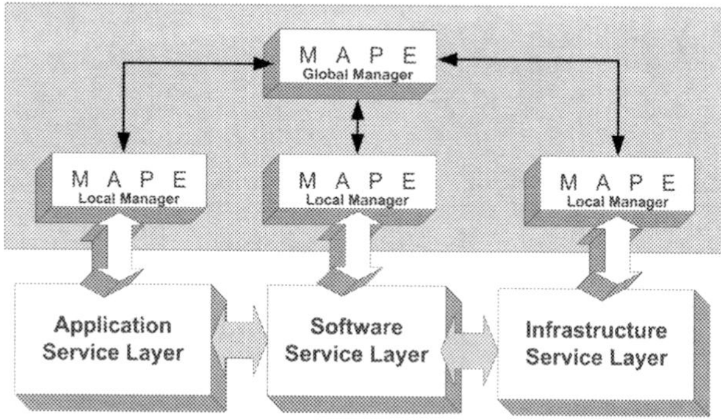

Fig. 1. Self-adaptation framework for CSBS

2.1 Adaptation Managers

The framework contains two types of adaptation managers, GAM and LAMs, which operate at different levels of abstraction and may operate at different time scales.

The LAM is concerned with a single, specific layer of the service-based system. It consists of all the MAPE components:(1) **M**onitor, which is responsible to determine the abnormality within the layer; (2) **A**nalysis, which is responsible to determine whether an adaptation is required and what needs to be adapted; (3) **P**lanning, which is responsible to plan the appropriate adaptation action for the layer; (4) **E**xecutor, which is responsible to execute the adaptation plan.

Meanwhile, the GAM is concerned with the overall service-based system. It consists of all the MAPE components: (1) **M**onitor, which is responsible to monitor the abnormality notification triggered by the local monitors; (2) **A**nalysis, which is in charge to determine the joint effect of the cross-layer adaptation; (3) **P**lanning, which is in charge to plan the appropriate adaptation strategy for the entire system; and finally,(4) the **E**xecutor, which is in charge to properly instruct the local executors to perform the adaptation.

2.2 Adaptation Interaction Process

The interaction among GAM, LAMs, and CSBS can be presented in terms of a UML sequence diagram as depicted in Figure 2. The adaptation process is perceived as a continuous activity of monitoring and adapting the CSBS.

Each LAM monitors the CSBS behavior at runtime, while the GAM monitors each LAM. If an abnormal condition is detected at a specific layer, the respective LAM Analyzer is executed and the respective LAM notifies the GAM. The LAM proceeds with the local planning and then waits to synchronize with the GAM's decision.

From the GAM perspective, it performs a global analysis upon receiving the notification. Then, the GAM analyzes the abnormal conditions to understand the

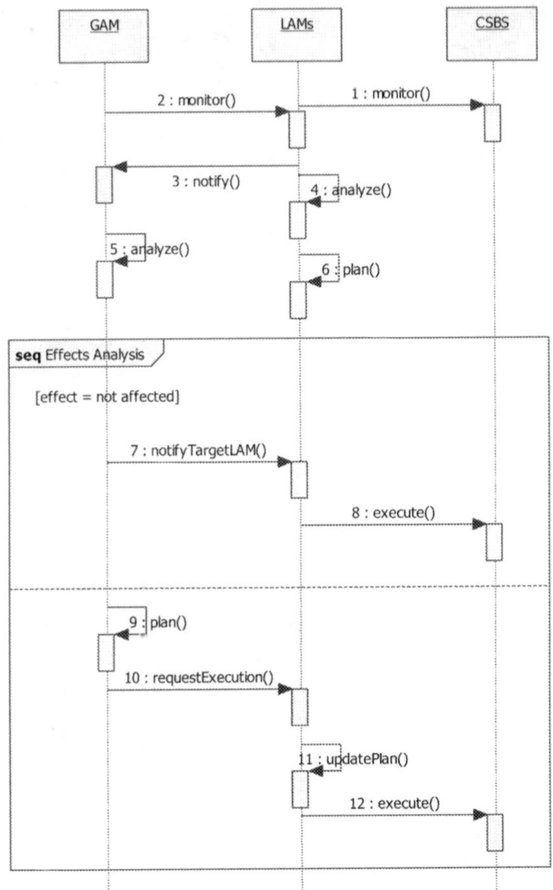

Fig. 2. Interaction model of the adaptation process

effect on the cross-layer system. The outcomes of the analysis may fall into one of these categories: (1) *Affected*, which is identified when more than one CSBS layer is affected; (2) *Not Affected*, which is identified when the other layers are not affected by the abnormal condition notified by the LAM.

Based on this outcome, the GAM performs either of the following: (1) let the LAM operate locally; (2) handle the situation. The first case is triggered if the GAM's analysis results in *Not Affected*. In this case, the GAM skips the planning activity and notifies the targeted LAM to perform the local adaptation. Upon receiving this notification, the respective LAM executes the established plan. For instance, if the LAM refers to the application layer, then a replanning process will be executed by invoking an existing planner, i.e., the MOSES planner [6,5].

The second case is triggered when the GAM's analysis results in *Affected*. The GAM performs a global planning which determines the adaptation actions for the multiple layers. Then, the GAM's executor instructs all the LAMs to execute the plan. Herein, the GAM decision will supersede the decision taken by the respective LAM. Hence, the LAM will update the existing plan with a new plan and execute the latter.

We provide the design for the planning component in the following section, while the remaining framework components are beyond the scope of this paper and are left to future work.

3 Adaptation Planning

In this section we present the adaptation planning component for the CSBS, first introducing the selected methodology and then analyzing how we determine the single and multiple planning strategies.

3.1 Overview of the Methodology

The technique we used to model the planning is based on decision-theoretic planning and specifically on Markov Decision Processes (MDPs), that provide a suitable framework to model the decision making process under uncertainty and to take forward-looking decisions [3,17].

The basic MDP model is also known as *centralized MDP* and is suitable to model a single planning problem. MDP has been applied in various application domains, including multi-robot coordination and sensor network management. The common MDP model consists of states, actions, transition probabilities, and rewards. In addition, the model can be associated with finite and infinite horizon. The optimal solution can be obtained by using stochastic dynamic programming algorithms such as value iteration and policy iteration.

The centralized MDP is also determined as fully observable, which means the agent has a full knowledge about the underlying state environment. However, in certain situations an agent may only have a partial information about the underlying state environment. Hence, a generalization of MDP was proposed, also known as Partially Observable Markov Decision Process (POMDP) [11]. In POMDP, the agent needs to establish its belief to the state environment in order to determine the appropriate policy.

Several variants and generalizations of MDP and POMDP models have been proposed in literature, especially related to the multi-agent decision processes. Cooperative multi-agent systems are often modeled by Multi-agent MDP, Multi-agent POMDP, decentralized MDP, or decentralized POMDP [18]. There are some common elements to model the multi-agent systems [12], which include the set of agents, the set of global states, the set of joint actions, the set of joint observation, the joint transition function, the global reward, and the set of belief states.

In this study, we identify two types of planning approaches (i.e., single and multiple) to support the adaptation planning process. The single planning approach concerns only a single layer of the CSBS. Hence, we model this type of planning based on the centralized MDP. On the other hand, the multiple planning approach deals with multiple layers of the CSBS and therefore we model this type of planning based on the *multi-agent MDP* (MMDP) [3], which is a generalization of the centralized MDP.

3.2 Single Planning

We first present the problem formulation of the single planning using a single MDP and explain how to achieve the optimal policy. The single planning will be executed by a LAM. The single planning problem is modeled as a single MDP with a tuple (S, A, P, R, H), where:

- S refers to the set of violation states associated to the services in a specific layer. There are three possible stati for the state: *normal*, *expected violation*, and *violated*.
- A refers to the set of possible adaptation actions to be executed associated to a specific violation state. The action to be taken will change a state to the next state. Herein, we consider a significative subset of adaptation actions that can be executed at a specific service layer. For instance, the actions that can be taken at the infrastructure layer include adding a new virtual machine instance or migrating a virtual machine instance from one physical machine to another machine. The possible actions at the platform layer may include updating or redeploying a Web server. Meanwhile, the actions to be considered at the application layer include replanting the workflow or rebinding to different component services (i.e., through service selection) that provide the same functionality but with different non-functional parameters (e.g., response time, cost, availability, reputation).
- P is a transition function $P : S \times A \rightarrow \Delta(S)$. $P(s'|s, a)$ denotes the transition probability (uncertainty effect) of taking action a in state s which results in a transition to state s'. For instance, a state s, e.g., *violated*, may change to the next state s', e.g., *normal*, if action a is taken with 0.9 probability.
- R is the reward function $R : S \times A \rightarrow \Re$. $R(s, a)$ denotes the reward obtained when action a is taken from a state s which a state transition to s' occurs. The reward can be viewed as a utility value of a specific layer in fulfilling the layer objective. For instance, the objective of the application layer can be to minimize the response time, and thus the utility value represents the response time of taking an adaptation action. The objective of the infrastructure layer can regard the minimization of the energy consumption and thus the utility value represents the energy consumed in taking an adaptation action. For simplicity, we assume the reward value takes either 1, 0, or -1. The reward 1 is assigned when state s' holds the *normal* status. The 0 reward is assigned for the *expected violation* status, while reward -1 is assigned for the *violated* status.

- H is the finite horizon during which the policy can be computed. This period is essential to ensure the proposed policy can maintain the quality assurance of CSBS. For instance, the adaptation cycle can take up to a maximum of t time to maintain the overall execution time.

Based on these elements, the optimal policy for the adaptation planning can be formulated. The optimal policy refers to the best adaptation action to be executed for evolving the state of a service to the next state. The policy is based on Bellman equation, given as follows:

$$\pi^*(s) = \arg max_{a \in A}\{R(s,a) + \sum_{s'} P(s'|s,a)V^*(s')\} \tag{1}$$

In Eq. 1, $\pi^*(s)$ is the optimal policy (the best action to be taken) for state s. The best action is obtained based on the maximum reward of the possible action rewards $R(s,a)$, the transition probability $P(s'|s,a)$ and the value function of the next state from the previous adaptation cycle $V^*(s')$.

In contract to reward, the V value represents the long term objective to be achieved by the specific layer through a set of adaptation cycle. Technically, the V value can be formulated as follows:

$$V^k(s) = \{R(s,a) + \sum_{s'} P(s'|s,a)V^{k-1}(s')\} \tag{2}$$

In Eq. 2, k refers to one of the steps in the finite horizon H. The optimal solution can be achieved by using the standard algorithms, namely, the value iteration in a finite horizon. In the algorithm, the initial V value of all states can be set 0. Then, for each k, the V value will be computed iteratively until the value converges, namely, $V^k(s) - V^{k-1}(s') < \epsilon$. After that, the best V value is used to select the best action at step k.

3.3 Multiple Planning

The multiple planning is implemented whenever two or more layers are analyzed as affected. This planning is essential to avoid conflicting adaptation objectives at the different layers. For instance, the local planning at the infrastructure layer aims to minimize the energy consumption by migrating some virtual machines. This decision may affect the application layer which aims to minimize the response time by replanning the workflow. Thus, a joint decision is needed and can be achieved through multiple planning.

We model the multiple planning problem as multi-agent MDP [3] with a tuple (I, S, A, P, R, H) where I is a set of agents, S is a set of global states, A is a set of joint actions, P is the global transition function, R is the global reward function and H is the horizon.

We map the elements in multi-agent MDP to the adaptation planning problem as follows:

- I is a set of layers, namely the local adaptation managers (LAMs).

- S is a set of global states of the CSBS. The global states can be factored into local states observed by LAMs such as, $S = S_i \times S_j$ where $(i, j) \in I$. This means, each LAM will have a full observation on the states within a specific service layer.
- A is a set of joint adaptation actions, $A = A_i \times A_j$ where $(i, j) \in I$. Each A_i represents the possible local adaptation actions available to a specific service layer.
- P is a global transition function $P : S \times A \rightarrow \Delta(S)$. $P(s'|s, a)$ denotes the global transition probability of taking joint adaptation action a in global state s which results in a transition to the global state s'. The global transition probability can be decomposed into a set of independent local transition probabilities, given as follows:

$$P(s'|s, a) = P(s_i'|s_i, a_i) \times P(s_j'|s_j, a_j) \tag{3}$$

- R is the global reward function $R : S \times A \rightarrow \Re$. $R(s, a)$ denotes the global reward obtained for taking the joint adaptation action a in state s and transitioning to state s'. The global reward is obtained by the following:

$$R(s, a) = \sum_{i \in I} R_i(s_i, a_i) \tag{4}$$

- H is the finite horizon during which the policy can be computed.

Based on the given model, the global optimal policy, which consists of a set of joint policies, can be obtained on the basis of Eq. 1. In the latter, the reward function refers to Eq. 4 and the transition function refers to Eq. 3.

4 Example and Discussion

In this section, we provide an example of scenario to show the practicality of the proposed approach. The scenario refers to the citizen service center scenario adopted from [1].

The public service center can be abstractly presented as a multi-layer service as shown in Fig 3. At the highest level there is the application service layer, which refers to the application of citizen service center. The middle layer is the software service layer which consists of composite health and mobility services. This composite service comprises of the booking service, healthcare service, and mobility service. The lowest layer is the infrastructure service later which refers to the actual service providers for each service in the software service layer.

Each of these layers is associated to the LAMs. For instance, the application layer is managed by a specific LAM. Meanwhile, all LAMs are controlled by the GAM.

To show the adaptation needs, let us assume that the infrastructure service layer is detected as having a problematic behavior by the LAM's monitor. The problem can be due to many reasons, such as one of the call center providers has

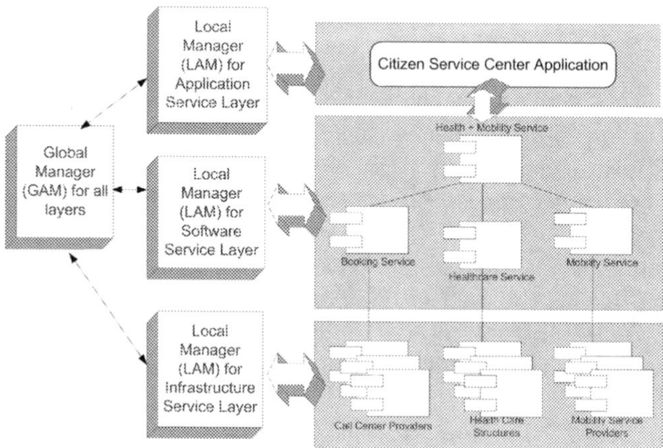

Fig. 3. Citizen service center considered as use case scenario

been detected as unavailable. Due to this problem, the LAM's analysis of the infrastructure layer will notify the GAM's monitor for a global analysis (refer to Fig. 2).

The GAM's analysis will assess the impact level of the problematic situation. Conceptually, there are two possible outcomes; affected or not affected. If the outcome is not affected, this means the other layers are not affected by the condition, that is in our example the booking service can behave as a normal service. In this case, the GAM will notify the LAM of the infrastructure layer to handle locally the adaptation problem.

If the analysis outcome is affected, it means the other layers may violate their QoS constraints due to the problematic condition, in this case the software service layer. Thus, the GAM performs a further analysis to identify the impact region (a set of affected services) which results in the booking service. Based on such outcome, the GAM performs a global planning to determine the appropriate adaptation action for each service in each layer, namely, the booking service and the respective call center provider.

In the context of local planning, the mapping between the scenario we consider in this example and the MDP can be viewed as follows:

- States: the state of the call center provider which is violated;
- Actions: renegotiating the SLA or replacing the call center provider;
- Probability: the effect value of taking the possible actions from the current state to the next state;
- Reward: the value assigned to the next state;
- Horizon: the number of iterations to address the problematic situation;
- Value: a value to quantify the goodness of the action.

By solving the MDP, a set of values will be obtained in relation to the possible actions. Thus, the best action that maximizes the objective (as specified in Eq. 1) will be selected and executed by the Executor component.

5 Related Work

Adaptivity is one of the most challenging research problems for service-based systems and the existing approaches can be mainly divided into three areas [4]: dynamic context-aware adaptation, user-centric adaptation, and multi-layer adaptation. In this paper, we address the multi-layer adaptation challenges.

The complexity and the uncertainty of a complex service-based system demand for a robust adaptation planning in order to decide the appropriate adaptation actions during the runtime operations. The approach by Pernici and Siadat [15] proposed a fuzzy-based solution to select the adaptation actions based on QoS satisfaction. It differs from our work since the uncertainty is associated to the service behavior rather than to the adaptation action effect. The works in [9,19,24] proposed and utilized Cross-layer Adaptation Manager (CLAM) to handle the complexity of service-based systems in the adaptation process. CLAM covers three aspects: first, the integrated platform to plug in existing adaptation and analysis tools; second, the cross-layer model of the service-based system as core input; third, the rule-based analysis to construct alternative cross-layer adaptation strategies. In contrast to our work, we address the uncertainty planning challenge in deciding the adaptation strategies/actions. This is essential since the actual effect of executing any adaptation action is unknown and cannot be guaranteed. In [16] Popescu et al. proposed a methodology for the dynamic and flexible adaptation of multi-layer applications that uses adaptation templates and taxonomies of adaptation mismatches. However, their approach focus on functional properties and cannot handle multiple mismatches that occur at the same time. Zeginis et al. proposed in [23] a framework that can deal with both reactive and proactive cross-layer adaptation of service-based systems. While they focus on a cross-layer monitoring mechanism, we investigate the adaptation phase.

The Model-based Self-Adaptation of SOA Systems (MOSES) framework [5] aims to dynamically adapt service-based systems according to non-functional QoS properties by acting at the SaaS layer. Our work aims to complement such framework with a planning mechanism that takes the complexity (i.e., the multi-layer model) and the uncertainty effect of adaptation actions into account.

6 Conclusions and Future Work

In this paper, we have proposed a conceptual architecture and interaction process for self-adapting a complex service-based system. The architecture consists of two adaptation managers to cater the global and local perspectives of the adaptation. Furthermore, we have proposed a planning model based on MDP techniques by considering the uncertainty and complexity factors of adapting a complex service-based system. Our study shows the viability of MDP techniques for realizing a multi-layer self-adaptation planning component.

In the future, we plan to analyze the performance of the proposed approach as well as its computational complexity with respect to the system scale. We also plan to explore reinforcement learning for realizing a decentralized multi-layer adaptation planning where full knowledge of system dynamics is not required.

Acknowledgement. This work is supported by the Fundamental Research Grant Scheme (600-RMI/FRGS 5/3 (164/2013)) funded by the Ministry of Higher Education Malaysia (MOHE) and Universiti Teknologi MARA (UiTM), Malaysia.

V. Cardellini also acknowledges the support of the European ICT COST Action IC1304 Autonomous Control for a Reliable Internet of Services (ACROSS).

References

1. Armellin, G., Chiasera, A., Frankova, G., Pasquale, L., Torelli, F., Zacco, G.: The eGovernment use case scenario service level agreements for Cloud computing. In: Service Level Agreements for Cloud Computing, pp. 343–357. Springer (2011)
2. Baryannis, G., Garefalakis, P., Kritikos, K., Magoutis, K., Papaioannou, A., Plexousakis, D., Zeginis, C.: Lifecycle management of service-based applications on multi-clouds: a research roadmap. In: Proc. of 2013 Int'l Workshop on Multi-Cloud Applications and Federated Clouds, MultiCloud 2013, pp. 13–20. ACM (2013)
3. Boutilier, C., Dean, T.L., Hanks, S.: Decision-theoretic planning: Structural assumptions and computational leverage. Journal of Artificial Intelligence Research 11(1), 1–94 (1999)
4. Bucchiarone, A., Kazhamiakin, R., Marconi, A., Pistore, M.: Adaptivity in dynamic service-based systems. In: Proc. of 1st Workshop on European Software Services and Systems Research - Results and Challenges, pp. 36–37 (2012)
5. Cardellini, V., Casalicchio, E., Grassi, V., Iannucci, S., Lo Presti, F., Mirandola, F.: MOSES: A framework for QoS driven runtime adaptation of service-oriented systems. IEEE Transactions on Software Engineering 38(5), 1138–1159 (2012)
6. Cardellini, V., Casalicchio, E., Grassi, V., Lo Presti, F.: Adaptive management of composite services under percentile-based service level agreements. In: Maglio, P.P., Weske, M., Yang, J., Fantinato, M. (eds.) ICSOC 2010. LNCS, vol. 6470, pp. 381–395. Springer, Heidelberg (2010)
7. Comuzzi, M., Kotsokalis, C., Rathfelder, C., Theilmann, W., Winkler, U., Zacco, G.: A framework for multi-level SLA management. In: Dan, A., Gittler, F., Toumani, F. (eds.) ICSOC/ServiceWave 2009. LNCS, vol. 6275, pp. 187–196. Springer, Heidelberg (2010)
8. Esfahani, N., Malek, S.: Uncertainty in self-adaptive software systems. In: de Lemos, R., Giese, H., Müller, H.A., Shaw, M. (eds.) Self-Adaptive Systems. LNCS, vol. 7475, pp. 214–238. Springer, Heidelberg (2013)
9. Guinea, S., Kecskemeti, G., Marconi, A., Wetzstein, B.: Multi-layered monitoring and adaptation. In: Kappel, G., Maamar, Z., Motahari-Nezhad, H.R. (eds.) ICSOC 2011. LNCS, vol. 7084, pp. 359–373. Springer, Heidelberg (2011)
10. Ismail, A., Yan, J., Shen, J.: Incremental service level agreements violation handling with time impact analysis. Journal of Systems and Software 86(6), 1530–1544 (2013)
11. Kaelbling, L.P., Littman, M.L., Cassandra, A.R.: Planning and acting in partially observable stochastic domains. Artificial Intelligence 101(1-2), 99–134 (1998)

12. Kaufman, M., Roberts, S.: Coordination vs. information in multi-agent decision processes. In: Proc. of 5th Workshop on Multi-agent Sequential Decision Making in Uncertain Domains, MSDM 2010 (2010)
13. Kephart, J.O., Chess, D.M.: The vision of autonomic computing. IEEE Computer 36(1), 41–50 (2003)
14. Marconi, A., Bucchiarone, A., Bratanis, K., Brogi, A., Camara, J., Dranidis, D., Giese, H., Kazhamiakink, R., de Lemos, R., Marquezan, C.C., Metzger, A.: Research challenges on multi-layer and mixed-initiative monitoring and adaptation for service-based systems. In: 2012 Workshop on European Software Services and Systems Research - Results and Challenges (S-Cube), pp. 40–46. IEEE Computer Society (2012)
15. Pernici, B., Siadat, S.H.: A fuzzy service adaptation based on QoS satisfaction. In: Mouratidis, H., Rolland, C. (eds.) CAiSE 2011. LNCS, vol. 6741, pp. 48–61. Springer, Heidelberg (2011)
16. Popescu, R., A., Staikopoulos, P.L., Brogi, A., Clarke, S.: Taxonomy-driven adaptation of multi-layer applications using templates. In: Proc. of 4th IEEE Int'l Conf. on Self-Adaptive and Self-Organizing Systems, SASO 2010, pp. 213–222 (2010)
17. Puterman, M.L.: Markov Decision Processes: Discrete Stochastic, Dynamic Programming. Wiley, New York (1994)
18. Pynadath, D.V., Tambe, M.: The communicative multiagent team decision problem: Analyzing teamwork theories and models. Journal of Artificial Intelligence Research 16, 389–423 (2002)
19. Siadat, S.H., Zengin, A., Marconi, A., Pernici, B.: A fuzzy approach for ranking adaptation strategies in CLAM. In: Proc. of 5th IEEE Int'l Conf. on Service-Oriented Computing and Applications, SOCA 2012 (2012)
20. Varshney, L.R., Oppenheim, D.V.: Coordinating global service delivery in the presence of uncertainty. In: Proc. of 12th Int'l Research Symposium on Service Excellence in Management (2011)
21. Weyns, D., Schmerl, B., Grassi, V., Malek, S., Mirandola, R., Prehofer, C., Wuttke, J., Andersson, J., Giese, H., Göschka, K.M.: On patterns for decentralized control in self-adaptive systems. In: de Lemos, R., Giese, H., Müller, H.A., Shaw, M. (eds.) Self-Adaptive Systems. LNCS, vol. 7475, pp. 76–107. Springer, Heidelberg (2013)
22. Zeginis, C., Kritikos, K., Garefalakis, P., Konsolaki, K., Magoutis, K., Plexousakis, D.: Towards cross-layer monitoring of multi-cloud service-based applications. In: Lau, K.-K., Lamersdorf, W., Pimentel, E. (eds.) ESOCC 2013. LNCS, vol. 8135, pp. 188–195. Springer, Heidelberg (2013)
23. Zeginis, C., Konsolaki, K., Kritikos, K., Plexousakis, D.: Towards proactive cross-layer service adaptation. In: Wang, X.S., Cruz, I., Delis, A., Huang, G. (eds.) WISE 2012. LNCS, vol. 7651, pp. 704–711. Springer, Heidelberg (2012)
24. Zengin, A., Kazhamiakin, R., Pistore, M.: CLAM: cross-layer management of adaptation decisions for service-based applications. In: Proc. of 2011 IEEE Int'l Conf. on Web Services, ICWS 2011, pp. 698–699 (2011)

Towards an Integration Platform for Bioinformatics Services

Guzmán Llambías, Laura González, and Raúl Ruggia

Instituto de Computación, Facultad de Ingeniería, Universidad de la República, Uruguay
{gllambi,lauragon,ruggia}@fing.edu.uy

Abstract. Performing in-silico experiments, which involves an intensive access to distributed services and information resources through Internet, is nowadays one of the main activities in Bioinformatics. Although existing tools facilitate the implementation of workflow-oriented applications, they lack of capabilities to integrate services beyond low-scale applications, particularly integrating services with heterogeneous interaction patterns and in a larger scale, ideally based on a Platform as a Service paradigm. On the other hand, such integration mechanisms are provided by middleware products like Enterprise Service Buses (ESB). This paper proposes an integration platform, based on enterprise middleware, to integrate Bioinformatics services. It presents a multi-level reference architecture and focuses on ESB-based mechanisms to provide asynchronous communications, event-based interactions and data transformation capabilities.

Keywords: Platform as a Service (PaaS), Scientific Platforms, Middleware.

1 Introduction

An in-silico experiment is a procedure that uses computer-based resources (local and remote) to test a hypothesis, derive a summary or search for patterns [1]. Bioinformaticians develop these experiments using Workflow Management System tools, specially adapted to the biological context, giving birth to scientific workflows.

Scientific workflow tools, notably Taverna [2], have revolutionized the way researchers perform experiments by enabling them to use powerful computational tools without needing a strong IT background. These tools enable to access external services via Web Services, perform data format transformations, execute queries on large databases and even request the execution of an experiment in the cloud [3]. Although the generalized use of Taverna is a clear success indicator [2], it does not provide suitable mechanisms to handle some particular characteristics of bioinformatics services [4] (e.g. the polling approach followed by most biological service providers and the use of different data formats in services). This fact turns the logic to be implemented by workflows more complex. Furthermore, it doesn't provide asynchronous message-oriented mechanisms and quality of service management.

On the other side, middleware technologies which have been evolving during the last years, provide abstractions and solutions to increasingly complex integration issues (e.g. asynchronous communications and interoperable communications over

A.R. Lomuscio et al. (Eds.): ICSOC 2013 Workshops, LNCS 8377, pp. 445–456, 2014.
© Springer International Publishing Switzerland 2014

the internet) related to the construction and integration of distributed applications. In particular, Enterprise Service Buses (ESB) and cloud-based Internet Service Buses (ISB) [5], are sophisticated middleware technologies which enable to integrate highly distributed and heterogeneous services. ESBs provide rich mediation capabilities (e.g. message transformation and intermediate routing) which can be used to address mismatches between applications and services (e.g. regarding communication protocols, message formats, interaction styles and quality of service) [6] [7].

This leads to the challenge of improving collaboration in bioinformatics community by enhancing service-based integration capabilities and reducing the complexity in the involved development. Such enhanced platforms should enable to integrate bioinformatics Web-based services (e.g. NCBI Web Services) and experiment-oriented workflow tools (e.g. Taverna) with general purpose mediation features and other value-added capabilities. The ultimate goal is to put into practice a Platform as a Service (PaaS) approach in the bioinformatics area, enabling an active participation of laboratories, researchers, and middleware and cloud computing suppliers and developers.

This paper addresses these issues and proposes a reference integration platform for the bioinformatics domain which, mediating between Taverna (Kepler[1], Galaxy[2], etc.) and bioinformatics services, provide mechanisms that facilitate the development of distributed scientific workflows and solve common challenges arising when performing this task. The proposed integration platform leverages mediation features of enterprise middleware (particularly ESBs), addresses identified integration requirements by improving asynchronous interactions, event notification and message transformation capabilities, and provide the means to implement other value-added services.

This paper, which is part of a larger work jointly developed with the Bioinformatics Unit of the Pasteur Institute at Montevideo, focuses on solutions oriented to medium and large-scale integration platforms potentially involving cloud resources.

The rest of the paper is organized as follows. Section 2 presents background. Section 3 presents a high level view of the proposed solution. Section 4 describes an ESB-based design which provides solutions for some identified scenarios. Section 5 presents related work and finally, Section 6 presents conclusions and future work.

2 Background

2.1 Cloud Computing and PaaS

According to NIST [8], *"Cloud computing is a model for enabling ubiquitous, convenient, on-demand network access to a shared pool of configurable computing resources that can be rapidly provisioned and released with minimal management effort or service provider interaction"*.

On the other side, Platform as a Service (PaaS) is one of the five service models that compose Cloud Computing. It provides the consumer the capability to deploy, in the cloud infrastructure, applications built on top of the elements (e.g. programming

[1] https://kepler-project.org/

[2] http://galaxyproject.org/

languages) supported by the provider. The consumer does not manage or control the underlying cloud infrastructure, but he has control over the applications he deploys and over configuration settings for the hosting environment [8].

2.2 Taverna and myGrid Project

myGrid[3] is an e-science middleware project, whose main purpose is to provide middleware based tools of high abstraction that can simplify the development of bioinformatics experiments. One of the tools developed in this context is Taverna: a tool that allows scientists to model their experiments as a composition of biological services, building in this way scientific workflows. The main contribution of Taverna is that it allows scientists with limited IT expertise, to be capable of developing their experiments using advanced technologies such as Web Services, BioMart, R, etc [2].

2.3 Enterprise Service Bus (ESB)

An ESB is an environment belonging to the platform middleware systems category, which provides sophisticated interconnectivity between services and enables to overcome issues related to reliability, scalability and communications. Service interaction using an ESB is based on a combination of the patterns: Asynchronous Queuing, Event-Driven Messaging, Intermediate Routing, Policy Centralization, Reliable Messaging, Rules Centralization and Transformation [9]. Additionally, interaction styles define the way each actor may behave using an ESB.

ESB Design Patterns. *Intermediate routing patterns* dynamically determine the message path according to different factors. More concretely, a content-based router defines the message path based on its content and a recipient list routes the message to a list of dynamically specified recipients.

Transformation patterns deal with the runtime transformation of messages. In [9] the authors identify three types of transformations: data model transformation, data format transformation and protocol bridging.

The *Asynchronous Queuing pattern* deals with the interactions of client and services when synchronous communication can affect performance and reliability.

Interaction Styles. In [11], eight ESB interaction patterns are identified. These patterns are abstract and define the way actors behave and interact in terms of synchronous/asynchronous interfaces, level of assurance of delivery, handling of timeouts, late responses, and error handling. In this paper, we focus on two interactions styles: 1) Synchronous update Request with acknowledgement and callback and 2) One-way with status poll for completion.

---

[3] `http://www.mygrid.org.uk/`

3 Towards a Bioinformatics Integration Platform

An environment for in-silico bioinformatic experiments includes, on one hand, local bioinformatic tools (e.g. *Taverna*) which enable researchers to implement experiments by composing resources. On the other hand, there are bioinformatic resources, especially external and distributed over the Internet (e.g. NCBI, EBI, DDBJ), which are accessible via APIs, Web Services SOAP and REST.

Although bioinformatic tools like *Taverna* provide user oriented development features, their lack of mediation mechanisms (e.g. asynchronous interactions, event management, declarative data transformations) and management functionalities (e.g. quality of service, service policy) limits their ability to integrate all the involved elements.

The proposed Bioinformatics Integration Platform provides features to implement an advanced interaction between bioinformatics applications and services (Fig. 1). Concretely, it enables to perform not only traditional synchronic function invocations, but also asynchronous interactions based on a request-response pattern and data transformation mechanisms.

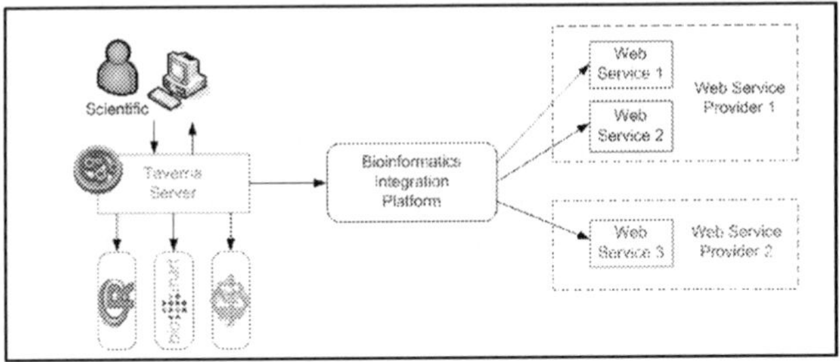

Fig. 1. The Bioinformatics Integration Platform in Context

The specification of the integration platform consists of several refinement levels. The highest level, shown in Fig. 1, is independent from technical approaches and laboratory application contexts. Specifications in a subsequent level are based on the technical approaches followed to solve integration requirements in different laboratory scenarios by using specific middleware technologies. The third refinement level introduces middleware product aspects related to specific implementations.

The following parts of this section focus on these aspects, starting with solutions proposed to integration requirements (asynchronous interaction, events and notification, and data transformation) and following with a classification of Laboratory scenarios characterized by their scale and service capabilities. The overall architecture, based on the multilayer refinement specification, is presented at the end of the section.

3.1 Integration Requirements

Asynchronous Interactions. Nowadays, many biological service providers design their Web Services using asynchronous communications due to the large amount of time and resources they use to perform data processing. After studying some Web Services of the NCBI[456], we can argue that they were designed using a response polling model, where clients send a job request to the Web Service and receive a jobId, to use afterwards and check for its status (waiting, running, finished). Only when the job status is finished, the client can poll the response. Fig. 2 presents this model.

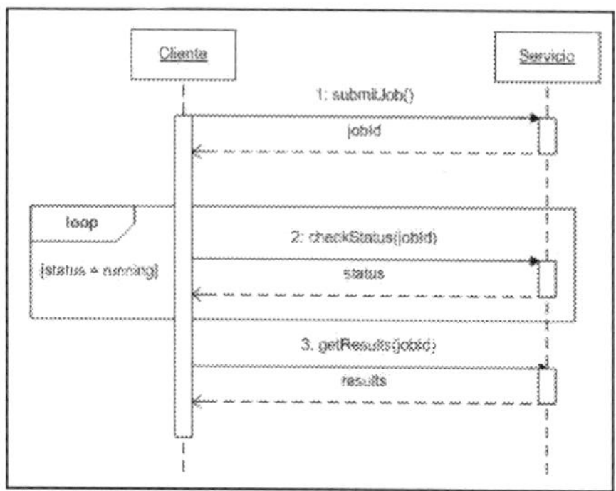

Fig. 2. Polling based asynchronous communication.

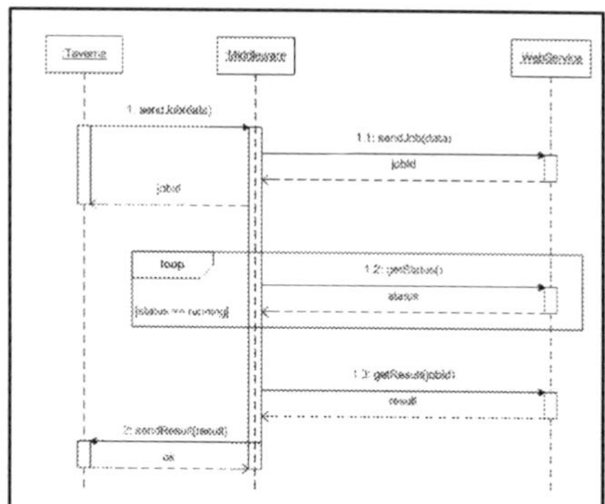

Fig. 3. Callback based asynchronous communication

Although the polling model is very effective, it is not too efficient as it requires three tasks and a loop to perform only one analysis. A callback approach as showed in Fig. 3 is much more efficient and equally effective as the polling model. This paper proposes that the design of asynchronous bioinformatics Web Services use a callback approach instead of the polling model. If this is not possible, middleware technologies should be used to mediate between client and service to reach this approach.

Events and Notifications. The completion of a workflow, the receipt of a message from an external system or a timeout to finish a task, are different types of events which are provided as natives features in many enterprise workflow management tools (WS-BPEL, Windows Workflow Foundation, JBPM, etc). As far as we know, Taverna does not have support for these features, and it has limited support for basic event notifications (Atom feeds, email, SMS, Twitter and Jabber when workflows are completed). The latter are very useful for human notification but are not suitable for machine to machine notifications or the integration of Taverna to other information systems. Some useful examples of notifications are Database updates (each update of the Genbank database could be notified to Taverna to rerun existing workflows), Receive notifications of available information from an external system (i.e. receive or

[4] `http://www.myexperiment.org/workflows/203.html`
[5] `http://www.myexperiment.org/workflows/210.html`
[6] `http://www.myexperiment.org/workflows/230.html`

wait WS-BPEL activities) and Workflow completion (notify external systems by more sophisticated means other than the ones supported nowadays).

This paper proposes the application of middleware-based technologies to provide a notification mechanism based on the Publish/Subscribe design pattern, which could allow Taverna to subscribe to events and notifications from external systems.

Transformation Services. As scientific workflows are usually based on the composition of third party services, scientists have to transform the output format of one service to the input format of the next service (e.g. transform a plain text output into a FASTA format input). A survey of 415 registered workflows in myExperiment found that 30% of the tasks involved in each experiment were due to format changes, while just 22% were due to task for invoking Web Services [12]. Therefore, shim services are needed to accomplish the parsing and transformation of data formats [13], but this task is hardened by the lack of accepted standards and data models. BioXSD [14] and PhyloXML [15] are two examples of standardization initiatives for sequence alignment and phylogenetic data, with yet, low acceptance by the scientific community.

In [14], three possible scenarios are analysed based on how much alignment exists between the input and output data formats. In the first scenario, services receive and return data in plain text using the data type xsd:string. It is necessary to use shim services to transform data formats. In the second scenario, services return and receive data in xml format but the output data model is different from the input model of each service. It is necessary to use shim services or xslt scripts to perform the transformations. Finally, in the third scenario, services use the same data model and xml format. There is no need for transformations and data flows smoothly from one service to the other.

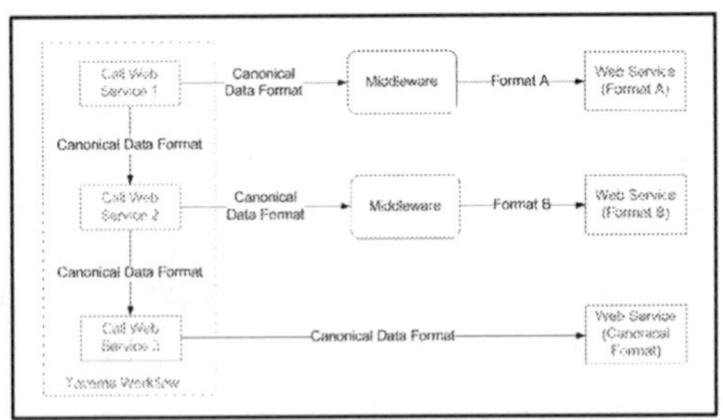

Fig. 4. Middleware-based message transformations scenarios

It would be desirable to reduce as much as possible the burden of shim services and try to seek for C scenarios, where there is no need for data parsing and transformations. Today, part of this objective can be achieved if the services use canonical data formats based on international standards. However, much work has to be done in this sense and in the meanwhile, alternative solutions are needed to achieve this goal.

This paper proposes to include intermediaries that provide standard service views to clients. The intermediate broker will offer the same service to clients but in a suitable data format performing the necessary transformations (Fig. 4).

3.2 Laboratory Scenarios

The characteristics of the Bioinformatics Laboratories, especially the ability to export new services, influences the way in which the Bioinformatics integration platform may be used. The following classification enables to instantiate this aspect:

- Laboratory type 1: Uses Taverna as a standalone tool, using the native connectors to consume biological services (WSDL, SoapLab, R).
- Laboratory type 2: Uses Taverna to consume biological services using the native connector, while uses point-to-point middleware to consume services not supported natively by Taverna. The number of middleware-based integrations is low.
- Laboratory type 3: Uses Taverna to consume compatible biological services while uses a platform middleware to consume other services not compliant with native Taverna integration. This type of laboratory is a large-scale service consumer.
- Laboratory type 4: Provides services to other laboratories while not necessarily consumes. It focuses on interoperability and accessibility features. Uses point-to-point or platform middleware depending on the number of provided services.
- Laboratory type 5: Provides Platforms as a Service (PaaS) and it doesn't focus on biological business aspects. One example of this type of Platforms is the Amazon SWF. This type of laboratories uses platform middleware.

3.3 Overall Architecture

Globally, the Bioinformatics Integration Platform can be defined as a domain-specific middleware, which provides abstractions and high quality services to solve common integration requirements in a bioinformatics context. Its architecture, shown in Fig. 1 at the highest abstraction level, can be refined by instantiating three dimensions:

- Integration functionalities: asynchronous interaction, events and notification, and data transformation.
- Laboratory scenarios: Laboratory types from 1 to 5.
- Middleware technologies: Web Services, Message Queues, ESB & ISB.

Characterizing solutions through these dimensions enables to specify and implement them, keeping the consistency with the overall architecture and with other differently instantiated solutions. Notably, Fig. 5 shows connections between specific architectures for laboratory scenarios (type 1 to type 3) based on different middleware technologies. In section 4, specific solutions are described for laboratories scenarios type 4 and type 5, using ESB as middleware technology.

4 An ESB-Based Bioinformatics Integration Platform

The Bioinformatics Integration Platform can be designed and implemented using various middleware technologies (Queues, Web Services, ESBs, etc). This section presents an ESB-based Bioinformatics Integration Platform, which is suitable for Platform as a Service (PaaS) development (Laboratory type 5 scenario), and shows how the requirements of Section 3 are supported.

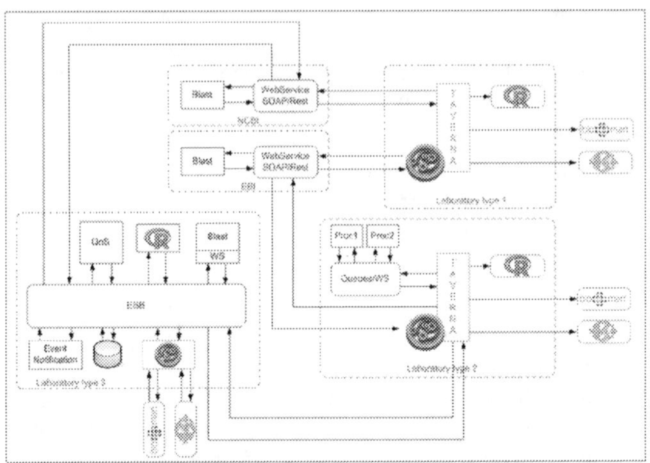

Fig. 5. Overall architecture instantiated in different laboratories

4.1 Asynchronous Communications

The proposed solution (Fig. 6) is ESB-based and follows the patterns: Asynchronous Queuing (i.e. ESB message queues), Intermediate Routing (i.e. Content Based Router, CBR) and Protocol Bridging (i.e. ESB Endpoints and ESB Connectors) [9].

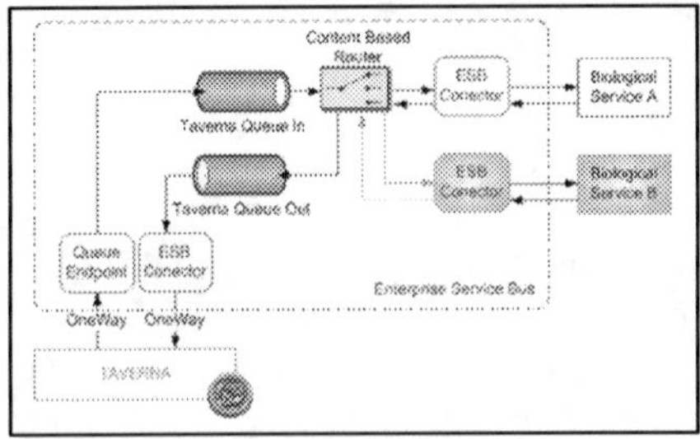

Fig. 6. Asynchronous communications based on ESB

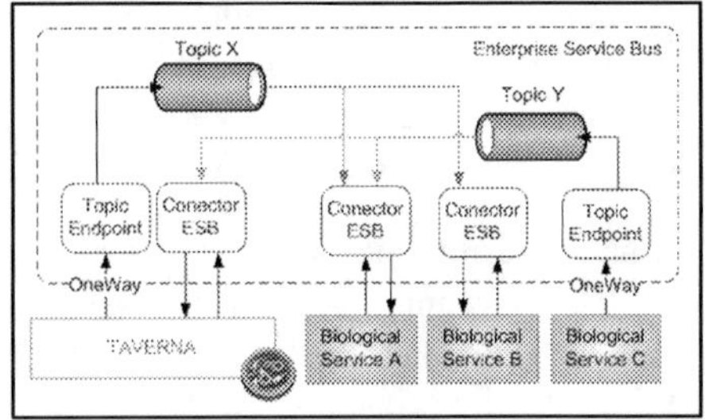

Fig. 7. Events and notifications based on ESB middleware

This solution involves defining two message queues in the ESB: one used to receive messages from Taverna (TavernaQueueIn) and the other to send the responses (TavernaQueueOut) from the ESB to Taverna. The only subscriber of the TavernaQueueIn message queue is a CBR, which inspects and routes messages to the biological service through a specific ESB Connector, and uses messages' content to identify the destination service. All request messages must specify a destination service, which should be registered in the Platform's Service Catalog. After processing the request, the service sends a response message to the TavernaQueueOut queue, whose only subscriber (ESB Connector) forwards the message to Taverna. Since there may be multiple instances of Taverna waiting for response messages, a replyTo attribute must be defined in the request messages to identify the destination instance.

4.2 Events and Notifications

The proposed solution is based on an ESB-oriented design and takes advantage of the Publish&Subscribe and Protocol Bridging (i.e. Topic Endpoints and ESB Connectors) design patterns [9]. This solution defines a topic in the ESB for each type of event or notification to be managed by the Platform. Each topic is identified by a TopicID and may have N publishers and M subscribers, where each subscriber may subscribe using two different types: synchronous or asynchronous.

To notify an event to the Platform, the publisher creates a message with business data and a TopicID, and sends it to the Endpoint Topic in the ESB. This component places the message in the corresponding topic according to the TopicID and acknowledges its reception. Each subscriber of the topic will receive a copy of the message according to the chosen subscription type. For asynchronous subscribers, the topic sends a copy to the ESB Connector associated with the service according to the communication protocols and specific data format. Synchronous subscribers instead, should query the topic through the Endpoint Topic for new messages.

4.3 Transformation Service

The design of this solution (Fig. 8) is ESB-based and applies the Content Based Routing, Canonical Data Model and Protocol Bridging (i.e. ESB Connectors and ESB Endpoints) design patterns [9]. The solution consists in automatically determining the format of the messages sent by Taverna and transforming them to the data format required by the service. To reduce the number of transformations to be configured, the Canonical Data Model pattern is applied, transforming incoming messages to a canonical data model and later-on back to the specific service data format. A Content Based Router is used to route incoming messages to the service. Native connectors are used (ESB Connectors) to perform the communication between the ESB and services.

4.4 Implementation Details

To show the feasibility of the proposed approach and to analyse key implementation aspects, prototypes were developed using JBoss ESB and NCBIs Web Services.

Concretely, Asynchronous Communications were implemented using JBoss's built-in features: ESB Queues and the CBR. Events and notification requirement were implemented using ESB's Topics. The transformation requirement was developed using the JBoss's CBR and XSLTs engines. The development of XSLT style sheets were needed to be used by the message transformation engine. The ESB Connectors used in all the scenarios were provided by JBoss's SOAP Proxy. Finally, the ESB Endpoint was also a JBoss's JMS Listener and HTTP Gateway.

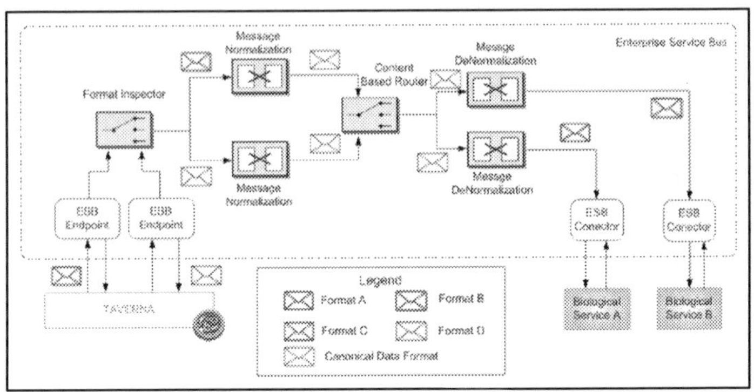

Fig. 8. Data/Model transformation based on ESB

5 Related Work

While different proposals have addressed asynchronous communications issues in scientific workflows, they present limitations. Particularly, [16][17] assume that biological Web Services have WS-Addressing support while this is not frequent (e.g. EBI, NCBI, DDBJ do not provide it). Our approach does not depend on this feature.

Notification mechanisms and events have also been addressed in Bioinformatics. In [17] Apache ODE, a WS-BPEL engine, is extended to send notifications in an e-science context. This solution has the limitation of being too coupled to Apache ODE. In [18] a Web Services based message broker is proposed to send notifications. The main difference with our approach is the scale of the solution: while this broker is lightweight and suitable to be integrated into other platforms, our mechanism is part of a wider integration platform for Bioinformatics built on top of an ESB. In [19] a WS-Eventing middleware is proposed to improve interoperability between workflows tools. This solution only allows synchronous subscriptions while ours also supports asynchronous ones. In [20] a notification bus is proposed integrating all the components. Unlike this proposal, our solution is based on a service oriented design and leverages an existing ESB infrastructure.

Regarding format transformation, the excessive use of shim services is addressed by automatically identifying which shim services are required to be included in the workflow [13]. Our work proposes reducing as much as possible, their use. In [21] the concept of Virtual Data Assembly Lines (VDAL) is presented to hide the use of shim services to scientists. While VDALs are locally defined in each workflow, our solution provides a global view of the transformed service to the whole organization.

Unlike the previously described work, our approach aims to provide a comprehensive domain-specific platform for bioinformatic services. This kind of platform provides building blocks and services adapted to a specific domain. The Open eHealth Integration Platform [22] is a platform middleware for e-health aiming at providing mechanisms to integrate e-health applications (e.g. HL7 message processing). In [23] an ESB-based platform is proposed in the context of geographic information systems. It uses mediation mechanisms (e.g. SOAP WMS-Wrapper) to facilitate the integration of geographic Web Services and enterprise applications. To the best of our knowledge there are not proposals of domain-specific integration platforms in the Bioinformatics domain using enterprise middleware technologies.

6 Conclusions and Future Work

This paper addresses the issues of improving Bioinformatics laboratory collaboration and proposes a reference integration platform which provides enhanced capabilities to implement distributed and service-based systems.

The implementation approach, based on enterprise middleware technologies (ESB, etc.), has shown to be capable of addressing the requirements of providing advanced integration features and adequately connecting to Taverna and other Bioinformatics services. Still, functionalities like processing very large data sets require further work.

The main contributions of this work consist in the analysis and identification of relevant features to be provided in a Bioinformatics integration platform, the proposed solution that can be applied to different types of laboratories, and the implementation of prototypes that enabled to validate technologies and the implementation approach.

The work also constitutes a step forward on carrying out a Platform as a Service (PaaS) approach for Bioinformatics.

Future work consists in extending the presented results with service composition and policy rules management mechanisms. On the other hand, it could include the conceptualization of Domain Specific integration platforms, beyond the Bioinformatics context, based on a PaaS approach as well as on the here applied framework.

References

1. Stevens, R., Glover, K., Greenhalgh, C., Jennings, C., Pearce, S., Li, P., Radenkovic, M., Wipat, A.: Performing in silico Experiments on the Grid: A Users' Perspective (2003)
2. Wolstencroft, K., Haines, R., Fellows, D., Williams, A., Withers, D., Owen, S., Soiland-Reyes, S., Dunlop, I., Nenadic, A., Fisher, P., Bhagat, J., Belhajjame, K., Bacall, F., Hard-isty, A., Nieva de la Hidalga, A., Balcazar Vargas, M.P., Sufi, S., Goble, C.: The Taverna workflow suite: designing and executing workflows of Web Services on the desktop, web or in the cloud. Nucleic Acids Research 41, W557–W561 (2013)
3. Dou, L., Zinn, D., McPhillips, T.M., Köhler, S., Riddle, S., Bowers, S., Ludäscher, B.: Scientific workflow design 2.0: Demonstrating streaming data collections in Kepler, ICDE 2011, pp. 1296–1299 (2011)

4. Llambías, G., Ruggia, R.: Taverna: un ambiente para el desarrollo experimentos científicos. Pedeciba Informatica
5. Ferguson, D.F.: The Internet Service Bus. In: Meersman, R., Tari, Z. (eds.) OTM 2007, Part I. LNCS, vol. 4803, p. 5. Springer, Heidelberg (2007)
6. Schmidt, M.-T., Hutchison, B., Lambros, P., Phippen, R.: The enterprise service bus: making service-oriented architecture real. IBM Syst. J. 44, 781–797 (2005)
7. Wiederhold, G.: Mediators in the architecture of future information systems. Computer 25, 38–49 (1992)
8. Mell, P., Grance, T.: The NIST Definition of Cloud Computing. NIST (2011)
9. Erl, T.: SOA design patterns. Prentice Hall, Upper Saddle River (2009)
10. Hohpe, G.: Enterprise integration patterns: designing, building, and deploying messaging solutions [..] [..]. Addison-Wesley, Boston (2003)
11. Enterprise Connectivity Patterns: Implementing integration solutions with IBM's Enterprise Service Bus products, `http://www.ibm.com/developerworks/library/ws-enterpriseconnectivitypatterns/`
12. Wassink, I., van der Vet, P.E., Wolstencroft, K., Neerincx, P.B.T., Roos, M., Rauwerda, H., Breit, T.M.: Analysing Scientific Workflows: Why Workflows Not Only Connect Web Services. (presented at the July 2009)
13. Hull, D., Stevens, R., Lord, P., Wroe, C., Goble, C.: Treating shimantic web syndrome with ontologies. University, Milton Keynes (2004)
14. Kalaš, M., Puntervoll, P., Joseph, A., Bartaševičiūtė, E., Töpfer, A., Venkataraman, P., Pettifer, S., Bryne, J.C., Ison, J., Blanchet, C., Rapacki, K., Jonassen, I.: BioXSD: the common data-exchange format for everyday bioinformatics web services. Bioinformatics 546, i540–i546 (2010)
15. Han, M.V., Zmasek, C.M.: phyloXML: XML for evolutionary biology and comparative genomics. BMC Bioinformatics 10, 356 (2009)
16. Perera, S., Gannon, D.: Enabling Web Service extensions for scientific workflows. In: Workshop on Workflows in Support of Large-Scale Science WORKS 2006, pp. 1–10 (2006)
17. Gunarathne, T., Herath, C., Chinthaka, E., Marru, S.: Experience with adapting a *WS-BPEL* runtime for eScience workflows. In: Proceedings of the 5th Grid Computing Environ-ments Workshop, pp. 1–7. ACM, New York (2009)
18. Huang, Y., Slominski, E., Herath, C., Gannon, D.: Wsmessenger: A web services-based messaging system for service-oriented grid computing. In: CCGrid (2006)
19. Alqaoud, A., Taylor, I., Jones, A.: Publish/subscribe as a model for scientific workflow interoperability. In: Proceedings of the 4th Workshop on Workflows in Support of Large-Scale Science, pp. 1:1–1:10. ACM, New York (2009)
20. Gannon, D., Christie, M., Marru, S., Shirasuna, S., Slominski, A.: Programming Paradigms for Scientific Problem Solving Environments. In: Gaffney, P.W., Pool, J.C.T. (eds.) Grid-Based Problem Solving Environments, pp. 3–15. Springer, US (2007)
21. Zinn, D., Bowers, S., McPhillips, T., Ludäscher, B.: Scientific workflow design with data assembly lines. In: Proceedings of the 4th Workshop on Workflows in Support of Large-Scale Science, pp. 14:1–14:10. ACM, New York (2009)
22. IPF Overview - Open eHealth Integration Platform 2.x - Confluence, `http://www.openehealth.org/display/ipf2/IPF+Overview`
23. Rienzi, B., González, L., Ruggia, R.: Towards an ESB-Based Enterprise Integration Platform for Geospatial Web Services. Presented at the GEOProcessing 2013, The Fifth International Conference on Advanced Geographic Information Systems, Applications, and Services (February 24, 2013)

Requirements to Pervasive System Continuous Deployment

Clément Escoffier[1,2], Ozan Günalp[1], and Philippe Lalanda[1]

[1] Université Grenoble Alpes, LIG, F-38041, Grenoble, France
{firstname.lastname}@imag.fr
[2] Dynamis-Technologies, Grenoble, France
clement.escoffier@dynamis-technologies.com

Abstract. Pervasive applications present stringent requirements that make their deployment especially challenging. The unknown and fluctuating environment in which pervasive applications are executed makes traditional approaches not suitable. In addition, the current trend to build applications out of separated components and services makes the deployment process inherently continuous and dynamic. In the last years, we developed several industrial pervasive platforms and applications. From these experiences, we identified ten requirements vital to support the continuous deployment of pervasive systems. In this paper we present these requirements and the associated challenges.

Keywords: Pervasive Computing, Continuous Deployment, Dynamism, Requirements.

1 Introduction

Pervasive computing aims to remove the barrier between users and computing systems by blending the computers into the users' environment [1]. This vision is becoming possible in the near future thanks to the recent evolutions in mobile, wireless and sensor technologies. However, the development, deployment and evolution of pervasive applications are difficult challenges [2,3,4]. Building a robust pervasive application does not only require the business logic but a large amount of code to deal with device heterogeneity and volatility, security enforcement and adaptability.

A multitude of works are providing smart execution environments dealing with the pervasive constraints at runtime on behalf of the application [5,6,7,8]. These approaches distinguish the execution environment from the applications. The platform deals with the device communication, manages the application scheduling, and provides different technical services, simplifying the application code. These approaches have proved their maturity reaching operational states [9]. A large part of these works are built upon the service-oriented computing paradigm. Indeed, pervasive applications are often subject to architectural reconfigurations at runtime to cope with the changeability of the surrounding environment. The

A.R. Lomuscio et al. (Eds.): ICSOC 2013 Workshops, LNCS 8377, pp. 457–468, 2014.
© Springer International Publishing Switzerland 2014

loose-coupling and dynamic management of the service-orientation [10] allows such reconfiguration, avoiding service disruptions [11].

Fewer works have been done on the deployment of such applications and platforms. Unfortunately, the pervasive environment characteristics lead to numerous challenges impacting the deployment process. The unknown nature and variability of the environment, in which pervasive applications are executed, discard traditional deployment approaches. The deployment process must not only install the application's components but also adapt them to the current and future context situations (i.e. available devices, users, computation resources...). In addition, continuous evolution of pervasive applications and platforms makes the deployment process even more complex. As a consequence, specific tools must be provided to manage the deployment of such systems in a robust and industrial way.

In the last years, we implemented pervasive platforms and applications in several industrial projects. Throughout these developments, we identified stringent requirements that must be fulfilled to successfully support the continuous deployment of pervasive systems. This paper presents the different requirements for pervasive system deployment and confronts existing tools with these requirements.

This paper is organized as follows. After having briefly remembered the pervasive environment characteristics and the pervasive system deployment scope, the different requirements are described. These requirements are organized in two categories: the deployment platform and the deployment process. These sections are followed by a comparison of industrial and academic works with these requirements. This paper concludes by giving perspectives to successfully implement a deployment support for pervasive systems.

2 The Pervasive Environment

Before presenting the key features of pervasive system deployment, let's first remind the characteristics of pervasive environment. The term 'Pervasive' is used as a synonym for ubiquitous, ambient, seamless and transparent: it is the extension of software systems in the physical world. Pervasive systems offer sophisticated services to users by relying on smart, communicative, autonomous and diffused objects. The 'how' such features are provided is remarkable. Pervasive systems are so melted with the environment that features are accessible seamlessly naturally and unobtrusively. This invisibility makes usages so easy that users are consuming them even without noticing the system. However, this invisibility makes the development of pervasive systems very strenuous.

Developing pervasive systems is not only a software development challenge. It is an integration problem between devices, software applications and platforms. This triptych is fundamental, but extremely delicate to achieve correctly. Indeed, it involves tough aspects as the device volatility, continuous context evolution, security enforcement, privacy protection, and the so difficult but essential melting of the user interactions with his/her environment. Supporting all these characteristics have an obvious consequence on the application complexity. Software engineering principles, methodologies, techniques and specific tools are required to support pervasive application development.

A common approach to deal with the inherent complexity of pervasive applications is the distinction between the execution framework and the applications (Figure 1). The execution framework is responsible for dealing with all non-functional properties, such as persistence, security and remote management, on behalf of the application. These applications running on such a platform are much easier to develop, manage, and maintain because they rely on the features provided by the specialized domain-centric platform. This architecture is not new, and widely used in other domains such as enterprise applications [12,13] and mediation platforms [14].

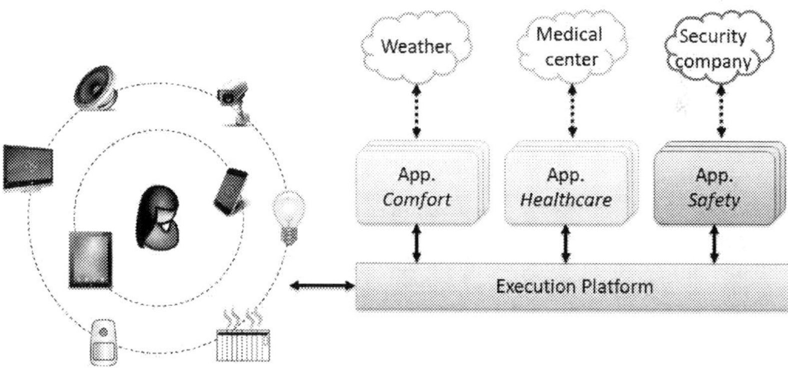

Fig. 1. Pervasive application server in its environment

In this paper, we define the *pervasive system* as the execution platform and the set of applications running on it. The surrounding *environment* is composed by the devices and users. Finally, the *context* is a set of data collected from the environment and the platform, containing all the required information to implement context-aware behavior [15].

3 Continuous Deployment of Pervasive Systems

Informally, the term software deployment refers to all the activities that make a software system available for use [16]. It's a post-production activity [17]. Generally, it is at this point in time that all user centric customization and configuration takes place. Traditional deployment facilities are able to install and activate *resources* (code, binaries, files, configurations...) on pre-defined sites. Different works use different terms for defining manipulated resources such as component, artifact and yet product. The deployment descriptor defines how the deployment process will proceed.

The deployment process also includes the update and uninstallation of the deployed artifacts [18]. The process can be triggered from the platform or remotely, but an agent, present on the platform, deals with all the on-site activities [19].

Recently, continuous deployment approaches are becoming very popular [20]. Software systems are continuously updated with new versions continuously improving the services provided to the users [21]. Continuous deployment opens several possibilities such as the reduction of service disruptions and migration between versions [22]. Although, providing these capabilities is intricate, continuous deployment is particularly interesting for pervasive systems. The characteristics of the pervasive environment induce unceasing installations, updates and removals of software components. First, the platform itself is remotely operated, and subject to regular updates. Second, applications are deployed on-demand, and are updated regularly. Finally, whenever a new device type is discovered, a software driver must be installed to correctly interact with the device. Unfortunately, despite the ability of most of the deployment technologies to manage some pre-defined variability, and drive adaptations [19,18], they are insufficient for pervasive systems. The pervasive environment and system exhibit a large degree of dynamism. Devices appear and disappear dynamically; users also arrive, leave, or modify their intents. This dynamism does not only require actions at installation time, but must keep these components continuously in-sync with the changing environment. This characteristic extends the deployment process with a continuously executed adaptation loop such as in [23]. The deployment agent has to monitor and adapt the deployed system to environment changes. Obviously these reconfigurations are only possible if the deployment descriptor enables enough flexibility.

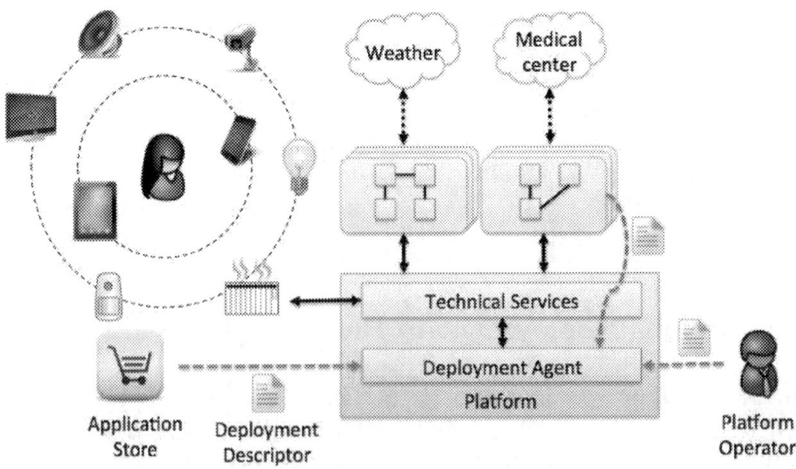

Fig. 2. Deployment agent on pervasive execution platform

Consequently, new deployment facilities must be provided to face the pervasive environment characteristics. The requirements described in this paper must be satisfied to successfully support pervasive application deployment (Figure 2).

4 Platform Requirements

The first category of requirement focuses on the deployment platform, i.e. the facilities that must be provided by the execution environment to support the continuous deployment of pervasive applications. The platform must provide the ability to deploy components separately at runtime in a continuous way. Because of the dynamism exhibited by the pervasive environment, the platform must also provide configuration, introspection, architectural reconfiguration and context mining capabilities.

4.1 Requirement PF.1 – Modular Dynamic Deployment Platform

Obviously, pervasive systems cannot be monolithic, the underlying execution platform must provide modularity support. Monolithic approaches would not be able to dynamically adapt themselves to unanticipated situations. The platforms and applications must be composed by distinct modules that can be deployed and updated individually. Modularity also requires dependency management. Modules declares dependencies that must be handled by the deployment process. The targeted entities can be a module, or be more abstract in order to introduce variability and constraints.

As the deployment of a module must not disrupt the services offered by other already deployed modules, the platform must offer dynamic deployment facilities. Modules can be installed, uninstalled or updated dynamically without requiring a restart of the platform and impacting the execution of unrelated components.

4.2 Requirement PF.2 – Configurability

The deployment process is not limited to transfer software components to the execution environment; it also includes configurations. This requirement is particularly important in pervasive environment, as the configuration is one of the most used levers to handle adaptations.

Because of the dynamic adaptations required by pervasive systems, the configurations must be updatable at runtime. The platform must provide mechanisms to store configurations, update and apply them dynamically.

4.3 Requirement PF.3 – Introspection

Managing modules and configurations is not enough. The platform must also provide information about the current modules and their states, and configurations. Having such introspection facilities is an absolute requirement to let the deployment process determines the changes to apply on the system.

The introspection layer must not be limited to the installed modules, but also represent system specificities, available services, computational resources and any data required by the deployment agent to drive the deployment process.

4.4 Requirement PF.4 – Architectural Reconfiguration Support

As stated above, pervasive applications often require architectural reconfigurations [24] to meet the changing environment constraints. The platform must provide all the required mechanisms to support such reconfigurations [25]. This includes the management of state integrity of modules [26] and the reduction of the service disruption [27]. Service-orientation is today widely used to support dynamic reconfiguration support as in [11].

4.5 Requirement PF.5 – Context access

Finally, the last requirement for the platform is the context representation. Pervasive applications are context-aware, but the deployment process also depends on the context. The continuous deployment process needs to consume contextual data and performs deployment tasks in respond to the changes. Therefore, the platform must provide means to retrieve and observe contextual information.

4.6 Related Work on Deployment Platforms

In this section we position well-known platforms and academic works against presented platform requirements and compare them (Table 1). Nearly all deployment solutions are built on existing platforms. They enhance standard functionalities on these platforms for providing deployment operations.

Package managers, such as RPM [28] built on Linux systems, are heavily used in the provisioning of industrial applications. The combination of the underlying operating system and the package manager allow the installation, updates and removal of packages dynamically. The package structure, their customization and how dependencies are expressed make them an interesting approach to build Linux-based pervasive systems. With the rise of Cloud Computing, new tools have emerged to ease deployment in large-scale [29,30]. Infrastructure as code [31] facilitates creating deployment descriptions. These systems support configuration and reconfiguration of different types of systems. However, they don not support architectural reconfiguration. Their context management is also limited to predefined data.

The OSGi service platform has become the de-facto modular layer for the Java Virtual Machine. OSGi defines a dynamic deployment platform fulfilling most of the platform criteria. With modular deployment capabilities, OSGi constitutes an important foundation for building Java-based deployment platforms. OSGi supports way to support architectural reconfiguration by promoting service-orientation. However it requires very complex code to manage it correctly. In addition it does not provide any context support.

In academia, early works such as [32] concentrated on defining bases of deployment platforms and stressed importance of modularity and the dynamic update of modules. Later, platforms that provide dynamic reconfigurability feature [33,34] gained focus as foundations for deployment in pervasive environments.

By default, all of these systems satisfy introspection requirement, which is absolutely necessary for any kind of deployment. However, they lack the context mining ability. Without a proper access to contextual information, they cannot be used for deploying pervasive systems.

Table 1. Positioning of deployment approaches against the platform requirements

Tools	Dynamic and Modular Deployment	Configurability	Introspection	Architectural Reconfiguration	Context representation
RPM w/ Linux	●	●	●	○	○
Puppet w/ Linux	●	●	●	●	◐
Chef w/ Linux	●	●	●	○	◐
OSGi	●	●	●	◐	○
JDrums[32]	●	●	●	○	○
Sofa 2.0[33]	●	●	●	●	○

5 Deployment Process Requirements

The previous section has constrained the execution platform. This section focuses on the deployment process itself. The pervasive environment imposes several characteristics to the deployment process.

Whether it is for an installation, update or uninstallation, the deployment process is initiated either from the system or externally. Then, it analyzes the deployment request and defines a deployment plan listing all the actions. This process includes the selection and/or refinement of the components to deploy. Because of the pervasive environment characteristics, the decisions taken during the deployment process may become invalid, and adaptations must be applied to keep the applications in an operational state.

5.1 Requirement P.1 – Pull and Push

The deployment process may be triggered either by system itself or push from externally. In the first case, the system discovers a new required resource, such as a device driver and asks the deployment agent to install the required artifacts. In the second case, the deployment process is triggered by an external entity. It can be the user having purchased a new application on a store, an application update pushed by the application vendor or the platform operator updating technical services.

The openness and uncertainty of the pervasive environment requires that the pull and push are supported. More interestingly, the source of the push is not unique. Multiple sources complexify the scheduling and prioritization of deployment requests.

5.2 Requirement P.2 – Determinism and Idempotence

Determinism is an essential property to make pervasive system deployment reproducible. For a particular environment, on a specific platform, a singular deployment process must always result to the same system. Such a capability is critical for making the deployment process testable, and improve the reliability of the deployment infrastructure.

In addition, the idempotence is also important. It implies that deployment of already deployed artifacts would not change the system. This property is rarely supported in traditional deployment platforms. Unfortunately, the multiplicity of deployment sources makes the idempotence a requirement necessary but difficult to satisfy.

5.3 Requirement P.3 – Transactional

The deployment process is constituted from a set of actions that change the pervasive system. However, one ore more of these deployment actions can fail. In this case, it is essential to rollback to an operational state, avoiding stale situations. As a consequence, all the deployment activities must be executed inside a transaction [35].

Many deployment technologies are supporting transactions, however in case of the pervasive environment and its surrounding dynamism, transactions are not only impacted by the deployment process but also by external events. This aspect makes the transaction support very complex to implement.

5.4 Requirement P.4 – Adaptability and Customizability

One of the main differences between traditional deployment and pervasive system deployment is unknown environment in which the applications are deployed. The constantly changing target site entails the process to adapt itself. These adaptations include variability in the resource selection, resolution and activation. This variability often relies on the dependencies and constraints expressed by modules or in the deployment descriptor.

In addition, the platform is an active actor in the deployment process. It often needs to participate to the resolution and decision making process to adapt the deployed resources and their configurations. The deployment process should be customizable according to platforms changing requirements and constraints. For instance, the platform may provide the process with configuration data and influence dependency resolution to fit the underlying system constraints.

5.5 Requirement P.5 – Continuous Adaptation

Deployment process adaptation does not only happen during the initial deployment. Throughout the lifetime of the system, adaptations are required such as in [36]. Environmental changes may require to adapt already installed resources. Newly installed applications may also ask for optimizations or reconfigurations on technical services provided by the platform.

This continuous adaptation process is similar to the autonomic computing loop proposed by [37]. In such paradigm, the deployment agent would be an autonomic manager handling deployment requests, and adapting applications when changes influence the component selection and/or configuration. Notice that pervasive applications are often autonomic [38,39] and application's autonomic manager collaborate with the deployment agent as proposed in [40].

5.6 Related Work on Deployment Process

In this section, we position well-known platforms and academic works against the presented process requirements. Table 2 summarizes this study.

Table 2. Positioning of deployment approaches against the process requirements

Tools	Pull & Push	Determinism & Idempotence	Transactional Process	Adaptable & Customizable	Continuous Adaptation
RPM w/ Linux	Pull only	●	●	●	○
Puppet w/ Linux	●	●	○	●	○
Chef w/ Linux	●	◐	●	●	○
OSGi	Pull only	◐	○	○	○
OSGi w/ Deployment Admin	Pull Only	●	●	●	○
OSGi w/ Apache Ace	Push Only	●	●	●	○
Software Dock [19]	Pull Only				
Constraint-based Approaches [41,34]	Pull Only	○	○	●	◐

Package managers enhancing the operating system are providing very customizable transactional deployment processes. Every module can extend the process with pre- and post- actions. Unfortunately, they do not support external push. In addition, they do not drive any continuous adaptation.

Tools like Puppet or Chef rely on package managers to support large-scale deployment. Using a centralized *master* server, they can trigger deployment remotely. Thanks to the resource-based model promoted by Puppet, it supports idempotence. However this feature makes the usage of Puppet much more complex for administrators, requiring to shift their mind to this new model.

Software Docks [19] proposes a deployment agent supporting a very customizable process. It can adapt deployed components to the current environment, and install additional components according to the current constraints. Unfortunately, they do not support continuous adaptation, and do not natively provide a dynamic deployment platform.

Many tools rely on OSGi to enhance its deployment capabilities. The deployment admin provide a transaction model. Apache Ace is based on the deployment admin and allow controlling deployments from a remote server. However both do not provide enough flexibility to support pervasive deployment.

Several projects have proposed autonomic deployment process such as [41] and [34]. The proposed approaches are based on constraint-solving to select the components to install. However, none of them is supporting transactions, and their support of the continuous adaptation is not deterministic.

6 Conclusion

The heterogeneity, uncertainty and dynamics of the pervasive environment are not only making developing applications harder but also the deployment. In addition, pervasive systems require advanced deployment scenarios, including continuous deployment initiated from different sources. Because of the pervasive environment characteristics, traditional deployment tools are not suitable.

This paper has presented ten requirements impacting the deployment platform and process for supporting the continuous deployment of pervasive systems. Unfortunately, existing tools do not fully match with these requirements. In the near future, we aim to provide a tool suite to fully support the continuous deployment of pervasive applications.

Trends such as infrastructure as code and resource-orientation are providing very interesting features that may be used to implement pervasive deployment facilities. However, variability must be infused within the language.

The context-awareness of the deployment platform is a very hard requirements. We believe that pervasive deployment must rely on a context engine supporting advanced context mining capabilities and runtime extensibility.

Finally, applying the autonomic computing principles to support the continuous adaptation is a very promising trend. It must go along with a platform supporting architectural reconfiguration. It looks clear that the service-oriented computing will play a central role in such platform.

References

1. Weiser, M.: The computer for the 21st century. In: Human-computer Interaction, pp. 933–940. Morgan Kaufmann Publishers Inc. (1995)
2. Banavar, G., Bernstein, A.: Software infrastructure and design challenges for ubiquitous computing applications. Communications of the ACM 45(12), 92–96 (2002)

3. Thackara, J.: The design challenge of pervasive computing. Interactions 8(3), 46–52 (2001)
4. Bhaskar, P., Ahamed, S.I.: Privacy in Pervasive Computing and Open Issues. In: AERES, pp. 147–154. IEEE Computer Society (2007)
5. King, J., Bose, R., Yang, H.I., Pickles, S., Helal, A.: Atlas: A service-oriented sensor platform: Hardware and middleware to enable programmable pervasive spaces. In: Proceedings 2006 31st IEEE Conference on Local Computer Networks, pp. 630–638. IEEE (2006)
6. Escoffier, C., Bourcier, J., Lalanda, P., Yu, J.: Towards a home application server. In: Consumer Communications and Networking Conference, pp. 321–325 (2008)
7. Helal, S., Mann, W., El-Zabadani, H., King, J., Kaddoura, Y., Jansen, E.: The Gator Tech Smart House: a programmable pervasive space. Computer 38(3), 50–60 (2005)
8. Schreiber, F., Camplani, R., Fortunato, M., Marelli, M., Rota, G.: Perla: A language and middleware architecture for data management and integration in pervasive information systems. IEEE Transactions on Software Engineering 38(2), 478–496 (2012)
9. Coll, J.F., Angskog, P., Chilo, J., Stenumgaard, P.: Industrial environment characterization for future m2m applications. In: 2011 IEEE International Symposium on Electromagnetic Compatibility (EMC), pp. 960–963. IEEE (2011)
10. Papazoglou, M.P.: Service-Oriented Computing: Concepts, Characteristics and Directions. In: Proceedings of the fourth International Conference on Web Information Systems Engineering, Los Alamitos, CA, USA, pp. 3–12 (December 2003)
11. Escoffier, C., Bourret, P., Lalanda, P.: Managing Dynamism in Service Dependencies. In: IEEE International Conference on Services Computing. IEEE Computer Society, Los Alamitos (2013)
12. Burke, B., Monson-Haefel, R., Szczepaniak, M., Ostrowski, K.: Enterprise JavaBeans 3.0., vol. 5. O'Reilly (2006)
13. Lowy, J.: Programming. NET Components: Design and Build. NET Applications Using Component-Oriented Programming. O'Reilly (2009)
14. Chappell, D.A.: Enterprise Service Bus. O'Reilly Media, Inc. (2009)
15. Dey, A.K.: Understanding and Using Context. Personal and Ubiquitous Computing 5(1), 4–7 (2001)
16. Object Management Group: Deployment & Configuration of Component-based Distributed Applications Specification - version 4.0. OMG (April)
17. Dearle, A.: Software deployment, past, present and future. In: 2007 Future of Software Engineering. IEEE Computer Society pp. 269–284 (2007)
18. Carzaniga, A., Fuggetta, A., Hall, R.S., Heimbigner, D., Van Der Hoek, A., Wolf, A.L.: A characterization framework for software deployment technologies. Technical report, DTIC Document (1998)
19. Hall, R.S., Heimbigner, D., Wolf, A.L.: A cooperative approach to support software deployment using the software dock. In: Proceedings of the 21st International Conference on Software Engineering, pp. 174–183. ACM (1999)
20. Humble, J., Farley, D.: Continuous Delivery: Reliable Software Releases through Build, Test, and Deployment Automation. Addison-Wesley (2010)
21. Feitelson, D., Frachtenberg, E., Beck, K.: Development and Deployment at Facebook. IEEE Internet Computing 17(4), 8–17 (2013)
22. Humble, J., Read, C., North, D.: The Deployment Production Line. In: Proceedings of the Conference on AGILE 2006, pp. 113–118. IEEE Computer Society, Washington, DC (2006)

23. Dong, X., Hariri, S., Xue, L., Chen, H., Zhang, M., Pavuluri, S., Rao, S.: Autonomia: an autonomic computing environment. In: IEEE Conference on Performance, Computing, and Communications Conference, pp. 61–68 (2003)
24. Oreizy, P., Gorlick, M.M., Taylor, R.N., Heimhigner, D., Johnson, G., Medvidovic, N., Quilici, A., Rosenblum, D.S., Wolf, A.L.: An architecture-based approach to self-adaptive software. IEEE Intelligent Systems and Their Applications 14(3), 54–62 (1999)
25. Mikic-Rakic, M., Medvidovíc, N.: Architecture-level support for software component deployment in resource constrained environments. In: Bishop, J.M. (ed.) CD 2002. LNCS, vol. 2370, pp. 31–50. Springer, Heidelberg (2002)
26. Kramer, J., Magee, J.: The evolving philosophers problem: dynamic change management. IEEE Transactions on Software Engineering 16(11), 1293–1306 (1990)
27. Vandewoude, Y., Ebraert, P., Berbers, Y., D'Hondt, T.: Tranquility: A low disruptive alternative to quiescence for ensuring safe dynamic updates. IEEE Transactions on Software Engineering 33(12), 856–868 (2007)
28. Bailey, E.: Maximum RPM. Red Hat Software Inc. (February 1997)
29. Turnbull, J., McCune, J.: Pro Puppet. Apress (2011)
30. Nelson-Smith, S.: Test-Driven Infrastructure with Chef. O'Reilly (2011)
31. Spinellis, D.: Don't Install Software by Hand. IEEE Software 29(4), 86–87 (2012)
32. Andersson, J.: A deployment system for pervasive computing. In: Proceedings of the International Conference on Software Maintenance, pp. 262–270 (2000)
33. Bures, T., Hnetynka, P., Plasil, F.: Sofa 2.0: Balancing advanced features in a hierarchical component model. In: Fourth International Conference on Software Engineering Research, Management and Applications, pp. 40–48 (2006)
34. Hoareau, D., Mahéo, Y.: Middleware support for the deployment of ubiquitous software components. Personal and Ubiquitous Computing 12(2), 167–178 (2008)
35. Coghlan, B.A., Walsh, J., Quigley, G., O'Callaghan, D., Childs, S., Kenny, E.: Principles of transactional grid deployment. In: Sloot, P.M.A., Hoekstra, A.G., Priol, T., Reinefeld, A., Bubak, M. (eds.) EGC 2005. LNCS, vol. 3470, pp. 88–97. Springer, Heidelberg (2005), http://dx.doi.org/10.1007/11508380_11
36. Medvidovic, N., Malek, S.: Software deployment architecture and quality-of-service in pervasive environments. In: International Workshop on Engineering of Software Services for Pervasive Environments, pp. 47–51. ACM (2007)
37. Kephart, J.O., Chess, D.M.: The vision of autonomic computing. Computer 36(1), 41–50 (2003)
38. Parashar, M., Liu, H., Li, Z., Matossian, V., Schmidt, C., Zhang, G., Hariri, S.: AutoMate: Enabling Autonomic Applications on the Grid. Cluster Computing 9(2), 161–174 (2006)
39. Diaconescu, A., Bourcier, J., Escoffier, C.: Autonomic iPOJO: Towards Self-Managing Middleware for Ubiquitous Systems. In: IEEE International Conference on Wireless and Mobile Computing, Networking and Communications, WIMOB 2008, pp. 472–477 (2008)
40. Maurel, Y., Diaconescu, A., Lalanda, P.: CEYLON: A Service-Oriented Framework for Building Autonomic Managers. In: 2010 Seventh IEEE International Conference and Workshops on Engineering of Autonomic and Autonomous Systems (2010)
41. Dearle, A., Kirby, G.N.C., McCarthy, A.: A framework for constraint-based development and autonomic management of distributed applications. In: Proceedings of the International Conference on Autonomic Computing, pp. 300–301 (2004)

Towards Structure-Based Quality Awareness in Software Ecosystem Use

Klaus Marius Hansen[1] and Weishan Zhang[2]

[1] Department of Computer Science
University of Copenhagen, Denmark
klausmh@diku.dk
[2] China University of Petroleum, Qingdao, China

Abstract. Software ecosystems – a group of actors, one or more business models that serve these actors in a possible wider sense than direct revenues, one or more software platforms that the business models are built upon and the relationships of the actors and business models – are gaining importance in software development as a way of increasing software innovation, decreasing internal development cost, and spreading software platforms. Software quality, not only of individual applications or components, but also of the software ecosystems as a whole is important, but has not received much attention so far. We here aim to explore to which extent composition of components from a software ecosystem influences software quality. We do this in order to provide groundwork for application awareness of software quality in a software ecosystem context.

We ran the same Maven build tasks in 15 simultaneous releases (including associated service releases) of Eclipse and measured time, energy, and memory performance. Based on an analysis of the plugins installed with the versions of Eclipse, we next found the structure of the subset of the Eclipse software ecosystem that was used in each version. The performance measurements and computed structure were then analyzed and compared. We found that performance and structure changed considerably throughout versions of Eclipse. While we found no direct correlation between the evolution of the two, our exploratory study warrants further study.

1 Introduction

Arguably, one of the reasons why Apple iOS and Google Android have gathered the main smartphone market share is the abundance of applications that are available for these platforms. The number of Android applications available is, e.g., rapidly approaching 1,000,000[1]. These applications are not developed by Apple or Google alone, but mostly by independent developers that use APIs, tools, and frameworks provided by Apple and Google. Having developed an application, developers can then choose to sell application (for a fee) using Apple's or Google's infrastructure (iOS App Store or Google Play). This symbiotic

[1] http://www.appbrain.com/stats/number-of-android-apps

A.R. Lomuscio et al. (Eds.): ICSOC 2013 Workshops, LNCS 8377, pp. 469–479, 2014.
© Springer International Publishing Switzerland 2014

relationship between actors (Apple, Google, developers, smartphone users) is instrumental in the platforms' success and the backbone of what has been termed "software ecosystems".

It is not only within the smartphone (application) domain that software ecosystems are becoming important and relevant. Another domain is software development itself, where development tools such as Apache Maven or Eclipse provide a base platform that is either a platform for an ecosystem or part of an ecosystem itself. In such situations, the composition of elements in the software ecosystem becomes important. Does one composition (or choice) of elements, e.g., lead to better performance, more defects, or better productivity? In this paper we provide an initial exploration of these questions in the context of the Eclipse software ecosystem by i) analyzing the structure of the networks of releases of the Eclipse software ecosystem and ii) by analyzing performance characteristics of releases of the Eclipse software ecosystem.

The rest of this paper is structured as follows: First, we provide background and point to related work (Section 2). We then (Section 3) describe the steps we took in our exploratory analysis, followed by a discussion of the results obtained (Section 4. Finally, we conclude and point to future work (Section 5).

2 Background and Related Work

This section introduces central concepts used in this paper and (very) briefly discusses related work.

2.1 Software Ecosystems

Software ecosystems [1,2] may be defined as [2]

> the interaction of a set of actors on top of a common technological platform that results in a number of software solutions or services

Furthermore

> Each actor is motivated by a set of interests or business models and connected to the rest of the actors and the ecosystem as a whole with symbiotic relationships, while, the technological platform is structured in a way that allows the involvement and contribution of the different actors.

Prominent examples of software ecosystems include Google's Android and Apple's iOS. Taking Android as an example, the common technological platform is the Android operating system and the software services that are built on top are manifested as applications on (in particular) Android-based smartphones. While Google is central in providing Android, another key actor is arguably Samsung[2]

[2] http://blogs.strategyanalytics.com/WSS/post/2013/05/15/Samsung-Captures-95-Percent-Share-of-Global-Android-Smartphone-Profits-in-Q1-2013.aspx

that sells the largest number of Android smartphones. In addition, independent application developers may develop applications ("apps") using Android's APIs, publish these on Google Play, and sell them, leaving a transaction fee (30%) for Google.

Research on software ecosystems is increasing, but so far there has been little research in the context of real-world software ecosystems [2]. This paper presents research on the Eclipse ecosystem (that we discuss next) and on network analysis of software ecosystems.

2.2 Eclipse

Eclipse[3] is a platform for integrated development environments that can be extended via *plugins*. One (the main) such extension is the widely-used Java Development Tools (JDT) version of Eclipse that supports Java development. Eclipse provides an API for extension via plugins and plugins be shared (and even sold) on the Eclipse Marketplace[4]. As such, Eclipse delineates a software ecosystem.

Plugins for Eclipse are written in Java and based on the OSGi specifications [3]. OSGi defines a dynamic component and service model for Java based on *bundles*. Bundles are JAR files that have added metadata describing among others their modularity in terms of imports and exports of Java packages. Bundles are loaded by an OSGi framework that manages their lifecycle (installing, starting, stopping, updating). The core of Eclipse is one such framework, *Equinox*.

While there have been many empirical studies of Eclipse (e.g., [4,5,6,7]), few have investigated the structure of the Eclipse ecosystem as a *network*. Kidane et al. [5] investigated social networks forming around Eclipse whereas we are concerned with networks of bundles (as defined by dependencies) in Eclipse.

2.3 Network Analysis

Complex structures often form *networks*, a pattern of connections among things [8]. Examples of networks include social networks (in which people are connected, e.g., through their communication), the Web (in which web pages are connected via links), and international trade (in which countries are connected through trade). Networks are most often modelled as graphs of *nodes* (or vertices) and *links* (or edges); in the social network example, a person would be represented by a node that would be connected to other nodes (persons) if those persons had communicated.

Given a network modelled as a graph, graph theoretical measures can then be applied for network analysis [8]. In this paper, we apply such techniques to analyse the Eclipse software ecosystem network of bundles. Manikas and Hansen [9] previously used network analysis to analyse the structure of two OSGi frameworks, but in this paper propose to compare the results of a structural analysis to a performance analysis.

---

[3] `http://www.eclipse.org`

[4] `http://marketplace.eclipse.org/`

3 Method

We analyzed 7 'simultaneous' releases of Eclipse (Europa, Galileo, Ganymede, Helios, Indigo, Juno, and Kepler) versions of Eclipse and 9 service releases of these (see Table 1) for the complete list. Throughout, we used the 32 bit Java EE versions of Eclipse. For each of the 16 versions, we performed a *dynamic performance analysis* and a *static structural analysis*[5].

Table 1. Summary statistics of Eclipse versions

#	Release	Version	Release date	#nodes
1	Europa	3.3	2007-06-29	173
2	Galileo	3.5	2009-06-24	247
3	Galileo SR1	3.5.1		248
4	Galileo SR2	3.5.2		249
5	Ganymede	3.4	2008-06-25	220
6	Ganymede SR1	3.4.1		221
7	Ganymede SR2	3.4.2		221
8	Helios	3.6	2010-06-23	249
9	Helios SR1	3.6.1		249
10	Indigo	3.7	2011-06-22	302
11	Indigo SR1	3.7.1		312
	(Indigo SR2)	3.7.2		394
12	Juno	4.2	2012-06-27	394
13	Juno SR1	4.2.1		394
14	Juno SR2	4.2.2		398
15	Kepler	4.3	2013-06-26	383

3.1 Dynamic Analysis

For each Eclipse release, we performed the same following compilation steps 9 times using JVM 1.6.20-b02 with Windows 7 (64 bit) as operating system and Thinkpad W700 T9400 2.53G CPU, 7200rpm hard disk, 4G DDR2 RAM as hardware. The software system compiled was the open source Net4Care framework[6] in version 0.4. The compilation steps performed were:

- Start the appropriate Eclipse version
- Run "clean" using Maven
- Run "install" using Maven
- Shut down Eclipse

For each run, we (manually) recorded the state of Eclipse: "starting", "started", "cleaning", "cleaned", "installing", "installed", "stopping", and "stopped" and

[5] We exclude Indigo SR2 from the dynamic analysis since our measurements for that version were outliers.

[6] `http://www.net4care.org`

the transition time between states. During the runs, we recorded energy consumption using a digital multimeter (a UNI-T UT71C Digital Multimeter). Furthermore, we measured CPU, memory, internet connection, file, and thread usage by the Eclipse process using the Python "psutil" module running in a separate process.

3.2 Static Analysis

We analyzed the JAR files of the plugins in each Eclipse release. The "#nodes" column in Table 1 presents a count of the number of plugins in each installation. We based our analysis on the manifest files of the plugins. Based on the "Export-Package" and "Import-Package" OSGi headers [3], we deduce that a plugin is dependent on another if the first exports a package (as specified in the "Export-Package" header) that the last imports (as specified in the "Import-Package" header).

In this way, we construct a network for each release with plugins as nodes and dependencies (as calculated above) as links. The networks were exported to GraphML and imported into the Gephi graph visualization platform version 0.8.2. Using Gephi, we calculated the following (average) metrics:

- *In-Degree:* the number of links to a node
- *Eccentricity:* the distance from a node to the node furthest away in the network
- *Closeness Centrality:* the average distance from a node to all other nodes
- *Number of Nodes*: the total number of nodes (i.e., plugins in our case) in the network
- *Number of Edges*: the total number of edges (i.e., package import dependencies in our case) in the network
- *Betweenness Centrality:* the sum of the proportions of shortest paths from all nodes to all others nodes that pass through a node
- *PageRank:* a directed variant of Eigenvector Centrality in which nodes linked to a node are considered ($p = 0.85, \epsilon = 0.0010$) [10]
- *Clustering Coefficient:* for a node, the proportion of actual links between the node's neighbors to possible links
- *Eigenvector Centrality:* a measure of importance/centrality for a node in which the centrality is proportional to the average centralities of its neighbors

Furthermore, we used download volumes (from `http://www.eclipse.org/downloads/packages/` (July 2013)) and defects counts (from `https://bugs.eclipse.org/bugs/query.cgi` (July 2013)) to calculate the following additional quality metrics [11]:

- *Rate Of Usage:* the number of downloads per day. For (gratis) open source software this is arguably a value-based quality metric
- *Open Defect Ratio:* the number of open defect to the number of open plus closed defects (plus 1). For Eclipse, we used counts of open defects in "JDT" and classified defects with a "STATUS" of "UNCONFIRMED", "NEW", "ASSIGNED", and "REOPENED" as "open". We classified "RESOLVED", "VERIFIED", and "CLOSED" defects as "closed".

4 Results

Figure 1 shows a typical run for our dynamic analyses. Eclipse initially allocates ressources file, thread, and connection ressources (no connections are allocated in this version). CPU usage is initially high, but then falls. Power usage remains at about the same level.

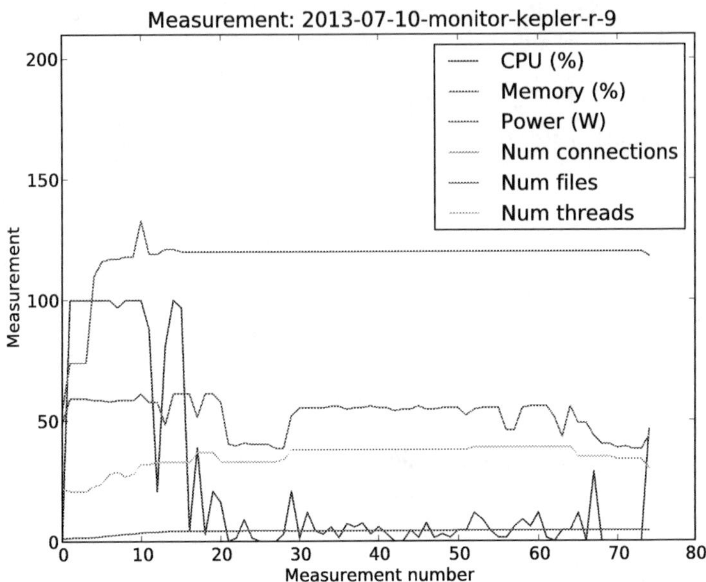

Fig. 1. Example of runtime measurements for Eclipse Kepler. Graphs are made with Matplotlib [12].

Focussing on power usage, Figure 2 shows box plots for each of the states of the experiment and for each version of Eclipse. In general, there appears to be little difference in the power usage among versions, but power usage is generally highest in the “starting” state.

Average execution time varied across Eclipse version with Ganymede and Helios being fastest and the most recent version, Kepler, being next (see Table 2).

Open Defect Ratio appears higher for later versions of Eclipse (Juno and Kepler) but is most probably due to these versions having high Rate Of Usage and having existed for shorter time (see Table 2).

Concerning the structure of the Eclipse dependencies, Figure 3 shows a visualization of the dependency network. The three nodes with highest in-degree correspond to org.eclipse.osgi (70), com.ibm.icu (52), and javax.xml (37). The four nodes with highest out-degree correspond to org.eclipse.equinox.p2.reconciler.-dropins (13), org.eclipse.ui.workbench (12), org.eclipse.equinox.p2.ui (12), and org.eclipse.equinox.touchpoint.eclipse (12).

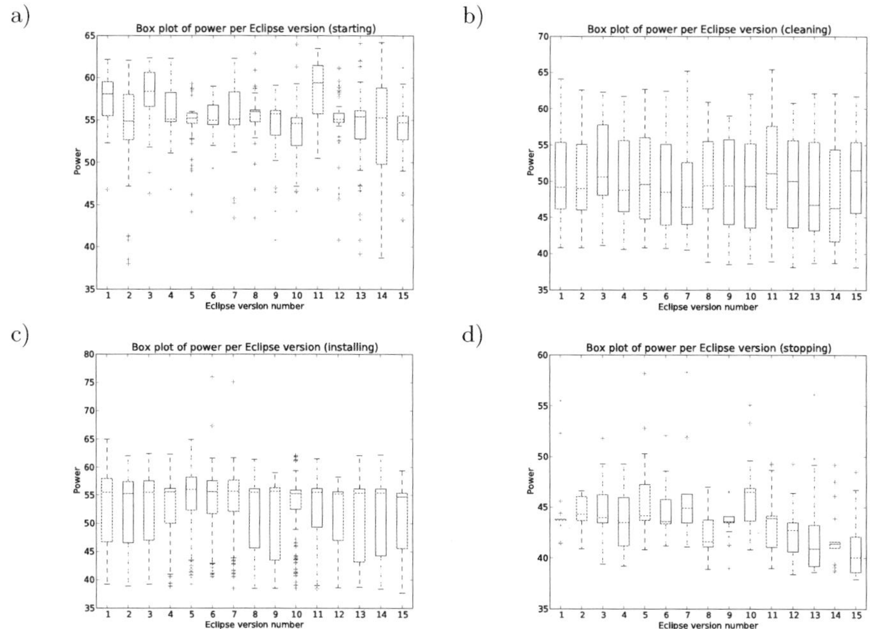

Fig. 2. Boxplots of power usage of Eclipse versions in different states: a) starting, b) cleaning, c) installing, d) stopping

Table 2. Quality data for Eclipse releases (July 2013)

Release	Rate Of Usage	Open Defect Ratio	Execution time (s)
Europa	n/a	0.19	91.33
Ganymede	n/a	0.26	76.38
Galileo	n/a	0.27	88.15
Helios	n/a	0.30	76.12
Indigo	3365.91	0.36	86.34
Juno	11600.39	0.83	84.11
Kepler	5899.60	0.65	82.80

Finally, Table 3 (page 477) shows a summary of the (average) metrics for the dependency networks. In general, the number of nodes (plugins) and edges (dependencies) are increasing with releases (and unsurprisingly also in every service release). The Kepler release is the only exception to this. Except for the earliest Europa release, the average in-degree and clustering coefficient appears stable, signifying that while new plugins are introduced these (and older plugins) keep being used.

Average betweenness centrality appears to rise, with a peak for Juno. Looking at Juno, there is a set of highly central nodes: org.eclipse.equinox.security (386.8), org.eclipse.jetty.servlet (360.1), org.eclipse.jetty.server (347.0), org.eclipse.osgi.-services ((315.1), and org.eclipse.jetty.util (306.2). Interestingly, the same is not

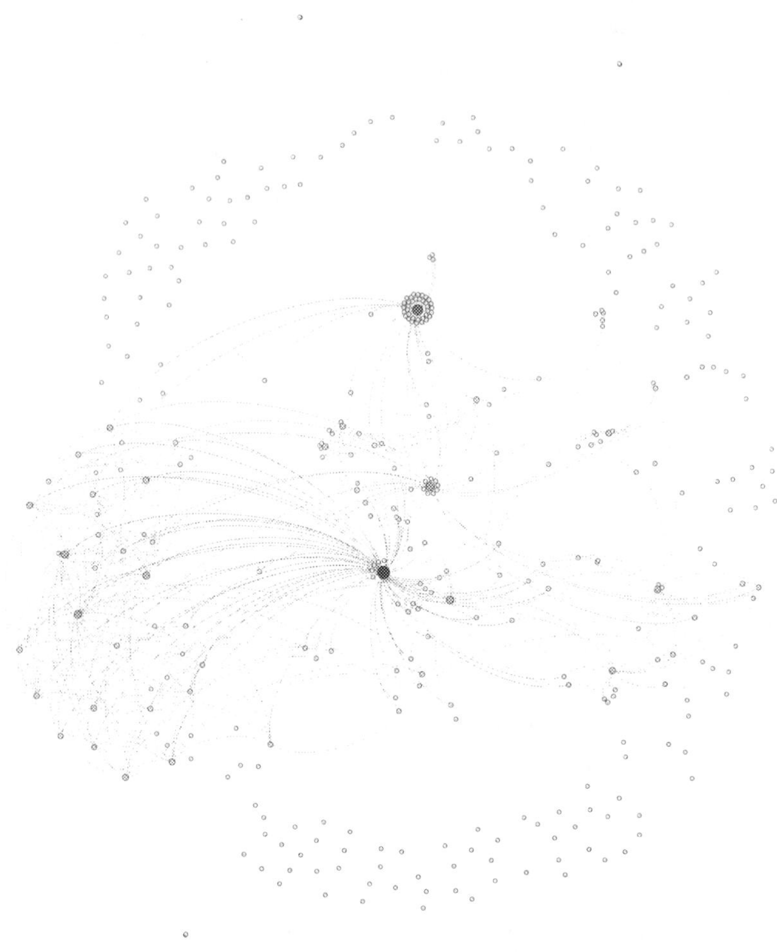

Fig. 3. Dependency network for Eclipse Kepler. The size and shade of nodes are proportional to their degree.

the case for the PageRank and eigenvector centrality. It should be noted that averages of some of the metrics are not necessarily a good characterization of their distribution since they may be scale-free [13].

We further plotted the dynamic measurements and static network metrics against each other. Figure 4 show the plots of CPU versus metrics. There appears to be some correlation for a), b), c), d), and e). However, more detailed analysis and measurements are necessary. For the memory measurements, the general picture of correlation was the same; for other measurements there appeared to be no correlations.

Table 3. Average network metrics for Eclipse releases

Release	In-Degree	Eccentricity	Closeness Centrality	# Nodes	# Edges	Betweenness Centrality	PageRank	Clustering Coefficient	Eigenvector Centrality
Europa	0.5491	0.3988	0.3718	173	95	0.1445	0.0058	0.0359	0.0186
Galileo	1.4818	0.7814	0.5665	247	366	1.2874	0.004	0.0738	0.0185
Galileo SR1	1.3468	0.6734	0.5207	248	334	0.9153	0.004	0.0713	0.0185
Galileo SR2	1.4699	0.7751	0.5619	249	366	1.2771	0.004	0.0732	0.0184
Ganymede	1.2364	0.7045	0.5043	220	272	1.1318	0.0045	0.0691	0.0181
Ganymede SR1	1.2308	0.7014	0.5021	221	272	1.1267	0.0045	0.0688	0.018
Ganymede SR2	1.2308	0.6968	0.4974	221	272	1.1312	0.0045	0.0685	0.018
Helios	1.498	0.8635	0.6416	249	373	1.5221	0.004	0.0768	0.0183
Helios SR1	1.506	0.8635	0.6415	249	375	1.5261	0.004	0.0775	0.0184
Indigo	1.4967	1.1623	0.7855	302	452	4.2384	0.0033	0.0912	0.0221
Indigo SR1	1.4519	1.0673	0.7271	312	453	3.3718	0.0032	0.0926	0.0221
Indigo SR2	1.4534	1.2283	0.7743	311	452	5.0836	0.0032	0.0939	0.0225
Juno	1.4137	1.4518	0.9233	394	557	9.1168	0.0025	0.0892	0.0175
Juno SR1	1.4289	1.4264	0.9067	394	563	8.8706	0.0025	0.0856	0.0181
Juno SR2	1.3442	0.9296	0.6519	398	535	2.6508	0.0025	0.0842	0.0145
Kepler	1.3864	1.1358	0.7142	383	531	4.4125	0.0026	0.0861	0.0147

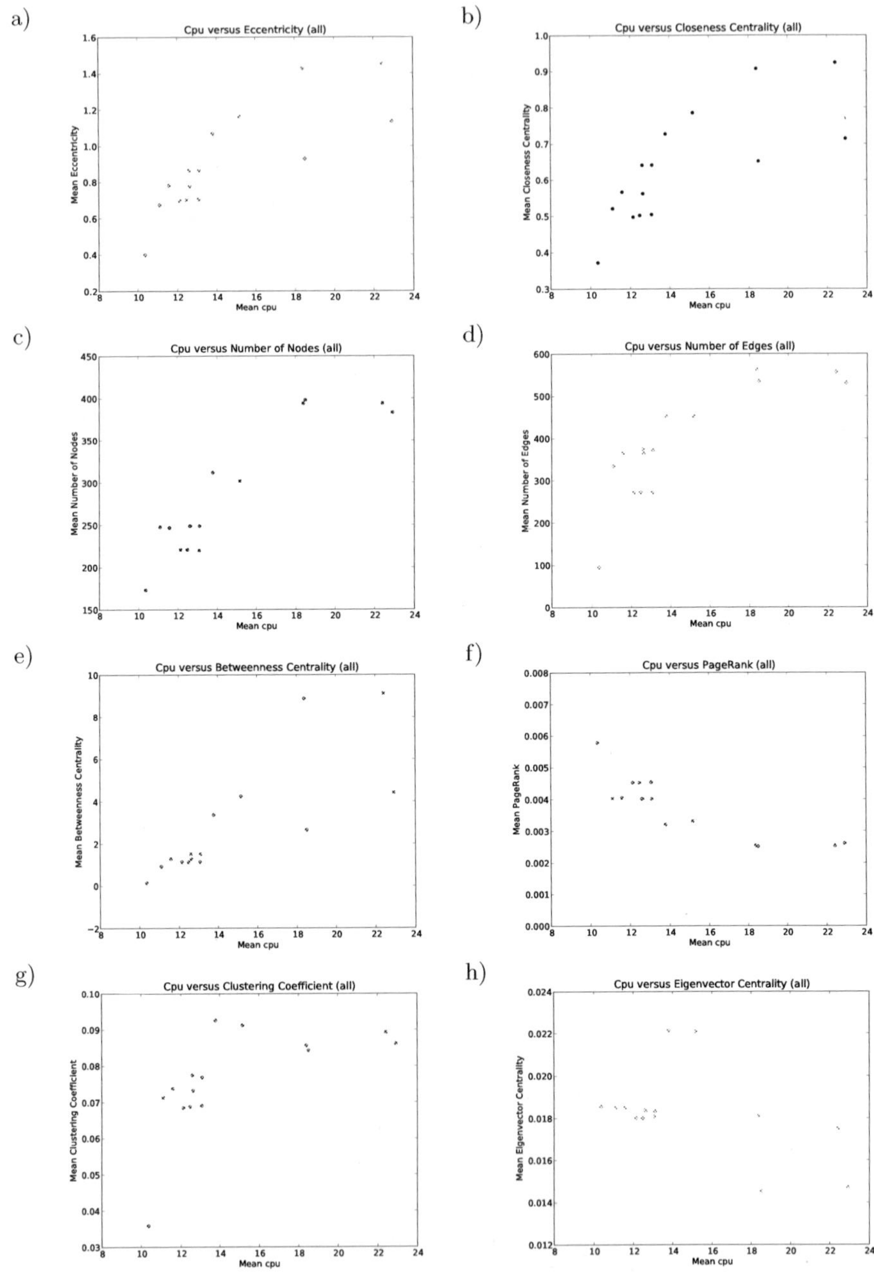

Fig. 4. Scatter plots of CPU usage versus network metrics for versions of Eclipse: a) eccentricity, b) closeness centrality, c) number of nodes, d) number of edges, e) betweenness centrality, f) PageRank, g) clustering coefficient, h) eigenvector centrality.

5 Discussion and Future Work

This paper has been concerned with software ecosystem and in particular the Eclipse software ecosystem. We analysed 15 (16) releases of Eclipse dynamically (through a performance monitoring of a specific compilation task) and statically (through analysis of the structure of the Eclipse software ecosystem as defined by dependencies among bundles in it). Future work includes more thorough dynamic analyses of software ecosystems such as Eclipse (e.g., with more and more realistic tasks) and more fine-grained monitoring (e.g., on a bundle level).

In conclusion, we found that performance and structure changed considerably throughout versions of Eclipse. However, we found no strong correlations between the two and as such our study is exploratory.

Acknowledgements. We thank Feifei Shi and Pengcheng Duan for help in performing the experiments that provided the data for this paper.

References

1. Bosch, J.: From software product lines to software ecosystems. In: Muthig, D., McGregor, J.D. (eds.) SPLC. ACM International Conference Proceeding Series, vol. 446, pp. 111–119. ACM (2009)
2. Manikas, K., Hansen, K.M.: Software ecosystems a systematic literature review. Journal of Systems and Software 86, 1294–1306 (2013)
3. The OSGI Alliance: OSGi Core Release 5 (2012), `http://www.osgi.org/Specifications/`
4. Zimmermann, T., Premraj, R., Zeller, A.: Predicting defects for eclipse. In: ICSE Workshops 2007 International Workshop on Predictor Models in Software Engineering, PROMISE 2007, p. 9 (2007)
5. Kidane, Y., Gloor, P.: Correlating temporal communication patterns of the eclipse open source community with performance and creativity. Computational and Mathematical Organization Theory 13(1), 17–27 (2007)
6. Mens, T., Fernandez-Ramil, J., Degrandsart, S.: The evolution of Eclipse. In: IEEE International Conference on Software Maintenance, ICSM 2008, pp. 386–395 (2008)
7. Zhang, H., Kim, S.: Monitoring software quality evolution for defects. IEEE Software 27(4), 58–64 (2010)
8. Easley, D., Kleinberg, J.: Networks, crowds, and markets, vol. 8. Cambridge University Press (2010)
9. Hansen, K.M., Manikas, K.: Towards a Network Ecology of Software Ecosystems: an Analysis of two OSGi Ecosystems. In: Proceedings of the 25th International Conference on Software Engineering and Knowledge Engineering (SEKE 2013), Boston, USA (July 2013)
10. Brin, S., Page, L.: The anatomy of a large-scale hypertextual web search engine. Computer networks and ISDN systems 30(1), 107–117 (1998)
11. Hansen, K.M., Jonasson, K., Neukirchen, H.: An empirical study of software architectures' effect on product quality. Journal of Systems and Software 84(7), 1233–1243 (2011)
12. Hunter, J.D.: Matplotlib: A 2D graphics environment. Computing In Science & Engineering 9(3), 90–95 (2007)
13. Goh, K.I., Oh, E., Jeong, H., Kahng, B., Kim, D.: Classification of scale-free networks. Proceedings of the National Academy of Sciences 99, 12583–12588 (2002)

An Adaptive Enterprise Service Bus Infrastructure for Service Based Systems

Laura González, Jorge Luis Laborde, Matías Galnares, Mauricio Fenoglio, and Raúl Ruggia

Instituto de Computación, Facultad de Ingeniería, Universidad de la República, Uruguay
{lauragon,mgalnares,mfenoglio,ruggia}@fing.edu.uy

Abstract. Service-based systems (SBS) increasingly need adaptation capabilities to agilely respond to unexpected changes (e.g. regarding quality of service). The Enterprise Service Bus (ESB), a recognized infrastructure to support the development of SBS, provides native mediation capabilities (e.g. message transformation) which can be used to perform adaptation actions. However, the configuration of these capabilities cannot usually be performed at runtime. To deal with this limitation, Adaptive ESB Infrastructures have been proposed which leverage their mediation capabilities to deal with adaptation requirements in SBSs in an automatic and dynamic way at runtime. This paper presents a JBossESB-based implementation of an Adaptive ESB Infrastructure and demonstrates its operation by describing their main functionalities. The paper also presents an evaluation of the implemented solution.

Keywords: enterprise service bus, service-based systems, adaptation, mediation.

1 Introduction

As service-based systems (SBS) operate in an increasingly dynamic world, they need adaptation capabilities to behave correctly despite unexpected changes. This becomes especially relevant in internet-scale systems and virtual service-oriented enterprises [1], where their massively distribution leads to several challenges regarding performance, availability and security, among others [2].

A widely recognized approach to deal with highly distributed services is based on Enterprise Service Buses (ESB) [3], which are a mainstream middleware to support the implementation of SBS. Within an ESB-based infrastructure, services communicate by sending messages through the ESB. This way, messages may be processed by mediation flows, implementing integration and communication logic, which apply different mediation operations to them (e.g. transformations). Furthermore, propositions like the Integration as a Service paradigm [4], and more concretely the Internet Service Bus (ISB) [5], aim to apply these integration technologies in the context of cloud-based and internet-scale SBS. ESB products usually support a wide range of mediation capabilities including message transformation and intelligent routing [3].

A.R. Lomuscio et al. (Eds.): ICSOC 2013 Workshops, LNCS 8377, pp. 480–491, 2014.
© Springer International Publishing Switzerland 2014

However, while mediation flows can be used to react to unexpected changes (e.g. a transformation can be set up to handle a change in a service contract), they usually have to be configured at design time, in a per-service basis and in a slightly static way. This restricts the rapid responsiveness of the system and the generality of the solutions. Furthermore, in large-scale internet SBS (e.g. Internet of Things, Internet of Services) is unreasonable to assume that every time a service changes (regarding its contract or quality of service), all its clients will rapidly adapt. This motivates implementing server-side mechanisms that reduce the risks of client incompatibility.

In order to address these limitations we proposed an Adaptive ESB Infrastructure [2,6,7], which deals with adaptation requirements in SBSs by leveraging its mediation capabilities and allowing them to be configured and applied dynamically and automatically at runtime. The adaptive infrastructure is based on messaging and integration patterns commonly supported by most ESBs, so it provides a generic solution which is likely to be implemented in most of these products. Although in our previous work we developed some prototypes to validate the technical feasibility of the conceptual solution, we had neither implemented the complete adaptive infrastructure nor evaluated it regarding, for example, performance issues.

This paper describes a complete JBossESB-based implementation of the proposed adaptive infrastructure and demonstrates its operation by describing their main functionalities including the configuration of the adaptive behavior of services and the runtime adaptation capabilities according to different situations (e.g. response time degradation). The paper also presents an evaluation of the implemented solution in terms of the overhead it introduces and the resources it uses.

The rest of the paper is organized as follows. Section 2 presents the Adaptive ESB Infrastructure and its main components. Section 3 describes details on how this infrastructure was implemented on top of the JBossESB product and demonstrates its main functionalities. Section 4 presents an evaluation of the implemented solution. Section 5 presents related work. Finally, Section 6 presents conclusions and future work.

2 The Adaptive ESB Infrastructure

This section describes the Adaptive ESB Infrastructure [2,6,7] which, leveraging the mediation capabilities provided by ESBs, has the ability to address adaptation requirements in SBS in an automatic and dynamic way at runtime.

2.1 Overall Approach

In order to address adaptation requirements within the infrastructure, services are invoked through Virtual Services deployed in the ESB, following Service Virtualization patterns [8]. Also, for each supported mediation capability the infrastructure hosts an Adaptation Service which performs a specific mediation operation (e.g. a transformation). Adaptation Services are generic given that their behavior is not fully specified at design time, but it depends on run time information (e.g a Transformation Service executes a different transformation logic for each incoming message).

The general idea to achieve adaptation at runtime is to intercept all ESB messages and, if an adaptation is required for the invoked Virtual Service, drive them through Adaptation Flows. These flows, composed by Virtual and Adaptation Services, include all the required mediations steps (e.g. transformations, routing) to carry out a specific Adaptation Strategy (e.g. invoke an equivalent service).

Fig. 1 presents a general overview of the proposed solution where a client application invokes a virtual service (SRV), which virtualizes an external Web Service.

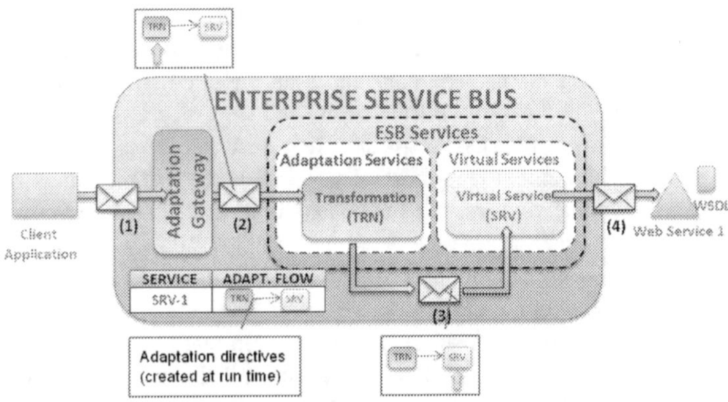

Fig. 1. Adaptive ESB Infrastructure [6]

First, the client sends a message through the ESB (1) to invoke the service SRV. The message is intercepted by an Adaptation Gateway following the Gateway pattern [8], which applies a common set of mediations to all incoming ESB messages. Given that there is an adaptation directive for SRV, the gateway attaches an Adaptation Flow to the message and routes it to the first step in the flow (2). This is supported by the itinerary-based routing pattern [3], which determines the message destination based on an itinerary included in the message itself. In this case, the itinerary (i.e. Adaptation Flow) consists of an Adaptation Service, which performs a transformation (TRN), and a Virtual Service (SRV). Thus, the message is routed to the TRN service which after performing the required transformation (specified in the message), routes the message (3) to the next step in the flow (SRV). Finally, the service SRV invokes the external Web Service (4) and, eventually, a response is returned to the client.

The infrastructure handles the conceptual elements of the S-Cube Adaptation and Monitoring Framework [9], which generalizes and broadens the state of the art in SOA adaptation. In particular, Monitoring Mechanisms refer to any mechanism to check if the actual situation corresponds to the expected one. They are used to detect Monitored Events (e.g. response time degradation), which represent the fact that there is a difference with respect to the expected system state, functionality or environment. Monitored Events trigger Adaptation Requirements (e.g. reduce response time) which represent the need of changing the underlying system, in order to remove the differences between the actual situation and the expected one. Finally, Adaptation Strategies define the possible ways to achieve these requirements (e.g. invoke an equivalent services) and they are realized by Adaptation Mechanisms (e.g. routing a request).

2.2 Logical Architecture

Fig. 2 presents the logical architecture of the solution which consists of internal ESB components and an Adaptation and Monitoring (AM) Engine.

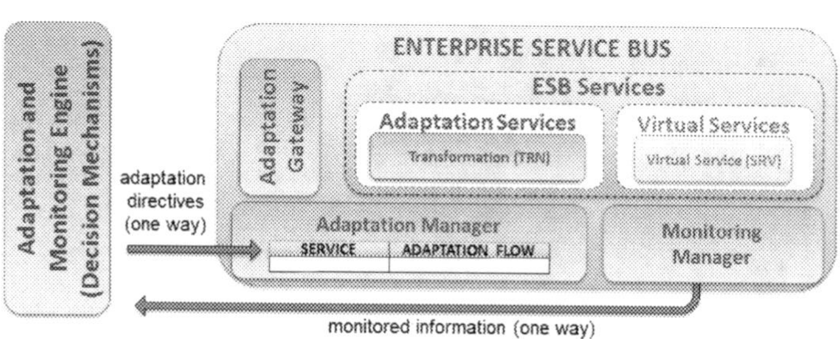

Fig. 2. Logical Architecture of the Adaptive ESB Infrastructure [6]

At runtime, the Monitoring Manager sends monitored information (e.g. the average response time of services) to the AM Engine, which is obtained by interacting with the built-in ESB Monitoring Mechanisms. When the AM Engine receives this information, it decides (based on services requirements and metadata) if an adaptation directive (implementing an Adaptation Strategy) should be created for a given service. If so, the directive (i.e. an Adaptation Flow) is sent to the Adaptation Manager which stores it, so it can be attached to all the incoming messages for the service.

2.3 Implementing Specific Adaptation Strategies

ESB products natively include different mediation capabilities (e.g. transformations) which are available as part of its execution environment. They can be configured based on specific requirements and can be combined to create mediation flows.

In the context of this solution, these mediation capabilities constitute the Adaptation Mechanisms supported by the infrastructure: transformations, routing, recipient list, aggregator, cache and delayer [6]. In particular, the transformation mechanism receives one message and returns another one, transformed according to a given transformation logic (e.g. data model transformation), and the routing mechanism dynamically determines the next service in the message path according to different factors.

In the proposed infrastructure, Adaptation Mechanisms are combined into Adaptation Flows to implement Adaptation Strategies. The infrastructure supports strategies to deal with Quality of Services (QoS) issues [6] and changes in service contracts [7] (e.g. Defer Requests, Distribute Request to Equivalent Services).

Adaptation Strategies are specified using YAWL [10]. Fig. 3 presents the load balancing strategy which was implemented using the routing and transformation mechanisms. In this case, messages are first processed by a routing mechanism which, according to a load-balancing strategy, routes the message to the invoked service (SRV-1) or to an equivalent service (SRV-2 or SRV-3). Given that services can use different data models, transformations to and from a canonical data model may be needed. This strategy can be used, for example, to overcome a service saturation situation.

Note that although the general structure of strategies is specified at design time, their configuration is performed at runtime according to the involved service/s.

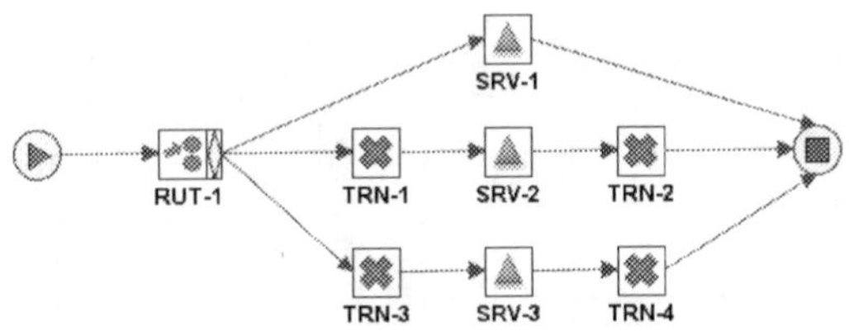

Fig. 3. Specification of the Load Balancing strategy using YAWL [6]

Fig. 4 presents all the elements, within the S-Cube Adaptation and Monitoring Framework, supported by the infrastructure which can be extended as needed.

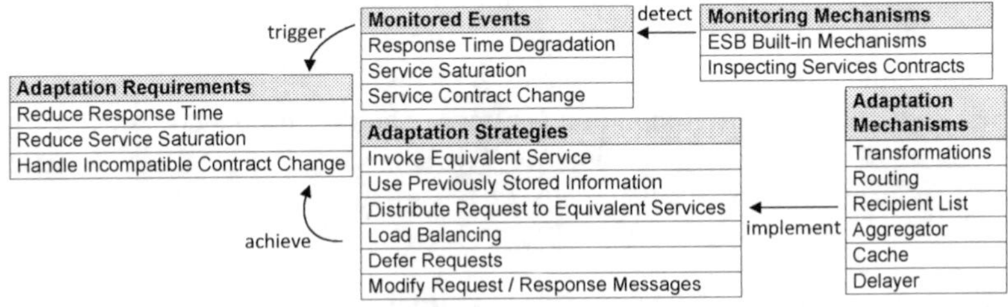

Fig. 4. Supported Adaptation and Monitoring Elements [2]

3 A JBossESB-Based Implementation

The infrastructure presented in Section 2 provides a generic solution to enhance general purpose ESB products with adaptation capabilities, by extending them with the components described in Fig. 2. This section presents a JBossESB-based implementation[1] [11] of the Adaptive ESB Infrastructure.

3.1 Internal ESB Components

This section describes the implementation of the Internal ESB Components.

Virtual Services. The implementation of Virtual Services requires a way to consume external Web Services and to expose them as Web Services through the ESB. Their implementation in JBossESB was based on the SOAP-Proxy component, natively provided by the product, which offers a direct way of implementing Virtual Services by exposing an external Web Service through the ESB.

[1] `https://code.google.com/p/esb-adaptativo/`

Adaptation Services. The implementation of Adaptation Services requires the adaptation mechanisms and a way to build ESB services based on these mechanisms.

Regarding adaptation mechanisms, JBossESB natively supports transformations, routing, recipient list and aggregator. However, given that they only support design time configuration (e.g. to use the transformation mechanism, the transformation logic has to be specified at design time in a configuration file), we enhance them to be able to obtain configuration values (e.g. the transformation logic) from the incoming messages. On the other side, the cache [12] and delayer mechanisms are not natively provided in JBossESB, but they were successfully implemented with the extensibility mechanisms provided by this product.

In order to create Adaptation Services based on the previous mechanisms, we used the native feature of JBossESB where each service is specified as an actions pipeline, in which each action performs a mediation operation (e.g. a transformation).

Itinerary-Based Routing Support. JBossESB does not natively support this pattern, so the product has to be enhanced with this capability. Our implementation uses a graph representation of an itinerary which can be included in the messages passing through the ESB. Also, Adaptation Services were built using a pipeline with two actions: the first one executes the mediation operation over the message, and the second one routes the message to the next step in the itinerary.

Adaptation Gateway. The Adaptation Gateway has to intercept all messages sent to the ESB. This component was implemented as an ESB Service leveraging the native HTTP-Gateway provided by JBossESB. In particular, an URL pattern was configured so that this service is the only entry point to the infrastructure. Fig. 5 presents the XML representation of the implementation of this component using this approach.

The Java class "GatewayAction" implements the specific logic of this component. In particular, it has to interact with the Adaptation Manager to check if there is an adaptation directive for the invoked service and, if so, it has to attach an Adaptation Flow (i.e. an itinerary) to the message. In order to specify the service to be invoked, clients has to use the wsa:To property of the WS-Addresing standard.

```
<service category="esb-adaptative" description="Gateway basado en HTTP localhost:8080/JBoss-Esb-Adaptative/http"
        invmScope="GLOBAL" name="ServiceGatewayHttp">
    <listeners>
        <http-gateway name="Http" urlPattern="/*"/>
    </listeners>
    <actions>
        <action class="org.fing.edu.uy.esbadp.action.gateway.GatewayAction" name="GatewayAction"/>
    </actions>
</service>
```

Fig. 5. Adaptation Gateway [11]

Adaptation Manager. The Adaptation Manager deals with the Adaptation Flows, received from the AM Engine, and it provides this information to the Adaptation Gateway when requested. The implementation of this component is based on an in-memory HashMap. So, given the identification of a Virtual Service, the corresponding Adaptation Flow (if any) can be obtained. As an additional feature, this component stores the history of the applied Adaptation Flows for each Virtual Service.

Monitoring Mechanisms and Manager. Monitoring mechanisms are used by the platform to check if the actual situation corresponds to the expected one.

First, we developed mechanisms which monitor Virtual Service invocations by leveraging the built-in monitoring features provided by JBossESB. In particular, JBossESB exposed monitored information as Java MBeans which can be accessed by clients with JMX support. This way, we implemented three Monitoring Mechanisms by interacting with the "MessageCounter" MBean and obtaining the values for the following attributes: messages successfully processed count, messages failed count and overall service time processed.

Also we developed mechanisms to monitor the contracts of the virtualized Web Services. They were implemented following the ideas of a tool[2] which compares two versions of a WSDL document and identifies the changes it suffered (e.g. a new operation). Also, we used the EasyWSDL[3] library which allows manipulating WSDL documents. When this mechanism is executed, it compares stored versions of WSDL documents with the current ones. This way, the infrastructure can detect which changes WSDL documents have suffered.

The Monitoring Manager interacts with the Monitoring Mechanisms to calculate Monitored Properties for each service. Our implementation supports four properties: number of invocations per time unit, ratio of successful responses, average response time and changes in service contracts. After calculating the values of the Monitored Properties, the Monitoring Manager sends them to the AM Engine.

Other Internal Components. Our implementation includes other internal components: Service Registry and Service Requirements Manager. The Service Registry allows registering services, specifying metadata for the services (e.g. XSLT transformations to and from the canonical data model of the platform) and specifying equivalent services. The Service Requirement Manager allows specifying requirements for the services which, along with the monitored information, allow detecting situations that need to be handled. Service requirements can be specified, for example, based on the monitored properties (e.g. average response time < 1000 ms).

3.2 AM Engine and Administrative Console

This section describes the implementation of the Adaptation and Monitoring Engine and the Administrative Console.

Adaptation and Monitoring Engine. The AM Engine receives monitored data from the Monitoring Manager, sends adaptation directives to the Adaptation Manager and takes the different adaptation and monitored decisions required by the infrastructure. This component also manages the Adaptation Events, Requirements and Strategies supported by the platform.

Every time the Monitoring Manager sends new values for the Monitored Properties for a given service, the AM Engine processes this information to generate, if needed,

---

[2] `http://www.membrane-soa.org/soa-model-doc/1.2/compare-wsdl-java-api.htm`

[3] `http://easywsdl.ow2.org/`

new adaptation directives for that service. This is done based on the monitored information, service metadata and service requirements. The AM Engine also knows which Adaptation Strategies can be used to deal with each Adaptation Requirement.

The engine also implements the required logic to select an Adaptation Strategy (currently in a random way) in case more than one is applicable to deal with a given Adaptation Requirement. As an additional feature, if more than one Adaptation Strategy has to be applied (e.g. a service has more than one Adaptation Requirement) the AM Engine combines various Adaptation Flows in a single one.

Administrative Console. The Administrative Console provides functionalities which facilitate the configuration of the adaptive infrastructure through a graphical interface. It also allows controlling and analyzing the adaptation processes generated for each service. The implementation of the Administrative Console was based in JSF 2.1 and in a set of components provided by the framework Primefaces 1.5. It is completely decoupled from the ESB and from the AM Engine: it interacts with them via JMX.

3.3 Demonstration of the Main Functionalities

This section presents the main features of the Adaptive ESB Infrastructure by means of the JBossESB-based implementation.

Fig. 6 presents the Administrative Console of the infrastructure which provides functionalities grouped in three main categories: Virtual Services management, Adaptive Server (ESB) configuration and AM Engine configuration. On the right side of the figure, three Virtual Services, virtualizing external Web Services, are listed.

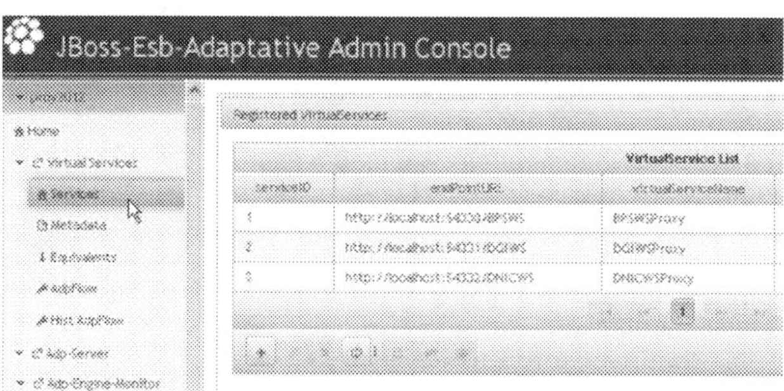

Fig. 6. Administrative Console: Virtual Services Management

The Administrative Console allows configuring basic information of Virtual Services (e.g. name, category), the transformations to and from the canonical data model of the platform and it allows associating equivalent services. It also allows configuring the adaptive behavior of services (e.g. the maximum number of invocations a service can support in a given period of time).

The adaptive infrastructure identifies and responds to different situations. For example, if a service is saturated by sending it more requests that the number it can handle, the solution detects this situation and applies a suitable Adaptation Strategy to handle it. Also, the current Adaptation Flows implementing the selected strategies for each Virtual Service are graphically visualized through the administrative console.

Fig. 7 shows the first two levels of the current Adaptation Flow for the service DNICWS, which implements a Load Balancing strategy and expires in 283 seconds.

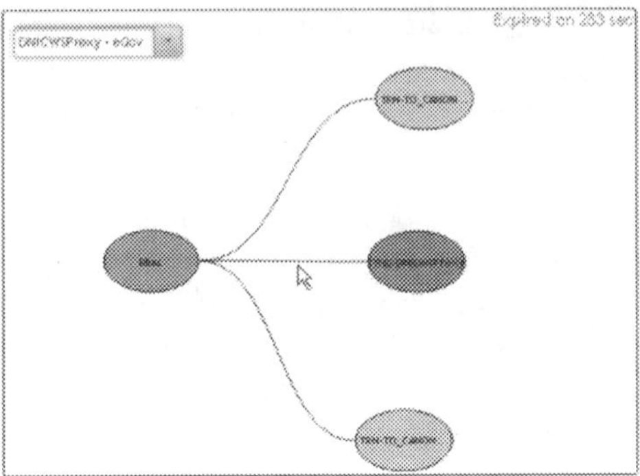

Fig. 7. Current Adaptation Flow for the Service DNICWS

Finally, the history of the applied Adaptation Flows for a given service can also be visualized through the administrative console.

4 Evaluation of the JBoss-ESB Based Implementation

This section presents an evaluation of the implemented solution. The SoapUI tool v4.5.1 was used to simulate service invocations and the VisualVM tool v1.3.5 was used to monitor resource usage. The platform was run on a desktop PC with 4GB of RAM and a dual-core processor of 3.2Ghz.

4.1 Overhead Introduced by the Infrastructure

We performed some tests in order to quantify the overhead in the invocations introduced by the infrastructure. Table 1 presents the results of the tests which were obtained based on 1200 invocations to a Web Service.

Table 1. Overhead in Invocations [11]

Adaptation Strategy	Average Time (ms)	Overhead (ms)
Direct invocation to the Service	18	N/A
Invocation through the Infrastructure	21	3
Invoke Equivalent Service	94	76
Use Previously Stored Information	6	N/A
Distribute Request to Equivalent Services	350	332
Load Balancing	129	111
Defer Requests	121	3
Modify Request / Response Messages	179	161

The first row in the table, correspond to a direct invocation to the Web Service. The second row corresponds to an invocation to the Web Service through the infrastructure but without applying any strategy. The rest of the rows correspond to invocations to the Web Service where the different Adaptation Strategies were applied. For a given strategy, the overhead value is calculated with respect to the time required for a direct invocation.

We believe that the obtained values are acceptable, given that for most of the strategies the overhead is less than 200 milliseconds.

4.2 Resource Usage

We also monitored the CPU and memory usage while the platform was operating and applying different adaptation strategies.

As presented in Fig. 8, the first interval (1) had a normal CPU usage of around 40%. However, in the second interval (2) the usage was increased because the "Distribute to Equivalent Services" strategy was applied, which requires performing various messages copies and transformations. In the third interval (3), after the execution of this strategy was finished, the CPU usage decreased to a normal use again.

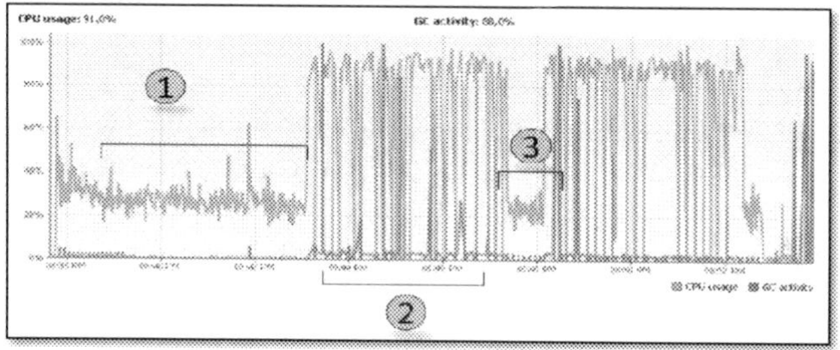

Fig. 8. CPU Usage [11]

Regarding memory usage, Fig. 9 presents similar characteristics, that is, the usage increased when the "Distribute to Equivalent Services" strategy was applied. It also allows visualizing that the solution does not present memory leaks, as the memory usage at the end of the test is very similar to the one at the beginning.

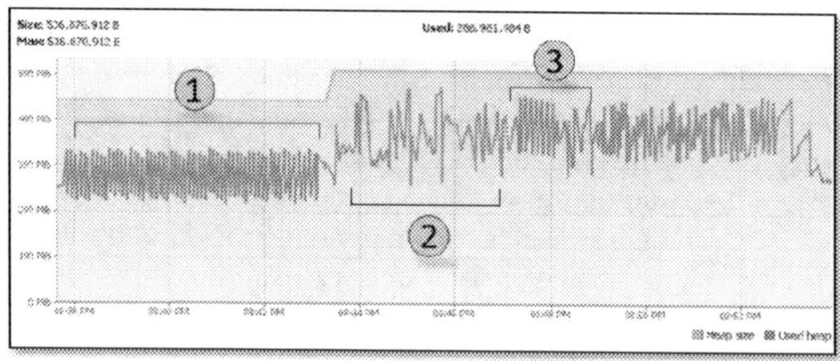

Fig. 9. Memory Usage [11]

5 Related Work

As stated in our previous work [1,6,7], dynamic adaptation in ESB has recently been addressed. Most authors propose solutions that allow applying or configuring ESB mediation capabilities in a more dynamic and automatic way. For example, a recent work [13] proposes an Adaptive ESB as part of an Adaptive SOA platform. The Adaptive ESB focuses on adapting service compositions by selecting at runtime (based on past invocations and QoS values) the services to be invoked.

Related proposals, although dealing with dynamic and automatic adaptation in ESBs, they use limited mediation capabilities, they are not extensible, and mediation flows to be followed by messages are defined at design time. In turn, our solution uses a wider and extensible range of mediation capabilities (e.g. cache and delayer). Also, it enables to select concrete mediation flows for messages at run-time, which enables to choose different strategies when an issue is detected (e.g. regarding response time). Finally, our proposal aims at enhancing general purpose ESB products with adaptation capabilities. To this, the proposed infrastructure is based on commonly supported ESB patterns and it is not restricted to the characteristics of specific ESB products.

6 Conclusions and Future Work

This paper presented a JBossESB-based implementation of an adaptive ESB infrastructure, which provides adaptation capabilities for implementing large-scale SBS. The experimental results show the feasibility of this approach through an implementation based on a general purpose ESB product.

The main contributions of this paper consist of the proof-of-concept implementation of the complete adaptive ESB solution, which provides experimental results concerning the development and the execution. Such results are crucial to better know about the behavior of the followed approach as well as to identify aspects to improve. Regarding the development, JBossESB features and other existing tools enabled a direct implementation of most of the components of the solution. However, some elements required significant ad-hoc development. Concerning execution, the overhead introduced by the solution, which is one of the most critical aspects, appears to be acceptable as preventing client execution failures. CPU and memory usage is also acceptable. However, applying adaptation strategies which require significant message copies and transformations increased this usage in a considerable way.

Beyond current results, this work aims at being a step forward for adding dynamic adaptation capabilities to Internet SBS, notably based on ESBs.

This work is currently being extended by implementing different strategies as well as by improving the overall system. The approach is being applied to implement do-main-specific integration platforms for Geographic Information Systems [14] and Bioinformatics. In addition, a research line on applying this kind of platform to Internet of Things scenarios [15] and context-aware service systems [16] is ongoing.

Future work consists in specifying and prototyping other Adaptation Strategies, addressing other Adaptation Requirements, as well as implementing the adaptive infrastructure with other ESB products. Other topic to be addressed concerns the application of Complex Event Processing mechanisms for the AM Engine.

References

1. Erl, T.: Service-Oriented Architecture: A Field Guide to Integrating XML and Web Services. Prentice-Hall (2004)
2. González, L., Ruggia, R.: Adaptive ESB Infrastructure for Service Based Systems. In: Adaptive Web Services for Modular and Reusable Software Development: Tactics and Solutions. IGI Global (2012)
3. Chappell, D.: Enterprise Service Bus: Theory in Practice. O'Reilly Media (2004)
4. Buyya, R., Broberg, J., Goscinski, A.M.: Cloud Computing: Principles and Paradigms. Wiley (2011)
5. Ferguson, D.F.: The internet service bus. In: Meersman, R., Tari, Z. (eds.) OTM 2007, Part I. LNCS, vol. 4803, p. 5. Springer, Heidelberg (2007)
6. González, L., Ruggia, R.: Addressing QoS issues in service based systems through an adaptive ESB infrastructure. In: Proceedings of the 6th Workshop on Middleware for Service Oriented Computing - MW4SOC 2011, Lisbon, Portugal, pp. 1–7 (2011)
7. González, L., Ruggia, R.: Addressing the Dynamics of Services Contracts through an Adaptive ESB Infrastructure. In: 1st International Workshop on Adaptive Services for the Future Internet, Poznan, Poland (2011)
8. Wylie, H., Lambros, P.: Enterprise Connectivity Patterns: Implementing integration solutions with IBM's Enterprise Service Bus products
9. Kazhamiakin, R.: Adaptation and Monitoring in S-Cube: Global Vision and Roadmap. In: Proceedings of the Workshop on Monitoring, Adaptation and Beyond (MONA+), Madrid, Spain, pp. 67–76 (2009)
10. Hofstede, A.H.M., ter Aalst, W.M.P., van der Adams, M., Russell, N.: Modern Business Process Automation: YAWL and its Support Environment. Springer (2009)
11. Laborde, J.L., Galnares, M., Fenoglio, M.: Implementación de una Plataforma ESB Adaptativa (2012), https://esb-adaptativo.googlecode.com/
12. Yan Fang, R., Ru, F., Zhong, T., Eoin, L., Harini, S., Banks, T., He, L.: Cache mediation pattern specification: an overview
13. Masternak, T., Psiuk, M., Radziszowski, D., Szydlo, T., Szymacha, R., Zielinski, K., Zmuda, D.: ESB-Modern SOA Infrastructure. SOA Infrastructure Tools, Concepts And Methods. Poznan University of Economics Press (2010)
14. Rienzi, B., González, L., Ruggia, R.: Towards an ESB-Based Enterprise Integration Platform for Geospatial Web Services. In: The Fifth International Conference on Advanced Geographic Information Systems, Applications, and Services, pp. 39–45 (2013)
15. González, L., Cubo, J., Brogi, A., Pimentel, E., Ruggia, R.: RunTime Verification of Behaviour Aware Mashups in the Internet of Things. Presented at the 3rd International Workshop on Adaptive Services for the Future Internet, Malaga, Spain (September 2013)
16. González, L., Ortiz, G.: An ESB based Infrastructure for Event Driven Context Aware Web Services. Presented at the 3rd International Workshop on Adaptive Services for the Future Internet, Malaga, Spain (September 2013)

Dynamic Adaptation of Business Process Based on Context Changes: A Rule-Oriented Approach

Guangchang Hu, Budan Wu, and Junliang Chen

State Key Laboratory of Networking and Switching Technology,
Beijing University of Posts and Telecommunications, Beijing 100876
{hgc,wubudan,chjl}@bupt.edu.cn

Abstract. In a dynamic environment, business process needs to be adjusted and evolved in response to the changeable internal policies and external environment. However, it is a time-consuming and laborious way by redesigning process model and executing the process instance. In this paper, we propose a rule-oriented approach to dynamically generate business process according to the current context at runtime. To enable dynamic and context-aware adaptation, the relationship between services and context is described as rules, which are then used to generate the solution with a mapping mechanism. Two algorithms are designed to generate the activity sequence at runtime, which is the solution of process adaptation. In order to achieve the preference selection, a process assessment strategy has been proposed to constrain the generated activity sequence. Simulation experiments have been conducted to demonstrate the efficiency of our approach.

Keywords: BPM, adaptation, dynamic assembly, service composition, context-aware.

1 Introduction

Service-oriented computing is a new computing paradigm. There are many advantages to organize business processes in the form of services [10]. A well designed business process can increase effectiveness and add value for the enterprise. However, the ability to respond to the changes in business processes is very small. The changes come from the adjustment of internal regulatory policy, as well as the impact of environment context change [5]. Due to the changes, a predefined business process may become unable to continue or no longer meeting the current business goals. So, business process needs to be adjusted and evolved in response to the changeable internal policies and external environment [14]. However, it will be a time-consuming and laborious work by redesigning process model and executing the process instance. Therefore, how to rapidly adjust the predefined business processes to meet business goals at runtime according to the current context is a meaningful problem. Especially in Internet of Things (IoT), the dynamic characteristics of the environment and the burstiness of services will directly affect the running process instances. It has practical significance to reassemble business activities to adapt to the changes by the way of dynamic planning at runtime.

A.R. Lomuscio et al. (Eds.): ICSOC 2013 Workshops, LNCS 8377, pp. 492–504, 2014.
© Springer International Publishing Switzerland 2014

The traditional workflow mainly concern to design business process model by analyzing business requirements at design stage, and execute the business process instances at runtime [18]. Both the definition of process logic and the binding of services can be realized at design stage. This kind of workflow is suitable for fixed business, and it is a static process, e.g. alarm process using WS-BPEL. But in a dynamic environment, the changing context or abnormal events will lead to the initial process instances cannot continue. And the changes of application requirements will lead to the initial business processes cannot meet the new business goals. Some changes are unpredictable, and it may only occur once, or only reappear under the certain situations. So, it is a time-consuming and laborious way to adapt to the changes by redefining the process models back to the design stage. And it is a good solution to generate a temporary process which meets business goals and user preferences by a rule-oriented approach according to the current context and various rules at runtime.

2 Related Work

The process is too rigid is the main problem in traditional workflow management systems (WFMSs). These systems are not suitable for handling rapidly evolving processes [7]. The case-handling paradigm, such as FLOWer, is usually considered as a much more flexible approach, which allowing users to modify the predefined model [1]. A new generation of adaptive workflow management systems are developed [8,19], such as ADEPT, which response to the demand of dynamic business process management. However, both in case-handling and adaptive systems, process models are presented in a process modeling language (e.g., Pi calculus, Petri nets [13], etc.), which precisely prescribes the algorithm to be executed. Although case-handling and adaptive systems allow for changes of models written in imperative languages, the result remains an imperative model. This can result in many efforts to implement various changes over and over again. In order to avoid the mandatory features of these modeling languages, Pesic et al. [11] proposes ConDec as a declarative language for modeling business process. Unlike imperative languages, declarative languages specify what not to do instead of specifying how to work. This leaves a lot of room for the maneuver of users who can make decisions and work in various ways with the same ConDec model. But this method strongly depends on the description of constraint. The flexibility is very weak when the description is insufficient [15]. And it cannot access the runtime state of the process [2].

There already exist many researches on the adaptability of business process in the field of business process management [4,12,17]. Bucchiarone et al. [3] defines abstract activities of process model according to business goals at design stage. The proposed method is fragment-based, and it gradually refines the implementation of abstract activities by a series of adaptation mechanisms at runtime. However, the adaptation mechanisms are relatively complex, and it cannot support manual intervention and adjustment for the generated business process. Moreover, this method does not support to user preferences. Yu et al. [20] uses the technology of aspect-oriented. And the proposed method can realize different user's preferences which are weaved in processes in the form of aspect. But the process logic of process model is fixed, and its variability only reflects in the replacement of a specific service according to different user at runtime. Mejia et al. [9] maps the business processes to a series of ECA rules. And the proposed method can realize process reengineering according to business requirements. However, this method is more dependent on the business experts. Due to services and process logic are bound in ECA rules, it has a lower flexibility to cope with the changes in the changeable environment.

Our research is based on the previously developed information service platform of heating system. The platform is an IoT application project about urban central heating and room temperature monitoring system. The architecture of this platform is shown as Figure 1. This paper is research on the adaptive module (the dashed rectangle of Fig.1) for BPM. We encountered a dynamic assembly problem between main process and sub-process at runtime, when we developed the application of the Maintenance Process with this platform. Based on this problem, we propose a rule-oriented dynamic planning approach (called RoDP) which can quickly respond to the changes at runtime. The RoDP approach can realize dynamic assembly and adaptive adjustment of the interrupted business process at runtime.

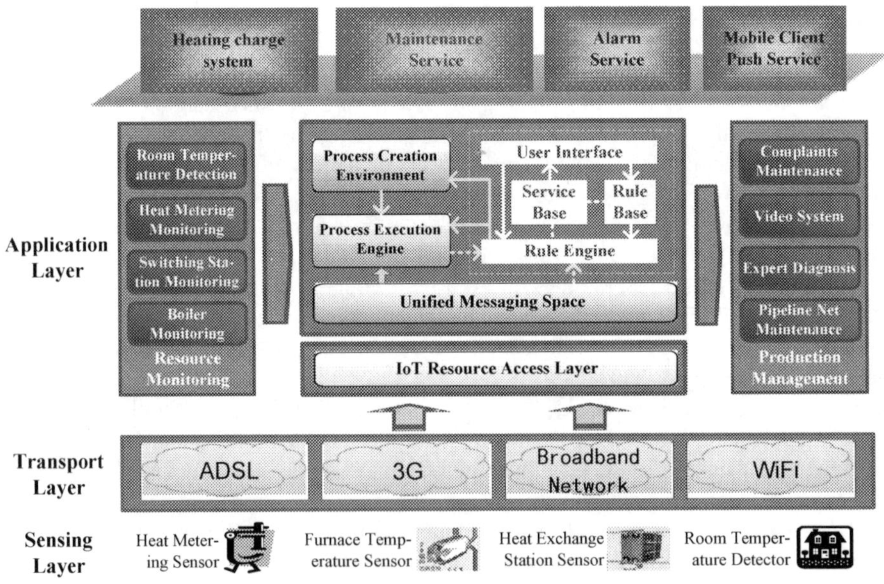

Fig. 1. Architecture of information service platform

3 Scenario and Problem Description

The following scenario is about heating maintenance process of the Maintenance Service. There are three ways to submit a maintenance request. When a request is submitted, duty manager assigns repairman to repair and confirms the result of the maintenance. The maintenance process is shown as Figure 2.

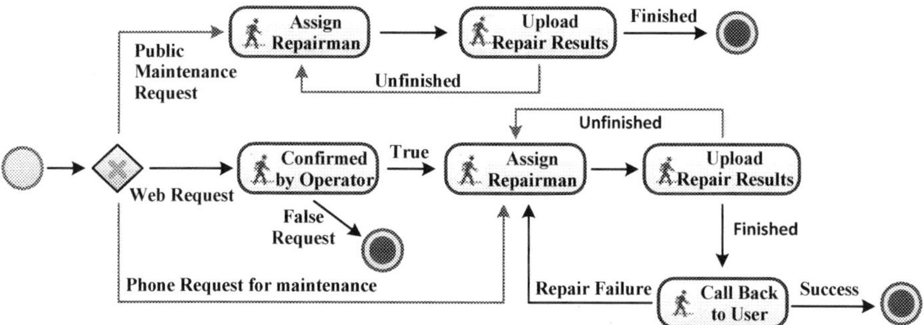

Fig. 2. Heating maintenance process of Maintenance Service

The changes of context information may interrupt an ongoing maintenance process instance. For example, if there is a lack of some materials during the maintenance period, the process instance will be unable to continue until the materials are supplemented. So, the main process instances need to dynamically assemble and execute the sub-process of procurement, and return to the process instances to continue until the total business goals are achieved. In addition, the heating maintenance process may not be suitable for some new requirements. For example, heating equipments or temperature sensors need to be replaced uniformly. So, a new process needs to be dynamically generated to achieve this new goal.

Therefore, one of the problems is how to dynamically assemble the relevant sub-processes and return to the main process when the execution of process instance is interrupted by some events. Another problem is how to dynamically generate the relevant processes to meet the new goals according to the current state, when new business requirements appear. Figure 3 shows the procurement sub-process about the event of lack of material. Figure 4 shows the new process about the new requirement of the replacement of heating equipments or temperature sensors. In conclusion, the general problem is how to rapidly organize business process to meet business goals at runtime according to the current context and the existing service, when the changes of contextual information or the emergence of new requirements affect the execution of process instances in the dynamic environment. The key to solve the general problem is to generate a related activity sequence to meet the business goals.

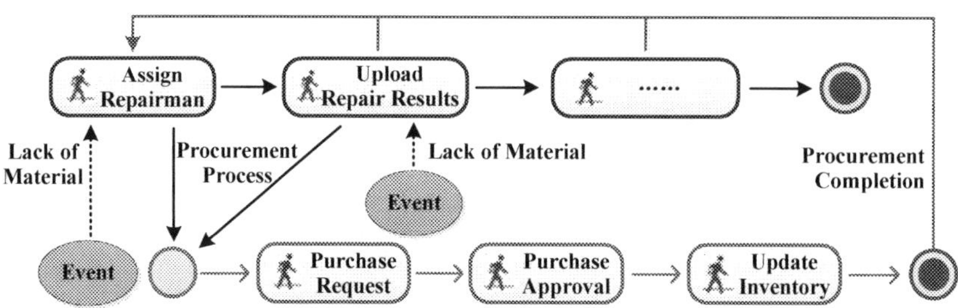

Fig. 3. Process of the procurement sub-process

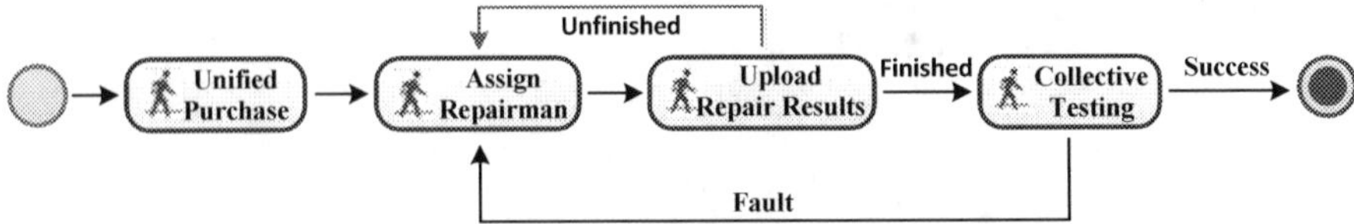

Fig. 4. Process of the replacement of heating equipments or temperature sensors

4 The RoDP Approach

In this section we propose our RoDP approach and discuss several key principles used in the design of this approach. First, we describe the adaptation architecture and the function of each component. Second, we introduce formal definitions of the elements of our adaptation architecture. Finally, we propose two algorithms to generate the activity sequence at runtime, and we conduct experiments and comparative analysis. In addition, we describe the mapping mechanism and assessment strategy in detail.

4.1 The RoDP Architecture

The adaptation architecture is shown as Figure 5. The predefined business processes are stored in the Process Model which is a part of the Process Creation Environment. Process instances are executed in the Process Execution Engine and receive the events from the Unified Messaging Space. In response to these events and new requirements, Rule Engine generates the corresponding activity sequence according to various rules which describe the relationships between states of resources and activities. Rules are stored in the Rule Base, and activities are stored in the Service Base. The relationship between services and rules is realized by the Mapping module in the User Interface. Different user preferences are realized by the module of Process Assessment.

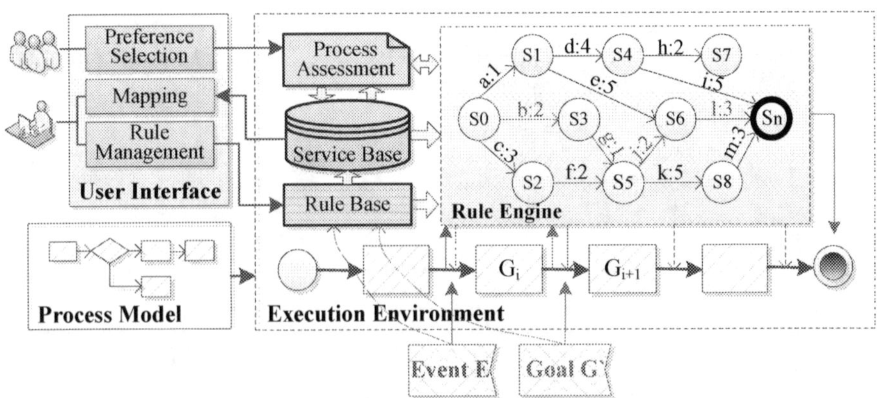

Fig. 5. The architecture of adaptive process

When the process instances are interrupted by events or new requirements, Execution Engine extracts the current states of the related resources and the objective states of the remaining activities. According to the current states, the objective states and the relevant rules, Rule Engine generates a weighted directed graph (called WDG), and then outputs the corresponding activity sequence according to assessment strategy. In addition, for the interruption caused by events, Execution Engine just return to process breakpoint or anywhere of the remaining activities in process model.

4.2 Definition

In this section we introduce formal definitions of the elements of our adaptation architecture.

1) *Context:* Context describes the current states of the resources. Many things can be seen as resources especially in IoT, such as sensor, material, person and other physical resources. Virtual resource can also be seen as an operable resource, such as data, Web service. Each resource has two or more states to mark the current feature of the resource. For example, the state of the material *I* is none (or yes), and the state of the Web service *J* is unavailable (or available).

Definition 1: *(Context)* S_o=<$\mathbb{E}_{id}(i)$|$\mathbb{E}_{id}(i)$.*State*, $i \in N$>, where: S_o represents the current states of related resources of the interrupted instances; $\mathbb{E}_{id}(i)$ is the serial number of resource *i*; $\mathbb{E}_{id}(i)$.*State* is the current state of the $\mathbb{E}_{id}(i)$ resource and *State(a)* represents the resource state, and $0 \leq a \leq \varepsilon$; ε is the quantity of the states of a specific resource.

2) *Activity*: Activity (or service) describes the input, output, a set of operations and the corresponding weight. In addition, the data which transmit between activities can be defined and accessed in the form of Artifact [16].

Definition 3: *(Activity) A=< $\mathbb{A}_{id}$, $\mathbb{E}_{id}$, Input, Output, Weight>*, where: $\mathbb{A}_{id}$ is the activity identity, and $\mathbb{A}_{id}(x)$ is the serial number of activity *x* ($0 \leq x \leq \mu$), μ is the total number of activities; *Input* represents the triggered state of activity or input parameter of Web service, and *Output* represents the changed state or output parameter; *Weight* represents the cost, response time, user expectation or other QoS parameters of the activity; the $\mathbb{A}_{id}$ and $\mathbb{E}_{id}$ of virtual resource is the same, and the $\mathbb{A}_{id}$ and $\mathbb{E}_{id}$ of physical resource is different.

3) *Business Goal:* Business goal describes the states, which the remaining activities of process model should achieve. Business goal is generated by extracting all the outputs of unfinished activities when the process instance is interrupted by events. And business goal is *G`* which represents the final states when a new business requirement *G`* appears.

Definition 2: *(Business Goal)* G=<S_x, S_{x+1},..., S_n>, where: $0<x<n$; and S_x represents the objective state which the first unfinished activity *x* should achieve, and S_x:= $\mathbb{A}_{id}(x)$.*State(b)*; S_{x+1} represents the objective state which the next activity *x+1* should achieve in the process model; S_n represents the final state which the last activity should achieve.

4) *Rule*: Rule is an abstract description of the activity, which describes the precondition, result and operation for performing an activity.

Definition 4: *(Rule)* $R=<\mathbb{R}_{id}, \mathbb{A}_{id}, precondition, result>$, where: $\mathbb{R}_{id}$ is the rule identity, and $\mathbb{R}_{id}(\alpha)$ is the serial number of rule α ($0\leq\alpha\leq$m), m is the total number of rules ; *precondition* is the condition that an activity is triggered; *result* is the result of implementation of the activity;

5) *Activity Sequence:* Activity sequence describes the ordinal relation of activities. According to the Process Assessment strategy, the activity sequence is generated by the RoDP algorithm and returned by the Rule Engine.

Definition 5: *(Activity Sequence)* $P=<\mathbb{A}_{id}(x), \mathbb{A}_{id}(y),\ldots, \mathbb{A}_{id}(z)>$.

4.3 The Rule Mapping Mechanism

Rule is an abstract description about the activities of the corresponding physical resource and services of the corresponding virtual resource. The state of a physical resource can usually be changed by an atomic activity which has the same input and output. For example, the procurement activity changes the state of material *I* from none to yes, and the input and output parameters are all about the change of material quantity. So, the precondition and result of the rule respectively are the states (before and after the change) of the resource. The state of a virtual resource represents that the corresponding service is available or not. And the precondition and result of the rule respectively are the input and output parameter of the service. If an activity or a service realizes the transition from one state to another, it can be expressed as follows:

Physical resource	Virtual resource
$\mathbb{A}_{id}(x)::\mathbb{E}_{id}(i).State(a)\rightarrow\mathbb{E}_{id}(i).State(b)$	$\mathbb{A}_{id}(y)::\mathbb{E}_{id}(y).State(a)\rightarrow\mathbb{E}_{id}(y).State(b)$
$\mathbb{R}_{id}(\alpha)::\mathbb{A}_{id}(x)$	$\mathbb{R}_{id}(\beta)::\mathbb{A}_{id}(y)$
$\mathbb{R}_{id}(\alpha).precondition:=\mathbb{A}_{id}(x).State(a)$	$\mathbb{R}_{id}(\beta).precondition:=\mathbb{A}_{id}(y).Input$
$\mathbb{R}_{id}(\alpha).result:=\mathbb{A}_{id}(x).State(b)$	$\mathbb{R}_{id}(\beta).result:=\mathbb{A}_{id}(y).Output$
$<\mathbb{R}_{id}(\alpha),\mathbb{A}_{id}(x),\mathbb{A}_{id}(x).State(a),\mathbb{A}_{id}(x).State(b)>$	$<\mathbb{R}_{id}(\beta),\mathbb{A}_{id}(y),\mathbb{A}_{id}(y).Input,\mathbb{A}_{id}(y).Output>$

Annotation: '::' represents associated relationship, ':=' represents the assignment operator.

The rule mapping mechanism is shown as Figure 6. In addition, in order to make full use of the existing process fragments (otherwise known as composite services), each fragment can be mapped to one rule. Developers or users can manage the entire Rule Base by the component of Rule Management in the User Interface. The changes of business policy could be achieved by modifying the relevant rules. When the current Rule Base is unable to generate solution, we can solve it by adding rules and injecting related services [6].

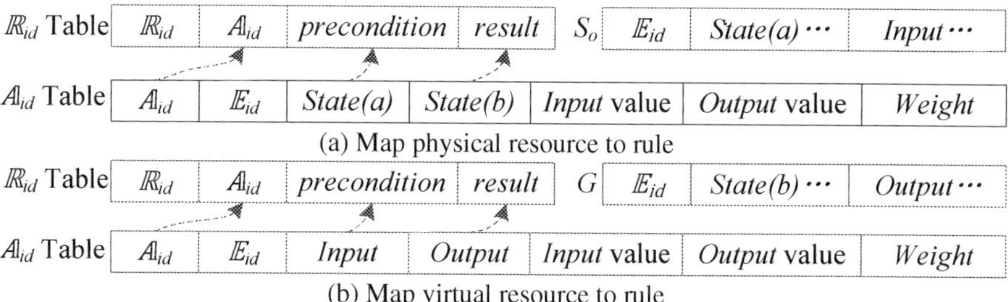

(a) Map physical resource to rule

$\mathbb{R}_{id}$ Table	$\mathbb{R}_{id}$	$\mathbb{A}_{id}$	*precondition*	*result*	G	$\mathbb{E}_{id}$	*State(b)* ···	*Output* ···

$\mathbb{A}_{id}$ Table	$\mathbb{A}_{id}$	$\mathbb{E}_{id}$	*Input*	*Output*	*Input* value	*Output* value	*Weight*

(b) Map virtual resource to rule

Fig. 6. The rule mapping mechanism

4.4 The RoDP Algorithm

The key problem of the RoDP is to generate the activity sequence to meet the business goals by matching the rules. The required activity sequence can be considered as the edge of the feasible path from current states to objective states in WDG. We propose two algorithms for generating activity sequence according to the number of the rules. One is a global approach that the Rule Engine creates WDG by matching all the rules and finds the optimal path from the current states to the objective states. The generated activity sequence is the optimal sequence in the optimal path. Another is a local approach that the Rule Engine matches the rule with the minimum weight from the current states to the objective states by greedy algorithm step by step. This approach is to solve the suboptimal path, when the number of the rules is very large, and the generated activity sequence is the suboptimal sequence.

The step to create the WDG is as follow: I. For the first rule, create the node S_{11} (S_{11}:=$\mathbb{R}_{id}(1).precondition$) and the node S_{12} (S_{12}:=$\mathbb{R}_{id}(1).result$) in WDG, then create the directed edge from S_{11} to S_{12}, and mark the edge with the weight $\mathbb{A}_{id}(x).Weight$ of related activity x; II. For the rule α (α>1), create the node $S_{\alpha 1}$ ($S_{\alpha 1}$:=$\mathbb{R}_{id}(\alpha)$. *precondition*) and the node $S_{\alpha 2}$ ($S_{\alpha 2}$:=$\mathbb{R}_{id}(\alpha).result$) in WDG, merge the same nodes, then create the directed edge from $S_{\alpha 1}$ to $S_{\alpha 2}$, and mark the edge with activity weight $\mathbb{A}_{id}(y).Weight$; III. Continue to II until α>m (m is the number of the rules).

1) Algorithm of optimal activity sequence (called RoDP-opt)
The key issue for generating the optimal sequence is to solve the optimal path from the current states to the objective states in the WDG. In our RoDP-opt algorithm, we use the Dijkstra algorithm to solve the optimal path.

The step to generate the optimal activity sequence is as follow: I. Extract the current states S_o (S_o::$\mathbb{E}_{id}(i).State$) and the objective states G ($\mathbb{A}_{id}(x).State(b)$, $\mathbb{A}_{id}(x+1).State(b)$, …); II. Create the $G(V,E)$ (namely WDG) according to all the rules; III. Label the nodes S_o and the nodes G in WDG; IV. Find the shortest path from S_o to S_n, and S_n is one of the elements of the set G; V. Output the optimal sequence based on the assessment strategy.

Algorithm 1. The RoDP-opt algorithm
```
capture the current context S_o and business goal G
receive user-preference
for rule R(α) (1≤α≤m)
    create V(G) and E(G), Edge[S_1][S_2]:= A_id.Weight
```

```
for S_i∈V(G) (1≤i≤|V(G)|)
    if S_o= S_i, then change the label S_i to S_o
    else if S_n= S_i, then change the label S_i to S_n
  P`:= activity of (path of (Dijkstra(S_o,S_n)))
  P:=Min (P`)
  return P
```

2) Algorithm of suboptimal activity sequence (called RoDP-subopt)
It is very difficult to create and manage the WDG when the number of the rules is larger. The RoDP-subopt algorithm generates a suboptimal activity sequence by a local optimum manner. The key issue is to support backtracking in the solving process for generating the suboptimal sequence. In the RoDP-subopt algorithm, it is realized by emptying the related rules of the unreachable path temporarily and selecting the remaining rules which can be matched iteratively.

The step to generate the suboptimal activity sequence is as follow: I. For the current states S_o, match the *precondition* of all the rules with S_o, then select the activity x with minimum weight from all the matching rules, put activity x into activity sequence P and assign the *result* of the related rule to S_o; II. If there is not any matching rules with S_o, then backtracking (flag=0); III. Continue to I until S_o⊆G or P=∅.

Algorithm 2. The RoDP-subopt algorithm

```
capture the current context S_o and business goal G
receive user-preference
do
{   for rule R(α) (1≤α≤m)
      if R_id(α).precondition= S_o, then add A_id(x) in P`
  A_id(y):=Min(P`)
  add A_id(y) in P, P`:=∅, S_o:= R_id(β).result, flag:=0
  for rule R(α) (1≤α≤m)
      if R_id(α).precondition= S_o, then flag:=1
  if (flag=0)&(S_o⊄G), then
      delete A_id(y) in P, delete R_id(β), S_o= R_id(β).precondition
} while ((S_o⊄G)&(P≠∅))
recover R_id(β)
return P
```

4.5 The Process Assessment Strategy

Because of the different user preference, the generated activity sequence is different. This paper assesses the generated activity sequence with service cost, respond time, user experience or other QoS parameters. Users set the Process Assessment strategy by the Preference Selection in the User Interface, and the RoDP algorithm receives these parameters and generates corresponding activity sequence. The activity sequence can be directly executed by the Execution Engine, or it can be modified by developer in the Process Creation Environment.

$$\text{Optimal}(P) = \text{Min}\left\{\sum_{i=1}^{\theta}(\delta_i + \lambda_i + (\Delta - \tau_i))\right\} \quad \text{s.t.} \begin{cases} \sum_{i=1}^{\theta}\delta_i \le C \\ \sum_{i=1}^{\theta}\tau_i \ge U \\ j \ne 3 j \le n \\ \dots\dots, \dots\dots \end{cases}. \tag{1}$$

Formula 1 is the mathematical expression for calculating optimal sequence or sub-optimal sequence. δ, σ, and τ respectively represent the cost, response time, and user experience; θ is the number of activities in each group; Δ is the full mark of user experience ($0 \le \tau \le \Delta$); j (j:: $\mathbb{A}_{id}$) is the serial number of the activity ($j \ne 3$ represents that no expect to use the activity which serial number is 3). Constrains (s.t.) provide more advanced assessment strategy for users. For example, if the preference is that users expect to choose activity sequence with minimum response time in the constraint that the total cost is not more than C, it can be expressed as formula 2.

$$\text{Optimal}(P) = \text{Min}\left\{\sum_{i=1}^{\theta}\sigma_i\right\} \quad \text{s.t.} \sum_{i=1}^{\theta}\delta_i \le C. \tag{2}$$

4.6 Experiment and Analysis

In this paper, we validate our RoDP approach by Matlab simulation experiment. We use service cost as the assessment strategy. To simplify the problem, we suppose that current state is S_o and objective state is S_n. The experimental data is shown as Figure 7, and the experimental result is shown as Figure 8.

$\mathbb{R}_{id}$	$\mathbb{A}_{id}$	*precondition*	*result*
0	29	S_o	S_1
1	14	S_o	S_3
2	9	S_o	S_2
3	21	S_1	S_4
4	36	S_1	S_6
5	1	S_2	S_5
6	11	S_3	S_5
7	13	S_4	S_7
8	6	S_4	S_n
9	23	S_5	S_6
10	5	S_5	S_8
11	31	S_6	S_n
12	17	S_8	S_n
...	...	...	...

$\mathbb{A}_{id}$	$\mathbb{E}_{id}$	*State(a)*	*State(b)*	*Weight*	activity
1	9	S_2	S_5	2	f
5	4	S_5	S_8	5	k
6	26	S_4	S_n	5	i
9	17	S_o	S_2	3	c
11	0	S_3	S_5	1	g
13	11	S_4	S_7	2	h
14	15	S_o	S_3	2	b
17	6	S_8	S_n	3	m
21	30	S_1	S_4	4	d
23	12	S_5	S_6	2	j
29	7	S_o	S_1	1	a
31	19	S_6	S_n	3	l
36	22	S_1	S_6	5	e
...	...	...	...	...	...

Fig. 7. The experimental data of RoDP

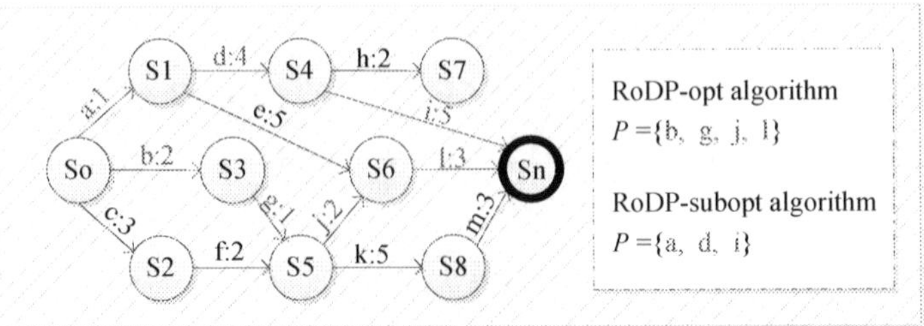

Fig. 8. The experimental result of RoDP

The computer configuration is that the CPU is dual-core 2.40GHZ and the memory is 4.00GB. We simulate the time consumption and space consumption while the rule number is 15, 50, 150, 450, 1350, and 4050, as shown in Figure 9. Abscissa indicates the number of rules. Experiments show that the time consumption is 7.162s for generating optimal activity sequence and the time consumption is 74.329ms for generating suboptimal activity sequence, when the number of rules is 1000. Through the experimental results, we conclude that we should use the RoDP-subopt algorithm to generate suboptimal activity sequence when the number of rules reaches 10^3 orders of magnitude. To avoid circular wait or infinite wait, we specify to execute the RoDP-subopt algorithm when execution time of the RoDP-opt algorithm exceeds 10s.

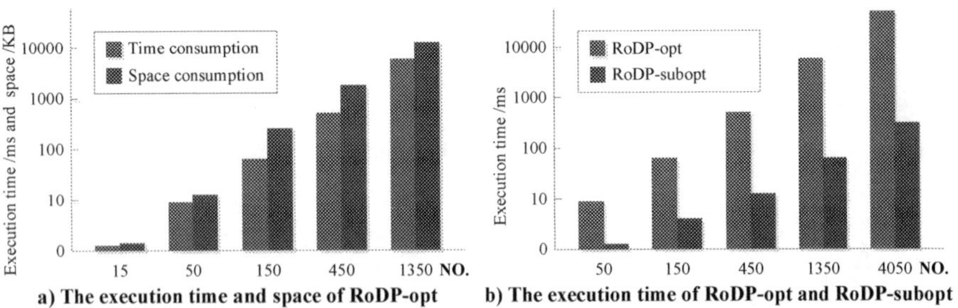

Fig. 9. The algorithm comparison under different number of rules

Table 1. The comparison of various methods

Method	Automatic Adjustment	Consistency Detection	Context Aware	New Requirement	User Preference	Manual Intervention
ADEPT		√			√	√
ConDec		√		√	√	√
Fragment-based	√		√			
Aspect-oriented			√		√	
ECA-based	√	√		√	√	
RoDP	√		√	√	√	√

Table 1 shows the comparison of various methods which were mentioned in the section of the Related Work. The major elements of comparison are as follows: whether to support the Automatic Adjustment at runtime; whether to support the Consistency Detection of the generated process; whether to respond to the changes of the Context and new requirement; whether to support the User Preference and Manual Intervention during the process of dynamic adaptation.

5 Conclusion

In the dynamic environment, it is an effective way to respond to the changes of environment information and application requirements by the dynamic planning approach. And the generated activity sequence of business process satisfies the business goals. This paper focuses on the dynamic assembly problem while we develop heating maintenance process based on the previously developed information service platform of heating industry. We propose the RoDP approach to adapt to the changes. The approach can realize adaptive adjustment of business process at runtime. The RoDP has high flexibility, because it is based on the rules. And we can also adjust the rules to respond to the changes. In addition, our approach supports user preference and manual intervention for the generated process. However, this paper does not focus on the data flow and the consistency detection which may lead to the problem of process inconsistency. So, we need to do further research on them. This approach not only solves the dynamic assembly problem between processes, but also proposes a general solution for the adaptation problem of business process in the changeable environment. The next step is to develop the corresponding components or tools.

Acknowledgments. This research is supported by the National Natural Science Foundation of China (Grant No. 61003067), National 973 Programs (Grant No. 2013CB329102, No.2012CB315802), and Key Project of National Natural Science Foundation of China (Grant No. 61132001), Program for New Century Excellent Talents in University (Grant No. NCET-11-0592), The technology development and experiment of innovative network architecture (CNGI-12-03-007).

References

1. Aalst, W.M.P., Weske, M., Grunbauer, D.: Case handling: a new paradigm for business process support. Data & Knowledge Engineering 53(2), 129–162 (2005)
2. Adams, M., ter Hofstede, A.H.M., van der Aalst, W.M.P., Edmond, D.: Dynamic, extensible and context-aware exception handling for workflows. In: Meersman, R., Tari, Z., et al. (eds.) OTM 2007, Part I. LNCS, vol. 4803, pp. 95–112. Springer, Heidelberg (2007)
3. Bucchiarone, A., Marconi, A., Pistore, M., et al.: Dynamic adaptation of fragment-based and context aware business processes. In: 2012 IEEE 19th International Conference on Web Services (ICWS), pp. 33–41. IEEE (2012)
4. Bucchiarone, A., Pistore, M., Raik, H., et al.: Adaptation of service-based business processes by context-aware replanning. In: 2011 IEEE International Conference on Service Oriented Computing and Applications (SOCA), pp. 1–8. IEEE (2011)

5. De, L.M.: Adaptive process management in highly dynamic and pervasive scenarios. arXiv preprint arXiv: 0906.4149 (2009)
6. Guinard, D., Trifa, M., Karnouskos, S., Spiess, P., Savio, D.: Interacting with the SOA-Based Internet of Things: Discovery, Query, Selection, and On-Demand Provisioning of Web Services. IEEE Transactions on Services Computing 3, 223–235 (2010)
7. Heinl, P., Horn, S., Jablonski, S., et al.: A comprehensive approach to flexibility in workflow management systems. In: ACM SIGSOFT Software Engineering Notes, vol. 24(2), pp. 79–88. ACM (1999)
8. Kammer, P.J., Bolcer, G.A., Taylor, R.N., et al.: Techniques for supporting dynamic and adaptive workflow. Computer Supported Cooperative Work 9(3-4), 269–292 (2000)
9. Mejia Bernal, J.F., Falcarin, P., Morisio, M., et al.: Dynamic context-aware business process: a rule-based approach supported by pattern identification. In: Proceedings of the 2010 ACM Symposium on Applied Computing, pp. 470–474. ACM (2010)
10. Papazoglou, M.P., Traverso, P., Dustdar, S., et al.: Service-oriented computing: State of the art and research challenges. Computer 40(11), 38–45 (2007)
11. Pesic, M., van der Aalst, W.M.P.: A declarative approach for flexible business processes management. In: Eder, J., Dustdar, S. (eds.) BPM Workshops 2006. LNCS, vol. 4103, pp. 169–180. Springer, Heidelberg (2006)
12. Pfeffer, H., Linner, D., Steglich, S.: Dynamic adaptation of workflow based service compositions. In: Huang, D.-S., Wunsch II, D.C., Levine, D.S., Jo, K.-H. (eds.) ICIC 2008. LNCS, vol. 5226, pp. 763–774. Springer, Heidelberg (2008)
13. Reisig, W., Rozenberg, G. (eds.): APN 1998. LNCS, vol. 1491. Springer, Heidelberg (1998)
14. Ruy, S.H., Casati, F., et al.: Supporting the dynamic evolution of Web service protocols in service-oriented architectures. ACM Transactions on the Web 2(2), 1–45 (2008)
15. Schonenberg, H., Mans, R., Russell, N., et al.: Process flexibility: A survey of contemporary approaches. In: Dietz, J.L.G., Albani, A., Barjis, J. (eds.) Advances in Enterprise Engineering I. LNBIP, vol. 10, pp. 16–30. Springer, Heidelberg (2008)
16. Vaculin, R., Heath, T., Hull, R.: Data-centric Web Services Based on Business Artifacts. In: IEEE 19th International Conference on Web Services, pp. 42–49. IEEE (2012)
17. Verma, K., Gomadam, K., Sheth, A.P., et al.: The Meteor-S approach for configuring and executing dynamic web processes. Lsdis Meteors project. Technical report (2005)
18. Wanf, Y., Yang, J., Zhao, W.: Change impact analysis for service based business processes. In: 2010 IEEE International Conference on Service-Oriented Computing and Applications (SOCA), pp. 1–8. IEEE (2010)
19. Weske, M.: Formal foundation and conceptual design of dynamic adaptations in a workflow management system. In: Proceedings of the 34th Annual Hawaii International Conference on System Sciences, pp. 1–10. IEEE (2001)
20. Yu, J., Han, J., Sheng, Q.Z., Gunarso, S.O.: PerCAS: An approach to enabling dynamic and personalized adaptation for context-aware services. In: Liu, C., Ludwig, H., Toumani, F., Yu, Q. (eds.) Service Oriented Computing. LNCS, vol. 7636, pp. 173–190. Springer, Heidelberg (2012)

Flexible Component Migration in an OSGi Based Pervasive Cloud Infrastructure

Weishan Zhang[1], Licheng Chen[1], Qinghua Lu[1], Peiying Zhang[1], and Su Yang[2]

[1] Department of Software Engineering, China University of Petroleum, No. 66, Changjiang West Road, Qingdao, China, 266580
[2] College of Computer, Fudan University, Shanghai 201203, China
zhangws@upc.edu.cn, lcchen.upc@gmail.com

Abstract. Task and service migration is an important feature for mobile cloud computing in order to improve capabilities of small devices. However, the flexible management of components migration between small devices themselves and powerful nodes in between is remaining a critical challenge for enabling mobile clouds. In this paper, we present a solution using OSGi component model based on the OSGi pervasive cloud (OSGi-PC) infrastructure we have developed. We have evaluated the component migration in different scenarios in terms of performance and power consumption to show the usability of our approach.

1 Introduction

The convergence of different computing paradigms, such as cloud computing, pervasive and mobile computing, makes the arising of a new computing paradigm called mobile cloud computing (MCC) [3]. The key idea of mobile cloud computing is to use backend powerful computing nodes from traditional cloud services to enhance capabilities of small devices. In order to realize this idea, computing tasks or services need to be shifted to and from different computing nodes, not only from small devices to the heavy weight computing nodes, but also in between different small devices, and from the heavy computing node to the light weight nodes. Therefore, how to effectively manage and conduct the migrations of software components in MCC is a critical problem.

So far, there are a number of MCC proposals, such as CloneCloud [2], Misco [4] and Hyrax [9]. CloneCloud [2] needs a modified Java Virtual Machine to work, which makes it unrealistic in practice [21]. Misco and Hyrax focus on making MapReduce [1] working on small devices, which did not address component migration among computing nodes. eXcloud [7][8] is a MCC middleware that supports fine granularity tasks migration from code snippets to a whole virtual machine from small device to the backend. From our experiences and understanding, the migration of tasks should not be done only from small devices to backend heavy weight nodes, but can be migrated in between all different kinds cloud nodes. Also, based on the context-awareness requirements[15][16] [19], the migration of too fine granularity tasks as code snippets may not be beneficial if the cost of migration needs to be taken into consideration.

A.R. Lomuscio et al. (Eds.): ICSOC 2013 Workshops, LNCS 8377, pp. 505–514, 2014.
© Springer International Publishing Switzerland 2014

Considering all these challenges and existing solutions, we are developing an OSGi based pervasive cloud (OSGi-PC) [18] that is based on the idea of flexible management of software components among cloud nodes for facilitating task migrations. The components can be migrated between OSGi frameworks on remote powerful nodes, but also between OSGi frameworks on small device nodes and remote powerful nodes. In other words, components can be migrated smoothly between any two frameworks of the OSGi-PC. We have done some preliminary evaluations of the OSGi-PC in terms of performance, power consumption, latency and usability.

The rest of the paper is structured as follows: we present an overview of the components migration in Section 2, we then discuss the implementation of it in details in Section 3. An evaluation of the components migration is shown in Section 4. After that we compare our work with the related work in Section 5. At last, conclusions and future work end the paper.

2 Overview of Component Migration

2.1 Simple Introduction to OSGi and R-OSGi

OSGi (Open Service Gateway Initiative)[1] is a module system and service platform for the Java programming language, which implements a complete and dynamic component model and has become a de facto industry component standard for Java platforms. The applications or components of OSGi (coming in the form of bundles for deployment) can be remotely installed, started, stopped updated, and uninstalled without requiring a reboot.

R-OSGi (Remote Services for OSGi)[2] was proposed to access services remotely from another OSGi service registry. It runs as an OSGi bundle and facilitates distribution for arbitrary OSGi framework implementations. All that a service provider framework has to do is registering a service for remote access with some specific properties. Subsequently, other peers can connect to the service provider peer and get access to the service. Remote services are accessed in an entirely transparent way. For every remote service, a local proxy bundle is generated that registers the same service. Local service clients can hence access the remote service in the same way and without regarding distribution.

2.2 Component Migration of OSGi-PC

As components are standard OSGi bundles, so they can be dynamically installed and uninstalled. Ideally, components should be easily migrated to any nodes inside OSGi-PC, as depicted in Fig. 1. An OSGi framework (deployed on different nodes, for example powerful PC nodes, or Android phones) can run any number of OSGi components. The components can smoothly be migrated from one framework to another without concerning about whether frameworks are deployed on remote

[1] `http://en.wikipedia.org/wiki/OSGi`

[2] `http://r-osgi.sourceforge.net/index.html`

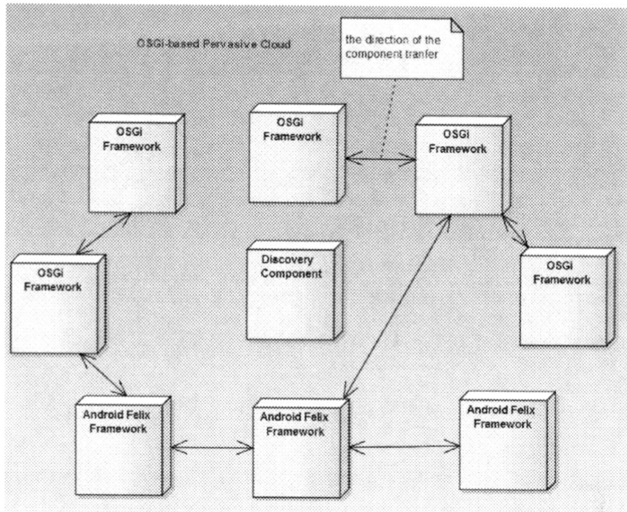

Fig. 1. Component migration model of OSGi-PC

powerful nodes or some small devices. We can see that component migrations can be classified into three different types: component migration between frameworks on remote power nodes, between frameworks on small devices and between the two kinds of frameworks above.

To achieve this goal, at first we need two services: one service is to determine which components need to be migrated to remote frameworks while the other service is to provide these components to specific remote frameworks according to the status of remote OSGi frameworks. At the same time, the framework receiving components have to register a remote deployer service before migrations (when OSGi framework starts), which makes it possible for the migration initiating framework to migrate components to the receiving framework, and to manage the migrated components after the migration. In the following, we will discuss the implementation based on this.

3 Implementation of Component Migration

Figure 2 is the core class diagram to show the design of component migrations between frameworks on OSGi-PC nodes. Class Redeployer is responsible for determining what components should be migrated and then it shuts down those components, and then it uses class ServiceProvisioner to deploy those component remotely. The ServiceProvisioner class looks for proper frameworks (in this first prototype, it will select one framework whose free memory is the maximum) to deploy components by utilizing the service RemoteDeployer. The RemoteDeployer has been registered as a basic service for all OSGi frameworks, and this RemoteDeployer service can can store, install and start components

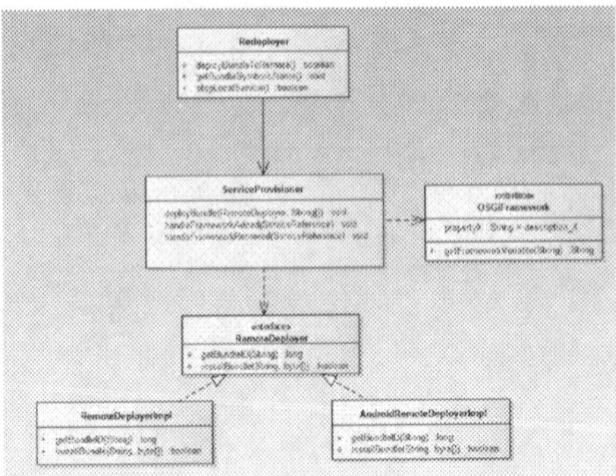

Fig. 2. Core classes of Component Migaration

migrated from other frameworks. According to different component migration types, there are different implementations of the RemoteDeployer interface. In our implementation, there are two kinds of implementation of this interface.

3.1 Component Migration between Frameworks on Remote Powerful Nodes

For this type of component migrations, the OSGi-PC uses Apache Distributed OSGi (DOSGi) where Zookeeper is used as as a discovery component. When a new framework joins in the OSGi-PC, the new framework will register itself to the discovery component with necessary information. Therefore, one framework can obtain information of all frameworks in OSGi-PC from the discovery component. Based on our former work [18], we can get one framework whose available memory is maximum, after that we can redeploy components to this framework.

3.2 Component Migration between Frameworks on Different Platforms

Because of the popularity of Android platform, we choose it as the front end of OSGi-PC. We use Apache Felix framework as the container of OSGi components. As Felix frameworks can only be used in one JVM, we need some communication frameworks to run across different JVMs. R-OSGi [11] is a lightweight and efficient communication component between distributed OSGi frameworks that can be tailored to run on Android [18]. Therefore we use R-OSGi for communication and component migrations between two frameworks within which one framework needs to be deployed on a small device.

But when one component has been migrated to target Android framework, it cannot be installed and started normally. This is because the Android platform cannot run java Jar files directly. The Dalvik virtual machine of Android can only read byte code compiled for it. Therefore when OSGi-PC needs to migrate components to an Android framework, the RemoteDeployerImpl service of OSGi framework running on power nodes will use a "dexShell" shell to convert components from java code to Dalvik code. Similarly, when components are migrated to framework running on power nodes (normal JVMs), the RemoteDeployerImpl service of it will use a shell named "undexShell" to convert the components back to normal Jar files. The shell uses dx.jar of google Android platform to complete this conversion. We illustrate these processes in Figure 3 and Figure 4.

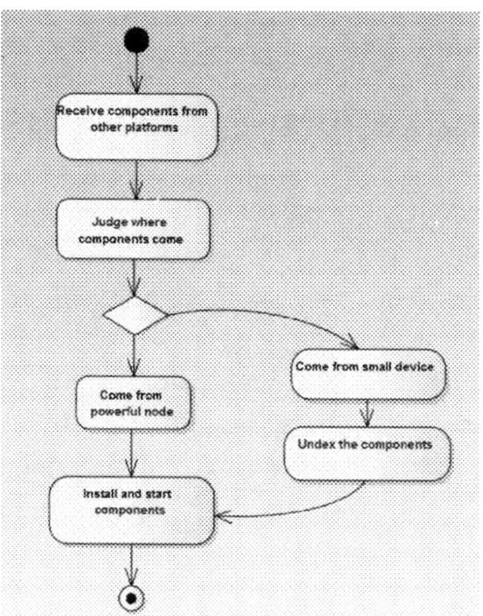

Fig. 3. Component migration from small device to powerful node

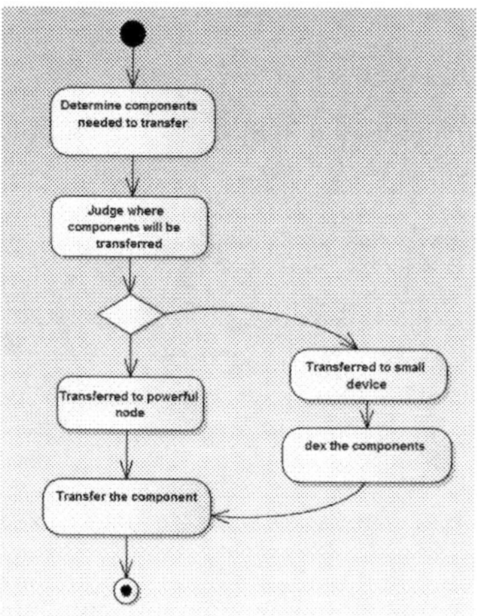

Fig. 4. Component migration from powerful node to small device

3.3 Component Migration between Frameworks on Small Devices

It seems to be simple to migrate components between frameworks running on Android platform. Because components migrated between them are Dalvik code which primarily converted from OSGi frameworks running on remote powerful nodes, what we do is just receive the components, install and start them. There are no differences between different Android devices.

4 Evaluation

To evaluate the performance of the component migration, we use FelixDroid[3] as the application console which can provide a UI of felix console to show the status of bundles at runtime. At the same time, we use PowerTutor[4] to evaluate the power consumption of the FelixDroid application when in the process of component migration. In this evaluation, we use two simple OSGi bundles as the components to migration.

From Table 1, we can see that the migration process from an Android phone to PC takes around 215ms to finish a whole migration process, which is quite good and usable in a pervasive computing environment. For the power consumption on Android phones, the CPU takes around 1.37 J during the process, which is acceptable also.

Table 1. Phone to computer power consumption(J)

	1	2	3	4	5	6	7	8	9	10	11	average
stop local bundles(ms)	5	6	8	7	7	5	7	7	6	6	7	6.45
uninstall local bundles(ms)	12	10	12	10	10	9	11	10	10	9	9	10.18
network transfer(ms)	148	89	126	80	95	122	98	112	92	94	106	105.64
install bundles remotely(ms)	25	25	28	22	30	25	23	58	30	27	23	28.73
start bundles remotely(ms)	89	64	67	89	66	68	70	30	61	69	33	64.18
CPU power consumption(J)	1.7	0.804	1.7	2	1.8	1.6	1.5	0.897	1.3	0.957	0.814	1.37
LCD power consumption(J)	11.2	9.6	10.1	8.5	8	8	8.5	9.1	7.5	9.1	8	8.87

From Table 2, we can see that the migration process from a PC to an Android phone takes around 1.60s to finish a whole migration process, which is OK. Another thing to note is that in a pervasive computing environment, this kind of migration is rare.

From Table 3, we can see that the migration process from one Android phone to another phone takes around 645ms to finish a whole migration process, which is good and usable in a pervasive computing environment. For the power consumption on Android phones, the CPU takes around 1.35 J during the process, which is acceptable.

[3] `http://www-irisa.univ-ubs.fr/CASA/dev/felixdroid/`

[4] `http://ziyang.eecs.umich.edu/projects/powertutor/`

Table 2. Performance of computer to phone component migration

	1	2	3	4	5	6	7	8	9	10	11	average
stop local bundles(ms)	3	3	2	3	3	3	3	3	4	2	3	2.91
uninstall local bundles(ms)	7	11	15	52	21	24	29	38	6	9	9	20.09
network transfer(ms)	1011	1030	1038	1180	1122	1373	1209	1206	1132	1167	1058	1138.73
install bundles remotely(ms)	38	38	39	44	41	40	37	39	40	37	43	39.64
start bundles remotely(ms)	323	185	591	784	177	752	216	593	182	371	175	395.36

Table 3. Phone to phone power consumption(J)

	1	2	3	4	5	6	7	8	9	10	11	average
stop local bundles(ms)	8	5	6	6	6	5	7	6	7	5	6	6.09
uninstall local bundles(ms)	11	13	11	10	9	11	21	9	12	10	17	12.18
network transfer time(ms)	386	334	276	357	376	358	331	309	289	331	347	335.82
install bundles remotely(ms)	75	56	49	45	62	47	46	48	66	56	67	56.09
start bundles remotely(ms)	437	187	229	226	213	279	185	233	205	160	227	234.64
CPU power consumption(J)	1.7	0.843	1.7	1.3	1.5	1.9	0.809	0.885	2.3	0.925	1	1.35
LCD power consumption(J)	5.9	6.9	6.4	6.4	5.3	5.3	4.8	5.9	4.8	5.3	5.3	5.66

When comparing three tables above, we can see that time consumption of stop and uninstall operation of OSGi frameworks on PCs needs less time than that of phones. But the time consumption of a migration, installation and start process of a phone is more less than that of PCs. This is because the migration from PC to phones needs to dex the components for running on Android platform before the migration to an Android phone, and this process is time-consuming. The LCD and CPU power consumption is acceptable. The migrations between phones are faster than that from computer to phone without dex process.

5 Related Work

There are quite a few work on mobile cloud computing [3] [5] targeting enhancing capabilities of small devices. Some are focusing on creating MapReduce frameworks for small devices, such as Misco [4] and Hyrax [9], in order to improve the performance of handhold devices. The components migration aims at transferring services and tasks among component nodes in order to utilize resources not available locally, which have higher flexibilities in terms of that this can be done at different levels, such as a bunch of services or a single service.

The work of eXcloud [7][8] is a MCC middleware that supports fine granularity tasks migration. As we have said, the migration should consider a number context and quality of service factors, for example the cost of network usage, the time taken for a migration, and so on. Therefore in our opinion, the migration should be conducted at a proper level, a too fine level may incur too much overhead comparing with the benefits it has. In OSGi-PC, we are working on task migration at component and service level (a number of components fulfilling a certain service).

CloneCloud [2] can clone the computation and data from mobile devices to backend heavy weight cloud nodes, and then return the computation results to the small devices which offload the tasks. The real problem with CloneCloud is that it needs a modified Java Virtual Machine for offloading code to the cloud nodes, which makes the approach unrealistic in practice [21].

CloudLet [12] makes use of virtual machine technology to instantiate services instances in nearby CloudLet, which may alleviate the latency of wide area networks, and limitations of network bandwidth. In our future work, we will investigate how to use this virtual machine technology without actually moving components in some situations, as an alternative for component and task migration.

The work on MCC-OSGi [6] uses OSGi Bundles as basic mobile Cloud service components, which can execute services remotely and run on different platforms. In our work on OSGi-PC, we have followed Remote Service specification for achieving the registration of services across different cloud nodes. We have also achieved components migration seamlessly on all different kinds of node in the OSGi-PC. This feature is very important when no remote services are available for the current request and there is a need to offload a task due to the nature of the task that is computation heavy.

In [13], the authors presented a middleware called OSGi4C (OSGi for the Cloud), which allows seamless deployment of locally non-existent OSGi bundles and services on demand without requiring any changes to the OSGi platform. Based on P2P platform JXTA, it realized remote bundles discovery service in a distributed manner. We will investigate in the future to include the P2P feature for component migrations based on our previous work [10].

6 Conclusion and Future Work

The convergence of cloud computing, pervasive and mobile computing can help to enhance capabilities of small devices, as what is focused on by the research of mobile cloud computing and pervasive cloud computing [19]. There are emerging research prototypes on middleware and frameworks to realize the idea of mobile cloud computing. But few of the existing ones are focusing on component based cloud infrastructure in order to facilitate inter-operability and ease the management of services and component migrations, following certain well-accepted standard. In this paper, we have proposed and developed a flexible component migration approach for an OSGi based pervasive cloud infrastructure (OSGi-PC). The advantages of this approach is that it can support flexible migration between any kind of cloud nodes, instead of only migration from frond end to backend as in other related work. We have shown the acceptable performance and power consumption features with evaluations.

We will deploy more services on OSGi-PC to make our system full fledged, for example context management [15], task migrations decisions support [3] based on our previous work on goal management [17][14][20] to make it really useful to develop applications in smart cities.

Acknowledgements. The research is supported by the National Natural Science Foundation of China (Grant No. 61309024). Weishan Zhang has been supported by "the Fundamental Research Funds for the Central Universities" and also the start up funds for "Academic Top-Notch in China University of Petroleum" professors.

References

1. Chu, C., Kim, S., Lin, Y., Yu, Y., Bradski, G., Ng, A., Olukotun, K.: Map-reduce for machine learning on multicore. Advances in neural information processing systems 19(281) (2007)
2. Chun, B., Ihm, S., Maniatis, P., Naik, M., Patti, A.: Clonecloud: elastic execution between mobile device and cloud. In: Proceedings of the Sixth Conference on Computer Systems, pp. 301–314. ACM (2011)
3. Dinh, H.T., Lee, C., Niyato, D., Wang, P.: A survey of mobile cloud computing: architecture, applications, and approaches. Wireless Communications and Mobile Computing (2011)
4. Dou, A., Kalogeraki, V., Gunopulos, D., Mielikainen, T., Tuulos, V.: Misco: a mapreduce framework for mobile systems. In: Proceedings of the 3rd International Conference on PErvasive Technologies Related to Assistive Environments, p. 32. ACM (2010)
5. Fernando, N., Loke, S., Rahayu, W.: Mobile cloud computing: A survey. Future Generation Computer Systems (2012)
6. Houacine, F., Bouzefrane, S., Li, L., Huang, D.: Mcc-osgi: An osgi-based mobile cloud service model. In: 2013 IEEE Eleventh International Symposium on Autonomous Decentralized Systems (ISADS), pp. 1–8. IEEE (2013)
7. Ma, R.K.K., Lam, K.T., Wang, C.-L.: excloud: Transparent runtime support for scaling mobile applications in cloud. In: 2011 International Conference on Cloud and Service Computing (CSC), pp. 103–110. IEEE (2011)
8. Ma, R.K.K., Wang, C.-L.: Lightweight application-level task migration for mobile cloud computing. In: 2012 IEEE 26th International Conference on Advanced Information Networking and Applications (AINA), pp. 550–557. IEEE (2012)
9. Marinelli, E.E.: Hyrax: cloud computing on mobile devices using mapreduce. Technical report, DTIC Document (2009)
10. Milagro, F., Antolin, P., Fernandes, J., Zhang, W., Hansen, K., Kool, P.: Deploying pervasive web services over a p2p overlay. In: 18th IEEE International Workshops on Enabling Technologies: Infrastructures for Collaborative Enterprises, WETICE 2009, pp. 240–245. IEEE (2009)
11. Rellermeyer, J.S., Alonso, G., Roscoe, T.: R-oSGi: Distributed applications through software modularization. In: Cerqueira, R., Campbell, R.H. (eds.) Middleware 2007. LNCS, vol. 4834, pp. 1–20. Springer, Heidelberg (2007)
12. Satyanarayanan, M., Bahl, P., Caceres, R., Davies, N.: The case for vm-based cloudlets in mobile computing. IEEE Pervasive Computing 8(4), 14–23 (2009)
13. Schmidt, H., Elsholz, J., Nikolov, V., Hauck, F., Kapitza, R.: Osgi 4c: enabling osgi for the cloud. In: Proceedings of the Fourth International ICST Conference on Communication System software and middleware, p. 15. ACM (2009)
14. Zhang, W., Hansen, K.: An Evaluation of the NSGA-II and MOCell Genetic Algorithms for Self-management Planning in a Pervasive Service Middleware. In: 14th IEEE International Conference on Engineering Complex Computer Systems (ICECCS 2009), pp. 192–201. IEEE Computer Society, Washington, DC (2009)

15. Zhang, W., Hansen, K.M.: Using context awareness for self-management in pervasive service middleware. In: Handbook of Research on Ambient Intelligence and Smart Environments: Trends and Perspectives, 1 vol., p. 248 (2011)
16. Zhang, W., Hansen, K.M., Fernandes, J., Schütte, J., Lardies, F.M.: Qos-aware self-adaptation of communication protocols in a pervasive service middleware. In: Green Computing and Communications (GreenCom), 2010 IEEE/ACM Int'l Conference on & Int'l Conference on Cyber, Physical and Social Computing (CPSCom), pp. 17–26. IEEE (2010)
17. Zhang, W., Hansen, K.M., Fernandes, J., Schutte, J., Lardies, F.M.: Qos-aware self-adaptation of communication protocols in a pervasive service middleware. In: Green Computing and Communications (GreenCom), 2010 IEEE/ACM Int'l Conference on & Int'l Conference on Cyber, Physical and Social Computing (CPSCom), pp. 17–26. IEEE (2010)
18. Zhang, W., Chen, L., Lu, Q., Rao, Y., Zhou, J.: Towards an osgi based pervasive cloud infrastructure. In: 2013 IEEE International Conference on Internet of Things (iThings2013), pp. 418–425. IEEE (2013)
19. Zhang, W., Hansen, K.M., Bellavista, P.: A research roadmap for context-awareness-based self-managed systems. In: Ghose, A., Zhu, H., Yu, Q., Delis, A., Sheng, Q.Z., Perrin, O., Wang, J., Wang, Y. (eds.) ICSOC 2012. LNCS, vol. 7759, pp. 275–283. Springer, Heidelberg (2013)
20. Zhang, W., Hansen, K.M., Kunz, T.: Enhancing intelligence and dependability of a product line enabled pervasive middleware. Pervasive and Mobile Computing 6(2), 198–217 (2010)
21. Zhang, Y., Huang, G., Liu, X., Zhang, W., Mei, H., Yang, S.: Refactoring android java code for on demand computation offloading. In: Proceedings of the ACM International Conference on Object Oriented Programming Systems languages and Applications, pp. 233–248. ACM (2012)

Hybrid Emotion Recognition Using Semantic Similarity

Zhanshan Zhang[1], Xin Meng[2], Peiying Zhang[2], Weishan Zhang[2], and Qinghua Lu[2]

[1] International School, Tongji University, No. 67 Chifeng Road, Shanghai, China, 200092
[2] Department of Software Engineering, China University of Petroleum, No. 66, Changjiang West Road, Qingdao, China, 266580

zhanshan@tongji.edu.cn, mengxin605@163.com, zhangws@upc.edu.cn

Abstract. It is challenging to know emotion status of people at run time as emotion can be influenced by many factors. Speech contents heart rates are used in our former work on hybrid emotion recognition approach. However, fixed emotional keywords is not enough as there may be unknown and new keywords arise. Therefore we add semantic similarity to emotional keywords recognition. After obtaining the content of the user, even if the emotional keywords are not in the knowledge base, we calculate the similarity between the keywords in the talk of the user and the words in the knowledge base. A hybrid similarity calculation algorithm is proposed to alleviate the problems that some words do not exist in HowNet knowledge base where we combine the similarity calculation method for Tongyici Cilin. If the similarity is greater than a threshold, then a corresponding emotion status will be recognized together with the heart rate of the user. The advantage of using semantic similarity is that it is much more flexible than the one with only fixed emotional keywords in the knowledge base, together with a higher recognition accuracy than before.

1 Introduction

Emotion status is an important factor that affects the health status of people. Therefore, recognizing emotion status is an important step towards the intervention of low emotion status. Currently, there are quite some emotion recognition technologies, such as the ones using physiological signals, or using facial expressions and voice contents. Due to the complexity nature of mind state which can be influenced by the health status of a person, external events, physiological changes, and many other factors, we proposed a hybrid emotion recognition approach which combines physiological signal (heart beats) and speech contents [18].

For speaking, different people may use different emotional keywords to express the same kind of emotion. At the same time, it is not rare at all that these emotional keywords may not be in the knowledge base designed for the emotion recognition, and new emotional keywords may arise. Therefore, to make the emotion recognition really practical using speech contents, it is necessary to identify the semantic similarity of emotion keywords spoken by different people or in different situations.

Therefore, in addition to the physiological signals for example heart rates, the semantic similarity of the emotional keywords in a speech should be taken into consideration during the process of emotion recognition. In our work, we first classify anger, joy, normal and sadness based on heart rates, then the emotion recognition is further improved

A.R. Lomuscio et al. (Eds.): ICSOC 2013 Workshops, LNCS 8377, pp. 515–526, 2014.
© Springer International Publishing Switzerland 2014

by emotional key words: first, we segment the sentence of the talk of the user, then depending on semantic similarity we will calculate the result of keywords recognition. We have initially tested the proposed approach and found that our approach indeed works well.

The rest of the paper is structured as follows: We show an overview of the proposed emotion recognition approach in Section 2. Section 3 discusses the implementation of our emotion recognition approach. We evaluated the proposed approach in Section 4. Related work is described in 5. Conclusions and future work end the paper.

2 An Overview of Emotion Recognition Using Heart Rate Monitoring and Emotional Key Words Identification

As we all know that the smart phones is increasingly popular, we adopt heart rate as one method to identify the emotional status of the user. In order to get the heart rate, we only need to use the built-in camera on the smart phones. The color for finger is changing continuously with the heart beats. Therefore the user will only need to shoot the finger to detect color changes, and henceforth to get the heart rates.

2.1 Heart Rate for Different Emotion Status

Usually people will have different heart rates when they are in different emotion status [18], as shown in Figure 1 below.

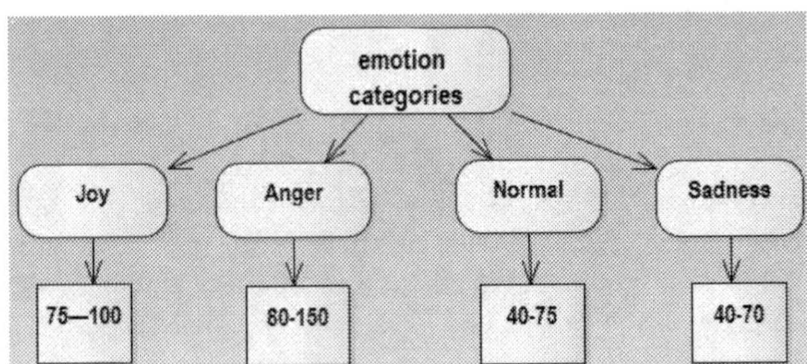

Fig. 1. Relationships of Heart Rates with Emotion

Only heart rate itself can not accurately decide the emotion status as we can see from Figure 1. It should be combined with other approaches, for example, identifying what a person is talking may help to recognize the emotion of the speaker.

2.2 Emotional Key Words

As a common sense, people in different emotional status may say different emotional words[4], which are called emotional key words. Based on the work done by Wu [13][12], we build our own emotional key words knowledge base, partially shown in Table 1.

Table 1. Some keywords of four categories of emotion

emotion	keyword1	keyword2	kerword3	keyword4	keyword5
joy	太 嘻嘻	高兴 哈哈	开心 了	快乐 心情	嘿嘿 –
anger	以为 滚开 闭嘴 死	回 敢 脑子 滚蛋	事 省 进 –	讨厌 省 水 –	烦 吧 去 –
normal	星期一 想 好 打算 周末	星期二 说 吧 不 星期六	星期三 这样 没什么 知道 –	星期四 吗 就 天空 –	星期五 也 结束 蓝 –
sadness	很 伤心 不 知道	不 为什么 开心 –	想 难过 一个 –	说 呜呜 人 –	话 失望 什么 –

2.3 Emotion Recognition Approach Overview

We show the proposed emotion recognition approach as shown in 2, similar as that in [18]. It is a hybrid emotion recognition approach combining physiology signal, obtained through the built-in camera and speech contents, obtained through the microphone on the smart phones.

First the user needs to shoot his finger around 10 seconds with the built-in camera. If the average heart beats is obtained successfully, then the preliminary emotion recognition will be conducted. After this, as the talking content will be continuously monitored, and then word segmentation is used to extract some keywords that can represent the emotion status of the user. Then semantic similarity is calculated to identify emotional keywords, which are reflecting the current emotion status of the user. Finally the recognition results will be further improved by using semantic similarity in keywords recognition process.

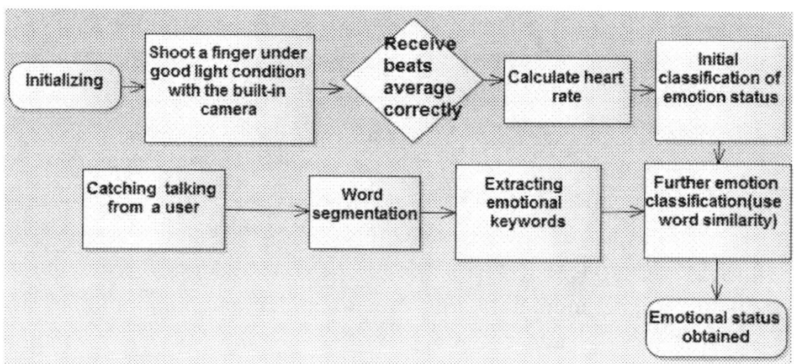

Fig. 2. Overview of the hybrid emotion recognition approach

3 Implementation of the Hybrid Emotion Recognition Approach

The emotion recognition can be considered as a sort of context-aware computing [1], where the contents of talks and heart rates are parts of contexts, and they are managed in a context-awareness framework based on our previous work [15][17][16]. The overall architecture of our hybrid emotion recognition application is shown in 3.

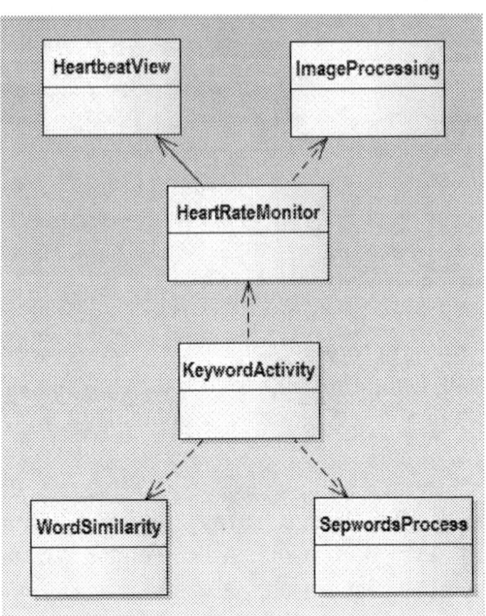

Fig. 3. Structure of the emotion recognition on Android smart phones

From 1, we can see that for heart rates, there are overlaps between different emotion states. The four emotional states can be largely classified as low rates (sadness and normal) and high rates (joy and anger). To show the decision making more clearly, a decision tree is shown in 4. We can see that it is not possible to differentiate emotion status at the third level in the tree. Here the emotional key words identification will help to improve the recognition process.

The main work flow of the mood recognition is realized in class KeywordActivity as shown in 5. During this process, the heart rate is used first to make decisions on which branch the recognition process will transverse 4. With the underlying speech content retrieved using a speech to text service from the context-awareness framework.

Then we make word segmentation, namely to segment contents of the sentence spoken by a user. After this, we can get the components in the content. For examples, we will know which are adjectives in the content, which are verbs in the content.

After the segmentation, we extract some specific components of the content that can represent the emotion of the user. Then by using a word similarity algorithm proposed in [11], we make comparison of the components and those emotional key words in the knowledge base.

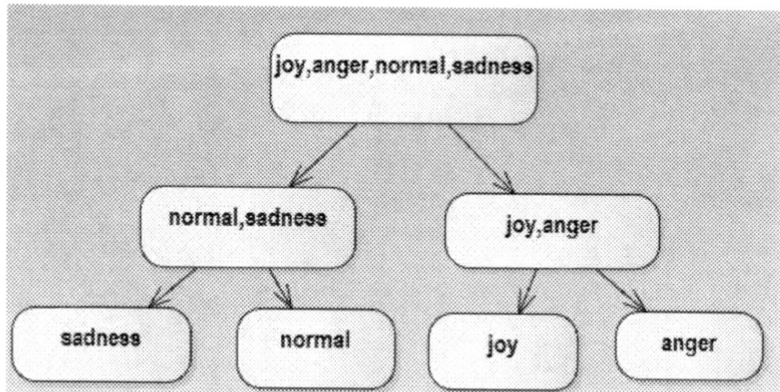

Fig. 4. Decision tree for heart rates based emotion recognition

3.1 Sememes Similarity

The calculation of word similarity based on sememes (smallest elements of HowNet knowledge base) in HowNet is using three basic components:

1. the depth of the sememes: Depth(seme1), where the first sememe is defined as seme1.
2. the overlaps of the sememes: Spd(seme1,seme2), where the first sememe is defined as seme2.
3. the dissimilarity of sememes(can be equals to the semantic distance): Dsd(seme1, seme2).

   The formula about the similarity of sememes is generally defined as follows:
   $Sim(seme1, seme2) = \frac{2*Spd(seme1,seme2)}{Dsd(seme1,seme2)+2*Spd(seme1,seme2)}$

   Or can be calculated using the following formula:
   $Sim(seme1, seme2) = \frac{2*Spd(seme1,seme2)}{Depth(seme1)+Depth(seme2)}$

3.2 Similarity of Words in HowNet

In HowNet, words can be classified as notional words and functional words. For us, the notional words are meaningful for knowing the emotion status. As in the HowNet, the words are described by $"\{thesememesofsyntax\}"and"\{thesememesof relationship\}"$, when we want to calculate the content words, we need to calculate the similarity of the two parts, when we calculate the function words, we only need to calculate the similarity of the two parts that without the braces. The algorithm is described in [11].

3.3 Similarity of Words Not in HowNet

When we calculate the similarity of the words that have not been concluded in the HowNet, we usually do as follows: as the concepts of the words can be segmented, just as $O_1, O_2, ...O_n$, include n concepts. We can calculate the similarity of the n concepts.

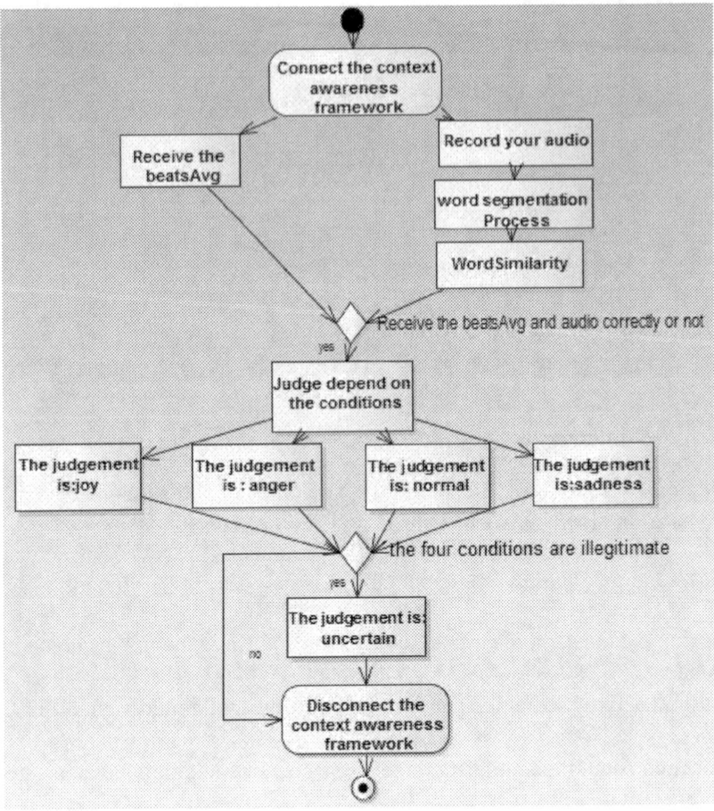

Fig. 5. Work flow of the emotion recognition on Android smart phones

We must be sure that all the n concepts are in the HowNet, then we can calculate the similarity as the calculation of the words that have been included in the HowNet, if any concepts in the n concepts that are not included in the HowNet, we must further make segmentation of the concepts, until every concept is in the HowNet. As we can see, the words similarity calculation depends on that all concepts are in HowNet. But this is not true from our experience, therefore, we need to handle the case where some concepts are missing in HowNet. In this case, we propose to use Tongyici Cilin to alleviate this problem.

3.4 Words Similarity Combining Tongyici Cilin

Tongyici Cilin[1] is another famous thesaurus taxonomy which organized by total different manner from the HowNet, but also in a tree way like how WordNet does. Therefore, We can utilize the tree structure of Cilin to measure the similarity among words as in [10]. Based on the HowNet-based Chinese word similarity algorithm, and Cilin-based

[1] http://download.csdn.net/detail/joy516688/4674656

Chinese word similarity algorithm, we propose a hybrid algorithm combined HowNet and Cilin, the formula is:

$$Sim(w1, w2) = \beta Sim(w1, w2)_{HowNet} + (1 - \beta)Sim(w1, w2)_{Cilin}$$

Where $Sim(w1, w2)_{HowNet}$ is the semantic similarity based on HowNet, $Sim(w1, w2)_{Cilin}$ is the semantic distance based on Cilin, and β is a restrain factor to adjust the weight of the two parts.

4 Evaluation of the Hybrid Emotion Recognition Approach

We have made experiments to evaluate the proposed hybrid emotion recognition approach as presented above. During the tests, we are using a Sony Ericsson LT 18i, with Android 4.1.2[2]. First we need to measure the heart rate of the user, the detail process of how to get the heart rate is defined in [18]. The speech of the user is recognized(include record the talk of the user, make word segmentation, use semantic similarity to judge the emotional status that the special words express)at the same time so that the hybrid recognition can work. In the following tables showing the measurements, we list the emotional key words first, following by the figure for a heart rate during the first test, and then by a 'Y' or 'N' to say whether the recognition of a corresponding emotion status is successful or not.

4.1 Accuracy

We have asked two people to test our system, we call them A, B. The tests for A are shown in Table 2 3 4 5. From these data, we can see that the total accuracy of emotion recognition can reach 71%, we can also see that there are some emotion key words could not be correctly recognized, which lower the accuracy of recognition.

The tests for B are shown in Tables 6 8 9 7. The tests for sadness is shown in the 7. The accuracy for the sadness is around 72%. The total accuracy of the test for B is only around 42%. It is much lower than the tests for A. One reason is that we do not make experiments for all the keywords in the knowledge base for B. So the result of the test for B can not represent all the conditions accurately. As in the test for A, B, the reason that some emotional keywords can not be recognized correctly is that we use the tool of speech to text of Google, so sometimes the unstable of the tool of Google results in that our keywords can not be recognized correctly. We regard this condition as an error, if this condition happens, we also regard it as the error of our work in the test. If we make experiments for B by using all the words in the knowledge base. The accuracy will be around the accuracy of the test for A, namely around 71%. If we do not regard the unstable of Google as an error, the accuracy of the test for A can be better than 71%, the accuracy of the test for B can also be improved.

4.2 Performance

To check the performance of our approach, we record the talk of the user and measure how long it takes recognize speech contents, and how long it takes to calculate the

[2] `http://freexperiaproject.com`

Table 2. Test of Normal for A

Keyword	first	second	third	forth
星期一	51 Y	49 Y	53 Y	41 Y
星期二	65 Y	53 Y	51 Y	71 Y
星期三	57 Y	47 N	71 Y	59 Y
星期四	61 N	59 Y	65 Y	59 Y
星期五	71 Y	53 Y	65 Y	65 Y
星期六	59 N	65 Y	71 Y	47 Y
周末	53 Y	59 Y	41 Y	59 Y
没什么想说的	59 N	47 N	56 N	65 N
好吧	65 N	59 N	51 N	47 N
就这样吧	71 Y	71 Y	53 Y	69 Y
我想说这样也挺好的	71 Y	56 Y	59 Y	65 Y
没什么打算	47 Y	41 Y	53 N	49 Y
就这样吗	65 Y	53 Y	65 Y	59 Y
不知道	59 N	65 N	65 N	65 N
天很蓝	47 N	53 N	65 N	53 N
没什么打算	47 Y	41 Y	53 N	49 Y
就这样吗	65 Y	53 Y	65 Y	59 Y
不知道	59 N	65 N	65 N	65 N
天很蓝	47 N	53 N	65 N	53 N

Table 3. Test of Sadness for A

Keyword	first	second	third	forth
我很难过	65 Y	53 Y	65 Y	41 Y
这是为什么	59 Y	65 Y	41 Y	59 N
好伤心	59 Y	59 Y	53 Y	65 Y
很失望	53 Y	53 N	59 Y	53 Y
好失望	65 N	47 N	59 N	48 N
很伤心	59 Y	53 Y	41 Y	59 Y
我不开心啊	47 N	65 N	53 N	41 N
我想一个人	65 Y	65 Y	59 Y	65 Y
什么都不知道	53 N	59 Y	47 Y	59 N
什么都不想说	47 Y	59 Y	41 Y	47 Y

Table 4. Test of Anger for A

Keyword	first	second	third	forth
真让我恶心	107 N	83 N	89 N	87 N
你怎么回事	83 Y	95 Y	83 Y	89 Y
你以为你是谁	107 N	90 N	94 N	107 N
我讨厌你	107 Y	83 Y	113 Y	107 Y
别烦我	95 Y	107 Y	107 Y	83 Y
滚开	90 Y	113 Y	119 Y	95 Y
你敢	83 Y	94 Y	90 N	107 Y
闭嘴	95 Y	107 Y	107 Y	113 Y
去死吧	107 Y	119 N	113 Y	107 Y
滚蛋	113 N	107 N	95 N	119 N

Table 5. Test of Joy for A

Keyword	first	second	third	forth
太高兴了	77 N	77 N	95 N	77 N
太好了	83 N	83 N	77 N	89 N
我的心情很愉悦	84 Y	90 Y	83 Y	77 Y
我的心情很快乐	90 Y	83 Y	77 N	95 Y
好开心啊	77 Y	83 Y	77 Y	89 Y
好快乐啊	89 Y	83 Y	77 Y	95 N
哈哈	84 Y	83 Y	89 N	83 Y

Table 6. Test of Normal for B

Keyword	first	second	third	forth
星期一	69 Y	71 Y	53 N	53 Y
没什么想说的	49 N	49 N	61 N	55 N
好吧	55 N	71 N	69 N	57 N
就这样吧	61 Y	65 Y	61 Y	59 Y
我想说这样也挺好的	57 Y	47 Y	51 Y	53 Y
没什么打算	73 Y	71 Y	71 N	65 Y

Table 7. Test of Sadness for B

Keyword	first	second	third	forth
我很难过	41 Y	51 N	55 Y	59 Y
这是为什么	55 Y	55 Y	59 Y	57 Y
好伤心	47 Y	43 Y	47 N	57 Y
很失望	65 Y	55 Y	51 Y	45 Y
好失望	43 N	51 N	61 N	63 N

Table 8. Test of Anger for B

Keyword	first	second	third	forth
真让我恶心	97 N	77 N	85 N	83 N
你怎么回事	77 Y	105 Y	103 Y	97 Y
你以为你是谁	97 N	89 N	103 N	119 N
我讨厌你	87 Y	77 Y	107 N	107 Y

Table 9. Test of Joy for B

Keyword	first	second	third	forth
太高兴了	87 N	77 N	94 N	85 N
我的心情很愉悦	94 Y	85 Y	83 Y	77 N
我的心情很快乐	89 Y	77 Y	79 N	95 Y
好开心啊	85 Y	77 N	87 Y	95 Y

Table 10. Performance tests

T1(s)	T2(s)	T(total)(s)
4.8	2.25	8.03
4.58	2.06	7.61
5.43	2.21	7.25
5.05	2.25	7.91
5.05	2.16	7.85
5.03	1.91	7.69
5.25	2.09	8.05
4.91	2.01	7.63
5.03	2.03	7.89

Table 11. Power consumption

Recognition		CA		
LCD(J)	CPU(J)	LCD(J)	CPU(J)	Total(mw)
35.3	20.5	6.3	6.1	927
36	20.9	6.5	6.3	934
35.9	20.3	6.4	6.1	927
35.6	20.9	6.3	6.4	940
35.3	19.8	6.3	6.2	925
36.3	20.5	6.7	6.3	934
36	21	6.2	6.1	936
35.9	20.9	6.3	6.3	925
35.6	21.2	6.5	6.2	927
36	20.8	6.7	6.1	930
34.9	20.6	6.2	6.1	925
34.8	20.4	6.6	6.4	927
35.6	20.5	6.4	6.2	936

semantic similarity, and how long for the whole mood recognition process takes. The tests are shown in Table 10, where the measurements for the time taken is denoted as T1, T2, and T3 respectively. We can see that it takes around 5s for speech recognition which takes the majority of the total recognition time. The process of word segmentation and semantic similarity calculation takes around 2s, which is reasonable for the current knowledge base. The total cost of the whole process that from recording the talk of the user to obtain the final result of emotion recognition is around 7s, which is OK for run time recognition purpose.

4.3 Power Consumption of the Recognition Application

Table 11 shows the power consumption while conducting the mood recognition process on a SE LT18i, the last column shows the power consumption of the context awarenss framework plus the emotion recognition application, which is less than 1 Watt, a reasonable power consumption for an application on Android. All the power consumptions are measured using the Power Tutor software tool[3].

5 Related Work

Using some wearable equipments in order to collect emotion-related physiological signals such as skin conductivity, heart rate and a skin temperature of the user [8]. There exist some emotion recognition systems that They used a base unit and gloves with sensor units in order to receive the data transmitted from sensor units. In our approach, we just avoid using these complex sensors, we make our work more convenient for people, not need to make the user to wear the equipments on their body, in our work we only use the built-in camera and microphone on the smart phone, at the same time, as our work use semantic similarity so we also need the help of the computer, in the future, we will make our work all on the smart phones, to use our work, just a smart phone and a computer are enough.

[3] `http://ziyang.eecs.umich.edu/projects/powertutor/`

There is an interesting work on collecting data only from key strokes which is presented in [5]. In their paper, they are also using the method of decision tree classifier for 15 emotional states, they classify six emotional states including hesitance, confidence, relaxation, nervousness, tiredness and sadness with around the accuracy of 80% successfully. For modern handhold devices, collecting key strokes are impractical where the main interaction method is touching screen, our work is more practical, as we use semantic similarity in our work, the accuracy of our work can be around 71%. We regard the unstable of Google as one of the errors in our work, If we not regard this as an error, the accuracy of our work can be better than 71%.

The recognition of speech emotion using Support Vector Machine is proposed in [3], where the classifier of Support Vector Machine is used to classify different kinds of emotional states such as sadness, anger, neutral, happiness, fear, from the Berlin emotional database. In this paper, it is surprising that it gives 93.75% classification accuracy for Gender independent case 100% for female speech and 94.7% for male. This high accuracy of the emotion recognition is compared with the work which is introduced in [7]. On the other hand, these research are exploring the emotion recognition off-line, not as what we are doing to recognize emotion status online at run time, they use the features of the voice, we now only use the key words by using semantic similarity. But in the future, we will consider more voice features definitely like pitch, rhythm and so on. In our work, we can recognize four kinds of emotional status, the gender has no influence on the accuracy of our work. Meanwhile by using the semantic similarity, the accuracy of our work can be 71%. It is reasonable.

The work proposed in [2] introduced automatic emotion recognition from speech using temporal features and rhythm. They use two kinds of methods to classify the features of voice, namely Support Vector Machine and Artificial Neural Network (ANN), both of them can achieve high accuracy of emotion recognition, by comparing with [7] and [3]. This emotion recognition is also off-line compared with our work. We now just use the key words in the talk of the user by using semantic similarity, the accuracy of our work is around 71%, to further improve the accuracy of our work. Fist we will try our best to improve the accuracy of the semantic similarity in our work. Then we would also make full use of the features of voice to improve the accuracy of recognition even contents may mislead the recognition sometimes.

A similar work that have been done in the paper that is proposed in [6], in this work where unobtrusiveness is emphasized as ours, as we use key words by using semantic similarity to judge the emotional status. we just use the feature of the voice, not the same as them. They collect and analyze user-generated data from different types of sensors by using the smart phones inconspicuously. These data include typing speed, frequency of pressing a specific key, maximum text length and so on; the features of the current environmental conditions around the user: average brightness, discomfort index, location, time zone and weather condition. Then they only choose ten features, by using the bayesian network to classify the features. Finally the average accuracy of seven kinds of emotion recognition is 67.52%. Meanwhile the accuracy of recognition about happiness, surprise, anger, neutral is around 50%. Because we collect the data from the smart phones. Then it is convenient for user to use. In this paper, both the direct features and the indirect features that have influence on people are taken into consideration. The disadvantage of the experiment is the collected data are not enough which result in low accuracy of the recognition of sadness and fear, and the experiment can not represent most people. We combined the physiology signal instead of only using those data as in [6]. Although we only use the semantic similarity in the recognition. We have tested that the accuracy of our work is better.

It is proposed that use a normal WebCam to measure physiological signals [9], where color channels in facial image caught on a webcam is utilized.By using this approach, it can obtain respiratory rate, heart rate and heart variability. This work does not need the attention of the user. To some special situations, it also has good potentials. It makes use of heart rate, just the same as us, in our work, we combine the heart rate and the key words(use semantic similarity), now our work just need a smart phone and a computer, in the future, we will move our work all on the smart phone and improve the accuracy of the semantic similarity to further improve the recognition accuracy of our work. But it needs the additional webcam.So our work is more convenient than it.

6 Conclusions and Future Work

It is very important for some people to understand the emotion status of a person. Especially those people that need health care service in order to keep them in good conditions. It is a great challenge that to recognize emotion status at run time. The existing approaches mostly work in an off-line way to identify emotional status[3][7], in our approach, we combine the voice recognition(first record the talk of the user, then segment the content, finally extract the special components of the content that can represent the emotional status of the user) and heart rate monitoring to recognize emotional states at run time. The experiments show that our hybrid approach can get high accuracy of emotion recognition with the feature of reasonable power consumption.

Our work that introduced in this paper is very simple for people to use. We have tested our work, the test showed very promising results. As our work still has some shortcomings. So we will extend our work in the future in a number of directions. First the recognition of voice contents, we extract only emotional keywords, then make segmentation, finally choose special components of the content that obtain special emotional status. In the future , we will make full use of the features of the voice, such as energy, pitch, rhythm and so on. Then use SVM, Bayesian and ANN to further classify features of voice. As the contents of the user may have different meaning, or totally different meaning in different situations, we will try our best to make our work more practical and more reliable by using pervasive cloud infrastructure [14].

Acknowledgements. The research is supported by the National Natural Science Foundation of China (Grant No. 61309024). Weishan Zhang has been supported by "the Fundamental Research Funds for the Central Universities" and also the start up funds for "Academic Top-Notch Professors in China University of Petroleum".

References

1. Abowd, G.D., Ebling, M., Hung, G., Lei, H., Gellersen, H.-W.: Context-aware computing. IEEE Pervasive Computing 1(3), 22–23 (2002)
2. Bhargava, M., Polzehl, T.: Improving automatic emotion recognition from speech using rhythm and temporal feature. In: Proceedings of ICECIT-2012, 139–147 (2012)

3. Chavhan, Y., Dhore, M.L., Yesaware, P.: Speech emotion recognition using support vector machine. International Journal of Computer Applications 1(20), 6–9 (2010)
4. Clore, G.L., Ortony, A., Foss, M.A.: The psychological foundations of the affective lexicon. Journal of Personality and Social Psychology 53(4), 751 (1987)
5. Epp, C., Lippold, M., Mandryk, R.L.: Identifying emotional states using keystroke dynamics. In: Proceedings of the 2011 Annual Conference on Human factors in Computing Systems, pp. 715–724. ACM (2011)
6. Lee, H., Choi, Y.S., Lee, S., Park, I.P.: Towards unobtrusive emotion recognition for affective social communication. In: 2012 IEEE Consumer Communications and Networking Conference (CCNC), pp. 260–264. IEEE (2012)
7. Pan, Y., Shen, P., Shen, L.: Speech emotion recognition using support vector machine. International Journal of Smart Home 6(2), 101–107 (2012)
8. Peter, C., Ebert, E., Beikirch, H.: A wearable multi-sensor system for mobile acquisition of emotion-related physiological data. In: Tao, J., Tan, T., Picard, R.W. (eds.) ACII 2005. LNCS, vol. 3784, pp. 691–698. Springer, Heidelberg (2005)
9. Poh, M.-Z., McDuff, D.J., Picard, R.W.: Advancements in noncontact, multiparameter physiological measurements using a webcam. IEEE Transactions on Biomedical Engineering 58(1), 7–11 (2011)
10. Tian, J., Zhao, W.: Words similarity based on tongyici cilin. Journal of Jilin University 006, 602–608 (2010)
11. Tian, X.I.A.: Study on chinese words semantic similarity computation. Computer Engineering 33(6), 191–194 (2007)
12. Wu, Y., Kita, K., Ren, F., Matsumoto, K., Kang, X.: Exploring emotional words for chinese document chief emotion analysis. In: Proc. of 25th PACLIC, pp. 597–606 (2011)
13. Wu, Y., Kita, K., Ren, F., Matsumoto, K., Kang, X.: Exploring the importance of modification relation for emotional keywords annotation and emotion types recognition. International Journal of Intelligent Engineering and Systems 4(4), 19–26 (2011)
14. Zhang, W., Chen, L., Lu, Q., Rao, Y., Zhou, J.: Towards an osgi based pervasive cloud infrastructure. In: 2013 IEEE International Conference on Internet of Things (iThings2013), pp. 418–425. IEEE (2013)
15. Zhang, W., Hansen, K.M.: Using context awareness for self management in pervasive service middleware. In: Mastrogiovanni, F., Chong, N.-Y. (eds.) Handbook of Research on Ambient Intelligence and Smart Environments: Trends and Perspectives, pp. 248–271. IGI Global (2011)
16. Zhang, W., Hansen, K.M., Bellavista, P.: A research roadmap for context-awareness-based self-managed systems. In: Ghose, A., Zhu, H., Yu, Q., Delis, A., Sheng, Q.Z., Perrin, O., Wang, J., Wang, Y. (eds.) ICSOC 2012. LNCS, vol. 7759, pp. 275–283. Springer, Heidelberg (2013)
17. Zhang, W., Hansen, K.M., Kunz, T.: Enhancing intelligence and dependability of a product line enabled pervasive middleware. Pervasive and Mobile Computing 66(2), 198–217 (2010)
18. Zhang, W., Meng, X., Lu, Q., Rao, Y., Zhou, J.: A hybrid emotion recognition on android smart phones. In: 2013 IEEE International Conference on Cyber, Physical and Social Computing (CPSCom 2013), pp. 1313–1318. IEEE (2013)

ICSOC PhD Symposium 2013

The 9th edition of the ICSOC PhD Symposium was held on December 2, 2013, in Berlin, as a satellite event of the 11th International Conference on Service Oriented Computing (ICSOC 2013). The aim of the PhD Symposium series is to bring together Ph.D. students and established researchers in the field of service oriented computing, to give students the opportunity to present their research, share ideas and experiences, and stimulate a constructive discussion involving experienced researchers. The Symposium is intended for active students whose research is still undergoing, where a problem has been clearly identified but whose solution is not fully developed or needs still major improvements.

The eight contributions accepted for publication cover many aspects of SOC, including Data Management, Big Data, Service Oriented Architectures, Service Level Agreement, and Workflows.

In addition to the standard review process, the accepted papers underwent an additional review round carried out by the students participating in the Symposium. This increased the participation of the audience and facilitated the exchange of ideas and suggestions among students, which resulted in interesting and fruitful discussions about the works presented at the Symposium.

These proceedings include the papers accepted for publication, revised by the authors based on the feedback received during the event.

February 2014

Fabio Patrizi
Boualem Benatallah
Ivona Brandic

A.R. Lomuscio et al. (Eds.): ICSOC 2013 Workshops, LNCS 8377, p. 527, 2014.
© Springer International Publishing Switzerland 2014

Towards the Automated Synthesis of Data Dependent Service Controllers

Franziska Bathelt-Tok and Sabine Glesner

Technische Universität Berlin, Germany
Software Engineering for Embedded Systems
bathelt-tok@soamed.de

Abstract. The treatment of data is a crucial step in service composition but it is currently done manually and informally. This makes the development process time-consuming, expensive, and error-prone, which is serious in safety-critical domains like the medical area. To overcome this problem, we present a novel approach for synthesizing data-dependent service controllers automatically based on composition and analysis methods for algebraic Petri nets. Consequently, our approach allows the automated, fast, and cost-efficient synthesis of correct controllers regarding data-dependent functional and safety-critical properties, which enables a reliable interoperability of medical devices.

1 Introduction

The idea of service-oriented architectures (SOAs) is to develop services with sophisticated functionality by composing simpler services appropriately. Services that are independently developed by different providers often cannot communicate with each other directly and cannot be adapted internally. Thus, it is necessary to develop another component, a controller, that routes and modifies messages depending on the exchanged data. It can be developed by a synthesis process that must ensure given data-dependent properties and, moreover, be correct with respect to safety-critical and functional requirements. Current approaches abstract from data and, consequently, model data-dependent choices as nondeterministic choices, which leads to invalid controllers. Thus, it is necessary to manually refine these controllers afterwards. This makes the controller development process expensive, time-consuming, and most of all error-prone.

To overcome this problem, we propose an approach to synthesize data-dependent controllers automatically based on algebraic Petri nets and a specification language that enables the presentation of causal dependencies of properties, which have to be fulfilled. It is ongoing work to show that the resulting controller is correct-by-construction and considers given data-dependent requirements. For our approach, we assume that, firstly, a formal representation as algebraic Petri nets of each service behavior is given. Secondly, we assume that the interface matching, which describes the mapping between the interfaces, is given. Thirdly, the set of data-dependent requirements to be fulfilled must be listed. Challenges of our work are the formal definition of the symbolic data treatment and the

A.R. Lomuscio et al. (Eds.): ICSOC 2013 Workshops, LNCS 8377, pp. 528–534, 2014.
© Springer International Publishing Switzerland 2014

generic data-dependency detection. To realize this and automatize the controller synthesis, we firstly translate the inputs into algebraic Petri nets as a uniform representation. This enables an easy understanding of the single component's behavior and of the causal dependencies between the single properties. Based on this, we compose the individual Petri nets to an over-all Petri net using the analysis methods Petri nets offer. As result, we achieve a single Petri net that fulfills all requested requirements, if it exists. Finally, we extract the required controller from this net. We have already implemented the translation step, and we are currently working on the implementation of the composition and the extraction step. The resulting controller

1. is synthesized automatically using the inputs,
2. handles different data types and considers data-dependent behavior,
3. ensures that all data-dependent properties are fulfilled,
4. is able to deal with synchronous and asynchronous communication, and
5. should be correct by construction w.r.t. safety-critical and functional requirements.

If we are able to verify the correctness, then we can apply our approach to safety-critical domains like the medical area, where different devices have to communicate with each other. As the single devices offer different functionalities that must be composed, we can shift the problem of enabling the interoperability of the medical devices to the more general problem of service composition.

The rest of this paper is organized as follows. Based on a running example we sketch the main formalisms on which our approach is based in Section 2. In Section 3 we present our approach. We then discuss related work in Section 4. Finally, in Section 5, we conclude and give an outline of future work.

2 Background

In this section, based on a running example we give an intuition of algebraic Petri nets [Rei91] and a specification language, which we use in our approach.

2.1 Running Example

As running example, we focus on a medical scenario known as artificial pancreas. The artificial pancreas comprises two components to be composed reliably, a glucose sensor and an insulin pump that should react on the sensor but isn't able to do so at the moment. Figure 1 shows an excerpt of the behavior of the sensor (Fig. 1a) and the pump (Fig. 1b). The chemical component of the sensor reacts with the blood glucose and offers a current flow that is measured (x), transformed in a digital signal ($f(x)$), and then stored internally (at p_5) and sent to the environment (y). The insulin pump compares the required amount of insulin recieved by the environment (y') with the amount of insulin that is still available in the pump (y). If not enough insulin is available a warn signal is sent to the environment, otherwise the requested amount is injected via a catheter.

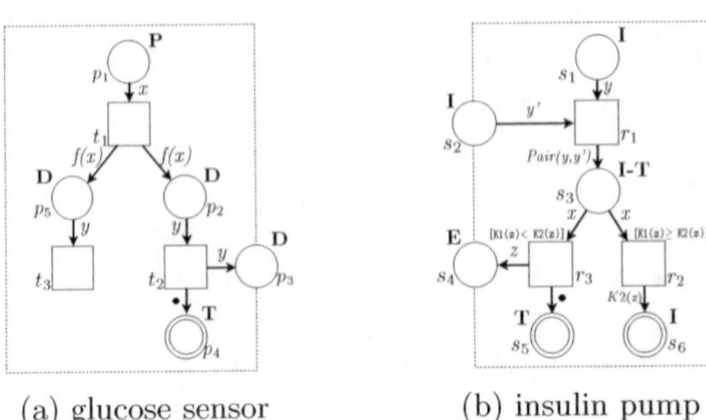

(a) glucose sensor (b) insulin pump

Fig. 1. Running example

2.2 Algebraic Petri Nets

The behavior of the components in Figure 1 is visualized by algebraic Petri nets. In this section, we give an intuition of their main elements using the representation of the insulin pump's behavior (see Figure 1b). Generally, *Petri nets* consist of places ($P = \{s_1, \ldots, s_6\}$), transitions ($T = \{r_1, r_2, r_3\}$) and a flow relation ($F = \{(s_1, r_1), (s_2, r_1), \ldots\}$). Transitions can be restricted by guards ($G = \{[K1(x) < K2(x)], \ldots\}$) that define in which case a transition is active and can fire. If the nets are inscribed by algebraic specifications, then they are called algebraic Petri nets. An *algebraic specification* is a 4-tuple $SP = (S, OP, X, EQ)$ comprising a set of: sorts S, operations OP, variables X and equations EQ. In our case, sorts ($S = \{I, I - T, T, E\}$) assigned to places represent the data types of the signals abstractly. The used variables ($X = \{y, y', x, z\}$) symbolically represent data values and operations ($OP = \{Pair : I \times I \rightarrow I - T, \cdot :\rightarrow T \ldots\}$) represent the modification of data. These elements are assigned to arcs. Apart from this, the set of equations ($EQ = \{Pair(y, y') = x, \ldots\}$) defines the relationship between the arc inscriptions and, thus, restricts the possible domains of the data types. Finally, places are marked with structured tokens, which are tokens with properties defined by the structure of the sorts. Thus, we can consider primitives as well as complex data types.

2.3 Specification Language

The interface matching and the requirements describe different states of markings and causalities. Thus, we need a specification language that is able to cope with state and run properties. For our approach, we use so called run properties [Rei13]. We just give an intuition based on the property '$(p_1.X_P) \mapsto (p_4.X_T \wedge p_3.X_D)$' of our example (Figure 1a). This property states that the interface and the final state is reached from the initial marking, i.e. the glucose sensor is deadlock-free. Here, three elements are represented. Firstly, the *state property* $(p_1.X_P)$ says that the place p_1 is marked with the data X_P. State properties can be combined using *propositional operators* $(\neg, \wedge, \vee, \rightarrow)$. This is the case in the second part $(p_4.X_T \wedge p_3.X_D)$. This states that there is a marking where X_T lies on p_4 and, at the same time X_D lies on p_3. Finally, we have the *leads-to operator* $\mapsto$ as temporal component. Thus, the whole expression states that *whenever* p_4 *is marked by* X_P *there exists a marking at the same time or in the future where* p_4 *is marked with* X_T *and* p_3 *with* X_D.

3 Synthesis of Data Dependent Service Controllers

Since the sensor must be replaced every 4-7 days, an automatic controller synthesis is necessary to enable a reliable and cost-efficient interoperability of these devices and, thus, enhance the quality of life of people with type-1-diabetes.

As shown in Figure 2, our approach starts from the formal representation of the involved services given as algebraic Petri nets. We begin by extracting the relevant service behavior using the initial representation. This *behavioral abstraction* (Sec. 3.1) leads to a set of properties, expressed by the specification language, which have to be fulfilled at least. The main challenge is to ensure that all important properties are extracted and all information and dependencies are retained. Thus, a formal model for storing data and data-dependencies is needed. Our aim is to combine the resulting behavioral abstraction, the interface matching and the requirements the controller must fulfill. For this reason, we transform the properties into algebraic Petri nets (Sec. 3.2) using our generic and data-related transformation algorithm. Finally, we apply the well-defined composition and analysis methods of Petri nets for our composition algorithm (Sec. 3.3). As a result, we obtain the requested controller if one exists.

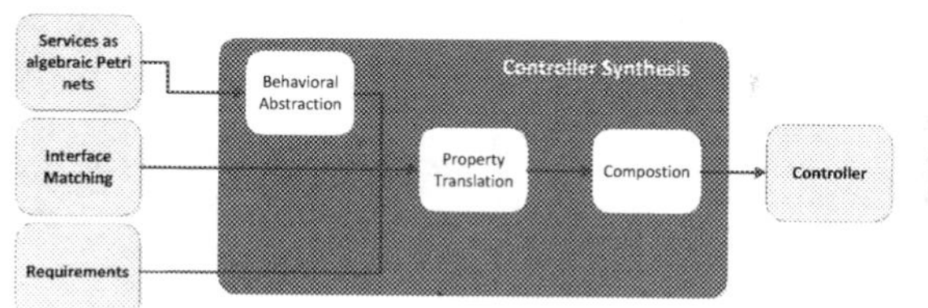

Fig. 2. Basic Idea of the Controller Synthesis Approach

3.1 Behavioral Abstraction

The formal representations of the services include their entire behavior and, thus, unused behavior as well, from which we abstract in this part. For our running example (Figure 1a) the internal storage of the measured glucose concentration, i.e., marking of p_5, is not important for the communication with the pump. To minimize the effort for the composition (Section 3.3), we just extract the properties that have to be fulfilled at least, especially the deadlock-freedom of the services, and define the set of equations w.r.t. the modifications of data. For this we use analysis methods for Petri nets, based e.g. on reachability graphs. This leads to a set of properties given in the specification language.

3.2 Property Translation

To get a uniform representation, we transform the properties into algebraic Petri nets. These properties are given by the result of the behavioral abstraction (e.g. deadlock-freedom), the interface matching (e.g. port p_3 is bound to s_2 (Fig. 1)) and the data dependent requirements (e.g. pump must inject if glucose value exceeds the limit G_{max}), and expressed in the specification language. For the translation, we already implemented a generic, data-related algorithm. Some of our defined rules describing the structural translation can be seen in Figure 3. These rules can be combined to form more complex rules. We have omitted guards restricting data domains and the inscription of arcs for reasons of clarity.

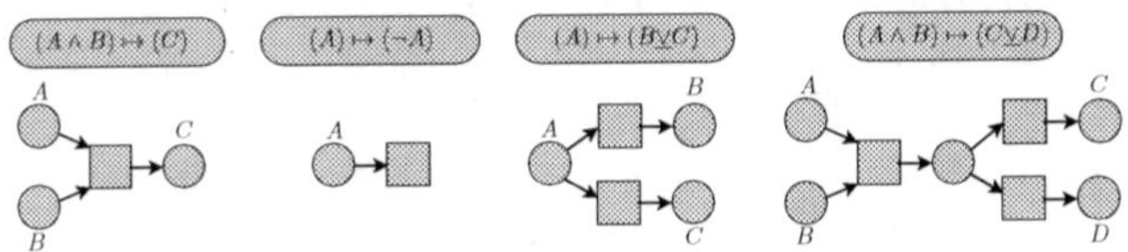

Fig. 3. Transformation rules

3.3 Composition

The basic idea of the composition algorithm (see Figure 4) is to compose the properties that are given as different algebraic Petri nets to an overall Petri net. Then, the controller can easily be extracted from this.

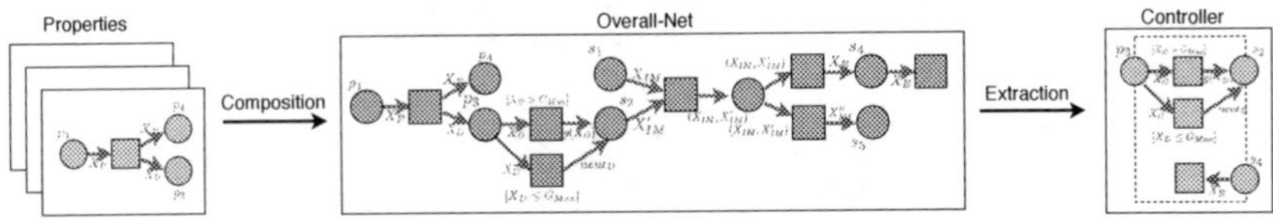

Fig. 4. Basic Idea of the Composition

In a first step, the algorithm chooses the smallest property (with the fewest places) out of the set of properties Pr and composes it with the empty set N. In each iteration, the smallest property $pr_{min} \in Pr$ that has at least one label (identifier of the place) that is present in N is chosen and composed to the net N. If there is exactly one label, the composition can be sequential or branching. Otherwise, if there is more than one match, we have to use the reachability analysis of Petri nets to decide if a composition is possible or not. Concerning this, we have to check if the reachability graph of the property pr_{min} is included in the reachability graph of N. The algorithm terminates if all properties are composed or if a property is found which cannot be composed. In the latter case, there exists no controller fulfilling all properties. In the first case, we can extract the controller from N by combining all elements between the interface places.

It is ongoing work to show that we get a reliable controller that fulfills all given properties, if it exists. The synthesis is done in three steps. Firstly, we derive necessary service properties using behavioral abstraction. The translation to Petri nets, which is already implemented, provides the basis for the composition. Within the composition, we are able to use the analyzing and composition methods Petri nets offer to decide if a property can be composed or not.

4 Related Work

There are several approaches dealing with service or component adaptation.

A controller synthesis process based on finite-state machines focusing on the protocol level is given in [YS97]. They do not consider data-dependent behavior and omit asynchronous communication. In [Bra05] a controller synthesis including the behavior-level that is based on the π calculus is presented, while the proposed approaches in [Aal09] and [Gie12] are based on Petri nets. However, the authors abstract from data and data-dependent behavior. Another approach [SG13] is based on model-checking and planning. It enables the time-related composition of services. They are able to represent clock values from type real, but this is not the kind of data we focus on. To the best of our knowledge, there is no approach that fulfills our requirements. In particular, the formal definition of data and data-dependencies are missing, so that an automated *data dependent* controller synthesis process is not available by now.

5 Conclusion and Future Work

In this work, we have addressed the problem of automatized controller synthesis based on data-dependent requirements. Our approach takes the formal representation as algebraic Petri nets of the involved services, the interface matching, and data-dependent requirements as inputs. The behavior of the services is reduced to the observable behavior, which is transformed to the specification language that we have introduced. Moreover, we have defined a translation from the specification language into Petri nets and have presented an algorithm for composing the abstracted behavior, the interface matching, and the requirements. We have already implemented the translation step and we are confident that with our approach, reliable service controllers can be extracted fully automatically, if they exist. Correctness-by-construction, which we still have to prove, makes our approach applicable in the medical domain.

In future work, we will formalize and implement our composition algorithm, the behavioral abstraction, and the controller extraction. Additionally, we will perform a case study, which is an extension of our running example.

References

[Aal09] van der Aalst, W.M.P., Mooij, A.J., Stahl, C., Wolf, K.: Service Interaction: Patterns, Formalization, and Analysis. In: Bernardo, M., Padovani, L., Zavattaro, G. (eds.) SFM 2009. LNCS, vol. 5569, pp. 42–88. Springer, Heidelberg (2009)

[Bra05] Bracciali, A., et al.: A formal approach to component adaptation. Journal of Systems and Software 74, 45–54 (2005) ISSN 0164–1212

[Gie12] Gierds, C., et al.: Reducing Adapter Synthesis to Controller Synthesis. IEEE T. Services Computing 5(1), 72–85 (2012)

[Rei91] Reisig, W.: Petri nets and algebraic specifications. Theoretical Computer Science 80, 1–34 (1991)

[Rei13] Reisig, W.: Understanding Petri Nets: Modeling Techniques, Analysis Methods, Case Studies, 230 p. Springer (2013) ISBN 978-3-642-33277-7

[SG13] Stöhr, D., Glesner, S.: Planning in Real-Time Domains with Timed CTL Goals via Symbolic Model Checking. In: IEEE TASE 2013 (2013)

[YS97] Yellin, D., Strom, R.: Protocol specifications and component adaptors. In: ACM Trans. Program. Lang. Syst. 19(2), 292–333 (1997)

Multi-agent Approach for Managing Workflows in an Inter-Cloud Environment

Sofiane Bendoukha*

Theoretical Foundations of Computer Science (TGI)
Department of Informatics, University of Hamburg, Germany
sbendoukha@informatik.uni-hamburg.de

Abstract. Despite the several attractive features that offers the cloud technology, managing, controlling processes and resources are among the serious obstacles that cloud service providers need to overcome. These issues increase when cloud providers intend to exploit services from several distributed platforms to satisfy client's requests and requirements. At this moment, they need to deal with some critical problems like heterogeneity, collaboration, coordination and communication between different types of participants.

In another side, the most known properties of an agent are: autonomy, pro-activity, cooperation and mobility. These features are attractive and have a great importance to design and implement software systems that operate in distributed and open environments such like cloud and grid. Our main goal through this thesis is to propose an approach and architectures to permit the integration of cloud/grid and multi-agent systems concepts and technologies for managing workflows in distributed service-oriented environments. Explicitly, in an Inter-Cloud environment.

Keywords: Cloud Computing, Workflow Management Systems, Workflow Petri Nets, Reference Nets, Multi-Agent Systems.

1 Research Issues and Objectives

Service-Oriented Computing (SOC) is the field of computer science that revolves around the concept of "service": Web services, grid services and recently cloud services. It allows the composition of loosely coupled services with different Quality of Service (QoS) constraints to achieve complex distributed applications even in heterogeneous environments [18]. Based on the Internet, cloud computing provides on-demand computing capacity to individuals and businesses in the form of heterogeneous and autonomous services.

Furthermore, we observed the emergence of the Inter-Cloud notion [8,1,20,16], which could be seen as a cloud of clouds [13]. The reason lies in the fact that one cloud infrastructure does not have unlimited resources to satisfy client's requirements and the latter may receive requested services from different cloud providers [8]. At this moment we need to deal with the problem of heterogeneity,

* Supervised by Dr. Daniel Moldt and Prof. Dr. Norbert Ritter.

A.R. Lomuscio et al. (Eds.): ICSOC 2013 Workshops, LNCS 8377, pp. 535–542, 2014.
© Springer International Publishing Switzerland 2014

communication, coordination and collaboration between all participants. Hence, the construction of complex systems remains a problem as soon as there are several independent / autonomous partners involved in the design and execution of these systems. Currently mainly data is stored in the cloud. (Web) services in the cloud are designed to be realized in a static fashion. What is missing is the support of processes in this environment. For complex systems with distributed partners, expressive and powerful software systems have to be provided.

MAS (Multi-Agent Systems) and workflow concepts are strong candidates to address this issue [23,17,7]. On the one hand, commonly accepted characteristics of agents are social ability, autonomy, pro-activity, adaptability, mobility and can be used as basic components for bringing intelligence in cloud systems to make them more adaptive, flexible in both resource management, service discovery/provisioning and in running complex applications. Also in this perspective, mobile agents are used to construct a cloud computing federation mechanism to permit portability and interoperability between different cloud platforms [3,24]. On the other hand, automation of processes and efficient coordination and collaboration between various entities are some advantages of workflow concepts.

However, WfMS (Workflow Management Systems) usually do not address the special aspects of cloud-based systems. Current inter-organizational WfMS are designed to control the autonomous entities (agents or web services) from another location. So it is not embedded within the systems. This causes problems with respect either to the autonomy of the participating partners or their efficient coordination. New concepts and constructs to overcome this problem are necessary.

In order to overcome the problems above cited, this thesis provides a conceptual and technical solution for the modeling and the design of complex systems in cloud-like environments with a special emphasis on processes. I aim to provide an agent-based WfMS, which supports definition, deployment and monitoring of distributed inter-organizational workflows for independent complex partners within cloud environments. The global objective is to investigate and propose approaches, techniques and tools that facilitate the integration between cloud environments and MAS for an efficient management and execution of workflows in environments qualified to be distributed and scalable. That means concretely, I strive to take advantage of concepts and technologies from agents and workflow domain in order to provide a powerful environment for the deployment of user's applications, which are based on multiple cloud platforms.

2 Approach and Methodology

For this research, I intend to exploit some techniques, models and tools, which are part of the PAOSE (PETRI NET-BASED, AGENT-ORIENTED SOFTWARE ENGINEERING) approach (see `www.paose.net`). On the basis of high-level Petri nets the above mentioned concepts like agents, workflows or services are integrated. The MULAN/CAPA (Multi-Agent Nets, see [21]; Concurrent Agent Platform Architecture, see [10]) framework and the RENEW (**RE**ference **NE**ts **W**orkshop) (see `www.renew.de`) modeling tool provide the technical background for this.

The description and implementation of this research will be carried out in several steps/phases, which are iteratively applied to have several prototypes. As the first step, a state of the art is continuously elaborated, which evaluates the existing theoretical basis of my work and technological solutions. The basic research areas are: Service-oriented computing, (Inter-) cloud/grid computing, workflow management systems, modeling techniques and tools, agent systems, Petri nets etc. The next step is to define the new requirements for modeling workflow execution in complex environments. I focus on the current issues in Inter-Cloud environments such as heterogeneity, communication, coordination and collaboration between the participants.

Taking into account the new defined requirements, I propose appropriate modeling techniques and concepts that should constitute a conceptual basis for the management of Inter-Cloud applications. UML (Unified Modeling Language) and Petri nets are the major modeling approaches that will be investigated to elaborate such techniques. This step also includes provisioning semantics based constructs that allow for an efficient design of process management of Inter-Cloud applications.

In order to evaluate and validate my results, I propose a direct modeling tool support, which will be implemented on the basis of RENEW for the elaborated techniques. The first version is based just on RENEW in terms of a drawing and simulation tool for Petri nets and UML models (see [6]). In this version, many refinements and extensions are proposed, in order to allow the future agent-based WfMS to manage interactions with the cloud. One of the main refinements is the introduction of a specialized *Cloud Task Transition* (CTT) (see Fig. 1).

Workflow modelers specify their requirements as parameters to the CTT in form of tuples (S, Q, I), which correspond respectively to the cloud service (S) to be used (it can be a storage or a compute service), the QoS constraints (Q) consisting of deadlines or costs and input data (I) consisting either of required files in case of a storage or scripts if modelers want to execute their codes on the cloud. Synchronous channels are used to make the connection with the WfMS, which controls the completion of the task. It either initiates the firing or cancels it and all input parameters are put back onto the input places.

The second version is based on MULAN and CAPA, which allow the simulation and the execution of agent-based systems. Due to the FIPA compliance also distributed execution is possible. An extension for workflows is provided by [12] for Petri nets and by [19] for workflow and WfMS. The third version is based on WfMS implemented on Grid/Cloud either using the Globus Toolkit[1] or existing cloud-based frameworks with a perspective to a future Inter-Cloud environments.

As a prove of concept for the conceptual solution proposed in the dissertation, a prototype distributed over above mentioned prototypes will allow for the investigation of heterogeneous implementation of the approach for the management of workflow in an Inter-Cloud environment. The solution is named Inter-Cloud Agent-based WfMS (IC-AgWfMS). The architecture that we propose is depicted in Fig. 2. It includes three basic layers from top to bottom:

[1] `http://www.globus.org/toolkit/`

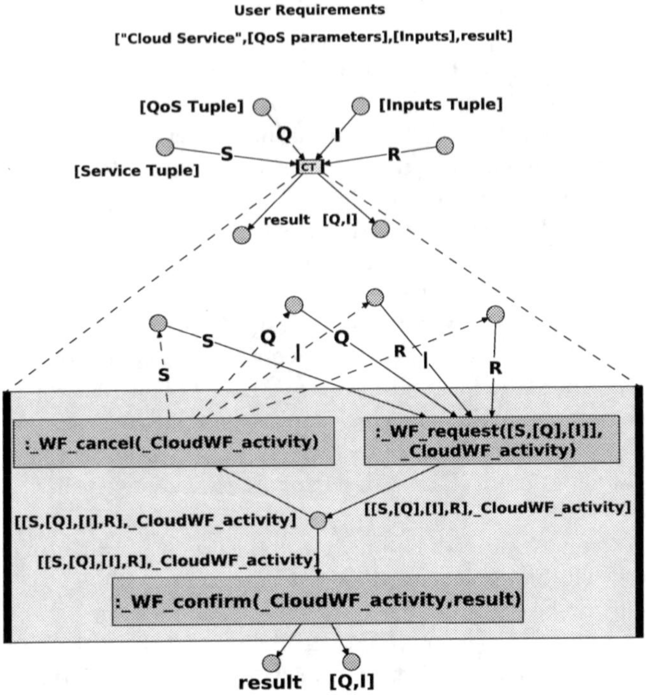

Fig. 1. The Cloud Task Transition

- *The User applications layer* (Ul): permits both managing users (access to the system) and monitoring deployed workflows,
- *The Middleware layer* (Ml): composed mainly of the workflow engine as well as the task dispatcher module (see step 4).
- *The Resource layer (Cloud infrastructure)* (Rl): This layer represents the resources used to excute the workflow tasks. They can be either compute or storage services. This depends on the workflow requirements.

As shown in Fig. 2, managing workflows can be broken down into a series of steps (indicated by numbered circles) and carried out by several components. More details about these steps can be found in [5].

3 Related Work

Much interesting work has been devoted to investigate the possible integration of agent paradigm, workflow concepts and cloud computing. For example, Pandey et al. [17] present a high-level architecture of a workflow management system for developing distributed applications on the cloud. Key components of the presented architecture are: A *Market-Maker broker* and a *workflow engine* to

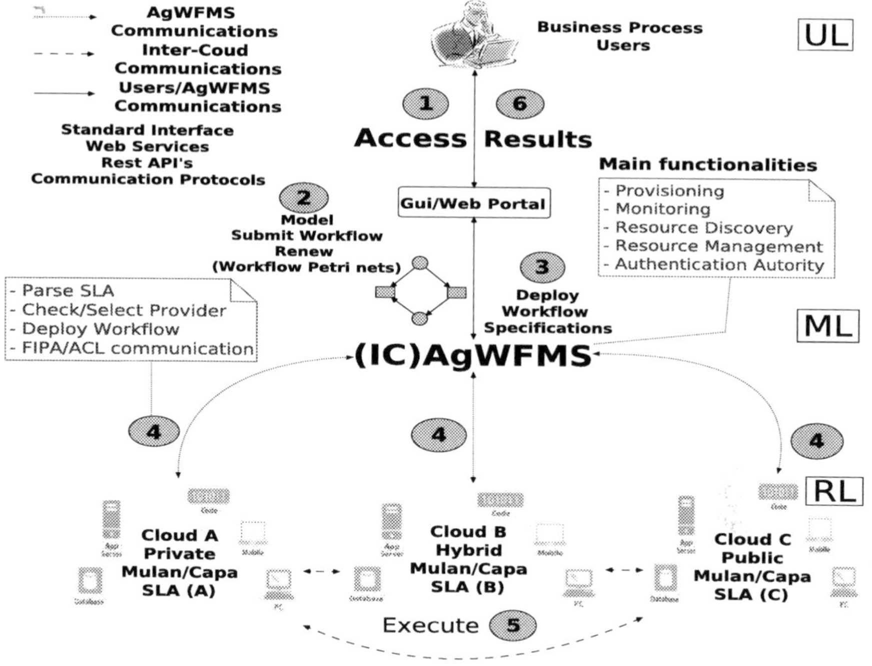

Fig. 2. Inter-Cloud Agent-based WfMS

schedule workflow tasks to the resources based on the QoS constraints. Liu et al. [15] outline three key issues in the design of cloud workflow systems: *system architecture* that decides how the system components are organized and how they interface with each other, *system functionality* that realizes the basic workflow system's functionality and manages the cloud resources, and finally *QoS* management. In [14], *SwinDeW-C*: a peer-to-peer workflow management system for cloud is proposed.

Concerning the Inter-Cloud, Buyya et al. [8] present the notion of federated cloud (Inter-Cloud) that facilitates scalable provisioning of services under variable conditions. In [11], the authors provide a classification of Inter-Cloud delivery models, which are *federated cloud* and *multi-cloud*. The EU-funded RESERVOIR[2] project [20] is the first initiative intending to provide open source technology to enable deployment and management of complex services across different administrative domains. The EU-funded mOSAIC[3] project [16] proposes a complementary solution based on software agents and semantic data processing. The mOSAIC approach is based on a *Cloud Agency* gathering client and provider agents in a brokerage process working with service level agreements. It is used as a Multi-Cloud resource management middle-ware, it plays

[2] `http://www.reservoir-fp7.eu/`

[3] `http://www.mosaic-fp7.eu/`

the role of run-time environment in the model-driven engineering project named MODAClouds [2].

In [24], the Mobile Agent Based Open Cloud Computing Federation (MAB-OCCF) is presented, where data and code are transferred from one device to another via mobile agents. Each mobile agent is executed in a virtual machine called Mobile Agent Place (MAP), and the mobile agents are able to move between MAPs, and also to communicate and negotiate with each other, realizing portability among heterogeneous cloud computing service providers. In [22], the concept of agent-based cloud computing is introduced. This concept is introduced to aid the development of software tools for service operations in the cloud using agent-based cooperative techniques. WADE (Workflow and Agent Development Environment) [9] is a domain independent platform built on top of JADE[4], it allows to develop distributed and decentralized applications based on the agent paradigm and the workflow metaphor.

4 Conclusion and Future Work

The first phase of the thesis is related to establish a study about the related work and the concepts, techniques and tools that are utilized to achieve the objectives. When some parts are well studied such as workflows and Petri nets, other domains still in their infancy and there is a lack of literature and standardizations. Therefore, they need more investigation such as the Inter-Cloud computing notion and agent-based workflow management in the cloud. Concerning the state of the art, many domains related to this research are investigated. This includes: Service Oriented Computing, web services, (Inter-) cloud/grid computing, Workflows, agent and Multi-agent systems, PAOSE approach, MULAN/CAPA framework and RENEW, A study about various modeling and composition techniques such as Petri-Nets, BPEL (Business Process Execution Language), Service-Oriented Architecture, WSCI (Web Service Choreography Interface), BPML (Business Process Modeling Language), BPMN (Business Process Model and Notation), WSCL (Web Service Choreography Language), etc.

The implementation of the several prototypes is in progress, this concerns at the first level the ability to invoke cloud services from Petri net models. The solution is based on the use of RESTful web services and cloud APIs. Many refinements and extensions are proposed to achieve this objective [6], which will allow the future agent-based WfMS to manage interactions with the cloud. An approach named Inter-Cloud Workflow Petri Nets (IC-WPN) is proposed [4], for enabling workflows in an (Inter-) Cloud environment. My future work includes finishing the prototypes of the proposed approach along two directions. The first direction is to provide the support modeling tool in Renew. This allows users to specify their workflows and the related QoS constraints through Petri net models. Second, I will use the latter results to implement the proposed models (see [4] for the IC-WPN and [5] for IC-AgWfMS).

[4] http://jade.tilab.com/

References

1. Aoyama, T., Sakai, H.: Inter-cloud computing. Business & Information Systems Engineering 3(3), 173–177 (2011)
2. Ardagna, D., Nitto, E.D., Mohagheghi, P., Mosser, S., Ballagny, C., D'Andria, F., Casale, G., Matthews, P., Nechifor, C.-S., Petcu, D., Gericke, A., Sheridan, C.: Modaclouds: A model-driven approach for the design and execution of applications on multiple clouds. In: 2012 ICSE Workshop on Modeling in Software Engineering (MISE), pp. 50–56 (2012)
3. Aversa, R., Martino, B.D., Rak, M., Venticinque, S.: Cloud agency: A mobile agent based cloud system. In: Barolli, L., et al. (eds.) CISIS 2010, Krakow, Poland, February 15-18, pp. 132–137. IEEE Computer Society (2010)
4. Bendoukha, S., Cabac, L.: Cloud transition for qos modeling of inter-organizational workflows. In: Moldt, D. (ed.) Proceedings of Modeling and Business Environment. International Workshop, ModBE 2013, Milano, Italy. CEUR Workshop Proceedings, vol. 989, pp. 355–356. CEUR-WS.org (2013)
5. Bendoukha, S., Moldt, D., Wagner, T.: Enabling cooperation in an inter-cloud environment: An agent-based approach. In: 4th International Workshop on Cloud Computing, Models and Services (CMS 2013) (2013)
6. Bendoukha, S., Wagner, T.: Cloud transition: Integrating cloud calls into workflow Petri nets. In: Cabac, L., Duvigneau, M., Moldt, D. (eds.) Proceedings of International Workshop PNSE 2012, Hamburg, Germany. CEUR Workshop Proceedings, vol. 851, pp. 215–216 (June 2012)
7. Bergenti, F., Caire, G., Gotta, D.: Interactive workflows with wade. In: Reddy, S., Drira, K. (eds.) WETICE, pp. 10–15. IEEE Computer Society (2012)
8. Buyya, R., Ranjan, R., Calheiros, R.N.: InterCloud: Utility-oriented federation of cloud computing environments for scaling of application services. In: Hsu, C.-H., Yang, L.T., Park, J.H., Yeo, S.-S. (eds.) ICA3PP 2010, Part I. LNCS, vol. 6081, pp. 13–31. Springer, Heidelberg (2010)
9. Caire, G., Gotta, D., Banzi, M.: Wade: a software platform to develop mission critical applications exploiting agents and workflows. In: Proceedings of the 7th International Joint Conference on AAMS, pp. 29–36. International Foundation for Autonomous Agents and Multiagent Systems (2008)
10. Duvigneau, M., Moldt, D., Rölke, H.: Concurrent architecture for a multi-agent platform. In: Giunchiglia, F., Odell, J.J., Weiss, G. (eds.) AOSE 2002. LNCS, vol. 2585, pp. 59–72. Springer, Heidelberg (2003)
11. Grozev, N., Buyya, R.: Inter-cloud architectures and application brokering: taxonomy and survey. Software: Practice and Experience (2012)
12. Jacob, T., Kummer, O., Moldt, D., Ultes-Nitsche, U.: Implementation of workflow systems using reference nets – security and operability aspects. In: Jensen, K. (ed.) Fourth Workshop and Tutorial on Practical Use of Coloured Petri Nets and the CPN Tools, vol. 560, Aarhus, Danemark (August 2002)
13. K. Kelly.: A cloudbook for the cloud (2007), `http://www.kk.org/thetechnium/archives/2007/11/a_cloudbook_for`
14. Liu, X., Yuan, D., Zhang, G., Chen, J., Yang, Y.: Swindew-c: a peer-to-peer based cloud workflow system. Handbook of Cloud Computing, 309–332 (2010)
15. Liu, X., Yuan, D., Zhang, G., Li, W., Cao, D., He, Q., Chen, J., Yang, Y.: Workflow systems in the cloud. In: The Design of Cloud Workflow Systems. SpringerBriefs in Computer Science, pp. 1–11. Springer-Verlag New York Inc. (2012)

16. Di Martino, B., Petcu, D., Cossu, R., Goncalves, P., Máhr, T., Loichate, M.: Building a mosaic of clouds. In: Guarracino, M.R., et al. (eds.) Euro-Par-Workshop 2010. LNCS, vol. 6586, pp. 571–578. Springer, Heidelberg (2011)
17. Pandey, S., Karunamoorthy, D., Buyya, R.: Workflow Engine for Clouds, pp. 321–344. John Wiley & Sons, Inc. (2011)
18. Papazoglou, M.P., Traverso, P., Dustdar, S., Leymann, F., Krämer, B.J.: Service-oriented computing: A research roadmap. In: Cubera, F., Krämer, B.J., Papazoglou, M.P. (eds.) SOC, Dagstuhl, Germany. Dagstuhl Seminar Proceedings, vol. 05462. IBFI (2006)
19. Reese, C.: Prozess-Infrastruktur für Agentenanwendungen. Dissertation, Universität Hamburg, Fachbereich Informatik, Vogt-Kölln Str. 30, D-22527 Hamburg (2009), http://www.sub.uni-hamburg.de/opus/volltexte/2010/4497/
20. Rochwerger, B., et al.: The reservoir model and architecture for open federated cloud computing. IBM Journal of Research and Development 53(4), 4:1–4:11 (2009)
21. Rölke, H.: Modellierung von Agenten und Multiagentensystemen – Grundlagen und Anwendungen. Agent Technology – Theory and Applications, vol. 2. Logos Verlag, Berlin (2004)
22. Sim, K.M.: Agent-based cloud computing. IEEE Transactions on Services Computing 5(4), 564–577 (2012)
23. Talia, D.: Clouds meet agents: Toward intelligent cloud services. IEEE Internet Computing 16(2), 78–81 (2012)
24. Zhang, Z., Zhang, X.: Realization of open cloud computing federation based on mobile agent. In: Intelligent Computing and Intelligent Systems, vol. 3, pp. 642–646 (2009)

An Information-Centric System for Building the Web of Things

Stefano Turchi*

Department of Information Engineering, University of Florence, Italy
{stefano.turchi,federica.paganelli}@unifi.it
http://www.dinfo.unifi.it

Abstract. In recent years, common-use devices has seen a leap transition in terms of equipped technology, introducing the so called "smart things" to the consumer market. This technological and societal revolution has underpinned the realization of the Internet of Things. To take full advantage of the opportunities arising from connectivity capabilities, smart things approached the application realm bringing the novel Web of Things vision to life. The Web, as a collaborative global space of information, is a critical asset to create value-added services. However, such a promising potential entails a number of challenges including data interoperability, data integration, information reuse and collaboration. This Ph.D. work focuses on a novel approach to take a smart thing to the Web, by representing it as graph of granular and individually addressable information called IDN-Document. IDN-Documents are simply structured web resources which can be aggregated, linked, reused and combined to build collaboration oriented, value-added services. IDN-Documents are managed by the InterDataNet middleware leveraging Linked Data and REST.

Keywords: Internet of Things, Web of Things, Information Modeling, Representational State Transfer, Linked Data, Information Reuse.

1 Introduction

The advances in electronics, informatics and communication sciences have paved the way for the widespread distribution of devices with considerable technological potential. Due to their capabilities, these objects are usually called "smart". This scenario motivates the Internet of Things (IoT) concept which is a transformation of the Internet from a network of computers to a network of heterogeneous devices [1].

Leveraging the existing Web technologies and standards including HTTP [2], URIs [3], etc., smart things can also enter the application realm, giving rise to the Web of Things (WoT) vision. To take full advantage of the WoT opportunities is essential to address issues including interoperability, data integration,

* This Ph.D. work is supervised by Dr. Federica Paganelli

A.R. Lomuscio et al. (Eds.): ICSOC 2013 Workshops, LNCS 8377, pp. 543–550, 2014.
© Springer International Publishing Switzerland 2014

information reuse and collaboration. These topics are definitely challenging because of the heterogeneity of smart things in a number of aspects such as device and application requirements, connection strategies, data representation, data management and many others.

This Ph.D. work proposes an approach to enable interoperability and data reuse between objects in the WoT. To this intent, I follow a two-steps methodology: first, a connection with the smart object is established via a dedicated adapter, and second the object is represented as a graph of granular, individually addressable data units called IDN-Document, leveraging an information model. Consequently, the object is put on the Web as an aggregation of information whose pieces can be dereferenced, consumed, reused, and managed with negligible effort. The smart object representation relies on the expressiveness and flexibility of the graph structure adopted by Linked Data [4], which has been chosen as the inspiring paradigm. In this work I refer to a more general interpretation of Linked Data, as the one provided by Wilde et al. [5], who define Linked Data as "the general concept of publishing interlinked data representations, without referring to the one specific way of implementing it that is often associated with that term as well".

The implementation of the IDN-Document is delegated to a middleware called InterDataNet (IDN) [6–9] which exposes RESTful [10] HTTP APIs for its management. This Ph.D. work covered the study and design of the information model, the study, design and implementation of the whole IDN core architecture, and the study, design and implementation of several applications on top of IDN, for validation purposes.

2 Motivation of the Work

Although the WoT is very promising, many problems remain to be solved [1]. Data should be produced and consumed easily, without worrying about formats and custom representations. Moreover, security concerns must be addressed to support collaboration around data. To fully benefit from the WoT concept, the author argues that the Web of Data [11] vision would contribute to effectively put a "thing" on the Web. Indeed, not only data produced by a smart object, but also the object itself can be represented as a graph of structured information to be exposed in the global space, where applications can use it and other objects can connect to, building a richer and more informative object. Zeng et al. [1] made a survey on the WoT and their analysis highlights several points of interest, which validate the approach proposed in this paper. First, they make a comparison of the WS-* and REST architectural styles and conclude that REST is the best choice because of its low complexity and loose-coupling stateless interactions. These features are particularly desirable because they take into account resource constrained devices. Also Wilde in [12] states that REST has substantial advantages over applications, having better performances in terms of testing, scalability, and integration with other applications with respect to state-based paradigms. Second, search and discovery capabilities are critical for

WoT, spanning from regular search to advanced search managing very transient data. In this paper, is presented a methodology for bringing an object of the real world to the Web as a graph of interlinked information pieces. Such information should be made available taking into account all the aforementioned issues. To fulfill these requirements I propose the InterDataNet middleware which leverages an adapter towards physical objects and supports a Linked Data oriented resources representation. Therefore, resources are exposed via RESTful APIs for their management. InterDataNet is also provided with transversal services such as a data-centric [13] security framework and a search service supporting semantics.

3 InterDataNet

InterDataNet (IDN) [6–9] is a middleware offering capabilities for representing and managing information units and their structural relations on the Web, in a RESTful way. For the sake of conciseness, in this paragraph a brief introduction of the IDN middleware is provided. Further details can be found in [6–9].

The main goal of IDN is to enable the easy reuse of globally web-addressable information units to support collaboration around data. To this end, IDN considers documents as first class entities. In the following, I refer to a document in IDN as an IDN-Document.

3.1 IDN Information Model (IDN-IM)

The IDN-Information Model (IDN-IM) defines the rules for organizing data in an IDN-Document.

Definition 1. An IDN-Document is a directed graph $G = (V, E)$ where V is the set of vertices and E is the set of edges. The elements of V and E are the nodes containing the granular information (IDN-Nodes) and the relations between IDN-Nodes, respectively. IDN supports two types of relations between IDN-Nodes: aggregation (i.e., containment) and reference.

Definition 2. An IDN-Node is a set $S = C, P$, where C is the set of content elements (i.e., data) and P is the set of properties (i.e., metadata) that characterize C.

Definition 3. The Aggregation Link represents a container-content relation. The node where the edge starts from aggregates and therefore contains the node the edge points to.

Definition 4. The Reference Link represents a pointer towards the referred resource. To better understand the Reference Link role, it could be somehow compared with the HTML `href` attribute.

Through the IDN-Information Model (Fig. 1) is possible to define an IDN-Document as an aggregation of data provided by different information sources. Indeed, an IDN-Node can be referred to by more than one IDN-Document, thus favoring the reuse of information across different applications. This is possible since each IDN-Node is associated with an information provider which is authoritative for the information the IDN-Node refers to. It is worth to mention that many efforts have been made to keep the IDN-IM as simple as possible, to lower the entry barriers for WoT developers. It is possible to see the IDN-IM as a projection of a RDF graph in an extremely reduced dimensional space (containment and reference dimensions). The definition of the container-content relation (Aggregation Link) serves well for the scopes of document composition, still not burdening the formalism. Consequently, data can be managed without requiring a query language such as SPARQL for RDF. Of course, when such simplification is not sufficient, it is possible to lift an IDN-Document to the RDF representation. That's why IDN-Documents support semantic annotations.

In addition, IDN-IM can be extended with metadata enforcing privacy, licensing, security, provenance, consistency, versioning and availability properties attached to IDN-Nodes and affecting IDN-Documents. Such features are crucial to support effective and trusted collaboration on real world scenarios.

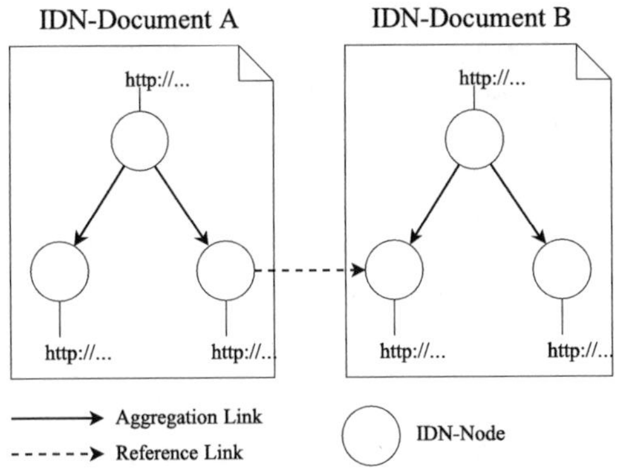

Fig. 1. The InterDataNet Information Model

3.2 IDN Service Architecture (IDN-SA)

IDN-Documents are exposed as resources through the IDN-Service Architecture (IDN-SA) API. The IDN-SA API is a set of generic REST interfaces for addressing, resolving and handling IDN-Documents. IDN-SA is the architecture that implements services needed to enforce the IDN-Documents properties and capabilities. IDN-SA has been designed with the separation of concern principle in mind and is organized according to a modular architectural pattern. IDN-SA has three main modules: Virtual Resource (VR), which provides RESTful APIs for accessing, creating, and modifying IDN-Documents; Information History (IH), which implements information versioning capabilities; Storage Interface (SI), which offers persistence capabilities. In addition, a set of horizontal services, including search and security management are defined.

A key role is played by the IDN-Adapter (ADPT), which is implemented as an independent module, detached from the core architecture. Its main task is to connect to external data sources and prepare the information with custom format to be used by the IDN-SA. As a consequence of the IDN-Adapter mediation, the IDN-SA can treat outer data as its own, and enable all the properties characterizing IDN-Documents, acting as a decorator. The IDN-Adapter is also designed with a modular approach, and includes three components: 1) a Transformer module that refines data served by the outer source (e.g., demultiplexing the information to achieve a more granular representation); 2) a Document Manager that assembles the outer information in a specific structure (associating it with a specific IDN-Document); 3) a Command Manager that translates commands coming from the IDN-SA interface in commands appropriate for the original data-source interface (e.g., a PUT request to IDN-SA could map to a POST request to the data-source).

From a system point of view, IDN is organized as a network of peers. Indeed, the top layer of the architecture, the Virtual Resource, is able to contact different instances of the same module to realize the distributed graph of information. In such way, IDN-Documents spanning through various domains can be interlinked and managed from a single access point. Fig. 2 shows a comprehensive picture of the InterDataNet system.

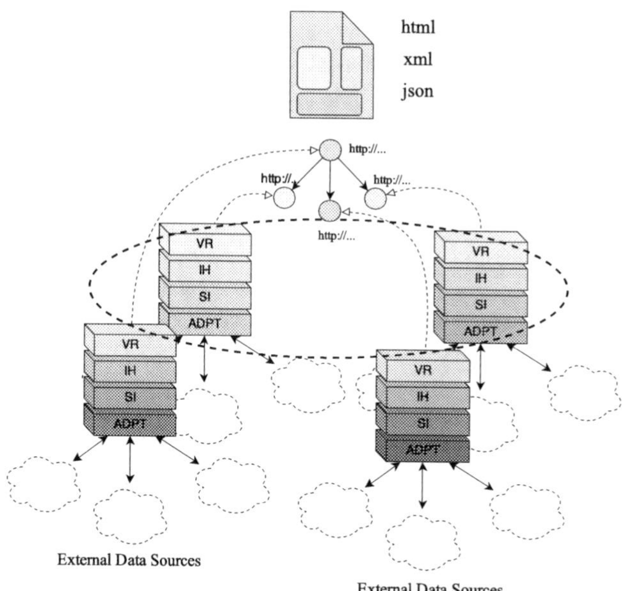

Fig. 2. An overall view of the InterDataNet system and the document resource

The system representation depicted in Fig. 2 includes outer data sources, components of a single InterDataNet instance, the network of peers, the information model and a representation of a document resource. The dashed clouds at the bottom represent outer data sources which provide information to the architecture in their own custom format. The adaptation layer (ADPT) interfaces with these data sources and performs a transformation of the information to comply with the InterDataNet formalism. Such information proceeds through the architecture up to the Virtual Resource (VR) layer, which implements the document abstraction. At this level, data are exposed as documents which can be composed to build new richer graphs (i.e., other documents).

InterDataNet is not limited to management of data coming from external sources. In fact, is possible to create InterDataNet native data using the RESTful interface. Analogously to the case of information coming from outer providers, these data will be exposed by the architecture in document form. The IDN-Document is depicted as a graph with four vertexes coming from different Virtual Resources to emphasize the distributed nature of the model. Finally, on top of the model, there is a representation of the document in one of the three data formats currently supported by the implementation: HTML, XML and Json.

4 SmartSantander: Enabling a Web of Sensors

This use-case is part of experimentation within the SmartSantader European project [14], where a number of different sensing devices were installed in the urban territory of Santander, Spain. The goal of the experimentation is to take a sensor and put it on the Web as a graph of resources manageable in an easy way, to support novel applications development such as the Virtual Sensor explained in the following.

The IDN-Document depicted in Fig. 3 represents a general sensor as an aggregation of structured information (web sensor). Leveraging this model, is possible to easily reach all the useful resources related to a particular sensor, e.g., measured data, accuracy, sensor location, and much more.

Since the chosen architectural style is REST, interacting with resources is straightforward: to get the representation of a particular sensor is sufficient to invoke an HTTP GET on the sensors name (i.e., the URI). The output of a particular sensor can be retrieved analogously. For example, the sensors output data could be retrieved issuing the following GET request:

```
http://.../sensor/{id}/data_production/data
```

while the location could be retrieved with an HTTP GET invoked on the URI:

```
http://.../sensor/{id}/location.
```

By leveraging the IDN-Document sensor representations I designed a new IDN-Document consuming sensors data. It is a Virtual Sensor, i.e. a sensor whose IDN-IM comprehends web sensors data and an analytical model which can be combined to produce new information. For instance, IDN-Documents representing temperature and humidity sensors can be combined to create a new heat-index virtual sensor IDN-Document.

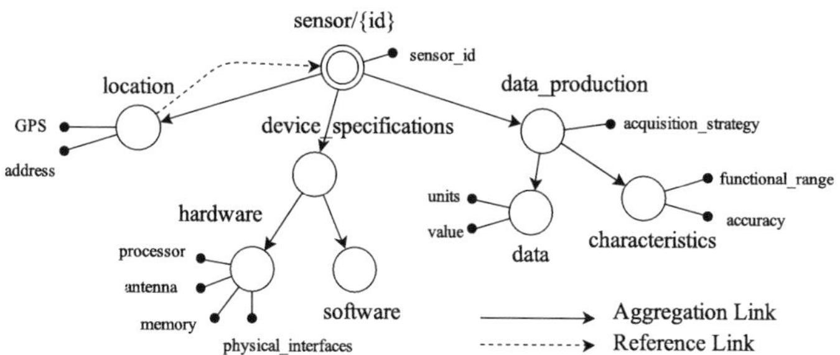

Fig. 3. IDN Information Model of a web sensor

5 Conclusions

In this paper, I propose an approach for enabling data interoperability and reuse in the Web of Things. To accomplish this task, I adopt a two-step methodology: 1) provide a connection with smart objects via a dedicated adapter, and 2) represent objects as graphs of granular, individually addressable data units. Expected benefits include easy sharing of objects related data and models across the Web, and support for the development of scalable applications. These principles have been put in practice by the InterDataNet RESTful middleware which leverages 1) an adapter for the connection to smart objects and 2) the IDN-Document formalism to turn objects into graphs of information.

Future works will include the integration of semantics into the IDN-IM and subsequent development of the IDN middleware to support semantic exploration of IDN-Documents as long as a security framework to secure information grains.

References

1. Atzori, L., Iera, A., Morabito, G.: The internet of things: A survey. Computer Networks 54(15), 2787–2805 (2010)
2. Fielding, R., Gettys, J., Mogul, J., Frystyk, H., Masinter, L., Leach, P., Berners-Lee, T.: Hypertext transfer protocol HTTP/1.1 (1999)
3. Masinter, L., Berners-Lee, T., Fielding, R.T.: Uniform resource identifier (URI): Generic syntax (2005)
4. Guinard, D., Trifa, V.: Towards the web of things: Web mashups for embedded devices. In: Workshop on Mashups, Enterprise Mashups and Lightweight Composition on the Web (MEM 2009). In: Proceedings of WWW (International World Wide Web Conferences), Madrid, Spain (April 2009)

5. Wilde, E., Kansa, E. C., Yee, R.: Web Services for Recovery. gov (2009)
6. Pettenati, M.C., Ciofi, L., Pirri, F., Giuli, D.: Towards a RESTful architecture for managing a global distributed interlinked data-content-information space. In: Domingue, J., et al. (eds.) The Future Internet. LNCS, vol. 6656, pp. 81–90. Springer, Heidelberg (2011)
7. Turchi, S., Ciofi, L., Paganelli, F., Pirri, F., Giuli, D.: Designing EPCIS through linked data and REST principles. In: 2012 20th International Conference on Software, Telecommunications and Computer Networks (SoftCOM), pp. 1–6. IEEE (September 2012)
8. Paganelli, F., Turchi, S., Bianchi, L., Ciofi, L., Pettenati, M.C., Pirri, F., Giuli, D.: An information-centric and REST-based approach for EPC Information Services. Journal of Communications Software & Systems 9(1) (2013)
9. Turchi, S., Bianchi, L., Paganelli, F., Pirri, F., Giuli, D.: Towards a Web of Sensors built with Linked Data and REST. In: 2013 IEEE 14th International Symposium and Workshops on a World of Wireless, Mobile and Multimedia Networks (WoWMoM), pp. 1–6. IEEE (June 2013)
10. Fielding, R.T.: Architectural styles and the design of network-based software architectures (Doctoral Dissertation, University of California) (2000)
11. Page, K.R., De Roure, D.C., Martinez, K.: REST and Linked Data: a match made for domain driven development? In: Proceedings of the Second International Workshop on RESTful Design, pp. 22–25. ACM (March 2011)
12. Zeng, D., Guo, S., Cheng, Z.: The web of things: A survey. Journal of Communications 6(6), 424–438 (2011)
13. Recordon, D., Reed, D.: OpenID 2.0: a platform for user-centric identity management. In: Proceedings of the Second ACM Workshop on Digital Identity Management, pp. 11–16. ACM (November 2006)
14. Sanchez, L., Galache, J.A., Gutierrez, V., Hernandez, J.M., Bernat, J., Gluhak, A., Garcia, T.: SmartSantander: The meeting point between Future Internet research and experimentation and the smart cities. In: Future Network & Mobile Summit (FutureNetw.), pp. 1–8. IEEE (June 2011)

Testing of Distributed Service-Oriented Systems

Faris Nizamic

Distributed Systems Group, Johann Bernoulli Institute,
University of Groningen, Nijenborgh 9, 9747 AG Groningen, NL
F.Nizamic@rug.nl

1 Introduction

We are experiencing an exponential growth of devices connected to the Internet and services offered through the web. Today, we are just a few mobile-clicks away using services which enormously simplify our life. Just think of how we are paying our bills, recharging our mobile pre-paid account, or how we buy tickets for the events we want to attend. It is all being done through web services. This increasing reliance on distributed service-oriented systems provided through the web places a high expectation on their reliability. To keep up with this growing trend that is embracing changes on a daily basis, the software development of the services has to be rapid and at the same time leaving not much space for software errors or failures.

In contrast with that, testing of distributed service-oriented systems is still a relatively unexplored area. In fully distributed environments, the costs of integration and testing are extremely high. The situation is even worse in large scale infrastructures where there is no single owner of the system and the various elements are highly decoupled. Sometimes even observing and monitoring the whole system is difficult.

In this research, we propose a framework where simulation environments are automatically built and maintained starting from existing process specifications of individual services, as well as available choreography and service behaviour knowledge. The proposed techniques, which are integral part of the software engineering process of building large scale, loosely coupled service-oriented systems, simplify the development by automating complex testing, verification and validation, thus resulting in more cost-effective reliable software-as-a-service solutions.

This paper is structured in the following way. In Section 2, we state the problem. Then, in Section 3 we define the research questions and research methodologies. Subsequently, in Section 4 we explain initial ideas and list the published work. In Section 5, we propose solution and then in Section 6 we discuss expected impact. In Section 7, we present preliminary results and the research plan. Finally, in Section 8 we list the envisioned research outcomes.

2 Problem Statement

Today, society's increasing reliance on services provided by web applications places a high demand on their reliability. Yet, significant amount of failures is

A.R. Lomuscio et al. (Eds.): ICSOC 2013 Workshops, LNCS 8377, pp. 551–556, 2014.
© Springer International Publishing Switzerland 2014

still being found [1]. That is due to poor engineering processes, unstandardised knowledge, and poor practices in software development and software testing processes. It is evident that the complexity of the software has drastically increased since the service-oriented architecture introduced. That was because the software became distributed across the network, which made many initial assumptions obsolete (shared memory and CPU, one owner of the system, etc.). Therefore, the new rules of the game are:

1. Software is distributed. Software systems are now distributed across different physical and/or logical locations. By means of network communication between system components (web services), certain functionality is being provided to end-users of a distributed service-oriented system. Yet, the testing of software still implicitly assumed full control over a system, which is not case in the reality.
2. System components are owned by different entities. To make the situation even more complicated, each service owner, be it individual, organization or company, uses its own development and testing standards, preferred technologies and methodologies, and has its own development schedules and policies towards their service consumers. Yet, from the end-user's perspective a final bill for eventual poor quality of provided service goes to overall service integrator (entity which provides a service by composing other services).
3. Testing tools and methodologies supporting automation of the software development life cycle are insufficient. Looking at software modelling tools going all the way to software testing tools, appropriate methodologies and tools supporting the automation of complete process of software delivery are rare or non-existing. That made communication and execution of tasks very difficult and imposed many issues for which the software engineering community did not find appropriate solutions yet.

3 Research Questions and Methodology

The main research question we therefore state is: *How can we simplify and automate testing of complex highly distributed and loosely coupled service-oriented systems to make them more reliable, robust and error-free?*

To answer this research question, a number of challenges needs to be addressed:

- **RQ1:** How to identify the constraints that limit the output of development, testing and integration processes for distributed service-oriented systems?
- **RQ2:** Which approach and techniques to use in order to tackle the identified constraints?
- **RQ3:** How to automate the creation and management of a testing environment?

In order to answer to **RQ1**, we plan to observe testing process of the newly developed distributed service-oriented system and that way to identify the constraints that industry encounters (high dependencies on external testing environment, not available test data, etc.) that slow the development process. To get a realistic state from the software engineering field, besides literature research a survey may be conducted among the companies or organizations that are concerned with development and testing process of such service-oriented software systems.

In **RQ2**, we concentrate on the observed constraints from **RQ1** that may be solved or whose effects can be minimized using our proposed approach and techniques. Namely, using service virtualization (web service simulation) to mimic system components are not owned or under control of test performing body. Thus, within **RQ2** we construct models formally describing simulated services, define approaches for their automated creation and maintenance, and their validation and verification against service description or against real services. Additionally, we plan develop new testing techniques which can result in more cost-effective reliable service-oriented systems. Energy and Banking sectors are the main application fields for the project.

In **RQ3**, we focus on the automation process of fully integrated environment for simulation and testing of service-oriented systems. To achieve full automation, we combine and/or customize existing tools and techniques. Once automation is achieved, we evaluate the proposed solution by comparing expected and observed improvements, that may be reflected in energy savings (Energy sector), time or money savings (Banking sector).

4 Related Work

In the paper *Testing for Highly Distributed Service-oriented Systems using Virtual Environments* [2], we show the risks of performing tests in production environment and propose how testing can be enabled using simulated services (virtual environment). To illustrate how this process, we use an example of a real system - WMO, based on the Dutch law for supporting people that have a chronic disease or disability.

Subsequently, in the paper *Policy-Based Scheduling of Cloud Services* [3], we address the questions of optimal scheduling for different partners competing for the available computing resources.

Finally, we propose a service-oriented system for making buildings more energy-efficient (*BernoulliBorg - The building of sustainability* [4]). The proposed project was awarded with a grant by the University of Groningen (Green Mind Award) and currently being implemented. This project being a source of valuable experience and inspiration, through which we have an opportunity to observe more constraints that encounter during development and testing of a service-oriented system and to experiment with possible solutions.

5 Proposed Solution

Taking into consideration diversity of work done until now, the integration of the previous work with current work will be done with the following approach. Firstly, we will finalize the implementation of the mentioned service-oriented system in order to gain the valuable knowledge from practice and to prepare the environment for experimentations to follow. Besides our own system, we will analyse other existing systems, not only to understand issues in external systems (i.e. banking applications), but also to understand differences and similarities among them. Furthermore, we will describe in detail how, by using the logic of theory of constraints [5], we can identify and remove the observed constraints. The evaluation will be done on our developed system [4], and potentially on one external system from industry. That way, we will gain the necessary insight and knowledge by going through the software development life cycle (SDLC) from the inside (by developing a service-oriented system), and from the outside (by observing a system developed by other company or organization).

Using gathered data, we propose a solution to solve some of the identified constraints in service design-time. To solve the identified constraints, we use use an approach of modelling and simulation techniques [6], [7] to substitute non-owned, non-developed or simply blocking parts of the system. That way, service under test can be properly tested before being deployed to production environment.

In our work, we first define the terminology of simulated services, explain the concepts and the processes around it. Subsequently, we propose the ways to create and model the simulated services and then we propose how to validate modelled services against the real services or against service description (interfaces and behaviour). Once modelled and validated, we show how executable simulated service should be modelled, maintained and deployed to both a design-time environment (for internal service consumers) and a run-time environment (for external service consumers). Further, we define a simulated service life cycle (SSLC), make a parallel with the SDLC, and propose how development cycles can be reduced and speed-to-market increased using service simulation. Finally, we introduce the a new testing technique, namely *Environment-based testing*, and present how it can make services under development to be more robust and error-free.

Finally, our proposed solution will be a process or technique for decoupling dependent services by providing simulated environment that supports automated changes. As a side effect, automated scripts or combined software solution supporting the process will be developed.

6 Expected Impact

This research will have impact on several different fields, namely: global service-oriented research community, software engineering industry, as well as local community in the North of The Netherlands.

The impact on the global service-oriented research community will be reflected through the fusion of simulation, system modelling and production management knowledge with the software engineering knowledge. The expected results of this fusion are that techniques, methodologies and approaches of service development will be proposed to reduce very high the complexity of service composition and integration.

Meanwhile, the impact on the global software engineering industry will be represented in decrease of time-to-market of service-oriented software products. This will be done by inclusion of simulated test environments auto-deployment within the overall test automation process. That way, there will be no constraints to use all currently unused time for automated testing in highly decoupled service-oriented systems.

Other side effects are expected as well. One of the side effects is that knowledge on automated simulation environments will suggest software engineers that concept like this can serve as a tangible communication mean to model services under development, but also to make an executable artefact which can be used for multiple purposes (e.g. documentation, traceability, environment state tracking, etc.).

Last but not least, the implementation of our energy-saving service-oriented system will definitely have a significant local impact on the University of Groningen. We expect that in case our developed system proves to fulfil the goals of energy saving, it will be deployed to more buildings of the North of The Netherlands.

7 Preliminary Results and Research Plan

The preliminary results are showed in a proof of concept *Sustainable Buildings* service-oriented system that is, at the moment of writing of this document, being deployed at the Faculty of Mathematics and Natural Sciences building where the Distributed Systems research group is located. The pilot project includes 15 office spaces, of which there are nine private working rooms, one meeting room, one social corner, two hallways, and two restrooms. There are 15 people working at the area. Consumption measuring wireless devices are used for 42 appliances, providing the ability to measure the electricity consumption and to control the appliances. At the moment, we have available preliminary results of the experiments showing if system like this makes a building more energy efficient, and what the actual savings are.

Current focus is on completion of the implementation of the afore-mentioned proof-of-concept system. Undoubtedly, once the system is in place, our proposed approach and techniques will be tested on the developed system through a number of experiments. That will subsequently lead to data analysis and publishing of observations and findings. Final part of the project will be devoted to publishing of final results and writing the thesis.

8 Envisioned Research Outcomes

The main envisioned outcomes of the research project are:

- **Out1** An observation report of the constraints in software engineering process of service-oriented systems based on industrial experiences

- **Out2** Techniques, methods and theoretical foundations for an automated testing using simulated services
- **Out3** A pilot prototype of automated service-oriented system deployment and testing
- **Out4** An evaluation report of the proposed techniques and methodologies for testing service-oriented systems in different areas
- **Out5** A PhD thesis that consolidates all above-mentioned outcomes

As this work can be considered to be applied research, the experience gained may also be considered as the potential basis for setting up a commercial enterprise exploiting such unique knowledge on energy-efficient buildings. Additional exploitation may be seen in the software testing consulting with the special focus on web service providers.

Acknowledgement. The author would like to thank to Prof. Marco Aiello, Dr. Alexander Lazovik and Dr. Rix Groenboom for their invaluable support in this research project. Faris Nizamic is supported by the JoinEU-SEE grant and Green Mind Award project.

References

1. Offutt, J., Papadimitriou, V., Praphamontripong, U.: A case study on bypass testing of web applications. In: Empirical Software Engineering 2012, pp. 1–36. Springer US (2012)
2. Nizamic, F., Groenboom, R., Lazovik, A.: Testing for Highly Distributed Service-oriented Systems using Virtual Environments. Postproceedings of 17th Dutch Testing Day 2011, EEMCS, 23–25 (2012)
3. Nizamic, F., Degeler, V., Groenboom, R., Lazovik, A.: Policy-Based Scheduling of Cloud Services. Journal on Scalable Computing: Practice and Experience 13(3), 187–199 (2012)
4. Nizamic, F., Nguyen, T.A.: BernoulliBorg - The building of sustainability (2012)
5. Cox, J., Goldratt, E.M.: The goal: a process of ongoing improvement. North River Press (1986)
6. Sargent, R.G.: Verification and validation of simulation models. J. Simulation 7(1) (2013)
7. Briand, L., Labiche, Y., Wang, Y.: Using Simulation to Empirically Investigate Test Coverage Criteria Based on Statecharts. In: ACM International Conference on Software Engineering, ICSE 2004, pp. 86–95 (2004)

Automation of the SLA Life Cycle in Cloud Computing*

Waheed Aslam Ghumman

Department of Computer Science,
University of Applied Sciences Zittau/Görlitz
{wghumman,jlaessig}@hszg.de

Abstract. Cloud computing has emerged as a popular paradigm for scalable infrastructure solutions and services. The requirement of automated management of Service Level Agreements (SLAs) between the cloud service provider and the cloud user has increased to minimize user interaction with the computing environment. Thus, effective SLA negotiation, monitoring and timely detection of possible SLA violations represent challenging research issues. A big gap exists between a manual/ semi-automated and a fully automated SLA life cycle. This gap can be bridged with formalization of generally existing natural language SLAs. Algorithms and strategies for SLA monitoring, management and SLA violation are directly dependent on a complete formalization of SLAs. The goal of the thesis is to analyze currently existing SLA description languages, to find their shortcomings and to develop a complete SLA description language. As next step, we plan to develop distributed algorithms for automated SLA negotiation, monitoring, integration and timely SLA violations detection for cloud computing.

Keywords: Cloud computing, service level agreement, automated SLA management.

1 Introduction and Problem Statement

The current trend in application service delivery is to move away from centrally located services towards structures of distributed services, dynamically bound to establish complex systems. With the emergence of cloud computing, businesses are focussing more to buy cloud services (on pay-as-you-go basis) rather than making one-time heavy investments on infrastructures and software licenses. Such an environment is governed by dynamically negotiated electronic contracts between the service providers and the service customers. A service level agreement (SLA) is a part of a service contract where different properties of the service are formally defined. It is very vital for users to obtain guarantees from providers on service delivery [1]. Typically, these are provided through SLAs, negotiated

* Advisor: Jörg Lässig
Department of Computer Science,
University of Applied Sciences Zittau/Görlitz

A.R. Lomuscio et al. (Eds.): ICSOC 2013 Workshops, LNCS 8377, pp. 557–562, 2014.
© Springer International Publishing Switzerland 2014

between the providers and end users. Generally, the SLAs are the only source of formal description of service contracts between the two parties. In e-business platforms, SLAs are essentially important for the service consumer as it compensates the consumer's high dependency on the service provider [2]. Consider a bigger company which purchases many different cloud services from multiple vendors and sells these services as composed products. Huge efforts in terms of human resources and computer systems (including softwares) are required to properly manage, negotiate and monitor this large set of SLAs. An *automation of SLA management tasks (i. e., negotiation, monitoring, integration and enforcement) strongly depends on the complete formalization of human readable SLAs. The definition of SLA specifications is needed in such a way that it has an appropriate level of granularity, namely a good tradeoff between expressiveness and complexity, so that they can cover most of the consumer expectations and are relatively easy to manipulate, verify and evaluate, and that they can be enforced by a resource allocation mechanism on the cloud.* The described goals might be easy to achieve for simple web service using SLA templates as e. g. presented in [3], however, this problem turns into a bottleneck with the growth in number and sophistication of cloud services. With our research, we aim to develop a state-of-the-art SLA based framework which can express regular SLAs in a machine readable format, can automate the negotiation process and is helpful for an automated SLA management, i. e., enforcement, monitoring and integration. The ultimate goal would be a framework which not only is useful to define, negotiate, integrate, enforce and monitor cloud services but also helps in system cost estimation and performance evaluation. In Section 2, we describe related work, state-of the-art techniques and shortcomings of existing approaches for different stages of the SLA life cycle. In Section 3, we describe methods and techniques towards a possible solution which we plan to develop during this research work. In Section 4, we give some concluding remarks about this work.

2 Research Challenges, Gaps and Related Work

In cloud computing environments, a service integrator provides a platform that allows to orchestrate independent service providers and services and cooperatively provide additional services that meet e. g. certain security requirements. The Web Service Level Agreement (WSLA) framework [4] is targeted at defining and monitoring SLAs for web services. The WSLA framework consists of a flexible and extensible language based on an XML schema and a runtime architecture comprising several SLA monitoring services, which may be outsourced to third parties to ensure a maximum of objectivity. But, this framework does not support a cost model for SLAs. WS-Agreement [5] is a language for advertising the capabilities of a service provider. WS-agreement does not define specific service level objective terms, nor does it possess a condition expression language to be used in specifying guarantee terms and negotiability constraints. Both of these languages (WSLA and WS-Agreement) do not specify the terms of the quality of services (QoS) and their attributes. Barros and Oberle [6] present the design of a Unified

Service Description Language (USDL), aimed at describing services across the human-to-automation continuum. A comprehensive USDL tool chain, including editors, stores and marketplaces, has been developed by SAP Research and partners and allows flexible deployment scenarios. Yet, more methods are required to fully exploit USDL, such as the integration with service engineering approaches. One possible solution to these problems is to create a formal declarative language to describe features and constraints of service providers [7]. It is in the interest of both parties (service user and service provider) to create and operate SLAs with a minimum of human interaction. Hasselmeyer *et al.* [8] describe a generic framework for negotiating SLAs. The components of the framework automate large parts of the negotiation process while at the same time letting the user retain control. Their framework however is not capable to implement scenarios which include different pricing models. Another negotiation mechanism [9] is designed for the dynamic resource allocation problem where multiple buyers and sellers are allowed to negotiate with each other concurrently and an agent is allowed to de-commit from an agreement at the cost of paying penalty. However, it fails to realize equilibrium strategies in dynamic resource allocation scenarios. Redl *et al.* [10] presented a method for finding semantically equal SLA elements from different SLAs by utilizing several machine learning algorithms. They assess the cost of SLA matching and provider selection with an SLA mapping technique and discuss methods for reducing this cost in Grid and Cloud marketplaces. They use the developed approach for automatic discovery of semantically equal SLA elements and the creation of SLA mappings that compensate differences in their syntax specification. Furthermore, using automatic SLA matching algorithms, it allows for autonomic provider selection in grid and cloud computing marketplaces. This approach, however, does not consider QoS metrics and also fails to automatically determine the influence of each individual parameter to the overall matching result. There is a large body of work considering the development of flexible and self-manageable cloud computing infrastructures. Most of the available monitoring systems rely either on Grid [11] or service-oriented infrastructures [12], which are not directly compatible to clouds due to differences in the usage models, or due to heavily network-oriented monitoring infrastructures. Comuzzi *et al.* [13] define a process for SLA establishment adopted within the SLA@SOI framework. The authors propose an architecture for monitoring SLAs considering two requirements introduced by SLA establishment: the availability of historical data for evaluating SLA offers and the assessment of the capability to monitor the terms in an SLA offer. But, they do not consider monitoring of low-level metrics and mapping them to high-level SLA parameters for ensuring the SLA objectives. Emeakaroha *et al.* [14] present the Detecting SLA Violation infrastructure (DeSVi) which senses SLA violations through resource monitoring. The detection of possible SLA violations relies on the predefined service level objectives and the utilization of knowledge databases to manage and prevent such violations. Their approach is, however, centralized and not capable to monitor a cloud environment with multiple data centers which is a major drawback of their approach.

3 Methods and Approaches towards Possible Solutions

In the previous sections, we have described the background, state-of-the-art techniques and existing shortcomings for SLAs description, negotiation, management, monitoring and enforcement. Now we move towards possible improvements and solutions in these directions. Starting with description languages, for instance, we have highlighted different problems like the inclusion of cost models and business process flows in SLAs. One possible idea might be to develop object oriented service level agreements in which SLAs are divided in different classes of objects based on their service type, usage, duration or any other property. We can then design an entity-relation or class-relation structure to define the relationships, business process rules/flow, price models and service requirements, etc. The SLAs, which are described using such ontological/object-based description languages for SLAs, can help in reasoning and automation processes. A similar approach is adopted by Ivanović *et al.* [15], in which a runtime based method to predict possible situations of SLA conformance and violation is presented for service orchestrations. The method is based on modeling QoS metrics of a service orchestration using constraints, based on assumptions on the behavior of the orchestration components. A violation of these constraints means that the corresponding scenario is infeasible, while satisfaction makes the scenario possible. The major challenge in this direction is to combine all important/critical language requirements (for cloud based SLAs) in one single language. Services are usually built by combining different smaller components or modules. Another approach might be to define a hierarchical structure for SLAs, where each smaller service component/object (leaf module) is bound with an SLA. The leaf SLA may include different service properties for the service object, e. g., service requirements, offering, computation cost, price model. We can then utilize these SLAs of smaller objects to build-up SLAs for the main service. There can be different approaches to utilize SLAs depending on the business flow and design model. For instance:

- Bottom-Up SLA: Attributes/properties in such SLAs are transferred from bottom to top, i. e., from child services to parent service. Such SLAs can be useful when integrating multiple services of different hierarchy.
- Top-down SLA: Attributes/properties in such SLAs are transferred from top to bottom, i .e., from parent services to child services. Such SLAs can be useful in different scenarios, e. g., to enforce a certain policy to all child services.
- Parallel SLA: Attributes/properties in such SLAs are transferred from left to right or right to left among SLAs of the same hierarchy. Such SLAs can be useful in situations where similar attributes are required in SLAs of the same hierarchy.

We aim to provide such a machine readable SLA description language which is capable to describe SLAs of major cloud service providers. We start by analyzing the textual SLAs of all major cloud service providers and define combined

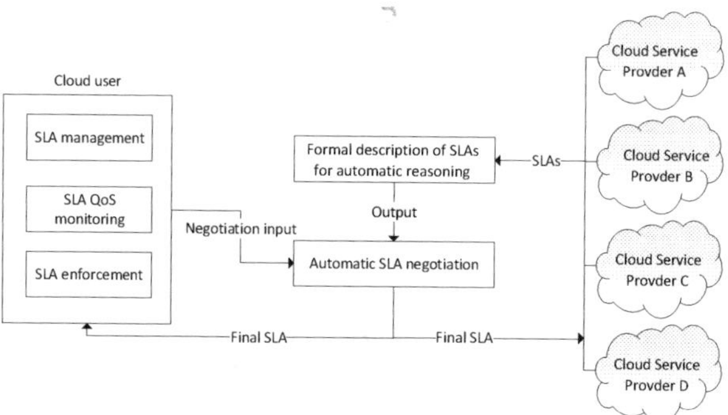

Fig. 1. The SLA automation process starts with a standardized SLA description. After that, an automated SLA negotiation between/among cloud service user(s) and cloud service provider(s) take place and successfully negotiated SLAs are communicated. Different distributed algorithms manage, monitor, enforce and integrate SLAs for reliable and error-free delivery of cloud services.

common and distinctive SLA attributes based on their static or dynamic behavior. In a next step, we plan to develop an SLA negotiation framework which can dynamically automate the negotiation process and generates an machine readable output of the negotiation process to be integrated with external information systems. A representation of this abstract idea is depicted in Figure 1. As next step, we plan to define scalable, accurate, and non-intrusive distributed algorithms for cloud monitoring based on SLAs. This step includes automatic SLA enforcement and management.

4 Conclusions

We have presented a research problem related to SLAs in cloud computing that emphasizes that the automation of SLA negotiation, management, monitoring and integration are a natural next step in service oriented computing. In general all steps in the SLA life cycle (from design to establishment of actual SLAs) are dependent on the capabilities of an SLA description language. We have discussed deficiencies in existing SLA description languages and methods with reference to SLA life cycle automation. We presented a brief overview of existing approaches, their drawbacks, research challenges and existing gaps. Also it has been discussed that SLA negotiation, management, monitoring and integration can be achieved to a certain extent after formalizing a description language for SLAs. Increasing requirements of smooth, flawless and reliable delivery of cloud computing services with little or no human-computer interaction is of much interest. In the planned thesis we give a possible solution to develop an SLA description language and to automate the SLA life cycle based on that description language.

References

1. Gong, Y., Ying, Z., Lin, M.: A survey of cloud computing. In: Yang, Y., Ma, M. (eds.) Proceedings of the 2nd International Conference on Green Communications and Networks (GCN): Volume 3. LNEE, vol. 225, pp. 79–84. Springer, Heidelberg (2012)
2. Ul Haq, I., Brandic, I., Schikuta, E.: SLA validation in layered cloud infrastructures. In: Altmann, J., Rana, O.F. (eds.) GECON 2010. LNCS, vol. 6296, pp. 153–164. Springer, Heidelberg (2010)
3. Rodosek, G.D., Lewis, L.: Dynamic service provisioning: A user-centric approach. In: Proceedings of the 12th Annual IFIP/IEEE International Workshop on Distributed Systems: Operations & Management (DSOM), pp. 37–48 (2001)
4. Keller, A., Ludwig, H.: The WSLA framework: Specifying and monitoring service level agreements for web services. Journal of Network and Systems Management 11(1), 57–81 (2003)
5. Andrieux, A., Czajkowski, K., Dan, A., Keahey, K., Ludwig, H., Nakata, T., Pruyne, J., Rofrano, J., Tuecke, S., Xu, M.: Web services agreement specification (WS-Agreement). In: Global Grid Forum, vol. 2 (2004)
6. Barros, A., Oberle, D.: Handbook of Service Description: USDL and Its Methods. Springer Publishing Company, Incorporated (2012)
7. Ortiz, J., de Almeida, V.T., Balazinska, M.: A vision for personalized service level agreements in the cloud. In: Workshop on Data Analytics in the Cloud (2013)
8. Hasselmeyer, P., Mersch, H., Koller, B., Quyen, H.N., Schubert, L., Wieder, P.: Implementing an SLA negotiation framework. In: Proceedings of the eChallenges Conference on Exploiting the Knowledge Economy - Issues, Applications, Case Studies (2007)
9. An, B., Lesser, V., Irwin, D., Zink, M.: Automated negotiation with decommitment for dynamic resource allocation in cloud computing. In: Proceedings of the 9th International Conference on Autonomous Agents and Multiagent Systems: Volume 1, pp. 981–988. International Foundation for Autonomous Agents and Multiagent Systems (2010)
10. Redl, C., Breskovic, I., Brandic, I., Dustdar, S.: Automatic SLA matching and provider selection in grid and cloud computing markets. In: Proceedings of the 2012 ACM/IEEE 13th International Conference on Grid Computing. IEEE Computer Society (2012)
11. Reyes, S., Muñoz-Caro, C., Niño, A., Sirvent, R., Badia, R.: Monitoring and steering grid applications with grid superscalar. Future Generation Computer Systems 26(4), 645–653 (2010)
12. D'Ambrogio, A., Bocciarelli, P.: A model-driven approach to describe and predict the performance of composite services. In: Proceedings of the 6th International Workshop on Software and Performance, pp. 78–89. ACM (2007)
13. Comuzzi, M., et al.: Establishing and monitoring SLAs in complex service based systems. In: IEEE International Conference on Web Services, 783–790. IEEE (2009)
14. Emeakaroha, V.C., Netto, M.A., Calheiros, R.N., Brandic, I., Buyya, R., De Rose, C.A.: Towards autonomic detection of sla violations in cloud infrastructures. Future Generation Computer Systems 28(7), 1017–1029 (2012)
15. Ivanović, D., Carro, M., Hermenegildo, M.: Constraint-based runtime prediction of SLA violations in service orchestrations. In: Kappel, G., Maamar, Z., Motahari-Nezhad, H.R. (eds.) Service Oriented Computing. LNCS, vol. 7084, pp. 62–76. Springer, Heidelberg (2011)

Towards a Dynamic Declarative Service Workflow Reference Model*

Damian Clarke

Department of Computer Science, University of Miami, Miami, USA
d.clarke6@umiami.edu

Abstract. Functional, nonfunctional, just-in-time approaches to composing web services span the sub-disciplines of software engineering, data management, and artificial intelligence. Our research addresses the process that must occur once the composition has completed and stakeholders must investigate historical and online operations/data flow to reengineer the process either off-line or in real-time. This research introduces *an effective reference model to assess the message flow of long-running service workflows*. We examine Dynamic Bayesian Networks (dDBNs), a data-driven modeling technique employed in machine learning, to create service workflow reference models. Unlike other reference models, this method is not limited by static assumptions. We achieve this by including the trend and time varying variables in the model. We demonstrate this method using a flight dataset collected from various airlines.

1 Introduction

In response to today's increasingly volatile business environment, web service workflows need to be agile and dynamic. The main cause of volatility is trend and time dependent, which are secondary but influential variables implicitly within the service workflow that affect the relationship between dependent variables and other independent variables of primary interest. Therefore, reference models [1] for service workflows must consist of trend and time varying constructs that efficiently and effectively capture dynamically identifiable changes in the information-processing functionalities. One method to dynamically identify changes is to infer meaning from data the service workflow consumes and produces and then be able to recommend action based on that meaning. With the inclusion of on-demand data intensive discoveries the model can now accommodate constructive feedback and forward interventions resulting in an agile representation that can more accurately reflect trend and time varying variables.

As a motivating scenario consider an *Airline Ticket Pricing Workflow*. Such a workflow consists of a Select Airlines service that takes origin and destination cities from the user and devises a list of air carriers who fly between the two cities. Subsequently, a Collect Prices service contacts the list of airlines and develops the best ticket price. The Collect Prices service may have many attributes that are not used in

* Supervised by Prof. M. Brain Blake.

A.R. Lomuscio et al (Eds.): ICSOC 2013 Workshops, LNCS 8377, pp. 563–568, 2014.
© Springer International Publishing Switzerland 2014

every instance of the workflow such as number of connections, time of day of departure, and time of day of arrival. In this service workflow and in others like it, the user may be able to leverage unused message types to find the most optimal price. For this scenario, the date and time of purchase and the time-of-day for the flight also may affect the optimal price. A more sophisticated example of this workflow is used in our evaluation section later in this paper.

In our work, our research contributes to the next step after a set of functionally-adequate workflows are created, on-demand, by a third party and in use. Given historical data and the ability to strategically poll these longer-standing workflows, we believe that, by using the real operational message data generated by the workflow logic which we call *constructive feedback*, a reference model of the workflows can be dynamically created. *A **contribution of our work*** is the introduction of a model that can encapsulate declarative and predictive features that can deal with uncertainty thereby facilitating *forward intervention*.

2 Related Work

Research projects related to the optimizations of web service workflows [2][3] can be classified into three areas, service engineering and modeling projects that focus on the web service specifications, similar service engineering projects that alternatively concentrates on the operational web services and their data, also the general body of work in workflow optimization and workflow decentralization. Largely, the state-of-the-art in web service discovery, composition, and mashup operates with the specifications and not the running operational systems [4][5]. As such, these projects are not related to our approach as we look at the real data content of messages as a method to re-engineer operational web service workflow systems.

There are other service engineering projects that investigate the real data content. One such work is in the area of automated or semi-automated web service testing. To automate testing of web services, related projects must evaluate if web service outputs meet tests plans and, in other cases, predict the specific data content that requires testing. These approaches must develop models to understand the data. The most relevant approaches develop models of data that extend SOAP [6] and UDDI data models [7]. These approaches try to perturb data from specifications and then execute them in operational mode. Unlike these approaches that tend to work on just one web service, models in our work leverages models across multiple services in a web service workflow.

3 Technical Approach

We introduce a reference model for service workflows created from the underlying messages collected during the actual service workflow operation. Our approach includes the implicit secondary trend and time varying variables to more accurately reflect a volatile business environment. This section describes how we formalize the model by proposing the use of *non-homogeneous semi-flexible dynamic Bayesian networks* [8].

3.1 Bayesian Networks

Static Bayesian Networks usually referred to as simply *Bayesian Networks* (BN) are a class of *graphical models* [9]. They allow a concise representation of the probabilistic dependencies between a given set of random variables X = $\{X_1, X_2, \ldots, X_p\}$ as a directed acyclic graph (DAG) G = (V,E) where each node $v_i \in V$ corresponds to a random variable X_i and E is the set of edges between connecting nodes. A random variable denotes an attribute, feature, or hypothesis about which we may be uncertain.

An important feature of Bayesian networks is that by instantiating vertices in the directed structure independences may change to dependences, i.e. stochastic independence has specific dynamic properties. This produces the concept known as "explaining away" [10] where the confirmation of one cause of an observed or believed event reduces the need to invoke alternative causes and/or confirmation of one cause increases belief in another.

Whereas static Bayesian Networks model multiple independent "snapshots" of the process, intuitively *Dynamic Bayesian Networks* (dBN) extend the fundamentals of Bayesian networks by modeling associations from the temporal dynamics between entities of interest. We refer the reader to [11] for a comprehensive review. Each variable in a dBN is represented by several nodes across time points. In addition, temporal signatures are useful in capturing possible feedback loops that are disregarded by static Bayesian Networks. A set of sufficient conditions for a model to be represented as a dynamic network are detailed in the following works [12] [13] [8].

By combining qualitative and quantitative event data (e.g. intra-service-workflow step messages) in a coherent way, a Bayesian statistical approach allows the representation of each event with its set of mutually exclusive and collectively exhaustive values as a random variable. Each node (perhaps defining a data point from a service messages) has assigned a function that describes how the state of a node depends on the parents of the node. The topology of the graph that relates the nodes defines the probabilistic dependencies between the node variables, by means of a set of conditional distributions. In addition, we can integrate different sources of information, for example domain expert knowledge, historical and polled event data, to give a unified knowledge that allows us to manage internal and external "causal" factors such as bottlenecks. In this context, a Bayesian network is augmented with two other types of nodes, then it is possible for actions to be decided based on given evidence. These two types of nodes are utility nodes and decision nodes. Utility nodes represent the value of a particular event, while decision nodes represent the choices that might be made.

3.2 Proof of Concept and Discussion

The intent of our experimentation is to demonstrate that the behavior in web service workflow operations vary in the nuanced ways that enable our approach to predict the content-based outcomes and perform forward interventions. When using a web service workflow to manage the airline ticket purchase workflow, we believe that the businesses have encoded their purchase operations and these operations might vary from airline to airline. This variation is the basis for why our data model would be important for optimizing workflow paths. Consider the workflow path in Fig. 1. We introduce a reference model that can:

1. *Predict when it is not necessary to check the availability of an airline ticket on a particular airliner, thus the overall BPEL workflow can be truncated*
2. *Predict when the purchase date for a ticket is too close to the departure date to get an optimal price*
3. *Predict that when a passenger is restricted for a particular time-of-day certain airlines will not have optimal pricing.*

In Fig.1, we see an exemplar model for the airline ticket shopping workflow. When a service provider receives a request through a Web Service Interface Service, then this would trigger the concurrent availability (Airline N: Check Availability Service) and price checks (Airline N: Check Prices Service) from the web services of the various airlines. The final step is a decision to buy a ticket from a particular airline (Airline N. Purchase). The shaded web services represent a truncated workflow determined using our data model.

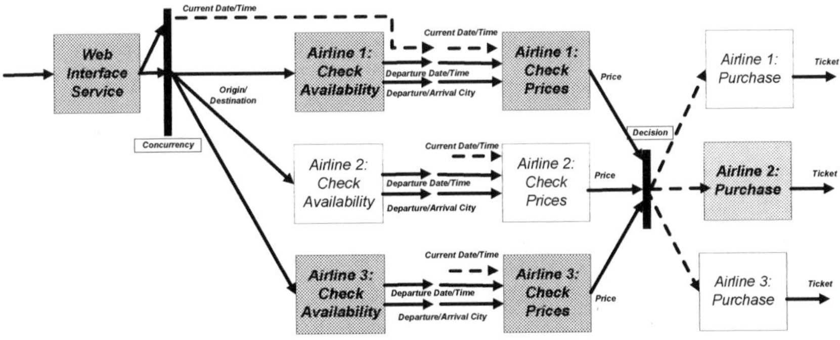

Fig. 1. An Example Airline Purchase Workflow

As a first part of our evaluation, we used 41 days of airline data from [14] where we anticipate that each airline is running a business specific workflow similar to that illustrated in Fig. 1. Consequently, when we analyze their data we saw different behaviors in how their airline prices are generated. It is evident that airlines modify their prices for the same ticket as the time to departure reduces. As we anticipated, these modifications fluctuate as the business operations for each airline differs.

Figure 2 shows a representation of a BN for the real airline pricing data for AA. Our model accurately predicts lower prices for polling dates further away from the actual flight time on 1/1/2003 and higher prices as the polling date gets closer to the flight time.

Figure 3 shows data collected from 10/12/2002 through 02/01/2003 for a United Airline's flight leaving on 02/02/2003. We demonstrate how our model behaves twenty-five time points in the future in the shaded region. The dotted lines show a gentle upward tick in the price. Figure 4, plots the data collected from 10/12/2002 to 17/12/2002. Our model accurately predicts a downward trend in the price and then a leveling off.

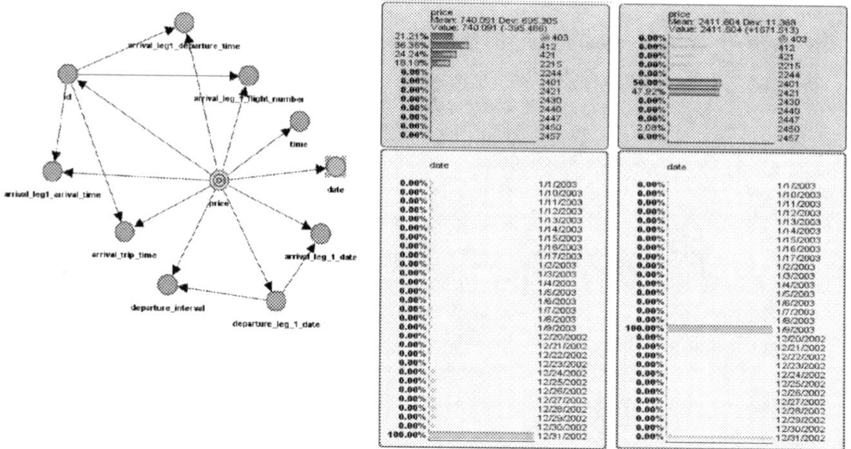

Fig. 2. An Instantiation of the BN for AA prices

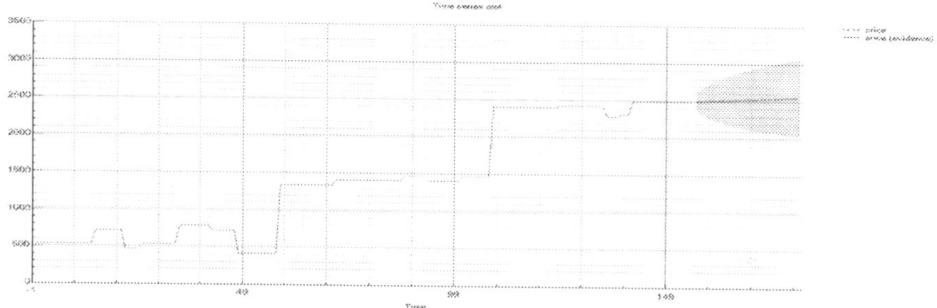

Fig. 3. UA prices (10/12/2003 to flight date on 02/01/2003) with 25 time point projection

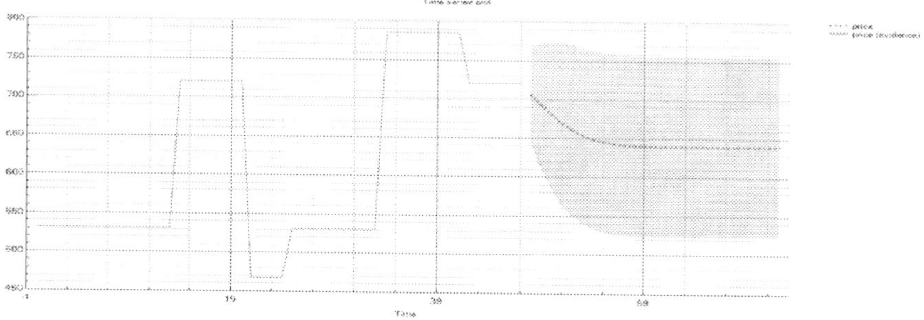

Fig. 4. UA prices taken from 10/12/2003 to 17/12/2003 with 25 time point projection

4 Conclusion and Future Work

The service workflow assessment vision that we explore in this paper is to completely automate the data centric service workflow model and to perform such assessments in a reliable, reproducible and efficient manner. The intention is that service workflow assessment can be deployed frequently and on demand. We have seen that this vision is promising with the inclusion of trend and time-varying features of a business environment. Unanswered questions such as polling rate still need to be explored.

References

[1] OASIS SOA Reference Model (SOA-RM) TC, `https://www.oasis-open.org/committees/soa-rm/faq.php`

[2] Blake, M.B., Huhns, M.N.: Web-Scale Workflow: Integrating Distributed Services. IEEE Internet Computing 12(1), 55–59 (2008)

[3] Blake, M.B., Gomaa, H.: Agent-oriented compositional approaches to services-based cross-organizational workflow. Decis. Support Syst. 40(1), 31–50 (2005)

[4] Liu, X., Hui, Y., Sun, W., Liang, H.: Towards Service Composition Based on Mashup. In: 2007 IEEE Congress on Services, pp. 332–339 (2007)

[5] Srivastava, B., Koehler, J.: Web Service Composition - Current Solutions and Open Problems. In: ICAPS 2003 Workshop on Planning for Web Services, pp. 28–35 (2003)

[6] Offutt, J., Xu, W.: Generating test cases for web services using data perturbation. SIGSOFT Softw. Eng. Notes 29(5), 1–10 (2004)

[7] Bai, X., Dong, W., Tsai, W.-T., Chen, Y.: WSDL-based automatic test case generation for Web services testing. In: IEEE International Workshop on Service-Oriented System Engineering, SOSE 2005, pp. 207–212 (2005)

[8] Dondelinger, F., Lèbre, S., Husmeier, D.: Non-homogeneous dynamic Bayesian networks with Bayesian regularization for inferring gene regulatory networks with gradually time-varying structure. Mach. Learn. 90(2), 191–230 (2013)

[9] Dawid, P., Lauritzen, S.L., Spiegelhalter, D.J.: Probabilistic Networks and Expert Systems: Exact Computational Methods for Bayesian Networks. Springer (2007)

[10] Wellman, P.P., Henrion, M.: Explaining 'explaining away'. IEEE Trans. Pattern Anal. Mach. Intell. 15(3), 287–292 (1993)

[11] Kim, S.Y., Imoto, S., Miyano, S.: Inferring gene networks from time series microarray data using dynamic Bayesian networks. Brief. Bioinform. 4(3), 228–235 (2003)

[12] Lèbre, S.: Inferring Dynamic Genetic Networks with Low Order Independencies. Stat. Appl. Genet. Mol. Biol. 8(1), 1–38 (2009)

[13] Lèbre, S., Becq, J., Devaux, F., Stumpf, M.P., Lelandais, G.: Statistical inference of the time-varying structure of gene-regulation networks. BMC Syst. Biol. 4(1), 130 (2010)

[14] Etzioni, O., Tuchinda, R., Knoblock, C.A., Yates, A.: To buy or not to buy: mining airfare data to minimize ticket purchase price. In: Proceedings of the Ninth ACM SIGKDD International Conference on Knowledge Discovery and Data Mining, New York, NY, USA, pp. 119–128 (2003)

A Context-Aware Access Control Framework for Software Services

A.S.M. Kayes, Jun Han, and Alan Colman

Faculty of Science, Engineering and Technology
Swinburne University of Technology, VIC 3122, Australia
{akayes,jhan,acolman}@swin.edu.au

Abstract. In the present age, context-awareness is an important aspect of the dynamic environments and the different types of dynamic context information bring new challenges to access control systems. Therefore, the need for the new access control frameworks to link their decision making abilities with the context-awareness capabilities have become increasingly significant. The main goal of this research is to develop a new access control framework that is capable of providing secure access to information resources or software services in a context-aware manner. Towards this goal, we propose a new semantic policy framework that extends the basic role-based access control (RBAC) approach with both dynamic associations of user-role and role-service capabilities. We also introduce a context model in modelling the basic and high-level context information relevant to access control. In addition, a situation can be determined on the fly so as to combine the relevant states of the entities and the purpose or user's intention in accessing the services. For this purpose, we can propose a situation model in modelling the purpose-oriented situations. Finally we need a policy model that will let the users to access resources or services when certain dynamically changing conditions (using context and situation information) are satisfied.

Keywords: Context-awareness, context, context-aware access control, situation, situation-aware access control, access control policy.

1 Introduction

In recent years, the rapid advancement of computing technologies has led to the world to a new paradigm of access control, shifted from fixed desktop to dynamic context-aware environments [15]. Such a shift brings with it opportunities and challenges. On the one hand, users demand access to resources or services in an anywhere, anytime fashion. On the other hand, such access has to be carefully controlled due to the additional challenges coming for the dynamically changing context information. For example, a doctor's request to obtain some patient information from a service through a desktop computer in his surgery may be very appropriate, but may not be so from his tablet on a public bus. Therefore, *the information about the changing environment, called context information, needs to be taken into account when making access control decisions* [7].

A.R. Lomuscio et al. (Eds.): ICSOC 2013 Workshops, LNCS 8377, pp. 569–577, 2014.
© Springer International Publishing Switzerland 2014

A security policy normally states that the particular information resources or software services can be invoked only for the specific purpose; and it describes the reason for which organizational resources are used [2]. For example, in the medical domain the American Health Information Management Association (AHIMA) identifies 18 health care scenarios across 11 purposes (treatment, payment, research, etc.) for health information exchange [4]. In the context-awareness literature (e.g., [1]), existing situation definitions typically describe the states of the specific kind of entities, such as user's state (e.g.,[16]). However, these works need to be taken into account the focus of access control-specific considerations in dynamic environments, where a user wants to access specific resources from a particular environment (e.g., a patient is in a critical health condition) for a certain purpose (e.g., emergency treatment purpose). Therefore, in order to specify situations, other than the states of the specific kinds of entities, *it is required to capture the states of the relevant relationships between entities*. Moreover, *it is required to identify the purpose or user's intention in accessing the software services*, when making access control decisions.

To point out some unique challenges in access control for dynamic environments, we start by considering an application scenario in the domain of electronic health records management system, requiring context-aware access control [9]. The scenario illustrates many of the key ideas of our research. As different types of dynamic information are involved in the scenario, some important issues arise. These issues and their related requirements are discussed in [8][9].

2 Research Challenges

In general, to achieve context-/situation-awareness and integrate the dynamic context/situation information into the access control processes, the following research challenges have to be addressed.

(1) Understanding and identifying the context information and associated context entities relevant to access control, thereby formulating an appropriate context model for capturing the dynamic context information.
(2) Developing a suitable reasoning technique to infer richer and more complex context information according to user-defined rules.
(3) Capturing the states of the context entities relevant to access control and the states of the relevant relationships between different entities, and identifying the user's intention in accessing the services, thereby formulating an appropriate situation model to determine the relevant situations.
(4) Developing a suitable reasoning technique to recognize a more complex or composite situation from the atomic situations using logic-based approach.
(5) Specifying and enforcing access control policies that use the dynamic information (context and situation) as the contextual conditions and make access control decisions based on the relevant dynamic information.
(6) Monitoring context/situation changes at runtime and managing reauthorization of access as changes of this dynamic information.

To address and tackle the identified research issues and challenges, the overall goal of this research is to develop a new access control framework, named *Context-Aware Access Control (CAAC)*, that can capable of providing secure access to information resources or software services according to the dynamic information in a context-aware manner; and can enable software engineers to improve privacy and security when building CAAC applications.

3 Related Work

A recent study [11] shows that the Role-based Access Control (RBAC) [12] approach has become the most widely used access control framework. It typically evaluates access permission through roles assigned to users and each role assigns a collection of permissions to users who are requesting access to the software services. On the other hand, the Attribute-based Access Control (ABAC) [14] approach grants accesses to services based on the attributes (e.g., user's identity - the attribute possessed by the user/requester) rather than direct role-based support. It is not applicable in large-scale domains because the identity-based approaches do not scale well in large open systems [10]. Towards this goal, in this research we propose a new Context-Aware Access Control (CAAC) framework that adopts and extends the traditional RBAC framework by incorporating the dynamically changing context/situation information.

Research continues to the present age to extend the basic RBAC framework in support of new policies to integrate dynamically changing contextual information (context/situation) into the RBAC policies. During the past decades, several research efforts (e.g., [3]) incorporate specific types of contexts as constraints in the access control policies, such as time and location. Recently, He et al [5] and Huang et al [6] have adopted and extended the basic RBAC solution, which provide useful insight to present user-role and role-permission assignment concepts. We compare our approach with them in [8][9].

Some situation-aware access control frameworks have been proposed in the access control literature (e.g., [16], [17]), each of them having different origins, pursuing different goals and often, by nature, being highly domain-specific. They consider the specific types of context information (e.g., the user's state) as policy constraints to control access to software services or resources. However, the basic elements of the situation-awareness in access control systems (i.e., the combination of the relevant *entity states* and the *relationship states*, and the *purpose or user's intention* in accessing the services) were not the focus to date.

4 The Approach: Context-Aware Access Control

Our work in this research is concerned with how to support and manage a fine-grained access control to software services in a context-aware manner. We show how the context-/situation-awareness capabilities and role-based access control (RBAC) decision making abilities can be integrated, allowing us to control the access to resources or services, while retaining the benefits of RBAC, such as

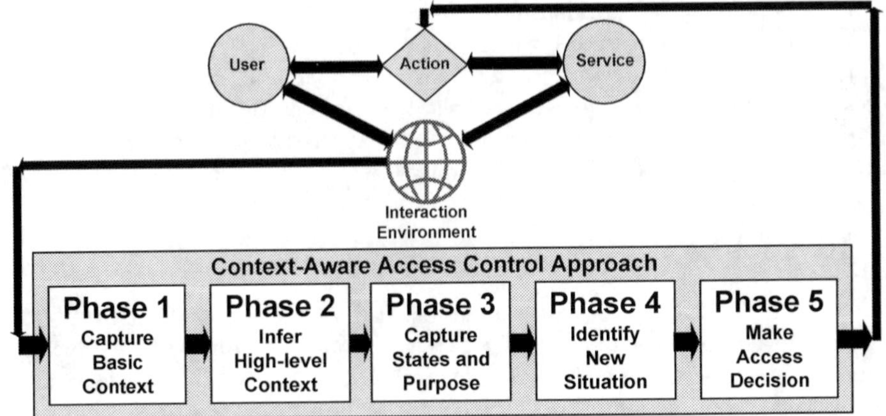

Fig. 1. The Proposed Context-Aware Access Control Approach

role hierarchy, role inheritance, etc. Towards this goal, in this section we present a high-level approach to context-aware access control for software services.

We propose a 5-phase Context-Aware Access control (CAAC) approach for providing context-specific access to software services (see Figure 1).

- *Capture basic context:* it is the process of capturing the basic context information (low-level information) from the interaction environment.
- *Infer high-level context:* it is the process of inferring high-level context information that are not explicitly specified, using phase 1 information.
- *Capture relevant states and purpose:* it is the process of capturing elementary information from the phases 1 and 2, both "states" of relevant entities and "purpose" of accessing services, brought together into an integrated whole to form the basic atomic situations.
- *Identify new situation:* it is the process of identifying new complex (or composite) situations from the basic atomic situations, using phase 3 knowledge.
- *Make access decision:* it is the process of making access control decisions based on the context/situation information captured in the previous phases and consequently take necessary action in a timely and effective manner.

5 Current Status of the Research

5.1 A Semantic Policy Framework for CAAC

Access control is a mechanism to determine whether a request to access the information resources or software services provided by a system should be permitted or denied. In this research, we adopt and extend the basic Role-based Access Control (RBAC) framework [12], and propose a new access control framework [9]. Figure 2 shows our CAAC framework and the relationships between its elements. The CAAC framework enables dynamic privileges assignment at two

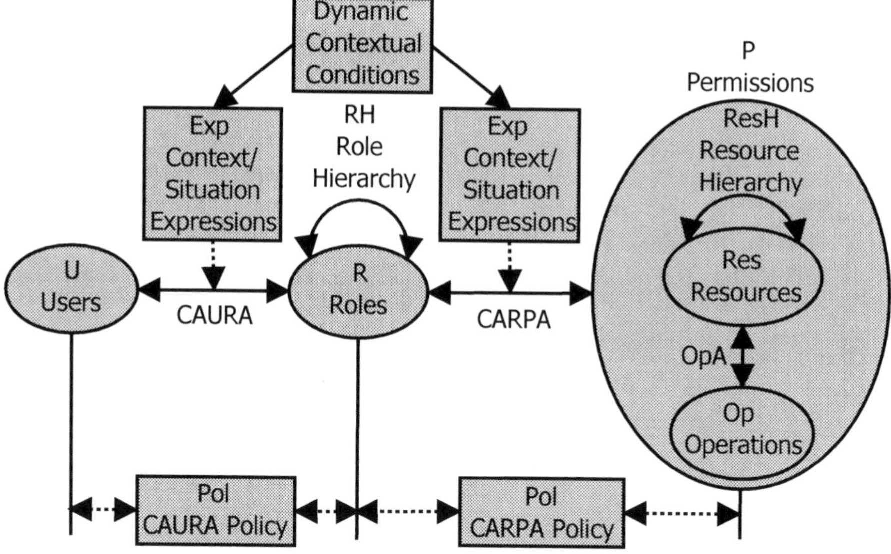

Fig. 2. Our Proposed CAAC Policy Framework

steps, letting users to access resources or services when a set of contextual conditions are satisfied. At the first step, the users are dynamically assigned to the roles when a set of contextual conditions are satisfied. At the next step, when a role is activated, then the service access permissions are dynamically assigned to that role when a set of contextual conditions are satisfied. Towards this end, we introduce two main concepts: *context-aware user-role assignments (CAURA)* and *context-aware role-permission assignments (CARPA)*.

Based on the formalization of the traditional Role-Based Access Control (RBAC) model [12], we present a formal definition of the CAAC model.

$$\begin{aligned} M &= (M_S, M_R) \\ M_S &= (U, R, Res, Op, P, Exp, Pol) \\ M_R &= (RH, CAURA, ResH, OpA, CARPA) \end{aligned} \tag{1}$$

First of all, we define the following seven elements of our CAAC model:

- ***Users (U):*** A set of users $U = \{u_1, ..., u_m\}$. The users are human-beings (who are service requesters) interacting with a computing system, whose access requests are being controlled.
- ***Roles (R):*** A set of roles $R = \{r_1, ..., r_n\}$. A role reflects user's job function or job title within the organization (e.g., healthcare domain).
- ***Resources (Res):*** A set of different parts of a resource $Res = \{res_1, ..., res_o\}$. Resources are the objects protected by access control. A resource represents the data/information container (the different parts of a patient's medical records).

- ***Operations (Op):*** A set of operations on the resources $Op = \{op_1, ..., op_p\}$. An operation is an action that can be executed on the resources, for instance, read and write.
- ***Permission (P):*** A set of permissions $P = \{p_1, ..., p_q\} = \{(res_i, op_j) | res_i \in Res, op_j \in Op\}$, where i = {1, 2, ..., o}, j = {1, 2, ..., p}, Res is a set of different parts of a resource, and Op is a set of operations on the resource parts. Permission is an approval to perform certain operations on resource parts, by the users who initiate access requests.
- ***Expressions (Exp):*** A set of expressions $Exp = \{exp_1, ..., exp_r\}$. An expression is used to express the contextual conditions (using relevant context/situation information) in order to describe the user-role and role-permission assignment policies.
- ***Policies (Pol):*** A set of policies $Pol = Pol_{CAURA} \cup Pol_{CARPA}$, the context-aware user-role assignment policies and context-aware role-permission assignment policies.

Originating from the above elements, the CAAC model has five other elements (using the relationships between the different sets of the above elements) of our model which are defined formally as follows:

- ***Role Hierarchy (RH):*** $RH \subseteq R \times R$ is a partial order on R to serve as the role hierarchy, which supports the concept of role inheritance. The role is considered in a hierarchical manner in that if a permission assigned to a junior role, then it is also assigned to all the senior roles of that role.
- ***Context-Aware User-Role Assignment (CAURA):*** It is a context-aware user-role assignment relation, which is a many-to-many mapping between a set of users and roles, when a set of dynamic contextual conditions are satisfied.

$$CAURA = \{(u_1, r_1, exp_1), (u_2, r_2, exp_2), ..., (u_m, r_n, exp_r)\} \subseteq U \times R \times Exp \quad (2)$$

- ***Resource Hierarchy (ResH):*** $ResH \subseteq Res \times Res$ is a partial order on Res to serve as the resource hierarchy, which supports a user to access the different granularity levels of resources. The resource is considered in a hierarchical manner in that if a user has the right to access a resource with the highest granularity level, then he also has the right to access the lower granularity levels of that resource.
- ***Operation Assignment (OpA):*** $OpA \subseteq Res \times Op$ is a many-to-many operation-to-resource mapping. Each operation could be associated with many resource parts, and for each resource could be granted to many operations. A set of operation assignment relations, $OpA = \{(res, op) | res \in Res, op \in Op\}$.
- ***Context-Aware Role-Permission Assignment (CARPA):*** It is a context-aware role-permission assignment relation, which is a many-to-many

mapping between a set of roles and permissions, when a set of dynamic contextual conditions are satisfied.

$$CARPA = \{(r_1, p_1, exp_1), (r_2, p_2, exp_2), ..., (r_n, p_q, exp_r)\} \subseteq R \times P \times Exp \quad (3)$$

5.2 Context Model

We introduce an ontology-based approach to context-aware access control (CAAC) for software services [8]. It includes an extensible *context model* specific to access control for capturing the basic contexts information, and a *reasoning model* for inferring high-level implicit context information based on user-defined rules, and an access control *policy model* incorporating context information from the context model. We also develop a CAAC application in the healthcare domain and present a case study, which shows the effectiveness of our CAAC approach. Using our approach, different users can access different services (by dynamically invoking different operations on resources at different granularity levels) depending upon the relevant context information.

6 Future Directions

6.1 Relationship Model

Due to the rapid advancement of social computing technologies [13], there is an urgency for different types of relationships. The relevant relationships with different granularity levels and strengths need to be captured for the purpose of access control decision making. For example, a doctor's request to obtain a patient's some health records may be possible, but by obtaining the relevant relationship between them (e.g., treating doctor-patient). Such new challenges require a new relationship-aware access control model.

6.2 Situation Model

In open and dynamic environments, access control applications need to capture and manipulate context information to identify relevant situations and need to adapt their behaviors according to the situation changes. In the literature, many researchers have attempted to define the concept of "situation" and "situation-awareness" (e.g., [16], [17]). In [16], Yau et al have defined the situation as a set of context attributes of users, systems and environments over a period of time affecting future system behavior. However, in addition to the states of the entities, there exists the states of the relationships between entities and a goal or purpose (i.e., user intention in accessing the services) in every situation. Therefore, it is necessary to represent and capture the purpose-oriented situations to provide purpose-specific access to software services. The situation model also needs the reasoning capability to infer a new complex situation based on the basic atomic situations. How to determine the purpose information based on the captured data is also an important concept to be considered.

6.3 Prototype and Evaluation

A comprehensive prototype framework for CAAC with a user-friendly front-end will be developed so that it can be used by developers to build the CAAC applications. We also plan to investigate experimental evaluation that can be used to check the feasibility of our framework.

7 Conclusion

In this work, we have presented the research agendas for developing a new context-aware access control (CAAC) framework for software services. By leveraging the dynamically changing context information, the context-specific control over access to services can be achieved. We have introduced with the basic RBAC approach a new access control policy framework that will be applicable in today's dynamic environments. Furthermore, we have presented a comprehensive context model specific to access control, in order to represent and capture dynamic context information. As a next step, we intend to further develop the relationship model and situation model. Subsequently, we will examine how to integrate these concepts into the access control policies and evaluate our framework.

References

1. Bettini, C., Brdiczka, O., Henricksen, K., Indulska, J., Nicklas, D., Ranganathan, A., Riboni, D.: A survey of context modelling and reasoning techniques. Pervasive and Mobile Computing 6, 161–180 (2010)
2. Byun, J.W., Li, N.: Purpose based access control for privacy protection in relational database systems. The VLDB Journal 17(4), 603–619 (2008)
3. Chandran, S.M., Joshi, J.B.D.: *LoT-RBAC*: A location and time-based rbac model. In: Ngu, A.H.H., Kitsuregawa, M., Neuhold, E.J., Chung, J.-Y., Sheng, Q.Z. (eds.) WISE 2005. LNCS, vol. 3806, pp. 361–375. Springer, Heidelberg (2005)
4. Dimitropoulos, L.L.: Privacy and security solutions for interoperable health information exchange: nationwide summary. AHRQ Publication (2007)
5. He, Z., Wu, L., Li, H., Lai, H., Hong, Z.: Semantics-based access control approach for web service. JCP 6, 1152–1161 (2011)
6. Huang, J., Nicol, D.M., Bobba, R., Huh, J.H.: A framework integrating attribute-based policies into role-based access control. In: SACMAT, pp. 187–196 (2012)
7. Kayes, A.S.M., Han, J., Colman, A.: ICAF: A context-aware framework for access control. In: Susilo, W., Mu, Y., Seberry, J. (eds.) ACISP 2012. LNCS, vol. 7372, pp. 442–449. Springer, Heidelberg (2012)
8. Kayes, A.S.M., Han, J., Colman, A.: An ontology-based approach to context-aware access control for software services. In: Lin, X., Manolopoulos, Y., Srivastava, D., Huang, G. (eds.) WISE 2013, Part I. LNCS, vol. 8180, pp. 410–420. Springer, Heidelberg (2013)
9. Kayes, A.S.M., Han, J., Colman, A.: A semantic policy framework for context-aware access control applications. In: TrustCom, pp. 753–762 (2013)
10. Lee, A.J., Winslett, M., Basney, J., Welch, V.: The traust authorization service. ACM Trans. Inf. Syst. Secur. 11(1), 2:1–2:33 (2008)
11. O'Connor, A.C., Loomis, R.J.: 2010 economic analysis of role-based access control. NIST report (2010)

12. Sandhu, R.S., Coyne, E.J., Feinstein, H.L., Youman, C.E.: Role-based access control models. IEEE Computer 29, 38–47 (1996)
13. Squicciarini, A., Paci, F., Sundareswaran, S.: Prima: an effective privacy protection mechanism for social networks. In: ASIACCS, pp. 320–323 (2010)
14. Wang, L., Wijesekera, D., Jajodia, S.: A logic-based framework for attribute based access control. In: FMSE, pp. 45–55 (2004)
15. Weiser, M.: Some computer science issues in ubiquitous computing. Commun. ACM 36(7), 75–84 (1993)
16. Yau, S.S., Huang, D.: Development of situation-aware applications in services and cloud computing environments. IJSI 7(1), 21–39 (2013)
17. Yau, S.S., Liu, J.: A situation-aware access control based privacy-preserving service matchmaking approach for service-oriented architecture. In: ICWS, pp. 1056–1063 (2007)

Description and Composition of Services towards the Web-Telecom Convergence

Terence Ambra[*]

Department of Information Engineering, University of Florence, Italy
{terence.ambra,federica.paganelli}@unifi.it

Abstract. Current research trends within a Next Generation Networks (NGN) are investigating the benefits and feasibility of developing integrated services in order to converge the Telco and Web worlds. These trends responds to the need to integrate features offered by heterogeneous subjects to provide new innovative value added services to end users on any device equipped with a web browser. This PhD work focuses on the study of service description models and mechanisms that facilitate and automate the interoperation and composition of heterogeneous services (Web and Telecom) within a NGN. The objectives of this research work are: first, creating a model for abstract and concrete service interface specifications for each service type and interaction model, second, defining a service creation environment (SCE) using a orchestration language to compose heterogeneous services, and third, developing a convergent platform for the orchestration and composition of heterogeneous services from different domains environments.

Keywords: Next Generation Network, Web-Telecom Convergence, Service Composition, BPMN, JSLEE.

1 Introduction

The providers of Telecom services are researching the development of value-added services leveraging on internet and telephony networks, i.e. the integration and composition of services offered by IT providers with Telecom operators towards the Web-Telecom convergence.

The major technical difficulty to achieve the convergence is that each service environment relies on specific protocols and architectures that are not natively interoperable. The web services are typically exposed with a synchronous interaction model (request-reply) and use Hyper Text Transfer Protocol (HTTP) [1] and Web Service Description Language (WSDL) [2], respectively, for message exchange between client and provider, and service description. The Telecom services, instead, are typically asynchronous and event-driven. In this case, international level specifications have been defined, e.g., applications based on the Session Initiation Protocol (SIP) [3] (e.g., call forwarding service) in IP Multimedia Subsystem (IMS) [4] and Java API for Integrated Networks Service Logic Execution Environment (JSLEE) [5], and

[*] This PhD work is supervised by Dr. Federica Paganelli.

A.R. Lomuscio et al. (Eds.): ICSOC 2013 Workshops, LNCS 8377, pp. 578–584, 2014.
© Springer International Publishing Switzerland 2014

Parlay X specifications [6], which define a set of Web service interfaces for the invocation of communication functionality.

This work aims at investigating the study of service description models and mechanisms that facilitate and automate the interoperation and composition of heterogeneous services towards the Web-Telecom convergence. The objectives of this research work are: i) to create a model for abstract and concrete service interface specifications for different service types, such as Simple Object Access Protocol, (SOAP) [7], Representational state transfer (REST) [8], and SIP services, and interaction models (i.e., input and output parameters, events and action related to an event), ii) to define a service creation environment that uses a orchestration language to compose Web and Telecom services, and iii) to develop a service orchestration platform based on the adoption of a standalone workflow engine to orchestrate heterogeneous services from different domain environments (e.g., SOAP and REST services, IMS-based and JSLEE-based SIP services).

I chose to adopt Business Process Model and Notation (BPMN) 2.0 [9] as orchestration language because it allows non-expert users to describe in intuitive and easy way any service type (Web or Telecom) by graphical notation.

Finally, to validate the proposed approach, my work includes also the implementation of a proof-of-concept of the above-mentioned Service Orchestration Platform. This prototype composes heterogeneous services provided by JAIN SLEE-compliant platform and simple IT web services developed by SOAP. This prototype leverages the Java Business Process Management (JBPM) [10] as workflow engine and Mobicents [19] as open source platform certified for JSLEE compliance.

2 Related Work

In literature there are different approaches for the realization of a convergent platform that provides an orchestration of heterogeneous services within the NGN.

TeamCom [11] project permits to define a service creation environment (SCE) in which each service is composed from one or more reusable service components. This approach employs BPEL to specify the composition and control flow of these service components. The BPEL scripts are analyzed and translated by a code generator into java code modules that can be deployed on a JSLEE execution environment. This approach permits to abstract the communication services, but is limited to compose and integrate only Telecom services on a JSLEE environment. Analogously, SewNet [12] platform proposes a solution that permits to abstract the communication services defining, in this case, an abstraction model for the Telecom functionalities.

Femminella et al. [13] propose to integrate a JBPM workflow engine inside the development environment of the JSLEE platform. This approach permits that service business logic can be separated by implementation issues and designed by non JSLEE experts. This solution is thus bounded to the JSLEE environment and supports the orchestration of services invoked through a variety of JSLEE Resource Adaptors. Analogously, Bessler et al. [14] integrate a BPEL orchestration engine into a JSLEE environment. This approach permits to create a service orchestration environment that uses deployable BPEL scripts to control and invoke service building blocks (SBB) or external entities via different protocols as SIP , Intelligent Network Application Protocol (INAP) [15] or SOAP.

OPUCE [16] implements a solution that uses a standalone BPEL orchestration engine. This approach permits to define, for the communication services, base services identified by three sets of elements: properties, actions and events. With respect to previous approaches, this solution allows developers to choose their preferred environment to develop and deploy the base services. However, base service exposure should adopt the Web service stack specification and a WS-proxy is needed for interfacing components that offers different APIs.

Among the above mentioned works, this PhD work shows some similarities with OPUCE, since I chose to adopt a standalone workflow engine. Therefore, I do not specify any constraint on the implementation and execution environment of the base services. In addition my original contribution permits that base services APIs shall not be necessarily exposed as SOAP web services. Services can be invoked through different protocols (e.g., SIP, HTTP) and message formats.

3 Service Orchestration Platform

In this section, first I describe the objectives of this research work, and second, I present the proposed solution for the orchestration of heterogeneous services.

The first aim is to create a model for abstract and concrete service interface specifications for different service types (e.g., SOAP, REST and SIP services) and interaction models [17] (i.e., input and output parameters, events and action related to an event).

The second aim is to define a service creation environment (SCE) that uses a business process orchestration language to orchestrate heterogeneous Web and Telecom services. In the most widely used current approaches [16], [14] and [11], BPEL is been used as orchestration language, although it is conceived to orchestrate only web services. In our solution, I chose to adopt Business Process Model and Notation (BPMN) 2.0 [9] because it allows non-expert users to describe any service type (Web and Telecom) in very intuitive and easy way by a graphical notation.

The third aim is to design and develop a service orchestration platform that is able to invoke heterogeneous services from different domain environments (e.g., IMS-based and Mobicents JSLEE-based SIP services, SOAP and REST services).

To this end, the proposed solution is based on the adoption of workflow engine that can be deployed as a standalone solution. The workflow engine interacts with heterogeneous services provisioned by different external service provider platforms, according to the interaction paradigm (synchronous/asynchronous), protocol (e.g., SOAP, HTTP, SIP) and message format, such as Extensible Markup Language (XML) [18] and Session Description Protocol (SDP) [3], specified in the service interface description. Fig. 1 shows the functional architecture of the service orchestration platform proposed in this PhD work. This platform provides three components:

- The Service Creation Environment (SCE) includes BPMN 2.0 as orchestration language to compose base services for offering composite services.

- The Service Execution Engine (SEE) includes a workflow engine that invokes the heterogeneous services provisioned by different external service provider platforms, and a component to select the provider services that optimize the overall Quality of Service (QoS) [19] [20], according to network requirements.
- The Service Repository holds the information about each the service instance including the service URI and capabilities description.

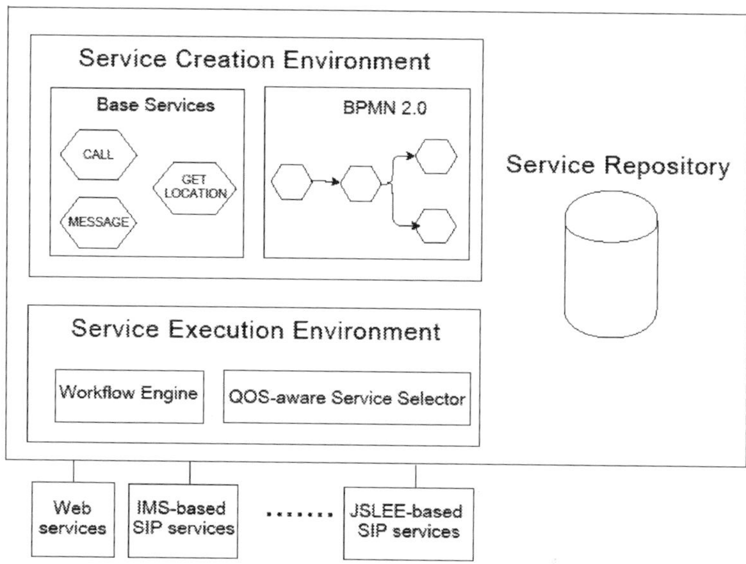

Fig. 1. Functional architecture of a Service Orchestration Platform

3.1 Proof of Concept

To validate the proposed approach, this PhD work includes the implementation of a proof-of-concept of the above-mentioned Service Orchestration Platform. Fig. 2 shows the prototype of this platform at the current state of development.

As orchestration engine I chose to adopt JBPM because it is open source, offers a strong interaction in Java environments and has a very simple graphical design tool. Moreover, JBPM allows to extend a default process constructs with domain-specific extensions that simplify development in a particular application domain. This permits also non-expert users to define domain-specific work items [10] for each type of service (also called service nodes), which represent atomic units of work that need to be executed. I embedded the JBPM workflow engine in a servlet container (Apache Tomcat [21]). In this way, an end user accessing a web application can trigger a composite service execution through a HTTP request.

As an example, I show the implementation of an "Expert on Call" service. In this scenario, a user having noticed a malfunction or failure of the business device, can contact a technician for assistance. The invocation flow is structured as follows:

first the user's personal data and location are retrieved, respectively by invoking a GetMember and GetLocation services. Then a GetCredit service is invoked to perform a check on the available user's credit. If the user's credit is enough to call, a GetLocation service is invoked to search the expert nearby and are retrieved the expert's personal data by invoking a GetMember service. Finally, a third party call service is invoked to establish a call between the user and the expert. Otherwise, if the user's credit is not enough to call, a message service is invoked to inform the user that the call can be not established. These service nodes can be combined as shown in Fig. 2. The base services have been implemented in two different environments. The third party call service is implemented as a JSLEE service that sends appropriate SIP signaling messages for the call setup between the two peers.

As JSLEE platform we chose to adopt Mobicents [22]. The Mobicents platform is built on top of the open source JBoss Application Server. The other services have been implemented as JAVA web services hosted on a JBoss Application Server.

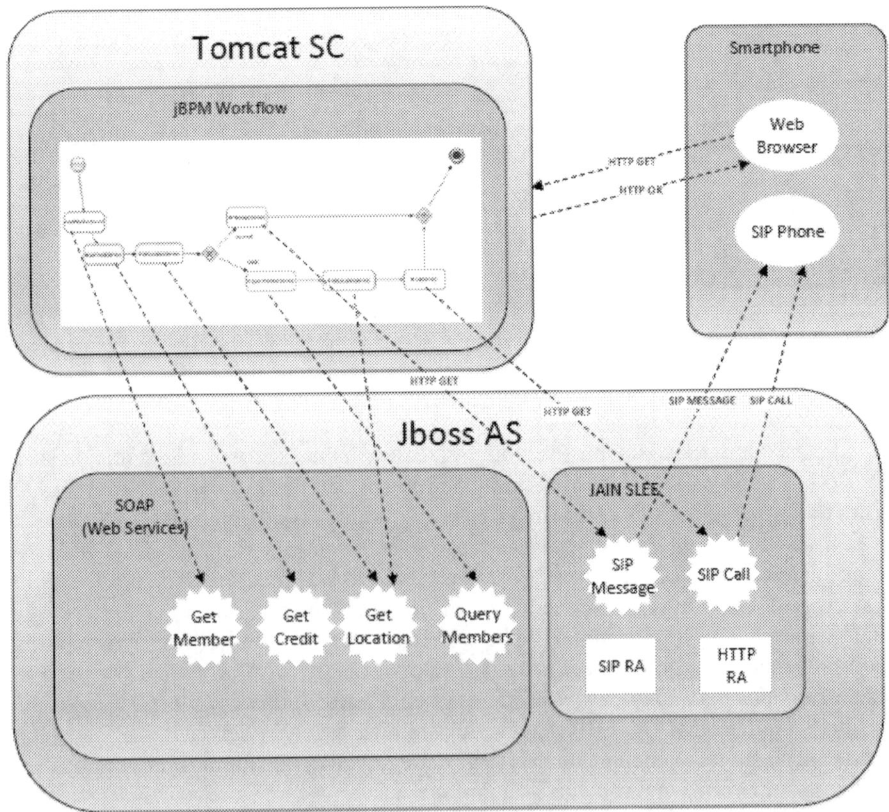

Fig. 2. Prototype of a Service Orchestration Platform

4 Conclusions

This PhD work focuses on the study of service description models and mechanisms that facilitate and automate the interoperation and composition of heterogeneous services (Web and Telecom) within a NGN. The objectives of this work are: i) to create a model for abstract and concrete service interface specifications for each service type and interaction model, ii) to define a service creation environment that uses BPMN 2.0 as orchestration language to compose Web and Telecom services, and iii) to develop a service orchestration platform based on the adoption of a standalone workflow engine to orchestrate heterogeneous services from different domain environments (e.g., SOAP and REST services, IMS-based and JSLEE-based SIP services).

At the current state of development, I implemented a prototype of Service Orchestration Platform which is able to compose heterogeneous services provided by JAIN SLEE-compliant platform and simple IT web services developed by SOAP. This prototype employs JBPM as workflow engine that permits to implement custom work items to define abstract service interfaces, and Mobicents as open source platform for the JSLEE services. I took into account a scenario for a "Expert on Call" service between a user and a expert, and I embedded JBPM in a servlet container (Apache Tomcat) so that an end user accessing a web application can trigger a composite service execution through a HTTP request.

Future work includes the study and development of a orchestration environment implementing dynamic binding techniques that comply with the binding information contained in the base service description, and the creation of a component to select the provider services that optimize the overall QoS, according to network requirements.

References

1. W3C, Hypertext Transfer Protocol – HTTP/1.1, W3C Note (June 1999), http://www.w3.org/Protocols/rfc2616/rfc2616.html
2. W3C, The Web Service description Language (WSDL) 1.1, W3C Note (March 15, 2001), http://www.w3.org/TR/wsdl
3. Rosenberg, J., et al.: RFC3261-SIP: Session Initiation Protocol. (June 2002), http://www.ietf.org/rfc/rfc3261.txt
4. Blum, N., Magedanz, T.: Requirements and components of a SOA-based NGN service architecture. Elek. und Inf. 125(7), 263–267 (2008)
5. Sun Microsystems, Open Cloud, JSR-000240 Specification, Final Release, JAIN SLEE (JSLEE) 1.1, SUN (2008)
6. The 3rd Generation Partnership Project (3GPP), Open service access (OSA) Parlay X web services (2008), http://www.3gpp.org/ftp/Specs/html-info/29-series.htm
7. W3C, Simple Object Access Protocol (SOAP) 1.1, W3C Recommendation, 2nd edn. (April 27, 2007), http://www.w3.org/TR/soap/
8. Belqasmi, F., et al.: RESTful web services for service provisioning in next-generation networks: A survey. IEEE Communications Magazine 49(12), 66–73 (2011)
9. OMG, Business Process Model and Notation (BPMN), http://www.bpmn.org/
10. JBPM User guide, http://docs.jboss.com/jbpm/v4/userguide/html_single/

11. Lehmann, A., et al.: TeamCom: a service creation platform for next generation networks. In: Proc. of 4 Int. Conf. on Internet and Web App. and Services, Venice/Mestre (2009)
12. Mittal, S., Chakraborty, D., Goyal, S., Mukherjea, S.: SewNet - A framework for creating services utilizing telecom functionality. In: Proc. of WWW Conf., pp. 875–884 (2008)
13. Femminella, M., Maccherani, E., Reali, G.: Workflow Engine Integration in JSLEE AS. IEEE Communications Letters 15(12), 1405–1407 (2011)
14. Bessler, S., Zeiss, J., Gabner, R., Gross, J.: An orchestrated execution environment for hybrid services. Fachtagung Kommunikation in Verteilten Systemen, 77–88 (2007)
15. ETSI, Intelligent network application protocol (INAP), ETS 300 374-1 (September 1994)
16. Yelmo, J.C., et al.: A User-Centric service creation approach for Next Generation Networks. In: ITU-T. Innovations in NGN - Future Network and Services, Geneva (May 2008)
17. Ambra, T., Paganelli, F., Fantechi, A., Giuli, D., Mazzi, L.: Resource-oriented design towards the convergence of Web-centric and Telecom-centric services. In: Second International Conference on Future Generation Communication Technologies (FGCT 2013), December 12-14, British Computer Society, London (2013)
18. W3C, Extensible Markup Language (XML), `http://www.w3.org/XML/`
19. Paganelli, F., Parlanti, D.: A Dynamic Composition and Stubless Invocation Approach for Information-Providing Services. IEEE Transactions on Network and Service Management 10(2), 218–230 (2013), doi:10.1109/TNSM.2013.022213.120229
20. Paganelli, F., Ambra, T., Parlanti, D.: A QoS-aware Service Composition Approach based on Semantic Annotations and Integer Programming. International Journal of Web Information Systems 8(3), 296–321 (2012)
21. Apache Software Foundation, Apache Tomcat (January 2008), `http://tomcat.apache.org/`
22. Mobicents Project, Mobicents: The open source VoIP middleware platform, `https://mobicents.dev.java.net/`

Author Index